ARMS AND ARMOUR
OF THE
IMPERIAL ROMAN SOLDIER

Arms and Armour
of the
Imperial Roman Soldier
From Marius to Commodus, 112 bc–ad 192

Raffaele D'Amato

Introduction, colour paintings and line drawings by Graham Sumner

Extra drawings and plates by Andrea Salimbeti, Elaine Norbury, Tomato Farm Studio

Frontline Books, London

Arms and Armour of the Imperial Roman Soldier: From Marius to Commodus

This edition published in 2009 by Frontline Books, an imprint of Pen & Sword Books Ltd
47 Church Street, Barnsley, S. Yorkshire, S70 2AS
www.frontline-books.com

Copyright © Raffaele D'Amato and Graham Sumner, 2009
Illustrations © Graham Sumner, 2009

ISBN: 978-1-84832-512-8

For more information on our books, please visit
www.frontline-books.com, email info@frontline-books.com
or write to us at the above address.

Typeset by JCS Publishing Services Ltd, www.jcs-publishing.co.uk

Printed and bound in China through Printworks International Ltd

~ CONTENTS ~

Foreword by Giorgio Ravegnani   ix
Introduction by Graham Sumner   xi
Sources and General Considerations   xiii

I FROM MARIUS TO AUGUSTUS 112–30 BC

Sources and Historical Outline	3
Events Timeline	3
Military Organisation	5
Weaponry	6
Shafted Weapons	6
Swords, Daggers and Belts	12
Shields	25
Helmets	32
Body Armour and Greaves	38
Auxiliary Troop Equipment: Bow and	
Arrows, Slingers	43
Special Equipment and Rank Symbols,	
Standards, Musical Instruments and	
Military Decorations	45
Cavalry Equipment: The Man	48
Spears and Javelins	48
Swords	49
Shields	49
Helmets	49
Armour	49
Cavalry Equipment: The Horse	52
Clothing	53
Tunics	53
Cloaks	54
Trousers	54
Other Garments	54
Shoes	56
Naval Equipment	57

II THE ROMAN EMPIRE IN THE AGE OF EXPANSION, 30 BC–AD 192

Sources and Historical Outline	63
Events Timeline	63
Military Organisation	64
Weaponry	66
Shafted Weapons, *Pilum* and *Hasta*	67
Swords, Daggers and Belts	80
Shields	101
Helmets	109
Body Armour	122
Leather, Linen and Felt Armour	135
Garments Worn Under and Over the Metallic	
Cuirass	144
Auxilia, *Numeri* and *Cohortes Equitatae*	152
Shafted Weapons	152
Swords, *Pugiones* and Belts	153
Shields	157
Helmets	158
Armour	159
Archers and Slingers	160
Numeri	164
Signa Militaria and the Equipment of Standard-	
Bearers	169
Medical Corps, Special Equipment, Musicians,	
Rank Symbols and Military Decorations	173
Medical Corps	173
Special Equipment	175
Symbols of Rank	175
Musicians	176
Military Decorations	177
Cavalry Equipment: The Man	182
Shafted Weapons	182
Swords	182
Shields	184
Helmets	184

II THE ROMAN EMPIRE IN THE AGE OF EXPANSION, 30 BC–AD 192 (CONTD)

Armour — 191
Cavalry Equipment: The Horse — 193
The *Hyppika Gymnasia* — 194
The Heavy Cavalry: The First *Catafractarii* — 198
The Imperial Guard and *Urbaniciani* and *Vigiles*
  Equipment — 200
  Shafted Weapons and Swords, Daggers and
  Axes — 200
  Shields and Helmets — 205

Armour — 209
Clothing — 212
  Tunics and Cloaks — 212
  Colour Evidence — 217
  Caps and Other Clothes — 218
  Trousers and Leg Coverings; Socks — 221
  Shoes — 222
Naval Equipment — 224

Conclusion — 229
Appendix: Further Details of milites, equites
  and weapons from the Arausius (Orange)
  Arch — 230
Notes — 235

Bibliography — 263
Glossary — 275
Acknowledgements — 279
Index — 283

~ PLATES ~

The colour illustrations include recent and specially commissioned artworks by Graham Sumner, some of which are published here for the very first time. Sumner's paintings are produced in gouache on board, recording in meticulous detail the painstaking research work carried out by Raffaele D'Amato. Together with the other two volumes this will form a unique collection of images documenting a radical new interpretation of the evidence for Roman military equipment.

PLATE I Roman *tribunus* and *milites* of the Late Consular age — 9
PLATE II Caesarian centurions — 31
PLATE III Caius Valerius Crispus, *milites* of *Legio VIII Augusta* — 69
PLATE IV Favonius Facilis, *centurio* of *Legio XX Valeria Victrix* — 83
PLATE V *Miles* or *centurio* of a *cohors voluntariorum* — 91
PLATE VI *Beneficiarius* of praetorian *cohors* — 119
PLATE VII Insus, *eques* of *Ala Augusta* — 181

To a small baby, who lived only three months inside his mother.
In spite of this, he will not be forgotten.

~ FOREWORD ~

The Roman army is perhaps one of the most striking fields in the study of antiquity, both for the importance it had in the history of each period – not only as element of power but also as sign of civilisation – and for the wide number and variety of sources that can make accurate research possible. In this context, it is especially important that the reconstruction of the equipment, armament and clothing of the Roman soldiers is conducted on the basis of the literary sources but above all in combination with the artistic and archaeological sources, so as to obtain a frame that could be as realistic and detailed as possible. Archaeology in particular can offer constant revisions in this and enrich the information that the historian already possesses with new elements through integration with less recent works devoted to the Roman armies.

The work done by Raffaele D'Amato is particularly praiseworthy, using this approach based on concrete elements to interpret ancient depictions of the soldiers, according to the reality of the time, not seeing them as simple artistic manifestations. Thus he has changed in a quite radical way the conventional research perspective. In this book these contemporary accounts and portrayals are in fact valued and accepted as a mirror of the time in which they were produced, always remembering the fact that we are dealing with simple artistic expressions and are deprived of a real correspondence to the framework from which they come.

This is an original vision originated by the assiduous evaluation and comparison of finds. Dr Raffaele D'Amato has long shown himself to be a valuable scholar of the Roman military, with a passion that pushes him to conduct researches in a capillary way, using any possible scientific contribution; at the same time he has a method that is directed to produce a different and more complete interpretation of the past.

Professor Giorgio Ravegnani
Professor of Byzantine History
University Ca' Foscari Venezia

～ Introduction ～

The Roman army is generally acknowledged as being one of the finest fighting machines of the Ancient World. It created and then defended an empire that lasted for almost a millennium. In spite of his rough and often cruel way of life, the Roman soldier nevertheless assisted the spread of Greco-Roman culture and civilisation throughout the entire Mediterranean basin. The *Pax Romana* that he helped to maintain, allowed first the rise and then ultimately the spread of Christianity until it was accepted as the state religion.

Fifty years ago reconstructions of the armour and equipment of Roman soldiers by the likes of Couissin, Racinet and Forestier were by and large based on interpretations of ancient sculpture and the few finds of equipment that had come to light. These representations found their way into popular art forms, such as the cinema, making the Roman soldier, at least of the first century AD, one of the most instantly recognisable characters even to modern eyes. With the discovery of the Corbridge hoard in 1964, and the subsequent reconstructions by H. Russell Robinson, of the armour known today as *lorica segmentata*, the picture of the Roman soldier was transformed. Soon afterwards this armour was reproduced in even greater numbers by the first Roman re-enactment societies and subsequently copied by modellers and book and magazine illustrators. As a result, the image of rows and rows of scarlet-dressed and iron-clad soldiers, which is frequently presented today as a depiction of the Roman army, while not an entirely fictitious portrait is probably also a somewhat misleading one. Not least because it reinforces the belief that only one type of armour was used throughout the Roman era.

In its development, which began with Indo-European Latin warriors on the Palatine Hill, and ended with the last defenders of Constantinople in AD 1453,[1] the Roman military structure was one of the most long standing and varied in history. Even though in some periods the appearance of standardisation was strong, it was necessary to adapt tactics and weapons of different enemies from various geographic locations, which resulted in a high degree of non-uniformity amongst the army, its equipment and clothing. Moreover, from AD 212 all the people living inside the boundaries of the Empire received, whether they wanted it or not, Roman citizenship. Therefore, what was once the enlistment of foreigners as auxiliaries became at the stroke of a pen the enlistment of citizens as citizen soldiers, who, for all that, retained their own distinctive regional characteristics and traditions that were now fused with the Roman ones. In addition,

in spite of rigid frontier defences the borders were not closed entirely, which allowed many other cultural influences to flow back and forth from places far beyond direct Roman control.

There remains to this day a huge amount of interest in the Roman army, its organisation and especially its armour and equipment. This interest is fuelled by films, television documentaries and numerous books. Many of these continue to show the familiar images that have defined the popular view of the Roman soldier at key stages in Roman history and one could almost guess what any new book might offer. Undoubtedly the pictures in such a book will include the many and varied scenes from Trajan's Column that depicts the imperial army at its height, the altar of Domitius Ahenobarbus that shows us the classic Republican soldier, while the ivory diptych of Stilicho illustrates the stereotypical warrior at the fall of the Western Empire. Although not ignoring these iconic images, D'Amato attempts to remind us that all these scenes only represent a single moment in time in one particular place and do not truly reflect what the Roman soldier may have been wearing elsewhere at the same period.

Therefore the purpose of this work is to throw new light on the examination of the equipment, armour and clothing of the Roman soldier – throughout both a thousand years of history and across the vast territories once encompassed within the boundaries of the Roman Empire. Following in the footsteps of pioneers such as Coussin and Forestier, D'Amato combines the use of written and artistic sources and compares both new and old archaeological finds that are often forgotten or ignored by modern scholars. He hopes to show in a clear way that the equipment of the Roman soldier comprised many rich and varied elements. The use of organic materials like leather, linen and felt as protective elements so often dismissed by today's scholars will nonetheless also be reassessed for their defensive qualities in comparison with the metallic forms frequently seen as far superior.

By travelling extensively D'Amato has brought back a collection of photographs of many rarely seen examples of military equipment, sculpture and mosaics that provide us with a unique snapshot of the past. In particular the pictures of finds from collections in Eastern Europe and the Middle East, so often inaccessible to all but the most determined traveller or scholar, will be both refreshing and hopefully a revelation.

Unfortunately, we too often presume to know more than the people who lived two thousand years ago and forget that the artisans or historians saw the ancient soldiers for themselves. The colour plates of this book have therefore been prepared on the basis of Roman period paintings – especially the portraits, mosaics, sculptures, coin depictions, written sources and, above all, the archaeological specimens that relate to each separate age of Roman history. The original Latin and Greek terminology is also used in preference to modern terms, with its own English translation.

So much rare and unpublished material was collected by D'Amato that the publishers realised at an early stage it could never be properly covered in a single volume. The decision was therefore taken to release the work in three separate books, each covering a distinct period in Roman history. This first volume deals with the most familiar period, including the age of Julius Caesar, the death of the Republic and the early Imperial era. Other volumes on the Republic and the later empire will follow. It is hoped that together these works will offer to the reader an image of the *miles Romanus* as close as possible to the overall archaeological evidence and to show Roman soldiers as they have never been seen for almost two thousand years!

Graham Sumner
Flint, 2009

~ Sources and General Considerations ~

The sources used in this work are mainly those used in any other book about the Roman military, that is, the literary evidence (including also papyri and epigraphical works), artistic representations (from the great variety of artworks of ancient times, like paintings, mosaics, sculptures, miniatures, friezes and tombstones) and the archaeological data. The interpretation of this material here, however, is radically different from many of the previous books on the subject. The present work will present evidence that the monuments of ancient times were the mirrors of their own age, and that the equipment and the clothing of the Roman soldier were faithfully reproduced, with some concessions to the limitations of stylistic conventions and the skills of the artist. Although it is absolutely crucial to be aware of the ancient authors' motives, background, language and audience, we should remember that they were not like modern artists or artists of the Renaissance. They were commanded to realise artworks, and they did so by copying the world before their eyes. Romans loved fantasy and invention, and they used it a great deal in the depiction of mythological subjects in artworks, but the representational evidence on the monuments of propaganda, or the portraits on the gravestones, were linked to the rigid necessity of realism.

The unhappy circumstance that not all the pieces of equipment illustrated on ancient monuments have been confirmed by archaeology can be explained by the limits of the excavations that have been carried out in many parts of the Roman world and that organic materials such as felt, leather or linen only survive in extreme and rare conditions. Even metallic equipment is only represented today by a tiny fraction of what originally existed. In spite of this, wherever possible, evidence will be used to prove that the ancient monuments show in almost photographic detail actual pieces of equipment and armour. Furthermore, we must remember that the monuments of the ancient world were lavishly painted and furnished with metallic and organic appliqués, now lost. What is left now before our eyes are the ruins of a magnificent and colourful world that had a mindset and vision of reality completely different from the modern one.

The ancient literary sources and their description of equipment are highly reliable against modern concepts that try to deny them. Ancient authors had access to the works of early historians and documents now lost. They saw with their own eyes the paintings (especially the *tabulae pictae* paraded in the triumphs and representing the military campaigns), mosaics and

artistic works when they were intact and colourful; moreover they had access to the oral and literary traditions of the great families. They could see for themselves the spoils of the ancient trophies preserved in the private houses and hung on the walls. They spoke with the veterans and the survivors of the battles. Above all, they could examine ancient armour and weapons, preserved in the temples, churches and mausoleums. Even if artists never saw a battle, soldiers were a highly visible presence in the ancient world, carrying out their duties as policemen, guards, supervising engineering projects or on ceremonial and religious parades.

This work will also emphasise the fact that Roman equipment was never standardised, although there were attempts at uniformity in fittings, weapons making, metallurgy techniques and manufacture, even of items such as boots and clothing. All the same this was a pre-industrial age and in military life just as the civil one, the tastes of each individual and the necessity to supply equipment according to the needs of the moment introduced many personalised military items, as we can clearly see from the soldiers' own tombstones.

It will also not be a surprise to discover that many generations of soldiers used the same helmets, armour and other items of equipment until they became unserviceable. So it is perfectly possible that at any one time arms and armour even two or three centuries old were still in use. Therefore in all periods of Roman history we can expect to find a mixture of brand-new equipment alongside quite battered pieces of armour, not only within the same theatre of operations but often within the same unit! This can help to explain why the soldiers represented on the monuments are sometimes differently dressed and equipped, even when a certain degree of uniformity seems to be stronger, as in the imperial propaganda monuments such as the columns of Trajan and Marcus Aurelius.

The impact of propaganda and ideology – linked to some dynasties – also influenced military equipment. Officers and soldiers liked to please their rulers or show their allegiance by purchasing arms and armour that celebrated the emperors or victorious generals by recalling the mythical origin of their families, or the glory of their ancestors. The whims and dictates of many powerful individuals could also exert their influence over military hardware, often with complete disregard to tradition or practicality.

Archaeologists often find high-quality ancient armour, arms and weapons that they classify as parade or ceremonial objects, not used for battle. However, the evidence tells us a different story. The concept of parade armour or helmets did not exist in the ancient world; even in Napoleonic times soldiers wore their best armour into battle. Of course the best pieces were displayed in parades and ceremonies, but at the same time they were displayed in front of their enemies and used on the battlefield, to show the richness and the glorious aspect of the wearer, who was protected by the gods whose likenesses were incised or chiselled into the armour and weapons. This custom continued into the Christian era.

Occasionally in the text I have used different terms to those usually found in modern works to indicate periods or classification. This was done because I wished to follow the terminology used by the Romans. So instead of 'Republican' I have used 'Consular' and instead of 'Hellenistic' I have used the adjective 'Hellenic' or more simply Greek. Hellenic/Greek has been used to refer to what the Romans considered objects, words and ideas deriving from the Greek world. The term Hellenistic has also occasionally been used in its modern meaning – Greek culture from the death of Alexander the Great to the defeat of Cleopatra and Mark Antony.

A last note: many archaeological finds of weapons are listed by a classificatory name given by the first place of discovery: for instance, the 'Montefortino' helmet type, the 'Corbridge' *lorica segmentata*, the 'Oberaden' *pilum*. While this is a logical criterion from the point of view of archaeological research and for that reason is sometimes kept in this book, it has nothing to do with the historical reality of Roman times. Therefore we can be sure that no Romans ever used such terms to indicate a certain kind of weapon, instead they called them by their generic name of *cassis, lorica, pilum*.

For the translations from Latin and Greek, I have mainly used the Loeb translations, but changed some words where the Loeb version does not use the specialist vocabulary for arms and armour.

~ I ~
From Marius to Augustus
112–30 BC

~ Sources and Historical Outline ~

Sources: Appianus, Atheneus, Gaius Suetonius Tranquillus, Cassius Dio Cocceianus, Marcus Tullius Cicero, Cornelius Tacitus, Decimus Junius Juvenalis, Gaius Julius Caesar, Gaius Plinius Secundus Maior, Gaius Sallustius Crispus, Isidorus of Seville, Joannes Laurentius Lydus, Lucius Annaeus Seneca, Marcus Annaeus Lucanus, Marcus Fabius Quintilianus, Marcus Valerius Martialis, Marcus Terentius Varro, Plutarchus, Polybius, Pomponius Porphyrio, Publius Annius Florus, Publius Virgilius Maro, Quintus Asconius Pedianus, Quintus Horatius Flaccus, Sextus Julius Frontinus, Sextus Pompeius Festus, Sextus Propertius, Strabo, Suidas, Titus Flavius Clemens Alexandrinus, Tiberius Catius Silius Italicus, Titus Livius, Titus Maccius Plautus, Valerius Maximus, Xenophon.

Events Timeline

146 BC After the destruction of Carthage, the Roman Republic began its military conquest across the Mediterranean area. The Romans, in a short period of time, conquered the ancient African and Spanish territory of the Punic Empire, then the Eastern Greek lands. In the last quarter of the second century BC, the Roman *Imperium* already comprised the following *provinciae*: Sicily, Sardinia and Corsica, Spain (divided into the two provinces of Hispania Citerior and Hispania Ulterior) Macedonia, Africa and Asia.

113 BC A Roman army was defeated by the Germans. At the same time, against the advice of the Senate, the Roman people (*plebs*) and Equestrians demanded the war against Jugurtha. After initial setbacks, command of the war was given to the Consul Caius Marius, of the Equestrian party.

112 BC Two stronger political parties evolved that would dominate Roman history for the next one hundred years; these two parties often fought each other violently and the clash would ultimately bring about the fall of the Republic and the rise of the Emperors. The first party was the old Patrician aristocracy, represented by the Senate (*Senatus*). The second party, the Equestrian, had evolved from the class rich enough to purchase a horse for military service, the so-called *equites* (cavalrymen).

112–105 BC In the Jugurthine War the King of Numidia, Jugurtha,

tried to free his kingdom from Roman influence; Italic and Roman colonists in Cirta (Constantina) were massacred. Almost simultaneously Rome experienced the menace of the Germans, with the invasion of the Cimbri and Teutoni in the south of Gaul.

107 BC Marius began the transformation of the army from citizens recruited by levy to volunteers, who owed their loyalty to their own generals who recruited them rather than to the state (*Res Publica*) itself.

105–101 BC Jugurtha was captured by Lucius Cornelius Sulla and was killed in the Mamertinus prison after the triumph of Marius. There followed the appointment of Marius as *Consul* for four consecutive years to deal with the invasion of the Cimbri and Teutoni. The Germans were eventually destroyed in the successful battles of Aquae Sextiae (Aix-en-Provence) and at the Campi Raudii, near Vercellae (perhaps the modern Macello near Turin, or Vercelli in Piemonte).

90–88 BC At the beginning of the first century BC the Italic allies, who had fought with Rome during the victorious Punic Wars and had participated in the conquest of the Mediterranean, pressed the *Res Publica* for the Roman citizenship. This resulted in the Social War, and although defeated, the Italic allies received citizenship. Mithridates, King of Pontus, tried to expand his kingdom into Asia and Greece. Sulla's appointment as commander of the war against Mithridates met with opposition from Marius and his supporters, leading to Rome's First Civil War. Rome was for the first time conquered by a Roman army, the army of Sulla. Mithridates was also defeated and sued for peace.

82–81 BC   A supporter of Marius, Quintus Sertorius, raised an army in Spain composed of citizens and Iberians, leading to the Second Civil War and the appointment of Sulla as Dictator. At the same time the new province of Gallia Cisalpina was created.

73–71 BC   In Spain, after many victories over the consular armies, Sertorius was murdered by one of his officers, and his army was defeated by the Consul Gaius Pompeius. During these years the revolt of Spartacus and his gladiators broke out, and Mithridates once more menaced the Roman East. Marcus Lucius Crassus defeated and killed Spartacus in battle.

70 BC   New provinces were constituted in Gallia (Narbonensis), in Asia (Cilicia and Bithynia) and in Africa (Cyrenaica). The campaign of Lucullus in the east against Mithridates was successful and the legions campaigned in Armenia.

69–67 BC   The heavily armoured Cataphracts of the Armenian King Tigranes were destroyed by Lucullus in the Battle of Tigranocerta. Pompeius, with five hundred warships, was given an 'unlimited power' to defeat the Cilician pirates, which he achieved in an astonishing three months.

64–62 BC   The conquest of the east continued. Mithridates, for long a thorn in the Roman side, committed suicide, and the Diadochia of Syria became a province, while a Roman protectorate was imposed on Palestine. In Rome the personality of Gaius Julius Caesar began to emerge. Although of an ancient aristocratic family, Caesar was linked to the popular Marian party.

60–59 BC   The first alliance[1] between Pompeius, now called 'magnus' (great), Caesar and Crassus began; Caesar was appointed Consul and received the government of Gallia Cisalpina and Narbonensis.

58–56 BC   Cyprus was conquered and annexed to Cilicia. The siege of Genaba (Geneva) by Divico and 210,000 Helvetii warriors was broken by Caesar, now Proconsul, with five legions and some Aedui auxiliary cavalrymen; 80,000 Helvetii were killed at Bibracte. The Germans invaded Gaul again but were defeated by Caesar. Eighty thousand Germans were killed and their leader Ariovistus was wounded. Caesar successfully subdues the Celtic Belgians; their cities were taken and the Nervii's tribe annihilated on the river Sabis with 53,000 Belgians reduced to slavery after the final conquest. Caesar defeated the Veneti of Armorica, who lost 220 ships in a single battle.

55 BC   Another horde of 430,000 Germans (Usipetes and Tencteri) invaded Gaul. Caesar not only defeated them but also built a grandiose bridge on the Rhine, and ravaged deep into Germanic territory. In the same year Caesar landed in Britain; after many battles, he decided to go back to Gaul before the winter.

54–53 BC   With four legions and 4,000 Celtic cavalrymen, Caesar made a second expedition against the Britons; the British King Cassivellaunus sued for peace. Caesar destroyed the rebellious Eburones and their Germanic allies the Treveri in revenge for the previous massacre of Roman *milites*. Crassus was killed and his army destroyed by the Parthian horse archers and cataphracts at Carrhae, in Mesopotamia. Only the courage of Cassius Longinus saved the province of Asia.

52 BC   Vercingetorix raised a major Gallic rebellion. In response to the massacre of Romans in Cenabum, Caesar destroyed Avaricum and killed 40,000 Gauls. In September Vercingetorix was besieged with 100,000 warriors in Alesia by Caesar and eleven legions who surrounded the city with a double system of fortification. Caesar defeated a Gallic relief army of a quarter of a million men and Vercingetorix surrendered.

49–47 BC   The civil war between Caesar and Pompeius and the senatorial faction began. In the decisive battle, at Pharsalus in Greece, in July 48 BC, Pompeius' army of 50,000 men was destroyed by the selected legions of Caesar's veterans. Pompeius escaped to Egypt, but was murdered by King Ptolemy XIV. There followed the brief campaign in Egypt, where Caesar supported the young Cleopatra against her brother Ptolemy. Caesar was besieged in Alexandria by the Egyptian general Achillas. In March 47 BC Caesar struck back after receiving reinforcements from Asia. The Egyptians were destroyed near the Nile by a charge of the Celtic and German cavalry and *legionarii*.[2] In July 47 BC Caesar overcame the new menace of Farnakes, son of Mithridates, with a lightning war in Pontus.[3]

46–44 BC   April 46 BC saw a fresh victory of Caesar in Africa at the Battle of Thapsus, against the reconstituted Senatorial and Pompeian forces allied with Juba I, King of Mauretania. The last confrontation with the sons of Pompeius took place on the Spanish battlefield of Munda, which Caesar won by putting himself in the front line. Caesar celebrated the triumphs in Rome. All was ready for an empire and an emperor, but on the Ides of March 44 BC Caesar was killed by a plot prepared by Cassius and Brutus. Marcus Antonius and Gaius Octavius inherited Caesar's legacy. After initial clashes they formed a Triumvirate with Marcus Aemilius Lepidus.[4]

42 BC   The army of Brutus and Cassius was destroyed at Philippi in Greece. In the following years Octavianus consolidated his power in Rome and Italy. Fascinated by the beautiful Cleopatra, Antonius shared with her and their sons the eastern territories he had won from the Armenians and Parthians.

32–30 BC The inevitable conflict between Antonius and Octavianus arose: the final victory was achieved by Octavianus and his general, Agrippa, in the naval clash at Actium in Greece, in 31 BC. In 30 BC Antonius and Cleopatra committed suicide, ending the last Hellenistic Kingdom, successor of Alexander the Great. Octavianus adopted the title of Augustus and so began the Roman Imperial Age.

~ MILITARY ORGANISATION ~

Each consular army (*exercitus*) was formed of four legions. Each legion comprised ten cohorts, each *cohors* was divided into three maniples.[5]

The *cohors* was created by Marius, who gathered under this denomination a maniple of *hastati*, a maniple of *principes* and a maniple of *triarii*.[6] At first the *cohors* comprised 300 men, which was increased to 500[7] or 600[8] when it was considered a permanent tactical unit.[9] The first *cohors*, which was made up of a body of elite soldiers (*electi milites*)[10] and defended the eagle of the legion and was under the command of the *primus pilus*, had twice the number of men of any other *cohors*.

Each maniple was subdivided into two centuries (*centuriae*), so each legion had sixty *centuriae* or *ordines*. The total number of soldiers (*milites*) in the standard legion was 4,200 men, but the number was sometimes raised or reduced, up to a maximum of 5,000 men or a minimum of 1,000.[11]

Attached to each legion were 300 cavalrymen or *equites*.

After Marius' reforms, the levy was not based on social classes but the *capite censi* (heads counted), i.e. it was enlarged to include the proletarians. The new method of recruitment provided a longer service, not seasonal, based more on the concept of the volunteer, to create a permanent and professional army. The reforms were in any case slow and not immediately extended to all the consular armies.

The Marian reforms appear to have abolished the light legionary infantrymen, the *velites*, that had been created during the Second Punic War. We find that the sources mentioned in their place light infantrymen called *antesignani*, supplemented with other skirmishers with a round shield, the *parma bruttiana*. For the most part the legionary (*miles legionis*) was now armed with a heavy shield (*scutum*), javelins and a sword. The standard Roman javelin, the *pilum*, was now carried without distinction by the *hastati*, *principes* and *triarii*, the latter having previously been equipped with the *hasta* (spear).

The levy system was of two types: the first, the *dilectus*, was the annual levy of the consul for his four legions, and the second, the *tumultus* was an extraordinary levy. Once the legions were created as a permanent military force, each legion was given a number,[12] related to the commander and to the other legions. The *exercitus* was under the command of the *consul*, the higher rank of the Republic. If necessary, the Senate could prolong the mandate of the commander, who was then called *proconsul*. The rank of *imperator* was given to the victorious commander directly by the soldiers if more than a thousand enemies were killed in battle. The *imperator* exercised the right of life and death over his soldiers (*imperium*).

A single *legio* was commanded by a *legatus*.[13] The *legati* came from the Senatorial order and were appointed by the Senate, after being proposed by the *imperator*. In the absence of the *imperator*, a *legatus* could substitute for him, taking the rank of *legatus pro praetore*. Sometimes an army could also be led by a *quaestor* who, if he received command of the army, was appointed *quaestor pro praetore*.

In the middle Consular Age six senior officers called *tribuni militum* alternated the command of the *legio*, each for one day. However, they were often dismissed by generals such as Caesar, who considered them more interested in a *cursus honorum*, a political career. The *tribuni* could be elected by the people (*tribuni militum*) or directly appointed by the *consul*[14] (*Rufuli*). They could be of senatorial (*laticlavii*) or equestrian (*augusticlavii*) rank.

A single *centuria* was under the command of the most famous officer in the Roman army, the *centurio*. In the manipular organisation the tactical unit was the maniple comprised of two *centuriae*: the *centuria* on the right side was commanded by the *prior centurio*; that on the left by a *posterior*. The centurions were named according to their old legionary speciality: *triarii* (or *pili*), *principes* and *hastati*. There were twenty *centuriones* with the rank of *pili* (ten *priores* and ten *posteriores*); twenty *principes* (ten *priores* and ten *posteriores*) and lastly twenty *hastati* (again equally divided into *priores* and *posteriores*).

The cohort to which the *centurio* belonged was indicated by his number in the *legio*, for example: *Decimus Pilus Prioris Centuriae* (Tenth Centurion of the Right *Centuria* of the *Pili*), *Decimus Pilus Posterioris Centuriae* (Tenth Centurion of the Left *Centuria* of the *Pili*), *Nonus Pilus Prioris Centuriae* (Ninth Centurion of the Right *Centuria* of the *Pili*), and so on. The junior centurion in the *legio* was called *decimus hastatus posterior*, the senior centurion of the *legio centurio prior*. This latter was called *Primus Pilus*. He was the senior in rank and commanded the *primi ordines*, who participated in the war council with the *imperator*, the *legatus* and the *tribuni*.

Under the centurions were ranked the junior officers, the *principales*: *aquilifer*, *signifer*, *beneficiarius*. The first two were standard-bearers. The *beneficiarii* were attendants of the officers, and as the so-called *immunes*, were excused from fatigues. Other *principales* were: the *tesserarius*, who received the password written on a tablet (*tessera*) from the tribunes; the *vexillarius*, another standard-bearer; the *cornicen*, the *tubicen* and the *buccinator*, who were musicians.

During the civil wars of the late Consular period special cohorts were formed by re-enlisted veterans, called *evocati*. At the Battle of Pharsalus 2,000 of them fought under their own commander, the *praefectus evocatorum*. Similar veterans acted as bodyguards for generals, fighting on foot, although during the marches they were on the horseback. During this tumultous period many regiments of bodyguards (*cohortes praetoriae*) were made up of non-Roman soldiers; Caesar had 400 Germanic cavalrymen in Gaul as bodyguards, and 2,000 Iberians in Rome in 44 BC.

After the Punic Wars the *auxilia* were composed of foreigners or troops recruited among the Italic allies (*socii*). The availability of foreigners increased in number after the Social War. These *cohortes auxiliariae* were commanded by their own officers or by *praefecti* of equestrian rank. Their number and ethnic composition varied: we find Celts (Aedui, Narbonenses, Belgii, Cisalpini, Aquitanians), Germans, Iberians, Illyrians, Norici, Cretan, Ruthenian, Syrian and Iturean archers and Numidians, Balearic slingers and Galatians, Greeks (Rhodians, Acarnians, Dolopians, Aetolians), Macedonians and Hellenised troops, Anatolians, Nabateans. The core of these troops, especially the Celts, formed the bulk of the Roman cavalry. Their tactical unit was the *ala* formed by 300–400 men and commanded by a *praefectus equitum*, if a Roman of senatorial rank. Each *ala* was divided into *turmae* of 33 men, commanded by a *decurio*, often a Roman. They were the basis of the *cohortes equitatae* of the Imperial period.

~ WEAPONRY ~

Shafted Weapons

Pilum, *gaesum* and *hasta* were the main shafted weapons of the Roman legionary.

The *pilum*, a javelin of Etrusco-Italic origin,[15] was the most employed shafted weapon[16] and was without doubt the most famous weapon used by the Roman soldier.[17] It is often mentioned in the classical sources, where the ancient authors discuss its efficiency, technical features and tactical use. The *pilum* was a close-range javelin, consisting of a wooden shaft around 1 m long in which was inserted or to which was attached a long thin metallic shank of approximately the same length.[18] Its penetrative power was determined by its weight. It was capable of wounding an enemy, but if the *pilum*, after piercing the shield, did not wound the enemy, it would have been broken by the impact at the junction of the iron shank and the wooden shaft, so that the opponent could not employ it again. The bent *pilum* stuck into the shield and could not be drawn out, so that the burdened shield was unserviceable and the enemy exposed to the slashing blows of the terrible legionary sword, the *gladius*.

In 101 BC, Marius made a new innovation by reducing from two to one the number of iron rivets fixing the iron part of the *pilum* to the shaft and putting in the place of the lower rivet a wooden peg[19] that could easily be broken. So the javelin, after striking the enemy's shield, would not stand straight out; the breaking of the wooden dowel allowed the shaft 'to bend in the iron head and trail along the ground, being held fast by the twist at the point of the weapon'.[20]

Two types of *pila* are mentioned by Polybius in 146 BC:[21] a stout one and a thin one. They have been confirmed by archaeological specimens of the first century BC (**1**). In the previous period they were given to *hastati* and *principes*, who used both categories of *pilum*. However, in the Battle of Pharsalus Caesar refers to *milites* carrying only one *pilum* instead

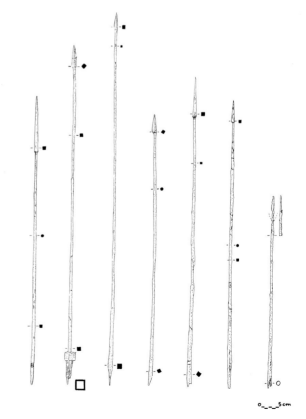

1 Roman shafted weapons, of *pila* type, first century BC–third century AD, from Saône, France (*ex Feugère; drawing by Andrea Salimbeti*)

of the two *pila* used in the second century BC,[22] so that it seems that every *miles* was provided now with a single *pilum*.

Some further modifications in the Caesarian period concerned the heavy *pilum*. Caesar ordered that the metallic part of the ferrule, the iron shaft under the point,[23] should not be hardened. Porphyrio recounts that just a slight blow could break the *pilum*, so that the enemy could not reuse it.[24] Not all the soldiers adopted these modifications, however: Caesar remembers quick-reacting Gauls throwing *pila* back to the *milites*.[25]

The *pila* heads (*cuspides*) were originally barbed, but usually in the late Consular period they have a bodkin or pyramidal shape, more suitable for piercing shields or armour, and are rarely leaf-shaped. The joint of the iron part with the shaft could be socketed, or with a tang inserted into the wooden shaft and fixed with wedges and/or collets. Many Late Republican *pila* were furnished with a small heart-shaped flat tang without holes; it was probably in the Caesarian age that the flat tang at the base was replaced by a tang not wider than the upper part and with one hole for a wedge. The collet (a ring-shaped metal cover) was also introduced to secure the attachment of the wooden shaft with the shank.[26]

At least eight specimens of Late Consular *pila* have been recovered in La Caridad (Caminreal), corresponding to the heavy and light *pila*. The two types are different in length and also in the shape of the socket: usually square or circular in cross section for the lighter type, rectangular for the heavier, but this is not a general rule.[27] The four heavier specimens are only incompletely preserved. The average complete length of the iron shank has been estimated to be 100 cm. The shanks are circular in section, with a diameter of 9 mm for more or less the whole weapon. The first three *pila* have pyramidal points; the fourth does not have a separate point, the shank just ends in a point.

The four light specimens are complete: their average length is 39.3 cm. The circular or square socket presents an external diameter of 2.6 cm. The shafts are circular, with a diameter progressively decreasing considering the shape of the weapon, i.e. narrower down its length. The *cuspides* are the natural continuation of the shaft, as in the medieval *verruda*, which was used in Sardinia until the fourteenth century AD.[28]

Caminreal's specimens can be compared with those from La Almoina (Valencia), Cerro de la Peladilla, Numancia, Arcobriga, Càceres el Viejo and Alesia. The *pilum* of Valencia (79–72 BC) is fitted with a pyramidal head and elongated rectangular flat tang, with two rivets without turned edges.

The battlefield of Alesia has been fundamental to the study of the kind of shafted weapons used in the first century BC. The large amount of spears and javelins found shows that these was the main weapons of both sides. The *pila* of Alesia, where forty fragments have been recovered, are often fitted with pyramidal heads and barbed points. Socket-mounted heads have been found as frequently as the riveted or tanged type.

The length varies from 25 to 70 cm; both types were furnished with butts.[29]

The use of the socketed long type, square in section, is attested by two specimens found in the investigations of Camp C. A complete specimen with leaf-shaped point has been found in Castellum 11.[30] Several other *pila* added a spiked tang with a rivet through it, representing an evolution of an early Italic type, still visible on some imperial specimens.

Pila of the socketed shorter type have been found in Alesia[31] and Urso (Osuna),[32] where the shorter type was about 15 cm long. Caesar mentions the so-called *pila muralia*, used by defenders to beat off an enemy attack.[33] They were obviously short-range weapons that were thrown down from the ramparts.

The distinction between the socketed and the flanged type was maintained, but since the first century BC the flat tanged *pilum* had become slimmer as in the Oberaden specimens of the early Principate,[34] whose prototype is a *pilum* of Alesia.[35] This last type[36] was a very sophisticated weapon with a round iron shaft in section, very thin, varying in length from 17 to 50 cm, with a point (*cuspis*) rhomboid in section, and ending with a flat tang fastened with two rivets in the wooden haft. The wooden handle has a thick upper dowel that is pyramidal or conical in shape, pierced laterally to accept round or square ferrules.[37] This kind of *pilum* is represented on the Glanum monument in Saint-Remy (**2e**, **2f**, **2g**, **2h**).[38] Several of these ferrules, used in the later imperial specimens to fasten the iron point to the haft, were found in Alesia.

This new method of fixing seems to have been developed at the end of the Gallic Wars.[39] A well-preserved example of this type, with a ferrule in addition, was recovered from the Saône at Ouroux (**1**).[40] It is 76.5 cm long, characterised by a long point of square section (15.3 cm); the width at the base is 10 mm and prolonged with a slender shaft (8 mm in diameter) and a squared tang of 25.8 cm. This last is pierced by an oval hole for the wooden dowel, probably fixed to the shaft with the usual round or squared ferrules.

The *gaesum*, a javelin of Celtic origin, was also employed by the Late Consular soldiers, as is visible on the Julii monument in Glanum (**2b**, **2f**). Antonucci suggests that it was especially used by the *milites* of Celtic origin, as part of their own armament (**PLATE I**). It was a heavy javelin, originally made of a thin narrow shaft of forged iron, also known by the Romans as *soliferreum*, of about 1.4 m in length. When thrown, like the *pilum*, it bent once it had hit the enemy shields, and could not be reused. Like the *pilum* it also wounded the enemy badly. The Romans kept the shape of the head, but changed its iron body to a wooden one.

Heavy javelins with cross-pieces, used especially by soldiers and officers on hunting activity, were already used in the Late Consular period, as represented in a late first-century BC fresco (**3**).

* * *

PLATE I *(from left to right)*

a *Tribunus* 58–44 BC: his head is covered by a helmet of Agen–Port type. The use of this kind of helmet by Caesar's legions is widely attested by many monuments.[i] Some original specimens have a *cannula* for the crest, and the Aquileia reliefs add lateral holders for the *geminae pinnae* sacred to Mars.[ii] A ring attached to the back of each cheek guard was used for the under-chin strap, secured by a rivet placed towards the rear of the lower edge.

He wears a muscled armour as his main body protection. These armours, of copper alloy, iron and bronze, were composed of two plates, joined at the sides by hinges and clasps, and their surface was often chiselled with mythological scenes or animals, although plain specimens, like this, are attested by sources and archaeology.[iii]

His cloak is fastened by a gold *fibula*, described by Pliny the Elder as being worn by the *tribunes* at the Battle of Philippi.[iv] Black was not a usual colour, but Crassus, on the eve of the Battle of Carrhae, wore a black *paludamentum*, which was – correctly – interpreted as a bad omen.[v] His shield, copied from a monument from the age of Sulla, is enamelled with *piyropus*, a gilded copper alloy that, used as a coating on precious shields, gave them a shining aspect.[vi]

Cicero and Valerius Maximus say that the officers and even Pompeius used to wear together the *Fasciae cretatae* with *caligae*.[vii] These were leg-bindings so called because of the mode of cleaning by rubbing them with a white sticky soil resembling our pipe-clay.

b *Miles* of *Legio V Alaudae*, 46 BC: a *Legio* of Caesar, the *V Alaudae*, was so called because of the special appearance given by the distinctive crest arrangement.[viii] According to an allusion in the *Aeneid*, such *milites* might have fought under the protection of Mars.[ix] A rather similar crest is visible on a middle Republican coin of the Aquilia family, representing an Agen–Port helmet with horsehair crest and two lateral feathers, and on a Coolus helmet engraved on a funerary monument from Sora (**128**). The two side feathers or *geminae pinnae* were sacred to Mars, since the god, according to the ancient religious beliefs, would appear with this ornament on his helmet.[x] During the Late Republic the helmet side-feathers were considered to be military decorations and the soldiers who bore them were called *insigniti milites*.

[xi] The man wears the kind of Coolus helmets shown on the monuments celebrating the wars of Ceasar.[xii] He has a *thorax linteus*. Fragments of a terracotta statue from Saint Gregorio al Celio show red-purple and yellow colours for this kind of armour.[xiii] The symbol of the *Legio V Alaudae* was an elephant trampling on a snake, as recorded by the Caesarian coins celebrating the Battle of Tapsus.[xiv] For their bravery against the Pompeian elephants, Caesar gave these soldiers the right to use this symbol as their distinctive sign.[xv] The man is armed with a javelin, *gaesum*, with a wavy-edged point like those shown on the Glanum monument (**2b, 2f**). Its shaft is in cornel wood, following Pliny the Elder: 'cornel, of which glossy yellow hunting-spears are made, marked with incisions for their further embellishment'.[xvi]

c Marius' *mulus*, 101 BC: The description of Quintilianus and a very important funerary frieze from Sora (**17**) of the first or probably second half of the first century BC have been the sources for the reconstruction of this warrior. He wears a Negau-type helmet with volutes on the upper skull and cheek guards closed at the front, like the Hellenistic helmets. A further decoration of the helmet is the badge of honour, the horns of *corniculum* attached on the skull-cap.

The *gallica* armour is copied from Samothracian fragments.[xvii] It is reinforced with broad shoulderpieces in leather, painted red and with a bronze fitting of a snake around a staff, like the one shown on the Altar of Ahenobarbus. It is worn over a *subarmale* of simple leather. He bears the name of the commander on his *scutum* (shield), whose decoration is copied from a Etruscan sarcophagus of Tuscania.[xviii] Waist-belts were important with long mail shirts, for they helped to spread their considerable weight. His *gladius hispaniensis* has been reconstructed from the Mouriès sword, integrated with elements of the Delos sword. *Fasciae* for the army, inserted inside the shoes, are attested for the marching uniform by Pliny the Elder, referring to the period of the Social War.[xix]

The historian Lydus, quoting Varro, describes a statue of Aeneas in military uniform of the first century BC, equipped with mail armour and wearing *fasciae* of black cloth on his legs, called *ufantai* in Greek These *fasciae crurales* were only worn at that time in particular weather conditions or on high ground.[xx]

---

i   Compare it with Robinson, 1975, p. 43, pl. 95; see the *metopae* of the Mausoleum of Plancus, at Gaeta (**11**) and the monuments of Narbonensis, see Antonucci, 1996, p. 15; see also the the Aquileia reliefs, executed perhaps in honour of Caesar's legions who were stationed there in 58 BC, in Scrinari, 1972, pl. 598b; Antonucci, 1996, p. 29.

ii   Baldassarre and Pugliese, 1993, cat. 3 (painting in REGIO IX of Pompeii); the god Mars is shown with an Italic type of helmet (Montefortino or Buggenum), with the *geminae pinnae* on both sides.

iii A copper-alloy original from the first century BC has been recently sold in the auction of the Axel Guttmann Collection. It had two clasps on each side and two clasps on the shoulders for fastening.

iv   Plin., *HN*, XXXIII, 12, recounts the old aristocratic indignation of Brutus at the gold *fibulae* worn by his tribunes.

v   Plut., *Crass.*, XXIII; black wool was produced in Pollentium (Pollenzo) see Mart., *Apoph.*, 157.

vi   Prop., *El.*, IV, 10, 21.

vii Val. Max., *Mem.*, VI, 2, 7: '.candida fascia'; Cic., *Ad Att.*, II, 3: '. . . in fact I do not like his *caligae* and *fasciae cretatae* . . .'

viii Suet, *Caes.*, XXIV, 1; Plin., *HN*, XI, 44, 121: '. . . praeterea parvae avi, quae, ab illo galerita appellata quondam, postea Gallico vocabulo etiam legioni nomen dederat alaudae . . .' (small wings, that, with a certain helmet called after them, in following times from a Gallic word had given also the name to the legion *Alaudae*); see Bishop and Coulston, 2006, p. 66.

ix   Virg., *Aen.*, VI, 779.

x   Val. Max., *Mem.*, I; 8,6; see Cantilena, Cipriani and Sciarelli, 1999, cat. I, 29–30.

xi   Varro, *DLL*, V, 142; Caesar remembers that due to the sudden attack of the Nervii his legionaries did not have the time to put on their *insignia*, i.e. the crests or the plumes of the helmets.

xii From Gaeta (**11**), Glanum (**2e, 2f**), from Narbonne and from Urso, see Antonucci, 1996, pp. 15 and 44.

xiii Andren, 1940, p. 350;

xiv Antonucci, 1996, p. 45.

xv   Caes., *BA*, LXXXVI, 3; App., Εμφ. Πολ., II, 95.

xvi Plin., *HN*, XVI, 62, 186; see also **41**.

xvii Horn and Rüger, 1979, fig. 196.

xviii Polito, 1998, p. 116, fig. 48.

xix Plin., *HN*, VIII, 82, 221: '. . . By gnawing the silver shields at Lanuvium, mice prognosticated the Marsian war; and the death of our general, Carbo, at Clusium, by gnawing the bandages with which he wrapped his shoes.'

xx   Quint. *Decl.* XI, 3, 144: '. . . *Palliolum, sicut fascias quibus crura vestiuntur et focalia et aurium ligamenta* . . .' (As regards the short cloak, bandages used to protect the legs, mufflers and coverings for the ears).

2 Roman *milites* and *equites* from the Julii mausoleum, in situ, Saint-Remy de Provence (Glanum), 30–25 BC (*author's photos*).

In the Glanum monument, executed in the Augustan period to celebrate the Gallic wars of Caesar, the shape of some Hellenistic helmets used by the Roman *milites* has a metallic crest of Phrygian type (**b, g, h**). The use of helmets of Macedonian and Thracian origin was a propaganda move by the armies of the Julii, to link them with the Trojan origin of Rome. A *miles* wearing a Greek corselet is clearly visible, armed with a *pilum* (**g, h**). A muscled armour is worn by a Roman warrior or officer while fighting (**a**). Some *milites* (**b**) and cavalrymen (above) on the Glanum reliefs are fitted with a double crest (*insignia*) or *cornicularius* horn, as decorations for bravery

2a

2b

2c

2d

2e

2f

2g

2h

2i

The pre-Marian army was equipped with a long spear (*hasta longa*) in its maniples of *triarii*.[41] It was one of the earliest types of offensive weapon in the Roman infantry, furnished with a point (*cuspis*) and usually with a butt. Many modern scholars have thought that the spear was completely replaced by the *pilum* in the legionary armament, but excavations have shown that this kind of weapon was still widely employed by the *milites legionarii*.

Since prehistoric times, the spear point was most commonly leaf shaped. For this reason it is generally difficult to determine the age of the spears found in excavations – and also whether they belonged to the Roman army – except when they are found in a precise archaeological context.[42]

The *hasta* is archaeologically well attested by iron spearpoints from Caminreal,[43] Urso[44] and Alesia.[45] The spears from Caminreal can be said to come from the war with Sertorius. A great range of spear points have been excavated in the locality known as La Caridad; the variety is probably a result of the different specific uses of the weapon or, maybe, of the different factory methods. Some of the specimens have a tubular socket that is quite long (17 cm) compared to the leaf of the *cuspis*. Other examples show a very large leaf-shaped point (34 cm) and an ordinary socket (9.5 cm).[46]

The Alesia and Urso weapons have an average length of around 10 cm and have a rhomboid or leaf point, with a cylindrical haft. These would have been strong stabbing weapons, many of them with a central rib down the middle of the blade. Two specimens, found at the edge of the plain of Grésigny, are leaf-shaped.[47] Excavations in Alesia have also revealed the butts of spears.[48] These kind of spears could be used in a phalanx formation.[49] According to Plutarch, Pompeius Magnus fought with a spear (*doru*).[50]

Swords, Belts and Daggers

After throwing the *pila*, the Roman legionary charged with a sword (*gladius*)[51] in his hand. This short sword was the standard weapon of the Roman *miles* from the Consular period until the second century AD. The Roman sword was one of the symbols of the military *imperium*: element of virility, military virtues and perseverance. Every *gladius* was composed of a hilt (*capulus*), a guard for the hand (*mora*), a blade (*lamna*) furnished with a point (*mucro*) and was enclosed in its scabbard (*vagina*).

The Iberian type, called *hispanus* or *hispaniensis*, had been used by the legions since the third century BC, according to Livy and Polybius.[52] The double-edged weapon was used both for edgewise cutting and especially for thrusting in dense fighting

3 Hunting scene, Roman landlord or officer with his retinue hunting a wild boar, fresco from Villa Rustica at Gragnano near Stabiae, end first century BC (*author's photo, courtesy of the Soprintendenza per I Beni Archeologici delle Province di Napoli e Caserta*).

In this exceptional painting from a villa recently found near the site of the ancient Stabiae, a Roman officer and his retinue are performing the myth of the hunting of Meleagros. Note the red-pink *tunica militaris*, the green *sagum* edged with yellow, the blue *cothurni* and the cross-pieces. One of the men has a *pilos* of a Greek type upon his head, and the warriors defend themselves with shields of the el-Fayoum type, edged with blue

4 Statue of Augustus at Prima Porta in full colour, reconstruction by L. Fenger, 1886 (*courtesy of Staatliche Antike Sammlung and Glyptotheke Anschrift Munich*).

In 20 BC Augustus obtains from the Parthian King Phraates IV the restitution of the *signa* of Crassus. The event represents the central episode of the decoration of the leather armour worn by Augustus, which was lavishly painted and decorated. The colours of the original statue have been recently restored by the Italian archaeologists Liverani, Spada, Santa Maria and Morresi.[i] The artist who executed the statue would perhaps have copied an actual suit of armour commissioned for Augustus. There are several features that indicate that this was a real breastplate made of leather. Boiled leather, or *cuir boilli*, can attain a very high level of detail, as can be seen in an excellent revivalist piece from the sixteenth-century armour of Charles V, and can be easily fitted with metallic painted decorations. The vivid white colour of the armour's ground suggests a painted leather, rather than a painted bronze

---

i   Glyptothek, 2004, p. 186 ff.

formations, a technique in which the *milites* were particularly trained. The main characteristic of this sword, according to the medieval Suda Lexicon, was essentially the pattern-welding of the blade (*lamna*), which was forged in several hard layers of steel.[53]

The earlier samples show a somewhat longer blade and more elongated point than the later types, but it is possible that the *gladius* underwent a double evolution, from the Celtic and Hispanic swords. Nine specimens, probably of the earlier shape of the *gladius hispaniensis*, have been recovered, in very poor fragmentary condictions, in the votive deposit of weapons at Gracurris in Spain.[54] Dated to the time of Sertorius' revolt, they attest to the uninterrupted use of the swords of the Šmihel type, dated to the first half of the second century BC.[55] Compared to the other first-century BC swords, the better-preserved specimens show a narrow blade, like the previous typologies, being 5 cm wide at the sloped shoulders and narrowing to 4.5 cm towards the point. The broadening of the swords' blades is not visible as it is in some later specimens.

The most complete specimen of *gladius hispaniensis* of this period, with its metal-framed scabbard, comes from Delos,[56] dated to about 69 BC. It was the precursor of the Mainz-type *gladii* of the Imperial era, 4 cm longer, with an overall length of 76 cm and a blade length of just over 60 cm, but without a pronounced midrib. The wooden handle was covered by bronze fittings. More than twenty similar specimens, including a exemple from Mouriés (**PLATE I**), were found in Gallia.

Other swords found in the Alpine region, like the specimens of Boyer and Gué de l'Epine, are very similar to the specimen from Mouriés, as well as the variously dated specimens from Giubiasco, in Switzerland and Berry-Bouy, near Bourges. The Boyer sword (58–20 BC) presents a blade (67.2 cm length) with its sides curved inwards from the hilt but broadening before narrowing to the point. This characteristic (waisted blade) can be seen to some degree in many specimens from the Late Consular age, for example in the swords from Giubiasco and Nidau.[57]

Two blades (*lamnae*) and a scabbard of *gladii hispani* have been found in Alesia.[58] These are very similar to the Celtic swords of the type La Tène III, with an extremely sharp point (*mucro*). The Osuna sword[59] dates from the time of Caesar's campaigns in Spain. Its slightly waisted blade is 6 cm wide. At the hilt it narrows to 5 cm and has sloped shoulders. Peter Connolly, feeling that the point should begin 45 cm from the sword's shoulders, presumed an average point of 19–20 cm and a total length of 64–5 cm. The same length is visible on a *gladius hispaniensis* found in the Saône River, which some authors consider as a possible Caesarian-period sword (**5b**).[60] Its shape is interestingly very similar to that of the sword brandished by the *centurio* of the Arc d'Orange (**6, 6c, 315c**).

Two very important specimens from Sisak and Kupa are preserved in the archaeological collection of the Museum of Zagreb.[61] One of them has an elongated, almost completely

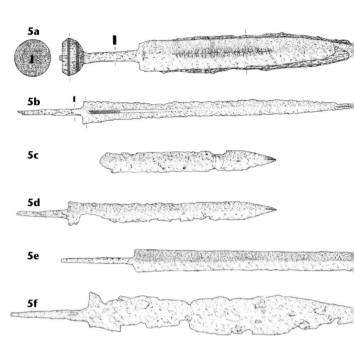

5 *Gladii* of the Mainz and Pompeii types, first century BC–first century AD (*Musée de Chalon, inv. 72.24.1/84.8.12/88.24.9/81.9.6/78.12.30; Musée de Mâcon inv. 193; ex Feugère; drawing by Elaine Norbury*).
    The second sword from the top, although badly corroded, was originally 64.2 cm long. Its shape is still that of the old *gladii*. The first sword still has in good condition part of its scabbard and pommel in lime wood; the pommel decorated by parallel lines. It is 55.9 cm long. The sixth sword – 67 cm long – still has the copper-alloy mouth fitting of its scabbard, showing traces of the alder wood used for the *vagina*. The Pompeii type swords are respectively 58, 48 and 31.8 cm long

preserved blade, relatively narrow and with a long point. It is slighty shorter than the Giubiasco specimen. It has a channel for the blood and the point is additionally reinforced, having a rectangular section. It is about 5 cm at its widest part. The second specimen is similar but longer, without a midrib on the blade and with the shoulders of the sword sloped, which is typical of the earlier Roman *gladii*. These swords were probably originally around 70 cm long. The swords have been dated by Radman-Livaja to 35 BC and to the first century BC respectively, but without ruling out the possibility of a slightly earlier origin.[62]

The dimensions of the swords mentioned generally show a blade less slim than the earlier specimens represented by the Šmihel swords. It seems that, from the time of the Delos specimen and until the last quarter of the first century BC, the blade underwent a rather gradual broadening, changing from 4.5 to 5 cm. All these swords confirm the statement of the Suda Lexicon about the steel manufacture of the blade, which was pattern-welded in layers and very strong.

The general employment of the *gladius hispaniensis* does not preclude the possibility that older short models of daggers were still in use: this is the case with the dagger found in the

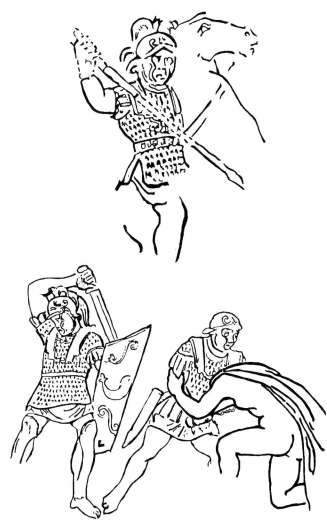

6 Roman *milites* and *equites* from the Arc d'Orange, 29 BC or AD 21 (*drawings above by Elaine Norbury, ex Coussin, author's photos overleaf*)

The carved reliefs of the Arc d'Orange are a mine of information about the Augustan–Tiberian army. Note the Roman centurion clad in ring-mail armour (**6, 6c, 315c**), the use of the cylindrical shield by the legionaries (**315r, 315x, 315z, 315aa**), the Roman cavalrymen equipped with the oval or even rhomboid shields complete with *umbo* (**6a, 6e, 315e, 315h, 315i, 315j, 315r**); following the Celtic models. Devices on the shields are the wings of Jupiter's eagle (**6a, 315r, 315z**), while the capricorn head on the centurion's shield probably indicates the *digma* of the *Legio II Augusta* (**6, 6c, 315c**). The shields of the *trophea* are marked with the names of the general, like MARIO, SACROVIR, DACURDO, CATUS, BODUACUS (**6g, 315b, 315u, 315v**), and a interesting mark (BO)UDILLUS AVOT (**6f**).[i] If some of the weapons in the *trophaea* are the representation of the booty taken at Actium by Agrippa, we can perhaps find there the devices of the marines of the fleet of Cleopatra and Antonius, or so it seems to be suggested by the hexagonal shield with the representation of an Ibis (**315b**). We should remember that the shields of the *classiarii* represented on Trajan's Column are also hexagonal.

On the arch, some legionaries and a centurion are already equipped with the new kind of helmet of the Weisenau typology (**6a, 6c, 315c, 315r, 315x, 315y**), alongside other infantrymen equipped with the Coolus–Haguenau and Buggenum helmet. Masked helmets (**315m, 315n, 315o, 315p**), Mainz daggers and worked leather belts (**315q, 315s**) are hanging from the various *trophaea*. Note the masked helmet embossed with hair and the whole face (**315m, 315n**), a prototype of the Kostol helmet (**271**)

grave of a Roman Legionary of Etruscan origin, found in his grave in Volterra, and variously dated to the second to first centuries BC (**7**).

The hilt (*capulus*) of the Roman sword was generally not metal, but made of bone or wood. An earlier hilt might be reconstructed in a hypothetical way (**PLATE I**) from the altar (*ara*) of Domitius Ahenobarbus – a monument executed shortly after the reforms of Marius[63] – where a *miles* shows a sword with a big pommel worn on the right side of the body,[64] and a sword's guard (*mora*) decorated with parallel lines. We cannot exclude, however, the presence of metal hilts as in the Celtic swords. The sword worn by the *milites* of the Osuna (Urso) relief is clearly a straight sword with a hilt and pommel of La Tène D1–2 typology, having metallic handguards (**8a, 8e**).[65] Particularly in Spain and in Gaul the first hilts of the *gladii* show a strong Celtic influence.

The metal frame scabbard (*vagina*) of Delos is very similar to those of previous Hispanic swords found in the graves of warriors who fought for and against the Romans during the Second Punic War, such as the scabbard from Osma.[66] But in this period the Romans, as shown on the Osuna sword,

---

i   I.e. *Boudillus fecit*, see CIL XII, 1231.

6a

6b

6c

6d

6e

6f

6g

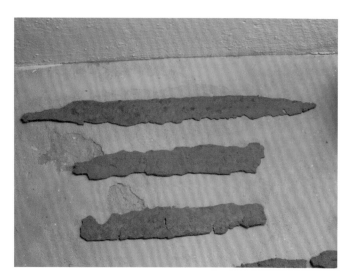

7 (Above, left and right) Tomb of *miles*, Volterra, with fragments of *umbo* and a well-preserved dagger blade, first century BC (*Volterra, Museum Guarnacci; courtesy of the museum*)

8 (Below and opposite page) Relief of Romano-Iberian *milites* from Urso (Osuna), first half of first century BC (*Cordoba, Museo Arquéologico Provincial; author's photo, courtesy of the museum*)
a) Detail of the sword, chain mail and felt armour. **b) c)** Details of the helmets. **d)** Detail of the sword. **e) f) g)** Details of the ring-mail armour, the *coactile* and the *subarmale*. **h) i) j)** Details of the greaves

8a

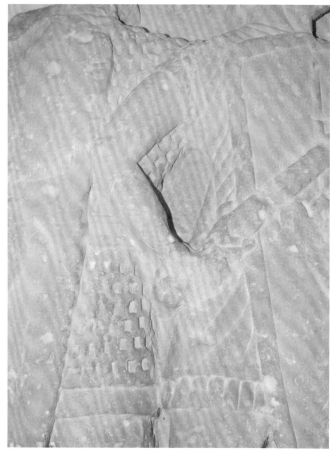

8b

8c

8d

8e

8f

8g

8h

8i

8j

added a fourth ring for suspension, so that it could be worn on either hip, with the front facing outwards. The Delos scabbard was made of leather-covered wood, wrapped by the surviving bronze wires. Other scabbards were made of iron. The Arch of Carpentras (Carpentoratum), erected in the first century AD to celebrate the victories of Caesar in Gaul, shows iron scabbards decorated with the Roman number X on the sheath, and with four suspension rings as on the scabbard from Delos (**9**). The number X might refer to the identifying number of the *legio*.[67]

The scabbard chape, a fitting that enclosed the scabbard structure to give it strength and uniformity, is rarely preserved in archaeological finds. Its triangular shape and round finial is, however, easily visible on the figurative monuments (**9g**). Important findings of first-century BC swords have come from Croatia. One of them is a piece of the scabbard chape, which, by comparison with other similar specimens found in

Magdalensberg, Comacchio and Kalkriese could be dated to the Late Consular or early Augustan ages.[68] The reticulate fitting, made of thin metal plate, corresponds with the carvings visible on the Arch of Carpentras (**9g**), and with a decorative relief from Croatia and today preserved in the museum of Split (**158**). This kind of fitting was not riveted, but attached by bending the arms around the wooden and leather finial of the scabbard.

As well as weapons, the belt was an essential part of the soldier's equipment. The legionaries, in the first century BC, wore a belt called *cingulum militiae*, formed by a leather core decorated by metallic fittings. *Cingulum* was the true name of the belt of the Roman soldier. It was used between the first century BC and the second century AD to indicate an indispensable part of military equipment, the belt, as an insignia that commanded respect and which designated a man who was subject to military discipline. To take the belt (*cingi*) was synonymous with being a soldier; to be deprived of it (*discingi*) meant to be reduced in rank, a military punishment that was applied to the single

9 (Below and opposite page) Details of Roman weapons and equipment from the Arch of Carpentras (Carpentoratum), last quarter of the first century BC (*author's photos*)

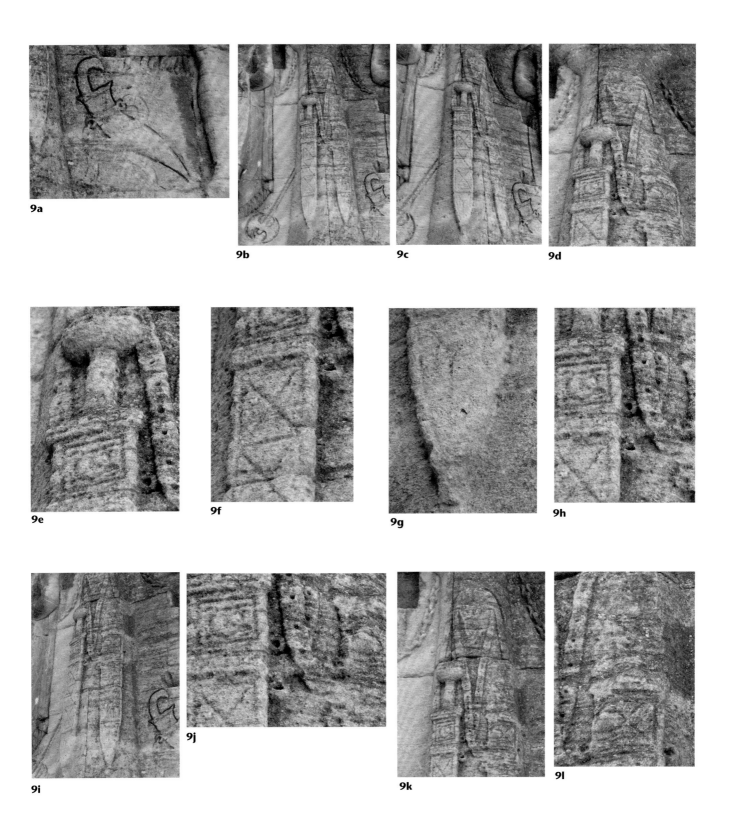

9a

9b

9c

9d

9e

9f

9g

9h

9i

9j

9k

9l

10 Roman weapons, carved reliefs from Avignon, first century BC–first century AD (*Museum Calvet, Avignon, author's photos, courtesy of the museum*)

The deeds of the campaign against Sacrovir are probably immortalised on a now lost monument, the fragments of which are now in the Museum Calvet in Avignon. Note the details of the centurion's greave and the highly detailed Mainz type sword

soldier, to the officers, to a *cohors* and even to a whole legion.[69] So when the Consul Gaius Curio, in 75 BC, was campaigning near Dyrrhachium in the war against the Dardani,

> and one of the five legions, having mutinied, had refused service and declared it would not follow his rash leadership on a difficult and dangerous enterprise, he led out four legions in arms and ordered them to take their stand in the ranks with weapons drawn, as if in battle. Then he commanded the mutinous legion to advance without arms and belts [*discincta legio*], and forced its members to strip for work and cut straw under the eyes of armed guards. The following day, in like manner, he compelled them to strip and dig ditches, and by no entreaties of the legion could he be induced to renounce his purpose of withdrawing its standards, abolishing its name and distributing its members to fill out other legions.[70]

The belt was useful in holding the heavy weight of the chain mail, when used (**315c, 315e, 315l**), and was at all times the symbol of military service, the *militia*. The soldier was immediately recognised as a soldier by wearing it, even without other parts of the military equipment.

The *cingulum militiae* was, in the first century BC, still of the type found in Numantia,[71] with ornamental bronze plates and buckles. This belt is visible on the soldiers of the Consular age represented on the Saint-Remy monument (**2, 2c, 2g, 2h**). Here, infantrymen and cavalrymen are wearing – together with the baldric (*balteus*) from which the sword is suspended on the left or right side – a wide belt that goes over the armour at waist height. Some of the warriors still show a system of double-crossed belts derived from Greeks and Etruscans. Sometimes the belts were simply fastened by central double buckles of Celtic derivation, corresponding to the last La Tène typology.[72]

The sword belt was often called *balteus* or *balteum* in the sources. Although this word is usually associated with the baldric – the belt slung across the body from one shoulder to the opposite hip, to which the sword is attached – the Roman sources use *balteus* or *balteum* to indicate the sword belt in general, regardless of whether it refers to the waist belt or to an effective baldric. So the words *balteus* and *cingulum* were both used to indicate the military belt to which the sword was attached.

The sword could in fact also be worn slung across the body or attached to the side belt (*gladio cinctum*).[73] This is clearly visible on the altar of Domitius Ahenobarbus and on many details of the Arch of Carpentras and the Arc d'Orange (**9a, 9b, 9c, 9d, 9e, 9k, 315s**), where the plates of the *cingula*[74] and the fastening buckles are clearly visible. With the Delos sword were found a plate, a belt buckle and two small buckles, which helped to reconstruct a possible system of attaching the sword to the side belt.[75] The same system could have been used for the Osuna sword, even though the buckles and the belt plate are quite different from those of Delos. The two small

11 *Metopae* reliefs from Munatius Plancus mausoleum, in situ, Gaeta (*author's photos*)

Munatius Plancus was Caesar's *legatus* Caesar in Gallia. The *metopae* of his funerary monument offer very interesting details of the Roman equipment. Agen–Port helmets of Robinson's type B and *gladii* with spherical pommels are clearly visible, as are the use of *baltei* or baldrics for swords buckles were used to strap the sword to the belt, without being visible from the outside; perhaps this is why the attachment system of the sword is never visible on first-century BC military tombstones. At other times the scabbard was fastened to the belt by passing the belt through an iron ring attached to the back of the scabbard.

The use of a baldric is clearly attested in many monuments, such as the *metopae* of Munatius Plancus on his mausoleum in Gaeta (**11**) and the reliefs of the Julii mausoleum in Saint-Remy (**2a**, **2c**, **2d**, **2g**, **2h**). This last monument seems to echo Caesar's descriptions of the brave centurions Vorenus and Pullo:[76]

> In that legion there were two very brave men, centurions, who were now approaching the first ranks, T. Pullo, and L. Vorenus. They used to have continual disputes between them over which of them should be preferred, and every year used to contend for promotion with the utmost animosity. When the fight was going on most vigorously before the fortifications, Pullo, one of them, says, 'Why do you hesitate, Vorenus? or what [better] opportunity of signalling your valour do you seek? This very day shall decide our disputes.' When he had uttered these words, he proceeds beyond the fortifications, and rushes on that part of the enemy which appeared the thickest. Nor does Vorenus remain within the rampart, but respecting the high opinion of all, follows close after. Then, when an inconsiderable space intervened, Pullo throws his javelin [*pilum*] at the enemy, and pierces one of the multitude who was running up, and while the latter was wounded and slain, the enemy cover him with their shields, and all throw their weapons at the other and afford him no opportunity of retreating. The shield of Pullo is pierced and a javelin is fastened in his belt [*balteus*]. This circumstance turns aside his scabbard [*vagina*] and obstructs his right hand as he attempts to draw his sword; the enemy crowd around him when [thus] embarrassed. His rival runs up to him and succours him in this emergency. Immediately the whole host turn from Pullo to Vorenus, supposing the other to be pierced through by the javelin. Vorenus rushes on briskly with his sword and carries on the combat hand to hand, and having slain one man, for a short time drove back the rest; pushing on too eagerly, slipping into a hollow, he fell. To him, in his turn, when surrounded, Pullo brings relief; and both having slain a great number, retreat into the fortifications amidst the highest applause. Fortune so dealt with both in this rivalry and conflict that the one competitor was a succour and a safeguard to the other, nor could it be determined which of the two appeared worthy of being preferred over the other.

The passage seems to support the circumstance that the sword of Pullo was worn with a baldric, as confirmed by the images of the Julii mausoleum, and that here the word *balteus* refers to a true baldric. However, the gravestone representation of Minucius Lorarius (**PLATE IIa**), a *centurio* of the Caesarian period, has the sword worn on his left side in its scabbard and

attached to a side belt, which gives us a clear picture of a possible alternative sword suspension system for the centurions.

In general the sword was usually worn on the right side for the *milites gregarii*, on the left side by the officers.[77] It was probably not an absolute rule, unless the Glanum monument and the Arc d'Orange represent officers only: many Romans engraved here wear the *gladius* suspended by a baldric worn on the right shoulder of the body, or attached on the left side (**2**, **315z**).

It seems that the military dagger, the *pugio*, was undoubtely of Iberian origin and adopted by the Romans during the fights against the Iberian tribes.[78] Roman specimens of the early first century BC come from Cáceres and Gracurris, as well as other sites in Spain.[79] It was generally a double-edged dagger, with the central part in many specimens narrower than the top and the bottom part. In the Late Consular period the midrib of the blade was very pronounced, in the shape of a rectangular bulge.[80] The handle consisted of a tang covered by a bone or wooden grip, and had metal fittings. The double-disc handle was the most ancient shape: it is visible on a late Republican specimen from Oberaden.[81] Other examples with a double-disc handle were discovered in the Saône River and in a blade from Alesia.[82] However, all these finds do not constitute a proof that the *pugio* was already fitted to all the *milites* as part of their standard equipment. The written sources[83] only refer to officers' *pugiones*. Based on this information, Antonucci has suggested that in Caesar's time the *pugio* was mainly given to the officers, and was worn on the right side of the body, as shown on the *stela* of the Centurio Minucius (**PLATE IIa**). This thesis is supported by the fact that, from the first century BC, the sword and the *pugio* were among the imperial insignia.[84] Antonius, according to Dio Cassio,[85] used always to appear in sword (*xiphos*) and purple garments, and was joined by his lictors and soldiers; in another passage, by Florus,[86] he is mentioned as having a Persian dagger (*akinakes*) and one gold staff (*aureum baculum*). Horace[87] also mentions the *medus acinaces* (Persian *akinakes*) used in warlike banquets! In any case, this type of weapon soon became a standard part of the equipment of the *milites*.

Some monuments from Narbonensis and Tauroentum (Le Brusq) show precious specimens of *pugio*, worn by officers. The first are virtually identical to the actual specimens from Alesia and Castra Caecilia. The second, showing a single-edged blade with the hilt in the shape of an eagle's head, confirms that these daggers already existed in the first century BC.[88] This was the so-called *parazonium*, a dagger or short sword of Greek origin, already visible in the hands of the *tribunus* of the altar of Domitius Ahenobarbus.[89] True swords of these type are visible among the trophies represented on the Arc d'Orange (**315q**, **315u**, **315v**). Their colour, in paintings from Pompeii, is sometimes rendered as yellow, probably representing a gold-plated hilt and scabbard, or white, perhaps to show an ivory hilt and scabbard.[90]

Shields

In general the legionary shield (*scutum*) was of the same typology and shape as that of the previous age; the texts are generally silent about the kind of *scutum* reserved to the legions in the first century BC. Polybius, however, gives a detailed description of the convex *scutum* used by the Romans in the second century BC: the *milites* were now equipped with a curved oblong *scutum*, furnished with *spina*, a characteristic of the Roman battleline, derived from the combination of Italic[91] and Celtic models.

Polybius uses the Greek word *thyreos* for the shield.[92] The convex surface measured 'two and a half feet' in width and 'four feet' in length (making it about 75×120 cm), the thickness at the rim was a 'palm's breadth'. It was made of two wooden planks glued together – using the technique of the reversed thread with natural ox glue, the outer surface being covered first with linen canvas and then with calf skin. Its upper and lower rims were strengthened by an iron edging that protected it from descending blows and from damage when rested on the ground. It also had an iron central boss (*umbo*) to turn aside blows by stones, pikes and heavy missiles in general.[93]

The grip of the *scutum* was perpendicular to the central spike, allowing the shield to be moved in any direction, as can be seen on the altar of Ahenobarbus.[94] This last sculptural source contains one of the most clear representations of the shield as described by Polybius.

A complete specimen of this kind of shield, larger, plywood, perfectly corresponding to the above-mentioned sculptures, has been found in the dry Egyptian desert, from Kasr[95] el-Harit,[96] in the oasis of el-Fayyum (**13**). It was recovered in an excellent state thanks to the climatic conditions. It measures 128 cm in length and 63.5 cm in width. Three layers of thin wooden laths (possibly birch wood) were glued together, laid with the outer ones horizontal, giving it the curved form that is also visible on the monuments (**2d**). There were nine vertical strips of between 6 and 10 cm wide (**13**), and forty horizontal strips that were between 2.5 and 5 cm wide. Originally a layer of lamb's wool felt, attached by stitching around the edge, would have covered the back and the front of the shield, which was

then lavishly painted. The inner felt covering overlapped the outer surface by about 5–6 cm.[97]

The shield was reinforced by a wooden 'barleycorn' boss with a vertical rib (*spina*) divided into three sections (**13**), fixed above and below by metal nails on the surface of the shield. This gave the shield much more strength in its central part, while the edges were less thick, giving more flexibility near the rim. The interior of the central boss was – as shown in the monuments – hollowed out and furnished with a horizontal handgrip. Remains of rings for the attachment of carrying straps were also found. No traces of metal *umbo* or the metal lining mentioned by Polybius to protect the rims or the edges were found on the shield, but the metallic *umbo* is also missing from the carved monument of Ahenobarbus. Bishop and Coulston suggested that the shield would weigh 10 kilos, which would not have been so difficult for a professional warrior to carry who was trained to march, fight and kill.

The colours have now disappeared from the leather fragments of the Fayyum shield but in the reconstruction by Racinet (**14**), who saw the traces of the colour on the altar of Ahenobarbus while they were still there, the shield is painted in red *carminium*, with the wooden 'barleycorn' painted yellow.[98] A similar shield of a warrior, from a painting in the necropolis of Porto, although scarcely visible today, is painted in yellow (**15**). The same yellow-brown colour is visible also on shields of the same type represented in a painting from Stabiae, where they are also edged with blue (**3**).

Today it is impossible to say if the Fayyum shield was a Roman one, a Ptolemaic model borrowed from the Romans or a shield of a Galatian mercenary in the Ptolemaic army, because the shield was discovered in 1900 by scholars looking for papyrus documents.[99] Whatever the case, the shape of this shield was that of the Roman army in the second and first centuries BC.

The reliefs at Urso (Osuna)[100] show a very interesting variation of the shield's shape: a long trapezoidal *scutum* that is wider at the top, not curving or oval in shape, and narrower at the bottom (**8**). This kind of shield is very similar to those described by Livy as carried in 310 BC by the Samnite warriors.[101] We should remember also that Sallustius[102] said that the Romans had copied from the Samnites '*arma et tela militaria*' i.e. the defences and the javelins (defensive and offensive weapons). Antonucci[103] suggests that, considering the high number of Pompeian soldiers enlisted in Picenum and Umbria, the reliefs at Urso represent soldiers that still preserved an ancient part of their heritage in their panoply. Many Italics, moreover were enlisted in the legions after the Social War, and this kind of *scutum* is perfectly visible on the warriors of a Late Consular painting from Esquiline (**16**). A variant of the rectangular *scutum* of the Marian or Caesarian period is visible on one monument from Sora (**PLATE Ic, 17**).

The *parma velitaris*, the typical shield of the light skirmishers known as *velites*, was replaced by Marius with the *parmula*

12 Detail of the fastening system of the mail armour from Cugir, first century BC–first century AD (*photo Museum Alba Julia; courtesy of the museum*)

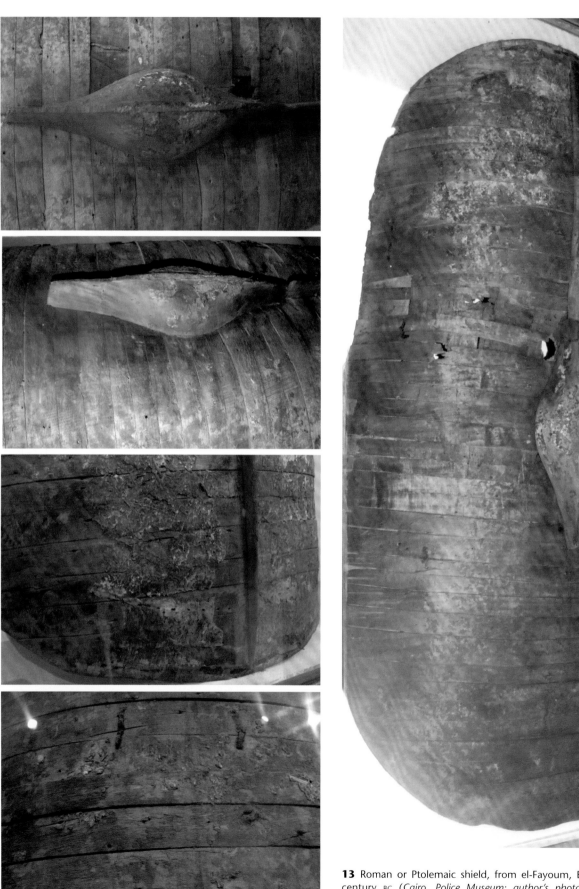

13 Roman or Ptolemaic shield, from el-Fayoum, Egypt, second–first century BC (*Cairo, Police Museum; author's photos, courtesy of the museum*)

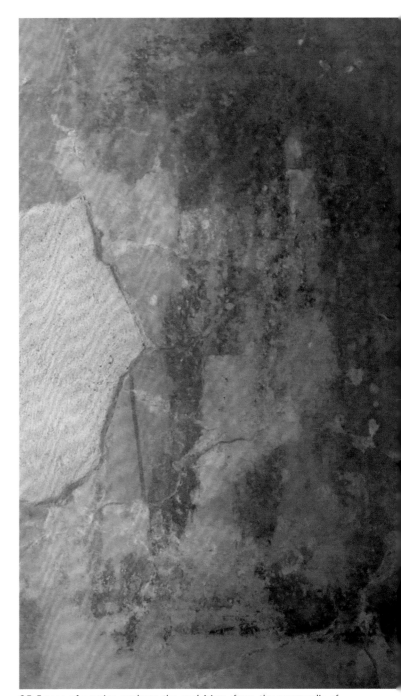

14 *Tribunus* of Altar of Domitius Ahenobarbus, Louvre Altar (*Ara*) (*ex Racinet, author's collection*).

The *milites* on the Louvre altar[i] wear helmets related to the Montefortino type and to the more elaborate Italic or Hellenic version of the Attic type. The Celtic helmet of the Agen–Port type is for the first time[ii] represented as being worn by *milites*. Racinet transformed the tribune of the Louvre relief into a *triarius* but kept the original colours. The armour is a linen one, with a rectangular *kardiophylax*[iii] over it, perhaps the same kind as provided for *hastati*, *principes* and *triarii* having a *census* (social rank) lower than 10,000 drachmae. The main armour was originally painted white, with the *pteryges* blue edged, and the pectoral in yellow

15 Fresco of warrior, perhaps the god Mars, from the necropolis of Porto, near Ostia, first century BC–first century AD (*author's collection*)

---

i   Liberati, 1997, p. 32.
ii Antonucci, 1996, p. 32.
iii Polybius, *Prag.*, VI, 23,14;

16 Fresco fragments from the Esquiline, Statilii grave, first century BC–first century AD (*Rome, Museo nazionale Romano, author's photo, by kind permission of the Ministero per I beni e le attività culturali – Soprintendenza Speciale per i beni archeologici di Roma*)

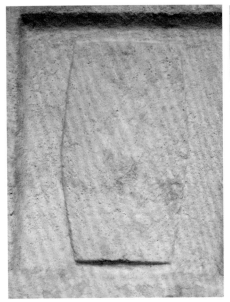

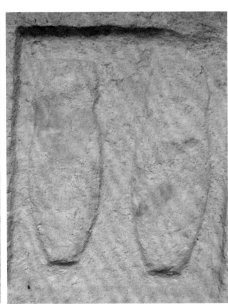

17 'Doric' frieze from Sora, in Valle del Liri, representing the weapons of a Marian or Caesarian *miles*, first or second half of the first century BC: *gladius*, *scutum* and masked helmet of Negau type with *cornicula* as distinctive badge (*author's photo, courtesy of D.ssa Alessandra Tanzilli*)

In the funerary reliefs arms and armours were engraved to show, through precise detailing of the uniform and weaponry, the *cursus honorum* of the wearer.[i] It is worth noting that the birthplace of this warrior was not far from the birthplace of the great Marius

i Franzoni, 1987, p. 105.

bruttiana when he created the auxiliary troops, giving the *parmula bruttiana* to the *leves milites* (light infantrymen).[104] It was a small oval shield that perhaps can be identified with the Lucanian shield by comparing it with coins of the second century BC from Bruttium.[105] The shield was made of leather-covered wicker. In fact Polybius describes this shield as *bursa*, i.e. tanned leather made of several layers, referring to the ox cover of the shield.

Shields were reinforced by a central metallic boss called the *umbo*. A rounded-oval specimen of an *umbo* has been found in a legionary grave of Volterra (**7**), dated to the first half of the first century BC. This circular *umbo* is very similar to the boss shown on the above-mentioned shields of trapezoidal shape, as it finds a good artistic parallel with the oval *umbo* of the Osuna relief (**8**). A lot of specimens of oval iron *umbones* were found in Gallia (Alesia) and Germania, which could have come from late versions of the Late Consular shield. These *umbones* were of the 'butterfly' type, with a central boss and two lateral wings, and of conical shape, bossed along the rim.[106] Remains of the iron rims described by Polybius that constituted the metallic framework have also been found in Alesia.

According to Vegetius, the shields of the ten cohorts of the *legio* were marked by a device (*digmata* or insignia).[107] This was already the rule in the Caesarian period; the X Legion could have the zodiacal sign of Caesar, the Taurus (bull), as *digmata*, recorded in the African campaign as *signum decumanorum*.[108]

A very important passage by Quintilianus describes in detail a *miles gregarius* of Marius, with the name of the general inscribed on the shield of each soldier ('the name of C. Marius inscribed on the shield').[109] Caesar also mentions names inscribed on the shields,[110] and this statement is further confirmed by the Arausio (Arc d'Orange) sculptures (**6**).

PLATE II (*from left to right*)

a Minucius T.F. Lorarius, *centurio* of the *Legio III Martia*, 40–30 BC: the reconstruction is taken from his *stela* preserved in Padua Archaeological Museum, while the colours of his dress are deduced from contemporary colour references. The *tunica militaris* visible on the monument follows the description of Quintilianus, and its colour is taken from the paintings of the Esquiline frescoes (**16**), where a possible centurion is represented amongst the other fighters.

The cloak (*sagum*) is fastened on his breast by a *fibula* of the Aucissa type, as is shown very clearly on his *stela*, a kind of *fibula* already widespread in the military sphere from the early Augustan period.[i] The wide belt at the waist has a series of laces for attaching weapons. Fastened in different places from the *balteus*, always by means of laces, its dagger or *pugio* is closed in a scabbard with metallic frame and spherical tip. Note his *gladius hispaniensis* with trilobate pommel: this shape finds analogies with *gladii* represented on other Roman monuments.[ii] The sword was worn on the left side, as shown also on the *stelae* of the centurions of the first century AD. As a symbol of his rank he carries the *vitis* or vine-branch staff reserved for centurions and *evocati*[iii] from the first Consular era. The *vitis* represented a staff of command, in some ways having the same function as the *virga* or *vindicta* of *lictores*. It was often used to inflict corporal punishment on the soldiers who were Roman citizens. His shoes are closed *calcei* probably furnished with an extra reinforced tip

b *Centurio* of the *Legio VII, VIII* or *IX*, Aquileia, 58 BC: among the arms sculpted on the Aquileia reliefs in honour of the *legiones* of Caesar stationed there in 58 BC, there are centurions' weapons,[iv] used in this reconstruction. The centurion has been equipped with an Agen–Port helmet furnished with a *crista transversa argentata*: Vegetius said that the plumes of the centurions' helmets were this kind of silver crest, so as to be easily recognised by his men on the battlefield.

On the Aquileia reliefs a *corium* is represented, an anatomical armour in leather (easily recognised because it is pleated on the left side in the original sculpture), here reconstructed, and furnished with *humeralia* and a small protective collar. It is worn over a second protection in linen with *pteryges*. Over the armour the brave *centurio* proudly wears his *dona militaria*, here copied from the Rubiera gravestone:[v] a leather harness supporting twelve decorated *phalerae* surrounding a winged Nike (Victory) where the straps cross on the breast. Professor Ortalli has interpretated the Victory as referring to the *signa* of the cohorts it belonged to, the praetorians. The monument of Rubiera is dated to the early Augustan age, so the *dona miltaria* of Caesar's legions would have been the same. The *gladius*, with silvered hilt and scabbard, is worn on the left side of the body, as shown on the Aquileia monument. On the Aquileia reliefs a pair of greaves are represented, fixed with a strap, and decorated at the knee with a gorgon's head

i   Franzoni, 1987, p. 46.
ii   Franzoni, 1987, pl. XIV, 3 and p. 47 no. 3, with reference to a similar *gladius* worn by the *tribunus militaris* L. Appuleius.
iii Daremberg and Saglio, 1873–1917, V, 1, col. 929.

iv   Antonucci, 1996, pp. 28–9.
v   Feugère, 2003, p. 55; Franzoni, 1987, p. 106; the great block upon which the harness with *phalerae* is engraved was part of a cylindrical funerary monument.

In the Spanish war Caesar tells of two *milites*, 'the devices of the shields shining in chiselled metal'.[111] Suetonius moreover states that Caesar wished his soldiers to be equipped with arms and armour decorated in gold and silver inlay, for a better psychological impact on the enemy, and because the soldiers were much braver if they were afraid to lose their valuable equipment.[112] Robinson has suggested that this only applied to the favourite X Legion, and so perhaps the other units had copper- and bronze-inlay panoplies.[113] Fragments of different friezes were excavated in Alesia in 1864,[114] showing both bosses and metallic sheets shaped like flames, that constituted both decoration and metal reinforcements on the shields. Thunderbolts and lightning symbols begin to appear on Roman shields as metallic appliqués; monuments from Narbonensis show these images, probably representing the winged thunderbolts of Jupiter, alluding to the *Imperium* of Caesar. In the Imperial age, these were popular devices on the legionary shield (**PLATE II, 6a, 315i, 315r, 315z**). In some coins of the Caesarian period similar shield devices are shown, such as eight- or five-pointed stars. Antonucci correctly suggests that these are representations of the *sidus Iulium*, the symbol of the Julii, the good stars under which Caesar was born. The device is clearly visible (**2g, 2h**) on a round shield carried by a *miles* on the Julii monument at Glanum (Saint-Remy). It was probably engraved on Octavianus' own shield, as shown in a coin of 32–29 BC.[115]

A less well-known section of the Palestrina mosaic shows a legionary shield hung on a pillar.[116] The shield has a white field, black blazon and yellow rim. This might represent the copper, the bronze and the iron of the metallic appliqués. These colours are also further confirmed in the descriptions of the Hispanic War. Other shields from Narbonensis are shown with a laurel crown chiselled all around the rim, and a single internal grip surrounded by rhomboid motifs.[117]

Many figurative monuments (**2a, 2c, 315z**) often show a double grip inside the *scutum*. Such handgrips are visible on the *metopae* of the Plancus monument (**11**) and on the Aquileia reliefs dated to the Caesarian period. The shield had a leather cover (*tegimen*), mentioned in Plutarch's description of the marching soldiers of Lucullus[118] and by Caesar on more occasions.[119] Upon it was often embroidered the *legio*'s symbol.

The old round or half-round *clypeus* of Greek origin, widely employed by the Romans of the Early Consular period, was still used ,[120] but it was mainly reserved for the officers, in the form of valuable specimens, often engraved and painted. A splendid example is visible on a sculpture from the Basilica Aemilia in Rome, where it is carried by a Roman officer depicted on a monument of the Jugurthine War. Engraved on the surface is a winged horse (Pegasus), a device that was probably linked with the old Sabine tribes of the Tities.[121] The officer on the Ahenobarbus altar, though, is furnished with a half oval *clypeus*.[122] Its use by the *milites gregarii* is still attested by the

Glanum monument (**2**), as well as by coins of Aquilius dated to 71 BC.[123]

Officers' shields were round following the Hellenistic style and often richly engraved with heads of gods and divinities to protect the wearer, as attested by the monument of the first century BC[124] from Colonia Zama (Kbor Klib),[125] which shows an *imago clipeata* of Diana or Artemis Tauropolos, of clear Hellenistic derivation. In the Pompeii House of the Impluvium similar shields (*clipei*) are painted with a silvered surface. Other frescoes show a shining bronze surface. A vivid depiction of one such shield, maybe decorated for the same Emperor Augustus, is given by Virgil in the description of Aeneas' shield.[126]

A wide range of engraved shields of this type are represented on the frieze from the Campidoglio or Theatre of Marcellus, a monument made *c.* 91 BC (**18**).[127] It shows a hoplite shield, having as blazon an eagle seated on a winged lightning bolt,[128] representing the eagle of Jupiter holding the palm of victory. The shield is decorated by two festoons made of laurel crowns. This was a genuine decoration of this kind of shield (*ornamenta triumphalia*), when it was carried in parade. A second shield is engraved with the image of a Dioscurus on horseback, armed with a spear (**18**). A third shield is decorated with the head of a goddess wearing an Etrusco-Corinthian helmet, perhaps the personification of Roma–Virtus (**PLATE Ia**). A fourth shield has got a peculiar quadrangular shape, and incised on its surface is the figure of a dragon.[129] This last may be a Numidian device, since the frieze was erected by Bocchus of Mauretania to celebrate the victory over Jugurtha, although other authors interpreted it as a Mithridatic device.[130] It was copied from an original that perhaps after the triumph was used by a Roman officer. Engraved bronze officers' shields with blazons of a Hellenistic typology are also visible in paintings.[131]

Helmets

In the first century BC a great variety of helmets (*galeae* or *cassides*)[132] came into use among the legions, heavily influenced by the Hellenistic world and the new patterns of Celtic derivation. According to Varro,[133] the two words originally indicated the leather helmet (*galea*) and the metallic one (*cassis*). In Caesar's works both words referred to the metallic helmet, but *galea* most probably was used with reference to a light helmet, *cassis* to the heavier helmet.[134]

The absence of the concept of mass production in the ancient world, and the constant need for the Roman army to equip its warriors with all the different parts of the panoply, created an infinite variety of helmets over the centuries, which cannot be linked to an absolute chronology or classification. A helmet could have been produced in the first century BC and used, with modifications and restorations, until the end of the first century AD, alongside new types of helmets in the same legion or military corps. In the first century BC the comparison

18 Weapons and armour from the Campidoglio monument, probably a dedication to Sulla from Bocchus of Mauretania for the victory over Jugurtha, 91 BC (*Rome, Musei Capitolini; Studio Tomatofarm*).

The symbol of the Dioscurii was linked with the equestrian order, favoured by Sulla. Two of the *loricae* represented are probably those of centurions, considering the crests of the helmets. The single *lorica*, of Hellenistic type, has a luxurious decoration with winged victories chiselled on the *humeralia* and a Gorgon appliqué at the centre of the breast. The high commanders had, following the Hellenistic style, the *zona militaris* knotted at the armour's breast: it was a purple band, a rank badge. The presence of simpler palm trees on the *humeralia* of the *centurio* armour is probably a rank badge. Both the *loricae* have lappets directly sewn on the borders

between the archaeological and the iconographical sources allow us to see the following models:

1.   helmets of Etrusco-Italic tradition;
2.   helmets of new Celtic pattern and derivation;
3.   helmets of Greco-Italic tradition;
4.   local varieties.

The Etrusco-Italic tradition of the Montefortino style of helmet (*galea*)[135] continued in use, as shown on the altar of Domitius

Ahenobarbus, preserving its ogival shape but showing a slow evolution with the neck guard increasing in size down to the Early Principate.[136] Generally the helmet was composed of a bronze bowl made from one piece of metal in a bulbous shape and drawn up to the apex to terminate in a hemispherical knob; the lower rim presents a short sloping neck guard and a bold border, often filled above with horizontal lines and flutings. The helmet was cast in bronze, and further shaped by a process of progressive hammering.[137] The conical shape of this helmet was probably designed to absorb the impact of strikes coming from above; it is no coincidence that in the military slang of that age it was called *conum* (cone).[138] The cheekguards, made of thick bronze, were attached by means of two rivets to the bowl.

A very rare specimen of this category comes from the dragging of the river Kupa, near Sisak.[139] It differs from the usual Montefortino type because the decorative knob was not cast together in one piece with the helmet (as in the other helmets of the same type), but riveted to it. This could be dated to the first half of the first century BC (**19**).

In Spain a helmet from Quintana Redonda (Soria)[140] from the war against Sertorius shows a scaled knob and waves on the neck guard, typical of the second-century BC Montefortino type, although the helmet comes from a first-century BC context. There is a similar helmet from the Celtiberian site of Piquete de la Atalaya, where the plates for the internal fastenings of the lost cheekguards are still visible (**20**).[141] The helmet, however, is without decoration. The production of these kinds of helmets of Italic tradition decreased in quality because of the demands of equipping huge armies, especially during the civil wars. The production was linked to the idea of achieving a simple and practical protection without many decorative elements,[142] so the fabrication of the helmets was often associated with low-quality workshops. The thin metal plate of the bowl of the archaeological specimens derived in fact from a simpler workmanship. The bad quality of these helmets is recorded by the sources describing how sometimes they were covered by wicker protections (*viminea tegimenta*), like those of Pompeius' soldiers during the siege of Dyrrachium in 48 BC, which were seriously damaged by the missiles of Caesar's slingers and archers.[143]

Very similar to the Montefortino type is the Buggenum type.[144] This is derived from earlier Etrusco-Celto-Italic types, but very much simplified in manufacture or decoration, which is very scarce or sometimes even missing on the lower rim. These helmets are from the mid-first century BC[145] and many examples have been found in south-western areas of France and the Iberian Peninsula.[146] In these helmets the apex is slighter smaller, round and empty to allow the insertion of the plume;[147] the neck guard is beginning to get bigger. The cheek guards in some specimens were attached to the bowl with only one rivet. One relevant specimen, from Kulpa near Sisak (Croatia), still bears on the neck guard the inscription *SCIP IMP*, allowing us to identify it as having belonged to the army of P. Scipio Cornelius Nasica, consul in 49 BC.[148]

From the Rhine near Mainz comes a helmet that is a further development of the Etrusco-Italic tradition.[149] Its shape is very similar to the helmets worn by the *milites* represented on a urn from Volterra, showing the siege of the city by Sulla in 88 BC, although ostensibly a depiction of the mythological episode of the Seven against Thebes (**21**). The helmet in the sculpture is worn in exactly the opposite way to what is commonly

19 Roman helmet from Sisak, first half of the first century BC (*Zagreb Archaeological Museum, ex Radman-Livaja*)

20 Roman helmet of Montefortino type C, from Beligiom (Piquete de la Atalaya), Spain, beginning of the first century BC (*Zaragoza, Museum; courtesy of the museum*)

interpreted,[150] with the part believed to be the neck guard worn at the front.

The process of simplification of the common legionary helmet is visible in the helmet of the Coolus–Mannheim type,[151] preserved in heavier and lighter types,[152] where the apex of the Montefortino helmet disappeared altogether. The helmet is always derived from the Italic tradition, but with a strong influence from Celtic armourers and metalworkers. The widespread distribution of these helmets throughout the army probably begins during the Gallic Wars, when Gallic armourers in the Coolus district were used to supply the legions.[153] The first specimen of this category is considered to be the one from Madrague de Giens, dated to about 70 BC, but many helmets of this type have been found in Gaul,[154] suggesting that this was one of the most widely used kinds of head protection by Caesar's *milites*.

The bowl of the heavier helmet is hemispherical, with a slight hint of neck guard on the back in some specimens. Sometimes a scarce decoration is provided on the lower rim. The lighter helmet shows a slightly globular shape, with two holes on each side of the bowl for the attachment of the chin strap (*vinculum*).

The first Coolus helmets were provided with leather chin straps; the cheek guards are often missing from the preserved specimens, just simple side holes suggest the use of a leather *vinculum* as an under-chin strap. However, in some examples the presence of two rings articulated on a riveted tubular clasp at ear height might suggest their employment both as attachment points for the leather *vinculum*, and for metallic cheek guards.[155] Cheekpieces – of the type shown on the Agen–Port specimens – were soon added to meet the exigencies of the Roman *milites*.

The expansion of Rome into the Celtic heartlands favoured the import into the army of other strong helmet types, such as the so-called Agen–Port specimens,[156] and the further evolution of the Coolus–Mannheim type into the Haguenau helmet. The presence of the Celts as auxiliaries in the Roman army was probably the route by which this import was made, which in turn determined the further evolution of these types into the imperial ones. The new models represented an improvement in both the fitting to the human head and for the cheek guard (*bucculae*) shape, which now covered the cheekbone and jaw without hindering the wearer's field of vision. These cheek guards were then standardised on many successive Roman specimens. In the Montefortino specimens the *bucculae* became in fact similar to the Agen–Port specimens, although much more simplified, being linked to an under-chin crossed strap (*vinculum*) in the Montefortino model.[157]

In the iron specimen found in Agen the bowl has vertical sides and the lower rim is strongly curved outward, with a more marked neck guard scored by two metal lines. An iron

21 Etruscan urn representing the scenes of the Theban Cycle, but probably inspired by the siege of Volterra by Sulla, 88 BC (*Volterra, Museo Guarnacci; courtesy of the museum*)

ring of triangular section is fixed in the bowl, 3 cm above the rim, to improve its regularity. The cheek guards are clasped in the space between the rim and the reinforcement ring, and they have the rings for the fastening of the chin strap positioned on the lower back edge.[158] The Agen–Port type, in iron, recovered as the Agen type on the battlefield of Alesia,[159] and shown on many monuments from the Caesarian period (**11**), is characterised by a hemispherical skull with two metallic volutes (eyebrows) on the frontal part that function as both decoration and reinforcement (**22**), and by a short neck guard (**PLATE Ia**, **PLATE IIb**) with two or three ridges.[160] Large cheek guards, sometimes decorated with Celtic patterns of the La Tène type,[161] were attached to the bowl by means of clasps.

The Haguenau specimen[162] typically has a more distinct flattened and peak-like projection to the neck guard, and a small browband protecting the skull. The hemispherical bowl of the Coolus type is slightly reduced, then furnished with a low and flat neck guard and reinforced, on the brow, by an additional brow piece in metal. This type, also called the Schaan type by modern scholars,[163] was probably developed during the Gallic Wars and became typical of the late first century BC. Heavier

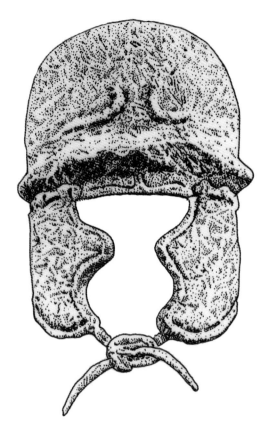

22 Funerary *cippus* of a *miles* of Italic origin, first century BC (*Aquileia, Museo Nazionale Romano, inv. n. 280, drawing by Graham Sumner*).
   The *cippus* represents an Agen–Port helmet with large cheek guards. The veteran of the *X Legio* mentioned by Caesar in *De Bello Africano*, XVI, 3, probably wore this kind of helmet

and lighter specimens were both cast.[164] The characteristic side-feathers of some specimens could allow us to date the first examples to the Caesarian period (**PLATE II**).

A noteworthy study of helmets of the Hellenistic type emerges from the iconography of the period (**23**).[165] We should remember that the conquest of the last kingdoms of the Greek rulers in Asia and Egypt brought a huge amount of Greek military equipment to the Roman legions, which was used by them especially during the chaotic period of the Civil wars. The Romans were highly influenced by Greek culture in many spheres, including in their military equipment. The elaborate models of the Greek world were often reserved for the officers and elite soldiers as a status symbol. The fact that these elaborate helmets are rare in the archaeology of the first century BC is a result of the scarce archaeological excavations conducted in the battlefields and in military fortresses of the Late Hellenistic age (**24**). In addition, many finds preserved in the stores of Near Eastern museums still await proper research. Last but not least, these helmets were of high quality and made of precious materials, and were used only by officers and elite

corps, so they were not as widespread amongst the troops as the mass production helmets of Montefortino type.

   The use of helmets of the Hellenistic type by the *milites* is widely attested by the figurative monuments of Glanum (**2**) and Narbonne,[166] and by Etruscan urns of the first century BC (**23**) and by the Pompeii frescoes, where helmets of the Askalon[167] type and other late-Hellenistic helmets are very well detailed. Helmets of a Beotian–Pseudocorinthian type are represented both on the relief of Sulla from the Campidoglio (**18**), and on the Julii monument (**2g**, **2h**). The Greco-Roman tradition of the Attic helmet style was widely continued in the first century BC. High-ranking officers often wore such helmets, as shown on the Sullan monuments (**18**) and coins.[168] Augustus, at the Battle of Actium, probably wore an Attic helmet with polished cheekguards decorated with embossed thunderbolts and, on the bowl, the embossed *sidus Iulium*, symbol of the *gens Iulia*.[169]

   The tradition of more elaborate helmets of Greco-Italic origin continued in the Roman army. The Attic and the Apulian–Corinthian helmets, often subjected to rich and elaborate decorations, continued for long time to be part of the panoply of high-ranking officers, generals and elite troops, as is shown in the iconography of the period.[170]

23 Romano-Etruscan *tribunus* in a mythological scene, represented on an Etruscan urn, second–first century AD (*Volterra, Museo Guarnacci; courtesy of the museum*)

24 Roman helmet of Hellenistic type, first century BC (*photo courtesy of Gian Baldo Baldi*)

On a funerary monument from the Cimitero dei Giordani, Rome[i], fighters on a Liburna are shown attacking with rectangular *scuta* and spears. Only the armoured oarsman on the right seems be equipped with muscled armour, and the details of a helmet represented on the side of the monument shows the employment of a composed Coolus type with Hellenistic marks. This specimen, recently exhibited in the Italian antiquary market, is virtually identical to that on the sculpture

* * *

Perhaps the first reference to a masked helmet in use by the *milites* is in Quintilian. The expression used – 'the face covered by the helmet'[171] – could equally refer to a helmet with *bucculae* firmly closed around the face, but the presence of a masked helmet is not astonishing, considering the great range of these helmets among the Hellenic and Etruscan armies since the sixth to fifth centuries BC. Moreover, a Roman triumphal sculpture of the period, from Sora, shows the presence of a masked helmet among other weapons (**17**).[172] The helmet depicted is of the old Negau type, of Etrusco-Italic origin, fitted with a mask made up of two embossed cheek guards (**PLATE Ic**).

In the provincial armies, the preservation of local forms by the Roman army is visible on various monuments, like the Osuna relief (**8b, 8c**). Here the *milites* wear a helmet similar in shape to the most common form of Iberian headgear, a close-fitting bascinet with reinforcement bands around the edge and leather cheek guards.[173] This was certainly a result of contamination by different equipment, a phenomenon that reached its peak during the Empire.

The inside of all helmets and cheek guards were lined with leather or felt. A helmet lining, formed by an off-white cap, is clearly visible on the head of a warrior in a very famous painting from Pompeii, representing a military doctor curing Aeneas' wounds.[174] A well-known first-century AD fresco from

Pompeii, copied from earlier paintings, shows a coif with a chin strap. The chin strap in the helmets of Montefortino typology was attached to a large iron rivet fixed on the inside of the neck guard, then fastened to the iron rings attached to each cheekpiece. A knot was tied under the chin, as can be seen on various iconographical sources.

The crests (*insignia*) were usually attached to the helmets shortly before fighting commenced[175]. Caesar reports that during a unexpected attack from the Belgii the *milites* were so caught by surprise that they could not even put the *insignia* on the helmets nor remove the *tegimenta* from their shields![176] The crest colour for the Roman *milites* shown in the Statilii tomb fresco is red,[177] but yellow crests are depicted in the Pompeii paintings.[178] A Montefortino-type fragment from Caminreal, with only the apex surviving in the knob,[179] shows a hole for the insertion of the plumes. The apex was filled by lead and then a hole was made in it for the plumes, usually of swan or duck.[180] The presence of a hole for the crest pin, on knobs of the helmets, leads us to suppose that the hair or plumes were put in by means of a *cannula*, then the crest tied together with a strap. The coins of this period still attest the use of the three feathers described by Polybius, of black and purple colour (**25**).

Vegetius wrote that the centurion's badge, the tranverse crest (*crista transversa* (**18**)), was silvered (*argentata*) so the men might see it in the chaos of the battle. Possibly it was only the crest-holder that was silvered and the horsehair (or feathers) were light grey. Many helmets did not have plumes or crests, as

25 Coins from Late Republican era: **1)** Servilia and Cornelia Gentes, second–first century BC; **2)** *Legatus pro praetor* P. Carisius, late first century BC (*ex Antonucci; drawing by Elaine Norbury*)

The axe as war instrument could be seen on a coin of the *Legatus pro praetor* P. Carisius, but this indicates a personal badge rather than generalised use

---

i   Liberati, 2003, p. 109.

attested by the archaeology – where the hole or other elements for the crest attachment are missing – and confirmed by the written sources.[181] During marches the helmets were covered by leather,[182] probably to keep them protected from the dust and to conceal the arrival of the army by hiding the shining of the metal.

Officers' helmets were probably also lacquered and painted. This is shown on a Pompeian fresco representing the god Mars whose helmet, of the Attic type, is painted red and yellow, with a red holder for the crest and yellow plumes.[183]

Body Armour and Greaves

The body protection of the Roman *miles* has a long tradition, passing through the Etruscans, the Greeks, the Italic peoples, the Celts and the Hellenistic commonwealth. The Roman protection of the body was generally called *lorica*.[184] In the *Commentarii* of Caesar the word *lorica* is used in referrence to officers and *legionarii*. If some of them were called *loricati* and others were not, it suggests that not all of the men were equipped with the armour.[185] On many monuments of the period, in fact, the *milites* are represented only clad in their belted tunic (**28, 315r**).

Many different kind of body protection were employed in the first century BC, even within the same *legio*. The main body protection was armour made of iron ring mail, linen and leather corselets, the muscled cuirass in iron and leather, and scale armour.

The ring or chain mail already in use at least since the third century BC[186] was the main armour of the *miles gregarius* in the first century BC (**PLATE I**). Varro, who was *legatus* under Pompeius in Spain, uses the word *Gallica* to designate it,[187] a word surely used in the military 'slang' of the soldiers. Lucanus, in his *Pharsalia*, gives the following description of chain mail: '. . . and the twisted armour offers heavy chains, the breast covered by the panoply . . .'.[188] The *gallica* was usually made of iron (*lorica ferro aspera*)[189] and protected the thighs – at the height of the thigh bone – and breast, if belonging to the long type visible on the Narbonne monuments,[190] or just the breast,[191] and was worn over a padded corselet. Short sleeves protected the upper arms.

It was a flexible protection, allowing the warrior freedom of movement. The employment of the *gallica* by the legionaries is attested on the arches of both Saint-Remy and Orange (**2d, 2e, 2f, 2h, 315c**). A fragment of a *gallica* of the Caesarian period comes from a Celtic *oppidum* near Berna:[192] it shows the usual construction of a linked series of five iron rings, with four rings linked to the central open one, then closed by a rivet.[193] This construction is identical to that of the chain mail depicted on the Osuna monument (**8a, 8e, 8f, 8g**).

Sometimes the armour was furnished with *humeralia* (shoulder pieces) that regulated the fastening system of the

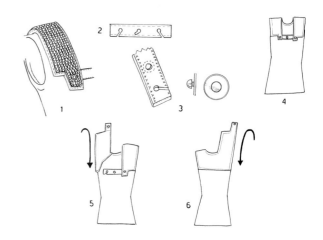

26 Fastening system of the Gallica, Caesarean era (*ex Antonucci; drawing by Andrea Salimbeti.*)

The *lorica* reaches to the mid-thigh and has no sleeves but is reinforced with broad shoulder straps made of mail or metal edged in leather, brought over from the back and fastened down on the breast, closed by a metallic button that secures the shoulder strap on the front of the shirt. The leather edging was made by rolling up the leather around the mail borders and sewing it down.

armour by means of pins passing through a bronze or leather piece placed horizontally on the upper breast (**26**). The shoulder pieces, always lined with leather, sometimes extended to cover the deltoid muscle, with a reinforcement piece fastened also on the back, and probably inspired by the structure of Greek linen armour.[194] Different types of shoulder guards are represented in the altar of Ahenobarbus, where the mail shirts of the *milites* are tighly gathered to the waist by the sword belts. One man, in fact, has short extensions projecting from under the shoulder straps over the shoulder bones; another has broad shoulder straps spreading over the upper arms.[195] The shoulder straps are linked by a horizontal strap going across the body from each side, and attached under the mail. It was probably towards the end of the Caesarian period that metal fasteners were introduced, formed by two metal plates that hooked onto the shoulder flaps of the chain armour, just under the chest, following a model derived from the Celts (**6**).[196]

Examining the monuments celebrating Caesar's victories, Antonucci has assumed the existence of chiselled metal shoulder plates.[197] The significant weight of the whole armour was partially mitigated by the presence of the *cingulum* around the waist – which helped to spread some of the weight on to the hips instead of the shoulders – and by the presence of the felt or leather under-armour garment.

Obviously the *gallica* could not be provided to all the *milites*. Its manufacture was expensive and the warrior was often supplied

27 Roman *miles* first century BC, from unknown monument (*drawing by Graham Sumner*)

with an organic armour. The linen armour (*linothorax*), derived from Greek and Etruscan models, an armour of stiffened linen equipped with shoulder guards fastened on the breast, was still widely employed in the late Consular age (**27**). It can be seen to be worn by the Roman soldiers depicted on coins related to the rebellion of the slaves in Sicily of 101 BC,[198] and by a *miles* on the Glanum reliefs (**2g**, **2h**). In the Roman army there was possibly a version in leather (*corium*) or felt (*coactilium*), both of which are mentioned by Caesar in the first century BC (**PLATE Ib**).[199]

The reliefs of Aquileia and Narbonensis often show armour with gorgets protecting the neck. A possible leather version of the *linothorax*, with gorget and short sleeves fixed to a padded garment with lappets, is visible on the Aquileia monument (**PLATE IIb**). This panoply, forming two superposed armours (one in linen and one in leather) can be related to the description by Valerius Maximus of the heroic *centurio* Caesius Scaeva in Britain, who, even though burdened by the weight of two *loricae*, saved himself by throwing himself into the sea with all the armament.[200] Sertorius saved himself in the same way by swimming in the Rhone wearing his armour. It is obvious that both descriptions are dealing with non-metallic armours. The use of leather armour is clearly attested by the sources. Lucius Calpurnius Piso Caesonius went to Macedonia (58–55 BC) with extraordinary powers to requisition all the

cattle or as much as necessary to provide equipment for the army in the form of hides to be shaped into armour, shields and horse trappings.[201]

Iron breastplates (*thoraka*) of the Hellenistic type are visible on the Gaeta reliefs (**11**); one of them, covered by a purple *exomis*, is worn by the wounded Aeneas dressed as a Roman officer, in the above-mentioned painting from Pompeii.[202] These corselets often show *pteryges* attached to the lower edge, in one[203] or two rows. This bronze or iron armour – as shown by the colours given to this kind of panoply on the Esquiline fresco (**16**) – could have the lappets directly attached to the lower rim, or could be worn over a linen garment fitted with *pteryges*.[204] More elaborate armours of this type, visible on the Sulla monument (**18**) were often reserved for officers. These were composed of two metallic halves fastened on the left side. A pair of *humeralia* (shoulder guards) was clasped on the back, from which emerged also a neck protector. An armour of this type was probably worn by Pompeius at the battle against the Albanians[205] in 65 BC, when Prince Cosis struck him with a javelin on the fold of his breastplate (*epiptyché thorakos*).[206]

Muscled plate armour, i.e. armour made in the form of a human torso, is attested in the monuments and artworks, and by some archaeological specimens (**29**), both in metal and in leather. Marvellous metallic specimens were reserved for generals, such as that represented on the statue of Caesar preserved at Campidoglio.[207] This armour is highly decorated on the breastplate in low relief, with embossed images of griffins which are combined with vegetal and volute decorations. The lower border of the armour is ornamented from round lappets, forming a double border (*cymation*) hinged to the main torso of the armour. A probably very similar armour (*thorax*), but decorated with British pearls, was offered by Caesar to the goddess Venus Genetrix.[208]

Simplified models (**PLATE Ia**) are shown on the monuments. A mural from Pompeii, representing perhaps the last onslaught against Spartacus, shows a Roman infantryman with Montefortino helmet and rectangular shield fighting a man in Samnite armour, also armed with helmet, cuirass, shield and sword.[209] A similar Roman infantryman is represented on the Glanum relief, although in this monument the baldric is worn on the right shoulder (**2a**). The image on the figurative monuments can be seen as evidence for the employment in battle of such armour not only for the high-ranking officers (**23**), but also for some ordinary legionary (*miles gregarius*) or, most probably, by junior officers or centurions.

On the Narbonensis reliefs a muscled armour, decorated with a rhomboidal decorative motif, is clearly copied from a leather original, worn with a padded garment with lappets at the arms, neck and waist. The same can be said of the armour worn by a officer, perhaps a *tribunus*, on a Etruscan urn from Volterra, where the *Sidus Iulium* is applied to the leather surface, probably as a metallic appliqué (**23**). Another muscled

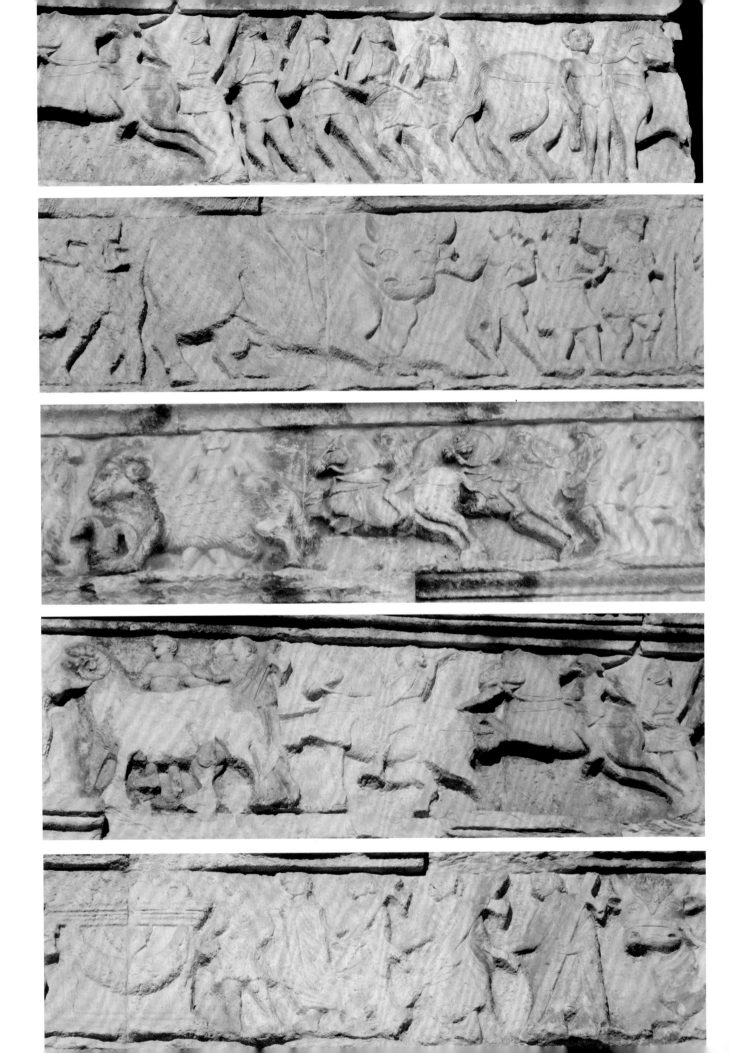

armour worn together with a 'Montefortino' helmet, shown on the Aquileia monument, evidences a rigid structure, mounted upon a trophy. This is clearly the representation of a metallic armour and also proof that the Roman artists copied different specimens of different materials. Sometimes the lappets were metallic parts of the armour, as on the statue of Munatius Plancus from Tivoli, today at the Museo Nazionale Romano.[210] The armours of this type were often furnished with shoulder guards, leather-lined on the metallic specimens, fastened on the breast by thongs attached to metallic hinges.[211]

Scale armour was also used. This armour, of Greek origin, was made up of small plates of bronze, iron, leather or horn cut in the desired shape and fixed upon a backing of leather or linen by means of wire or leather laces. The scales were attached in parallel rows to overlap each other like fish scales or roof tiles.[212] Plutarch[213] remembers the *thorax lepidotos*, i.e. a a steel breastplate of glittering scales, worn by Lucullus at the Battle of Tigranocerta.

The trophies of arms clearly show the protective tunic or garment worn under the armour, the so-called *subarmale*. This was often a linen garment, provided with the usual *pteryges* protecting the limbs. Often the *pteryges* were fringed, in gold or silver silk. The linen garment worn under Caesar's armour in the statue mentioned above, visible on the waist down, is divided into strips (*pteryges*) with fringed terminals.[214] Caesar describes garments of leather (*ex coriis*), felt (*ex centoniis*) or padded cloth (*coactis*) used for added protection (*tegimenta*).[215] These garments, worn with or without the armour, are often visible as quilted on the Caesar's coins celebrating his

28 (Above and opposite page) *Milites* and *equites* from the Arch of Augustus, in situ, Susa, 14 BC (*author's photo*).

The peace with Cotius was celebrated on the arch of Augusta Seguvina (Susa). Roman *milites* in *lorica segmentata* are shown on a Roman monument for the first time, together with *equites*, *tubicines* and *leves armaturae* (light infantryman). The *equites* are performing an equestrian *decursio*

triumphs. The relief of Urso that depicts a couple of *milites* provides evidence of the use, in the same unit, of different kinds of body protection: beside a *miles* wearing the *gallica* a second *miles* wears a felt quilted protector, made of separated strips of felt stitched together (**8, 8a, 8e, 8f**).[216] The same kind of quilted tunic is also worn by a soldier joining a *victimarius* in another relief from the same locality (**30**).

The use of organic armour by the legionaries is described also by Plutarch, who, speaking about the defeat of Crassus at Carrhae, said:[217]

And when Crassus ordered his lightly armed troops to make a charge, they did not advance far but, encountering a

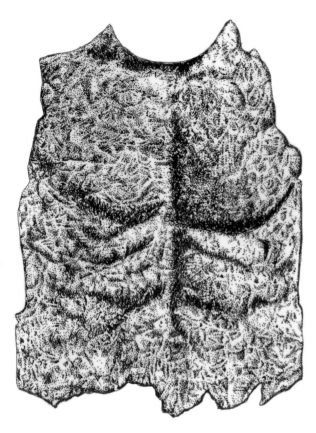

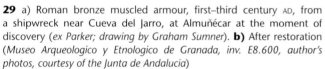

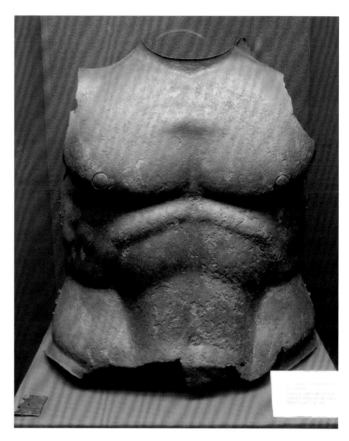

29 a) Roman bronze muscled armour, first–third century AD, from a shipwreck near Cueva del Jarro, at Almuñécar at the moment of discovery (*ex Parker; drawing by Graham Sumner*). **b)** After restoration (*Museo Arqueologico y Etnologico de Granada, inv. E8.600, author's photos, courtesy of the Junta de Andalucia*)

The *lorica* is one of the few surviving bronze muscled armours of the Roman Imperial age that has been published until now. This kind of *thorax stadios* is simple and linear, and the fastening system, with a staple (still preserved) through which the hinge joint pin passed, is much simpler than the older Greco-Italic, Samnite and Etruscan models. The fastening system is clearly the same as that represented on the equestrian statue of M. Nonnius Balbus from Herculaneum

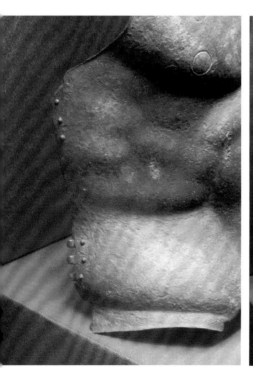

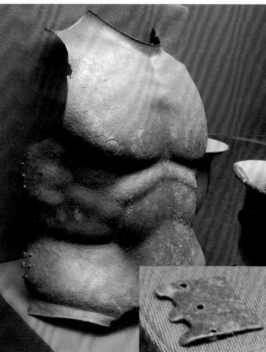

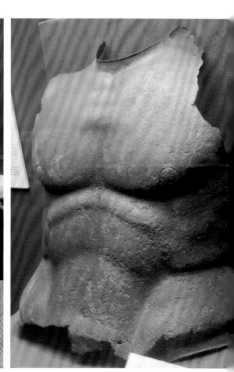

multitude of arrows, abandoned their undertaking and ran back for shelter among the men-at-arms, among whom they caused the beginnings of disorder and fear, for these now saw the velocity and force of the arrows, which fractured armour, and tore their way through every covering alike, whether hard or soft (*antitúpou kai malakou stegásmatos*).

The Greek word *malakos* is usually used to refer to works or materials in leather or organic and flexible material. Here Plutarch underlines the difference between the rigid (*antitupos*) protection and the flexible one (*malakos*) protection, i.e. between the metallic and the organic armour.

The protection of the legs was entrusted to metallic greaves (*ocreae*). Derived from Greek and Etruscan prototypes, the greaves were usually made of a single sheet of bronze, and shaped around the calf, as is visible on the legs of an officer on an Etruscan urn (**23**). Greaves are depicted on various monuments, but the Aquileia reliefs show for the first time the kind of greaves equipped with a clasp that divided the knee protection from that of the leg, as in the subsequent Imperial specimens.[218] These are fitted with an embossed *gorgona* on the centre of the knee, so perhaps the artist was representing officers here. Simpler plain greaves are shown on the Urso (Osuna) reliefs as worn by *gregarii* on each leg[219] and on Pompeian frescoes.[220] In the Urso reliefs the greaves are no longer simply worn by wrapping around the legs, like the old specimens of Greek origin, but are held on by a couple of leather straps under the knee and at the height of the heel (**8h, 8i, 8j**).

The historian Iohannes Lydus describes a statue of Aeneas dressed in first-century BC uniform: bronze helmet (*perikefalaia kalkì*), chain mail (*thorax krikotòs*), a short wide sword (*xifos platì*) hanging on the left thigh, two javelins (*akontia*) with a wide point (*cuspis*), greaves (*periknemides*), *fasciae* of black cloth

30 Relief with a *miles* and a *victimarius*, from Urso (Osuna), first half of first century BC (*Cordoba, Museo Arquéologico Provincial; author's photo, courtesy of the museum*)

on the legs and the footwear called *garbulai* or *crepidae* by the Romans or *arbulai* by the Greeks.[221]

~ AUXILIARY TROOP EQUIPMENT: BOW AND ARROWS; SLINGERS ~

The Roman army of the first century BC was a multi-racial force. The XIII and XIV Legions of Caesar in the campaign against the Belgians were supported by German Suebs, Celtic Elingones, Carnuti and Aedui, Numidians, Balearic slingers and Cretan archers. Pompeius' army on the eve of the Battle of Pharsalus was composed of five legions, the *legio gemella* formed by the unification of the legions of Cilicia and Bithynia, a legion of Cretan and Macedonian veterans, an Asiatic *legio*, fifteen Illyrian cohorts, 1,200 slingers and 3,000 archers from Sparta, Pontus and Crete, 7,000 horsemen, including Piceni shepherds, Germans, Gauls, Galatians of King Deiotarus, Cappadocians, Thracians and Commagene archers of King Antiochus. In the civil wars there are also mentions of Iturean, Syrian and Rhutenian archers, Iberian infantrymen and Greek mercenaries from Acarnania, Etolia, Rhodes and Dolope. All these peoples fought with their own weaponry and equipment, as well as the weapons borrowed from the Roman arsenals.

Germans: The Germanic spear weapon was the short *framea*, whose point was often engraved with magical symbols in runic inscriptions.[222] Tacitus[223] mentions the use by some Germans of short swords and round shields, often painted in lavish colours. When the Germans fought in a phalanx formation, they also used the big Celtic shield made of wood planks, like that shown on the Mondragon sculpture,[224] preserved at the Musée Calvet of Avignon. The use of helmets and armour was very rare,[225] but a certain protection was afforded by garments called *rhenones*, made of wild animal skins and reinforced by scales of Atlantic fish.[226]

Celts: Caesar mentions[227] the use by the Celts of javelins with sharp and wavy points, the *matara* and *gaesa*, and of the long spear called *tragula*[228] fitted with the *amentum*, a throwing strap wrapped around the shaft. Experiments conducted by order of Napoleon III in 1864 showed that such a weapon could reach a range of more than 80 m!

The sword of the Celtic warrior was the typical long blade of La Tène III. Many specimens, complete with their iron scabbards, have been found on the battlefield of Alesia.[229] These *gladii*[230] were usually worn with chains, but the Gauls serving in the Roman army also used *cingula*, as shown in the famous statue of the *auxilia* cavalryman from Vachères.[231]

The Celtic shields were furnished with *umbones* that were round or with a wooden *spina* reinforced with metallic fittings and a central *umbo* of butterfly shape. Metallic appliqués were often used to reinforce and decorate the shields, painted with bright motives. Many shields captured in Alesia were '. . . adorned with gold and silver . . .'.[232]

The coin of Dumnorix, the Celtic leader allied to Caesar,[233] shows the use of a Montefortino type of helmet, fitted with a central horsehair and a pair of lateral 'wings', probably made from real feathers. The decoration of the helmet shows the attack of a predatory bird, exactly as the ornament of the famous helmet of Ciumesti.[234] The coin also shows a leather coat reinforced by metallic bosses, with a frontal opening, whereas other coins represent chain mails. The Vachères statue shows a mail armour (*gallica*) fitted with a double-hook fastening plate, presumably in bronze, attached to the breast of the mail shirt for securing the shoulder pieces, lined with leather. This system, of Celtic origin, was at that time widely adopted by the Roman Imperial army.

The Galatian infantrymen of Deiotarus wore a typical Hellenistic armament, mixed with Celtic equipment, as illustrated by terracotta figures from Myrina in Asia Minor.[235] They show swords with bilobate pommels of the La Tène III type, worn by means of a baldric of brown colour; helmets (*galeae*) of Askalon type, muscled armours of a Greek type painted iron-blue and wide Celtic *scuta* painted lavishly.

Balearic: Helmets and armour are not mentioned for the Balearic slingers, the most famous slingers of the ancient world, who had been used in the Roman army since the time of the Punic Wars. They probably fought in tunics and cloaks, although around their legs they wrapped some bandages made of esparto fibres (**31**).

It is only in the Trajanic period that we have any documentation of the way the Balearic slingers carried their ammunition. During this period it is likely that they used the same method as the other ancient slingers such as the Rhodians and the Thessalians: carried in a shoulder belt purse, or in the folds of their cloaks.[236]

A statuette of a Rhodian warrior of the Consular armies has been found in Pompeii.[237] The man is naked and fitted with

31 Fragment of *esparto*, second–first century BC (*Zaragoza, Archaeological Museum; author's photo, courtesy of the museum*)

an Attic helmet. He has a sling (*sphendone*) extended between his hands, with the sling straps wrapped around the palm of the right hand and the missile (*glans* or *molubdis*) on the other hand. He wears around the body a small baldric, to which was originally suspended the small leather purse (*diftera* or πηρα λιθων) containing the missiles. The projectiles could be of different material: in lead (*glandes*) or in pottery or stone (*lapides missiles*). Sometimes they were marked with the name of the general (**32**).[238]

Cretans: The *Cretae sagittarii* formed the core of the best archers in the Roman armies, and their equipment is represented on a coin of Metello Scipio forged during the Civil War: a simple helmet of Coolus–Mannheim type with a short neck guard, a tunic of quilted leather, a short dagger (*pugio*), and a bow and curved quiver (*pharetra*),[239] probably used also as a bow-case. Two helmets in bronze of the type illustrated on the coin have been found by the archaeologists in Vieille Toulouse,[240] and are linked to the Caesar campaign in Gaul.[241] They are also fitted with a pair of rings for the under-chin strap.

Among the forty arrowheads found in Alesia, three specimens have been identified as Roman: their points have a rectangular section, presenting one or two barbed spikes.[242] The Roman arrow points found in Gaul are of iron, with dimensions around 7.8 cm long and 2.5 cm wide. The Urso excavations have shown various tapered or swallow-tailed arrow points.

Iberians: The Hispanic infantry were formed by the *scutati*, i.e. equipped with a big *scutum*, and recruited in Hiberia Citerior,

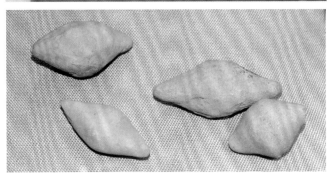

32 Lead *glandes* and *lapides missiles* from Spain, second–first century BC, from various localities (*Zaragoza Museum; Cordoba, Museo Arquéologico Provincial; author's photos, courtesy of the museum*)

and the *caetrati*, i.e. equipped with a round leather shield, enlisted in *Hiberia Ulterior*. Beside the *soliferreum* they used the *lancea*, a light spear with a *cuspis* that could reach 50 cm in length, which was also employed by the Celtic *equites*.[243] It was the prototype of the late-Imperial weapon used by the *lanciarii*. The *falcata* or *machaira* was the best sword of the Iberians, derived from a Greek prototype but further perfected by the excellent Celtiberian sword manufacture. This single-edged blade, of slightly curved shape, was worn in a leather scabbard with bronze fittings and hung from a baldric. The hilt was often ornamented with an engraved animal's head. A specimen from the first century BC was found in the military camp of

Caminreal, 60.4 cm long and assigned by the archaeologists to the Roman auxiliary troops.[244] The employment of these kinds of swords by the *milites gregarii* is in any case attested by the reliefs of the Carpentras Arch (**9a**).

Greeks: The late-Macedonian and Hellenistic equipment was widely used by the *symmachoi* of Greek armies and Eastern Hellenistic vassal kingdoms of Rome. The beauty of this equipment, that for the officers showed late Attic helmets with red crests and plumes, bronze muscled cuirasses and shining shields in silver and gold, is reflected in Pompeian paintings.[245]

~ SPECIAL EQUIPMENT AND RANK SYMBOLS; STANDARDS; MUSICAL INSTRUMENTS AND MILITARY DECORATIONS ~

With Marius' reforms in 106 BC, it was ordered that all the *milites* carry their personal equipment (*impedimenta*) that used to be loaded onto the pack mules; therefore they were nicknamed 'Marius'mules' (*Mules Mariani*).[246] The regular marching pack of the soldiers was called *sarcina*.[247] Among the recorded *sarcina* carried by the soldiers are a goatskin bottle (*uter*) and various tools such as the *ligo* (hoe) and the *rutrum* (rake).[248]

A very important instrument for the entrenching works was the pickaxe called *dolabra*, which has occasionally used like a sharpened and deadly weapon. Lucanus in fact mentions the use of the *bipennis* (double axe).[249]

Statuettes representing the victory (*Nika*) began to be fixed to poles and used in the triumphal processions of the victorious general, following the Hellenistic custom. The presence of twelve lictors for each consul was a sign of the *imperium* (**33**); their institution derived from the Etruscan age when twenty-four *lictores* escorted the Consul or the Dictator, carrying the symbol of supreme power (*imperium*), the double axe. The rods (*virgae*) linked to the axes (*secures*) were made of olive or birch wood and were symbolic of union and strength, and for this reason were linked by a purple ribbon (*infula*).[250] The *lictores* also used a staff (*vindicta*) for police service.

In the triumph the dictator wore a crown and the *vestis triumphalis*, i.e. the *toga picta*, dyed purple and embroidered with gold. The quantity of purple used determinated the degree of luxury of this garment. The ritual aspect of the *triumphator* was accentuated by strewing his body with red *minium* colour, which was also put on the statue of Jupiter Capitolinus – the god embodied by the *triumphator*. Caesar always wore the old-fashioned bright red boots called *calcei* or *mullei* to symbolise his divine origin from Iulus, son of Aeneas.[251] A *hasta summa Imperii* is mentioned as being carried by Octavianus at Actium.[252] It was the symbol of the authority of the Roman kings, magistrates and emperors.

Pliny the Elder[253] states that Marius, during his second consulship in 104 BC, replaced the old standards (*signa*) of the legions – the wolf, minotaur, horse, boar and bull – with the legionary eagle (*aquila*). Each legion received its own eagle. The claws of the holy eagle of Jupiter usually rested on a pedestal, while its wings were spread out. Cicero[254] says that it was made of silver, a piece of information confirmed by Pliny the Elder, who remarked that all the *signa* were silver because their shining meant that they were visible from afar.[255] Sometimes the eagle had other military decorations on the shaft, such as discs (*phalerae*).

The eagles of Crassus lost in the Battle of Carrhae are visible on coins and on the armour of the Augustus of Prima Porta (**4**),[256] which also gives us the colour of the *signum*. Equipped with a butt, it has a handle for the bearer in the middle of the shaft. The colour of the *phalerae* as restored today is blue, which is also the colour of the eagle, representing blue silver,[257] with a brown shaft. The different version of the restoration of the statue's colour by Fenger showed the *phalerae* and eagle in gold, but the moment of the discovery of the standard is described by Amelung:[258] '. . . blue are also the two discs of the battle *signum* . . .'. A second eagle of the Crassus legions is represented on a coin of Augustus minted in 20 BC.[259]

Similarly represented on coins are the eagles of Caesar's army, one of them on a shaft composed of spheres and the other fitted with a double handle and a small laurel leaf in front of the eagle's beak. The shape of an eagle is visible on a *denarius* (coin) struck by Valerius Flaccus in 82 BC,[260] as well as on a coin of A. Postumius Albinus, dated to 81 BC.[261] The eagle of the VIII Legion of Marcus Antonius, flanked by two military *signa*, is represented on a coin of 32–31 BC. The shaft of the *signa* is composed of small spheres and a handle.[262]

The single legionary eagle instituted by Marius was flanked by the other *signa militaria*.[263] Each *legio* had its *vexillum*. On coins from Imperial period[264] we can still see the *vexillum* of the X Legion, surmounted by a bull and ornamented by two silver *phalerae*. Dio Cassio[265] describes the *vexillum* of Crassus at the Battle of Carrhae as embroidered with the name of the *legio* and the commander in purple letters, often in archaic Latin.[266] Antonucci suggests therefore a white or light red colour for such *vexillum*. It was raised in front of the praetorian tent of the *Imperator*, as a war signal. The historians refer to the *vexillum* as a purple tunic or *phoinikon chitòn* fluttering ahead the commander's tent;[267] called by Virgil the *signum belli*.[268]

The *signa* existed in two versions: one for the maniple and one for the *cohors*.[269] The coins mentioned earlier show the *signum* of the *cohors* with the *cohors*' number on its *vexillum*.[270] A simple *signum* comes from a coin representing an oath and dated to 91–82 BC. Flaccus' coin also shows two *signa*: one related to a maniple of *hastati*, the other to a maniple of *principes*, as indicated by the letters H and P on the drapery. Similar *signa* are sometimes represented as having handles.

The *signa* were composed of a pointed shaft with ribbons, *phalerae*, crown and half-moon (*lunulae* or *cornicula*), as represented on the coins[271] related to Crassus' *signa* and Marcus Antonius' legions. A butt was provided, as is shown by the coins and by the episode remembered by Suetonius,[272] telling how Caesar menaced fugitive men with the *cuspis* (point) of a *signum*. It was a cause of great shame to lose the *signa* in battle; sometimes the commanders or officers would throw it into the enemy lines, to incite the soldiers to move forward to recover it.[273]

No source or iconographical image shows a particular uniform for the *signiferi* in the first century BC. The *auxilia* had their own *signa*, such as the tribal boar represented on the coin of Dumnorix. The shafts of such *signa* were often painted with bright colours.

Roman military instruments of the period were the *cornu*, the *tuba* and the *buccina*.[274] The *cornu* was a curving horn made of bronze, and derived from the horns of the prehistoric ox.[275] It was shaped like the letter G, ended in an auricle and had a metallic cross-brace (**33**).

The *tuba* was a long bronze funnel-shaped tube. An example of a *tuba* of the period is represented on the Pompeii fresco showing the Spartacus defeat, where it is played by a man (with

33 (Opposite) *Lictores* and *buccinatores*, musicians and standard-bearers from triumphal scenes of a magistrate's procession towards the Underworld, from Etruscan urns, first century BC (*Museo Guarnacci, courtesy of the museum*).

These representations of triumphal processions, that depicted the magistrate on his *currus* in triumphal pomp, preceded by *lictores* and other *apparitores*, like *praecones*, *viatores* and *tibicines*, escorted by cavalrymen, aid understanding of the rank of the dead and his insignia

grotesque face) dressed in simple tunic and cloak. The *buccina* was similar to the *cornu* but smaller, and without a cross-brace. Often the body was engraved with a wavy decoration.

On marches, the soldiers were almost certainly kept in step by means of a rhythm; one can imagine the noise and the psychological effect this would have had on the enemy in the battlefield. Lucanus describes the hoarse bass sound of the *cornu* and the deep thundering one of the *tuba*.[276] The *tuba* called the *milites* to battle, to the march and to guard duties (*vigiliae*), to assembly and to work duties,[277] as well as being a signal to strike camp.[278] The *buccina* was the signal for night guard duties.[279] According to Varro, it sounded like a human voice.[280]

* * *

In the Consular period, great importance was given to the *dona militaria*, i.e. the gifts and the military decorations given to the soldiers for their bravery. Many of them, from the earliest Roman times, consisted of items captured in battle,[281] such as the *torques* of the Gauls. *Torques*, *armillae* (bracelets) and *phalerae* often adorned the breast armour of the bravest warriors, as a reward for their acts of courage (**PLATE IIb**). Crowns were among the *dona militaria*, divided in various types according to the heroic action performed: the siege crown (*corona obsidionalis*), the civic crown (*corona civica*), the naval crown (*corona classica, rostrata*), the mural crown (*corona muralis*), the ramparts crown (*corona vallaris*) and the gold crown (*corona aurea*). The *corona obsidionalis* was made of grass. The *civica*, of oak leaves, was awarded to a soldier who saved the life of a Roman citizen. The *classica* or *rostrata* was awarded for the capture of a enemy ship. The *corona muralis* was in gold, and awarded to the first man over the enemy's wall during a

siege. The *corona vallaris* was also made of gold and given to the first man over the rampart during a siege. The *corona aurea* was awarded to centurions of high rank.[282] Other awards were based upon the tradition of the Roman army, such as the *hasta pura*, the ceremonial spear of the officer with the rank of *beneficiarius* and the *vexillum*. Minor awards were a simple cup (*patella*) or a *corniculum* (small bugle).

We do not have many original specimens of *dona militaria* from the Late Consular period. However, the coinage supplies a very good depiction of it, as in the coins of Marcus Arrius Secundus (second half of the first century BC) where a crown, a *hasta donatica* and a leather support for *phalerae* are perfectly represented.[283] It is hard to find representations of these *dona militaria* on monuments that can be related to the Late Consular age; perhaps the oldest monument showing it is the *stela* of C. Vibius Sextus Macer,[284] which seems to echo the words of Marius: 'I cannot, to justify your confidence, display family portraits or the triumphs and consulships of my forefathers; but if occasion requires, I can show spears, a banner, trappings and other military prizes . . .'[285]

In the *ovatio* – a victory ceremony inferior to the triumph – the victorious general celebrated with the sacrifice of a sheep on the Mons Albanus, and entered Rome on horseback, crowned by myrtle. Musicians playing pipes and flutes accompanied the general in parades, preceding men holding processional squared gold embroidered standards[286] (**33**). The palm tree and the laurel crown were the symbols of military victories. According to the historians, Caesar refused from Marcus Antonius the gold crown (*corona aurea*), symbol of the monarchy.[287]

~ CAVALRY EQUIPMENT: THE MAN ~

The cavalry of the Late Consular period was mainly composed of Romans and Celts. Strabo, in his *Geographica*, considered the Gauls, in particular the Belgii, to be the best cavalry force in the Roman army.[288] The high quality of the Gauls as cavalrymen favoured their permanent introduction into the Roman army as *auxilia*.[289] Numidians in light armour were also widely employed in the Gallic War, fighting as skirmishers and riding small but fast horses. According to Strabo they rode bareback, only controlling the animals with a small staff, called *virga* by Lucanus.

Spears and Javelins

The long *hasta* or *doru* was the cavalryman's main weapon, as can be seen on a small figurine of the first century BC, preserved

in the Ascoli Piceno Museum, representing a charging Roman cavalryman (**34**). If the fresco from Pompeii mentioned above represented the defeat of Spartacus, the Roman cavalryman who wounds him in the thigh (*Felix Pompeianus*) has a long cavalry spear as his main weapon, together with a wide circular shield (*parma*). An ornamented spear (*hasta donatica*), a symbol of rank, is worn by a Romano-Etruscan cavalryman of the beginning of the first century BC represented on a Volterran funerary urn (**38**).[290]

The Moorish and Numidian cavalrymen fought with javelins and spears: *iacula* according to Lucanus,[291] who also speaks[292] about the use of *lanceae*, and *akontia* according to Strabo, who gives a very detailed description of their appearance, dress and weapons.[293]

34 Charging cavalryman, first century BC (*Museo of Ascoli Piceno; Studio Tomatofarm*)

Swords

The cavalrymen were also equipped with the *gladius hispaniensis*, which was a much more efficient length than the older swords.[294] It is possible that a *gladius* found on the Alesia field, longer than the described specimens of *gladii hispanii*, was of the type provided to the cavalry. The narrow blade plugs into the under-portion of the scabbard, which is also made of iron and enclosed by a round chape decorated by volutes.[295] This is clearly an evolution of the La Tène type III swords. The total length is 68 cm.

Many officers were still fitted out with the Hellenistic *parazonium*, which had a scabbard (*vagina*) and a hilt of white ivory, like that shown on the fresco from the Fabius Rufus House in Pompeii representing a mythological subject. It is worth noting that in this fresco the pommel of the sword has a bilobate shape.

Shields

The round-shaped *parma* that according to Livy[296] was the main shield of the Roman cavalry from the third century BC continued to be the typical shield of the cavalryman (**35**), as mentioned by Sallustius.[297] Horatius, who participated in the Battle of Philippi in 42 BC, was equipped with a small *parmula*.[298] This shield, which was about 80 cm in diameter,[299]

is easily visible on a monument from Via Latina, probably the grave of a Roman cavalry officer.[300] Here two Roman *equites* equipped with wide helmets of Coolus and Haguenau types, spears and the traditional *parma equestris* are fighting Germanic warriors.[301] On the left and on the right sides of the battle scene are a *gladius* or *parazonium*, whose shape is very similar to the Celtiberian prototype, and a muscled armour. This is the typical weaponry of a cavalry officer.

Many officers used the *clipeus* from horseback as an alternative to the *parma*, At the funeral of Sulla they carried golden standards and silver shields of this typology.[302] An original specimen from the Castra Caecilia[303] has a diameter of 42 cm. But Caesar and other *legati* used[304] the long infantry *scutum* more often. For the cavalry we also have information that the name of the commander was written on the shields: some Augustan coins show the name of Caesar and the *sidus Iulium* on the cavalry *parmae*.

The Celtic cavalryman used his long *scutum* from horseback. The stele of Loredan I from Padua represents one of these Roman auxiliaries[305] charging a naked Celtic warrior. The shields had a trapezoidal or hexagonal shape, as shown on the Cecilia Metella tomb where the weapons of the Celtic cavalrymen of Publius Crassus are represented[306] (**36**) and on the *metopae* of Plancus in Gaeta (**11**).

Helmets

There is a wide range of cavalry helmets (*cassides*).[307] The Glanum reliefs (**2**) show Hellenistic helmets in use among the Roman cavalry, very similar to the actual specimens preserved in the Ashmolean Museum at Oxford and to the sculptures reproduced on the Pergamo Altar.[308] These models were distinguished by a horizontal neck guard and a skull embossed with a diadem, echoing the late Attic and Beotian types (**37**).

The Altar of Domitius Ahenobarbus portrays a lightly armed Roman trooper with a possible Beotian helmet,[309] corresponding to the helmet worn by the above-mentioned *eques* from Ascoli Piceno. The helmet of the Volterra cavalryman (**38**) seems to be a simplified Italic version of the Beotian category.

A funerary stone from north Italy shows Celtic auxiliary cavalry among two cavalry *signa* (standards), wearing round medallions or *phalerae* on the horses' harness.[310] The sword is worn on the left side, and the round *parma* as well as a trapezoidal *scutum* are in evidence. They are equipped with strong iron helmets of Agen–Port and Coolus–Mannheim types, as are shown on the Glanum monument (**2**), which also depicts a high crest with a double tuft of horsehair (*insignia*).

Armour

The Glanum reliefs show the use of linen breastplates, or Hellenistic short cuirasses of metal (**2**), both of which might

be painted in bright colours. Instead, the Romano-Etruscan cavalryman from Volterra (**38**) is wearing a mail shirt with shoulder guards knotted on the breast by laces and two rows of *pteryges* coming out of the *gallica*, perhaps belonging to a cuirass undergarment. Wrapped around the *lorica* the man wears his mantle or *sagum*, fastened in a practical way. On the Altar of Domitius Ahenobarbus a cavalryman can be seen in full chain mail without shoulder guards.[311]

The use of an officer *thorax* of Hellenistic type is attested by a funerary monument of a cavalryman from Avellino (**39**).[312] The armour, furnished with short *humeralia*, comes down to the waist, from which – separated by a small border of fringed short lappets (*cymation*) – a range of decorated linen *pteryges* protects the man's limbs. The badge of this officer is also a *parma equestris*, with a lion's head embossed on its centre and a spear (*doru*), together with a short *parazonium*. The funerary stele is dated to the turn of the second and first centuries BC.

The same kind of armour is visible on a series of six torsos of cavalrymen, from the Lanuvium sanctuary and linked to an inscription concerning Licinius Murena, consul in 62 BC and *legatus* under Lucullus in the third Mithridatic War, in which fierce cavalry fighting took place. A silk or linen *zonì* designating officer rank is knotted on the armour breast of the cavalrymen. The armour is worn together with a Greek tunic leaving the right

38 (Above) Etruscan urn of *eques* (*Volterra, Museo Guarnacci; courtesy of the museum*)

37 (Above) Roman helmet of Hellenistic type, end of the first century BC (*Hamburg Museum, inv. 1917.173, courtesy of the museum*)

35 (Opposite, top) Mettius Curtius relief, Roma, Palazzo dei Conservatori, first century BC, (*author's photo, by kind permission of the Sovraintendenza per I Beni Culturali del Comune di Roma*)
The cavalryman is represented with the old style *parma*, the typical shield of the horsemen of the early period, the *popanon* of Polybius[i]

36 (Opposite, bottom) Trophy reliefs of weapons, from the Caecilia Metella tomb, in situ, Rome, second half of the first century BC (*author's photo*)

i   Pol., Prag., VI, 25, 7.

shoulder uncovered; this is the *exomis*, here used as a decorative garment. A very rare coin minted by Crassus represents a cavalryman dressed in a similar *exomis* and with a helmet of the Coolus type fitted with a *cornicularius'* badge, plus the usual round *parma*. This kind of tunic was of the type fashionable in the Diadochoi armies[313] and was sometimes draped over the cuirass, as in the Gaeta *metopae* (**11**). Its colour was red *carminium* over faded purple, and it was sometimes knotted on the breast by a silk fade purple *zona militaris*,[314] as shown in the painting of the wounded Aeneas from Pompeii.[315]

The Hellenistic form of corselet was, of course, the distinctive symbol of the high commanders fighting from horseback: often it was a metallic corselet with *pteryges* and a gorgon's head on the breast, perhaps as a charm, since Sulla kissed his cuirass decorated with a deity's head before going into battle. Pompeius probably had a similar armour in 65 BC.[316]

39 Roman *eques*, from a funerary monument in Avellino, first century BC (*drawing by Graham Sumner*)

A very rare and exceptional cavalry armament is shown on a fragment of a lost monument from the Sanctuary of the Fortuna Primigenia in Praeneste, which belonged to one of Marcus Antonius' naval officers. The fragment, today in the Vatican Museum,[317] shows a very damaged image of Roman cavalryman armed with spear and oval shield (*scutum*), completely covered by a breastplate and with his left arm protected by an armoured laminated *manica* of Hellenistic type. The monument is dated about 30 BC. The use of a laminated protection for the arm was usual for Persian cataphracts and for late Hellenistic elite cavalrymen, as attested by the Pergamon monument and many other figurative works of the Seleucid and Ptolemaic Empires.[318] A specimen of these *cheira* (litt. 'the hands'[319]) has been recovered at Ai Khanum.[320] The Romans met and defeated the cataphracts of the Hellenistic world so it is unusual to find a Roman cavalryman equipped in such a way. Perhaps the man represented was an *evocatus* of Antonius equipped in Romano-Ptolemaic armour. In any case this is the earliest true image of a Roman cataphract cavalryman and it is, to my knowledge, the first representation of an armoured *manica* in a not-gladiatorial context.

The armament of the auxiliary *equites* tended to be that of their ethnic heritage.

~ CAVALRY EQUIPMENT: THE HORSE ~

In the artistic sources various horse harnesses can be seen, because the harness depended very much on the wealth of the owner. Plutarch describes Pompeius' horse[321] in the Sertorian War of 76 BC as particularly rich in gold fittings, having golden headgear and ornamented trappings of great value, which would be a rich booty for the enemy. Usually the *imperatores* rode white stallions, also used in the triumphs. Nine precious *phalerae* cover the head of the horse of the Volterra cavalryman (**38**), a trapping already seens on the horse of the *evocatus* on the Louvre Ara. The *phalerae* in this period were often copied from Celtic ones.

The four-horned saddle began to be introduced in the Roman cavalry in the first century BC. One of the first monuments which show it are the reliefs of Glanum (**2**). The saddlecloth (*ephippium*), on the other hand, was imported from the Greeks[322] and was much more decorative rather than practical for the cavalryman. A painting in the House of the Cryptoporticus in Pompeii shows an interesting example of the period.[323]

Protection for the horse is visible on the monuments. The Capitolium monument shows a rich Greek-fashioned *prometopidion* or frontal (*chamfron*) for the horse's head (**18**),

with a transverse crest with horsehair falling down on the sides. The horse of the funerary stele from Avellino has a leather-covered breastplate (peytral) – similar in shape to that worn by Alexander the Great's horse in the famous Issos mosaic[324] – embroidered with a lion and showing a metallic heart-shaped protection for the front (**39**). A Romano-Etruscan cavalryman from another Volterran urn has a very large and fringed protective peytral for his horse, probably of leather in the original, and very similar to harnesses of the contemporary Hellenistic cavalry: the red colour of it is still visible on the Alabaster sculpture. (**40**)

Celtic horsemanship was already at a high level when it began to be adopted by the Roman army. The horses were fitted with precious *phalerae* and a snaffle bit (*frenum*). The Celtic horses were also covered by Greek-type *ephippia*, as is shown on the Glanum monuments. The Gauls used iron shoes for the horses and wore spurs (*calcares*).

Germanic cavalrymen played an important function in Caesar's army. The harnesses of their horses was very simple, sometimes only having a decorative collar, like the specimen from Harmstorf.[325] The Germans in fact considered it effeminate

to ride a horse covered in decoration. They preferred to use Celtic horses,[326] because their own horses were ill-shaped and ugly, although they were accustomed to heavy duties by daily exercise. Caesar mentions, however, that in cavalary actions the Germans frequently leaped from their horses and fought on foot, while their horses were perfectly trained to stand in the very spot on which they were left, to which the soldier retreated when necessary.[327] In one occasion Caesar gave the Germans the horses of the *tribuni*, *evocati* and Roman *equites*.[328] The Iberian cavalry used horses similar to the Numidians but put harness on them.

The levy of horses took place in the conquered territories: Caesar bought the horses for his *equites* in Gallia and in Iberia[329], whereas the centurions at the beginning of the Civil Wars offered to pay for the equipment for the *equites*.[330] During the Gallic Wars Caesar even requisitioned the horses of the Celtic auxiliaries in favour of the *milites* of the X Legion.[331]

Pack mules were used as well: in Alesia Caesar ordered that a large quantity of baggage should be taken out of the camp, and commanded the muleteers (*muliones*), fitted with heavy cavalry helmets (*cassides*), to ride round the hills giving the appearance and guise of horsemen.[332]

~ CLOTHING ~

Tunics

The Statilii grave, on the Esquiline, depicting legendary events of the *gens Iulia*,[333] shows a battle between soldiers in white tunics and other men dressed only in short white kilts. Other warriors in the same fresco are wearing crimson tunics (**16**). The above-mentioned passage by Quintilianus about the Marian *miles* states that he wore 'the terrible dress of the god of the war', i.e. Mars. The tunic of Mars shown in Pompeian frescoes of the first century BC[334] and in the third-century AD mosaic preserved in the Villa Borghese – perhaps a copy of a Late Republican mosaic – where Salii priests are offering a sacrifice before the statue of the god, is red.[335] The red tunics of the circus factions were also dedicated to Mars; so this passage refers to red tunics worn in battle by the soldiers, at least at the time of Marius,[336] confirming the appellative of '*russati*' given to the *milites*.[337] This is also why a red tunic was hung before the tent of the general as a battle sign.[338] The image of this kind of tunic comes from the tombstone of Centurio

Minucius of *Legio III Martia* from Padova, which shows a short sleeveless tunic[339] coming just over the thighs, belted tightly around the waist.[340] The tombstone also supports the statement of Quintilianus[341] that the centurion's dress was a tunic worn above the knee (**PLATE IIa**).

For officers the colour of tunics could be pure white (*albus*, **16**), but also red or red-pink. This is clearly attested by an exceptional painting recently discovered near Stabiae, a city buried by the Vesusius in AD 79. Here a Roman landlord, dressed as a military officer (perhaps a *centurio* or even a *tribunus militaris*) is engaged with his men in a ferocious fight against a wild boar. The man is wearing a sleeveless pink-red *tunica*, identical in shape to that of the Centurio Minucius (**3**).

The repeated use of a sky-blue colour for the tunic in the depictions of officers could lead us to suppose that this colour was indicative of the rank of some officers, at least in Marius' and Caesar's age. We should remember, though, that the Romans considered everything coloured in light-blue or *caeruleus* as emblematic of heavenly deities.[342] The wounded

Aeneas, in the famous Pompeian painting, has a sleeveless tunic in this colour,[343] and the *zona militaris* that he wears linked around his armour is also blue. But much more interesting is the representation of a Roman officer painted in the House of Vettii in Pompeii,[344] which seems to be the coloured parallel of the so-called *tribunus* of the Altar of Ahenobarbus.[345] There is the same kind of tunic, painted in blue; the same short officer sword or *parazonium* with its scabbard, painted in yellow and white (probably intended to represent gold and ivory); the same mantle or *paludamentum*, painted crimson; the same armour, with the main torso painted in gold and the upper part, with the *cardiophylax*, shown in blue with a *gorgoneion* at the centre. The *subarmale* has two rows of white *pteryges*, as in the Altar of Ahenobarbus. The only difference in the garb is the presence of white *cothurni* at the feet. Both scenes represent military leaders – Aeneas and Agamemnon – and we should remember that *tribuni* could be appointed commanders of a *legio*. So if the models for the portrayals of these mythological leaders were Roman *tribuni*, or commanders of a *legio*, the blue colour could be indicative of their high rank.

In literary language the *milites* were also called *pratextati*, i.e. decorated with the *toga praetexta*, the toga with the purple border, which was worn by the honourable men.[346] A centurion who distinguished himself in the war against the Cimbrians was allowed to perform a sacrifice in *toga praetexta*, as an honorific reward.[347] The shining white *toga praetexta* or *pura* was worn as a symbol of peace.[348] Sometimes a punishment for the soldier was to stand all day outside the headquarters of the camp, barefoot and with the belt of his toga cut and his tunic ungirt, until the nightwatchmen came.[349]

Cloaks

In the army there was a clearly apparent difference between the cloaks worn by the simple *gregarius* and those worn by the officers (*paludati*).[350] The *paludamentum* of the senior officers was a woollen draped cloak fastened on the right shoulder by a golden *fibula*.[351] Quintus Caecilius Scipio, commander of Pompeius' forces in Africa, wore a purple cloak,[352] which was the usual colour for Roman generals, but this cloak was nevertheless a *sagulum*, i.e. a simple cloak of the *miles*. Plutarch called the fringed cloak of Lucullus by its Greek name *krossenos ephestris* and a similar mantle is visible on the Munatius Plancus statue in Tivoli.[353]

The Hellenised taste was borrowed from the Greeks and transmitted to the conquered people. This was true also for the weapons and garments. According to Plutarch, Sertorius, in fitting out his Hispanic followers, 'used gold and silver without stint for the decoration of their helmets and the ornamentation of their shields, and by teaching them to wear flowered cloaks and tunics'.[354]

The *sagum* or *sagulum gregalis* was instead the main cloak of the *milites* (**PLATE IIa**). It was essentially a square of heavy wool

cloth, draped and fastened with a *fibula*. According to Varro, it was in use from the fourth century BC, a fact confirmed by Livy.[355] The Etruscan urns of the first century BC help us greatly by picturing such military cloaks (**41**, **42**). There were different colours for the soldiers and the officers, and we have a good representation of green *sagula* (those of the officer edged with yellow) used by soldiers in hunting activities (**3**).

From the Etruscans the Roman soldier also derived the *paenula* (**43**). This was a thick cloak, chiefly used by the soldiers in travelling, as a protection against the cold and the rain.[356] Hence we find the expression '*scindere paenulam*' used in the sense of urging a traveller to stay at one's house.[357] The *paenula*'s shape is perfectly visible on first-century BC Etruscan urns: it appears to have been a long cloak without sleeves, and with only an opening for the head. From the alabaster sculptures in the Volterra Museum it would seem that the top half of the garment was sewn together at the front, and was divided into two parts, which might be thrown back by the wearer so as to leave the arms comparatively free: it must have been put on over the head, like a poncho (**43**).[358]

Trousers

Traditionally Romans despised trousers or trouser-like garments as barbarous or effeminate .[359] But the necessity of the army, especially in the northern regions, prevailed over old-fashioned Roman austerity. As well as tunics, Caesar mentions other protective elements for his soldiers during the hard winters of Gaul, which he calls generically *tegimenta*.[360] This is probably a reference to the use of Celtic trousers or other native protective garments (*gallici habitus*). The *milites* were originally accustomed to fight from March onwards, especially in a Mediterranean environment. But they began to adopt local garments against the severity of the climate in places such as Gaul and Germany, where the wearing of trousers was widespread. Caesar also used this kind of garment in Germania to disguise himself and reach his besieged men.[361] As could be seen on the Gundestrup cauldron, Celtic and Germanic trousers were often *bracae* in twill woven cloth.[362]

The *subligaculum* or *campestre* was a sort of girdle or apron which the Roman youths wore around their loins when they exercised naked in the Campus Martius, hence the name. The *campestre* were sometimes worn in warm weather in place of the tunic as well as under the tunic and the toga.[363]

Other Garments

Catullus and Valerius Maximus[364] both mention a kerchief (*sudarium*), already used in the first century BC. This might be the precursor of the *focale*, the customary scarf worn by the Imperial *miles gregarius*, but mufflers known as *focalia* are previously described by Quintilian in the above-mentioned passage.

41 (Above and below) Romano-Etruscan urn representing the myth of Meleagros, second–first century BC (*Volterra, Museo Guarnacci; courtesy of the museum*)

Shoes

The most famous military shoes of the Roman army, the *caliga*, of Etruscan origin, begin to be used in the second to first centuries BC, as attested by Quintilian and Cicero,[365] where their use by Pompeius is remembered, together with the *fasciae cretatae*. Service in the ranks was also named after this article of attire: Marius was said to have risen to the consulship *a caliga*, i.e. from the ranks.[366] It was a strong and heavy shoe, composed of a thick multi-layer sole, designed to avoid blistering, and characterised by an interlaced web of straps that covered the foot. The sole of the *caliga* was thickly studded with hobnails (*clavi caligarii*).[367] Their first representation can be seen on the Etruscan urns of the period (**43**).

The *stela* of Minucius is evidence for the use of enclosed boots (*calcei*) derived from early prototypes (**PLATE IIa**). Officers wore splendid closed *cothurni* of various colours, like those made of blue leather and worn by the officer represented on the Stabiae fresco (**3**), or white shoes of interlaced leather, the *carbatinae*, similar to *caligae*.[368]

The most common type of footwear during Caesar's era were the closed-top boot of buckskin called *pero*, and the *carbatina* made of soft hide interlaced with tongues. The shape of this latter type is perhaps preserved by the *ciocie* made in modern Lazio.[369]

Generals wore the so called *calcei patricii* or *mullei*, soft boots of senatorial rank. The senators wore such *calceus* or *aluta*, fastened on the instep with four thongs (*quattor corrigiae*).[370] They were usually black (*alutae nigrae*)[371] and decorated by a crescent. Marius wore crimson boots in triumphal processions.

42 (Above and below) Procession of cavalrymen from an Etruscan urn, first century BC (*Volterra, Museo Guarnacci; courtesy of the museum*)

43 (Left and below) Detail of Etrusco-Roman clothing from first-century Volterra urns: *paenula*, *cucullus* and *caligae* (*Volterra, Museo Guarnacci; courtesy of the museum*)

～ NAVAL EQUIPMENT ～

At the beginning, the employment of a Roman *miles* on a warship was seen as a punishment, because the Roman soldiers did not like to fight at sea. At Rome, service as oarsmen on warships was generally fulfilled by freemen, and only in exceptional circumstances by slaves. It was a normal military duty and often *nautae* (sailors,[372] who could be armed), *milites classiarii* or *propugnatores*[373] (i.e the professional soldiers of the fleet) and sometimes also the *remiges* (oarsmen)[374] were engaged in land battles.

Expansion across the Mediterranean gave a decisive impetus for the creation of a permanent military fleet, from the First Punic War. Etruscans and Greeks constituted the bulk of the Roman naval forces. From the Punic Wars there was a certain degree of difference in the equipment of the soldiers fighting at sea rather than on land. The Etruscan urns representing sailors and dated to the third and first centuries BC show the use of a much lighter accoutrement for sea fighting, in particular *piloi* felt caps and padded or quilted garments (**44**).

The monuments of the Late Consular period show mariners clad in simple tunics and armed with oblong shields (*scuta*) and spears, and wearing helmets of the Montefortino and Buggenum types.[375] They were probably part of the ship's equipment, to be used if necessity arose. Other artistic sources of the first century BC show the rectangular *scuta* and javelins, as well as helmets of the late Hellenistic type, complete with cheek guards. Singularly, the helmsman is sometimes shown as armoured, probably because of his vulnerability to enemy strikes. Oval *scuta*, on the ship, are disposed in a horizontal row under the deck, to protect the oarsmen. This image is a good depiction of the hoplites on the ships under the command of Annius, one of Sulla's generals.[376]

44 Detail of sailor's equipment on an Etruscan urn representing Odysseus and the Sirens, third century BC (*Volterra, Museo Guarnacci; courtesy of the museum*)

In the Albenga ship, dated to the early first century BC, eight fragments of bronze helmets survived, mainly of the Italic type (Montefortino–Buggenum), and a fragment of a bronze muscled cuirass (*thorax stadios*). The presence of a piece of armour suggests there were soldiers on the ship, to protect it against the pirate activity of the early first century BC.

The soldiers depicted on the *bireme* from Praeneste, a relief representing a warship with its crew[377] part of the above-mentioned funerary monument of a *navarcha* of Marcus Antonius and related to the Battle of Actium, wear Greek-type Attic helmets, sometimes with metallic crests, a feature that in the Augustan period is also typical of the officers of the *Gemma Augustea*. Some *classiarii* wears the Etrusco-Corinthian helmet. However, only two of the helmets shown were part the original sculpture, the others were restored in the nineteenth century,

although they imitated the originals. One original, still in place, shows the use of side-feathers on a helmet of Etrusco-Corinthian type.

The shields are oval *scuta*, having as blazons volutes, a hand holding Neptune's trident and the wings (*alae*) of the eagle. Their grip system, clearly visible, is a double grip, with a leather strap in which the arm passed through, and a second grip in line with the shield's *umbo*. As the Praeneste ship relief represents a ship of Antonius surrendered to Octavianus the shield blazons of some warriors could correspond to those of Antonius' legions, and the others – with vegetal volutes and wings, showing similarities with the shields meantioned above from *Narbonensis* – are probably devices of the *Legio V Alaudae* and of the XI Legion of Caesar that were now fighting for Octavianius. The shield with Neptune's trident is certainly the device of a *legio* of *classiarii*, because the same device is still visible in the Imperial age on monuments representing mariners.

Various armours are illustrated on the relief. The warrior with the Etrusco-Corinthian helmet wears the big muscled armour moulded in leather with a simple row of linen lappets (*pteryges*), as does a second man on the prow of the ship. The senior officer on the second row – maybe a *praefectus classis* – wears a splendid Hellenistic *thorax lepidotos* or scale armour, fitted with a double skirt of fringed *pteryges* and having, knotted on his breast with a Heracles knot, a cloth officer belt. The cuirass has shoulder-pieces and he wears greaves made of two pieces, one protecting the knee and the other the leg.[378] Much more importantly, he is the only one armed with a sword, which he wears from a baldric on the right shoulder. Similar weaponry is worn by Pompeius on a coin of 46–45 BC[379] that shows him on the deck of a warship.

The use of leather armour by the fighters at sea is clearly linked to the mobility required for fighting on board, so that they were more lightly equipped than the ordinary infantry *milites*,[380] but no less usefully: Octavian's men at Actium were well protected by their armour[381] against enemy blows. A *hasta navalis* is mentioned among the various types of *hastae* in use in the Late Consular age. Its shape is perhaps visible on an interesting relief dating to the first half of the first century BC, showing a group of Roman *classiarii* equipped with shields furnished with *umbo* and *spina*, wearing Montefortino helmets and armed with a spear with a wide triangular blade.[382] The same blade is also visible on the spears of the Praeneste monument.

Pila were also used in naval clashes.[383] Lightly armed troops such as archers and slingers were often used on board, and Antonius, in his morale-boosting speech before the Battle of Actium, reminds his soldiers how the towered ships of Cleopatra were well defended by a large number of slingers (*sphendonitai*) and archers (*toxotai*).[384] During the battle Antonius' men used spears (*kontoi*), axes (*axinai*) and stones against the Augustan sailors.[385]

Specific colours identified the *nautae*, the *classiarii* and the naval commanders: Sextus Pompeius, who received in 43 BC from the Senate the title of *Praefectus Classis et Orae Marittimae* (Admiral of the Fleet and Roman Shores), wore a mid-blue cloak. According to both Appianus[386] and Cassius Dio[387] this *venetus* was the colour sacred to Neptune.[388] The same colours are mentioned for Agrippas, but Plautus, speaking about the ordinary sailors,[389] talks about tunics in iron-grey, giving a very specific description of the *nauta*'s dress:

> Take care to come here dressed in the garb of a master of a ship. Have on a broad-brimmed hat [*scutula*] of iron-grey, a woollen shade [*lanea*] before your eyes; have on an iron-grey cloak [*palliolum*] – for that is the seaman's colour – have it fastened over the left shoulder, your right arm projecting out, your clothes some way well girded up, pretend as though you are some master of a ship.

Among the military decorations, the *corona navalis* was assigned to the *imperator* who was victorious over the enemy fleet. So Agrippa, *artefix* of the Imperial destiny of Augustus through the victory at Actium, is shown on many coins with the naval crown on his head.[390] Specific naval *signa* are recorded by the sources.[391]

~ II ~
The Roman Empire in the Age of Expansion
30 BC–AD 192

~ Sources and Historical Outline ~

Sources: Aelius Herodianus, Ammianus Marcellinus, Appianus, Aulus Gellius, Caius Suetonius Tranquillus, Cassius Dio Cocceianus, Claudius Aelianus, Cornelius Tacitus, Decimus Junius Juvenalis, Digestum seu Pandectae, Dionysius of Halicarnassus, Flavius Josephus, Flavius Renatus Vegetius, Gaius Julius Caesar, Octavianus Augustus, Gaius Petronius Arbiter, Gaius Plinius Secundus Maior, Gaius Valerius Catullus, Gaius Valerius Flaccus, Hesychios Alexandrinus, Isidorus of Seville, Lucianus of Samosata, Lucius Apuleius Platonicus, Lucius Flavius Arrianus, Marcus Aurelius Antoninus Augustus, Marcus Terentius Varro, Marcus Valerius Martialis, Pausanias, Phaedrus, Publius Ovidius Naso, Publius Papinius Statius, Publius Vergilius Maro, Pseudo-Hyginus, Quintus Horatius Flaccus, Res Gestae Divi Augusti, Rutilius Taurus Aemilianus Palladius, Sextus Julius Frontinus, Sextus Propertius, Scriptores Historia Augusta, Talmud, Yôḥānān (Saint John the Evangelist), Xenophon.

Events Timeline

29 BC — The Egyptian *praefectus* Cornelius Gallus imposed on the Kushites a vassal Roman state between the first and second cataracts of the Nile. Octavianus – now called *Imperator Caesar*[1] *Augustus*[2] – received the title of *Princeps Rei Publicae*.[3]

29–12 BC — The submission of the whole Alpine region was begun. After the campaign against the Salassi, a peace treaty was concluded with Cotius, King of the Celtic Cotii, in 14 BC (**28**). Rome annexed the last pieces of free Spanish territory. On the eastern frontier, a wise policy of vassal states[4] and annexations[5] created the buffer zone against the Parthians. In the Roman campaign on the Arabian Gulf Aden was sacked and the land of the Sabeans invaded.

16–15 BC — New *provinciae* were added in Raetia,[6] Vindelicia[7] and Noricum.[8]

8–6 BC — Pannonia and Moesia[9] were incorporated into the Empire by Tiberius Claudio Nero, son of Livia, who was the wife of Augustus.

7–5 BC — Tiberius began further penetration into Germania.

AD 9 — The *legatus* Varo and the XVII, XVIII and XIX Legions, together with nine auxiliary cohorts, were destroyed in the Teutoburgus Forest, near modern-day Kalkriese, by the Cherusci and the Chatti, led by Arminius. There followed bloody punitive expeditions by Drusus and Tiberius in Germany.

AD 21 — Under Tiberius (AD 14–37) a new Gallic insurrection by Sacrovir was crushed. During the rule of Caligula (AD 37–41) the military expeditions against Britain and Germany were aborted.

AD 41 — Caligula was killed by a conspiracy of Praetorians, and to avert the rage of Caligula's Germanic Guards, the Praetorians elevated Caligula's uncle Claudius to emperor (AD 41–54). Mauretania became a *provincia*. The *signa* lost by Varus were recovered.

AD 43–50 — Britannia was invaded by Aulus Plautius and transformed into a *provincia*; the British leader Caratacus was defeated.

AD 58 — Under Nero (AD 54–68), the campaign against the Silures and the Ordovices in Britain was completed.

AD 61 — Boudicca, Queen of the Iceni, raised a revolt, destroying the city of Camulodunum (Colchester), but her army was crushed by Suetonius Paulinus on the battlefield at Mancetter with detachments of XIV and XX *legiones*.

AD 66 — The revolt of the Jews took place, in Judaea, and the Sarmatians raided across the Danube. Following brilliant campaigns by Corbulo in Parthia, Nero crowned Tiridates Helios King of Armenia.

AD 68–9 — After the suicide of Nero, civil war tore the empire apart, leading to AD 69 being called the Year of the Four Emperors with Galba, Otho, Vitellius and Vespasianus all claiming the throne. The outcome of the war was decided after the titanic battles of Bedriacum and Cremona, Vespasianus' ultimate victory. In a side-effect of the civil war, Civilis, a

Batavian commander of *auxilia*, took advantage of the chaos and tried to form a coalition against Rome of Batavians, Germans, Gauls and Roman deserters. After some initial successes the rebellion was crushed.

AD 70–3   The revolt in Judaea was finally put down with the complete destruction of Jerusalem by Titus and the capture of Masada.

AD 75–96   In the remote Caucasus there was the First War against the Alani; military operations in the west brought the conquest of the Campi Decumani, a wide area around the Neckar and Lake Constance. After the rule of Titus (AD 79–81), his brother Domitianus (AD 81–96) conducted successful campaigns against the Chatti and created two provinces in Germania (Inferior and Superior). Agricola conquered the territory of southern Scotland. After two unsuccesful campaigns against the raids of King Decebalus of Dacia, between AD 85 and 88, and an undecisive campaign against the Sarmatians in AD 92, Domitianus was killed in a plot.

AD 96–8   Under Nerva victorious campaigns were undertaken in Pannonia and in Germania Superior.

AD 98–117   Under Trajan the Roman Empire reached its zenith: in two successive campaigns (AD 101–2 and 105–7) Dacia was conquered and Decebalus, King of the Dacians, committed suicide. In AD 106, with the conquest of Arabia Petraea, the Romans had under control all the caravan routes to India and the Far East. From AD 114 to 116 Trajan invaded Parthia, Armenia, Mesopotamia and Assyria, reaching the Persian Gulf. The Parthian capital Ctesiphon was conquered and new provinces of Assyria and Mesopotamia were created.

AD 117   These new provinces were soon lost, and upon the sudden death of Trajan his heir and successor Hadrian

(AD 117–38) began a policy of strengthening the frontiers. Examples of this new policy were the creation of Hadrian's Wall in Britannia, the Limes in Germania and the regionalisation of the army.

AD 132–5   A second Judaean revolt, named after its leader, Bar Kochbà,[10] broke out. Jerusalem was captured and Bar Kochbà was proclaimed Prince of Israel. The revolt was put down after three years by Lusius Quietus and his Moorish cavalrymen; 520,000 Jews were put to death. A new city of Aelia Capitolina was erected on the site of Jerusalem.

AD 138–61   Under Antoninus Pius the northern border with Scotland was extended with the construction of a new wall between the Firth of Forth and the Clyde.

AD 161–80   The reign of Marcus Aurelius was a period of continuous war. The invasion of Armenia by the Parthians in AD 161 was halted by the troops of the co-emperor Lucius Verus and his general, Avidius Cassius. Roman strongholds on the Euphrates, such as Dura-Europos, protected the caravan routes to Persia. But on the Danube a powerful confederation of Germanic and Iranian peoples (Quadi, Marcomanni, Lombards and Jazyges) attacked the empire in AD 166. They raided throughout Raetia, Dacia, Noricum, Pannonia and the Balkans, ravaging north Italy as far as Aquileia. A vigorous Roman counter-attack was mounted in AD 172 and the Barbarians were driven out of the empire, massacred and forced to capitulate.[11] In AD 175 Marcus Aurelius successfully defeated the insurrection of Cassius in the east.

AD 180–92   During the final phase of the Danubian War (AD 177–80), Marcus Aurelius died and was succeeded by his son Commodus, who concluded the peace with the Barbarians. After his murder by a plot in AD 192, with no obvious successors, the throne was once again open to powerful military leaders.

~ MILITARY ORGANISATION[12] ~

After the distribution of land to the veterans, Augustus began the demobilisation of the army, from fifty to twenty-eight legions, keeping a permanent army of about 150,000 men to defend the 8,000 km of the Roman Empire's borders. The number of legions varied at around thirty to thirty-three until the third century AD. The ethnic composition of the force slowly changed as provincial recruits began to increase in number.

A single *legio* was composed of sixty *centuriae*. The *centuria* was now a unit comprised of eighty *milites gregarii*, under the *centurio*[13] (*hekatontarchês* in the eastern part of the empire[14]). Junior officers were the *aquilifer* (standard-bearer of the eagle, only in the *primus pilus'*[15] *centuria*), the *signifer* (standard-bearer), the *optio* (*centurio*'s deputy),[16] the *cornicen* and the *buccinator*

(trumpeters) and the *tesserarius* (officer of the watch). The *custos armorum*, usually a *veteranus*,[17] was responsible for keeping the arms of the *legio* secure. Other ranks were the *semaforos* (signaller), the *hydraularius* (musician who played the water pipes), *speculator* (scout, then bodyguard) (**294**), *molendarius* (man turning the millstones), *siphonarius* (fire-fighter) and *aquarius* (responsible for the water-sources).[18] The *beneficiarius* was the soldier or junior officer acting as bodyguard or charged with special duties by his senior officer; he was exempted from heavy duties.

Three or more[19] *centuriae* were formed into a *cohors*, a military unit of about 240–500 men.[20] The *cohors prima* was under the command of the *primus pilus* and had twice the number of men.[21] So it usually numbered 1,000 men and consisted of five double *centuriae*. As before, the *primus pilus* was the commander of the first *centuria* on the right of the first *cohors* of *pili*, and the senior in rank of all the centurions.

Each *cohors* was still comprised of three maniples, so usually there was a total of thirty maniples in a *legio*. Normally ten *cohortes* made up a *legio*,[22] so the maximum strength of the *legio* was around 4,800–6,000 men. The *antesignani,* known from the Consular period, are still mentioned in the sources of the Imperial era, together with *postsignani*.[23] Special light troops from the legions called *levis armaturae* (lightly armoured infantry) controlled the provincial borders.[24] They were under the command of legionary officers from the nearby *castra*.

The *tribunus* was the *cohors* commander.[25] The commander of the *legio* was the *legatus*,[26] usually still of senatorial rank, and assisted by six *tribuni*. The second-in-command was an officer from the senatorial order, the *tribunus laticlavius*. The other five *Tribuni* held the rank of *tribuni angusticlavi*, and were of the Equestrian order (*ordo equestris*). Beside the *legatus* the senior experienced officer was the *praefectus castrorum*, usually a former *primus pilus* with responsibility for the whole camp, who took over as second-in-command in absence of the *legatus* or the senior *tribunus*.[27] Lower-ranking *principales* acted as *optiones* of centurions.

45 *Centurio* and his *calo* (servant), fragment of *stela*, first century AD (*Turin, Museo of Antichità, drawing by Graham Sumner*)

To each *legio* about 120 servants (*calones*) were attached per *cohors*. They were sometimes armed (**45**) and responsible for defending the camp.[28] From 13 BC until the middle of the first century AD the veterans, after serving for sixteen years, were transferred to the *vexillum veteranorum*, for a further four years of service.[29] With a strength of about 500 men plus officers, they were used for independent duties[30] or attached to the legion. The numerical title for each *legio* was kept, sometimes with a duplication because of period of the civil wars.[31]

The cavalry force of each *legio* had an average strength of 120 men.[32] The *seviri equitum Romanorum* were at the command of the single *turmae*, composed of thirty men.

The *praetoriani* constituted the Imperial Guard together with the *Germani corporis custodes*, the *equites singulares Augusti* and the *evocati Augusti*. Augustus formed an elite body of nine[33] *cohortes praetoriae*, each *cohors* comprised 500 to 1,000 men, paid three times as much as the regular troops and with a reduced service time (sixteen years as opposed to the thirty or forty of the other soldiers). They were based in Rome or in its surroundings, constituting, together with the other Imperial Guards, the only armed force in Italy,[34] under the command of a special officer of equestrian rank, the *praefectus praetorii*.

The *equites singulares Augusti*[35] were a body of picked men (*ala milliaria*), separate from the praetorians, and from different units.[36] The *Germani corporis custodes* were a *cohors* of ferocious Batavi, loyal to the person of the leader and considered more reliable than the other guards. They were disbanded by Galba, for their blind loyalty to Nero.[37]

The *evocati Augusti* were created by Augustus, as attested by the inscriptions[38] and by the sources.[39] They were recruited from the troops based in Rome, i.e. especially the praetorians, the *urbaniciani*,[40] and the marines of the *classis Misenatis*, a detachment of which were based in Rome.[41] Under the command of the *praefectus praetorianus*,[42] they did not, however, constitute a particular military body organised in a regular way or furnished with a particular *vexillum*; they were of inferior rank to those of the *primipilares* who were attached to the emperor, and they camped with them in the *castrum*.[43] They were reserved for missions and duties of particular importance.[44] Others were attached to the legions and spread across the Roman world.

The *urbaniciani* were soldiers of the urban *cohortes* under the command of a senator of *consularis* rank who governed the *praefectura urbana*.[45] They were divided into four *cohortes* with numerical designations following on from that of the praetorians (i.e. X, XI, XII and XIII), comprised of 1,500 men each, under the command of a *tribunus* chosen from the *primipilares* of the legions. In the second century they passed under the command of the *praefectus praetorii*. As well as them, seven cohorts of *vigiles* were raised, who from AD 6 had duties of policing and fire-watching. They were under the control of the *praefectus vigilum*, with their *tribuni* (one for each cohort), a *princeps* and seven centurions.[46] All the junior officers (*principales* and *immunes, optio ballistarii*) as well as the *praefectus vigilum* came from other bodies of the army, so we can suppose they kept their own uniform.

The *auxilia* were now formed from various races.[47] They were generally *peregrini*, i.e not *civites Romani*,[48] and divided into formations of cavalry (*alae*, of about 120 men) and infantry (*cohorts*, of about 350 men) or mixed cohorts of cavalrymen and infantrymen (*cohortes equitatae*)[49] commanded by *tribuni* and *praefecti* (*tres militiae equestres*).[50] They were also divided into *centuriae*.

Under Trajan and Hadrian the soldiers began to serve in the provinces or locality where they were recruited. Another innovation was the use of a special permanent corps, the *numeri* or *symmacharii*, made up from border peoples (*nationes*) who fought under the command of their own tribal leaders. Since the time of Augustus, the defence of the desert-frontier was delegated to the caravan cities of the Nabataeans, such as Palmyra and Petra, who formed regiments of cavalry archers, which were transformed into *numeri* under Hadrian. *Numeri* of Jazyges and Germanic cavalrymen were employed to put down the rebellion of Avidius Cassius, and possibly *numeri* of Dalmatae cavalrymen are also mentioned in *Historia Augusta* under the command of the *tribunus* Clodius Albinus.[51]

The *auxilia cohortes* and *alae* and sometimes *cohortes alares*[52] were also numbered, named and distinguished by different criteria.[53] The cavalry *alae* were divided into *turmae*.[54]

The *vexillationes* were detachments of a unit operating independently, recruiting under the same *vexillum* soldiers belonging to different bodies of the army. The usurper Pescennius Niger is recorded in a letter of Antoninus Pius as being appointed to the command of 1,400 men, 300 Armenians, 100 Sarmatians and 1,000 Romans.[55]

Sometimes gladiators were employed as soldiers, as the gladiatorial army from Cyzicus that supported Marcus Antonius and was crushed in 30 BC by Didius, legatus of Octavianus in Syria.[56] At the time of the Marcomannic War, gladiators and slaves were also enlisted, an unknown move since Hannibal's invasion of Italy. *Diogmitai*, the police corps of Asia Minor and the Hellenistic world, were sometimes also employed as regular troops.[57]

Private slave armies are occasionally seen, like those used by Sabinus in AD 4,[58] flanked by four regular cavalry *alae*.[59] Auxiliary *cohortes* (*voluntariorum Civium Romanorum*) were recruited in emergency situations, such as after the defeat of Varus.

The *imperator* was now the supreme authority of the Roman state. The government of the *provinciae* and the army's command was reserved for officers of senatorial rank, those of the fleet (*praefecti classium*), praetorian guard and of the *cohortes vigilum* for men of equestrian rank. The Roman *provinciae* were divided into imperial – defended by a regular army and ruled by an Imperial *legatus* – and senatorial, ruled by *proconsules*. An exception was Egypt, where two legions were commanded by a *praefectus* of equestrian rank.

~ WEAPONRY ~

Even though permeated by characters of pure classicism and substantially inspired in form and proportion by Greco-Hellenistic stereotypes, the figures adorning the monuments of the first and second centuries AD are a true mirror of Roman military equipment of that age. The precision of details, often confirmed by archaeological and literary data, reveals clear knowledge and personal observation of the army of their age on the part of the sculptors and artists.

Under the Trajanic Empire (AD 98–117) the Roman world attained the peak of its power. Among the Trajanic achievements, the conquest of the Dacia was certainly the most famous, not least for the iconographical celebration it received on monuments that, exalting the empire's glory, adorned the Imperial Fori in Rome. Among them are Trajan's Column and the great frieze that today can still be admired on the Constantine Arch. The rough but realistic images on the Adamclisi monument in Dacia (modern Romania) add more knowledge and quality to the understanding of the early Imperial equipment, and constantly receive more support from archaeology.

Recent works on the monuments of the Trajanic and Antonine periods have put forward the idea that, notwithstanding the high degree of realism sometimes shown, the artists who sculpted it were too permeated with Hellenism and too far removed from the knowledge of effective military equipment; so the subjects they portrayed were only partially representative of the reality of the Roman *milites legionis* and *auxilia*.

The present author thinks instead in a different way. The historical accuracy of Trajan's Column and other monuments of the Trajanic era, for instance, is attested by the conception and execution of Apollodorus of Damascus, a Syro-Greek architect well known as the architect who built the bridge across the Danube, as depicted also on the column, and who planned the whole of Trajan's Forum with the Trajan Markets (*mercati Traianei*), giving them their urban schema. He himself followed the Emperor Trajan in the Dacian expeditions, and one of the reliefs of the column is thought to represent him in Trajan's headquarters, in front of his monumental work of engineering. Therefore he was an eye-witness and the scenes he ordered to be represented on the Trajanic monuments were probably taken from life. Apollodorus knew very well the realities of his time: he may never have been on the front line, but his reliefs could be considered as sketches and information taken down on the spot. A detail shown on the Great Trajanic Frieze (a heap of fallen Dacians) can be seen as something like modern photographic reportage; it does not show idealised Hellenistic influence. It is enough to observe with attention and free from every prejudice the great number of Dacian bodies heaped one over the other, to understand that they are a true portrait from life.

Almost certainly, Trajan's Column depicts true Roman uniform and armour in the Dacian Wars. An example can best give an idea of what we are talking about. The column depicts most of the legionary infantrymen with the iron laminated armour known under the modern name of *lorica segmentata*, while most of the *auxilia* are portrayed clad in ring-mail armour or leather corselets. The reliefs have been executed in such a way for two reasons: first, the *lorica segmentata* was much more attractive from an aesthetic point of view, and so visibly preponderant; secondly, it was necessary to fix a general principle of distinction between the different bodies of the military.

It is true that the artisans at the centre of the empire were much less informed about the different kind of equipment and it was logical that they were so, although their work can be highly appreciated from an artistic point of view, the work of their colleagues of the frontier regions is much more reliable, with all the limitations that are imposed by carving stone; they have the Roman *milites* in sight every day. So perhaps the carved *metopae* of the Adamclisi monument preserve a certain rigidity, undoubtedly linked to the lack of expertise of the sculptors; they are, though, not idealised, and so provide useful records of the 'uniforms' that are not visible on the column.

Even though it was the workshops of Rome that executed the Column they are certainly were not short of first-hand material upon which to base their representations. They could have simply copied the armours of the troops based in Rome[60] which were, after all, the actual weapons of their age. These were all elite troops, with top quality equipment: the praetorian cohorts (infantrymen and cavalrymen); the *equites singulares*; the urban cohorts; the *vigiles* and the *evocati Augusti*.

Shafted Weapons: *Pilum* and *Hasta*

The *pilum* is attested, at least until the end of the second century AD, as the main shafted weapon, even used by the emperor.[61] There were changes in the *pilum* of the Late Consular age, but these concerned only the weight and the length of the weapon, and the system of attaching the metallic body to the wooden shaft; the basic shape, tanged and socketed, was kept untouched. The general length reached 2 m, with a long iron shank of about 40–90 cm and a pyramidal or barbed head.[62] By the Augustan time the junction was based on a narrow tang

46 Reconstruction of C. Valerius Crispus of *Legio VIII Augusta* (ex Coussin; author's collection)

at the end of the shank, generally perforated with two or three rivet holes[63] and fastened at the top with a pyramid-shaped metal collet.[64] *Pila* collets in iron and a fragment of an iron *pilum* have been found on the field of the Battle of Teutoburgus, near Kalkriese.[65]

The predominant form of the Early Principate *pila* is represented by three tanged specimens from Oberaden, preserved with a part of their wooden haft, showing intact heads, shanks, collets and a substantial portion of the wooden shaft.[66] The iron part is respectively 70, 60 and 49 cm long. The slim trapezoidal tang was secured in the haft by three rivets in the longer specimen, two rivets in the shorter ones. All present a square section in the lower iron part of the shank, becoming round as it tapers towards the point. Their main characteristic is the iron ferrule or collet used to secure the junction of the wooden shaft and iron shank. The ferrule was fitted after the head was riveted in place by a pyramidal expansion of the shaft. Four small iron wedges were then hammered down the inside of the ferrule to tighten the fit. The shaft narrowed below the junction to form a handgrip. The Hod Hill *pilum* has the same characteristic, showing that this weapon was used by the legions in Britannia. This kind of heavy *pilum* is shown on the gravestone of Valerius Crispus,[67] *Legio VIII Augusta* (**PLATE III, 46**).

Two other kind of *pila*, socketed and tanged, are often recovered in archaeological contexts.[68] Light specimens of socketed *pila* were found on the Rhine frontier, confirmed also by the sculptures of this corner of the empire (**48**), like the specimen preserved in Mainz Museum,[69] where the blade is

PLATE III C. Valerius Crispus, *miles* of *Legio VIII Augusta*: the leather suit of this famous *miles legionarius* from his gravestone in Wiesbaden is a revision of its standard reconstruction as a mail armour suit. It is reconstructed following the Vindonissa finds. Valerius wears a leather corselet, close fitting to the body, with fastened shoulder guards, and short sleeves. He wears short breeches or *feminalia* of leather, reaching the upper half of the knee. This reconstruction, already the subject of previous studies (**180, 46**), then refuted as an artistic convention, is proposed again here, following the Vindonissa finds, which attest the high level of the use of leather in the Roman army.

Essentially it is a tanned leather suit including a pair of short breeches of semi-rigid leather. Some authors have interpreted the leather trousers as furnished with two rows of *pteryges*, but similar trousers are worn by other soldiers represented on Rhine tombstones.

On his tombstone Valerius is represented with a Weisenau-type helmet, very similar to one specimen in the former collection of Axel Guttman (**127**) here used for the reconstruction. The helmet has three crest attachments: a central knob welded on a round base and back and front bosses with split pins.[i] The crest colour, of red-pinkish plumes, has been copied from a Pompeian fresco. The Weisenau helmet could be protected by leather cheek guards and covers,[ii] like the specimens found in Vindonissa. Around the neck he wears his woollen or felt *focale*. He is belted at the waist, with a simple but wide *cingulum*, metal plated and fitted with aprons (*baltea*). To the wide *balteus* is attached, at the right side of the body, the sword – here copied from the famous specimen from Mainz,[iii] held in a scabbard decorated using the *opus interrasile* technique.

His heavy broad-tanged *pilum* is copied from the Oberaden specimen: the iron part is 67 cm long. The lateral edges of the tang were hammered over at the point where they were fitted into the wooden haft to reinforce the junction of the iron with the wood. The trapezoidal iron tang was locked into the wood by means of two rivets; four nails were further inserted to lock the collar in position.

The typical rectangular shield of the Augustan age, fitted with a metallic *umbo*, is carried in the left hand. The curved rectangular shield is bordered and its face is decorated. The framework decoration of the shield was yellow-painted spirals and vegetables, as suggested by some fragment from Vindonissa.[iv] The two front corners have L-shaped digamma motifs framing the central area, while an ansate panel stretches horizontally between the boss and the border of the shield. An *umbo* located within a painted *tabula ansata*, upon which is inscribed the name of the *legio*. The rectangular boss plate is also decorated with a border and a saltire, at the centre of which is the boss. The L-shaped digamma motifs at the corners are visible also on the painted *umbo* of the second century, but useful in the style of the different decorative patterns. The boss itself is in the form of an animal's head in relief, evidently horned and so possibly intended to be a bull, symbol of the *Legio VIII Augusta*.[v] This last could have had a shape similar to some pendants from Augst[vi]

---

i   Mattesini, 2004, p. 118; Robinson, 1975, p. 46.
ii   *Galeatus*, as in Petr., Sat., 9-LIX, could also refer to a man wearing a leather helmet or an iron helmet completely covered by leather.
iii Vujovic', 2001, pl. 10.
iv   Gansser-Burckhardt, 1948–9, fig. 5.
v   Daremberg and Saglio, 1873–1917, see Legio, col. 1084.
vi   Deschler-Erb, 1999, pl. 31, no. 604.

47 (Right) Armoured *milites* and standard-bearers attacking with *pila*, Adamclisi relief, *metopa* XII, first half of second century AD (*Museum of Adamclisi; author's photo, courtesy of the museum*).

The Adamclisi monument represent an unusual use of the *pilum* as impact weapons, which is perfectly understandable considering the little equipment and nudity of the Dacian warriors. The *pilum* was a throwing weapon, but it could be used as a spear in hand-to-hand combat. The Roman extra-heavy armoured legionaries are protected with a *squama*, worn over a *subarmale*, which has the *pteryges* visible, and semi-cylindrical *scuta*, segmented helmets of spangenhelm construction and a *manica* protection on the right arm. The three standard-bearers (*signiferi*) behind them are probably carrying the *signa manipularia* and are also protected by scale armour, but very interestingly have a *focale* around their necks. All the warriors are wearing *caligae* on their feet

48 (Above) Military *stela* of unknown *miles*, first–second century AD, detail of the aprons (*Bonn, LandesMuseum; courtesy of Stefano Izzo*).

Note the frontal aprons studded with rows of eight studs and ending with *lunulae*. We can imagine the impression that thousands and thousands of these small belts made when the army was marching, and the psychological impact on the enemy[i]

i   Dante Alighieri, visiting Rome in AD 1301, remembers the soft sound produced by the wind on the metallic elements (still in place) on Trajan's Column, among which were also many metallic *balteoli* still attached to the sculptures.

49 (Opposite, bottom) Armoured *milites*, *signiferi* and *aquilifer* attacking with *pila*, Adamclisi relief, *metopa* XIII, first half of second century AD (*Museum of Adamclisi; author's photo, courtesy of the museum*).

The main difference from the previous *metopa* is the presence of the legionary eagle carried by the central standard-bearer. The eagle is mounted upon a pole and has thunderbolts on the base. Note the short beard of the left *signifer*, similar to many figures on Trajan's Column, and his manipular standard, a *signum* of an open hand and *phalerae*. Unusually, it is mounted upon a structure similar to those of the decorative *phalerae* of an armour

50 (Above, left) Marching legionaries, probably praetorians, Adamclisi relief, *metopa* XXXIX, first half of second century AD (*Museum of Adamclisi; author's photo, courtesy of the museum*).

The identification of these marching warriors as members of the praetorian guard could be supported by many elements of their

equipment, comparing it to contemporary monuments: the decorated volute scabbard, similar to those on the Great Trajanic Frieze;[i] the shape of the *pilum*, furnished with the spheroid (today lost) and *amentum*, like the *pila* of the praetorians of the Cancelleria relief,[ii] the shape of the shield and the form of the *caligae*, that, as on the Cancelleria relief, seem be furnished with an open-heeled woollen sock

51 (Above, right) Marching legionaries, probably praetorians, Adamclisi relief, *metopa* XLIV first half of second century AD (*Museum of Adamclisi; author's photo, courtesy of the museum*).

The scene is similar to the previous one, but here the spheroid parts of the *pila* are still preserved. The soldiers are covered with short *paenulae*, similar to that of the Cancelleria relief. Note the pyramidal head of the *pilum*, corresponding to the description by Arrian

---

i   Antonucci, 1994, fig. 8b; Touati, 1987, pl. 21, fig. 64.

ii   Rankov, 1994, p. 47.

52 Triumphal sculpture and details, representing two legionaries or praetorians with *scutum*, *paenula* and *pilum*, Trophaeum Trajani, Adamclisi, first half of second century AD (*Istanbul, Archaeological Museum; author's photo, courtesy of the museum*)

69 cm long, with a squared four-cornered tang, of pyramidal shape, from which the iron shank has a round section towards the pyramidal point. The tang is movable and was also used to cover the shaft handle. The iron tongue, which ends the lower part of the blade, was inserted in the tang and secured by rivets. A similar specimen was found in Carnuntum.[70] A second *pilum*, found in the *castra* of Hofheim,[71] has an iron square-sectioned shank 1.06 m long and a tang that is 20 cm long and 11 cm wide. The light type of *pila* were mainly used by legionary skirmishers. The first of these light *pila* is very similar to the representation of the *pilum* held by the *miles* Quintus Petilius Secundus, *Legio XV Primigenia*, dated to the second half of the first century AD.[72]

The *pila* were typically fitted with a pyramidal point. Arrian,[73] a Roman officer and historian of the second century

AD, mentions the length of the *pilum*'s iron point as being a third of its total length. Examples of *pila* having such a point have been found in Newstead from the pits,[74] and are visible on the Adamclisi monument (**47**, **49**, **50**, **51**) and on the well-known Croy Hill relief,[75] which probably represents *milites* of the *Legio II Augusta* that were at that time quartered in Scotland.[76] In Newstead other *pila* heads have been found near the Antonine barracks, and are up to 7 cm long.[77] Further examples come from Bar Hill, with square-sectioned pyramidal heads and square-sectioned shanks.

Appian says the *pilum*'s tang of its time was rectangular. This is in fact the shape of many specimens dated to the second century AD and found in Mainz; some others are cylindrical, such as the specimens from Gran San Bernardo.[78] Appian[79] notes, moreover, how, in his time, the iron shank was flexible, and he confirms that, because of this characteristic, the shank bent once the point had penetrated its target or had fallen to the ground. On some original specimens we can note that the point is in fact in steel,[80] with a shank of soft iron.[81]

Josephus, in his description of the weaponry of the Roman army in the age of Vespasianus, said expressly that 'those footmen also that are chosen out from amongst the rest [*epilektoi pezoi*] to be about the general himself, have a lance [*lonchês*] and a buckler; but the rest of the foot soldiers have a spear and a long shield.'[82] To underline the importance that the *hasta* had in the armament of the *milites gregarii*, we should furthermore remember the distinction made by Arrian between *kontophoroi* and *lonchoforoi*, in his description of the battle order against the Alans:[83] the first, as well as a long spear (*kontos*) usually reserved for the cavalry,[84] were armed with *pila*, the second with *hastae*.

The heavy *lonchês* or *lancea* and *hasta*,[85] the typical thrusting weapon of the Roman legionary, has an iron point called the *cuspis*.[86] The forged iron head of this period was nearly always

socketed, and the wood used for the shaft was usually hazel or ash.[87] Thousand of specimens of iron spearheads have been recovered from all over the empire's territories. Some models of the early first and second centuries AD still present the characteristic shape of the La Tène Celtic period: they generally have long and massive spearheads.[88] The spearhead has many shapes.

One common form has a leaf-shaped section, sometimes pistilliform, sometimes pinnate or sometimes lanceolate, but usually simple leaf-shaped,[89] and an oblong[90] or broad-shouldered blade and long socket (**53**, **54**, **55**, **56**).[91] These

54 Spearheads, spear butts, javelins and bolt points, from Ulpia Traiana Sarmizegetusa, end first–third century AD (*Museum of Ulpia Traiana Sarmizegetusa; courtesy of the museum*).

Some of these shafted and throwing weapons could now be dated to the beginning of the second century AD by comparison with similar specimens found in Augst (Augusta Raurica)[i] and Vindonissa,[ii] but we cannot discount the dating proposed by Ilies, i.e. second–third centuries AD. Note the elongated spearhead,[iii] with its long and narrow blade and a slight accentuated midrib. The lanceolate point also has a triangular midrib[iv]

53 Spearhead and arrow point from Ulpia Traiana Sarmizegetusa, first–second century AD (*Museum of Ulpia Traiana Sarmizegetusa, Romania; courtesy of the museum*).

The spearhead has a long and narrow blade with a slightly accentuated midrib and slightly thicker point merging without interruption into the cylindrical protective sleeve. It could be dated by comparison to a similar spearhead found in Augst (Augusta Raurica)[i]

i   Deschler-Erb, 1999, p. 21 and p. 133, pl. 5, cat. 60, no. 615.

i   Deschler-Erb, 1999, cat. 61 (spearhead), 82–3 (butts), cat. 23 (pyramidal iron bolt), cat. 15 (squared pyramidal bolt).
ii   Unz and Deschler-Erb, 1997, p. 20 and pl. 16, no. 250 (foliate spearhead).
iii Ilies, 1981, pl. I, no. 2, p. 416; the spearhead measures 29 x 2.5 cm; see a similar specimen in Coussin, 1926, p. 361, fig. 109.
iv   Ilies, 1981, pl. I no. 6, p. 416; the spearhead measures 10.5 x 3.1 cm; see a similar specimen in Coussin, 1926, p. 361, fig. 108.

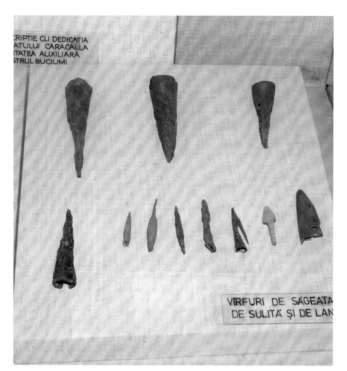

55 Roman spear butts and arrow points, from the military camps of Porolissum and Buciumi, second century AD (*Zalau Museum, Romania; author's photo, courtesy of the museum*)

56 Roman spearheads from the military camps of Porolissum and Buciumi, second century AD, (*Zalau Museum, Romania; author's photo, courtesy of the museum*).

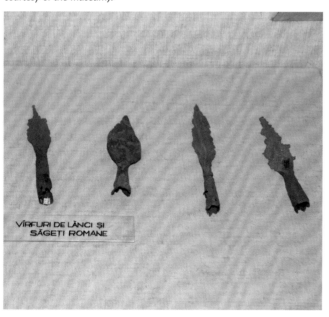

heads show an interesting similarity to the spear held by the *miles* P. Flavoleius Corduo, of the XIIII Gemina, dated to the first century AD.[92] Moreover, the spear of Flavoleius is a *hasta amentata*, i.e. furnished with the *amentum*, a central strap fixed in the middle of the shaft and used to increase the propulsion of the throw. This special throwing device was used to increase the range up to 60 m.[93]

Some first-century specimens have long and narrow-shouldered heads that are at their widest about halfway along the blade and reaching as much as 50 cm in length![94] We can imagine the kind of wounds that such spears would have inflicted on the enemy.

A central midrib is usually present on the middle of the blade. Leaf-shaped points of similar typology have been found in various military contexts of the first and second centuries AD, having either a slightly pronounced rib[95] or a slightly more pronounced portion of the leaf.[96] Others, dated to the first century AD, have a round-edged leaf shape, gradually tapering towards the top,[97] or are narrow and elongated with a slightly pronounced rib.[98] Specimens from Newstead are different in their size, but here a central midrib is also usually present on the middle of the blade.

A second shape for the spearhead has an elongated rectangular section. This form is often frequent in some archaeological contexts, but could have been used for javelins, or bolts.[99] Various heads of javelins and spears of this type, complete with butt, were found on Kalkriese.[100]

A third form is the rhomboidal section. The spearheads of this category are massive, with a strong midrib, and the length[101] of some specimens could probably support the identification of such spears with those worn by the *kontophoroi* mentioned by Arrian. An example from the second century also comes from Ulpia Traiana Sarmizegetusa.[102] On the column of Marcus Aurelius these kinds of spears are clearly visible (**57**).

The blades of the spears were often damascened, following the Celtic tradition. Specimens have been recovered from the graves in Sremska Mitrovica (ancient Sirmium) characterised by outstanding decorative work from the top to the bottom of the blade, always presenting a marked longitudinal rib.[103]

The length of the spear varied according to the speciality and the use in battle: as well as the longer specimens, the *milites gregarii* used short spears without butts in hand-to-hand fighting (**57, 59, 61, 63, 64, 65**).

The presence of a butt (*spiculum*),[104] i.e. the metallic reinforcement of the shaft end, in infantry spears is well documented in archaeological fields, but seems to be declining in the second century, because it is scarcely visible on the spears of the soldiers on Marcus Aurelius' time (**66**).[105] It was used to fix the spear to the ground when not in use, thus sparing the wood of the shaft, but it had also a effective function in battle, because if the spear was broken, the butt could be used as a improvised spearhead.[106] The most usual butt shape in the first to third centuries has with a polygonal or hemispherical

57 The miracle of the rain, scene from the Marcus Aurelius column, in situ, Rome (*ex Becatti, by kind courtesy of Editoriale Domus S.p.A.*).

The miracle is recorded by ancient authors, both pagans and Christians.[i] The soldiers represented are members of the Christian *Legio XII Fulminata*, as shown by the cruciform *digma* on the shield

---

i   Cassius Dio, *Rom.*, LXXI, 8–10; Euseb., *HE*, V, 5.

58 (Above) Armoured legionary fighting Dacian warrior, Adamclisi relief, metopa XXI, first half of second century AD (*Museum of Adamclisi; author's photo, courtesy of the museum*)

59 (Below) The army sortieing from Carnuntum, scene from the Marcus Aurelius column, in situ, Rome (*ex Becatti, by kind courtesy of Editoriale Domus S.p.A.*).

The Roman triumphs in the Marcomannic War were celebrated on the reliefs of the Marcus Aurelius column, and hundreds of other figurative monuments in the empire. All the forces of the empire were engaged in this deadly fight, a true 'Vietnam' of the ancient Romans. Here the army is going out from the fortress of Carnuntum upon pontoons (*scaphae*): notice the different armours worn by the *milites legionis* (*squama* or chain mail or *lorica segmentata*); the *vexilliferi* and the *cornicines* have their caps covered by a bearskin

60 (Above and details below) Roman warrior in padded or scale armour fighting Dacian warrior, Adamclisi relief, *metopa* XXIX, first half of second century AD (*Museum of Adamclisi; author's photo, courtesy of the museum*).

It is possible that here – with a system used for representing of the armour of Calidius – the warrior is shown clad in a padded *coactile*. Note the lack of armoured *manica*

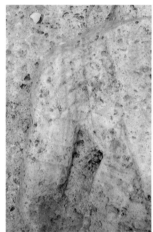

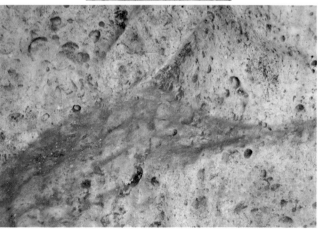

61 (Right) Roman *miles gregarius* fighting a Dacian warrior, Adamclisi relief, metopa XXXI, first half of second century AD (*Museum of Adamclisi; author's photo, courtesy of the museum*).

The *metopa* shows the use of the heavy *hasta* in man-to-man combat. The Roman wears a helmet with a cross-brace, probably fitted with a pointed *apex*, a mail shirt, heavy spear, short sword and rectangular convex *scutum*. The mail shirt is worn over a *subarmale* with two layers of short *pteryges*

62 (Above and right) Emperor Trajan in full armour joined by his bodyguards, Adamclisi relief, *metopa* XXXII, first half of second century AD (*Museum of Adamclisi; author's photo, courtesy of the museum*).

Trajan is here represented escorted by two possible *equites singulares*, who, according to Josephus, were chosen to be with the general.[i] They are protected by round shields (*aspides*) and armed with spears.

Trajan wears, attached to his armour, the *zona militaris*, which was usually embroidered in gold and in red leather (*puniceus*), a symbol of the Romano-Hellenic high ranks and typical *insignia* of the *praefectus praetorii*. On his feet he wears *calcei*, usually in gold with lion's-head lapels in natural leather, with red laces and tied ribbons.

i   Josephus., *BJ*, III, 5, 5, 97.

63 Roman troops raiding the villages, scene from the Marcus Aurelius column, in situ, Rome (*ex Becatti, by kind courtesy of Editoriale Domus S.p.A.*)

64 (Opposite, top left with details right) Armoured *miles* attacking a Dacian cart, Adamclisi relief, *metopa* XXXV, first half of second century AD (*Museum of Adamclisi; author's photo, courtesy of the museum*).

The Roman extra-heavy armoured legionary wears a *manica* protection on the right arm, defending his body with a rectangular *scutum* and a helmet of Sarmatian type, similar to the segmented helmet of some auxiliaries represented on Trajan's Column. Note the killing method, with the short *lancea* stuck into the clavicula of the Dacian warrior. The spearhead is similar to some specimens found in the military camps of Dacia (see **56**)

64 (Above, caption on opposite page)

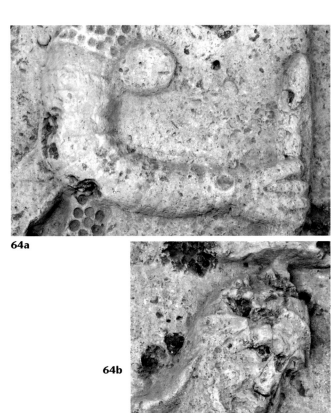

64a

64b

65 (Below) Marching *legionarii* in *lorica segmentata*, scene from the Marcus Aurelius column, in situ, Rome (*ex Becatti, by kind courtesy of Editoriale Domus S.p.A.*)

66 (Above) *Miles* in *lorica segmentata* of Stillfried type, scene from the Marcus Aurelius column, in situ, Rome (*ex Becatti, courtesy of Editoriale Domus S.p.A.*)

67 (Below, left) Spear butts, first–second century AD (*collection of Museum Het Valkhof, Nijmegen; courtesy of the conservator*)

68 (Below, middle) Extra-heavy armoured legionary fighting Dacian warriors, Adamclisi relief, metopa XX, first half of second century AD (*Museum of Adamclisi; author's photo, courtesy of the museum*)

terminal (**54**, **55**).[107] They are usually made of iron,[108] but bronze specimens have also been found along the Danubian *Limes* and from the Netherlands (**67**).

Pila and spears were sometimes punched with inscriptions, allowing the identification of the owner, or of the unit. This was because, contrary to what is usually thought, Roman soldiers did not live and sleep with their weapons, except during war time. The weapons were stored and kept in the armory supervised by the *custos armorum*. So most of the weapons (spears, but also swords, helmets, shields) were marked with the name of the owner who should receive it at the moment of need.

Swords, Daggers and Belts

Josephus tell us that 'the [Roman] infantrymen . . . have swords on each side; but the sword which is upon their left side is much longer than the other; for that on the right side is not longer than a span . . .'[109] It is clear that Josephus, in saying that the *milites* are wearing swords (*machairophorountes*), refers to the use of the dagger (*pugio*) and to the *xiphos* or *gladius*. What it is strange is that he seems to be telling us that the *gladius* is worn on the left side of the body, and the *pugio* on the right!

The iconography of the Roman *miles* in the first two centuries of the Principate shows instead, for the most part, the longer *gladius* worn on the right side of the body (**48**, **59**, **63**, **64**, **66**, **70**, **247**), while the shorter dagger or *pugio* is worn on the left side, except for the officers, where Josephus' rule is followed (**PLATE IV**, **71**, **72**, **73**). However, the wearing of the

69 (Below, right) Extra-heavy armoured legionary fighting a Dacian warrior armed with *falx-rhompaia*, Adamclisi relief, metopa XVII, first half of second century AD (*Museum of Adamclisi; author's photo, courtesy of the museum*),

Note the singular way of wearing the *gladius* scabbard and the use of a sword of the old type

period.[112] The specimens of the early Principate were still more or less the same as those of the Late Consular era.

Three specimens of Roman *gladii* from the last quarter of the first century BC were found in late Celtic graves of the Mokronog group at Mihovo (Slovenia).[113] They are all variants of the so-called Mainz type, considered to be the typical sword of Late Consular and Early Imperial ages.

The Berry-Bouy sword (20 BC), with its 75.7 cm blade, has a metal frame scabbard with suspension rings and related bands that are totally compatible with the Mainz sword typology. The latter, well attested for all of the first half of the

70 Legionary in mail armour, Trajan's Column, scene XXVII (*cast, Roma, Museo della Civiltà Romana, author's photo, courtesy of the museum*).

This scene is the proof that on this monument legionaries are represented also clad in mail armour, and not only in laminated armour. The shield was usually carried with the left hand to allow the right hand to use the offensive weapons freely. The kind of helmet worn by this legionary is very difficult to interpret, although it seems to be a simplified version of the old Italic type of Buggenum typology.

longer sword on the right side has some interesting exceptions in a monumental relief. Two standing legionaries (probably praetorians) of Adamclisi (*metopa* XXVIII) wear the *gladius* on the left side of the body.[110] So the *gladius* on the right side of the body was not the universal rule. Still, a relief from Turin (Italy), representing a centurion with his *calo*, shows this last servant with a military dagger hanging on the right hip (**45**).

The large number of sword (*gladius, ensis*)[111] specimens related to this age gives a very wide range of typology, often difficult to date. Moreover, during war time, many Roman soldiers supplemented their stocks with equipment of local origin, and this can help to explain why many swords or sword fittings of local production and Celtic derivation have been found in Roman settlements of Alpine regions and in the Noricum subjected to the Roman conquest in Early Principate

71 Trajan with military officer and *miles*, Adamclisi relief, *metopa* X, Trajanic age (*drawing by Graham Sumner*).

The reliefs of Trajan's Column and the *metopae* of Adamclisi have echoes of the glorious campaigns against the Dacians. The *Optimus Princeps* wears here a leather or metallic muscled *lorica* with bronze and gold appliqués, a symbol of the divine heroic emperor. He is represented bare-headed, his helmet being visible only on the Great Trajanic Frieze held by a guardsman.[i]

i   Antonucci, 1994, fig. 1, p. 4; the helmet is Attic in shape, embossed in silver and with gold cheek guards. It has on the top the 'rose of life' (known also as the 'Rose crown of Ecates') like the helmets of the praetorians on the same frieze. Two purple feathers were inserted on the helmet sides, flanking the rose of life.

PLATE IV (Right) Favonius Facilis, *centurio* of *XX Legio Valeria Victrix*, mid first century AD (AD 43–9): this is a totally new reconstruction of the *centurio* of the XX Legion from his gravestone, found in Colchester in 1868 (**72**).[i] On it he is represented bare-headed but dressed in the complete uniform of a centurion, carrying a *vitis* in his right hand. The *centurio* Facilis has been restored from his tombstone as clad in a leather corselet. The leather body of its *lorica* is semi-rigid but soft on the shoulders, to allow the movement of the arms, and has very

long and wide *humeralia*, probably of leather. The leather edge of these is thick and does not have a smooth surface, but it is slightly bossed to give more substance. The armour is lined at the edges by doubled leather, and it is clearly worn over a *subarmale* of linen or leather, equipped with *pteryges*. The equestrian rank of the *centuriones* is expressly stated by Martial in the Flavian age, as well as his rank symbol, the Latin *vitis*.[ii] According to Apuleius,[iii] the knobbed end of the *vitis* was called *nodulus*.

72a Detail of the Mainz *gladius*

72b Detail of the leather embossed belt

72 Details from the armour of Marcus Favonius Facilis (*courtesy of the Colchester Museum; photos by Stefano Izzo*)

i   Phillips, 1975, p. 102.

ii   Mart., *Ep.*, VI, 58; X, 26.

iii Ap., *Met.*, IX, 43: 'The souldier unable to refraine his insolence, and offended at his silence, strake him on the shoulders as he sate on my backe; then my master gently made answer that he understood not what he said, whereat the souldier angerly demanded againe, whither he roade with his Asse? Marry (quoth he) to the next City: But I (quoth the souldier) have need of his helpe, to carry the trusses of our Captaine from yonder Castle, and therewithall he tooke me by the halter and would violently have taken me away: but my master wiping away the blood of the blow which he received of the souldier, desired him gently and civilly to take some pitty upon him, and to let him depart with his owne, swearing and affirming that his slow Asse, welnigh dead with sicknesse, could scarce carry a few handfuls of hearbs to the next towne, much lesse he was able to beare any greater trusses: but when he saw the souldier would in no wise be intreated, but ready with his staffe to cleave my masters head, my master fell down at his feete, under colour to move him to some pitty, but when he saw his time, he tooke the souldier by the legs and cast him upon the ground: Then he buffetted him, thumped him, bit him, and tooke a stone and beat his face and his sides, that he could not turne and defend himselfe, but onely threaten that if ever he rose, he would choppe him in pieces. The Gardener when he heard him say so, drew out his javelin which hee had by his side, and when he had throwne it away, he knockt and beate him more cruelly then he did before, insomuch that the souldier could not tell by what meanes to save himselfe, but by feining that he was dead'

72c Detail of the leather armour (*corium*)

72d Detail of the *pugio*

72e Detail of the *pteryges*

72f Detail of the greaves

first century AD, was the last version, in the Imperial sword typologies, of the old taper-bladed *gladius hispaniensis*. It is well represented on Augustan monuments, such as the Arc d'Orange (**315s**).

In the Mainz typology, the blade of the sword began to be shortened and to transform into the slim type with a characteristic elongated point, then it evolved into the Julio-Claudian broad-bladed sword, with its width gradually tapering from the top downwards. One of the most famous specimens is the so-called 'Felicitas Tiberii' gladius, preserved in the British Museum.[114] The short and broad-waisted blade with a long tapering point was usually between 40 and 56 cm, excluding the tang, with a width around 5.4–7.5 and 4.8–6.0 cm.[115] A very unusual specimen of *gladius* of Mainz type comes from Dubravica

73 Trajan and Sura(?), Adamclisi relief, *metopa* XL first half of second century AD (*Museum of Adamclisi; author's photo, courtesy of the museum*)

74 Roman armoured officer holding a Dacian warrior, Adamclisi relief, *metopa* XXXIII, first half of second century AD.

(Serbia), and it is kept in the collections of the Belgrade War Museum (**75**).[116] The sword has a very well-preserved blade with a midrib.[117] The tang of this sword is almost unique – only one similar sword has been found, in Croatia in 1912[118] – having a rectangular cross-section and button-shaped tip, below which it expands into four rectangular loops placed in a shape of a cross, each containing a smaller copper-alloy ring. The rings were decorative, but also functional: this was how the chain was linked to the *miles'* wrist, as for a similar *gladius* of Mainz type from Rheingönheim.[119]

The sword from Rheingönheim has a silver cover to the hilt, and it is 72 cm long and 7.5 cm wide. The blade, which is very well preserved, shows, punched on the top of the handle the exceptional indication of the weight of the silver employed and the name of the smith.[120] We should remember that, at least in the first period of the Principate, the armourers were private people who received commissions from the army. Many tombstones from the Rhine show this type of sword hanging from the right side of the *milites*.[121]

After the middle part of the first century, maybe for a change in the fighting style, the so-called Pompeii type[122] *gladius* was manufactured with the edges of the blade parallel along the entire length of the blade to a short triangular point. To this type belonged, with slight variations, various specimens from Pompeii,[123] Newstead,[124] Hod Hill, Gusca[125] and other localities (**5**).[126] This type is the main one represented on Trajan's Column (**247**) and also on the Adamclisi monument (**64**, **74**), but its use decreased after the first half of the second century This kind of sword was much more suitable than the older Mainz type for the fight against the Germanic tribes, allowing the legionary to deliver equally successful blows by stabbing (**74**, **76**) and chopping (**68**).[127] It is possible that a transition type sword between the Mainz and Pompeii types could have existed: the specimen from Poiana (Romania) is a *gladius* with a broad blade (5.8 cm) with parallel edges and a long point.[128] Similar specimens have been found in first- and second-century AD layers of Sirmium, one of them having a length of 42 cm with very long tang.[129] In any case, the continuing use of the old type alongside the new typology is evidenced until the beginning of the second century AD.[130] On the famous Adamclisi *metopae* some of the extra-heavy armoured legionaries are armed with the old sword of the Mainz type (**58**, **60**, **69**), and its distinctive scabbard, ending with a circular pommel, shows a interesting correlation with a scabbard fragment recently found in Alba Julia-Apulum (**77**), *castra* of the *Legio XIII Gemina*. The find shows that the old typology of scabbards and swords was still in use in the *provincia Dacica* in the second century AD, and this is also confirmed by the iconographical sources.

The new kind of sword has been found in many specimens from many different localities, with local variations. A very little-known example from Dubravica and preserved in Belgrade War Museum has a blade with a longitudinal tip, and a small metal plate on the tang protecting the hilt guard.[131]

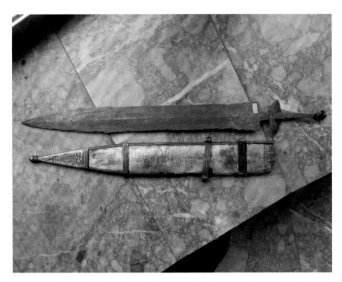

75 *Gladius* sword from Singidunum, having on the scabbard the inscription *LEVIS ARMATURA*', first century BC–first century AD (*Belgrade, War Museum inv. 16073; courtesy of the museum*).

The *gladius*, considered to be of the Mainz type from the shape of the blade, has its scabbard preserved, the wooden body of which was enclosed in a iron foil coating. On the mouth of the frame the scabbard has a very important inscription, shallowly engraved with a sharp object in two lines: the upper line features the name of the owner (ANIVALVS), the lower one (L(EVIS) A(RMATURA) (LEGIONIS) IIII (SCYTHICAE)) marks the military unit he served in. It is probable that Anivalus was a *miles* of possible Macedonian origin who was part of a special unit of light infantry of the *Legio IIII Scythica* that served as border *militia* in the *Limes* at the mouth of the Morava.[i] The tang has a copper-alloy plate like the terminal part of the lost pommel, the lower side of which was

adorned with engraved concentric circles. The pommel, handgrip and hand guard, lost today, were probably of an organic material, such as wood, bone or ivory. The ellipsoid copper-alloy plate at the base of the tang, with the edge profiled in an angular manner towards the lower section, was certainly used as a fitting for the hand guard. The scabbard had a wooden lining reinforced by metal fittings and covered with thin iron sheets. It comprised a (now missing) copper-alloy mouth adorned with stylised vegetal ornaments, like those of the surviving chape made by the *opus interrasile* technique. The iron elements were formerly coated with a tin layer, and certain fittings were made of copper alloy. The sides of the surviving suspension rings, of copper alloy, are ornamented with shallow fluting. The upper suspension band is missing, but it has been reconstructed by Dr Vujović on the basis of the similar scabbard from Rhine regions[ii]

i   Vujović, 2001, pp. 123–6.

ii   Vujović, 2001, p. 126, pl. 11.

76 Fighting between Roman *miles* and Dacian warriors, Adamclisi relief, *metopa* XXII, Trajanic age (*drawing by Graham Sumner*)

Note the killing technique used by the Roman warrior who uses his *gladius* for stabbing

78 Openwork bronze fragmentary scabbard fitting, second half of first century AD (*ex Guttman collection, Christie's photo*).

The fragment is from a Pompeii type sword scabbard, with remains of two front panels, decorated with battle scenes. The horse officer is wearing a pseudo-Corinthian helmet. It is 14 cm long

Traces of a midrib are still visible on the blade, as is the metal plate protecting the hand guard.

The swords of the Pompeii type evolved, especially after the second half of the second century AD, into longer specimens (**61**), transitioning towards the general use of the longer *spathae*. Traditionally reserved for *auxilia* and cavalrymen, these were now given to the *milites legionarii*, as a result of the enlistment of Germans and Celts into the army especially during the Marcomannic Wars. The evolution can be seen on two swords from the territory of Dacia, probably from the Antonine

period: one from Capidava (**79**) and one from Tibiscum.[132] The blade on both these is parallel-edged but narrower, and the tang is very long. Two further important specimens, one from Greece (**80**) and one from a Bulgarian grave of Commodus' time in Svilengrad (**PLATE V**), are representative of late longer specimens of such swords. This type is also depicted on monuments relating to the wars of Marcus Aurelius (**82**).

During the second century AD a new sword was introduced, influenced by the Germans and the Sarmatians, with a tapering blade,[133] and a grip assemblage composed of an iron

77 Scabbard chape of a *gladius*, from Apulum, first half of second century AD or last quarter of second century AD (*Museum Uniri, Alba Julia; courtesy of the museum*)

79 Roman *gladius* with scabbard, middle of the second century AD (*Constanza, Archaeological Museum; courtesy of the museum*)

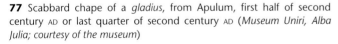

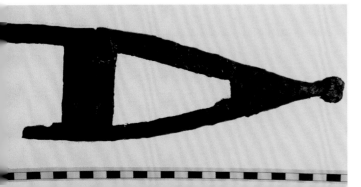

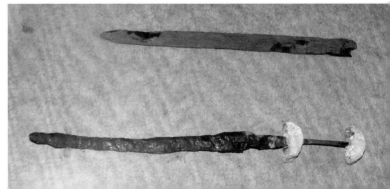

80 Late *gladius hispaniensis* of second half of second century AD (*Museum of Komtinì, Greece; courtesy of Dr Andrea Babuin*)

81 Sarmatian-type sword from from the territory of Bosnia, second half of second century AD (*Sarajevo, Zemalisky Museum, inv. 2471; courtesy of the museum*).

The sword was found on the road between Ljubuski and Vitine, in Bosnia-Herzegovina. It measures 62.5 cm in length and the diameter of the pommel is 4.3 cm

82 Details of battle between Romans, Quadi and Jazyges, frieze from a triumphal monument, last quarter of the second century AD (*Chiusi, Museo della Cattedrale; drawing by Graham Sumner*).

The Roman cavalrymen represented on the Chiusi frieze are probably clad in leather or horn scales. The frieze, probably made to commemorate some episode of Marcus Aurelius' war, presents some interesting details, such as the helmets with appliqué hair, the cataphract horses, and sword pommels identical to those found in the Danish bogs

tang, guard and open ring pommel at the top.[134] This kind of sword – called *ringknaufschwert* or ring-pommel sword by the modern scholars – spread first to the auxiliary troops, probably Sarmatians and Germans, and then, during the second century AD, was common also among the *milites legionis*. The shape of the blade is similar to the Pompeii type, but a slightly less acute angle characterises the transition from the blade to the short point.

There were longer specimens similar to the *spatha*, marking the beginning of the transformation of the legionary *gladius* to the longer *spatha* specimens of the succeeding period, and also shorter examples.[135] A very important dating element for earlier specimens is the sword from the Matrica grave in Pannonia, dated to exactly AD 147 from the other grave goods.[136] Specimens of the second half of the second century AD are known from Wehringen and Geneva (AD 180). An example from Bosnia (**81**) could be chronologically assigned to the same period, although this kind of swords became much more widespread for infantry and cavalry in later times. However, this kind of sword has been recently associated by Kovács[137] with the rank of the provincial officers who used them, to whom were also given miniature versions of the swords to be used as pendants as the *insignia* badge of the staff of the provincial governors.[138] This was connected with the already-mentioned image of the sword and of the dagger as symbols of Imperial power.[139]

The handle of the Roman swords was formed by a pommel, handgrip and hand guard, fastened together by a copper-alloy rivet.[140] The handle of the *gladius* was designed for thrusting,[141]

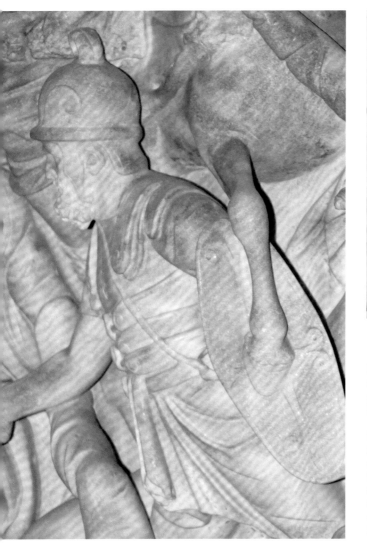

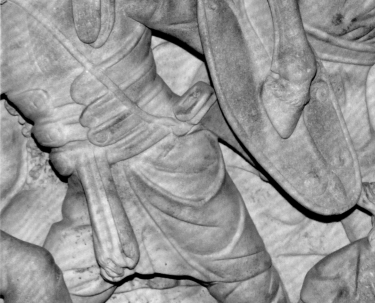

83 *Centurio* or officer of *cohors volontariorum*, from the Portonaccio Sarcophagus, Rome (*Museo Nazionale Romano; author's photo, by kind permission of the Ministero per i Beni e le Attività Culturali, Soprintendenza Speciale per i Beni Archeologici di Roma*).

The sarcophagus of the general of Marcus Aurelius, known as the Sarcophagus of Portonaccio after the place in which it was found, shows very interesting details of what was probably a *cohors* of eastern *civites voluntariorum*. This officer has a Hellenistic helmet fitted with leather cheek guards and neck guard. The most interesting part of his equipment is the leather *lorica segmentata*, corresponding to some original fragments of girdles found in Egypt. Note that the skirt (*zoma*) of the tunic is folded and passes over the last leather segment of the *lorica*, forming an apron in cloth

PLATE V *Miles* or *centurio* of a *cohortis voluntariorum*, AD 180. This is an attempted reconstruction of a Roman officer from the Portonaccio sarcophagus (**83**). The helmet is a simplified version of Weisenau late typology, with Attic elements. The crest system is made of embossed plumes arranged to form a 'round rose' placed horizontally on the top, forming a decorated complex of fake feathers laid out like a rose. The man has been reconstructed as a *centurio*: so the crest is silvered. The cheekpieces are of leather, with a leather edge, decorated (and reinforced) by two small bronze rivets. A leather lace, fixed to the ends of each check guard, formed the *vinculum* under the chin.

The tunic has been copied from the Bar Kochbà cave in yellow saffron with light purple *clavi*. These tunics were used throughout eastern Greece and especially by the irregular soldiers recruited in the times of emergency of the Marcomannic Wars. The tunic is 100 cm long and 115 cm wide, and is a single rectangular yellow sheet with two parallel bands woven of weft threads.

The banded armour is a leather one, in leather natural colour, made of rawhide like the specimen from Egypt (**191**). The leather corselet is closed on the breast with four buttons. Buttons (4 cm in diameter) of a possible banded leather armour have been found on the battlefield in Bedriacum. The corselet is reinforced on the abdomen by three extra leather girdles, linked by thongs and fastened by bronze buttons. Similar leather segments are visible on the shoulders, three for each side, and are fastened to the corselet by means of the same bronze buttons; here two of the leather segments are overlapping. Looking

the reference sculpture, all the girdles are leather lined (**83**).The breastplate of the leather corselet is closed with four buttons; note also the dividing line between the upper and lower parts of the armour. The buttons fastening the girdles are shown as if they are fastened to some leather backing. Identical armour is shown, as an isolated specimen, on the Marcus Aurelius Column.[i]

In his right hand the soldier holds the *gladius* from Svilengrad, a specimen dated to the late Antonine period.[ii] His round *clipeus* has rivets holding the metallic embossed parts on the surface. There is a border of silver and copper alloy all around the shield, gilded, and riveted with small oval rivets. At the centre of the shield we have put a bronze *umbo*, with the figure of Minerva, in tinned copper alloy (**286**).

The warrior wears short calf-length *bracae*, as do the other soldiers on the same sarcophagus.[iii] On his feet he wears wool socks, copied from Egyptian specimens.[iv] The recently found *calceus* from Dydimoi[v] corresponds to the shoes illustrated on the sarcophagus. They were dark brown leather, almost black. The fastening system was by means of linen threads. The *calceus* was slightly high on the ankle, the two sides fastened by two holes through which the threads passed. Two pieces of leather, with decorative cut-outs, were sewn on either side at the height of the ankle. The *calceus* covered the whole foot, from the instep to the ankle and ended with a point formed by a double thickness of the leather, sewn in front and on the sides to the internal vamp. A external vamp, thicker, was sewn to the internal vamp. The heel is reinforced by a sort of 'Gendarme cap' shaped leather extra-piece

i   Coarelli, 2008, pl. XXX
ii Welkov, 1937, p. 160.
iii Bianchi-Bandinelli, 1969, fig. 344–8.

iv Various, 1998, fig. 312: length 30 cm, From heel to toe, 22 cm, from heel towards the leg. 26 cm in circumference.
v   Leguilloux, 2006, pls 42–3, 28–9: length: 26.7 cm; width 12.3 cm.

having grooves for a better grip (**85**). In the Mainz type the pommel had a flattened ovoid appearance and the handgrip had an octagonal section; in the Pompeii type the pommel was a sphere. The pommel was usually made of wood (**5**),[142] but was sometimes silver-plated,[143] bone (**79**) or ivory;[144] the handgrip was made from bone[145], or wood, sometimes covered with leather, bronze, silver or gold[146]. The ring-pommel was of iron, often with inlaid niello decoration.[147] It is interesting to note that in the period of Marcus Aurelius some grips still preserved the shape of ancient models (**57**).

The early scabbard was composed of a framed metallic body, in iron but sometimes also in bronze, with a wooden core of lime or alder wood (**5**) and metallic fittings. Around the scabbard mouth was usually a fitting of openwork technique, in copper alloy (**84**).[148] Thin metal-plate cross bands were functional fittings to join the front and the back plates of the scabbard, with a loop on both ends through which passed the suspension rings used for the leather straps of the *balteus* or *cingulum*.[149] There were usually two such fittings placed below the handle at a short distance (8–10 cm) from each other. There were four suspension rings, and judging from the figurative sources the sword was hung from four, three or two rings.[150] A scabbard similar to the typical slim shape of the Mainz sword, is visible on a monument from Sora.[151] The carved scabbard is divided into three zones, the middle one is fitted with the suspension rings. This is visible on scabbards of the Mainz type: the metal construction consists mainly of vertical gutterings with U-shaped copper-alloy binding along the edges[152] with profiled suspension elements and loops for suspension rings. Thin iron sheets covering the wooden core have been mainly preserved on the front side of some specimens.

The decorative motifs were executed using the openwork technique in both types of swords (Pompeii and Mainz) as well as embossed relief motifs, as is visible on specimens from all over the empire, as a result of the merging of the Celtic and Greco-Mediterranean tradition of workmanship.[153] Samples of officers' scabbards have embossed motifs in place of openwork decoration, and the suspension bands are decorated with a laurel-wreath motif, as in the so-called Tiberius sword and in specimens from Colchester and Chichester.[154] Sword scabbards of AD 9 from Kalkriese have a series of clasps around the body, often fitted with an intaglio or cameo or a setting for precious stones.[155] A scabbard from Fulham[156] in particular is decorated by volutes and a beautiful silver or tin pattern, whereas the Pompeii type shows a new kind of scabbard, covered in leather and thin wooden sheets (**79**), fitted only with metal binding and chape and punched, embossed or engraved plaques of copper alloy attached.[157]

The chapes of the Mainz sword type usually consisted of a triangular copper-alloy plate with the edges completely protected, adorned with a stylised vegetal ornament executed in openwork technique (*opus interrasile*), including rings and fluting (**75**).[158] The bottom was closed by a massive spherical or

84 Scabbard locket plate of Pompeii type sword, first–second century AD (*collection of Museum Het Valkhof, Nijmegen; courtesy of the conservator*)

semispherical button, connected to the metal edges by a ribbed neck.[159] The chapes of the Pompeii typology were V shaped with palmettes at the sides and a button-shaped terminal. Usually, a palmette-like decoration was placed immediately above the scabbard chapes.[160] They were often adorned with embossed ornaments or openwork motifs.[161] The front side of the fittings were also adorned by a longitudinal band with decorative rivets, as in one specimen from Vindonissa,[162] and one unpublished specimen from the Danube, preserved in Kladovo Museum (**87**).

The use of the Greek sword called *parazonium*, reserved for emperors, generals, officers and guardsmen, and worn on the left side of the body by means of a *balteus* (baldric), is widely attested from the iconographical sources (**45**, **62**, **86**, **88**, **89**, **90**, **129**). It was linked with the ideology of the sword as a symbol of supreme power, inherited from the Greek world.[163] The grip of such a sword, in bronze, was often shaped like an eagle, as is also visible on the Arc d'Orange (**315u**, **315v**), where the *parazonium* is attached to a plated *balteus*. The Arc d'Orange also shows the *parazonium* scabbard having, around the mouth, the same copper-alloy openwork plate that is visible on some specimens from Mainz.[164] Original specimens of the first century AD, probably found in Pompeii, are preserved in the National Museum of Naples.[165] The hand guard was often rectangular, following the ancient models.

The now-lost grip of the sword of the Domitian triumphal monument today in Campidoglio was probably that of a

85 Triumphal sculpture and details, representing the armour of a centurion, probably praetorian, Trophaeum Trajani, Adamclisi, first half of second century AD (*Museum of Adamclisi; author's photo, courtesy of the museum*).

The wonderful armour used as a model for this sculpture was probably of highly decorated leather, and the fact that the companion statue of the Constantinian period represents an officer with a *crista transversa* could induce us to interpretate that this armour was the armour of *primipilus* or senior centurion of the praetorian guard

86 (Above) Officer from the House of Vettii, Pompeii and praetorian *miles* or 'Hector' from Domus Aurea, Claudio-Neronian age, in situ, Pompeii and Rome (*paintings by Graham Sumner*).

The officer – perhaps a *tribunus* – from the House of Vettii – is shown clad in a white leather armour reinforced by shoulder bands and a leather *zonì*, probably red lacquered, in the Hellenistic style, similar to that of Favonius Facilis. Note his Montefortino helmet and the employment of bronze greaves. His rank of *tribunus* might be indicated by the *parazonium* sword worn on the left side of the body.

The Hector representation was based upon an actual guardsman of the Claudio-Neronian period. He seems to be wearing a bronze *lorica segmentata*, whose segments and hinges are clearly visible. Many details of the equipment represented are confirmed by actual archaeological sources. The pseudo-Corinthian helmet correspondes to the Autun specimen,[i] the greaves to finds from Pompeii and the bronze *lorica segmentata* is finally confirmed by recently discovered specimens from Novae, Bulgaria. The green colour of the tunic is linked to the *prasina* faction in the Circus, favoured by Nero. The personal tastes of both praetorians and emperors existed in an age where there were no modern concepts of uniform

i   Robinson, 1975, pls 413–16.

87 Chape of a sword of Pompeii type, from Statio Cataractarum Diana (Davidovac, near Kladovo), end of the first century AD (*Iron Gates Museum, Kladovo; author's photo, courtesy of the museum*)

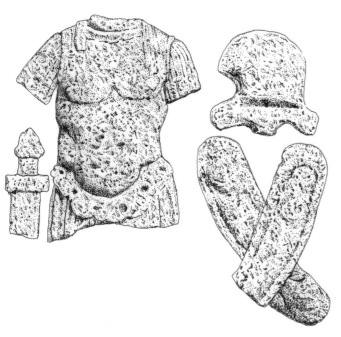

88 (Above) Fragment of great military stele, first century AD, Rome (*drawing by Graham Sumner*)

90 (Above) Representation of the Roman military salute, from the grave monument of T. Flavius Mikkalus, Perinth, Flavian era (*Istanbul, Archaeological Museum, author's photo, courtesy of the museum*).

As in the Altar of Domitius Ahenobarbus,[i] on this monument the *salutatio militaris* was also made by raising the right hand to helmet level, as modern armies do. The salute or *salutatio* differed according to the situation: the *milites* greeted by raising the right arm near the forehead with the fourth and little fingers bent, in a gesture later adopted by the Christian liturgy

89 (Left) Stele of Quintus Sulpicius Celsus, *praefectus* of *Cohors VII Lusitanorum*, with (*parazonium*) eagle pommel sword, *corona civica* and *vallaris*, first century AD (*Rome, Palazzo dei Conservatori, author's photo, by kind permission of the Sovraintendenza per I Beni Culturali del Comune di Roma*)

---

i   Antonucci, 1996, p. 8.

91 Daggers (*pugiones*) in their scabbards decorated in brass and enamel, from the site of Sisak (Roman Siscia), last decades of first century BC–first half/middle of first century AD (*Zagreb, Archaeological Museum, photo courtesy of Ivan Radman-Livaja*)

parazonium (**92**). The monument gives a good idea of how the decoration of a imperial scabbard might have appeared, with engraved figures of *putti* running along vegetal spirals. The monument is not artistic fantasy, and it is far from being the apogee of stylisation and fanciful invention in the *congeries armorum* genre. A similar scabbard, for a *parazonium* or a dagger, was in fact published by the archaeologist Ferrer in the 1930s.[166]

The soldier emperors such as Trajan also wore practical and effective swords of legionary type on the battlefield, as is shown on the Adamclisi monument (**71**, **73**).

The double-edged dagger (*pugio*)[167] is clearly attested now as the sidearm of the *gregarii* and officers as a standard part of military equipment (**PLATE IV**, **72**). The *pugio* was used in hand-to-hand fighting, probably as a spare weapon, and was usually worn on the left side of the body, attached to the *cingulum* by means of the two upper rings.[168]

Its shape did not generally change during this whole period.[169] It usually had a waisted blade with a scabbard provided with a suspension system identical to that of the *gladius*. The size varied between 25 and the 35 cm in the first century AD. The

92 Scale armour from the triumphal monument of Domitian, in situ, Rome, Campidoglio (*author's collection*)

dagger blade of the early Principate, as in Late Consular period specimens, had a pronounced rib in the shape of a rectangular bulge (or according to other scholars, a triangular section on the top and bottom of the blade) that from the age of Tiberius changed to a rib shaped like two parallel channels.[170] Narrow blades without a waist, with a mildly pronounced rib or single central channel, are typical of the specimens of the second half of the first century AD.[171] Four specimens of the Julio-Claudian age from Sisak (Siscia) have massive double-edged blades and a prominent central rib (**91**).[172]

The handle was the same as a sword handle, made of iron covered in ivory,[173] bone or wood, often fitted with richly decorated metal plates.[174] The bone or ivory plates were attached to the tang on both sides and fixed with an outer iron fitting that was shaped as a inverted letter T, riveted to the hilt. The daggers of the Early Principate show the presence on the hilt of rivet holes for hilt fittings.[175]

The old type of the Late Consular age, with flat tang and oval swelling in the middle, the top ending in a semicircular shape and with a pronounced midrib, is still attested by some Italic specimens,[176] by some specimens from Siscia;[177] and – for the scabbards – by sheaths found in Exeter (Britain), and Titelberg (Germany), similar to the old Spanish framed types.[178] But generally in the Augustan age the double-disc handle was modified and the tang, at least from the age of Claudius, was shaped like a massive rectangular-sectioned rod.

A dagger perhaps showing the transition from the old models to the new is one of the often-mentioned specimens recovered in the Kupa near Sisak (Siscia) (**91**).[179] The blade is not waisted as in previous models, the edges are in large part parallel and the hilt tang seems to be a massive rod, but has traces of rivet holes. The midrib is still pronounced by two blood channels, deep and wide, running on either side. This example has been dated by Professor Radman-Livaja to the middle of the first century AD.

New scabbard types were developed for the *pugiones*. They consisted of two iron plates lined with wood or leather[180] soon followed by a complete highy decorative scabbard with organic material (wood or leather) covered by silver or copper-alloy plates.[181] The scabbard plates were frequently decorated with fine niello and enamel inlays (often in brass or a yellow metal[182]), silver[183] or bright metal,[184] representing vegetal and geometrical motifs (rosettes, laurel wreaths, laurel twigs, crosses with interlaced leaves, herring-bone patterns, and even small stylised temples or *aediculae*[185]). Usually the early Principate specimens present inlay decorations in brass and enamel,[186] in silver and enamel,[187] in silver, brass and enamel.[188] The decoration of the scabbard plates was usually divided into four fields, occasionally into one field.[189] They were initially engraved and then inlaid and enamelled, also on the rivets. Some of these were also decorated with the name of the *legio*.[190] High-ranking officers had elaborate and luxurious daggers, such as a unique specimen with the sheath completely decorated with scenes from mythology.[191]

93 Roman dagger, with copper-alloy hand guard, from Statio Cataractarum Diana (Davidovac, near Kladovo), second century AD (*Iron Gates Museum, Kladovo Museum; author's photo, courtesy of the museum*)

Towards the end of the first century AD the scabbards begin to have a limited number of decorative motifs, with inlay only in silver.[192] The specimens of the second century are shorter, introducing the daggers of the period of military anarchy. The handle was T-shaped and, from the second century, ended with a crescent-shaped pommel. Interestingly, elements of the early daggers, such as the flat rectangular tangs, the waisted blade and the riveted hilt fittings, are again visible on the second-century specimens. This means that the modifications were only a decorative part in the history of such a weapon; the old tradition of *pugiones* was never dismissed. A specimen from Inveresk has been recovered complete, and some fragments from Bar Hill and Tuchyna.[193] The latter is 40 cm long and 7.4 cm wide, its framed scabbard is decorated on the front with concentric circles.

Various other forms of daggers were also in use. Nine examples of daggers with a wide haft and narrow blade, similar to the Celtic specimens of the late La Tène period, have been recovered in four Roman graves from Bobowk near Kranj (former Yugoslavia), variously dated between the first century AD and the age of Antoninus Pius.[194] Their rhomboid profile and the oval ring at the top of the hilt, fixed by pins, are also similar to a knife recovered in Neviodunum (Drnovo, Slovenia).[195] As well as from the possible auxiliary dagger of Mehrum,[196] there is also a similar specimen with simple triangular blade

94 Detail of Antonine-age belt and *culter*, from the military camp of Viminacium, second half of second century AD (*Narodni Muzej Požarevac, Serbia; author's photo, courtesy of the museum*)

but copper-alloy hand guard from the Iron Gate region (**93**), preserved in Kladovo Museum.[197] Daggers introducing the *culter venatorius*[198] of the late empire begin to appear in the Antonine period (**94**), sometimes with their bone handle still preserved.

The belt or *cingulum*, symbol of the *militia*, was a fundamental part of the Roman equipment in the Imperial period. In the Augustan time those centurions who had fought without honour were deprived of their sword belts.[199] Martial[200] calls the belt of a *tribunus* the '*decus militiae*'. As the wearing of the belt was synonymous with military service, to be deprived of it (*discingere*) meant to be reduced in rank.[201]

The general word to indicate the military belt, apart from *cingulum*, was *balteus/balteum* or *baltion*.[202] This was not used specifically to indicate only the baldric of the sword, but more often to indicate the military belt or belts in general (*baltea*)[203] with metallic fittings. The word *cingula* is, however, always used by Statius with reference to military equipment, meaning waist belts and baldrics.[204] This was a massive wide belt, generally made of leather.[205] Common elements were ordinary belt-plates, plates with a hinged buckle and plates with frogs for the attachment of a dagger or sword (**315s, 315u**; **210**). It could be simple, or could have gold fittings (*aureum balteum*) and be closed by a buckle (*fibula*) cast with gems, obviously this last for emperors and officers.[206]

The belt, during the first and second centuries AD, was decorated by rectangular metal fittings (**PLATE III, PLATE IV, 315c, 315s**), made of copper alloy[207] and often tinned or silvered,[208] or even made of solid silver.[209] The plates were usually in a series of different dimensions, the smaller designed to fasten the daggers, the larger to fasten the sword.[210] They were decorated with various motifs, or not decorated at all; many motifs found in archaeology reflect those of the tombstones:

1. imperial portraits or the Capitoline she-wolf, as in the specimens from Vindonissa, Risstissen;[211]
2. images of the sun god and the moon goddess, and other gods, probably worn in conjunction with a scabbard decorated with astral symbols such as sunrays, *lunulae*, globes and *baytiloi*;[212] splendid specimens have been found in Pompeii;[213]
3. lotus flowers; some specimens have been found in Augusta Raurica and are visible on the gravestone of an unknown *miles* from Bonn (**48**);
4. concentric circles, often in relief using with the repoussé technique[214] or engraved;[215] the specimen from Rheingönheim[216] corresponds perfectly with the belts engraved on a unknown *miles*' gravestone from Cassaco;[217]
5. geometrical and vegetal motifs.

95 Bronze buckles with leaf, relic of silver pearl-like twisted wire and stamped decorations, second half of the first century AD (*From Kostolna pri Dunai (district of Galanta), Sladkovicovo and Nitra; ex Kolnik, with kind permission of the Library of the Archaeological Institute of Belgrade*).
   The length of the three belt buckles is 6.1, 8.7, 7.9 cm. respectively

96 Aprons of military *baltea*, first century AD (*Cordoba, Museo Provincial; courtesy of the museum*)

97 *Miles* in Newstead armour, Trajan's Column, scene LXXX (*cast, Roma, Museo della Civiltà Romana, author's photo, courtesy of the museum*)

98 *Miles gregarius* in leather *lorica*, relief from Villa Albani, in situ, Rome, late Flavian era (*photo DAI*)

99 Detail of legionaries in leather *lorica segmentata*, Trajan's Column, scenes XXXVI, LXXXII, LXXXIII, (*cast, Roma, Museo della Civiltà Romana, author's photo, courtesy of the museum*)

99a

99b

99c

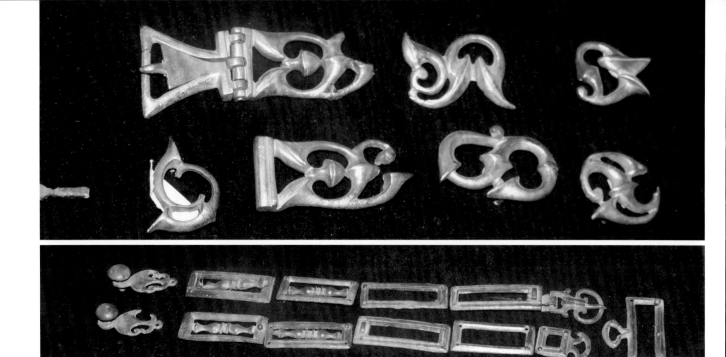

100 Antonine-period belts in openwork pattern fittings, from Constanta, Black Sea, second half of second century AD (*Archaeological Museum, Costanta ; courtesy of the museum*)

The belt was fastened by means of a buckle, often joined by a hinge with a belt fitting (**95**), which is typical of the first to second century AD.[218] The belt fittings were often decorated in niello with vegetal or geometrical motifs, which are useful to the scholars for dating purporses.[219]

The primary purpose of the belt was to carry the legionary's sword. The first system of carrying the scabbard was to suspend it from the side of the military waist belt (**50**, **51**, **59**, **73**). Methods for attaching the swords to side belts are clearly visible on many monuments.[220] Button-shaped fasteners with a single or double loop of circular or trapezoidal shape were often used in the first two centuries for hanging swords or daggers on the belts.[221] The complex attachment system for side belts for the *milites* shows two belts crossed on the belly, the *pugio* worn hanging on the left hip and attached through the upper rings of its scabbard to the upper belt, while the lower belt is used for fastening the sword and the central protection of the abdomen, constituted by a rows of vertical aprons called *baltea*.[222] Pliny the Elder describes the *baltea* as silvered; they were formed by leather belt terminals or straps decorated by round or squared tinned or silvered studs,[223] ending with small half-moons[224] (*lunulae*- (**48**, **96**), hearts or rhomboids hanging down.[225] These clink together with some small chains (*catellae*) – also fixed to the main *cingulum* – with the soldier's movement. As far as it is possible to judge from the sculptures, there could be as many as eight straps with sixteen studs each. Isidorus, writing in the sixth century AD, clarifies their purpose, as well as the distinction between *balteum* and *balteus*.[226]

On Trajan's Column marching *milites* are sometimes wearing two or even four overlapping *cingula* (**247**). Quite apart from the practical logic of it, that it enabled marching soldiers to carry more objects – such as purses with coins – inside the belts, I do not see why this image should be dismissed as a fantasy of the artist or as an artistical convention, considering that it is a system still used in the modern armies! The system of wearing the *cingula* crossed over the belly does not appear on second-century AD gravestones, and a double *balteus* means simply a belt for the sword and a belt for the dagger.

During all this period the sword could be hung from either shoulder, with the help of a shoulder belt or baldric made of leather (*e corio*),[227] with a four-ring suspension system, usually[228] resting on the left shoulder for the legionaries (**57**, **70**, **97**, **98**, **99**) or on the right for the officers (**PLATE IV**, **PLATE V**, **72**, **89**, **101**). The suspension baldric was often connected to the scabbard gutterings by means of two copper-alloy rivets.

An imperial *balteus* of the Domitianic period is represented on the Campidoglio monument (**92**). The fastening buckle of the baldric is identical to the typical belt buckles of the first century AD (**95**), except the plate to which it is attached is decorated with a horse that was probably embossed in the original specimen.

A golden officer's baldric fitted with clasps and pendants like those of previous ages is described by Virgil as being made of woven fabric and closed with buckles (*fibulae*).[229] A soldier's wife is remembered as making purple strips[230] for her husband's sword. On the Fayoum second-century portraits the *balteus* is often dyed red-purple (*fucatus*), or pink-red, and also dark blue, decorated by alternate silver and gold bosses or *bullae*[231] (*cingulum bullatum* (**PLATE IV**, **PLATE V**, **101**)). The borders of the baldric were often reinforced and doubled, and the leather was finely decorated (**85**, **89**, **92**).

From the Antonine period the belt fittings begin to change, now incorporating many openwork patterns, rectangular or cross shaped, under a strong Celtic influence (**100**, **104**).[232] Some buckles were no longer hinged to the belt fitting, but an extension of the belt plate passed through a loop on the back of the buckle and was bent back behind the frame and riveted or soldered to its fitting.[233]

A military belt cast in bronze, with an openwork pattern, with six fittings plus the buckle, has been found in the Apulum necropolis, the camp of the *Legio XIII Gemina*, and could be dated to the second half of the second century AD.[234] Similar belts have been found in the Black Sea regions (**100**). The system of attaching side belts is still visible on the figurative monuments (**59**, **65**, **66**), but the system of the baldric was always more widespread, and generally adopted at the end of the second century AD.

Shields

Continuing his description of the Roman army's weaponry,[235] Josephus said, '. . . those footmen also that are chosen from among the rest to be around the general himself have a lance and a buckler [*aspis*]; but the rest of the foot soldiers have a spear and a long buckler [*thureos*] . . .' He makes a clear distinction between the main shield used by the legionaries (the long *thureos*) and the round shield of the bodyguards (*aspis*). For the Greek speakers, the *thureos* was the main wooden shield of the Roman *milites*, the *scutum*.

The reliefs of the triumphal monuments and the funerary sculptures allow us to recognise the shape, size and decoration of the first- and second-century shield (*scutum*).[236] It was probably under Augustus that the *scutum* of the Late Consular age was transformed into a curved rectangular model, a shortened version of the previous one (**PLATE III**, **46**). The two models of shield are both visible on many monuments of the Augustan period (**106**, **315c**, **315x**, **315y**, **315z**, **315aa**), while a Novalesa monument[237] related to the wars in the Alpine area shows clearly the new concave rectangular shape. A very unusual kind of shield is represented on the early Principate monuments (**103**, **105**): it is rounded in the lower part, and concave at the top. The shield seems to have been a part of the transition from the old type of the Late Consular period to the rectangular shield.

The rectangular shield was half-cylindrical (**47**, **49**, **50**, **51**, **58**, **60**, **61**, **64**, **68**, **69**, **247**), rounded at the corners and thicker at the centre than at the edges. It was made of light plywood planks, joined by organic glue and covered by linen and leather. The shield sometimes had a bar for the arm, held by disk-headed iron nails, and a horizontal handgrip (*ansa*),[238] as well as shoulder straps. We can suppose an average of 125 cm in

101 Portrait of a officer, from el-Fayoum, Trajanic period (*Egyptian Museum of Cairo, inv. CG 33257; courtesy of the museum*)

102 Veteran or farmer picking olives, first century AD (*Seville, Museo Arqueologico, courtesy of the museum*)

104 Antonine-age belt and *culter*, from the military camp of Viminacium, second half of second century AD (*Narodni Muzej Požarevac, Serbia, author's photo, courtesy of the museum*)

103 Roman *milites* from a frieze in Arelatum (Arles), AD 21 (*Arles, Musée de l'Arles et de la Provence Antiques, photo Agostino Carcione, courtesy of the museum*).

Milites and officers of the Gallic legions are represented clad in muscled leather armour, scale armour, Hellenistic corselets fitted with *pteryges* and heavy padded tunics. The helmets are of Montefortino or Coolus type with high plumes and the *gladii* are worn on the right and left sides of the body. A *signifer*, clad in muscled armour and wearing a lion skin on his head, shows the remains of a *signum* and carries a round shield under his left arm

105 (Above and opposite page) Trophy relief, from Gardun, Croatia, first century AD (*Split Archaeological Museum; 1) T. Seser's photo 2) author's photo, courtesy of the Split Archaeological Museum*).

The relief shows a kind of leather armour similar to that of Favonius Facilis, with short sleeves and *humeralia*. Note the example of *falcata*, still used in the Gallic wars of Augustus and Tiberius, as shown by the Julii Mausoleum sculptures

106 Trophy relief with weapons, first century AD (*Turin, Museo di Antichità; photo DAI*).

The relief was a part of a bigger monument recently dated to the Julio-Claudian age.[i] Amongst the represented weapons a helmet of the Weiler type is clearly visible, with embossed hair. The embossing of the helmet's hair was done separately, and perhaps applied to a cloth surface covering the skull of the helmet. This seems be suggested by the remains of a similar helmet found in Xanten-Wardt, but a second possibility is that real hair was attached over the textile part of the helmets, as attested by a specimen from Vechten (**276**) and by figurative monuments (**82**). Note also the Attic helmet with griffin's head, identical to the actual specimen found in Nemi and dated to the rule of Caligula (**298**)

109 Circular *umbo* with punched inscriptions, from the territory of Macedonia, mid second century AD (*Skopjie Museum; courtesy of the museum*)

107 Shield borders in brass, from Ulpia Traiana Sarmizegetusa, first half of second century AD (*Museum of Ulpia Traiana Sarmizegetusa, author's photo, courtesy of the museum*)

108 *Milites legionis* et *auxilia*, Trajan's Column, scene CXIV (*cast, Roma, Museo della Civiltà Romana, author's photo, courtesy of the museum*)

110 Fragments of the Marengo treasure, silver belt with army trophy, c. AD 170 (*Turin, museo di Antichità, courtesy of the Ministero per i Beni e le attività culturali, Soprintendenza per i Beni Archeologici del Piemonte e del Museo Antichità Egizie*).

The treasure is dated to the time of Lucius Verus. Shown here for the first time is, on the silver belt, the shield of the *Legio II Italica*, created during the Marcomannic Wars. The device on the shield is identical to that of the later *Notitia Dignitatum*, mentioning such a *legio*[ii]

---

i   Torelli, 2003, p. 151ff. The author considers the represented weapons conventionally treated by the artist, not considering the importance that they have for the correct dating of it to the Julio-Claudian Age!

ii   Barker, 1981, p. 98, n. CXXXI

height and 78 cm in width. With these shields the legionaries were able to form special formations such as the *testudo* (*tortoise*), in which they were all covered by the overlapping shields. The centre of the shield was often reinforced by the usual iron or copper-alloy protruding metal plate, the *umbo*, which was circular (**57, 63, 109, 110**)[239] or rectangular.[240] When it was rectangular it curved around the central hemispherical boss (**47, 49, 60, 61, 68, 69, 70**). It was fixed to the shield's wooden planks with rivets (**109**). The dimensions of the circular *umbones* varied from 19 to 26 cm across.[241] The *umbo* protected the handgrip and was positioned in a circular opening made in the middle of the shield.[242]

The border of the shield was sometimes edged with brass bindings with a U-shaped section (**PLATE III, 58, 70, 107**), a style most often found in first- and second-century archaeological contexts,[243] and nailed to the wood with brass rivets inserted through lobate expansions on either side of the binding.[244] The nails sometimes had a flat surface and were highly decorated.[245] Iron bindings have been found in Ulpia Traiana Sarmizegetusa.[246] Although no complete specimens of shields survive for the period of the early Principate, many fragments have been recovered in different localities. A Romano-British original was found near Doncaster. Different examples of *umbones* came from Vindonissa,[247] Blümlein[248] and other localities, where metallic fragments of shields have been recovered (borders and appliqués, for example), but there is still no complete specimen like the Fayoum prototype.

The rectangular shields from Vindonissa had a leather-covered wooden frame, probably furnished with stout mountings. The dimensions varied, but generally we can assume a length from knee to shoulder, as is visible on Trajan's Column (**70, 247**). Usually the heavily armoured infantry of the early Principate had concave rectangular shields, as for most of the legionaries of Trajan's Column and the Adamclisi monument (**76, 108, 247**). On the Adamclisi monument the concavity of most of the represented shields is highly accentuated (**47, 49, 58, 60, 61, 64, 68, 69**), as it is on some specimens from Trajan's Column (**111, 112**), while flat rectangular shields seem to be carried by some marching legionaries (**50, 51**).

Oval shields, like those on the tombstone of Cordus and Castricius,[249] were also provided to *milites gregarii* from the first to second centuries AD (**105, 113**),[250] and the oval or circular shield is the main legionary shield on the Marcus Aurelius column (**57, 59, 63, 65, 114**)[251] and on the monuments of the Antonine period (**PLATE V, 110, 115, 116, 117**). They were probably entirely made from three layers of plywood, as shown by the specimens from Dura-Europos. The oval shield seems to have slowly replaced the rectangular by the end of the second century AD. The rectangular shield was not completely abandoned, however; it is still visible on the monuments (**65**), and archaeological specimens of it are still attested in the third century AD, all from Dura-Europos.

The Marcus Aurelius column also shows trapezoidal shields used by the legionaries (**65**), probably some transitional type part-way between the rectangular and the oval model.

The centurions were sometimes armed with the same concave rectangular shield as the *milites gregarii*. The grave of Blattius, a *centurio* of the Flavian age, of the *IV Legio Macedonica*,

111 (Below, left) Detail of legionary in *subarmale*, carrying his shield and personal equipment (*cast, Roma, Museo della Civiltà Romana, author's photo, courtesy of the museum*)

112 (Below, centre) *Signifer* and *milites* in composite armour, *lorica segmentata* and chain armour, Trajan's Column. Note the *signum manipularis* surmounted by a hand (*cast, Roma, Museo della Civiltà Romana, author's photo, courtesy of the museum*)

113 (Below, right) *Milites* or *auxilia* marching with round shields and swords, Adamclisi relief, *metopa* XIV, Trajanic age, first half of second century AD (*Museum of Adamclisi; author's photo, courtesy of the museum*)

114 Detail of *miles* in *lorica segmentata*, scene from the Marcus Aurelius column, in situ, Rome (*ex Becatti, by kind courtesy of Editoriale Domus S.p.A.*)

115 Detail of the general represented on the Portonaccio sarcophagus, second half of the second century AD (*Roma, Museo Nazionale Romano, courtesy of the museum*)

116 *Praetoriani* and *milites legionarii* from the Aurelian panels of the Constantine Arch, AD 180 (*author's collection*).

The sculpture is rich in detail of arms and armour of the Antonine period. It shows three excellent representations of a variety of Roman equipment. The first praetorian is wearing a *squama*, the one to the left of him is wearing a so-called *lorica segmentata*, and the one to the left of him has diaper-patterned armour, probably felt reinforced by metallic bosses. This last armour, as represented in the sculpture, could not be a convention for showing chain mail, because the chain mail is very well represented in other panels from the same monument, and it is clearly identifiable. Romans loved realism, especially in the representation of military gear

117 Panoply of *miles*, end of the second century AD. Present location unknown (*drawing by Graham Sumner*)

118 *Umbo* with Medusa's head, from Blerick, second half of the second century AD (*collection of Museum Het Valkhof, Nijmegen; courtesy of the conservator*)

from Fregole (Monselice) shows him armed with a rectangular *scutum*, *gladius*, *ocreae* and *vitis*.[252]

As a reward for special bravery in war, officers might be given the *clipeus virtutis*, a round gilded and engraved shield (**105**, **110**).[253] A magnificent specimen is represented on a relief from Amiternum,[254] dated to around the end of the first century BC and the beginning of the first century AD, showing a finely chiselled *gorgoneion*.[255] *Umbones* shaped like the head of the Gorgon Medusa were very common and are confirmed both from artistic works (**105**) and archaeology (**118**). On the Scafa frieze are visible, together with round shields, two rectangular specimens still fitted with a 'butterfly' *umbo*.[256] On these is clearly visible the internal horizontal handgrip and four other bars, probably metallic, to reinforce the internal wooden frame of the shields. The leather straps on circular shields are easily visible on the Marcus Aurelius column (**63**).

An episode belonging to the civil wars in Italy, in AD 69, mentioned by Tacitus,[257] teaches us that the *auxilia*, the legionaries and the praetorians were distinguished by their own *insignia*. Tacitus specifies, adding the Latin substantives '*galeis scutique*', that the word *insignia* referred to the helmets and to the shields. The Roman historian thus clearly explains these attributes as helmet crests and shield blazons. The passage from Tacitus should be connected with the already mentioned episode of the Gallic Wars, where Caesar recounts that the Romans were so surprised by a Belgian attack that they were

unable to arrange the *insignia* on their helmets, and to remove the shield-covers (*tegumenta*), as prescribed in the battle order.[258] These signs were also referred to by the Latinised term *digmata* (from the Greek *deigmata*) by Vegetius,[259] were apparently unit badges. Again Tacitus mentions two praetorians who, after taking two enemy shields from the ground, infiltrated their opponents and performed an act of valour.[260]

Therefore all these elements – together with the unit's standards or *signa* – could help us to recognise the various corps depicted on the Roman monuments. A certain type of dress or a kind of armour would not have been a very useful means of identification for the unit, considering that in the same body of troops dress could change very often and that different kinds of protective armour were worn within the same corps. Tacitus speaks certainly of 'helmets and shields taken in a hurry from a store [*armamentarium*]' and does not mention particular uniforms that varied according the unit.

Further confirmation is given by the tombstones of the first century AD, on which the military dress (*ornatus*) of the deceased appears indistinguishable for both *legionarii* and *auxilia*. The elements that allow us to identify the soldiers as legionaries or auxiliaries are the inscriptions and – when present – the unit *insignia*, i.e. the shield devices and the unit standards. The military clothing (*vestis militaris*) was certainly worn under different rules and symbols, according to the soldiers' rank and duties, but the loss of most of the colour elements – essential for the identification – on the gravestones and monuments leaves us with the shield blazons as the main criterion for identifying the Roman units.

The leather surface of the shield was lavishly painted with the *digmata* of the *legio*, thus allowing the identification of the troops on the battlefield (**PLATE III**, **57**, **63**, **110**, **247**). Some shield fragments from Masada preserve, for instance, traces of paintings.[261] The *digmata* were symbols, often of religious or mythical significance, such as the wings of the birds sacred to the gods or the winged lightning bolts of Jupiter (**315i**, **315r**, **315z**). The presence of an eagle nearby undoubtedly signifies a legion (**119**). Often also the name of the unit and the commander (**6f**, **6g**) was painted on the shield or engraved on the *umbo* (**109**). Some rectangular *umbo* samples, such as those from Carnuntum, have the name of the unity written on them:[262] (CENTURIA) AVIDI QUINCTI (of the *centuria* of Avidius Quinctus). The most famous specimen from Britain, found in the Tyne and dated to the time of Hadrian, is inscribed with the name of the *legio*, and indicated the name of the unit and of the owner![263]

The decoration of the shield was not only painted. Metallic appliqués of Jupiter's lightning bolts (*fulgures*) were a very common device, especially among the *milites gregarii* of a particular legion (**6**, **28**, **58**, **59**, **106**, **111**, **112**, **121**). The *milites* of the *Legio XII Fulminata* were probably identified, at least at the beginning, by the lightning bolts chiselled on their shields (**98**).[264] A very interesting description of it is given

119 Danubian *numeri* and Roman legionaries, Trajan's Column, scenes XLVI–XLVIII, details of helmets, shields and armour (*cast, Roma, Museo della Civiltà Romana, author's photo, courtesy of the museum*)

by the poet Valerius Flaccus, in his *Argonautica*: '. . . all the phalanx wears embossed on the shield the Jupiter device, and the spread fires of the trident-shaped [*trifida*] lightning bolts and You, Roman soldier, are not the first to wear on the shields the rays and the shining wings of the flashing thunderbolt . . .'.[265] This is clearly a reference to a metallic appliqué , which is further supported by the passage in Virgil that describes the working of the weapons in Vulcan's forge[266] Other metallic appliqués were shaped like vegetal ornaments (**57**, **63**, **105**, **110**). A bronze Capricorn, part of a shield appliqué decoration, has been found in Emlichheim. Legionary shield appliqués probably also had the L-shaped edges often represented on the shield borders (**PLATE III**, **46**, **69**, **70**, **111**, **247**). The metallic appliqués were not only for decoration; they also reinforced the whole wooden structure.

Trajan's Column, considering the huge amount of the devices of the shields represented there, can help in the identification of some units of the Roman army of the Trajan period. The unique example of number and title easily recognisable can be that of the cohorts of the legions bearing the name *victrix*: these

scuta bore, painted or embossed, a *corona aurea*. Other legionary cohorts have the shields adorned with a *corona civica* (**247**).

The reconstruction of the colours of some Roman shields from the Middle Imperial era can only be conjecture given the actual level of our knowledge. A very important document that can help us is the *Notitia Dignitatum*: many regiments mentioned in this fourth–fifth-century document had been in existence for some time when it was composed, and other regiments were simply the evolution of the old Roman legions, so that their colour and *digmata* can be useful in proposing some hypotheses for the colour and blazons of the old units too. It is in fact very probable that the legions of the late Roman Empire preserved the main ground colour of the shield that had previously belonged to the ten cohorts mentioned by Vegetius. We do not know, however, with certainty which colour originally signified the *cohors* number.

It is probable that the Imperial battle shield was painted with an identifiable colour, probably a dark red or violet purple ground combined with gilded or gold appliqués. Valerius Flaccus, in his *Argonautica*, however, refers to the shield of Jupiter as *nigrans* (black),[267] a probable reference to a true *scuta* or *clipea* painted in such a way.

The shield cover was made of ox leather, or occasionally of goatskin; beautiful fragments of *tegumenta* have been found in the military camp of Vindonissa (**120**). These fragments correspond to the typology shown on the monuments: rectangular (Trajan's Column), oval (Marcus Aurelius column) and round. This was the 'ordnance cover' of the legionary shield, whose shape corresponds perfectly to the descriptions in the sources and to the figurative monuments. The fragments usually show the mark of a band of constant size slightly impressed on the surface, and also many traces of the *tabula ansata*, where the name of the *legio* was written (**120**).[268] The *tabula ansata* was often also painted on the shield surface (**PLATE III**, **46**, **60**). Sometimes the leather cover was decorated with appliqués representing the *genius* of the *Legio*, or the protective divinity, as on the fragment from Bonner Berg, which is decorated with the image of Minerva, tutelary goddess of the *Legio I Minervia*. It is probable that this image was also painted or attached to the actual shield.

The rich repertory of Vindonissa can be explained by seeing the camp as a production centre for shields, as attested by the find of a small wooden tablet, reporting the name of the *scutarius* (shieldmaker) Valerius.[269] The fragments help us to recognise the shape of the shields. A fragment of rectangular shield cover, in dark ox hide, measures 75 cm, so Gansser-Burckhardt could deduce a general shield size of about 120–5 cm.[270] On the edge of the shield cover the wooden frame had left a mark of about 3.5 cm, where the rounded corners follow the shape of the shield. Around the edge are still visible the traces of a stitched seam of 2–3 cm, implying that the wooden frame of this shield was not nailed but probably sewn to the leather cover. This formed a solid structure for the shield, better than a nailed edge. The original shield was probably similar to that visible on the Basel tombstones. The decorative motif cannot be discerned anymore, although the general impression is very similar to those visible on some scenes of Trajan's Column.[271]

A fragment of a shield cover for an oval shield was 60 cm wide and had a maximum height of 17 cm, with a similar band on the edge. From it we can deduce a general measurement of 60–70 cm for the shield. A third fragment came from a round shield (**120**).

Helmets

The helmet continues to be called *galea* or *cassis*,[272] with no distinction as to what it was made of, but may have indicated some distinction as to its weight.

The use of the Montefortino–Buggenum and Coolus helmet continued uninterrupted (**86**, **103**), which were now manufactured by spinning and hammering them all around. The Italic and the Celtic tradition combined to create a form of helmet that was in use at least until the end of the first century AD: this was a calotte-shaped helmet with shorter horizontal or slightly slanting neck guard, forged from one piece of sheet bronze.[273]

Bronze helmets of the Buggenum type, furnished with inscriptions, are attested from Njimegen, Millingen, Olfen, Wardt-Luttingen, Neuss and various localities of the first

century AD.[274] They were probably still produced in regions such as Campania and Etruria, which were highly specialised in bronze work. In Anatolia this helmet is still evidenced until the end of the first century AD, not only by the centurion on the *stela* of Flavius Mikkales (**90**), but also by a contemporary specimen coming from Bithynia and preserved in Istanbul Museum (**122**). The cheekpieces were still made of leather in some specimens (**123**, **125**), and linked under the chin. Otherwise, they had cheek guards and brow guards following the Coolus model.

The Coolus–Haguenau type[275] (**124**, **126**) was now more widespread, and was used at least until the end of the first

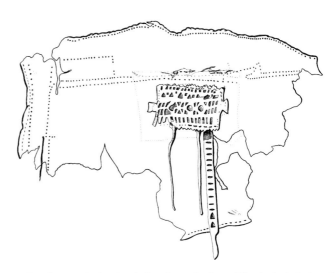

120 Shield cover fragments: **a)** rectangular; **b)** oval **c)** round; **d)** *tabula ansata* (*ex Gansser-Burckhardt, courtesy of Vindonissa Museum*).

A very interesting specimen[i] shows the *tabula ansata* still in place with the bindings intact, made from a darker oxhide for its attachment onto the shield cover. The *tabula*, which was perhaps also glued to the

surface,[ii] presented not only the denomination of the *legio*, but also of the cohort: LEG. XI. COH. I or COH. III. Some of the *tegimenta* found in Vindonissa still have fragments of side leather bindings. A specimen was finally found with the cover of the *umbo* incorporated[iii]

i   Gansser-Burchardt, 1942, pp. 84-85 figg. 59-60;
ii Like in the Masada fragments, s. Bishop-Coulston, 2006, p. 92;
iii Gansser-Burchardt, 1942, p. 87 fig. 62;

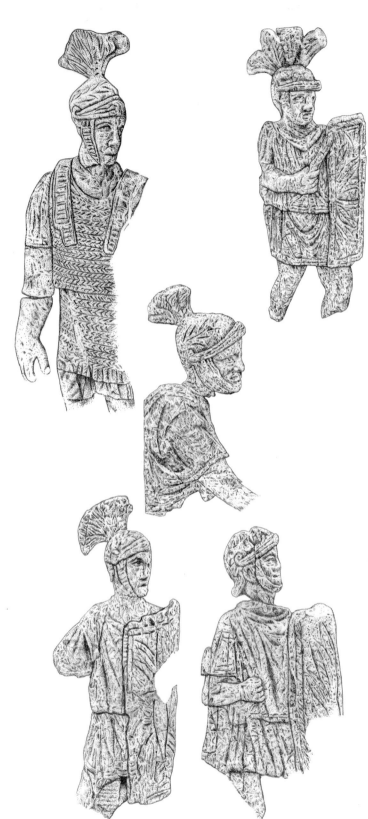

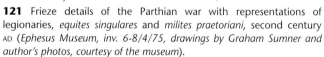

121 Frieze details of the Parthian war with representations of
legionaries, *equites singulares* and *milites praetoriani*, second century
AD (*Ephesus Museum, inv. 6-8/4/75, drawings by Graham Sumner and
author's photos, courtesy of the museum*).

The bodyguards of the Emperor Trajan, legionaries and *levis
armatura milites* are perfectly represented on this small ivory artwork,
celebrating the victories of Trajan in Parthia. Note the detail of the mail
armour, still fastened with shoulder guards or *humeralia* hinged on the
breast. One of the represented figures is a scout (*exculcator*). According
to Josephus, they had no helmets (*kranos*) or armour (*thorax*)[i]

---

i Josephus, *BJ*, V, 2, 2.

122 Helmet of Buggenum–Montefortino type, from Anatolia, end of the first century AD (*Istanbul, Archaeological Museum; author's photo, courtesy of the museum*)

124 Helmet of Coolus typology, from the river Sava near Srem (Sirmium), first century AD (*Novi Sad, Museum of Vojvodina, inv. A/727; author's photo, courtesy of the museum*).

This bronze helmet was found in the Sava River and bears the inscription '(CENTURIA) FLAVI, C(AI) PIMI' (of Caius Pimus, Centuria of Flavius); it is 28 x 20 cm, the browband is 21 cm long

century AD.[276] It was cast in a single piece of bronze and was further shaped by a hammer, a lathe was often also used, the rotation creating a more balanced work.[277] Sometimes surmounted by a button[278] – like some Italic specimens – it shows an ever-growing neck guard; in some specimens the neck guard has exaggerated dimensions.[279] Following the interpretation of Peter Connolly, the development of the neck guard was linked to a particular fighting style of the *miles*, who, 'forward couched', was well protected against blows from above and could easily use his *gladius* in a more effective way. The browband – riveted to the dome on each side – was part of its reinforcing structure, protecting the legionary from direct blows, and with the rounded cheek guards[280] completely closed the face of the warrior. The hinges of the cheek guards, as well as

the frontal browband, were sometimes hammered, sometimes cast. The attachment of the chin strap was by means of a small ring attached on the lower edge of each cheekguard. This development shows a constant attention to a greater protection of head, neck and shoulders of the warriors.

In the specimens shown on the Narbonne reliefs the browband of the Coolus type is made by decorated volutes, as shown on some Italic monuments (**128**): it is probably the outcome of a mixed type, echoing the later specimens of Weisenau typology that show the same decoration (**PLATE III**, **127**). Some Coolus–Haguenau helmets – in a similar way to the Hellenistic specimen preserved in Hamburg,[281] and like the specimens visible on the Scafa relief and many other monuments of the late first century BC–early first century AD (**28**) – were fitted with an embossed *diadema* like the Attic helmets.

125 Detail of sculpture of Attic *diadema* helmet with leather cheek guards, from a statue of a deity, Hadrianic period (*author's photo by kind permission of the Sovraintendenza per I Beni Culturali del Comune di Roma*)

This sculpture shows very clearly the use of leather cheek guards on Roman helmet, perhaps confirmed archaeologically by the Vindonissa specimens

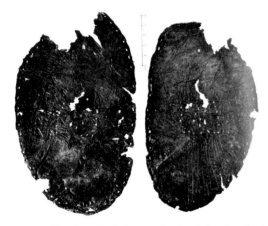

123 Fragments of leather cheekpieces or leather lining for cheekpieces from Vindonissa, first half of the first century AD (*Vindonissa Museum, ex Gansser-Burckhardt, courtesy of Vindonissa Museum*).

A leather-covered *galea*, fitted with leather cheek guards fastened under the chin, is visible on the Niger Aetonis monument. from Bonn.[i] Propertius also mentions leather helmets for the cavalry[ii]

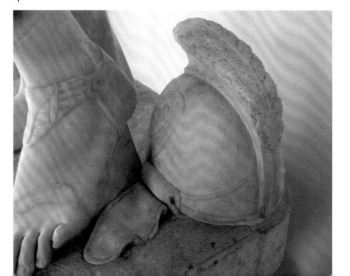

i Gansser-Burckhardt, 1942, fig. 28c.
ii Prop., *El.*, IV, 12, 8.

126 Helmet of Coolus–Haguenau type, type E of Robinson's classification, first century AD (*Belgrade, National Museum; courtesy of the museum*)

127 Bronze Imperial Gallic helmet, first half of first century AD (*ex Guttman collection, Christie's photo*).

This specimen of the Weisenau helmet type, of copper alloy, corresponds to the model worn on the Arc d'Orange and to that of C. Valerius Crispus on his monument in Wiesbaden. It has moulded eyebrows that curve downwards, a short flanged horizontal neck guard with two occipital ridges above and three crest attachments: a central knob welded on a round base and front and back bosses with split pins. The curved cheekpieces – which offer no protection to the ears and the skull of the helmet – show decorative red enamel studs (17) on the brow, on the sides and on the neck and cheekpieces

The Italic tradition of Greco-Attic helmets became one of the most popular in the eastern legions (**82**, **121**, **129**), where it was used also as part of the legacy of the Hellenic tradition of weaponry, and was often depicted on Imperial monuments. It is a current idea that this kind of helmet was reserved for the officers or only for the elite corps, but in reality the figurative monuments have plenty of illustrations of this kind of helmet being worn by *milites gregarii*, often, but not exclusively, in parade or triumphal processions.[282] One intact specimen, still with the ring that is shown on the Imperial monuments (**57**, **63**), is preserved in Hamburg Museum (**130**).

A much-debated helmet is that preserved in the Museum of Toledo, said to be from the Syrian Necropolis of Emesa. This is a typical Hellenised helmet, of Attic shape and furnished with a *diadema* and a ring on the top of the skull (**135**). This type

is represented on Trajan's Column (**97**, **112**, **131**) and on the troops fighting the Parthians (**129**) represented on the Nawa helmet, dated to the Hadrianic era. Many doubts have been raised about the authenticity of this helmet, and the general

128 (Above, above right and opposite page, bottom left) Frieze from funerary monument of a centurion(?), *c.* 20 BC, in situ, Church of San Domenico, Sora author's photos, (*courtesy of Professor Alessandra Tanzilli*).

The romanisation of the Liri valley and its centuriation (the Roman practice of formally dividing up the countryside – *territorium* – around newly established *coloniae* into blocks as allotments for the occupants of the colony) by veterans of a *IV Legio*, after the battles of Philippi and Actium, is widely attested by the funerary friezes with weapons, found

in Sora and in the nearby territory.[i] The gravestone of a officer, later incorporated in the medieval crypt of the Chuch of San Domenico,[ii] shows a pair of greaves, a round *parma* or *clypeus*, a padded *thoracomachus* or armour, and the *balteum* of the sword, closed by a buckle on the front, beside a Coolus–Haguenau helmet with embossed volutes in Hellenic style. Note the side feathers of the helmet, probably indicating that the wearer previously belonged to the *Alauda legio*. The sword hilt, in Celtic late La Tène *antennae* style, is visible on the back

i   Tanzilli, 1983, p. 37.

ii   Tanzilli, 1982, p. 81.

129 (Above and below, right) Roman *milites* and officers, from the helmet of the Nawa necropolis, second century AD (*ex Abdul-Hak; drawing by Graham Sumner*).

130 Bronze and iron helmet of a legionary, Attic type, second century AD (*Hamburg Museum, courtesy of the museum*).

This is for the moment the only known helmet of Attic shape preserved in bronze and with a ring on the top like those on the Marcus Aurelius column, to which it is identical in shape. The helmet has been found in an unspecified place in Germany in the twentieth century. With its similarity to the helmets on the Marcus Aurelius age it could be dated to the second half of the second century AD

inclination is that this specimen is a nineteenth-century fake,[283] although it was recently included in the exhibition on Antioch.[284] However, the great amount of silver used for the patina surface of the helmet is very unlikely for a work of the nineteenth century, and there is not sufficient reason to discount its antiquity, although some restoration or additions could have been carried out more recently. In spite of any doubts over its authenticity, this kind of helmet, continuing the Greek tradition, could easily have been produced in the factories of the Eastern Roman world, where helmets of this shape still existed at the time of Justinian.[285]

The tradition of the pseudo-Corinthian helmet was strong in Greece and in the Hellenised world, as attested by a *stela* of a Roman legionary, preserved in Patrasso Museum, from the end of the first century BC or the early first century AD (**132**), and by the famous sarcophagus of Meleagros, from Durrës (Albania), preserved in Istanbul Museum.[286] Magnificent specimens of this type of helmet were still worn by high commanders, as shown on the statue of a general from the Nerva Forum (**312**). An original specimen of such a helmet, in gilded bronze[287] dated to the end of the first century AD, has been recovered in Autun, in south-east France. Some scholars have interpreted the Autun helmet as clearly (*sic*!) from a statue and not as a practical piece of armour for military use. I do not see why. As outlined by Robinson and Simkins, this helmet could be an effective piece worn probably by high commanders in parade

or triumphal and religious processions. There is nothing in the helmet's manufacture that excludes its practical use as a piece of military equipment; even its dimensions fit very well with a human head.

The other principal category of helmet used by the *miles* in the first and second centuries AD was the Weisenau type (**PLATE III**, **PLATE VI**, **46**, **127**, **133**, **134**). The Weisenau type was the direct heir of the Celtic workmanship of the Agen–Port helmet, also combining elements of the Attic type. This kind of helmet – which Robinson had divided in the various categories of Imperial-Gallic and Imperial-Italic – is already visible on the Arc d'Orange as worn by legionaries and centurions (**6**);[288] its use already by the Augustan period is furtherly confirmed by the finds from Idria Pri Baci and Novo Mesto, dated to 30/10 BC.[289] A tripartite helmet of the Novo Mesto/Agen–Port type that belonged to a Roman legionary, and is dated to the very end of the first century BC, was found in cremation grave 25 in Siemechòw (Poland), used as an urn for the cremated bones of the deceased.[290] The helmet has a hemispherical bowl with three small ribs at the bottom and a large one where the bowl is joined to the forehead and neck guards. A prominent rib appears on the front of the forehead guard. The neck guard and the forehead guards were joined at the sides by means of rivets, two rivets for each one, a fixing that also was used for the cheekpieces. A fixture for a strap was attached to the inside. Although this is considered a variant of the east Celtic helmets, it is clear that these kinds of helmets were widely used by the Romans and transformed in the one-piece helmet of the first–second century AD.

131 Detail of *milites* in composite armour, *lorica segmentata* and a possible ring armour protecting the chest (*cast, Roma, Museo della Civiltà Romana, author's photo, courtesy of the museum*)

132 *Stela* of unknown officer from Actium (Patrassus), first half of the first century AD (*Patrassus, Archaeological Museum; author's photo, courtesy of the museum*).

Maybe this unknown officer was the Greco-Roman commander of a ship. Note that his equipment is similar to that on the Praeneste relief: pseudo-Corinthian helmet, leather *lorica* fastened on the breast by laces linked to the *humeralia*, embossed greaves with the head of a Gorgon. On his left arm he carries a *parazonium*

133 (Above) Roman helmet of Weisenau type, first century AD (*Sofia, National Museum, inv. #34176; by courtesy of Professor Lyudmil Vagalinsky*).

The reinforcing peak, the ear openings and the pronounced neck guard were the main characteristics of this typology of helmets Their superior technical features made them the most used specimen in the imperial army, especially during the second century AD. Inscriptions on the helmets were widely attested in Imperial period, as in this magnificent bronze specimen in Sofia Museum, which once belonged to a *miles* of the *Legio V Macedonica*[i]

134 (Above) Tinned bronze imperial Gallic helmet, first half of the first century AD (*ex Guttman collection, Christie's photo*).

The helmet is fitted with a pair of prominent curved eyebrows flanking two riveted bosses. Note the decorative beaded browband, the horizontal neck guard with flanged rim and central boss for fastening the chin strap. The cheekpieces are decorated by a winged thunderbolt (*fulmen*)[ii]

i   Peeva and Sharankov, 2006, p. 25ff.; this helmet was fashioned by hammering.

ii   Junkelmann, 2000, pp. 138–9, pls 65–6, XII and back cover.

135 (Above) Silver helmet, AD 50–100, from Tell Abou Saboun, Syria (*Toledo Museum of Art*).

This kind of helmet is largely visible on Trajan's Column and on the monuments from the time of Marcus Aurelius. However, doubts about the authenticity of this example have been often raised

136 (Opposite) Centurion's helmet from Sisak, found near the Kupa River, second quarter of the first century AD (*Zagreb, Archaeological Museum, ex Radman-Livaja, by kind permission of Professor Radman-Livaja*).

The helmet shows three layers of decoration, in silver and gilded metal, done at three different times in its use; the small ring preserved on the side of the helmet, and the hole on the other side where a second ring is today missing show a system for attaching the decorative crest transversely: so, with all probability, this was the helmet of a centurion, highly decorated and silvered, having a *crista transversa* as attested by the sculptures and by the literary sources

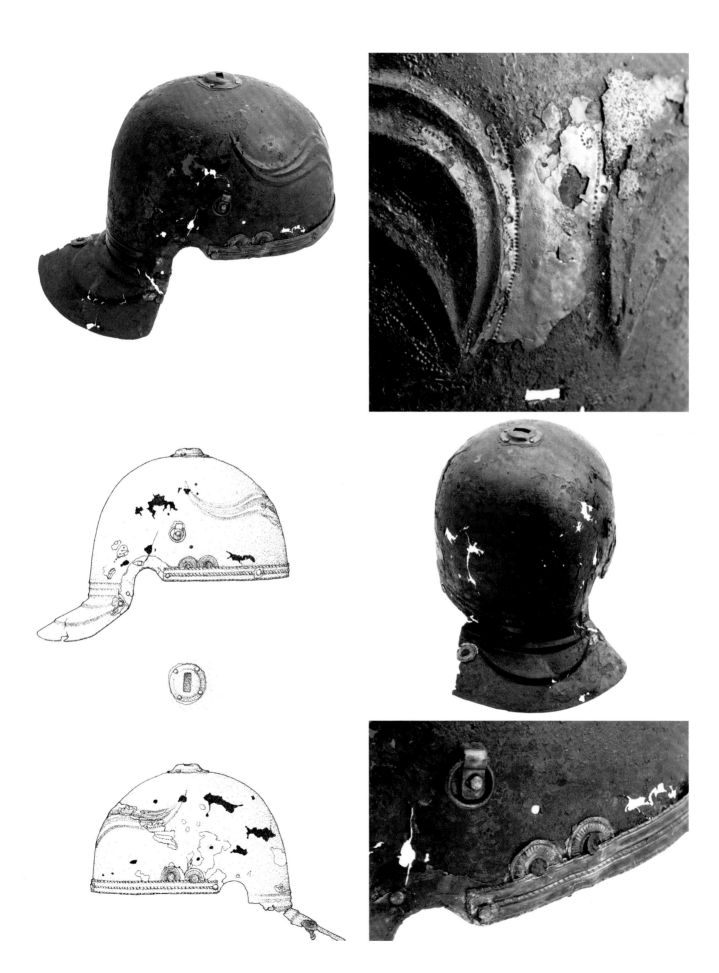

PLATE VI *Beneficiarius* of praetorian *cohors*, Trajanic period: the *beneficiarius* is covered by the Hebron helmet, a development of the Weisenau type.[i] The helmet is iron, with a hemispherical bowl with recesses for the ears. It has browbands of thin bronze, soldered to an applied strip of iron, *lunulae* of thin bronze soldered to the skull on the upper corners of the quarterings and an iron reinforcing peak with applied bronze strip (punched with dots, in alternating bosses and circles) on the lowerflange. It has flat cheekpieces with shallow raised central panels with semicircular devices below the hinges. Two chin-tie rings are on each plate: one for the point of the chin, the other situated at the rear edge below the ear recesses, where they are fastened. We have added the carrying handle like that of the Imperial Italic helmets in bronze.[ii]

The tunic of the warrior has been copied from one specimen of the Bar Kochbà cave,[iii] in red with dark purple *clavi* bordered in black. The tunic is a single rectangular red sheet with two parallel bands woven of weft threads. The bands ran from selvedge to selvedge, with an ample space between them. The two identical parts of the tunic were joined together along one selvedge; the section between the bands was left unsewn, forming a slit between the two sheets, which served as neck opening.

The *lorica* of the warrior is the typical laminated armour. Under it is worn a *subarmale*, so the positioning of the backplates was not like in the modern re-enactments, but the presence of the padded doublet was a level base for shoulderguards and raised the neck aperture of the collar plates above the trapezium muscle.[iv] All the segments of the armour have a leather lining, as show in the Great Trajanic Frieze (**291**). The garment worn under the cuirass has been copied from the fragments of the Nahal Hever leather garment. Essentially two large fragments of leather garments have been found: one of them seems to be composed of parts sewn on the borders with reinforcements strips.

The shield is painted in crimson on the inside, as the shield of the Palestrina mosaic. The metallic grip was probably wrapped with a rope for a better handhold. The badge of rank is the *beneficiarius* spear, copied from the Cancelleria relief. The leather-interlaced *caliga* are copied from a specimen from Pompeii.[v]

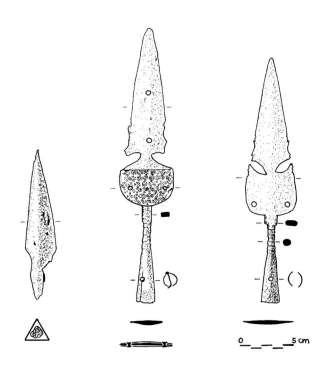

137 Roman shafted weapons and *beneficiarii hastae*, first–third century AD from Saône, France (*ex Feugère; drawing by Andrea Salimbeti*)

i   Robinson, 1975, pls 175–8 and fig. 100; Mattesini, 2004, p. 113; Bottini et al., 1988, fig. 5.1.
ii Robinson, 1975, pls 166–9.
iii Yadin, 1971, p. 71; Yadin, 1963, pl. B1.
iv Bishop, 2002, 163, p. 80.
v   Avvisati, 2003, p. 78.

138 Fragment of cheek guard for an imperial helmet of Weisenau type, first century AD (*collection of Museum Het Valkhof, Nijmegen; courtesy of the conservator*)

139 Cross-bar reinforcement helmet scene LXXXVIII, calco from Trajan Column, (*Museo della civiltà, Roma, author photo, courtesy of the museum*)

The Weisenau helmet, mainly made of iron and silver, presents a single-piece skull and drum and generally a small cut-out for the ears, usually reinforced by a riveted band. As in the Agen–Port type, the shape of the neck is reinforced with rounded edges, and on the front hammered volutes are often present, reinforced by a strong iron circle, fixed to the sides by two rivets. The neck guard is in a lower position in respect of brow line, compared to the Haguenau type, thus providing better protection of the head: it broadens into a very wide slanted part, slightly bent (**111**). The cheek guards are very wide and protective (**138**). From the Flavian period they also had a hinged handle for carrying the helmet, while in previous models of the second quarter of the first century AD decorative rivets, bent into a circle on the interior side of the neck guard, hold the strap or chain for carrying it.[291] Some examples of Weisenau helmets were made of bronze (**PLATE III**, **127**), probably to combine the Italic tradition of casting bronze helmets with the advantages of the Weisenau technical solutions.[292].

During the first and second century AD the neck guard of such helmets grew longer, forming an angle of about forty-five degrees with the drum. At the start of the second century the helmet shows a very important innovation: the crossed external bands riveted on the skull, as are visible on Trajan's Column (**108**, **139**, **247**), which corresponds perfectly with the archaeological evidence of the helmets of Brigetio,[293]

Berzovia[294] or Hebron.[295] The types of Mainz–Weisenau[296] and Theilenhofen[297] – this last dated to the Antonine time – represent a further evolution of this helmet, with their bronze or copper-alloy decoration or their simple iron structure with its comparatively shallow neck guard. On the Marcus Aurelius column both the Attic and Weisenau specimens of Theilenhofen type are well represented (**57**, **59**, **63**, **65**, **114**): many of them, of both types, have the embossed ring crest decoration, others have plumes inserted inside the top knob.

Some Weisenau helmets, such as a specimen from Sisak (**136**),[298] show impressive silver decoration, with silver frontal bands, rosettes decorated in enamel over the rivets holding the cheekpieces. Sometimes the whole helmet was covered in

140 Monument of the Tiberian period from Noviomagus, detail of the helmet with the *geminae pinnae* and central crest (*collection of Museum Het Valkhof, Nijmegen, courtesy of the conservator*)

142 a and **b** Details of helmets of extra-heavy armoured legionaries, Adamclisi reliefs, *metopae* XVII and XX, first half of second century AD (*Museum of Adamclisi; author's photo, courtesy of the museum*).
Note the helmets of *spangen* construction of Sarmatian origin

141 Eastern *auxilia* archers, Trajan's Column, scene LXXXVIII (*cast, Roma, Museo della Civiltà Romana, author's photo, courtesy of the museum*)

further layers of decorative sheet metal, showing successive restorations and decoration in its re-employment.

There is a further type of helmet, represented on the Imperial monuments and used by the legionaries of Trajan: it is of spangenhelm construction, sometimes furnished with a neck guard made of scales.[299] This helmet, made of metal plates positioned like segments around a metal or leather framework, and ending in a conical or pointed apex (**69**), was of Sarmato–Danubian origin and adopted by the Romans during the Dacian Wars. The extra-heavy armoured *milites* of Adamclisi are for the most part wearing it (**47**, **64**, **76**, **142a**, **142b**), and its shape – often wrongly confused with some stylisation of the Imperial-Gallic type – is characterised by a segmented construction of the skull, often surmounted by an apex. For comparison, it is sufficient to look at the same helmets worn by the eastern *auxilia* represented on Trajan's Column (**141**). The protection offered by such helmets against the heavy *falces* of the Dacians was proababy why the extra-heavy armoured legionaries were equipped with them, and gave the Romans inspiration for the reinforcing cross-bars on the Weisenau helmets.

The crest, in ancient warfare, always played a prominent part in the composition of the helmet. The crests were not only used in parade ceremonies but were also effectively used on the battlefield to make a psychological impact on the enemy. Plumes or crests made of horsehair or feathers were inserted along the length of the helmet, or directly in conical holes on the top of the helmet's bowl, or in special settings, inserted in

the front, centre and back. The buttons of some helmets were pierced to allow the insertion of the crest.[300] Other helmets have a pair of tubes on the sides, at the temples, allowing the insertion of the *geminae pinnae* dedicated to Mars (**140**).[301] In one Coolus specimen in Zagreb Museum, the decorative crest was probably tied with a string to the crest knob on the top of the skull, because the knob does not show traces of piercing or notching. In other specimens two laths to support the crest were soldered at the middle and immediately above the neck guard.[302] In some Weisenau helmets, the crest was worn upon a mount inserted in a ribbed plate on the crown (**PLATE III**, **127**).[303] On the Scafa reliefs we have evidence of pheasant plumes used by the warriors, shown by small lines incised on the feathers.

The *crista transversa* of the centurions is well attested for all the first century AD, and also archaeologically documented (**136**), but disappears from the iconography at the begin of the second century AD. At this time these officers were probably distinguished from their subordinates by means of the *vitis*, or the presence of particular features on the helmet or on the 'uniform' (**PLATE IV**). Some helmets of the Coolus–Haguenau type had a ring for hanging and carrying the helmet, attached under the neck guard.[304] But on the Rhine–Weisenau specimen the ring was attached over the wide neck guard. Helmets usually had a leather lining, fragments of which have been found in Vindonissa.

The helmet was also a way to identify the unit, by means of the punched inscriptions on them (**124**). The inscriptions were executed by simple tools, probably by the owner, and usually referred to the name of the unit and the owner.[305]

Body Armour

The protection of the body (*lorica* or *thorax*)[306] was the main concern of the Roman *miles*. Josephus states that 'the footmen are armed with breastplates and headpieces [*thôraxin tephragmenoi kai kranesin*], and have swords on each side . . .'[307] The Imperial Roman army was very rich in armour. Although a certain degree of standardisation was usual for this age, different and various shapes of armour were in use, both metal and leather or other organic material.

Metallic Armour

The Muscled Cuirass

In contrast to the flexible cuirasses more commonly worn by the junior officers and the *gregarii*, the metal muscled cuirass, descendant of the Greco-Hellenic and Etrusco-Italic tradition, was still worn by senior officers, high-ranking generals and commanders and, of course, by the emperor (**62, 71**). It was the preferred armour among the equestrian and senatorial ranks of Rome and ultimately of the emperor himself. The armour, that in the Consular era had been one of the armours of the Patrician hoplite and *miles*, was now a symbol of prestige and glory. Without neglecting the utilitarian needs of battle, it became a symbol of the virtues of the *militates* or military castes of ancient Rome. Every high commander and emperor had himself represented in such an armour as an embodiment of his rule and power.

This armour was called θώραξ στάδιος or στατός (*thorax stadios* or *statos*), because, when placed upon the ground on its lower edge, it stood erect. As a consequence of its firmness it was even used as a seat to rest upon.[308] Pausanias, writing at the time of the Emperor Antoninus Pius, describes a bronze specimen of it painted in the temple of Delphi, in such a way: 'On the altar lies a bronze corselet. At the present day corselets of this form are rare, but they used to be worn in days of old. They were made of two bronze pieces, one fitting the chest and the parts about the belly, the other intended to protect the back. They were called *guala*. One was put on in front, and the other behind; then they were fastened together by buckles . . .'

The words of Pausanias confirm the existence of bronze corselets still at the time of the Antonine emperors, but by that time they were very rare and so reserved for the upper ranks. The corselet consisted principally of the two γύαλα, the breastplate (*pectorale*) – made of bronze or iron, or sometimes more precious metals, which covered the breast and abdomen – and the corresponding plate which covered the back.[309] Both of these pieces were shaped to fit the human body. The anatomical details of the breast, like the belly button and the nipples, were sometimes embossed. The *thorax* worn by the Roman emperors and generals were usually ornamented on

the upper breast by a Gorgon's head[310] and, very often, two griffins, deities,[311] winged victories[312] or other fantastic animals underneath it (**144b**). Acanthus leaves and scrolled tendrils complete the decoration.[313] These could be embossed or, more often, metallic appliqués on the armour, fixed with small rivets and solder. A similar armour is worn by Trajan on the *metopa* X of Adamclisi,[314] with an eagle embossed on the centre and scrolled tendrils in the lower part. It is worn over a padded garment fitted with four rows of *pteryges* below the waist and two rows from the shoulders (**71**).[315]

The two plates were joined on the right side of the body by two hinges, as seen in many statues and in various parts of bronze cuirasses that survive.[316] On the other side, and sometimes on both sides, they were fastened by means of buckles (περόναι/*perónai*). There are, however, clear fasteners on the *thorax stadios* on many sculptures, as well as shoulder fasteners. There are some very rare images of the muscled cuirass with buckle fasteners, instead small strap hinges and simple ties tended to be used.[317] The breastplate and the backplate were further connected by shoulder straps passing over the shoulders and fastened in front by means of buttons or of ribbons tied in a bow (**132**). A ring over each breast was sometimes intended to fulfil the same purpose. Bands of metal often took the place of the leather straps, or covered them and became very ornamental, finishing in a lion's head, or some other appropriate figure on each side of the breast. In the most

143 Harness or armour pendant with the inscription *LEGIO IX HISPANA*, from Noviomagus, second century AD (*collection of Museum Het Valkhof, Nijmegen; courtesy of the conservator*).

The personal equipment and armour of the Roman soldier was often marked either as personal or official property given to the soldier. These inscriptions were frequently composed of the personal name of the soldier, the name of a junior officer and of the military unit.[i] Here only the name of the unit has survived.

i   MacMullen, 1960, 23–40.

precious specimens represented in the sculptures the shoulder guards are embossed with lightning bolts, sphinxes or other elements from the Greco-Roman repertory. In Roman statues we often observe the Hercules knot as a cloth band going round the waist and tied in front, so forming the so-called *zona militaris*.

The longer type of such armours reached the hips at the sides and curved down over the abdomen in the front. Sometimes the lower part of the armour had a dentilated border (*cymation*), composed of small lappets attached by hinges to the lower edge of the armour and decorated with small metallic appliqués such as discs, heads,[318] figures and floral motifs (**143**). A head of Medusa, preserved in Carnuntum[319] Museum, possibly came from such a cuirass border. Some small *phalerae*, from the territory of Serbia (**144**), could also have perhaps been part of the ornament of the armour borders. On Roman armour, continuing the Hellenistic tradition, these lappets are usually rounded and highly decorated. One fragment perhaps of these lappets, highly decorated, has been found in the legionary fortress at Caerleon, Gwent. This bronze piece is, however, 26.2 cm long, and we cannot preclude that it was destined for a bronze statue, rather than for actual armour.[320]

Shorter and more practical metallic breastplates were also used, like that represented in a marble frieze with depictions of weapons, preserved in Turin Museum,[321] and the Louvre relief traditionally said to represent praetorians but more probably legionaries of the Emperor Claudius. In this case the muscled armour is worn by a junior officer, with a *gorgoneion* and the fringed *cinctorium*; he is probably a *centurio* because a similar short armour, although clearly made of leather, is worn by a *centurio* on a gravestone from the Rhine grave and preserved, at least in the nineteenth century, in the Museum of Graz.[322] But according to some authors the figure on the Louvre frieze could even be the Emperor Claudius.[323] The emperors and the Imperial high officer on both the columns (Trajan and Marcus Aurelius) are wearing this kind of short metallic corselet (**145**, **146**, **147**, **148**). In the monuments it is not always easy to distinguish between the leather and metallic muscled cuirasses: on the same monument or artwork, for instance on the *Gemma Augustea*, both the types are well represented.

Around the lower edge of the cuirass were attached lappets or *pteryges* of linen, leather, felt and silk (as it seems to be in the Louvre relief), sometimes covered with small plates of metal. These straps served part as ornaments, and partly also to protect the lower region of the body. Appendages of a similar kind were sometimes fastened by hinges to the *lorica* on the right shoulder, to protect the part of the body which was exposed by lifting up the arm when throwing the spear or using the sword.[324]

Luxurious specimens of *pteryges* are sometimes recorded in figurative art. In a statue from Industria, dated to the third century AD but in style and decoration much more akin to the

144a

144b

144 *Phalerae* from the *cymation* of muscled armour, second–third century AD (*Belgrade Archaelogical Museum, courtesy of the museum*)

first century AD, are represented elaborate *pteryges*, copied from originals in leather or linen, which were probably painted. Inside each *pteryx*, lavishly inlayed in gold and niello, is represented a Roman *miles ostensionalis*, a soldier in dress uniform, [325] with muscled armour (**149**), very similar to the *milites* of the Louvre relief. This means that linen *pteryges* were often decorated in lavishly colours.

Scale Armour

Scale armour was widely used; there is evidence from the Augustan age[326] of sleeveless coats with broad reinforcing shoulder straps tied on using rings on the breast, as for the mail breastplates. The complete shoulder straps were leather-edged and had cut-away corners. At the neck, the armour was also leather-edged.

145 (Above left) Trajan and his headquarter, Trajan's Column, scenes XII–XIII (*cast, Roma, Museo della Civiltà Romana, author's photo, courtesy of the museum*)

146 (Above second from left) *Legatus*, Trajan's Column, scene XVII (*cast, Roma, Museo della Civiltà Romana, author's photo, courtesy of the museum*)

147 (Above third from left) Musicians, Trajan's Column, scene XLI (*cast, Roma, Museo della Civiltà Romana, author's photo, courtesy of the museum*)

148 (Above right) Trajan and *legati*, Trajan's Column, scene XXXV (*cast, Roma, Museo della Civiltà Romana, author's photo, courtesy of the museum*).

The emperor is often represented bareheaded in the figurative monuments, but this is not an artistic convention. Historians recount that many emperors, such as Caesar[i] and Hadrian,[ii] appeared or rode at the head of the troops *capite detecto*, whatever the weather, so that they could be easily recognised

149 (Below) Fringe of armour of bronze, part of a statue from Industria, first–third centuries AD (*Turin, Museo di Antichità, courtesy of the Ministero per i Beni e le attività culturali, Soprintendenza per i Beni Archeologici del Piemonte e del Museo Antichità Egizie*).

Albeit part of a statue, the embossed decoration reproduces in every detail the *pteryx* of an armour, with a possible representation of a *miles praetorianus*, as far as it is possible to tell from the device on his shield.

The scales were commonly bronze (**150, 152**),[327] copper alloy (**151**) or iron.[328] In Roman military language there was no differentiation in terminology, as there is today, to distinguish between scale armour or lamellar armour: the word *squama* was used indiscriminately to indicate either construction. The basis of the cuirass was sometimes a hide, or a piece of strong linen (*lorica lintea*) to which the metallic scales, or 'feathers', as they were also called, were sewn. Sometimes this backing had a muscled shape, forming, as in the cuirass shown on the Domitianic monument on the Capitoline Hill (**92**), a scale-covered muscled cuirass.[329] Imperial scale armours had a Gorgon's head on the breast. Leather and cloth were in fact the normal backing of the heavier *loricae* of scale and mail; linen the backing of the lighter armours of the same material.

In the Eastern language of the legions the epithet λεπιδωτός (*lepidotós*), as applied to a *thorax*, was opposed to the epithet φολιδωτός (*folidotós*).[330] The former denotes a similarity to the scales of a fish (λεπίσιν), the latter to the scales of snakes (φολίσιν). The resemblance to fish scales (*squamae piscis*), is shown on the bronze armour of the *centurio* Q. Sertorius Festus from Verona, from which the costume historian Hottenroth probably copied the original colours (**157**). Here the scales are similar to plumes (*plumatae*), flat and rounded but ending with a point and characterised by a groove down the middle.[331] The armour has short sleeves, ending in two rows of overlapping scales, and is worn over a *subarmale* or a doublet garmet worn under the cuirass with *pteryges*. The scales are worn attached to a leather backing, which gives to the whole body a slightly muscled shape. Scales like these have been found in Nekrasovskaya Stanitsa, in a Sarmatian context of the first to second centuries

---

i Suet., *Caes.*, 57.
ii SHA, *Hadr.*, 17, 9; 23,1.

AD.[332] Other Roman specimens come from Hod Hill in Dorset, each 2.6 cm long, plated with white metal.[333] A cuirass from Ham Hill shows tinned scales alternating with scales left in their natural brass colour.[334]

In the period of the Dacian and Marcomannic wars, this kind of armour became more widespread among the infantrymen, because it was the usual alternative to the laminated or mail armour. An example of the type of scale armour that had long and narrow or squared scales, like the scales of a snake, could be seen on the specially equipped Trajanic legionary represented on the Adamclisi monument (**47**, **49**, **69**).[335] They give the warrior an iron-clad appearance, especially when we also consider the presence of the laminated vambrace on the right arm and the greaves. Scale corselets usually finish at hip height, with a double range of short *pteryges* at sleeves and skirt. Shoulder plates are sometimes present,[336] sometimes the armour encloses the body like a bronze or iron box, sitting on the shoulders like the old Trasimenus style armour.[337] This is already visible in monuments of the Augustan age (**158**).

The scales varied in size. The small scales visible on *metopa* XVI[338] and XX (**155b**), rounded at the lower ends, are similar to the small rounded bronze scales found in Vindonissa, slightly convex in section, which could be attached to a leather backing (**152**). Some of these scales[339] are in bright yellow bronze.[340] Here the upper edge of each scale is pierced with a pair of square holes, for lacing to the flexible backing. The scales are wired together horizontally, as are most of the first-century scales. In *metopa* XXIX (**60**)[341] a *miles* is wearing a scale corselet covering his whole torso, coming down a little over the thighs and showing traces of the doublet with the *pteryges* only on the arms, so we can suppose the use of a flat leather garment under it. The sleeve of the armour is very similar to that of Sertorius Festus.

The armoured man of *metopa* XXXIII (**74**) – which is very interesting for the personalised way of wearing the scabbard of the sword, attached to the top right side of the breast[342] – shows the use of a single shoulder guard or laminated protection on the shoulder, edged by leather, or even entirely of metallic material.[343]

150 Fragments of scale armours of different sizes, from Sirmium, first–second century AD (*Museum of Vojvodina; author's photo, courtesy of the museum*).

Specimens of this armour type has been recovered from locality 36 in Sirmium. The armour consisted of over 900 plates of different shapes, and was probably stored in Sirmium where the workshops for production or repair of weapons may have been situated[i]

151 Fragments of scale armour, second century AD (*collection of 'Museum Het Valkhof, Nijmegen; courtesy of the conservator*)

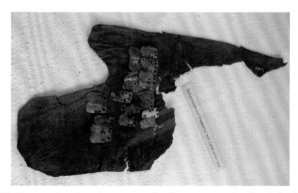

152 Fragments of scale armour fixed upon a not related leather backing, probably a part of a *subarmale*, second century AD (*photo Vindonissa Museum[ii]*).

In Vindonissa fragments of two scale armours have been found. The small scales were attached to a linen or leather backing. Fragments of leather have been found attached to the scale-armour

i   Dautova Rusevljan and Vujović, 2006, p. 43, fig. 19.

ii   Gansser-Burckhardt, 1942, p. 47.

153a

153b

153c   **153d**

154a   **154b**

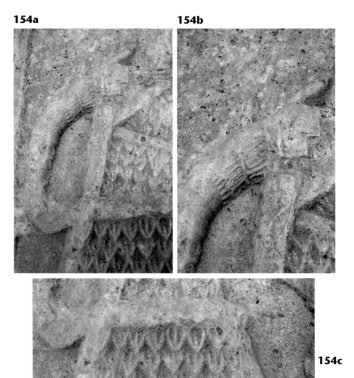

154c

154 (Above) Details of scale armour of extra-heavy armoured miles, Adamclisi reliefs, *metopae* XXXIII, first half of second century AD (*Museum of Adamclisi, author's photo, courtesy of the museum*)

153 (Above) Various fragments of scale bronze armour, from Buciumi, second century AD (*Zalau, Archaeological Museum; author's photo, courtesy of the museum*).

In the military camps of Dacia have been found fragments of the same *squamae* that is visible on the Adamclisi monument. Compare **a**, **b** and **d** with *metopae* XX–XXXIII (**155b, 154a**), **c** with *metopae* XII, XIII, XVII and XXIX (**47, 49, 59, 155a**)

155a   **155b**

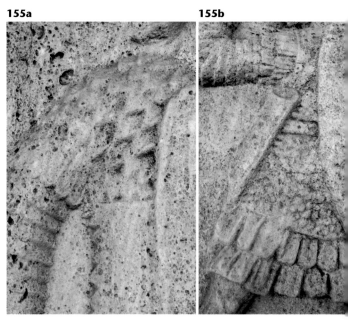

155 (Right) Details of scale armours of extra-heavy armoured legionaries, Adamclisi reliefs, *metopae* XVII and XX, first half of second century AD (*Museum of Adamclisi, author's photo, courtesy of the museum*)

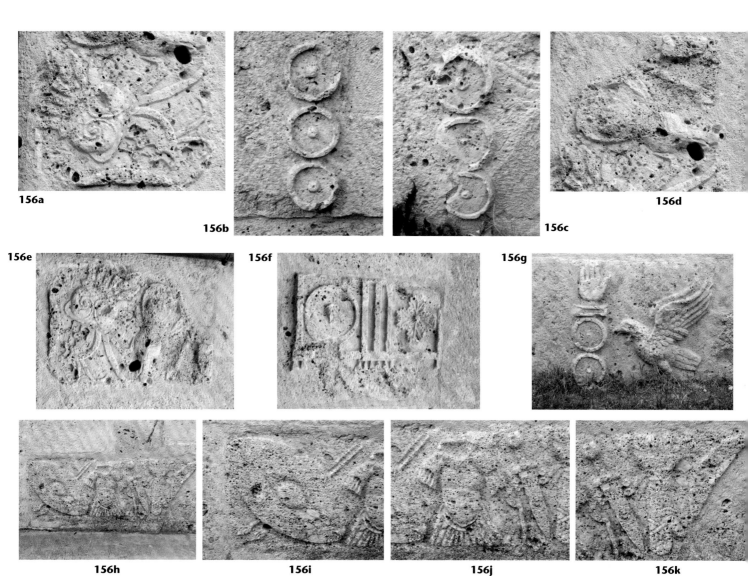

156a

156b

156c

156d

156e   **156f**   **156g**

156h   **156i**   **156j**   **156k**

156 (Above) Frieze of Augustan date from the Abbazia of San Domenico in Sora (*reproduced by kind permission of Professor Tanzilli*).
a) Helmet of Coolus typology with *bucculae*, feathers and crest, volutes decoration on the skull. **b)** and **c)** *Signa militaria* decorated with round *phalerae*.[i] **d)** Unidentified weapon, perhaps the upper part of a gladiatorial shoulderpiece. **e)** Helmet, unidentified weapon and ovoid *scutum*, **f)** Frieze fragment with cavalry *parma*, **g)** Legionary eagle and manipular *signum*. **h)** *Hasta*, *pilum* and *scutum* of oval shape, *lorica* or *thorax stadios*, *gladius* in its *vagina* and a *cestus*, a *parma* seen from the side. **i)** Detail of shield and shafted weapons. **j)** Detail of the *lorica*. **k)** Detail of the *cestus*

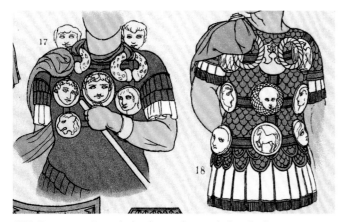

157 Reconstruction of the lost colours of the Caelius gravestone (Mainz) and Q.S. Festus (Verona) (*ex Hottenroth, author's collection*)

158 Decorative frieze from the territory of Salona, representing a scale armour (*squama*) and a *gladius* of late Consular or early Imperial age, late first century BC (*Split, Archaeological Museum; T. Seser's photo, courtesy of the museum*)

---

i   Tanzilli, 1982, pp. 79–81.

On the monuments of the Antonine period again we see *squamae* with scales of different sizes and shapes. The *milites gregarii* wear scale armour on the column of Marcus Aurelius, alongside laminated armour and mail amour.[344] The scale armour is usually hip length, very often made up of large *squamae* (**57**, **63**). Identical *squamae* have been found in the military camp of Carnuntum, made of bronze and iron,[345] attesting the high degree of detail made by the Roman artists in their representations. A *miles* has an armour composed of nine rows of scales overlapping like roof tiles.[346] Most of these armours, attached to a base of leather or linen, have dentilated lower edges. The same armour is visible on the scene of the *adlocutio* of the troops by Marcus Aurelius (**116**), incorporated in the Constantine Arch in the fourth century.[347] Two different *squamae* are represented on the reliefs: a *lorica* fitted to the body of a *hastiliarius*, probably worn over a leather tunic that gave to the wearer a much more muscled aspect; and a very rigid iron or bronze scale armour, with rounded scales, worn by a *miles* of a *legio*, perhaps the *XXX Ulpia*, in the scene of the reception of the prisoners.[348]

These kinds of armour could be fastened on the left side of the body by means of leather laces,[349] with an opening from the left armpit to the bottom hem. Hovewer, in the Antonine period a new fastening system began to be introduced, composed of two small decorated breastplates, fixed at the centre of the breast and closed by turning pins.[350] Bronze fragments of embossed plates, found together with the scales in a specimen from Buciumi, are maybe early examples of such plates, but these might also be side torso parts of a composite armour, made from metal plates and scales (**153**), which deserves closer study. Infantry scale armour of the old type was in any case employed alongside the new models, until the end of the Eastern Roman Empire in AD 1453.

161 Fragment of *squama* shoulderplate with the fastening hinge preserved, from Statio Cataractarum Diana (Davidovac, near Kladovo), second century AD (*Iron Gates Museum, Kladovo; author's photo, courtesy of the museum*)

Semi-rigid scales of a new type, wired on four sides to each of their four neighbours, were introduced from the Antonine period, as attested by the specimens from Carlisle (in iron), Musov,[351] Aquincum, the Iron Gate region, Sirmium (**150**) and other localities. The fragment in Kladovo Museum from the Iron Gate region is very important in understanding a part of the fastening system of such armour: it is probably a part of the shoulder protection, or lateral fastening, where the hinge to which the leather straps were linked is still in place (**161**).

Mail Armour

Mail protection appears in the legionary equipment as the mail shirt, as chain mail or ring mail. The mail shirt continued to be the ordinary armour of the *miles* (**61**, **64**, **70**, **76**).[352] Its shiny appearance is perhaps recorded by Propertius when he describes the ordinary soldier shining in deadly weapons.[353] Propertius also remembers an armour[354] burning the upper arms; he simply calls it *lorica*, but he must have had in mind iron armour: apart from leather corselets, the only heavy armour coming down over the upper arms at that time was mail armour.

At the beginning of the Augustan period the armour shape was still the typical Celtic one, with mail shoulder guards edged by leather or metallic elements. The shoulder doublings, leather backed, were attached to the back, just below the armholes. On the Arc d'Orange the chain mail has short sleeves emerging from under the shoulder protection. On this monument it is worn by all the infantrymen, even the centurion (**6c**, **315c**).[355] The centurion's cuirass is hip length and is decorated by an appliqué in the shape of Medusa on the breast, and shows that the Celtic fastening system has became the standard, with a pivot attached to the breast and hinged to the edges of the *humeralia* (shoulder guards). The chest fastener had various different designs (**159**, **160**). The double hooks, S-shaped and usually with snake-head terminals, were secured by a central rivet on the chest (**159**, **160**). The system allowed excellent freedom of movement, giving greater protection to the shoulders and the arms.[356] Similar fasteners for infantry mail have been found on the Kalkriese battlefield, some of

159 (Above, left) Double fastening hooks for *humeralia* of mail shirt of cavalry and infantry, first century AD (*collection of Museum Het Valkhof, Nijmegen; courtesy of the conservator*)

160 (Above, right) Right parts of fastening hooks for *humeralia* of mail shirt, first century AD (*collection of Museum Het Valkhof, Nijmegen; courtesy of the conservator*)

them are also decorated with niello and inscribed with the *miles'* name.[357]

A unique example of chain mail or scale armour worn on the Arc d'Orange still shows the shape of the Hellenic short armour with attached *pteryges* (**6**, **6e**): the other mail armours are worn in a looser way, held in at the waist by the *cingulum*, continuing the tradition shown on the Etruscan urns and the Altar of Domitius Ahenobarbus.

From the first century to the end of the second century AD the armour was composed of between 30,000 and 100,000 iron rings, with a diameter varying from 3 mm to 10 mm. This might very well explain the expression used by Statius in his epic poem *Thebaid*: '. . . where with iron weft the slender chains form the many-folded *thorax* . . .'.[358] The specimens from Newstead shows the construction of alternating rows of rings punched-out from sheet metal (*circuli*) interlocked with wire rings butted and riveted (*hami*).[359] The weight of a complete shirt can be calculated to have been 9–15 kg in the first century AD[360] and 6–10 kg in the second century. By wearing the belt such a weight was transferred from the shoulders, but generally this armour was relatively light to wear although very strong. These data have been arrived at by analysis of numerous fragments from the Rhine frontier, where complete specimens such as the armour from the *vicus* outside the fort at Rainau-Buch (Kastellvicus des Rainau-Buch), have been found.[361] Mail was usually made of iron rings, but bronze and gilded specimens have also been found, which is inevitable when we consider that decorative trims were often used (**162**). A fragment in bronze has been recovered at Avenches[362] and several Roman chain mail were recovered from the Saône River, with the lower rows of rings in bronze.

The mail armour was usually worn over a leather jerkin or doublet, sometimes fitted with *pteryges*. This undergarment had the advantage of providing extra protection against arrows or stabbing thrusts. Moreover, it made it easier to put the mail over the cloth garments, keeping the woollen or linen tunic clean and also protecting it from chafing by the metallic mail.

The shape of the mail also depended on the garment over which it was worn: sometimes this gave a muscled shape, as in the late Augustan trophy relief in Marseilles Museum,[363] with short sleeeves and small shoulder straps. These *loricae* could be sleeveless or short sleeved. Generally, a shorter (**70**) and a longer shape (**64**, **76**, **113**) are represented on the monuments. Towards the second century AD, the chain mail gradually abandoned the metallic shoulder guards, to assume the shape of a mail shirt, short or long, with dentils on the lower edges and on the shoulders.

On the Adamclisi monument all the types are visible: the long shirt without shoulder guards and worn over flat garments,[364] the waist-length type with shoulder guards and *humeralia* and worn over a doublet equipped with *pteryges*,[365] and the type that was dentilated at the bottom hem, which is also visible on Trajan's Column (**70**) and on the Marcus Aurelius column (**57**, **59**, **63**), where it is worn by many legionary unit, such as the men of the *Legio XII Fulminata* in the scene of the miracle of the rain.[366] On the column of Marcus Aurelius the mail shirt is the most common armour, worn as an alternative to the laminated and scale armour in the same unit[367] of *stratiotai*.[368] The lower dentilated edges could have a triangular[369] or rounded indentation.[370]

Three kinds of mail armours were used: the simplest had a flat surface (*licia*); a more sophisticated type had the rings sewn inside the cloth (*tela*); and finally there was the multi-layered mail armour. This last is visible on the famous Treasure of Marengo (**110**), showing weapons of the period of Lucius Verus. Here an embossed belt shows a mail armour with shoulder guards, and worn over a first *subarmale* with *pteryges* and a second of simpler cloth. Considering also the oval shield represented next to it, which bears the *digma* of the *Legio Secunda Italica*, identical to the later *digma* visible on the *Notitia Dignitatum*, this *lorica* could be associated with this legion, rasied at the time of the Marcomannic Wars.

The use of mail by the eastern legions is confirmed by the group of soldiers engaged in a battle against the Parthians, represented on the richly embossed helmet from Nawa (**129**). Here the warriors and the officers are wearing short waist-length mail breastplates, worn together with a padded garment with *pteryges* reinforced by metal plates. This equipment is dated to the time of the Bar Kochbà revolt, and attests that the Hellenistic style of such breastplates was still strong in the Hellenised regions of the empire. Mail remained widespread in the east as it would have been cooler to wear than laminated armour.[371]

Due to the rubbing action of the rings the mail shirts were largely self cleaning, so that, as recorded for the Consular times, they were often passed down from generation to generation.[372]

162 Fragments of very thin bronze ring armour, second century AD (*photo Vindonissa Museum; courtesy of the museum*).
The small rings were presumably attached to a linen backing. The fragment is about 10 cm in length and 1 cm wide. It is composed of six rows of bronze rings of 0.5 cm diameter and 0.5 mm thick. This is all that it is left of a very finely-worked mail armour

i   Gansser-Burckhardt, 1942, p. 47.

Laminated Armour

The ancient *lorica* of the Romano-Etruscans, made of strips of leather, appears again at the end of the Consular age in a metallic form. Lighter than mail armour, for two centuries it became the specific armour of the *miles gregarius*. It was simply called *lorica* by the Romans; modern scholars generally know it as *lorica segmentata*.

The main reason for its introduction was the combination of protection and manoeuvrability offered by the articulated armour. It was very effective against strikes and bodily injuries, especially against the arrows of the Parthians.[373] For this reason we should not discount the possibility that Caesar, in preparation for the Parthian campaign, might have contributed to the spread of such armour among the *milites*. But this is only a hypothesis; we do not know exactly when it was first made and distributed to the troops. Another explanation may be that it was an armour created to resist the terrible blows of the Germans and Celts.

All the metallic armours of the Roman world were worn over a protective garment, to absorb the force of the impact of the enemy's weapons. But the metallic strips of the *segmentata* were much more able to withstand hits, and especially provided better protection to the shoulders. This armour is no stylish design. It was an armour with a practical purpose only; maybe it was conceived by a mechanic rather than an armourer. Of course it was more economical than *squama* and mail, and it was easier to dismantle and repair, being composed of separate and detachable parts. From the aesthetic point of view, though, it was not an attractive sight: anyone wearing it would have looked like a mechanical automaton!

The first image that attests its use is from the Susa arch (**28**), dated to about 14 BC. It is worn by the Augustan soldiers who participated in the war in the Alps against the Celts of Cottius; the archaeological specimens are fragments of this kind of armour found on the battlefield of Kalkriese (**164**), showing it being worn by Varus' legions.[374]

Various finds from the provinces[375] show the continued use of various different types of this kind of *lorica* through the whole first and second centuries AD,[376] and important iconographic evidence of this laminated armour is shown on triumphal monuments and reliefs,[377] tombstones (**304**), coins,[378] paintings,[379] mosaics,[380] small statuary,[381] attesting its widespread use by the legions in the High Empire.

We are deeply indebted to scholars such as Webster, von Groller, Robinson, Poulter and Bishop for their deep analysis of the surviving fragments, who have made it possible for us to identify some of the types used. The high level of detail of Roman sculpture in the representation of this armour teaches us, however, that a great deal of further study needs to be conducted to reveal all the possible types of laminated armour used by the Romans.

163 Publius Helvius Pertinax, as *praeses daciae*, in *habitu militari*,[i] statue *loricata* from Apulum (Alba Julia), second century AD (*Alba Julia Museum, courtesy of the museum*)

Essentially these armours were composed of iron plates and laminated parts – a breastplate, a mid-collar plate, backplates, upper and lower shoulder guards and girth hoops – interlocked with internal leather straps and fastening elements (hooks, rivets) in bronze or copper alloy. The girth hoops overlap

---

i   SHA, *Macr.*, VI, 8.

horizontally and enclosed the trunk. On the front and back the plates were fastened by hooks and laces. On the inside the single plates were attached together by means of leather and rivets. The shoulder guards protecting the upper body were fastened by clasps; the breastplate and the backplate were hinged by means of clasps and leathers to the other parts of the armour.

In his most recent work on the subject, Dr Bishop has enlarged on the work of Robinson and categorised[382] the types of laminated armour, tracing a chronological evolution. The main differences between the types are based on the method of connecting the individual sections:

1. The Kalkriese, Dangestetten and Vindonissa (**164**) types, dated to about 9 BC–AD 43; it seems that here there was a complex method of section joints, and more buckles than in the later specimens; specimens of three-horned sub-lobate hinges from this kind of armour were recovered from Sisak, as well as hingeless buckles.[383] The sub-lobate hinges with rounded scalloped ends characterised this kind of armour.[384]

2. The Corbridge and Carnuntum type, with three different variants (conventionally called A, B and C), dated to a period around AD 69–100;[385] these kinds of armours are composed of about forty articulated iron plates (type A),[386] comprising two breastplates (**165**, **167**, **168**), six backplates (**166**), sixteen overlapping shoulder guards and sixteen girth hoops enclosing the body and back (**169**). The laminated parts were riveted with the help of three vertical leather straps, the shoulder pieces by copper-alloy lobate hings (**170**, **171**), the other parts by rectangular copper-alloy tie-hoops, clasps, hinged buckles (**173**, **174**, **175**) and circular rivets with embossed decorative washers that were sometimes flower-shaped (**172**, **175**). Clasps allowed the fastening of half-circular girth hoops with the help of leather laces.

   There are many variants of this kind of armour, however. The Carnuntum armour has still not received a satisfactory reconstruction because of its fragmentary status. The girth hoops are about 5–6 cm wide[387] and some of the shoulder fragments appear to be rounded at the edges, like the numerous specimens on Trajan's Column.

   The Gamala armour, which still has not had a proper publication, shows a unique system of sliding rivets to join the backplates, similar to the armour represented on many monuments.[388] So perhaps it would better to consider that there were many different types of *lorica segmentata*, not all with the same numbers of fittings.

3. The Newstead type, dated to a period around AD 164–80.[389] Made of forty-eight elements, this kind of *lorica* is simpler than the Corbridge typology; this is the main

164 (Top) Fragment of a shoulder guard of Kalkriese type, retaining a portion of a hinged sub-lobate fitting, from Vindonissa, first century BC–first century AD (*Vindonissa Museum;*[i] *courtesy of the museum*)

165 (Middle) Part of a virtually complete breastplate of *lorica* of Corbridge, type A, from Vindonissa, first century AD (*Vindonissa Museum; courtesy of the museum*)[ii]

166 (Bottom) Part of the upper backplate of *lorica*, retaining one of the hinged buckles used to join it to the plate on the other side, first–second century AD (*Vindonissa Museum;*[iii] *courtesy of the museum*)

i   Unz and Deschler-Erb, 1997, p. 28 and pl. 30, no. 615; Thomas, 2003, p. 133, fig. 83, no. 106; Bishop, 2002, p. 27, fig. 4.5.

ii Unz and Deschler-Erb, 1997, p. 28 and pl. 30, no. 616; Thomas, 2003, p. 132, fig. 83, no. 107.

iii Unz and Deschler-Erb, 1997, p. 28 and pl. 31, no. 629; Thomas, 2003, p. 134, fig. 83, no. 120.

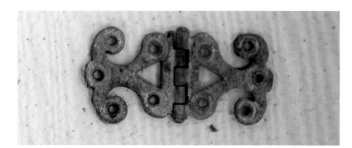

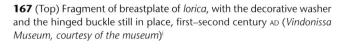

167 (Top) Fragment of breastplate of *lorica*, with the decorative washer and the hinged buckle still in place, first–second century AD (*Vindonissa Museum, courtesy of the museum*)[i]

168 (Middle) Fragments of back and breastplates of a *lorica*, retaining the hinged strap fittings, rivets and hingeless buckle, first–second century AD (*photo Vindonissa Museum;*[ii] *courtesy of the museum*)

169 (Bottom) Parts of girdle plates, retaining leather washers, tie-hooks and rivets at the top edge for securing the internal leather strips, first–second century AD (*photo Vindonissa Museum;*[iii] *courtesy of the museum*)

170 (Top) Copper-alloy lobate hinges for *lorica* shoulder guards, Vindonissa, first–second century AD (*photo Vindonissa Museum;*[iv] *courtesy of the museum*)

171 (Middle) Copper-alloy lobate hinges for *lorica* shoulder guards with parts of the iron plate and copper-alloy decorative washer, first–second century AD (*photo Vindonissa Museum;*[v] *courtesy of the museum*)

172 (Bottom) Copper-alloy lobate hinges for *lorica* shoulder guards, one still with parts of the iron plate preserved, and copper-alloy decorative washer, first–second century AD (*photo Vindonissa Museum;*[vi] *courtesy of the museum*)

---

i   Unz and Deschler-Erb, 1997, p. 29 and pl. 31, no. 636; Thomas, 2003, pp. 16 and 115, figs 3, no. 56 and 72, no. 23.
ii   Unz and Deschler-Erb, 1997, p. 28 and pl. 31, nos 631, 632, 634; Thomas, 2003, p. 132, fig. 122.
iii Unz and Deschler-Erb, 1997, p. 28 and pl. 30, nos 623–4, 627; Thomas, 2003, p. 134 and fig. 83, nos 114, 115, 118.
iv   Unz and Deschler-Erb, 1997, p. 31 and pl. 34, nos 832; Thomas, 2003, p. 65, fig. 19.
v   Unz and Deschler-Erb, 1997, p. 31 and pl. 34, no. 821 and p. 29, pl. 31, no. 639; Thomas, 2003, p. 70, fig. 49, no. 53.
vi   Unz and Deschler-Erb, 1997, p. 29 and pl. 31, no. 645; p. 31, pl. 34, no. 823; Thomas, 2003, p. 70, fig. 49, no. 55; inv. no. 28.2632, unpublished to my knowledge.

173 (Top) Copper-alloy tie-hooks and hingeless buckle of *lorica*, first–second century AD (*Vindonissa Museum; courtesy of the museum*[i])

174 (Middle) Copper-alloy and bronze hingeless buckles and hinged buckles of *lorica*, first–second century AD (*photo Vindonissa museum,*[ii] *courtesy of the museum*)

175 (Bottom) Copper-alloy and bronze tie-hook and hinged straps of *lorica*, first–second century AD (*photo Vindonissa museum;*[iii] *courtesy of the museum*)

i   Unz and Deschler-Erb, 1997, p. 29 and pl. 32, nos 693, 709; Thomas, 2003, pp. 94, 101, figs 61, no. 45 and 63, no. 94 (tie-hooks); inv. 4116 is unpublished to my knowledge.

ii   Unz and Deschler-Erb, 1997, p. 30 and pls 32–3, nos 733, 762, 772; Thomas, 2003, p. 19, fig. 8, no. 3 (hinged buckle) and bibliography; pp. 49–50, fig. 32, nos 37 (wrongly indicated as 633) 41, 45.

iii Unz and Deschler-Erb, 1997, pp. 29–30 and pl. 32, nos 688, 728, 730 ; Thomas, 2003, p. 101, fig. 63, no. 69; p. 27, fig. 15, no.35; p. 24, fig. 14, no. 40; inv. 2831347(?) is unpublished to my knowledge.

armour represented on the Trajan and Marcus Aurelius columns.[390] The breast and backplate fastenings were of three different types:

a) by buckles and straps,[391] with the small hole near the top in each of the back and breastplates used for fastening a copper-alloy edging strip around the neck opening; or

b) by turning pins, like those used for scale armour, each turning pin was held in place with its own split pin, attached to the collar by means of a thong; or

c) by tie rings, a method used also for the fastening the girth hoops;[392]

Very important and well-preserved fragments of this *lorica* have been recovered from Stillfried,[393] where the armour was found together with large parts of an internal leather still in place. The width of the girth hoops (**176**) is about 7 cm. The central fastening of the girdle hoops of the armour is virtually identical to those represented on the Marcus Aurelius column (**66**).[394]

Vertical fasteners were attached to the inside of the upper girth hoop and the hook passed through a hole in the plate to the outside, the single hook at the front coinciding with a pair of leathering rivets. This explains the rivets shown on the outer surface of some *loricae* on the Marcus Aurelius column.

The Stillfried armour, which appears to be a further development of the simpler Newstead type, shows the following characteristics:

a) A complete series of girth hoops, overlapping right over left: one half of the girth hoops was equipped with cast loops (tinned) and the other had small rectangular slots through which these loops fitted, each slot being furnished with a riveted rectangular copper-alloy plate (a rivet in each corner (**176**)) similar to the slot guards on the breast and backplates.[395]

b) The form of the copper-alloy plates around the girth hoops provided a tie ring: the use of tie rings (as in the specimen of Caerleon[396]), secured to their girth hoops through square roves, passing through slots, meant that the girth hoops were, like the upper elements of the cuirass, fastened with the aid of split pins; so the armour was more rigid in the torso area.

c) An inverted vertical fastener in the middle of one of the upper girth hoops, on the wearer's side, was for an unknown purpose.[397]

d) Vertical fasteners were attached to the inside of the upper girth hoop, and the hook element passed through a hole in the plate to the outside, the single hook at the front coinciding with a pair of leathering rivets.

e) Copper-alloy binding was used for the bottom edge of the lower hoop and the top edge of the top hoop (**176**), while the upper hoop was not narrowed under

176 Fragments of *lorica*, from Stillfried, second half of second century AD (*Traismauer, Museum für Frügeschichte; courtesy of Professor Clemens Eibner*)

the armpit, but was the same height for its entire length.

f) The breast plate could be fastened either by a turning pin[398] attached to the collar by means of a thong, or by means a tie ring like those used on the girth hoops.

The shoulder guards were not preserved in the Stillfried find, and I am convinced that the lobate hinges were not universally used in these specimens of *lorica segmentata*, neither are they visible on the monuments related to the Marcomannic Wars (**65**, **66**, **114**).

The earlier form of this *lorica* was sometimes found to be very oppressive and cumbersome.[399] The problem of this armour was that there were too many hinges, laces and clasps, which could explain the simplifications of the evolved Newstead model. The armour was usually worn, as were all the metallic armours, over a padded doublet, probably the *subarmale* mentioned in various sources, which improved the protection offered by the armour in absorbing the shock of the blows.[400] A clear example of this kind of armour being worn over a doublet is on scene LXXII of Trajan's Column (**177**), where the scalloped sleeves of such a garment emerge from above the *lorica*. *Milites legionarii* wearing their packed equipment, with their rectangular shield and the single *subarmale*, are also perfectly visible on the column (**111**). The lower edge of a scalloped garment worn under the cuirass is visible also on the Marcus Aurelius column.[401]

177 *Miles subarmale* and *lorica* details, Trajan's Column, scene LXXII (*cast, Roma, Museo della Civiltà Romana, author's photo, courtesy of the museum*)

Leather, Linen and Felt Armour

The Muscled Cuirass

Many monuments and statues *loricatae* show the great muscled armour, furnished with *pteryges* and laps, or worn over a doublet with *pteryges*, in leather versions (**4**, **103**, **163**).[402] Roman artists depicted the majority of the muscled armours of the Imperial age, continuing the tradition of the Consular period, giving the impression of leather cuirasses, often painted and sometimes adorned with beautiful metallic appliqués.[403] A statue from Adana, preserved in the local museum, shows a relief decoration with two winged griffins looking at an eagle with lightning bolts in its claws. Every circular element of the *cymation* is decorated by an animal head: a lion, in the centre, flanked by two griffins, a tiger, a panther, and two vegetal decorations. The main body of the armour is clearly made of leather, but the embossing of the appliqués reveals metal fittings.[404] In the Imperial specimens, the metallic fittings were also sometimes painted, or left in their natural bronze or silver colours to contrast with the painted surface (**4**). A bronze fitting of this kind of cuirass, once attached to the lower rim lappets of the armour (*cymation*) has been found in the military camp of Vindonissa (**178**).[405]

The statue of Augustus of Prima Porta (**4**) is very important in showing the way in which such armours were fastened, with details that can only have been copied from real life. The side seams are clearly visible. There are hinges on the opposite side, under the left arm, and strap hinges pull the seams together. Four hinges are represented in the detail under the right arm, they were probably made of leather or fabric, because they flex at certain points of the anatomy. On the right side, the second hinge from the bottom closes the seam of the cuirass at the narrowest point on the torso just below the ribcage. Since the second hinge from the bottom bends right at this juncture, it must be made of leather or a similar flexible material, otherwise it would prevent the cuirass from opening. This means that critical parts of this armour, as well as of many metallic specimens, must have been made of leather or fabric.[406] At the top of the seam on the right side of the statue, directly underneath the arm, a small tie is perfectly visible. This is the only obvious fastener and seems adequate to attach a piece of armour of this size and complexity, if it is made of leather. Following Dr Travis Lee Clark, 'the hinges appear to be straps threaded through the back and breast plates'. He suggests that if there were leather straps on the armour used by the artist as a model for the sculpture, then the ties or fasteners might be internal to the cuirass, which would have provided two benefits: to keep the fasteners from unintentionally catching on items while in battle; and to allow for the cuirass to be adjusted and tightened more easily. The shoulderpieces of the armour (different from the main body) were probably made of bronze.

178 Appliqué of *cymation* of muscled armour, first–second century AD (*photo Vindonissa Museum; courtesy of the museum*)

The muscled leather armour was reserved, as was its counterpart in bronze or iron, for emperors, generals and officers, or for some special corps. The presence of leather armour can be easily identified on monuments from many indications. First of all there are traces of colour still present on the gravestones and other sculptures, or copied by nineteenth-century artists when the colour was still visible. Second, the artist has clearly represented the folded leather and its characteristics. This is the case with the monument of the *centurio* Marcus (or Manius?) Caelius, of the *XVIII Legio*, killed in the Varus disaster in AD 9, where traces of the brown colour of the leather muscled armour were still visible in 1888 to be copied by Hottenroth (**157**). The armour of Caelius[407] is clearly a leather corselet with attached *phalerae*, as can be interpreted from the attached shoulder coverings, which are not possible in a metallic *thorax stadios*, and from the *umbilicus* shaped on the belly, which precludes the possibility that it was painted to represent mail. The armour had short sleeves, to which were directly attached – probably by sewing – two rows of short *pteryges*, of the same brown colour. The use of brown (probably leather) *pteryges* attached to a muscled leather armour is further confirmed by the painting of the 'dancing *centurio*' from the Villa of Varanus at Stabiae, dated to the first half of the first century AD (**179**).[408]

The gravestone of a second *centurio* or *evocatus*,[409] once preserved at the Museum of Graz, shows better details of a similar armour or *corium*, with leather shoulder guards shaped like those of an old linen armour and a metallic plaque on the central breast representing a Gorgon (*gorgoneion*). The short extensions covering the upper arm, shaped as two small true sleeves, are clearer. This aspect can also be seen very clearly on a sculpture of an unknown *miles* in action from a Flavian monument in Villa Albani, where the short sleeves of the leather armour have at their extremities a scalloped edge instead of *pteryges* (**98**). The *Gemma Augustea* shows a tribune or senior officer in a similar muscled *lorica*[410] with short sleeves. A reconstructed *centurio* on show in the Museo della Civiltà

Romana[411] shows leather armour fitted with short sleeves which do not restrict the movement of the arm: it is enough to use soft leather and hardened leather in different points of the same armour.

This is probably also the way in which the armour of M. Favonius Facilis, *centurio* of the *Legio XX Valeria Victrix* was made (**PLATE IV**), represented on his gravestone from Colchester (**72**). Robinson considered this armour to be mail, because it is constructed to fit over the shoulders and on the upper arms:[412] but his reasoning – that a thick leather would have prevented the man from raising his arm above the elbow – did not take into consideration the presence of the short sleeves, not very clearly shown on the unfinished tombstone, but clearly visible in other monuments where the same armour is represented (**105**). Moreover, what was considered a broad-plated *cingulum* was probably a leather decoration of the armour, applied as a reinforcement piece and fitted with metallic appliqués. This is clearly shown on a painting from the House of Vettii in Pompeii, where a similar belt, painted red, upon an identical armour, is worn by an officer, a *tribunus* or *centurio* (**86**). This kind of belt, created in this period and attached directly to the armour, survived long into the Byzantine period.

A small miniature of a leather armour similar to that of Favonius is shown on a triumphal relief from the first century AD, related to the *Legio VII Pia Fidelis* from Gardun (ancient Tilurium, Dalmatia, modern-day Croatia)[413] and preserved in Split Museum (**105**). The holes of the sleeves of the leather armour are perfectly visible, as are the row of padded[414] *pteryges* at the lower edge. Finally, the statue of a general of the Antonine period from the museum of Bergama (ancient Pergamon) in Turkey clearly shows a muscled *lorica* made of

leather.[415] The lower abdomen of the cuirass holds the shape of a human abdomen, but the material is obviously flexible, probably boiled or treated leather.

Another element useful in interpreting whether the sculpture represents a metallic or leather muscled *lorica*, is the shoulder guards. Quoting Dr Travis Lee Clark: 'In nearly every case they appear the same: flexible straps without hinges that are pulled over the shoulder. They often are decorated with low relief, as in this example with the lightning bolt, which is common. They are also tied off with straps and the straps are attached to the harness with a simple knot or lark's head.'

These armours were designed for a much more practical use than those of generals and emperors, so their decoration was a little less luxurious, sometimes reduced just to the typical *gorgoneion* at the centre of the breast and the lightning bolt appliqués on the shoulder guards. The plain leather muscled armour seems to be the standard for the second-century *optiones* on the gravestones and figuratives monuments. This is the case of the *optio* killing a Germanic prisoner on the Marcus Aurelius column,[416] which could be compared with the gravestone of the *optio* C. Septimus from Aquincum.[417] Neither of these armours, furnished with a single row of *pteryges*, have shoulder guards, that would have been attached separately by means of hinges and straps. The muscled shape of this armour was very stylised on the front and back; we can assume a fastening system on the shoulders and on the sides by mean of small straps passing through a buckle.

Hottenroth, in reconstructing this kind of armour from ancient monuments that still had traces of colour (**157**), represented red decorations and fittings. These armours were probably decorated with bronze metallic fittings of semi-barbarous shape as a result of the contact with the work of Germanic craftsmen, in their turn influenced by Greco-Roman art, which they adapted to their own taste.

Some scholars contest the existence of leather muscled armour by pointing out the scarcity of related finds: but this scarcity is not a good reason to consider the armours represented on the monuments as fantasies of the artist.[418] The monuments were very accurate in the representation of different shapes, and especially in clearly rendering the distinction between the muscled leather armour – represented as folded and pleated in many reliefs[419] or statues – and the corresponding metallic specimens – represented as rigid and never folded.[420] A typical example of leather armour is visible on the frieze from Lutetia, preserved at the Musée Carnavalet of Paris,[421] where the folds of the belly part are clearly evident. Here the short metallic laminated shoulder pieces and the small round lappets (*kremasmata*) at the lower edge and on the shoulders, to which a single range of *pteryges* is attached, are also useful to date the cuirass.[422] The square opening at the neck of the muscled armours that appeared only in the Trajanic period and lasted until the late Antonine period also represents a chronological discrimination.

179 The 'dancing *centurio*', fresco from Stabiae, first half of the first century AD (*Naples, Museo Archeologico Nazionale, author's photo, by permission of the Soprintendenza per I Beni Archeologici delle Province di Napoli e Caserta*)

Apart from the circumstance that many metallic fittings still need to be classified in an appropriate way, we have also to consider the difficulty of the preservation of the organic material, except in exceptionally dry climatical conditions, as in Egypt, Palestine and Africa, or cold conditions, as in marshy places like the Danish bogs.

Other authors have been sceptical about the possibility that muscled armour could be moulded in leather, because of the poor protection that such a cuirass would seem to offer. On the contrary, hardened leather, as the *cuir-bouilli* protection of the Middle Ages have widely demonstrated, was very effective against cutting blows.[423] Moreover this kind of armour was much more comfortable to wear than the metallic type. It was, however, less protective against sharpened point, so the body needed to be protected by a wider shield, such as the oval shown on the Marcus Aurelius column or the hexagonal one shown on the Caius Septimius tombstone.

This armour was probably achieved by the padding technique, where a quantity of tanned leather was treated in warm water,[424] where it was given a specific shape. Then the leather was stretched on a stone to dry. Rawhide could be worked in the same way, and the temperature of the water raised until the leather was consolidated. Then it was put on the pressing mould, which set the hardened leather into the desired shape. The same method was presumably used to produce the shoulder guards of the leather corselet, and the leather part of helmets, the leather lining of shield bosses, and the lining of greaves.

Leather Corselets

As well as moulded armour, the Romans used leather corselets as true armour. Leather corselets and leather doublets are very clearly represented on gravestones, on Trajan's Column and on other figurative monuments as well. Noteworthy fragments of this kind of leather armour, perhaps belonging to an armour like that worn by the *miles* C. Valerius Crispus on his stele

180 Fragments of possible leather armour from Vindonissa, first half of the first century AD (*Vindonissa Museum, ex Gansser-Burckhardt, courtesy of Vindonissa Museum*)

181 Reconstruction of C. Valerius Crispus by Alma-Tadema, in his *A Silent Greeting* (1889) (*Tate Gallery, London*).

The wonderful rendering of the leather armour of Crispus from the most famous Victorian artist of scenes from ancient Greek and Roman life shows that the leather protection of the body is comfortable and effective. Leather armour was possible and it would be tough, yet light and flexible. The leather could be hardened by being left in the tanning process for two years. Brine, grease, oils and tallow could be used to make it supple and waterproof. There might also be a combination of different types of leather, for example leather edged with rawhide

preserved in Wiesbaden,[425] have been found in Vindonissa (**180**, **181**).[426]

The reasoning used by the late Russell Robinson to argue that the corselets represented on the tombstones were mail armour and not leather armour was principally based on the fact that some of the corselets resemble the typical mail armour in shape (why could they not be scale armour, then?) and that the smooth surface was in ancient times painted grey or grey-blue to represent the metal. Tombstones, as all the monuments, were certainly painted: but the surviving colour on the flat surfaces of similar armour[427] represented on the tombstones has rarely, at my knowledge, revealed the iron-grey colour or the yellow colour of the metal. Instead, green examples have survived, albeit on a cavalry monument, representing the colour of the so-called Cymmerian tunic or of the leather surcoat.[428] When the corselet is in mail this is clearly visible, for instance on Trajan's Column, very clearly distinguished from the other flat corselets that are doublets of leather. The same flat doublet, with slits on the side to allow ease of movement, could be worn, for example, by a Roman soldier on the base of the Mainz column – probably an *optio* or a centurion because his sword is worn on the left side of the body[429] – although we cannot exclude here the possibility that it was originally carved as a mail armour that has been effaced by erosion over time.

The observation of Robinson and successive authors that to be effective against cutting and thrusting the corselets shown on the monuments, if in leather, had to be made of hardened leather thus making all the necessary movement impossible does not consider two main factors. First, leather jerkins, corselets and armours made of rawhide were used as effective protection for warriors from the Bronze Age until the seventeenth century AD and beyond, without making movement impossible. The problem could be solved by using leather of different thicknesses in different parts of the armour; the most striking examples are the *spolas* of the ancient Greeks,[430] which was a leather armour fastened on the shoulders, probably a true leather corselet,[431] and the leather coats of the English cavalry in the Civil War,[432] resistant to any fencing, thrusting or cutting hit.[433]

Second, leather armour is in any case some protection, maybe less effective than a metallic one, but always more effective than a simple tunic. However, there are examples where the *miles* – probably a *levis armatura* – is represented fighting with sword, shield and a simple tunic, as on the Chiusi frieze (**82**) or on the Ephesus monument (**121**).

Robinson was certainly right when he said that someone observing the memorials of the Imperial conquests on the Roman monuments can tell exactly what was intended. In fact, when you look at Trajan's Column and the other monuments

182 *Equites*, Trajan's Column, Scene XXVII, (*cast, Museo della Civiltà Romana, Roma, author's photo, courtesy of the Museum*).
The leather doublet of the cavalry on Trajan's column is similar to that of the infantry. Its use alongside mail armour is clearly visible, even in the same scenes

183 Fragment of leather armour from Vindonissa, perhaps a part of a shoulder guard, first half of the first century AD (*Vindonissa Museum, ex Gansser-Burckhardt, courtesy of Vindonissa Museum*)

from 2 cm away[434] and not from a photo, they reveal, in the same scene, made by the same hand, that leather corselets were used alongside mail armour (**182**).

Some auxiliary troops on Trajan's Column are clearly depicted in ring-mail armour, and others are clearly not, in the same scene. The extensive modern literature on the subject says that the chiselling of mail surfaces on auxiliary figures was a separate process in the creation of the reliefs, dependent on the sculptor's attention to detail. This does not appreciate, though, that the same hands worked on the same scene. Why would auxiliaries be depicted differently in the same scene? So the work of an artist that represents cavalrymen charging the Dacians and shows one man with chiselled mail and the man standing behind him without chiselled mail cannot be considered unrealistic. It is much more likely that different armours were used, mail and leather, by the warriors copied in the same scene by the artist.

This leather corselet may also have simply been called *corium* in the sources. Leather corselets, as the Vindonissa finds show, were mainly of goat or sheep leather. The stronger corselets or the stronger parts of it were made, however, of calf or chamois leather, rigid and strong. The leather armour made of chamois leather anyway gave much more flexibility and was worn like the coats of the Swedish or Imperial officers in the Thirty Years War.[435] These examples of leather coats appear in figurative monuments as rigid and without folds, giving the impression of hardened leather. Tacitus says that the German and Celtic tribes understood the making of leather armour and helmets, a circumstance confirmed by archaeological finds at Vindonissa.

Leather armour was generally sleeveless, the shoulder were, however, protected by strong leather shoulder guards, probably of calf leather (**183**), similar in the shape to those of mail armour. They were sometimes hinged down on the shoulders, or simply laced down, reaching half-way to the elbow, protecting the breast (*brachialia*) at the same time. They sometimes had small cuts to allow a better movement of the upper arm. This leather corselet was therefore a true armour, as is visible on the Caius Crispus monument (**PLATE III**). Metallic armour was not worn over the rigid leather armour. Looking closely at the detail on the Roman monuments it is easy to distinguish rigid leather armour (hardened leather) from the half-rigid leather doublet or other flexible soft leather corselets. So, for example, an unknown soldier in the Landesmuseum Bonn[436] wears a half-rigid rough leather armour without shoulder guards, fitted to his body (**48**). This kind of armour, worn by many imperial soldiers alongside or in combination with metallic armour that afforded more protection, was fastened by means of leather laces and buckles.[437] The main fastening points were probably on the shoulders.[438]

This is not, however, to exclude the possibility that some leather corselets were worn over the mail armour of the same shape, to protect it from rain and rust.[439] In this case the soldier was in some way covered by two armours: the metallic one (*thorax*) and the leather one (*lorica*).[440] We can therefore sum up that the leather corselet was sometimes worn over or in combination with a metallic armour, and was sometimes worn as the only body protection.

The shape of the leather corselet evolved during the first two centuries of our era: in the first century AD it is often long, the torso being cut straight, without scalloping, sometimes fitted with *pteryges*; it also had wide shoulder guards. In the second century, as with most of the soft leather protection, it became shorter, losing the shoulder guards and having the shape of a loose shirt; this is how it appears on the Imperial monuments (**184**). It is usually scalloped on the shoulders and on the lower edges but without *pteryges*. Sometimes it is reinforced by embossing (**184b**, **184c**). These kinds of jerkins were probably put on like chain mail, with which they are often confused, but not fastened at the back in the way proposed by Lindenschmit,[441] otherwise the fastening system would be visible on the monuments.

Linen and Felt Corselets

The linen corselet, called *thorax lineus*, *lorica lintea* or λινοθώραξ (*linothorax*), was still occasionally worn by the Romans of the early Imperial age, although it was considered a much less effective defence than a metal cuirass. Suetonius describes the Emperor Galba wearing such a corselet just some minutes before he was assassinated by his own soldiers.[442] Linen breastplates were judged by Pausanias[443] to be not so effective in combat, for:

> They let the iron pass through, if the blow be a violent one. They aid hunters, however, for the teeth of lions or leopards break off in them. You may see linen breastplates dedicated in other sanctuaries, notably in that at Gryneum, where there is a most beautiful grove of Apollo, with cultivated trees, and all those which, although they bear no fruit, are pleasing to smell or look upon.

However we can consider the possibility that armour made of organic materials such as leather and linen was used much more in the Hellenised provinces of the east, where they were already widespread before the Roman conquest, and where the hot weather favoured the employment of such armour instead of a metallic one. This is widely attested by the figurative monuments from Egypt, Syria, Greece and Asia. Aelian wrote of a linen cuirass dedicated to Athena in her temple at Rhodes;[444] he, or maybe a glossator, says that it could not be damaged by stones or iron weapons! Whether it was as resistant as that or not, its prominent dedication to the goddess argues that it was of some use; that is was dedicated to Athena rather than Artemis suggests that it was of use more in war than in hunting, at least traditionally.

The figurative monuments are also rich in representations of a second type of organic armour, made of strips of padded material, which were used both as protective equipment on their own or in combination with metallic elements, so forming a composite armour. This armour is clearly represented on a monument dated to the first years of Augustus' Empire, from Modena,[445] where the corselet – probably a *thoracomachus* – is associated with a round shield of an officer and with a structure for the wearing of the *phalerae*. The *humeralia* are shaped as metallic shoulder guards, and the breast fittings appear to be metallic, applied to an armour made of vertical and horizontal strips. The padding of the represented material is underlined

184a   **184b**

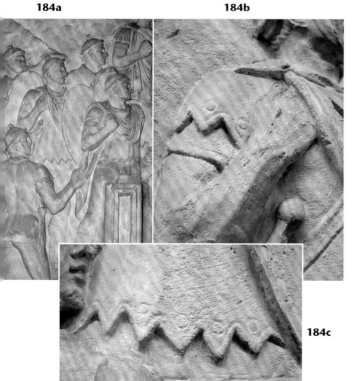

184c

184 *Auxilia* in *sagia* and leather corselet, reinforced by bosses at the scalloped borders, Trajan's Column, scene LI (cast, Roma, Museo della Civiltà Romana, author's photo, courtesy of the museum).

Wilson, studying ancient Roman costume, confirmed that of the 100 *milites* represented on Trajan's Column, two thirds are covered by a *sagum*, one third have the *paenula* – except, of course, the emperor, the high officers and the ten centurions[i]

i   Levi-Pisetzky, 1964, I, p. 33.

by the strong thickness of the figure, which shows a kind of armour that could also be worn without a second *lorica*. It is likely that felt is represented here, and that this padded armour was a kind of *coactile*.

This kind of armour, similar in the structure to the Hellenistic waist-long corselet, was probably used by officers, for its appearance is limited to private monuments of the Late Consular age or the first Imperial age, where it is depicted together with distinctive signs like the *phalerae*. A second funerary frieze, preserved in the church of San Domenico in Sora,[446] represents in fact a similar armour, this time completely padded and not furnished with metallic elements. The front of the cuirass is composed of eight rows of padded material, divided from the second half by a belt. The lower part is composed of rows of the same material, protecting the limbs like true *pteryges*. The armour is engraved on the stone beside a possible Coolus helmet, a round shield and a pair of greaves, maybe indicative of the rank of centurion (**128**). This monument could be also dated to the early Augustan period.

The Arc d'Orange shows a similar padded armour (**315a**); it is represented among a trophy of shields, so it was probably worn by a Celtic warrior equipped with Roman armour, or by some officer of the *Legiones* of Antonius and Cleopatra. The surface of this padded corselet is divided in rhomboidal stripes, and short *pteryges* hang from the lower part. An interesting detail is shown on the left side of the armour: it is open all down its length and the internal part of its back is perfectly visible. This means two important things: that this doublet was copied from a real specimen, and that it was fastened, probably by linen laces or leather thongs, on the left side. Its rhomboidal surface has four holes for each of the rhomboid spaces; when the Arc d'Orange was at the height of its glory, and completely painted, as all Roman monuments were, it is probable that metallic inserts were put there, to represent the nails that reinforced the surface of such padded armours.

The next example of padded armour comes from a more famous monument, the gravestone of the *centurio* T. Calidius Severus of the *Legio XV Apollinaris*. This has been always interpreted as a *squama*, a scale armour.[447] But if it is a scale armour, why are the scales suddenly cut off at the lower edge of the corselet? On the monuments where the scales are effectively represented, the last line of scales overlap the visible part of the *subarmale* or undertunic (**69, 315d**).[448] Instead, the armour of Calidius is completely cut at the borders and its surface is divided into the same rhomboidal spaces as the example represented on the Arc d'Orange. The rough carving shows the intention was to represent padded and thick material,[449] a probable *coactile*. The monument of Calidius can thus be inserted in the tradition of the padded doublets.

A unique specimen of organic armour, although reinforced with nails, is represented on a monument of the Antonine period, on the Constantine Arch (**116**).[450] A Roman legionary of the Emperor Marcus Aurelius, perhaps a man of the *Legio VIII*

Augusta, is protected by what seems to be a leather (*corium*), felt (*coactile*) or heavy padded wool (*cento*) jerkin divided in squared spaces, reinforced by small bosses[451] inserted in the centre of each squared space. This was also the interpretation of Colonel Le Clerc, who reconstructed such an armour for the Musée de l'Artillerie. Coussin, on the other hand, interpreted it as an armour of metallic squared scales.[452] The sculpture is of such high quality that there is no doubt about the interpretation: the doublet has scalloped borders and its shape is anatomical, contrasting with the Newstead type of armour worn by the man next to this. Moreover, the plates of the armour are reinforced by circular bosses, which would be pointless if the armour was completely in metal. It seems that here, as in the previously mentioned specimens, we are looking at a kind of armour made of organic material and made in the way described by Pliny the Elder,[453] speaking about the armours done with organic materials: 'They realise also a garment of wool pressed between its layers and, if vinegar is added, it even resists iron.'

There were probably special factories designated to the production of such armours. We have mention of a corporation of *lanarii coactores* operating in the city of Brixia (modern-day Brescia)[454] who were familiar with the process of straining and rubbing of wool. From Pompeii we also have mention of a certain M. Vecilius Verecundus who had a factory *coactiliaria*, and three other *officinae coactiliariae* are recorded for the period linked to the destruction of the city.[455] They produced felt by compacting animal hides: the raw material was worked in warm water vessels until a compact dough emerged, perhaps with the help of a curdling fluid. The felt so obtained was like oilskin and strong, and used to make hats, slippers, gloves and half-rigid corselets for the soldiers.[456]

It seems that this kind of armour has been used continuously in the succeeding period. It is clearly visible on the god Mars represented on the panel consecrated by a detachment (*Vexillatio*) of the *XX Legio Valeria Victrix* in Bremenium,[457] on Hadrian's Wall. Mars is beardless and wears a composite cuirass with shoulder plates and vertical strips made of padded material. On his head is a plumed helmet and his legs are protected by greaves. He holds a spear in his right hand and the rim of his shield in his left. It has been suggested that the relief belonged to the original Antonine dedication slab at the East Gate of the fortress. Although very crude, the detail of the armour is clearly the same of those represented on the above-mentioned monument from Sora. Considering the armament of Mars as probably copied at least from that of man having command duties, we have proof of the wearing of such armour by an officer and of the definitive use of organic armour in the Roman Imperial army.

A last important mention about organic armour comes from Suetonius. He said[458] that in winter the Emperor Augustus 'protected himself with four tunics [*tunicae*] and a heavy toga, as well as an undershirt [*subucula*], a woollen protection [*thorax laneus*], short trousers [*feminalia*] and wraps for his

185 Detail of *auxilia*, Trajan's Column, scene XXVIII (*cast, Roma, Museo della Civiltà Romana, author's photo, courtesy of the museum*)

186 Detail of leather armour worn by an auxiliary, over a probable *lorica lintea* or *thorax laneus*, (*cast, Roma, Museo della Civiltà Romana, author's photo, courtesy of the museum*)

Their breastplates they make in the following fashion. Each man keeps many mares, since the land is not divided into private allotments, nor does it bear any thing except wild trees, as the people are nomads. These mares they not only use for war, but also sacrifice them to the local gods and eat them for food. They collect their hoofs, clean, split, and make from them as if they were python scales. Whoever has never seen a python must at least have seen a pinecone still green. He will not be mistaken if he likens the product from the hoof to the segments that are seen on the pinecone. These pieces they bore and stitch together with the sinews of horses and oxen, and then use them as breastplates that are as handsome and strong as those of the Greeks. For they can withstand blows of missiles and those struck in close combat.

The author adds that the *loricae* made of these horny scales are much stronger and more impenetrable than linen

shins [*tibialia*] . . .' These garments were also used as further protection by the *milites*, as is visible on Trajan's Column where, under the leather corselet, many soldiers seem to be wearing a second fringed jerkin, maybe the *thorax laneus* mentioned from Suetonius (**185**, **186**).

Scale Armour

Scale armour made of organic material was also known in the Greek and Etruscan era, and their legacy passed to the Romans. But a wider spread of scale armour made of leather and other organic material was accelerated by contact with the Barbarians. Tacitus, in discussing the armament of the noble Sarmatians in AD 35, mentions scale armour made of metallic plates or hardened leather: '. . . *tegimen, ferreis lamminis aut praeduro corio consertum, ut adversus ictus impenetrabile ita impetu hostium provolutis inhabile ad resurgendum . . .*' (an armour, made of metallic plates or hardened leather, that is not possible to pierce with any blows, but allows the unseated cavalryman the possibility of getting up again). Tacitus' text does not specify, however, whether the leather armour was made by hardened scales – which could be interpreted from the following passage from Pausanias – or just a corselet of banded hardened leather.[459]

Horn and hoofs were employed as well. In AD 175, Pausanias,[460] talking about the Sarmatian breastplates, after mentioning a *thorax* preserved in the Temple of Aesculapius at Athens, mentions a variant of scale armour made of horn:

187 Roman scale armour fragments, in bone or ivory, Pompei, about AD 79 (*author's photo, courtesy of the Soprintendenza Speciale per i Beni Archeologici di Caserta e Pompei*).

This unique piece of armour, hidden in the National Archaeological Museum of Napoli, has been recently shown in an exhibition of the arms and armour found in Pompei. It was originally gilded

188 *Miles* in *lorica plumata*, relief, first century AD (*Turin, Museo di Antichità; Studio Tomatofarm*)

cuirasses. Ammianus Marcellinus, writing in AD 358 about the Sarmatians raiding Pannonia and Moesia, wrote that '. . . These people have . . . cuirasses made from smooth, polished pieces of horn, fastened like scales to linen shirts, extended like feathers on the bird's body . . .'.[461]

Although there has as yet been very little published on leather or horn scales amongst excavated artefacts, these kinds of armour were widely used by the Romans. Scales of bone are preserved at Naples Museum, from the excavations at Pompeii (**187**).[462] These were originally gilded,[463] and linked by means of metal wires passing through pair of holes cut on the upper edge of each scale; the fastening system was not visible when the scales were completely attached, for the lower rim of each row covered the upper edge of the one below.[464]

The Romans called the Sarmatian armour described above *plumatae*; also visible on the *loricae* depicted on many monuments, these scales with a midrib imitate the feathers of a bird (**82**, **188**). The scales on the above-mentioned armour of Domitian on the Capitoline Hill are represented in this way. The armour has no shoulder guards, but is highly decorated with a rich *cymation* of lappets disposed in two rows and very heavily embossed with heads. Two ranges of fringed *pteryges* protect the groin (**92**). Whether this is an official copy of the famous armour of scales made from boars' tusks worn by the Emperor Domitian in the Dacian Wars, or just a copy of a bronze or iron scale armour is hard to say.[465] This kind of armour, though, made its appearance in Roman military equipment from the time when the Romans met Sarmatians and Dacians in battle. The use of this armour in the Marcomannic War is clearly attested by many monuments, among which is a still-unpublished frieze

preserved in the museum of the Cathedral of Chiusi (**82**). Here a legionary engaged in battle with Quadi or Jazygian infantry and heavy cavalry[466] wears a distinctive loose-fitting *lorica plumata*, covered in what seems to be horn or leather scales. Each scale has a midrib. The scales follow the movement of the body, and the whole armour is tightly closed at the waist by a belt from which short aprons (today without details, lost through the ages) are hanging down. The scale coat is represented as very soft and allowing movement of the body; it has got short sleeves coming down to the elbow and letting the arms move freely. The clear detail precludes, in my opinion, any possibility of artistic convention, also bearing in mind that the man's sword is very close in shape to the archaeological specimen of Svilengrad, a *gladius* dated to the late Antonine period (**PLATE V**).[467]

Banded Armour

The existence of a leather version of segmented armour among the *milites* is a very highly debated topic in the study of the Roman army equipment. However, from the earlier studies on this subject, eminent personalities such as Lindenschmit[468] supported the thesis of the existence of the two variants of the banded armour, in metal and leather. The analysis was at first focused on Trajan's Column, but then many other figurative monuments and archaeological elements were taken into account to support or disprove the thesis.

The old definition of Varro, that the *lorica* was made of strips (*lori*) of leather,[469] referred to the first *loricae* of these types, mainly of Etruscan origin, which were of course also the prototypes of the metallic versions. But there are strong elements supporting the thesis that banded *loricae* made of leather were still produced and used in the early Imperial age. The images coming from the figurative monuments are very clear in the illustration of both types, and if the tendency of leather to decay has, for the time being, revealed very few fragments of this armour, we cannot discount the possibility that many clasps and hinges and buckles found in the military camps were originally used for the leather version of the banded armour.

We should remember the considerations that we have already discussed for the previous types of described leather armour and protection. Leather armour is the easiest to produce, and it is sometimes the best solution especially if it is necessary to equip thousands of men. Leather is in any case a good defence and some hardened leathers are impenetrable to blows, as the Sarmatian experience taught to the Romans.

Close observations of Trajan's Column indicate that it was the intention of the artist to show that the banded armour was made of different materials. For example, a *miles* working in the fields (scene LXXXIII (**99c**)) is bending over and his *lorica* is clearly compressed by his body, showing the folds of the leather. In other scenes the *milites* seen from the back have the bands of the armour following the movements of the body, fitted to the back muscles of the man (**99a**). This is very different when a metal armour is seen from the same perspective (**97**). In scene XIII a soldier wears a *lorica* that seems to be too flexible to be made of metal (**99b**).

It seems that this kind of *lorica* was composed in a very similar way to the metallic types, with a torso more fitted to the body. It possibly had a breastplate and backplate, closed at the back by metallic clasps and at the front by buckles, composed of several protective bands and with shoulder plates made of the same organic material. The leather segmented armour usually has four shoulder guards for each shoulder, created by bands made from one solid piece, not clasped on the upper shoulder as in the metallic versions, but fastened by buttons. Lindenschmit supposed that the shoulder guards would be fastened to the main armour body by means of buckles, and that the single shoulder bands would be linked together by small laces, taking into account their length and the different and various movements of the body and of the arms. The girth hoops are around five to six in number, closed by clasps on the back, but very often buttoned in front. The back clasps were fastened along a vertical opening.

Interestingly, the leather *loricae* illustrated on the Column are worn mainly by soldiers engaged in camp or entrenchment works, or working in the fields. This does not exclude the possibility that such *loricae* was used as lighter protection by those soldiers who had both to protect themselves and to engage in work where heavy armour would have been more of a hindrance. We should also remember the distinction between the *milites levis armaturae* (*psilon-peltastikon*) and the *milites gravis armaturae* (*oplitikon*), mentioned by Arrian[470] in his *Tactica*:

> . . . The *gravis armaturae* are equipped with armours [*thoraka*], round [*clipei/aspidai*] or long shields [*scuta/thureoi*], and swords [*gladii/machairai*] and spears [*hastae/dorata*], like the Greeks, and long spears [*sarissae*] like the Macedonians. But those of *levis armaturae* are exactly at the opposite; and, dismissing any armour, shield and greaves, they use the throwing weapons, like arrows, javelins, stones that could be thrown from slings or hands; instead those who used the small shields [*peltae*] are [armed] lighter than the *gravis armaturae* . . . but heavier than the *levis armaturae* . . .

189 Fastening buckles, first–second century AD (*collection of Museum Het Valkhof, Nijmegen; courtesy of the conservator*)

190 Legionary in leather(?) *lorica segmentata*, showing the system of fastening the central breastplate, Trajan's Column, scene VII (*cast, Roma, Museum of Civiltà Romana; author's photo, courtesy of the museum*)

So in the Roman army the *peltastai* could well be equipped with a lighter *lorica*. It is interesting to note that on Trajan's Column the fastening system of the leather-banded armour is shown through representations of buckles and hinges corresponding to actual archaeological specimens. So some buckles, identical to the *cingulum* fastening buckles, are represented as the main fastening element of the breastplate of a *lorica* in scene IX (**189**, **190**).

Lighter versions of this *lorica* existed and are archaeologically documented. A later kind of banded *lorica* appears on the famous Portonaccio sarcophagus, which belonged to a general of Marcus Aurelius and is today preserved in the Museo Nazionale Romano. It is worn by infantrymen and cavalrymen, and it is very clearly visible on an officer (maybe a *centurio*) of some *cohortes* of *Civium Volontariorum* or *Diogmitai* recruited in the eastern provinces (**83**). His armour is composed of two separate pieces, comprising segments that are clearly made of leather, fixed to a cloth backing (**PLATE V, 83**). The upper part is made up of shoulder pieces, each composed of three bands attached by metallic buttons on the undergarment, and lined with leather as well. The protection of the waist is entrusted to a belt made of three segments of thick but unhardened leather, laced at the front of the body (**83**). The upper torso is protected by a breastplate buttoned at the centre. A fragment of the lower part of a similar armour has been recovered in Egypt (**191**), from the Roman level of the fortress of Qasr Ibrim, and

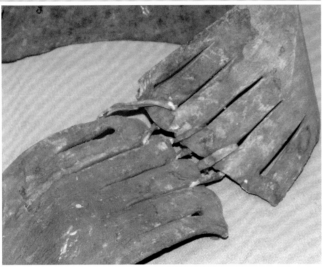

193 (Above) City guardsman from a linen shroud of the Hadrianic period, Egypt, second century AD (*Pushkin Museum, Moscow; author's collection*)

191 (Above) Fragment of the lower part of a leather banded armour, Roman, second century AD, from Qasr Ibrim (or Kasir-Ibrahim), Egypt (*London, British Museum, inv. QI, 80 1.21/75, courtesy of the museum*).

This exceptional specimen is, for the moment, the only known fragment of Roman banded armour in leather. Its shape is similar to those of such a banded protection visible on many funerary monuments of the Greco-Roman east and on the sarcophagus of the general of Marcus Aurelius known as the Sarcophagus of Portonaccio

192 (Below) Small votive hexagonal shield with engraved image of a warrior in leather *lorica segmentata*, second half of second century AD (*Museo Nazionale della Civitella, Chieti, by kind permission of the Soprintendenza Archeologica per l'Abruzzo*).

A leather *lorica segmentata* is visible on the warrior reproduced on the votive shield, perhaps a *bestiarius* or a *gladiator*

preserved in the British Museum.[471] The similarity with the Portonaccio armour is striking and demonstrates the accuracy of the Roman artists in the representation of their world.

Is is possible that this kind of armour was used mainly in the eastern provinces, where leather was easier to wear and more practical as body defence. Further confirmation of this is in a small and hidden detail of the famous Romano-Egyptian linen shroud of the Hadrianic age preserved in the Pushkin Museum in Moscow.[472] A city guardsman, painted in front of a door, wears the same armour at the Portonaccio *miles* (**193**). Last but not least, other monuments of Diogmitai from Asia Minor attest similar banded protection of leather around the waist and on the shoulders. The most significant monument is that of M. Aurelius Diodorus, from Hierapolis (modern-day Pamukkale), where the leather *lorica*, clearly visible, is worn by all the members of the family, among whom are a horseman (Julian – Ioulianos) and two infantrymen, armed with spears and a single-edged *machaira* and joined by hunting dogs. The leather armour is worn over a *subarmale* of thick *pteryges* (**203**). A similar *lorica* is worn by a gladiator or fighter represented on a small bronze plaque from the Bruttium, in south Italy (**192**).

Garments Worn Under and Over the Metallic Cuirass

Under or over the metallic armour and in any case over the tunic the soldier sometimes wore a doublet or jerkin made of leather or other organic material. When worn under the armour, it was probably the same kind of garment as that called *subarmale* in many sources, and so represented on Trajan's Column in many places.

Normally, it was always worn under the muscled armour; it was worn under and sometimes over the mail shirt, and under the scale and the laminated armour. Leather doublets, worn under the *lorica segmentata*, are visible on some scenes on Trajan's Column (**177**). In one scene *milites legionis* clad in leather jerkins are wearing on their shoulders *sarcinae* with the rectangular shield, and it is possible that their laminated armour is packed in the closed sack over their shoulders (**111**). So either this is a representation of legionaries protected only by a leather jerkin, or it is a clear representation of the kind of *subarmale* worn under the laminated armour.

The most usual type, with hangings strips (*pteryges*) of linen, leather, silk, felt or other organic material is visible, when the armour is worn, only at the shoulder and from the waist down, with various shape and decoration in the *pteryges*, according to the iconographical sources. Sometimes the strips are simple and plain, with a slightly rounded shape, as in the Adamclisi reliefs (**47, 49, 61, 62, 68, 69, 76, 154a, 154b, 154c**), sometimes they are fringed at the extremities (**149, 163**), and richly decorated according to the rank of the owner (**4**). It is also possible that the number of strips denoted rank. On the Domitianic armour from the Capitoline Hill (**92**) there are five overlapping rows of *pteryges*, including those directly attached to the armour border: two rows of rounded *pteryges* (*cymation* or *kremasmata*), one row of rectangular *pteryges* and two rows of fringed *pteryges*. It is probable in fact that, in many plate armours, the first row of the hanging elements was attached

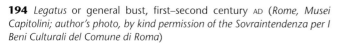

194 *Legatus* or general bust, first–second century AD (*Rome, Musei Capitolini; author's photo, by kind permission of the Sovraintendenza per I Beni Culturali del Comune di Roma*)

195 Statue of a *tribunus*, second half of second century AD (*Alba Julia Museum; photo courtesy of the museum*).

The *paludamentum* of the officers was often of doubled silk, like the marvellous example visible on a painting from the House of Fabius Rufus in Pompeii. Fringed cloaks were also used by the emperor, as shown on the equestrian statue of Augustus recovered from the Euboia Sea in 1979, which also shows a pretty decoration on its surface[i]

i   *Archeologia Viva*, 1990, no. 9, p. 8.

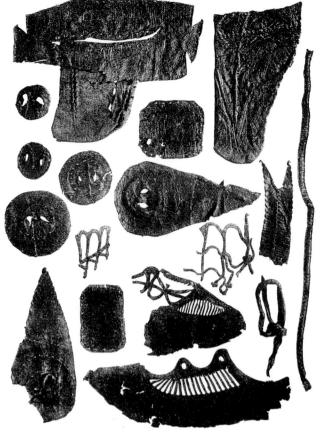

196 Fragments of possible leather doublet from Vindonissa, first half of the first century AD (*Vindonissa Museum, ex Gansser-Burckhardt, courtesy of Vindonissa Museum*)

197 Fragments of leather jerkin worn under the cuirass, shoes and tunics from Newstead, second century AD (*ex Curle*)

directly to the armour itself by stitching, and the overlapping of the armour and of the *subarmale* made different rows visible in the pictorial sources. Sometimes the rows of *pteryges* come directly from the scalloped edges of the *subarmale* (**194**), as in the statue of the *tribunus* from Apulum (**195**), where the doublet is worn under a leather muscled armour. In the same locality a statue has been found that possibly belonged to Pertinax. It shows rectangular fringed *pteryges* attached to a *subarmale* with scalloped edges worn under a muscled armour, clearly made of leather (**163**). The hanging elements were often thick and contiguous, offering good protection against blows. Certain *subarmales* were probably in the shape of the padded garment visible in numerous sculptures (**128**), so the strips would have been held together by sewing and were not hanging, but formed a unique compact garment.

Plain simple doublets, with notched and scalloped borders, were used more often with the armour of interlinked rings and the laminated *lorica*. Numerous fragments of this doublet have been found in Vindonissa (**196**), showing it as usually composed of soft leather, most probably goat, sheep or chamois (*camox*).⁴⁷³ Because of its composition, the doublet was more or less fitted to the body. Logically the doublet itself could not offer the same protection as an armour, but it was used as protection against bad weather, as a further protection over the linen or woollen tunic. In its composition, however, the doublet was essentially a leather version of the military tunic (**198**). We can

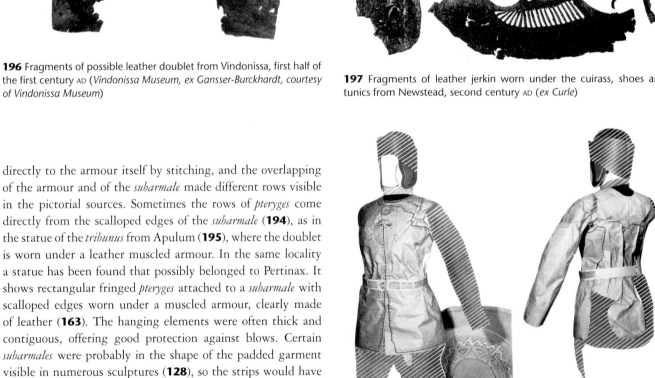

198 Reconstrution of the leather garment from Vindonissa fragments, first half of the first century AD (*Vindonissa Museum, ex Gansser-Burckhardt, courtesy of Vindonissa Museum*).

A clear example of a long-sleeved leather tunic worn under the armour is visible on a gravestone from Eining, on the Danube.ⁱ The Rhine tombstones also sometimes show the presence of sleeves, fragments of which have been found in Vindonissa and are from a leather tunic. Maybe this was a winter dress, worn in the northern regions of the empire. The type reconstructed by Gansser-Burckhardt in Vindonissa from many fragments might correspond to camp dress, used under or over mail armour and under scale, laminated and muscled armour

i   A leather tunic with sleeves is visible also on the Flavius Bassus monument, see Robinson, 1975, pl. 302.

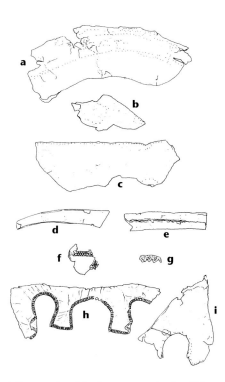

199 (Above) Fragments of leather garments, Bar Hill, second–third century AD (*drawing by Andrea Salimbeti ex Robertson, Scott, Keppie*)
a) Fragment of shield covering (33 x 100 mm). **b)** Fragment of shield covering (150 x 70 mm). **c)** Fragment of shield covering with stitch holes. **d)** Perhaps the lining of a pocket, or from a bag or purse. **e)** Possibly a sheathing for a blade. **f)** Fragment of belt with seam down the back. **g)** Fragment of belt, with elaborate cut-outs. **h), i)** Fragments of the tunic of an auxiliary soldier

easily recognise it in the iconographic sources from the draping and related folds, and from the clear circumstance that in some monuments its presence is signalled by a smooth surface with folds, very different from the mail worn in the same figurative sources. When the artist wanted to represent interlinked rings, he chiselled it on the surface of the sculpture, but in many scenes, made by the same hand, clear examples of mail armour and smooth surfaces are pictured side by side (**182**).

Curle correctly suggested that the Roman soldier was 'clad in leather' and published numerous fragments of leather remains from garments found in Newstead (**197**). He has often been criticised because he was an archaeologist and not a military expert. Although Curle was not an armour specialist, his viewpoint was not challenged until Robinson. Robinson was an armour specialist and he said that leather armour was impractical. However, he said the opposite in his book on oriental armour, and also discussed the employment of Roman leather armour from Pecenegs in the tenth and eleventh centuries AD, as borrowed from Byzantium.[474] Apparently he forgot all about this when he wrote his book on Roman armour!

Two bigger fragments from Vindonissa have been identified by Gansser-Burckhardt as the lateral side and rear of such a garment. The size of these two fragments would fit a slim

200 (Below) Armours and *subarmales* from the base of Trajan's Column, beginning of second century AD (*drawings by Graham Sumner*)

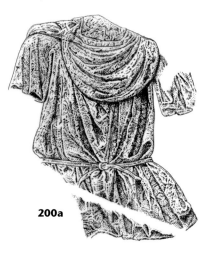

200a

200b

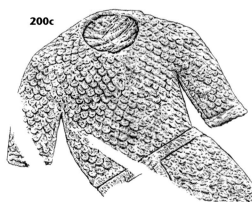

200c

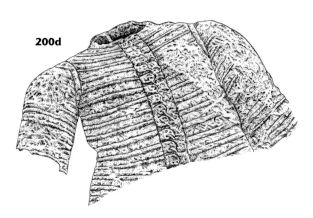

200d

201 (Left) Portrait of a *miles*, possibly in *subarmale*, Hadrianic or Antonine period, el-Fayoum, Egypt (*Oriental Institute of Chicago*).

This exceptional encaustic portrait from Egypt shows a Roman officer of Greek origin dressed in a pink garment, which seems be embossed on the shoulders. It could be a representation of part of the *subarmale* worn under the armour

202 (Above) Fragments of leather pieces from bags and garments, first half of the first century AD (*Vindonissa Museum, ex Gansser-Burckhardt; photo Vindonissa Museum*)

203 Detail of the funerary monument of Markos Aurelios Diodoros ex Hierapolis of Phrygia, from his sarcophagus, preserved in the courtyard of the museum of Pamukkale (*drawing by Andrea Salimbeti*).

Note the leather banded *lorica* and the thick *subarmale* worn under it. In the city of Asia Minor the police duty was performed by local militiamen (Διωγμιται) partially at foot and partially on horseback (ιππεις)[i]. The shown equipment is well exemplificative of the *Diogmitai* weaponry

---

i   Pio Franchi de Cavalieri, 1928, p.204;

person of medium height. The sleeves were partially cut on the shoulders in the shape of an indented edge. Special hides were used for the manufacture of these doublets: the front part was composed of two halves (two half-hides) and a breast part with a wide opening for the passage of the neck. The back was made of a single piece of hide. The dividing point of the foreleg took up the position of the armhole and it was notched. The flank section, i.e. the weak point of the leather used to made the garment, was positioned in the less exposed parts.

Gansser-Burckhardt also identified a collar fragment, composed of two reinforced double parts, made of two similar leather sections, whose sides were sewn together (**196**). The whole collar was made of a frontal piece and a neckpiece, both

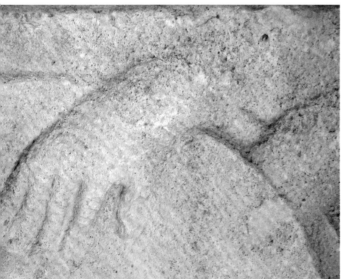

204 Decorative fragment of a probable funerary monument, with representations of various weapons, late first century BC–early first century AD (*Split, Archaeological Museum; T. Seser's and author's photos, courtesy of the museum*)

of them doubled. A fragment of a second possible collar made of two halves sewn in the middle was always found in Vindonissa (**196**), with a military badge superimposed. Fragments of similar leather doublets have been found in Bar Hill (**199**).

The scalloped edges visible on many doublets on the figurative monuments are possibly archaeologically attested by some leather fringes and notched fragments found in Vindonissa (**202**). Sometimes the surfaces of these doublets were studded by bosses (**184**).

Garments could be worn over the mail to protect the metal against rain and bad weather or also for the psychological impact of suddenly revealing the shining of the armour to the enemies when the covering was removed. This is clearly visible on numerous Rhine tombstones. So it is not out of the question that C. Valerius Crispus is wearing a metallic mail under his leather corselet.[475] On some leather fragments from Vindonissa there are grating marks, sometimes triangular, left from metallic armour. These recall the shape of the leather structure used for the *phalerae*.

Josephus describes the garment worn under the cuirass as a sort of simple tunic worn by Roman soldiers.[476] This is also attested by the pedestal of Trajan's Column, where, together with other pieces of armour, simple tunics of heavy material are represented (**200**). A further representation of a possible *subarmale* is in a portrait of the Antonine period from Fayoum, in Egypt (**201**). This seems to be a pink leather garment reinforced by bosses.

Leg Guards and Arm Guards

Limb protection is widely attested in the archaeology as well as in artworks of this period. The protection for the arms (*manica*) was composed essentially of laminated plates, specimens of which have been recovered from Newstead, Carnuntum and, recently, a complete one from Carlisle.[477] Examples of *manicae* are already visible on the Scafa relief,[478] of the first Imperial age, but it is not clear whether they refer to a gladiatorial context or to booty taken from the army of Sacrovir in the campaign of AD 21, to which the monument could referred. The *manicae* of Scafa have no gauntlet; in other monuments, such as a frieze from the Church of Saint Domenico in Sora (**156**), protective gauntlets are visible, with *manicae* completely covered by *squamae* or interlaced rings, or even plain,[479] like those represented on a relief of the Hadrianic era from Cuma and preserved in Berlin Museum. Protective gauntlets can also be seen, together with a complete *manica*, on a funerary relief from Croatia (**204**).

It is probable that laminated arm protection derived from that worn by gladiators. The *milites* adopted such equipment from the late first century AD to protect the sword arm – the only part of the body exposed in fighting when the shield was held in front of the body – probably as a result of the unlucky Dacian campaigns of the Emperor Domitian. The protection

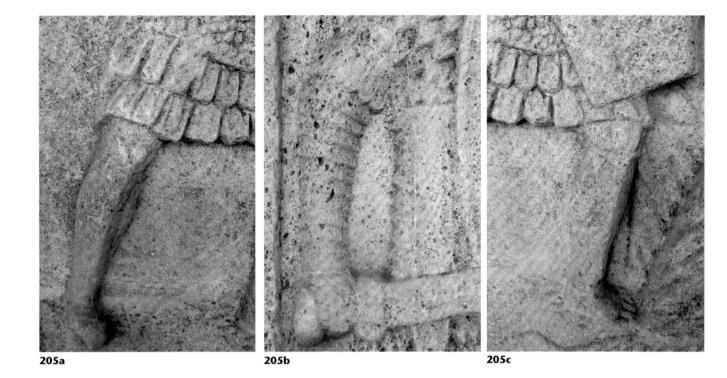

205a　　　　　　**205b**　　　　　　**205c**

205d

205 Details of leg and arm protections of extra-heavy armoured legionaries, Adamclisi reliefs, *metopae* XVII and XX, first half of second century AD (*Museum of Adamclisi, author's photos, courtesy of the museum*)

was extended to the *milites gregarii* because of the need to protect the arm from the terrible blows of the Geto-Dacian weapons. This is well represented on the Adamclisi reliefs, where laminated tubular defences for the right arm are worn by the legionaries especially equipped to deal with the long-handled Geto-Dacian *falx* or *romphaia*, which was furnished with a blade like a hedging hook (**47, 49, 64, 76, 154a, 154b, 155a, 155b, 205a, 205b, 205d**).

The specimen from Newstead is made of bronze, mounted on internal goatskin straps.[480] At the end of each plate are single punched holes for the fastening of the internal lining. The arm protection from Carnuntum, better preserved, has allowed further understanding of the construction of the arm protection: it was fixed internally over a leather backing; each small plate was secured to the leather backing by five small rivets that were positioned horizontally; the single plates were positioned over vertical leather strips which, corresponding to the rivet points, meant that there was a doubled leather backing. Probably at the height of the elbow, to allow ease of movement, was the bigger plate, leaving a space through which the leather backing could be seen. The whole structure of the arm guard was fastened under the armpit. Scholars have proposed two different interpretations: either it was a true armoured sleeve in leather, completely closed, with the plates riveted, or it was an armoured sleeve, fastened on the internal part of the arm by means of intelaced thongs. It is possible that both systems were used.

* * *

Leg protection was important too in Roman defensive equipment. The greaves (*ocreae*) of the officers still followed the old Greek model: those of the superior officers were often highly decorated with lightning bolts, as, for instance, those visible on a statue of Mars from Earith from the second half of the second century AD, preserved in the British Museum,[481] or with Gorgons' heads on the knee (**85**). The fastening method shown by the artist of the Earith statue is very interesting because of the three laces spanning the wide space between the edges of the greave. The *ocrae* represented on a funerary relief in Amiternum perhaps belonged to a centurion; this shows the interesting system of binding the *ocrae* by two crossed laces.[482] The most evident example of greaves worn in action by a centurion are on the relief of the Arc d'Orange (**6c**, **315c**), where they have a clear classical form. On the fragments of a monument, preserved in the Musée Calvet in Avignon, are another set of greaves, probably from a centurion of Tiberius' army (**10**). Other triumphal monuments show different examples of greaves: embossed on the knee with a Medusa head and decorated by vegetal grooves on the main body, like in the earlier Imperial monument from Perigueux;[483] some military greaves, represented on a relief from Turin, show the insertion of a small protective disk over the kneecap,[484] which is confirmed by a pair of actual specimens found in Pompeii and often considered to be gladiatorial greaves.

An embossed officer's greave is visible on a sculpture of the Great Trajanic Trophaeum of Adamclisi, showing on the knee a decoration with Medusa's head inside vegetal designs,[485] surmounted by a leaf crown on the rim (**85**). Usually the shape of these greaves is similar to the old Etruscan and Greek 'spring-on' greaves that were fitted on to the leg and not tied on with

206 Fragment of a possible greave of leather or of a lining of greave, first–third century AD (*photo Vindonissa Museum; courtesy of the museum*).

The accuracy of the reconstruction by Gansser-Burckhardt of this exceptional specimen has often been contested, but we do not see why the original piece restored by him could not be effectively a greave, or a lining of a greave

i   Unz and Deschler-Erb, 1997, p. 24 and pl. 21, nos 404, 406, 409, 410.

207 Fragment of a possible leather lining for greave, first-third century AD (*Vindonissa Museum, ex Gansser-Burckhardt, courtesy of Vindonissa Museum*)

laces. But, as shown by the Amiternum relief and the above-mentioned statue, many specimens were tied across the back at the ankle, calf and knee.

The centurions, on their *stelae*, are always represented with greaves: sometimes plain, as in the Favonius monument (**PLATE IV**, **72**), sometimes decorated only on the knee, as on the Calidius Severus gravestone,[486] echoing the old Etruscan greave pattern, sometimes highly embossed, as in the Q. Sertorius Festus *stela*.[487]

On the Arc d'Orange the greaves are worn only by a single *miles*. Arrian in his *Tactica*[488] states that the legionaries put a greave on the left leg. This statement, valid for the Hadrianic period, is confirmed in many details from the Adamclisi reliefs. Here the legs (sometimes both, sometimes only the left) are shown as protected by metallic greaves starting below the knee (**47**, **49**, **74**, **205a**, **205c**). It is notable the greaves of the soldiers were shorter than those of the officers, and that the fastening system was partly different. The knee protection was usually missing: the upper part of the greave was cut horizontally just under the knee and fastened by means of a complicate lacing system at the back of the legs. The Adamclisi specimens have been confirmed by archaeology in later specimens datable to the third century AD.

Leggings of oxhide or strong leather, probably in the form already described and designated by the same word both in Greek and Latin, were worn by agricultural labourers[489] and by huntsmen.[490] A very interesting piece of leather fashioned as an officer greave of classical type has been recovered from the military camp of Vindonissa (**206**). The leather surface was attached to a linen backing,[491] forming a very hard protection. It is under discussion whether this could be a greave lining or a true leather greave by itself.

Another possible leather lining of a soldier's greave has been always found in Vindonissa (**207**). It follows exactly the shape of greaves found in successive chronological contexts, such as the specimens of Künzing[492].

~ *AUXILIA, NUMERI* AND *COHORTES EQUITATAE* ~

The regiments of infantry and cavalry flanking the legions were generally called *auxilia*. From the period of Claudius Roman citizenship began to be given to the provincials extensively, especially easterners and Celts. Many subjects of the empire chose a military career in order to gain citizenship, which was also given to the family of the *auxiliarius*.[493] They were generally armed more lightly than the legionaries, or they constituted units with particular equipment and weaponry. An important distinction between the units on Trajan's Column is the armament of *auxilia* and legions: Tacitus clearly says that the first were armed with *hasta* and the latter with *pilum*. But the bronze arms once inserted in the appropriate holes on the monument are now lost.

Generally, on most of the monuments of the first and second centuries, we can see a very high level of standardisation of *auxilia* equipment. This is partly true because of the general tendency of the Roman military structure to issue uniform equipment, where possible.[494] In many units, though, the ideal of having standard military gear was only partially achieved, and especially in the east a wide range of national dress and weaponry was maintained, with a consequent influence on standard Roman military equipment. In many places the presence of infantry troops within *cohortes equitatae* is attested, as in Tekija (Serbia), where many pieces of first- and second-century equipment have been found, such as *fibulae*,[495] parts of armour and helmets, elements of belts,[496] parts of swords,[497] shields,[498] pieces of horse harness[499] and a bushel (*hemina*).[500]

The presence of the Gallo-Romans in the auxiliaries of the cavalry is widely attested by sources, archaeology and figurative monuments. One striking example is the trunk of a cavalryman from Saintes, dated to the turn of the first to second centuries AD,[501] represented with a scale armour, a wide Celtic shield and a helmet decorated by a high crest and laurel crown, reminiscent of the shape and ornamentation of the helmet of Rennes or Xanten-Wardt.[502] A characteristic *torques* is worn around the neck, a Celtic legacy preserved in the Roman army.

Shafted Weapons

The spear (*hasta*) was the main weapon of the auxiliary infantryman, together with the sword (*spatha*). This is clear from many reliefs of the first century AD, like that of Annaius Daverzus, of the *Cohors IV Dalmatorum* from Bingen in the Rhineland,[503] and it is well represented on the second-century monuments, such as Trajan's Column and the Marcus Aurelius column (**57**, **59**, **63**, **185**). Daverzus is represented holding two long spears (*hastae*), that are of an identical shape to those found on the Limes: these last have a blade which is sometimes sharp, bare and with a middle ridge that is sometimes lighter, and straight-sided or oval-sectioned towards the point.[504] The

auxiliarius Licaius, of the *I Cohors Panoniorum*,[505] is similarly armed on his tombstone.

Javelins were used too, as is shown in the Mainz reliefs. In the first two centuries of the empire, they were primarily used by the *auxilia*, and by the cavalrymen.[506] The Romans used javelins on a large scale and of varying shapes. They were – as befitted their primary function of throwing weapons – lighter than the spears.[507] Aulus Gellius gave us eighteen different names for shafted weapons,[508] but, as is correctly underlined elsewhere, it is very difficult to make a classification using the often interchanging terminology of the Roman authors.[509] Generally the javelins were called *iacula*, like those used by the very skilful Silei of Hispania.[510] The *gaesum*, the *veru* and the *phalarica* were kinds of javelins, as was the *lancea*, interestingly recorded in a source as *lancea pugnatoria*, i.e. battle javelin.[511] A *veru* or *verutum* point, corresponding to Vegetius' descriptions, has been found in Mainz. It is triangular and 17.8 cm. long.[512] The *venabulum*[513] was the typical javelin used for hunting, an exercise often recommended for the soldiers. Generally the shape of javelin heads found in archaeological contexts are leaf-shaped or pyramidal (**55**, **56**, **208**).[514]

In Vindonissa and other localities javelin heads have been found, similar to earlier Consular specimens, dated to the

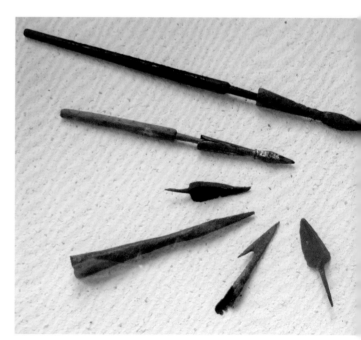

208 Late Republican and early Imperial arrow points, *ballista* bolts and spears from the military camp of Vindonissa (*photo Vindonissa Museum; courtesy of the museum*)

---

i   Unz and Deschler-Erb, 1997, pp. 23, 25–6 and pls 20, 23, 24, nos 338, 339, 372, 494, 497, 540.

209 Spear or javelin point from Salona, variously dated to between the first century BC and the fourth century AD (*Split, Archaeological Museum, inv. No. 1423; T. Seser's photo, courtesy of the museum*).

    The spearpoint is 20.2 cm high and 3.7 cm wide. Note the gilded impression on the metal blade

210 Fragment of armour or *pugio* clasp, first century AD (*collection of Museum Het Valkhof, Nijmegen, courtesy of the conservator*).

    Although the shape of this clasp is substantially identical to that of the belt attachments of the *pugiones*, it is movable and attached to a bronze and iron fragment of a rounded shape, that we cannot discount from being designed to fasten a *lorica*

mid-first century AD. A very unique specimen comes from Salona, classified as a medium-sized weapon, and more suitable for throwing than for use as thrusting weapon. It is unique because it shows the existence of engraved metal on the blade (**209**). The Croatian archaeologists have dated it to a broad timespan, to somewhere between the first century BC and the early Christian period.[515]

In Tekjia two main cavalry spear-point types have been found: the typical leaf-shaped type and the triangular squared type, with shoulder reinforcements. The first is the typical thrusting weapon, the second could be used for the same purpose, but also for throwing.[516]

The spear was usually fitted with a butt, as shown in the Giubiasco grave.[517]

Swords, *Pugiones* and Belts

The Romanisation of the Alps, culminating with the *pax Romana*,[518] has also left traces in the Celtic graves of the period. From Giubiasco come important specimens of *gladii*: one, complete with metal frame scabbard, is 81 cm long (grave 119); the second, whose metal framed scabbard is much more fragmentary, is 69 cm long (grave 471).[519] To these swords should be linked the sword from Nidau (total length 74 cm), characterised by a waisted blade and very long point (*mucro*[520]).

The presence of Roman swords in the Giubiasco graves should not be surprising considering (apart from trade) both the possibility of captured weapons and the large number of Alpine Celtic mercenaries in the Roman armies of the last Republican times.[521] The general impression that emerges from

these swords is that the *auxilia* had a longer sword (*spatha*) than the *gladius* of the *legionarius*. Tacitus expressly compared the *gladius* of the *legionarii* to the *spatha* of the *auxilia*,[522] meaning, in this case, a true *gladius hispaniensis* when he used the term *gladius*. This was not the general rule; many monuments of the first and second centuries show the *spatha* as well as the *gladius* at the side of infantry auxiliaries.

On his monument, Annaius Daverzus wears a longer *gladius* (on the right side)[523] and a short *pugio* (on the left) suspended from two waist belts (*cingula*) decorated with plates and with the usual long aprons visible on the legionaries' belts, here composed of eight strips of leather covered by metal bosses and ending in pendants shaped like small pots. The apron extends from the middle of his belt to the bottom of his tunic. On the tombstone of Annaius the plates of the *cingula* are clearly visible, with a big button attached (**210**) – circular fittings were used to fasten the daggers on the left side of the body.[524] Both the plates together with the round circular fittings were attached on either side of the dagger scabbard. Licaius, instead, shows a similar system of crossed plated belts with six hanging studded aprons, and a *pugio* on the left side, but his sword is clearly a *gladius* of Pompeii type.

The three advancing *auxilia* on the Adamclisi monument are all armed with *spathae* with the scabbard of the sword worn on the left side of the body, as recounted by Josephus in his description of Roman infantrymen (**113**). As for the *gladius*, the hilt of the *spatha* mainly constituted an ivory, bronze or bone handgrip of a cylindrical shape with four troughs, corresponding to the four fingers, for a better handling of the weapon. The form of the finds confirms the high level of

211 Relief with weapons, from Nomentana, last quarter of the first century BC, preserved in the *lapidarium* of Saint Agnese Basilica, in situ (*Rome, author's collection*)

An entire dotation for Romano-Celtic Cavalrymen, probably *auxilia* in a late Roman Consular army, is represented here. Note the *gladii* with bilenticular pommel (**a, b, f, g**), the cavalry parma (**c**), the two *vexilla* (**e, f, g**) and the Celtic horned helmet (**d**)

211a

211b

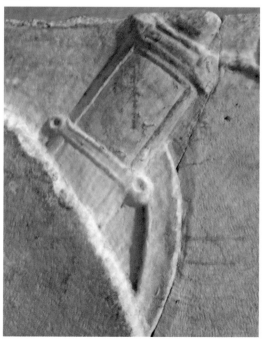

211c

211d

211e

211f

211g

212 Detail of *eques* and horse, Trajan's Column, scene XXVI (*cast, Roma, Museo della Civiltà Romana, author's photo, courtesy of the museum*)

213 Cavalry sword handguards, from Vindonissa, early second century AD (*photo Vindonissa Museum, courtesy of the museum*).
The handguards, made of bone, are identical to those represented on sculpture, attesting the realism and the authenticity of the artists of Trajan's Column

214 Roman *auxilia* fighting with Dacian warriors, Trajan's Column, scene LI (*cast, Roma, Museo della Civiltà Romana, author's photo, courtesy of the museum*)

detail in the sculptures (**212**, **213**). The handguard is usually rounded or rectangular, of any thickness but with an impressive appearance. Monuments and original specimens are also identical in this case. The pommel is wide and spherical, but, sometimes, especially on the swords of the auxiliaries of Celtic or Germanic origin, we meet the bilenticular pommel (**211**), obviously a legacy from the La Tène swords. A double-edged sword from a cremation pit at Blanchs Hotel, Bornholm, is furnished with a copper inlay on both sides, perhaps showing a plumed helmet.[525]

On Trajan's Column the *auxilia* use *gladii* as well as *spathae* (**214**). They are carried mainly by means of a baldric, often covered by studs (*bullatum*). The swords were enclosed in leather-covered wooden scabbards, the fittings of which were strongly influenced by the local manufacture.[526] Towards the middle of the second century there begins to be a general tendency to substitute the *gladius* with the *spatha*, in the weaponry of the legionaries as well as the *auxilia*,[527] But this was be consolidated only during the third century AD.

Specimens of knives in use amongst the *cohortes equitatae* and the infantry troops stationed along the Danube demonstrate the use of the *culter* amongst them. Four different types of *culter* from Tekjia[528] show three different types: a type with a grip longer in the middle, and a long narrow blade; a type with a raised blade, found also in the military camp of Intercisa; and a type with a curved blade, the forerunner of the kind used by the Romans in the Byzantine age.

215 Shield *umbo*, probably of an auxiliary, from Noviomagus, second century AD (*Museum Het Valkhof, Njimegen; courtesy of the conservator*)

Shields

The old *parma bruttiana* is still visible on some auxiliaries represented in the pictorial sources. But the early representations of *auxilia* show the employment of an oblong shield, not curved like the legionary shield but as flat as a board. The exceptional find at Doncaster of a similar specimen, reconstructed by traces in situ, has revealed after laboratory analysis a rectangular and slightly convex shield, made from three layers of wood glued together. It had metal fittings applied to its surface (plates and rivets) and a hemispherical central *umbo*, protecting a large vertical reinforcement on the inside used as a handgrip. The shield is 125 cm high and at its widest point is 64 cm across, with a thickness of 1 cm It was composed of three layers of oak and alder slats, glued at right angles, covered with linen or cow-leather, and with metallic rims protecting the edges.[529] Buckland has assigned it to the auxiliary troops, but this is a matter of debate.[530]

This sub-rectangular shield, sometimes with rounded corners, was in fact widely used by the legions, and both legionaries and *auxilia* used the oval shield. Generally the auxiliaries are not represented with rectangular curved shields constructed of glued layers, but their rectangular shields show a simpler construction, maybe just layers of planks.[531]

Shapes varied from oval to hexagonal, this last being of clear Germanic derivation. The shield used from an *auxilium* on the Mainz relief is typically oval,[532] with the *umbo* very similar to a plain specimen (**215**) preserved in the Van der Kops Museum of Njimegen (Noviomagus). The *umbones* of the *auxilia* shields could also be very elaborate, as is the specimen found in Kirkham in Lancashire, decorated with a series of military subjects around the central figure of Mars.

On the inside the shield was held by a grip, often in bronze.[533] Shield *tegimenta* in leather recovered from the fort of Valkenburg (Netherlands) show that the oval auxiliary shield in the first century AD would have been about 92 x 46 cm.[534]

Trajan's Column shows the *auxilia* invariably carrying the oval flat shield (**185**, **214**, **216a**, **216b**, **217**), as opposed to the rectangular shield of the legionaries. This general impression is confirmed by the Adamclisi monument (**113**),[535] but on the same column many units, usually considered by scholars to be auxiliaries, are in fact likely to be identified as *milites legionis*. A soldier in scene XLVIII, near a carved tree, with an oval shield and the 'typical uniform of an auxiliary', has, as device on his oval shield, the she-wolf with the Gemini, and a eagle on lightning bolts and staff – clearly legionary *digmata*. Behind him there is a warrior armed with a light *pilum*, the only image of such a javelin in the whole column. This must be a

216 Germanic *numeri*, Trajan's Column, scenes XXV–XXVI (*cast, Roma, Museo della Civiltà Romana, author's photo, courtesy of the museum*)

216a

216b

217 (Above and above, right) Roman auxiliaries with Dacian head, Trajan's Column, scene LII (*cast, Roma, Museo della Civiltà Romana, author's photo, courtesy of the museum*)

representation of *milites legionis*, although they are dressed like 'auxiliaries' (**119**).

On the Marcus Aurelius column all the *milites* are carrying oval and round shields (**57**, **59**, **63**, **65**). A grave of an auxiliary soldier from the age of Marcus Aurelius, near Serdica, has revealed a very similar oval shield with part of the wooden structure still in place.[536] The shield was covered by white leather,[537] and has the iron *umbo* intact, fixed to the middle of the shield, corresponding with a wooden tranverse bar attached to the shield by means of four metal fasteners, each fixed by two rivets on the outer surface. The circular *umbo*, fixed to the wood by five rivets, measures 20 cm in diameter[538] and, in section, is slightly pointed. The shield, reconstructed from the fragments and the traces of its outline still in place, was 84 cm long and 120 cm wide. In the same grave two spears were also found, each 2.08 m long, with leaf-shaped points 50 cm long and butts of 10 cm, and a sword 76 cm long and with its metallic scabbard of copper alloy still intact![539] The exceptional find, which gives us a good idea of the weaponry and dress of a Thracian *auxilium* in the second century AD,[540] corresponds perfectly to the pictorial sources.

Helmets

The comparison of the surviving helmets with figurative monuments is a general way to understand whether a certain helmet typically belonged to an *auxilium* or to a *miles legionis*. It is not a rule, however, because some categories of helmets were used by both forces. Other criteria for the distinction should be the place of provenance, the reported inscriptions and the weapons found in the grave if the warrior's finds come from a funerary context.

The Coolus helmet is well represented on the Mainz column showing an *auxilium* advancing with two javelins and a spear.[541] Bronze helmets of this type are often found with inscriptions, and those with a Latinised form – and not a pure Latin *nomen* and *cognomen* as we would expect from a Roman citizen – could be identified as *auxilium* helmets. As we have already seen, in the early Imperial age most of the legionary helmets bore the inscriptions of the name of the owner, the *centuria* and the name of the centurion. If this is missing it could be confirmation that it belonged to an auxiliary *cohors*.

The Fluren helmets, in the Museum of Bonn, very simple in shape, were identified by Robinson as helmets of auxiliary infantry.[542] The helmet, in both the preserved versions, shows a very similar shape to the Imperial type developed from Italic models, but it lacks many embossed details and applied fittings that characterised the prototypes, even on the cheekpieces.[543] Perhaps Robinson was correct in thinking that simpler helmets were given to the *auxilia*, but we should remember that after the first battle a soldier who had lost his helmet would have looked for the best helmet he could find on the battlefield! The Romans did not worry about the classification of helmet type, or about whether a certain kind of helmet could be worn by a legionary, an auxiliary or a cavalryman: they were people who needed to solve problems in a practical way, to save their lives!

On Trajan's Column the auxiliaries are wearing a helmet that has a hemispherical bowl and strong upstanding cross-reinforcements, terminated at the same level on all four sides (**141**, **214**, **229**). The helmet is used by both *milites legionis* and *auxilia* (**108**). A bronze skull-piece, from Florence, confirms the existence of these helmets, although with some differences. The reinforcing peak in the actual specimen is flat and crescent shaped,[544] riveted at each side and secured by a central tongue turned over through a slot in the centre of the brow. The helmets on the column always have a knob on the top, or sometimes a ring, which is missing on the original specimen. No crest attachments are visible for *auxilia* helmets, but the presence of rings or knobs on the *milites'* helmet is indicative of an element that was used to attach a crest.[545] This fixed ring is placed vertically on the helmet bowl, and it is also visible on the helmets of legionaries on both columns. Apart from the debated helmet in the Toledo Museum of Art (**135**) the only existing specimen, to my knowledge, that has such a ring still in place on the helmet bowl is preserved in Hamburg Museum (**130**). As well as its practical use, the ring was a representation of a solar symbol, a supernatural protection.

The *auxilia* helmets also sometimes had a carrying handle.[546] On the Marcus Aurelius column and on the reliefs from the Antonine period *sarcophagi* the *auxilia* helmet is identical to those of the legions (**57**, **59**).

Armour

The body protection of the auxiliary troops would usually have been lighter than that of legionaries. Tacitus, speaking about the German campaigns in the reign of Tiberius, emphasises the character of the *leves cohortes* (light cohorts) positioned in the middle of *Legio XX*,[547] but it is not clear if he is referring to the *auxilia*. On the Rhine *stelae* of the first century AD their equipment shows little defensive armour, but we cannot know if this was the gear used on the battlefield, or simply the standard equipment. Arrian remembers that the breastplate was not usually worn over the parade dress during the *Hippika Gymnasia*. Moreover, on the equipment of a private of the *Cohors II Raetorum* a leather breastplate appears worn over a fringed *subarmale*,[548] and a similar protection is also visible on other auxiliary gravestones.[549] The gravestone of an auxiliary from Bonn–Bad Godesberg shows, instead, the possible use of a leather corselet, with the *pugio* interestingly worn on the right side of the body.[550] This man wears two garments on top of each other, maybe a leather *subarmale* over a tunic. The outer corselet could also be coloured, like the garment worn on the *stela* of Silius Attonis, of the *Ala Picentiana*.[551] Chain mail was, however, widely employed, often with different shapes and sizes of chest fasteners, which were locally influenced, as in that from Usk, which shows evident Celtic patterns.[552]

On Trajan's Column the *auxilia* are furnished with leather corselets (**184**) and with mail shirts (**214**). Some *milites* are wearing two corselets (**186**), perhaps a leather corselet worn over a woolen one, and often those are reinforced by studs on the rims (**184**). Mail armour is worn over *subarmales* furnished with *pteryges* (**113**) or plain leather doublets, and on Trajan's Column it is usually fashioned with scalloped edges. The Adamclisi monument also shows auxiliaries clad in chain mail,[553] but without scalloped edges. A fragmentary suit of Roman mail armour that ties in with the Adamclisi monument has been recovered in good condition in Romania, in the cremation burial of a Dacian aristocratic horseman warrior, perhaps an enemy, perhaps an auxiliary of the Roman army. This spectacular fragment of chain mail (**12**, **218**, **219**) has come from the site of Cugir, and was found together with cheekpieces from a helmet, also belonging to the Celto-Roman auxiliary weaponry (**220**).[554] The fastening system of the mail was positioned on the back of the armour, and was composed

219 Detail of the rings and the fastening button still in place on the Cugir *lorica*, first century BC–first century AD (*photo Museum Alba Julia; courtesy of the museum*)

218 Mail armour from Cugir, first century BC–first century AD (*photo Museum Alba Julia, inv. 4647; courtesy of the museum*). The dimensions of the fragments are 16 x 10 x 11 cm

220 Cheekpieces of an auxiliary helmet from Cugir, first century BC–first century AD (*photo Museum Alba Julia, inv. D 4648; courtesy of the museum*).
The helmet could be of a Thracian provincial type, with strong similarities with a proto-Weisenau specimen. The cheek guards are 10 cm high and 7.5 cm wide

of metallic buttons of 4.5 cm diameter, fastened by hingeing the metallic bar (12 cm long) to each side button.

It is a matter of great debate whether laminated armour was used only by the *milites legionis* or also by the *auxilia*. The famous relief from Saintes representing a group of warriors clad in such *loricae* and wearing the helmet of the Weiler type[555] could be a possible positive answer, but the helmet is not a definitive way of classifying a Roman warrior as an *auxiliarius* or *miles legionis*; instead their belonging to *auxilia* could be deduced by the circumstance that at Mediolanum (Saintes) no legionary *vexillationes* or detachments are recorded for the period that the relief belongs to (the beginning of the second century AD).

Recently, in any case, some scholars have correctly supported the thesis of the employment of *lorica segmentata* by *auxilia*, in particular on the basis that many fragments of it were actually found in auxiliary forts. The most striking example is the fragments from Tekjia, where parts of two different shoulder hinges where found, together with a buckle and perhaps a tie loop of an unusual shape.[556] The presence of battle detachments (*vexillationes*) composed by mixed elements from *milites legionis* and *auxilia* formed the basis of many permanent garrisons and contributed to the wide dispersal of this armour perhaps originally reserved for the legionary citizens only.[557]

Archers and slingers

The best archers were easterners, often recruited from Crete, Commagene, the Near East and also the Danube area, although from the sources we know that all soldiers might shoot arrows and engage in competitions in use of arms.[558] Herodian remembers that Commodus' trainers were the most skilful of the Parthian bowmen and the most accurate of the Moroccan javelin-throwers.[559]

The best representation of archers of the period can be found on Trajan's Column. It has been said in recent works

on the subject[560] that the depiction of archers in the Roman forces on that monument was misdirected, because the archer figures evolved as the work progresses up the column and involved a progressively increasing incorporation of barbarian *spolia* (notably scale armour, segmented helmets and bows) and that the archers thus represent an entirely artificial figure type created by the sculptors and continually modified as work progressed (sic!). I do not see why. The Romans could very well distinguish on the column the different ethnic units, as they did, for instance, with the Moorish cavalrymen of Lusius Quietus. So why would a Roman artist use artifice to represent the archers? They are very well represented and distinguished with their conical helmets and scale cuirass or leather corselets. The conical and the segmented helmets, as well as their weapons, are confirmed by archaeology related to the period.

On Trajan's Column the archers are represented clad in a long leather coat (**222**), and scale armour (**141**, **229**), wearing conical or segmented helmets (spangenhelms) and composite bows (*arcus*).[561] These archers retain part of their own equipment mixed with Roman elements, so they could also be part of irregular *numeri*. A problem arises over their identification: they are carrying Asiatic composite bows (παλιντονα τοξα/*palintona toxa*) so they could be identified as the Palmyrene or Commagene or Iturean and Hemeseni[562] *auxilia* who participated to the Dacian campaign. Cichorius, probably because some of them (**227a**, **227b**, **227c**) appear very similar to the Jazyges cataphracts (**223**, **225**), points to a Danubian origin of some of these units.[563]

They appear to be different from the regular *cohortes sagittariorum*, who also appear on Trajan's Column clad in a more typical auxiliary dress, differing only from the other regular *auxilia* because of the lack of a shield.[564] On the gravestones of the first century AD they are dressed in what is possibly off-duty uniform of tunic with sword and dagger belts.[565]

Composite bows constructed of sinew and wood with stiffeners of bone or iron have been found in many military camps (**221**) and fortresses.[566] The quiver (*pharetra*) rested on both shoulders, as mentioned by Propertius in his description

221 Fragments of composite bow in iron and bone, second–third century AD (*photo Vindonissa Museum; courtesy of the museum*[i])

i   Unz and Deschler-Erb, 1997, p. 24 and pl. 21, nos 404, 406, 409, 410.

222 (Above and detail below) German and eastern *auxilia*, Trajan's Column, scenes LXXXII–LXXXIII (*cast, Roma, Museo della Civiltà Romana, author's photo, courtesy of the museum*)

222a

223 (Above) Details of Rhoxolani cataphracts, Trajan's Column, scene XXVII (*cast, Roma, Museo della Civiltà Romana, author's photo, courtesy of the museum*).

In the Danube region armour begins to cover the legs of the horsemen and the horses were likewise protected by a metal shirt of scale armour, fitted with eye plaques of the Cretan archers, who used hooked arrows (*hamatae sagittae*).[567] Notched stiffeners are usually the only surviving evidence of the bow, but arrowheads are frequently found, of many different shapes and dimensions;[568] they are tanged and socketed, sometimes made of bronze. Three categories are the most documented: the flat-bladed type, the triple-bladed type and those designed to carry incendiary material (**208**). The arrow plumes or flights were called *harundines*.[569]

The conical helmets represented on Trajan's Column are generally of three types,[570] all fitted with cheek guards, corresponding to three main types of auxiliaries:

1. A high cylindrical helmet with no neck protection (**227a**, **227b**, **227c**); unlike the others, it seems to have a typical segmented construction in iron, and its similarity to the helmet of the Rhoxolani cavalrymen on the same monument (**225**) could confirm the interpretation of these of a *numerus* of Jazyges or other Sarmatian tribe allied with the Romans; like their counterparts on horseback, these archers are clad in scale armour (*lorica plumata*).

2. A conical helmet of spangenhelm construction, with or without pointed apex; this is worn by Levantine archers clad in scale armour (**141**, **229**); curiously, some of them have the *vinculum* (chin strap) of the helmet passing under their hair. This helmet is the same as that worn by the extra-armoured infantrymen of the Adamclisi reliefs (**47**, **64b**, **76**, **142a**, **142b**).

3. A conical helmet worn by eastern auxiliaries, perhaps Syrians, clad in leather and ring-mail corselets, under which appears a long flowing tunic (**222**, **224**, **226**); these *tunicae* were called *kitoneh* in Aramaic, from the Greek *chiton* and they followed the Oriental tradition, going back to the time of the pharaohs.[571] Their shoes are true sandals in the eastern fashion (**222a**).

On the Antonine column the archers are represented wearing simple felt caps. The men are dressed in a simple long-sleeved tunic and are wearing wide oriental trousers.[572]

The type of helmets described is well represented by the precious helmet in gold and silver recovered from the Karaagatsch tumulus,[573] dated to the end of the first century AD; conical in shape, it is richly embossed with the figures of gods (**228**). It was found together with the remains of aventail neck protection made of bronze scales and its appearance would have been very similar to some helmets represented on the pedestal of Trajan's Column.[574] The bronze *squamae* formed overlapping rows linked together by copper-alloy wires; the upper row was attached to the bottom edge of the helmet. With the helmet were found spearheads, a shield *umbo*[575] and a fragment of a sword,[576] so it is quite difficult to ascertain whether the Thracian warrior in the grave, an auxiliary of the Roman army, was an archer. However, his highly decorated equipment and the other rich goods recovered from the grave

225 Rhoxolani cataphracts helmet detail, Trajan's Column, scene XXVII (*cast, Museo della Civiltà Romana, author's photo, courtesy of the museum*)

226 Eastern *auxilia* detail, Trajan's Column, scene LXXXIII (*cast, Roma, Museo della Civiltà Romana, author's photo, courtesy of the museum*)

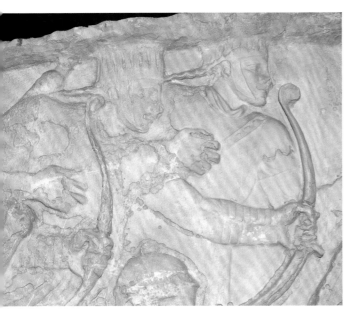

224 (Opposite, above and above, right) Levantine archers with leather coats, mail armour and segmented fluted helmets, Trajan's Column, scene L (*cast, Roma, Museo della Civiltà Romana, author's photo, courtesy of the museum*).

The column shows the evidence for the use of a leather bracer on the left forearm, used by Levantine archers. This is worn by Syrian(?) archers wearing leather corselets, a helmet with wide neck protection extending behind and closed quivers (*pharetrae*). One of them is wearing a *cingulum bullatum*

227 Danubian *numeri*, Trajan's Column, scenes XLVI–XLVIII (*cast, Roma, Musee della Civiltà Romana, author's photos, courtesy of the museum*)

227a   **227b**   **227c**

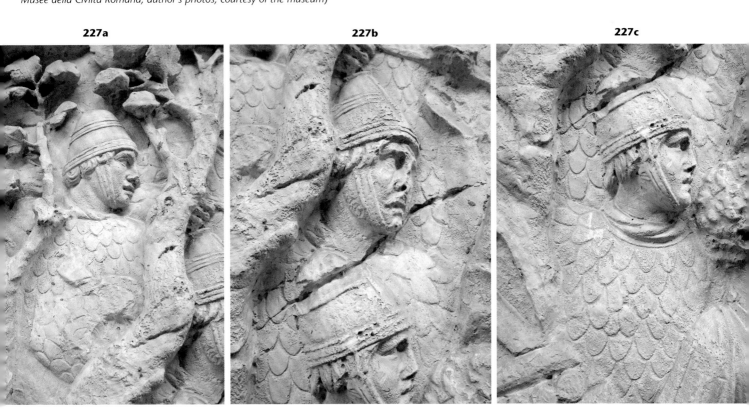

might suggest that an officer was buried here. This is not to exclude the possibility that the archers were also armed with javelins (*iacula*): the most famous example is the epitaph of the *miles* Soranus,[577] of the Hadrianic period, who was unbeatable in the use of the bow (*arcus*) and the javelin (*iaculum*); he was able to shoot at missiles thrown on the air and cut them in two pieces with an arrow, and able to cross the Danube *sub armis* – with his armour on. We can therefore imagine him clad in a leather corselet like those represented on the column.

A Syrian archer of the *Cohors Hamiorum Sagittariorum*, which was garrisoned at Housesteads in the early second century AD,[578] is portrayed in a conical helmet and possibly wearing mail armour or, more likely, a leather corselet.[579] On his back is slung a quiver of arrows and on his waist belt, at the right side, hangs a large knife. A bow – of a recurved composite type – and a small axe complete the equipment. His helmet type is confirmed by a splendid specimen of an Eastern Roman helmet dated to the second-third century AD, which has a conical shape and a low frontal band embossed with three deities (**230**).[580]

228 Helmet of Eeastern origin from Karaagatsch, end of first century AD (*Sofia, Archaeological Museum, Studio Tomatofarm*).
The conical helmet, found in a hill nearby the ancient city of Anchialus, is highly decorated with images of Zeus, Apollo, Athena, Hermes, Ares and Nike. Embossed vegetal interlaces and small decoration of armies' *trophea* are visible all around the helmet. The embossed Apollo has some characteristics of the future *sol invictus*, with a radial nimbus around the head. It was found together with spears and sword fragments, and it is dated to the end of first century AD. The diameter of the helmet is 21 cm, its height is 19.7 cm and its width is about 16.7 cm.[i] A neck protection of small bronze scales completed the helmet

i   Welkow, 1929, pp. 15 ff.

229 Eastern *auxilia* archers, Trajan's Column, scene LXXXVIII (*cast, Roma, Museo della Civiltà Romana, author's photo courtesy of the museum*)

The horse-archers, especially the easterners, usually carried no shields, little or no body armour and often wore a cap made of heavy cloth or leather in place of a helmet.[581] The *equites* of *Cohors VI Commagenorum* were skilful in the use of bow and arrows and sling, as reported in a speech by Hadrian to the African army.[582]

The sling (*funda*) with its lead missiles (*plumbea pondera*)[583] was used by special *funditores*, well illustrated on Trajan's Column. They are dressed simply in broad tunics with no armour, but carry a shield (**231**). Their cloak or *sagulum* acted as an ammunition bag. Maybe these figures could still be considered Balearic slingers, although we have not mention of *cohortes funditorum* (slingers) or *libritorum* (stone-throwers) coming from the Balearics (*Baliarium*) at this time. Both the specialities of slingers and stone-throwers are illustrated on Trajan's Column (**231**).[584]

Numeri

The *numeri* fought with their own weaponry and used their traditional tactics. Of course they also received a good range of weapons from the Imperial arsenals. We cannot exclude the possibility of the presence of regular cohorts that had

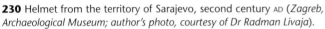

230 Helmet from the territory of Sarajevo, second century AD (*Zagreb, Archaeological Museum; author's photo, courtesy of Dr Radman Livaja*).

The helmet shows a strong similarity with some helmets on Trajan's Column and with the helmet of the Hamian archer from his *stela* in Housesteads. Note the holes on the lower rim for the attachment of scale or mail armour fixed upon a leather backing

231 *Funditores*, Trajan's Column, scene XLVI (*cast, Roma, Museo della Civiltà Romana, author's photo, courtesy of the museum*).
The effectiveness of the slingers was unquestionable and much appreciated, especially against elephants. Celsus, writing towards the end of the second century AD, remembered how a slingshot wound was more dangerous and harder to treat than one inflicted by an arrow

wearing their national dress. They are half-naked, clad only in long loose breeches and sometimes with a *sagum*.[587] Their breeches are virtually identical to the actual wool specimens found in the Danish bogs, further proof of the high fidelity of Trajan's Column as a historical and archaeological source. They are baggy trousers, with the top rolled down. Like the trousers found in Germanic sites (Thorsberg), they were fastened by belt-loops girdled around the waist. Sometimes Germanic *bracae* could have socks or even boots attached!

232a (Below) and **b** (Bottom) Germanic *numeri*, details of scenes XXV–XXVI (*cast, Museo della Civiltà Romana, author's photo, courtesy of the museum*)

been allowed to retain their own dress, but the wide range of different uniforms shown on Trajan's Column as well as the ordinary types, attests the picturesque and varied appearance of a Roman campaign army of the second century AD.

There are representations of warriors who wear – instead of the ordinary helmet – an animal skin arranged over the head and shoulders (**216a**). Tacitus, in his *Histories*,[585] mentions the fright of civilians in Rome before the Germanic auxiliary troops of Vitellius: 'Nor were the men themselves a less frightful spectacle, bristling as they were with the skins of wild beasts, and armed with huge lances.' Other warriors are represented marching behind the Emperor Trajan with their head covered by open helmets of the Teutonic pattern, identical to a specimen found in Britain and often considered to be just a religious crown (**216b, 232b**).[586]

Representations of Germanic *clavatores* (soldiers armed with clubs) on Trajan's Column also prove that these *auxiliarii* of the Imperial army fought with their national weapons and

Their traditional weapon was the club, but these *symmachiarii* appear armed with club only in some scenes (**234**), while in others they bear a staff, without the typical bulge of the club. In fact, Tacitus discusses[588] a German tribe, the Aestii, armed with this kind of staff, called *fustis*. Thus it is probable that in the Trajanic army there was a *numerus aestiorum* for which we do not have – for the time being – epigraphic evidence. This kind of weapon was also used by auxiliaries from Britannia, as shown on the *stela* of Catavignus (**233**). Although for artistic reasons the staff represented on the column is reduced in size, in real life it was very effective, being made of tough and hard wood (oak or olive), and was very useful, albeit primitive, as a striking weapon. It was even able, in hands of warriors like these, to knock down an armoured enemy.

Other Germans represented on the column are half-naked too but they are fighting with Roman weapons or with shafted weapons (javelins, *hastae*) which were reproduced in bronze on

234 Germanic *clavatores*, Trajan's Column, scene XXVII (*cast, Roma, Museo della Civiltà Romana, author's photo, courtesy of the museum*)

233 *Stela* of Catavignus, son of Ivomagus, of the *Cohors III Britannorum*, *centuria* of Gesate, AD 69 (*Cuneo, Museo Civico, by kind permission of the museum*).

Catavignus was a *miles* in the army of Raetia, who came to Italy in AD 69 to support Vitellius, commander of the legions of Germania Inferior, and proclaimed emperor after the death of Nero. He died after six years of military service at the age of 25.

He is represented with a club, the typical weapon of the troops from Britannia, clad in a *sagum* (cloak) covering the left part of the body and a military tunic. He wears light armour, probably of leather, with *pteryges* on the shoulders and with a small collar protecting the neck (compare with **PLATE IIb**). Note that his hair is coated with gypsum, and stands up in spikes, following the typical Celtic hairstyle of the British warriors.

the original monument and so are now lost, exactly like the *pila* and the *hastae* of the legionaries (**216**). Their oval shields may identify them as *parmae*, whose *digma* or *episema* is a four- or six-pointed star, vegetal motifs or interlaced rings, perhaps representing *torques*.

The Numidian *auxilia* horsemen are represented on Trajan's Column in their national equipment, substantially unchanged since the Battle of Zama: a spear and a small round buckler (*cetra*), riding horses without saddle or bridle but simply with a halter around the neck.[589] The costume of a Numidian prince of the first century AD, represented on a *stela* from Chensour Abbassa, is substantially the same: it differs only in the presence of low shoes and a cloak fastened on the right shoulder.[590] His horse has a low saddle covered by a cloth, and some harness. But Mauri cavalrymen dressed in tunics decorated with Egyptian embroidery (*picti tunica Nilotide*) are mentioned as escorts of the Emperor Trajan, together with other *equites*.[591] These tunics were probably similar to the African tunics represented in some mosaics from Tunisia, such as the red embroidered dress of the Muse near Virgil, preserved in Bardo Museum,[592] or the multi-coloured tunics of the *venatores* from Sousse.[593] These long-sleeved tunics were forerunners of the elaborate tunics of the late empire.

Pliny's description[594] of hippopotamus-leather helmets found confirmation in a unique procession of a local Egyptian *numerus*, from Tell El-Herr (**235**). These *numeri* and *cohortes equitatae* – who defended the *praesidia*, such as those of the

236 Relief with *signifer*, from monument of late Neronian–early Flavian period, second half of the first century AD (*photo DAI*)

235 (Above and top, left) Relief with soldiers wearing elephant helmets, Tell el-Herr (Egypt), second–third century AD (*ex Breeze, drawing of Graham Sumner*).

The cavalrymen and the infantrymen are a good representation of the irregular *numeri* defending the *praesidia* in the Egyptian desert. Note the rectangular shields, worn by both infantry and cavalry as well as small bucklers. The men wear boots like those found in Dydymoi,[i] and their helmets confirm the words of Pliny the Elder about wild animal leather made into helmets

237 (Opposite, left) Torso in lamellar armour, Hadrianic period (*drawing by Graham Sumner*)

238 (Opposite, centre and right) Relief fragment with cult scene representing the gods Iarhibol and Szokai as *dromedarii* officers, Palmyra, second century AD (*Damascus, National Museum, drawing by Graham Sumner*).

The representation of the god Iarhibol in Dura is probably a reflection of the officers of the garrison, with muscled cuirass, cloak, trousers, high boots[ii] and a spear.

---

i   Leguilloux, 2004, p. 137.

ii   Baur-Rostovtzeff, 1933, pl. XIX, 2.

Egyptian desert,[595] against the attacks of nomadic riders – were mainly composed of locals,[596] as attested by the names of the soldiers recorded on the *ostraka* found in various places. They were under the command of a *curator praesidii*, and very often their equipment was poor and mainly manufactured in leather and other organic material.

Among the eastern auxiliaries the use of lamellar armour was widespread; for the Romans it was just a variation of the usual *squama*. It was common among Palmyrene and strongly Hellenised *numeri* of the near east, as is shown by the fact that this kind of armour is well detailed on one of the provinces sculpted for the Hadrianic temple of Venus and Rome (**237**). This kind of protection of the body was not unknown to the Romans, who derived it from the Etruscans. Unlike scale armour, which was composed of *squamae* attached to a backing of cloth or leather and wired or linked each other, the lamellae *squamae* were laced to the backing in rigid horizontal rows. The individual pieces were longer and slimmer than the usual

scales, and so formed an even stiffer form of defence.[597] They were mainly made of metal, but considering the finds related to the later age, a form of lamellar armour in rawhide would also have been used.

Obviously this armour was first employed by auxiliaries and *numera*, and perhaps the fragments of fine lamellar armour found in Corbridge belong to them. Like the other pieces of armour, lamellar armour was used together with doublets fitted with leather or linen *pteryges* at the shoulder and around the waist. Statues of Palmyrene officers, gods and generals are a good source of evidence for the design of these armours, showing in their dress a strong Hellenistic influence.[598]

Eastern horse-archers also very often wore the *lydia*, the Phrygian cap,[599] made of felt, instead of the helmet. Easterners such as the Palmyrenes and Osroenes, armed following Greco-Parthian influence, were enlisted in the *numeri* of *dromedarii* who patrolled the desert frontier against the Parthian enemy (**238**).

~ *SIGNA MILITARIA* AND THE EQUIPMENT OF STANDARD-BEARERS ~

The *aquila* (eagle) of the *legio*, which contained the spirit (*genius*) of the whole army, was carried by the *aquilifer*, who would die in front of the *rostrum* (beak) of his eagle, rather than lose it.[600] *Aquilae*, cast in gilded bronze or silver,[601] are represented on the monuments with raised or open wings (**156**, **241**),[602] sometimes linked by wreath crowns,[603] and their claws resting on lightning bolts. Often the pole-shaft has a mounting for carrying the *signum*, positioned halfway up. As suggested by Lindenschmit,[604] this hook could also be used to draw out the *signum* from a body: so the butt of the

shaft could act as an effective weapon in the hand of an expert warrior.

Various *signa* were carried by the *signiferi* and acted as identification standards for *cohortes* and *manipuli*. Simple *signa*[605] decorated by *phalerae* are visible on the Scafa reliefs and from the Church of San Domenico in Sora (**156**). Usually the manipular *signum* were surmounted by an open hand (**239**).

The *imago*, carried by the *imaginifer*, was a pole upon which was mounted, enclosed in a small *aedicula*, a bust of the emperor, in bronze or silver.[606] Some busts in gold or silver have been

239 Manipular *signum* fragment, second century AD (*photo Vindonissa Museum, courtesy of the museum*)

241 Relief with *signum* from Villa Mattei, first century AD (*photo DAI*)

240 Detail of the *signa* of the *metopae* XIII, Adamclisi Relief, first half of the second century AD (*Adamclisi museum, author's photo, courtesy of the museum*)

242 *Vexillarii*, Adamclisi relief, *metopa* XLIII, Trajanic age, first half of second century AD (*Museum of Adamclisi; author's photo, courtesy of the museum*)

243 Praetorian *vexillifer*, Rome, second century AD (*Villa Medici, Studio Tomatofarm*)

found, and they were probably fitted on the top of the *imago* standard. In the bust, the emperor usually wore scale armour in the shape of a *squama plumata* with a *gorgoneion* in the centre of the breast.[607] They were about 25–30 cm high.

Different from the *imago* were the *imagines* carried on the *signa*, often inscribed in silver or gilded *phalerae*. They could be head only or bust with portrait (**241**). On a *signum* there were a wide variety of combinations: standards with *coronae* and *imagines*, standards with *phalerae* and *imagines*, and so on (**236**).[608] The manipular *signum* was also combined with *phalerae* or *imagines* on the same standard (**240**).

The praetorian *signa* represented on Trajan's Column[609] (**290a**) bear the *imago* of Trajan in their *phalerae*, combined with crowns, eagles in laurel wreaths and surmounted by *lunulae*. They are advancing on the battlefield preceded by the *signum* bearing the praetorian eagle. *Vexilla*, of a trapezoidal shape and fringed at the extremities, were used both by cavalry and infantry (**65**, **211**, **242**) and Praetorians (**243**).[610] A simple cavalry *vexillum* is visible on a coin struck in 12 BC; it has only two *phalerae*, and a drape with a fringed edge. An exceptional fragment of a *signum* or a *vexillum*, an iron cross-bar of about 13.70 cm long and 7.5 cm wide has been found in Ulpia Traiana Sarmizegetusa.[611]

In the face of the silence of the previous figurative sources, the equipment of the *vexilliferi*, *aquiliferi*, *signiferi* and *imaginiferi* is now widely represented and well documented from the archaeological and artistic point of view. In first-century AD tombstones the sword – and sometimes also the *pugio* – is usually worn together with a plated *cingulum*, sometimes on the left[612] and sometimes on the right of the body.[613] The side sword attachment is the rule. When a transverse strap or *balteus* is also visible across the breast of the man, it belongs to the strap used for carrying either the *signum* or the oval shield.[614] The sword is the typical legionary *gladius*. The aprons or *baltea* of the *cingulum* usually end in leaf-shaped metallic fittings. When two *cingula* are crossed over the belly, the lower is plain, the upper decorated with embossed plates with floral or vegetal motifs.

The helmets were the same as those of the legionaries, but sometimes covered by skins and heads of lions and bears, with the paws crossed on the breast (**290a**). This is visible especially on the second-century reliefs, and echoes the description of Vegetius, who describes, at the end of the fourth century, the armies of previous periods.[615]

On the gravestone of the standard-bearer Q. Luccius we find moreover a complete representation of a mask helmet, made of two separate parts, the skull and the visor.[616] This last corresponds perfectly with the famous specimen found on the Kalkriese battlefield,[617] probably belonging to a *signifer* who lost his life in the *Clade Variana*. A very similar helmet, preserved in the ex-Axel Guttmann Collection,[618] was found with the skull still intact: it shows that these masked helmets had a composite construction, with a stylised human face mask of iron, silver or copper alloy attached separately, with narrow eye-slits, pierced nostrils and mouth. The attachment to the skull was achieved by means of holes and rivets at each side and a hinge on the brow (**245**).

Shields are usually oval and of a smaller size than the normal legionary shields. On Trajan's Column it is possible see *signiferi* covered by bearskins, marching with a small *parma* under the arm (**244**), a way of holding the shield still visible centuries later in the Eastern Roman army of Byzantium.[619]

The mail shirt was the most commonly used body protection. The *lorica hamis conserta* was probably worn by Genialis Clusio under a rigid leather corselet, furnished with folded rigid shoulder guards, linked by a central hinge.[620] The lion's skin paws lie on his left shoulder, a symbol of the rank of *imaginifer*; along the neck edge can be seen the border of the head covering, probably shaped like a lion's head. A leather-fringed garment is visible also on the Pintaius monument, preserved in Bonn.[621]

The *aquilifer* Cn. Musius of the *XIIII Legio Gemina* wears a double-fringed *subarmale*, probably with the purpose of supporting the hardened-leather corselet better, over which are displayed nine *phalerae* and two *armillae* as military decorations.

244 (Above) Detail of *praetoriani signiferi* and *aquilifer*, Trajan's Column, scene XXXVII (*cast, Roma, Museo della Civiltà Romana, author's photo, courtesy of the museum*)

245 (Below) Mask of a possible *signifer* helmet, first half of the first century AD (*private collection, Christie's photo*).

This exceptional specimen, with the ears directly attached to the mask, is virtually identical to that represented on the Q. Luccius gravestone in Mainz. It shows the usual way of attaching the mask to the helmet, by hingeing the full face mask to the centre of the brow head. This kind of fastening is characteristic of the first- to the late second-century AD category of Roman mask helmets

246 (Above) Details of *subarmale* worn under the chain armour of a *signifer* (*cast, Roma, Museo della Civiltà Romana, author's photo, courtesy of the museum*)

This structure was fixed to the undergarment by means of two pins visible on the shoulders. Following the remains of the colour on the tombstone the subarmale was brown (leather?) with red fringes attached to the *pteryges*.[622]

Scale armour in the shape of a *plumata* is attested for the *aquiliferi*.[623] In the Verona gravestone of L. Sertorius Firmus[624] the scale corselet ends in a very similar way to the *plumata* of the centurion Q. Sertorius Festus,[625] but the final lappets are alternately covered by *squamae* or decorated with bronze embossed apotropaic heads, forming a single row overlapping the undergarment furnished with *pteryges*. Small metallic shoulder guards are hinged on the armour.

A protection completely made of leather is visible only on the above mentioned monument of Q. Luccius Faustus from Mainz[626]. The corselet is very similar to the leather protection of C. Valerius Crispus: the main differences are the three rows

of *pteryges* on the shoulders, and the single row of *pteryges* visible under the lower edge of the corselet. The shoulder guards are, however, wider, and the corselet has small cuts along the sides to allow for ease of movement, as does that of the officer on the Mainz column.

The standard-bearers of the second-century monuments wear a very varied range of protective armour: chain mail, scale, leather. Particularly interesting is the corselet of a *signifer* on Trajan's Column, which, clearly made of mail, is worn over a doublet with stud reinforcement on the scalloped rims (**246**).

The *signa* of the *legio* were kept, when not carried, in a special place in the camp called *aedes*. This was the *sacellum* or shrine of the standards. It was usually in the central part of the *principia*, and under it was the strong-room that held the unit's money and treasures.

~ MEDICAL CORPS, SPECIAL EQUIPMENT, SYMBOLS OF RANK, MUSICIANS, MILITARY DECORATIONS ~

Medical Corps

In the *castra* during the Empire there were quarters for the wounded *milites* (*valetudinaria*). Many sets of medical instruments used by military doctors have been recovered from Thracia,[627] Dacia, Pannonia and various provinces. The most used were:

1. probes (*specillum, auriscalpium, lingula, spathomela, μήλη*) made of iron, of various sizes but usually somewhere between 3.8 and 18.7 cm;[628]
2. scalpels (*scalpellum, σμίλη*), made of copper, from about 6 to 7.6 cm long; these were a sort of lancet used for blood-letting (*ad mittendum sanguinem*), and perhaps sometimes also for opening abscesses;[629]
3. knives, usually made of copper, the blade generally around 6.5cm long, and in the broadest part 2.5 cm or eight lines in breadth; the back was straight and thick, and the edge sometimes much curved, with a very short handle. When the edge was so curved and had such a straight thick back, the instrument might be struck with a hammer, and so used to amputate fingers, toes and other parts. Other knives had triangular blades and a straight back; these may have been used for enlarging wounds, for which they would be particularly fitted by the blunt point and broad back;

4. iron elevators, for raising depressed portions of the skull – generally 12.5 cm long, and very much resembling those used in the present day;
5. different kinds of forceps (*vulsella*),[630] furnished with a moveable ring, exactly like the *tenaculum forceps* employed in today. They were used for pulling out hairs by the roots (*τριχολαβὶς/tricholavìs*), or extracting foreign bodies that had stuck in the oesophagus or in a wound;
6. *spatulae* and tweezers (*volsella, vulsella*),[631] hooks (*hamuli*),[632] needles (*acus*).[633]

Roman physicians had boxes (*loculi*) of wood, bronze or ivory to keep their instruments and store medicines.[634] In small squarish boxes of bronze, with handles,[635] the instruments were kept in the upper compartment and the medicines underneath. Boxes with more small compartments were also used, as well as small cylindrical boxes (*pyxides, theca vulneraria*).[636]

On Trajan's Column we have the first representation of the Roman medical corps. They are armed very lightly, having a leather corselet worn over two tunics, and only a short *pugio* on the right side of the body (**248**). Interestingly, amongst the medical *instrumentarium* from Reims, an iron flask has been found.[637]

247 (Above and top, right) Trajan Column, marching milites, scene IV (*cast, Museo della Civiltà Romana, author photo, courtesy of the museum*).

Following Cicorius, the scene represent soldiers of the Legio I Adiutrix, identified by the *digma* on their shield (a crown of laurel leaves). In march (in agmine) the milites went usually bare-head. On the column are represented bare-head also the working milites, although the armour and the sword is always with them because of the danger of some ambush or attack. This was a prescription punished with the death if violated.[i] Although the general shield used by the legionaries on the Trajan column is the typical concave rectangular one, the soldiers crossing the bridges are often carrying shields of different shapes

i   Tac., Ann., XI, 18: "…At the outposts, on guard, in the duties of day and of night, they were always to be under arms. One soldier, it was said, had suffered death for working at the trenches without his sword, another for wearing nothing as he dug, but his poniard…"

248 (Above) Medical corps, Trajan's Column, scene XXIX (*cast, Roma, Museo della Civiltà Romana, author's photo, courtesy of the museum*)

~ Special Equipment ~

In the *Historia Augusta* it is said that when the Emperor Hadrian called men to military service, he always supplied them with horses, mules, clothing, the cost of maintenance, and indeed their whole equipment.[638] In the *Metamorphosis* of Apuleius[639] the unlucky Lucius, transformed into a donkey, is obliged to bear the heavy military equipment of a *miles*:

> The next day how my master the Gardener sped, I knew not, but the gentle soldier, who was well beaten for his cowardise, lead me to his lodging without the contradiction of any man: Where he laded me well, and garnished my body (as seemed to me) like an Asse of armes. For on the one side I bare an helmet (Galea) that shined exceedingly: On the other side a Target (scutum) that glistered more a thousand folde. And on the top of my burthen he put a long spear (lancea), which things he placed thus gallantly, not because he was so expert in warre (for the Gardener proved the contrary) but to the end he might feare those which passed by, when they saw such a similitude of warre. When we had gone a good part of our journey, over the plaine and easie fields, we fortuned to come to a little towne, where we lodged at a certaine Captaines house. And there the souldier tooke me to one of the servants, while he himselfe went towards his captaine; who had the charge of a thousand men

The regular set up (*sarcina*)[640] is clearly visible on Trajan's Column (**247**).[641] It was made up of a T-shaped stake (*furca*), from which hung a linen bag (*sacculus*), the leather haversack for the fifteen–twenty days' supplies (*trinum nundinum*) and personal effects, a pot (*ollula*), a cup (*patera*), and a basket for working in the fields. These were used for the usual dietary needs of the soldiers, such camp-fare as bacon, cheese and vinegar.[642] Tents (*papilla*) with their pegs are well documented in archaeological excavations, which have also attested the use by the soldiers of suspension hinges for vessels, *situlae* and *paterae*.[643]

Precious vessels have been found, like the *patera* decorated with a lion's head, belonging to an officer of the *Legio VI Ferrata* stationed in the fortified camp south of Megiddo (Israel), destined to become the fortress of Maximianopolis.[644] Normal work instruments such as the sickle (*falx*) have been confirmed in a military context and use.[645] Drinking equipment such as a bushel for vinegar and a bronze bucket to draw water from wells and springs have been found in different bases.[646]

The pick-axe (*dolabra*) was a fundamental tool in legionary life and was sometimes used as an effective weapon. Possible proof is the fragment of an iron *dolabra* found in a hoard at Ulpia Traiana Sarmizegetusa, together with fragments of helmets, shields, belts and other weaponry. Here probably a Roman *vexillatio* composed of *auxilia*, *milites* and *equites legionis* was engaged, in AD 105, in a bloody fight against the Dacians, and the Romans, who defended their wooden barracks or tents, used all the weapons they could against the sudden attack by their enemies.[647] When not in use the blades of the pick-axe heads were often kept in a bronze case, like the specimens found in the military camp of Vindonissa (**249**, **250**).

Tabellae were hollow wooden tablets, spread with a thin layer of wax, on which were incised short letters, messages and passwords by means of a pointed stylus with a rounded edge to delete the writing. They are shown in the hands of many soldiers on various tombstones.

Symbols of Rank

The gold chariots (*inaurati currus*)[648] for the *triumphator*,[649] with the horses decorated with laurel leaves, are still recorded for this time.[650] The Imperial age has given us beautiful specimens of carts used by generals and governors, highly decorated with bronze fittings representing divinities, animals, vegetal scrolls and flowers. Some of them have been recovered in Thrace, such

249 Pick-axe (*dolabra*) case of copper alloy, second century AD (*photo Vindonissa Museum; courtesy of the museum*)

250 Pick-axe (*dolabra*) in its case of copper alloy, second century AD (*photo Vindonissa Museum; courtesy of the museum*)

as the specimen preserved today in Stara Zagora Museum, ornamented with images of Hercules in the form of busts and *phalerae* on the horse harness.[651]

The *sceptrum eburneum* (ivory sceptre of the *triumphator*) is recorded by Virgil.[652] The twelve *fascii* borne by the *lictores* were always the *insignia* of the consul and followed him right to his house door, where one *lictor* knocked with a staff.[653] Usually, as the emperor was the *perpetuus consulatus*, the *lictores* escorted him (**145**).

The vine branch symbol of centurions (*vitis*)[654] is represented in different versions. It could be a curved or twisted vine branch, as on the tombstone of Facilis (**PLATE IV, 72**) and of Minucius Lorarius from Padua. Sometimes the *vitis* was straight, like that of M. Caelius.

Signet rings were given to officers charged with imperial duties, such as the centurion of the *Legio XV Apollinaris* who accompanied the Emperor Titus (while still a prince) on his journey to Palaepaphos on the island of Cyprus. The ring, found by the archaeologists in Paphos,[655] was engraved with a legionary eagle and with the inscription of that legion.

Musicians

The *tuba* is always mentioned as the military instrument par excellence making a gloomy sound.[656] The *bucina*[657] and the hoarse sound of the *cornu* playing the *classicum* is also noted by

251 Stele of the *cornicen* C. Coponius Felicio, beginning of the second century AD (*Mantua, Palazzo Ducale; Studio Tomatofarm*)

252 Stele of *cornicen* Victor, of the *collegium* of *liticines* and *cornicines*, from Sezze Romano, second century AD (*Museo di Sezze; courtesy of the museum*)

Propertius.[658] In Aquincum a local dedicatory inscription to his wife was left by a mercenary of the *Legio II Adiutrix*, who was a professional water-organ player. He may have played the organ for the legions during the gladiatorial games; in Aquincum a complete portable organ (*hydra*) has been recovered intact.[659]

Several funerary monuments of Roman military musicians survive. One of the best preserved is that of the *cornicen* C. Coponius Felicio from the late Flavian period, where the man is represented clad in a simple *tunica* and a military cloak (*sagum*) pinned on the right shoulder (**251**). Similar equipment is shown on the funerary relief of Victor, a soldier member of the corporation (*collegium*) of *liticines* and *cornicines*, found during the excavations of a villa in Crocemoschitto, near Sezze Romano (Roma). He holds with his left hand a *lituus*, while his *cornu* with the typical cross-bar for the grip is perfectly represented at his feet (**252**).

On the Trajanic monuments,[660] where all these instruments are represented, *cornicines* are equipped with mail shirts, probably because with the mail the soldier was able to take deeper breaths than with plate armour. The wearing of these by *buccinatores* is also confirmed from the Adamclisi monument.[661] The only main difference is that, on Trajan's Column, the heads of some musicians are covered by animal skins, like the standard-bearers (**147**).

Complete specimens and fragments of musical instruments are quite rare, but not entirely absent: a complete *lituus* from Salzburg, made of bronze and 74 cm long;[662] a bronze *tuba* from Zsámbek, quite well preserved and originally 148 cm long;[663] mouthpiece fragments from Vindonissa, perhaps from *tuba* and *cornu*;[664] a fragment of *cornu* from Strageath;[665] and various pieces of *tuba/bucina* and *cornu* probably from Augst (Augusta Raurica).[666] Various parts of *cornu* braces have been found in Trier, Stuttgart, Strasbourg, Murrhardt.[667]

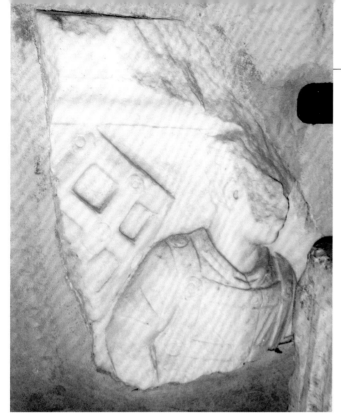

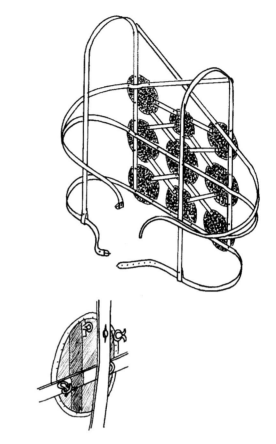

253 Relief with *miles phaleratus ostensionalis,* from the Cloister of the Basilica of San Paolo fuori le Mura, in situ, Rome (*author's collection*)

Military Decorations

Juvenal tells us that the early soldier or *miles* had decorations just on his armour and not on his dress, as the 'dandies' of the Imperial age did (**253**). This reference could well refer to the custom of wearing a rich suit of *phalerae* with its straps directly attached to leather garments or doublets. The most evident example can be seen on the gravestone of Musius, where the *phalerae* are worn over a leather structure (**254**) like a doublet over the *subarmale*. The wearing of a double-padded armour under the doublet provided twice as much protection for the warrior and enhanced the *phalerae* worn over the doublet. The magnificent *phalerae* from Lauersfort (**255**), echoing the decoration visible on the gravestone of the *centurio* Caelius who wears a *corona civica*[668] on his head, are the best-known silver military decorations of the early Imperial age (**157**). *Phalerae* of glass were made too, with images of generals and *principes*.[669]

Coronae and gold *torques* decorate the grave of C. Julius Macer, to which his companions dedicated a shield and a tombstone in the first century AD.[670] The *corona muralis*, as we can see on some sculptures of this age, has the shape of a fortified rampart crowned by a laurel *diadema*. In triumphs the spears of the marching soldiers were often decorated with laurel leaves,[671] and the soldiers crowned with different kinds of crowns.[672] The *torques* was composed of twisted rods of precious metal: gold for the Roman citizens and silver for the foreign allies.[673] It was flexible and ended with heads of wild animals, rosettes and so on. According to Pliny the Elder, the *armillae* (bracelets) were given only to Roman citizens,

254 Roman *phalerae* fastening system, first–third century AD (*ex Bruhn; reconstruction of Andrea Salimbeti*)

255 Lauersfort *phalerae*, first century AD (*photo DAI*)

256 (Above) Funerary monument of S. Vibius Gallus, from Amasia, AD 115–16 (*Archaeological Museum of Istanbul; author's photos, courtesy of the museum*).

Sextus was a *tricenarius*, *primipilarius* and *praefectus castrorum* of the *Legio XIII Gemina*. He is shown in action, on horseback, attacking Dacian warriors armed with *falces*. The momunent is impressive for all the *dona militaria* listed and represented here

and not to the allies. The gravestone of a cavalryman from Lancaster shows him in battle with a Celtic bracelet on his wrist, but perhaps this was the booty from the man he had just beheaded! (**PLATE VII, 257**)

The base of the statue of S. Vibius Gallus (**256**), from Amasia, who fought in the Dacian Wars, is a festival of Roman military decorations: two *vexilla*, three *coronae murales*, five *hastae purae*, a *corona aurea* and two *coronae vallares*. The dedicatory inscription also mentions *torques*, *armillae* and *phalerae* given as gifts for his military bravery. Interestingly, the inscriptions on his monument are in Latin and Greek, so we have preserved also the corresponding Greek and Latin terms for the military decorations:[674] *vexillum* (ουηξιλλος), *coronae murales* (στεφανοι

257 (Right) Tombstone of Roman *eques*, first century AD (*courtesy Lancashire Museums – Museum of Lancaster*).

This exceptional recently found gravestone from Lancaster shows the tombstone of a Roman cavalryman of Celto-Germanic origin, as could be attested by the long-sleeved tunic and the *armilla* on the right wrist, but especially by his trophy of an enemy's head. The inscription has been interpreted by the archaeologists as: 'To the gods of the Underworld. Insus, son of Vodullus, citizen of the Treveri, cavalryman of the *Ala Augusta*, *turma* of Victor, Curator. Domitia his heir has this set up'.[i] Note his three-fold crested Coolus helmet, the short trousers or *femoralia* and the *caligae*, as well as his wide *gladius* worn on the right side

---

i   Bull, 2007, p. 10.

πυργωτοι); *hastae purae* (λογχαι καθαραι); *corona aurea* (στεφανοs χρυσουs); and *coronae vallares* (στεφανοι τειχωτοι).

A symbol of imperial power was the *hasta summa imperii* often visible in the hands of generals and emperors. The *praefectus castrorum* had a *lancea* planted in front of his tent as a military insignia.[675] The *hasta* and its military use as badge of rank from the *beneficiarii* (**259**) and other officers of the staff of the emperor, or of the provincial governor,[676] can be followed in the age of the Principate thanks to real specimens and comparing them with those depicted on the monuments. These lances belonged to a special group of spear ensigns.[677] This kind of spear symbolised the supreme authority of the empire, sometimes the *domus divina* and the emperor himself.[678] As shown on the monument of the Cancelleria in Rome, where a praetorian *beneficiarius* is represented in the triumphal procession (*profectio*) of Domitian,[679] these were spearheads with broad-shouldered blades and two circular perforations or oblique incisions (**137**).[680] Some specimens were simply leaf-shaped *hastae* of large dimensions.[681] They were not used as weapons, having no tips, and they usually finished in rounded or acorn-shaped balls (*pila*)[682] or were palmette shaped.[683] Standards or bronze *tabulae ansatae* with inscriptions were sometimes attached to the holes perforated inside the blade.

Miniature versions of the *hasta summa imperii* in bronze and silver come from many corners of the empire, and a still unpublished specimen comes from the Iron Gate region in the Balkans (**258**). They were used by the officers and soldiers serving in the provincial *officia*, who received it on the occasion of their promotion, together with the rings and gems representing such insignia, and worn in the military belts (*cingula* and *baltei*).

Generally we can distinguish three different variants of such *hastae* in the first two centuries of the empire:

1. Those with a blade with long slots, with drilled holes in the metal and ending near the middle groove in small holes; this is visible for instance on the Cancelleria

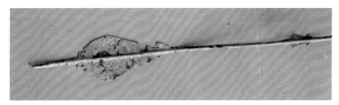

258 *Beneficiarius* miniature bronze spearhead, from Statio Cataractarum Diana (Davidovac, near Kladovo), second century AD (*Iron Gates Museum, Kladovo; author's photo, courtesy of the museum*).

This miniature spearhead is very similar to the first-century actual example from Kleinwinterheim, and has diagonal slots and holes for attaching to a military belt or baldric. It was a rank badge of officers belonging to the *officium consularis* of the *provincia* – such as *beneficiarii*, *speculatores*, *immunes*, *frumentarii* and sometimes *centuriones* as well – that were charged with political, tax collection, traffic control and inspection duties[i]

i   Kovacs, 2005, p. 956.

259 *Beneficiarius* of a Flavian *legio*, from the Templum Gentis Flaviae, AD 95 (*Museo Nazionale Romano and Ann Arbor Museum, drawing by Graham Sumner*)

This extraordinary piece of sculpture from the *Templum Gentis Flaviae* is thought to represent a *beneficiarius* of the praetorian guard of the Emperor Domitianus, who built the temple around AD 94–5. However, it could also be a representation of a *beneficiarius* of the legions who joined the emperors Vespasian and Titus in the Judaean campaign when we consider that the Templum Gentis Flaviae was a celebration of the glory of the Flavian dynasty and of the victorious war against the Jews, culminating in the destruction of Jerusalem in AD 70. The warrior wears an Attic helmet with a richly embossed frontal *diadema* and a *lorica segmentata* of the Corbridge (Corstopitum) type

relief, on a specimen from the Sanctuary of Mars in Kleinwinterheim[684] and on the miniature specimen from Kladovo (**258**).

2. Those with wide hollows, which are deep in the upper part of the spear and again, near the middle groove, end in small holes; examples of this are the miniature spear from Vindonissa Museum, the 30-cm long spear from Sarszentmiklos[685] and a spear from the Saône River, variously dated to the first and the third centuries AD (**137**).[686]

3. Those with short slots and big holes without a direct connection; a early specimen[687] of this category is a miniature lance from Mainz, represented on a military silver *fibula*, probably belonging to one of the officers *insigniti* with the right to wear such a spear. In this specimen, the miniature spearhead is represented between two miniature ring-swords of Sarmatian type, also a rank badge.[688]

PLATE VII Insus, Roman *eques* of *Ala Augusta*, second half of first century AD: this cavalryman has been copied from the gravestone of Insus, a Roman cavalryman recently found in Lancaster (**257**). The most striking feature of the gravestone is the helmet, which is unlike any other represented on a Roman tombstone found in Britain. It has a round bowl with a wide but thick brim marked with two parallel lines, and there are two well-defined cheekpieces. There is a central front-to-back crest that appears to be of horsehair and two side plumes. Although the left plume is damaged, the right is clearly rendered to look like a feather. The use of side tubes with feathers on first-century AD helmets was the continuation of the ancient tradition of the warriors dedicated to the god Mars, wearing the so-called *geminae pinnae*. The only other Romano-British cavalry tombstone that has them is that of Flavinus, *signifer* of the *Ala Petriana*.[i]

The helmet could be of Agen–Port type, with a rounded bowl with a wide although narrow brim and cheekpieces that are a good match for those on the Lancaster tombstone. The cheekpieces also, however, suggest that the Lancaster helmet did have Gallic origins. Alternatively, the helmet might be of the Coolus type, as we have chosen in the reconstruction. The closest parallel to the Lancaster helmet is the type Robinson called type E. The type E has a rounded bowl and three examples have been found in Britain, one from Berkhampstead, another from St Albans and the third from the Thames in London, all dating to the early part of the first century AD.[ii] The ones from London and St Albans both have side plume-tubes and a central crest holder. These helmets have a narrow brim but are also fitted with a reinforcing peak or browband above, which is perhaps what the artist of our tombstone may have been attempting to show. The cheekpieces of the Coolus type E are undecorated and have a cut-out at the rear that would leave the ears uncovered. Again this is a close match to the Lancaster type but is of further interest because Robinson identified those cheekpieces that had covered ears as belonging to cavalrymen. However, the Arc d'Orange shows cavalry *c.* AD 21 wearing Coolus helmets (**315e, 315g, 315h, 315i, 315j, 315k, 315r, 315t**), so there is a real possibility that the Lancaster helmet is of this type and in particular the E variant.

The sword brandished by the cavalryman on his tombstone appears to be an infantry *gladius*. That the sword is seen fully drawn is another unusual feature as the classic cavalry pose is stabbing the fallen Barbarian adversary with a spear or *hasta*. Nevertheless sword lengths on cavalry tombstones vary and those of Dannicus from Cirencester and that on the un-inscribed cavalry tombstone from Ribchester are even shorter. A sword baldric strap is shown passing over the left shoulder and down to the soldier's right side where one would expect to see a scabbard but none is visible, nor is there any indication that one was intended.

There is no indication of body armour on the man's torso. A sculpted edge below the man's waist and resting on his upper right thigh would appear to be the lower edge of this armour. There is also no suggestion that he is not wearing armour of some sort as there is no attempt to show any folds that might imply he is simply wearing a leather tunic, as on the tombstone of Silius of *Ala Picentiana*.[iii] We cannot however exclude the possibility that he was wearing a plain leather corselet,

like those represented on many cavalrymen on Trajan's Column, clearly distinguished from the cavalrymen wearing mail armour. The scalloped borders of such corselets were often rounded, as seems to be the case on the Lancaster tombstone, and often reinforced by bosses at the edges.

Around the only visible wrist of the Lancaster cavalryman is a feature that could be interpreted as an *armilla*, a military award. The most likely example is the version that looks like a small Celtic torque, from which these awards probably derived. However, the torque is a ring with two knobbed terminals, which does not look entirely like what we can see on the tombstone. Instead, a Celtic or Pictish bracelet booty of war could be a possible explanation. The Achavrail armlet, preserved in Inverness Museum, matches perfectly with the bracelet represented on the gravestone.

The cavalryman also has a possible leather tunic, with the turned-back cuffs of a long tunic sleeve. The same feature can be seen on the tombstone of T. Flavius Bassus from Cologne,[iv] but is illustrated even more dramatically on the sculpture of a Romano-Celtic warrior now in Avignon Museum.[v] Furthermore in this particular example a decoration in the form of a zigzag line extends from the cuffs up the wrist, highlighting that the band around the wrist is indeed a cuff.

It is not surprising to discover that the Lancaster cavalryman wears short trousers, called *bracae* by the Romans, which would be eminently suitable for riding. They were probably wool, like the tunic, although examples in leather have also been found. It may have been up to the individual as to which type they preferred and there is no clear indication which type is illustrated on the tombstone.

Around his shoulders the soldier wears a cloak of a type called a *sagum*, again most likely of wool. This is fastened by a large distinctive brooch shaped like a rose. It is possible this was bronze, with each petal filled with coloured enamel. The Romans believed the *sagum* had Gallic origins and there is no modern evidence to dispute this. It would be blanket shaped and probably doubled up as such on campaign. The cloak was edged on all sides with tablet weaving and on two sides by a fringe, a feature that can also be observed on some Roman cavalry cloaks but not, alas, on ours. A number of colours can be associated with military cloaks, including red, blue and white, but the most popular colour was a yellow-brown that may have been a natural wool colour retained to keep the natural waterproof lanolins. The boots on the Lancaster tombstone show no ridge, so there is every possibility that he has chosen to wear the enclosed type of boot. In the reconstruction they have been copied from a specimen found in Vindolanda.

Although the saddlecloth is visible on the original sculpture, the Roman saddle, with its distinctive four horns, is not, but it has been incorporated into the reconstruction. There are no elaborate *phalerae* on the harness junctions, only three strips hanging from the rear haunch strap. There is, however, a fringed breastband called, with a modern word, a peytral. These had both decorative and protective functions. A possible leather peytral has been identified at Vindolanda, while an almost identical example is displayed on another tombstone from Ribchester, not far from Lancaster.

i   Robinson, 1976, pp. 4–5.
ii   Robinson, 1975, pls 54–5, 58.
iii Junkelmann, 1992, fig. 46.

iv Junkelmann, 1992, fig. 84.
v   Robinson, 1975, pl. 461.
vi Dixon and Southern, 1992, fig. 39.

~ CAVALRY EQUIPMENT: THE MAN ~

Josephus gives us a detailed description of cavalry weaponry:[689]

> . . . The horsemen have a long sword [*machaira*] on their right sides, and axes or a long pole [*kontos*] in their hand; a shield [*thureos*] also lies by them obliquely on one side of their horses, with three or more darts [*akontes*] that are borne in their quiver, having broad points, and not smaller than spears. They have also headpieces [*kranê*] and breastplates [*thôrakes*], in like manner as have all the footmen. And for those that are chosen to be about the general, their armour in no way differs from that of the horsemen belonging to other troops; and he always leads the legions forth, this is the duty of the general. . .

Shafted Weapons

For the cavalry the primary weapons were the spear and the javelin, which received different denominations according to their different sizes:[690] *hasta*, *contus*, *lancea*,[691] *speculum*, *jaculum*[692] and *tragula*. The blade shape varied notably: leaf-shaped, three-cornered, four-cornered, always with spouts and a slim shaft, and were principally made of ash, cherry or hazel wood (**260**). The longer specimens were usually fitted with a butt (**67**), which allowed the cavalrymen to insert the light javelins into a quiver at the side of the saddle (**280**).[693] The usual length of the spear blade varied from 10 to 35 cm,

as is visible in many spear points from Newstead, Scotland, and dated to the first to second centuries AD.[694] The *pilum* was used by the cavalrymen only in the defence of their fortified camps.

Swords

The *spatha* had now consolidated its position as the weapon of cavalry (**182**, **212**, **261**, **267**). Its origin must be somewhere in the mix of the characteristics of the La Tène III sword with the new Roman *gladius* of the Pompeii type, which was longer and reduced in width, but it always kept its effectiveness for use mainly as stabbing weapon. This is apparent if we compare two sword blades from Newstead:[695] the infantry *gladius* is 49.5 cm long and 5.4 cm wide; the cavalry sword is 64.3 long and 3.6 cm wide, and it is lighter in weight than the infantry sword. It is worth mentioning that a Mainz specimen, 76.5 cm long, has the name of the swordmaker (*Sabini*) stamped on the surviving tang.[696] This specimen is more similar to the previous Late Republican sword of the

260 Cavalry spear points and butt from Vindonissa, first–second century AD (*photo Vindonissa museum; courtesy of the museum*).
    On the original specimens we can see that more attention was spent in the production of the long spear blade, while the points of mass-produced javelins and small missiles were much more roughly made. Usually the long blades had a middle ridge and sharpened edges. When such a blade was inside a body, it created serious wounds even if the hit was not immediately fatal

261 *Eques*, Trajan's Column, scene XXVII (*cast, Roma, Museo della Civiltà Romana, author's photo, courtesy of the museum*)

Alesia type. Other early Principate cavalry specimens are from Camelon and Rottweil.[697]

The general length of the first- and second-century cavalry *spathae* was of about 60–70 cm, on average 63 cm, with a width of 3.5 cm and a rhomboid section.[698] The grip was made of bone, ivory or wood, as that of the *gladius*. The handgrip had six grooves down it and four horizontal grooves for the fingers. The handguard had a leaf plate, but not of course true *quillons*. The pommel was large, mainly spherical or oval in section. The extraordinary correspondence between actual specimens of handguards from Vindonissa (**213**) and Trajan's Column (**182**, **267**) confirms the precision of the Roman artists in the execution of the military fittings on triumphal monuments. The *spatha* was enclosed in a scabbard or *vagina* with bronze mounts and fittings.

Single-edged swords were also in use. A gravestone of a cavalryman from the territory of Bosnia-Herzegovina shows a Thracian auxiliary cavalryman using his short single-edge sword, which corresponds perfectly to a specimen from Vindonissa, both dated to the first century AD (**262**). The Lancaster cavalryman mentioned above seems to have preferred a *gladius* of the old type for hunting heads (**PLATE VII**, **257**)!

262 a) (Top) Roman auxiliary cavalryman with Thracian sword, first–second century AD (*from a panel in the Zemalisky Museum, Sarajevo; drawing by Elaine Norbury*). **b)** Roman auxiliary cavalryman's Thracian sword, first–second century AD, (*from Vindonissa, photo Vindonissa Museum, courtesy of the Museum*)

264 (Below) Cavalryman holding the head of a Dacian warrior, Adamclisi relief, *metopa* VII, Trajanic age (*drawing by Graham Sumner*)

263 Detail of *eques* helmet, Trajan's Column, scene XXVII (*cast, Roma, Museo della Civiltà Romana, author's photo, courtesy of the museum*).

Shields

The old *parma* was still mentioned[699] and used at this time (**156, 211**). A *denarius* of Augustus celebrating his nephews Caius and Lucius Caesar as *principes juventutis* show the *parma* or *aspis* given to them[700] as *exemplum virtutis* of the young and noble Roman cavalrymen.[701] New shield shapes also appeared, as a result of the introduction of Celtic horsemanship, equipment and manpower in the cavalry. The shield of the cavalry (*thureos*[702]) was now mainly of a hexagonal[703] or oval shape,[704] sometimes obtuse (**262, 264, 315e, 315i, 315j, 315r, 315t**).[705] The oval shield was the commonest, with a construction similar to those of the infantry shields (**182, 212, 261, 267**). They were not curved like the legionary shield, but flat. They must have been rather large and heavy, as shown by the remains of some shields, very similar to the infantry *scuta* of the Republican time. The average shield's dimensions were 114 × 66 cm. In the middle of its wooden structure there was a hole of about 10 cm in diameter for the passage of the handgrip, usually made of iron or wood covered by leather, and protected on the outer surface, by a circular *umbo*, whose flat rim was fixed to the wooden surface by four or more rivets.

The shields were fitted with carrying straps. A passage of Josephus[706] says that, during marches, the Roman *equites* of Vespasianus had their shields attached to the saddle, hanging from the horse's sides. This is confirmed by numerous funerary reliefs.[707]

A good specimen of a leather *tegimen* for a cavalry shield comes from Valkenburg; it is oval in shape.[708] It was made of two separate but identical pieces of leather, joined in the middle by laces. As with the infantry shields, these covers helped to protect the shield against damp; they were usually made of goatskin and had *tabulae ansatae* applied to them, indicating the owner and the unit.

The surface of cavalry shields was lavishly painted or decorated by embossed appliqués (**265**).

Helmets

The typical shape of the Coolus–Haguenau helmet is perfectly visible on the Arc d'Orange (**315e, 315g, 315h, 315i, 315j, 315k, 315r, 315t**)[709] and possibly also on the Lancaster gravestone (**PLATE VII, 257**), but a new type also began to appear: the helmets of pseudo-Attic shapes, which are the most commonly represented on the first- to second-century monuments. They are clearly visible on the Rhine tombstones, furnished with a *diadema* and entirely covering the head, with an underdeveloped neck guard.[710]

265 Detail of *eques*, Trajan's Column, scene XXVIII (*cast, Roma, Museo della Civiltà Romana, author's photo, courtesy of the museum*).

Although they used bridles, in battle the Roman cavalrymen would have relied on leg control, since their hands would have been engaged in fighting and holding the weapons[i]

---

i   Dixon and Southern, 1992, p. 63.

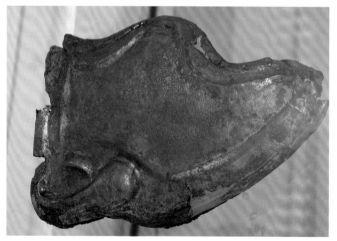

266 Cavalry helmet cheek guards from Njimegen, first–second century AD (*collection of Museum Het Valkhof, Nijmegen; courtesy of the conservator*)

267 Detail of *eques*, Trajan's Column, scene XXVII (*cast, Roma, Museo della Civiltà Romana, author's photo, courtesy of the museum*).

Note the ring-mail armour and the pommel of his sword, identical to the Vindonissa finds (**213**)

268 Bronze helmet from Lunca Mureşului, end of second century AD (*Museum Unirii, Alba Julia, replica; courtesy of Professor Radu Ciobanu*)

These correspond archaeologically to different specimens found in various localities, commonly designated by scholars to be like the Koblenz-Weiler-Bubenheim type.[711] Sometimes, on the sculptures, they are represented as plain, and in this way they correspond to the simple helmet found in Newstead fort, a very simple Attic helmet now missing the *diadema*.[712] But on many tombstones[713] and original specimens the skull is decorated in the shape of hair, and the embossed cheek guards include a representation of the ears.[714] The cheek guards (**266**) are usually cut from an iron plate and covered by a gold or silvered sheet, glued to the iron backing with a special gum (resin).

A splendid specimen of this type, belonging to an officer, was found in Xanten (Germany), completely made of iron but covered by a silver sheet and decorated on the *diadema* with a small *clypeus* representing the Emperor Caligula.[715] The bowl of the helmet was decorated by embossed hair, and a relief of a laurel crown was on the hair as well. Helmets with embossed hair are visible on the Arc d'Orange (**315f**), on the Julio-Claudian army relief from Turin (**106**) and a laurel crown embossed on the skull is perfectly represented on Trajan's Column (**182, 212, 261, 263, 267**).[716] A similar helmet in iron covered by gilded silver and embossed on the *diadema* with a lion inscribed in the *clypeus* has recently been found in Market Harborough, together with a hoard of 3,000 coins.[717]

The use of this kind of helmet begins to decline during the second century AD, in favour of a new helmet, the Guisborough type (**268**).[718] It was still a helmet of pseudo-Attic type, but the tendency of the cheek guards, fitted with ear protections and richly embossed,[719] was always to enclose the face of the individuals more, leaving only the central part of it visible, and so creating an open mask helmet. It was the beginning of an evolution that continued in the succeeding period.

The passage between the two typologies could have taken place during the second century AD. A helmet from the Iron Gate Museum (**269**)[720] could be the linking element, because the helmet (although very fragmentarily preserved) still shows elements linked to the Weiler typology as well as new characteristics of the Guisborough type. The iron helmet is of pseudo-Attic shape, and still preserves the frontal *diadema* in good condition, covered in gilded silver, and richly embossed on the whole surface with the curls of human hair. The small fragments of the bowl show that the whole surface was decorated with lines representing human hairs. *Diadema* and bowls of these types are visible on the monument of Flavius Bassus, for instance, or on the sculptures from Lake Fucino (**279**).[721] But unlike the Weiler types, the surviving back is deep, and it terminates in a medium-sized sloping neck flange, like the helmet from the Sava River, dated to the beginning of the first century AD.[722] From under the browband are riveted the rather shallow ear guards, not made in one piece with the rest, as in most part of the later specimens of the Guisborough type, but attached separately. So the helmet seems to be a transitional type from the Weiler to the

269 Fragments of a helmet of Attic shape with embossed browband, from Egeta (Brza Palanka, near Kladovo), second century AD, (*Iron Gates Museum, Kladovo; author's photo, courtesy of the museum*)

270 (Opposite, left) First-century AD type cavalry helmet from a Thracian tumulus at Philippopolis, iron and silver (*Sofia Archaeological Museum; courtesy of Professor Lyudmil Vagalinsky.*)

The helmet was found together with a sword, an *umbo* and a very rich hoards of silver vessels from Campania.[i] It was probably used by a Roman Thracian elite cavalryman armed as a heavy *contarius*

---

i   Junkelmann, 1996, fig. 50, p. 31.

Guisborough–Niederbieber type. It is difficult to say what is the purpose of the ring attached upon the brow: perhaps it was used for fixing some kind of crest, perhaps for attaching a visor or, simply, to help putting it on.

The most beautiful helmet of the new typology is the Theilenhofen helmet, which belonged to different men during the second half of the second century AD.[723] Other kinds of helmets could be ascribed to cavalry use, such as the Witcham helmet,[724] but generally it is not easy to distinguish whether a helmet was used by infantry or cavalry.

The helmets of cavalrymen were often fitted with splendid visors or masks (**270, 271, 274, 275, 276**), and a wide range of mask helmets have been found in the graves of Roman cavalrymen or in military bases. The common opinion, that these helmets were used only in games and combined with sporting equipment should definitely be rejected: it is absolutely contrary to the ideology of the ancient warrior. The exhibition of precious arms in front of the enemy was an element of psychological terror and corresponds to the will to show the invincible power of Rome. It will be enough to quote Josephus:[725]

. . . So the soldiers, according to custom, opened the cases wherein their arms before lay covered, and marched with their breastplates on, as did the horsemen lead their horses in their fine trappings. Then did the places that were before the city shine very splendidly for a great way; nor was there anything so grateful to Titus' own men, or so terrible to the enemy, as that sight. For the whole old wall, and the north side of the temple, were full of spectators, and one might see the houses full of such as looked at them; nor was there any part of the city which was not covered over with their multitudes; nay, a very great consternation seized upon the hardiest of the Jews themselves, when they saw all the army in the same place, together with the fineness of their arms, and the good order of their men.

Moreover, many mask helmets have been found in graves together with weapons and equipment definitely equipped for fighting (**272**).[726]

A particular kind of helmet comes from Ostrov in Romania: it is tall, in the shape of a Phrygian cap, with the curving apex shaped like an eagle's head (**273**). The whole helmet crown is embossed with a feather pattern. Robinson dated it to the second half of the second century AD, to the rule of Antoninus

271 (Above) First–second-century AD masked helmet from Kostol, iron and silver (*Belgrade, National Museum, courtesy of the museum*).

The helmet was found near the Trajanic bridge of Kostol (Serbia), and it has often been debated whether this helmet belonged to some late Hellenistic army or to the Roman elite warriors. This last theory has prevailed.[i] The helmet has a shallow skull reaching just below the tips or the ears. The lower rim of both skull and mask is pierced for the attachment of a lining. According to Robinson, the mask was made by a very specialist sculptor of portraiture[ii]

i   Junkelmann, 1996, fig. 33, p. 23.
ii   Robinson, 1975, pl. 309, p. 112.

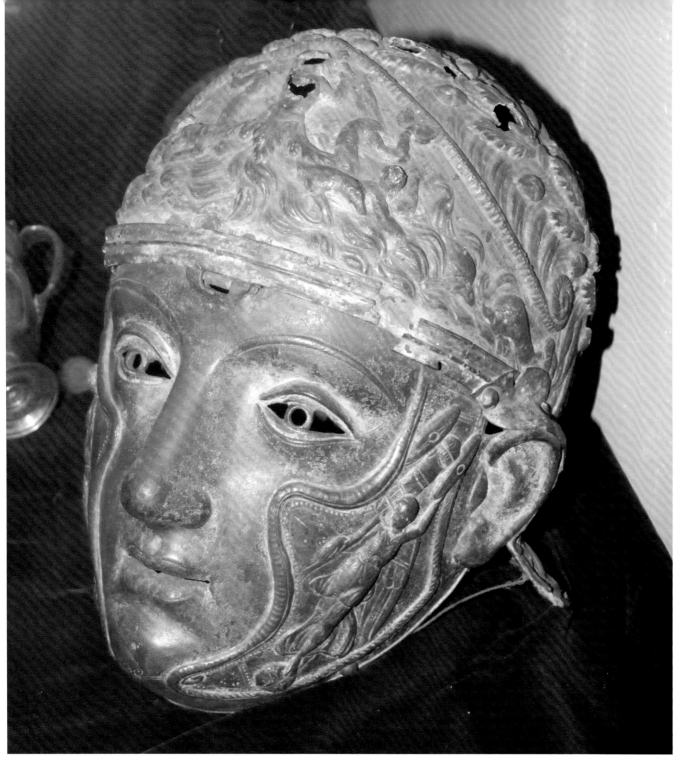

272 (Above) Helmet of a Thracian Chieftain, AD 45, from his grave in Vize, Thrace, Istanbul (*Archaeological Museum, author's photo, courtesy of the museum*)

The helmet has got the form of a first-century cavalry helmet of Attic type, furnished with a mask visor. It is highly embossed with a decorated brow-plate, the embossed hair is decorated with a *corona civica* of oak leaves and the mask is embossed with check-pieces[i]

273 (Opposite page) Bronze helmets from Ostrov, second half of second century AD (*Constanta, Archaeological Museum; courtesy of the museum*).

a) (Top half of page) The helmet is 26 × 22.4 × 16 cm. The tall helmet shows a central line ending in an apex shaped like an eagle's head. At the side are two snakes with heads meeting on the front of

the helmet. Under it, on the front of the brow, is the god Mars, flanked by two victories. On the back is embossed a Medusa's head. On the surviving linked cheekpiece is embossed one of the Dioscuri (Castor or Pollux). The whole helmet is decorated with an embossed feather pattern.[ii]

b) (Bottom half of page) The helmet has been preserved in three parts. The visor is missing; probably it never had one. The bowl has a tripart metallic crest, the median one running over the neck guard in the shape of a boar's head, flanked by two sphinxes surmounted by Minerva and a Leo. The neck guard is decorated by embossed victories and laurel crowns. The front of the open mask is embossed with hair, and under the ears there are holes for fastening to the bowl.[iii] The helmet measures 20 × 24.5 cm

i   RR, 1975, p.118, pls. 341–4

ii   Garbsch, 1978, p. 73 pl. 32
iii Garbsch, 1978, pl. 27.

273a

273b

274 Waal helmet from Njimegen, second half second century AD (*Leiden Museum, author's photo, courtesy of the conservator*).

Among other splendid specimens of the early Imperial age a precious helmet from Nijmegen, was decorated with the *diadema* with a prominent laurel-embossed decoration,[i] and has a mask attachment. Helmets distinguished by prominent peaks projecting from the rim of sometimes richly embossed skull pieces are typical of the late first century and beginning of second century AD, like the specimens from Ribchester and Newstead

275 Cavalry visor mask for helmet, first century AD (*collection of Museum Het Valkhof, Nijmegen; courtesy of the conservator*)

276 Reconstruction of cavalry helmet with mask and attached hair, first century AD (*collection of Museum Het Valkhof, Nijmegen; courtesy of the conservator*).

The psychological terror of enemies facing such a vision make it unlikely that the helmet was merely decorated for games. A distinction between a 'parade' helmet and a 'war' helmet was not conceivable in the ancient world: both could be used for war, with the most beautiful specimens used also for parades and games

i   Junkelmann, 2002, fig. 160; late first–begin of the second century AD.

Pius, and attributed it to a Sarmatian origin. The original Sarmatian shape was transformed by a Roman smith with artwork decorated with motifs linked to the classical heritage of Greece and Rome: the god Mars, the head of Medusa, the Dioscuri on the cheekpieces. Perhaps it is this tall kind of helmet that is represented on the tombstone of the auxiliary Sarmatian cavalryman from Chester (Deva) (**277**).[727]

Armour

As a result of the need to combine mobility with protection, the *eques* or *ippeus*[728] mainly used two kinds of armours: mail and the leather coat.

The chain mail, in the Augustan age (**315e**, **315g**, **315h**, **315i**, **315l**, **315r**, **315t**), enlarged on the Celtic system of a double hook fastening in bronze[729] and iron. The double hooks are always of serpentine form (**159**, **160**),[730] hooking behind further buttons on the shoulder guards. Sometimes, as in the relief from Mavilly,[731] the hooks are riveted inside the shoulder straps, to connect with other rivets on the shirt.

On the second century monuments the shoulderpieces slowly disappeared from cavalry mail (**261**, **278**) but are still visible on the Ephesus ivory panels (**121**). The mail was now worn like a shirt, often over a leather coat with scalloped edges. It is a matter of debate whether the so-called *segmentata* was also worn by cavalrymen. Laminated shoulder guards worn in combination with leather or mail[732] armour are attested by the Arlon monument.[733] The iron laminated *lorica* could also have been worn on horseback, considering that the cataphracts wore similar tubular and banded iron armours

278 (Above) *Equites* with *vexilla*, Adamclisi relief, *metopa* III, Trajanic age (*drawing by Graham Sumner*)

277 (Left) Sarmatian auxiliary (Rhoxolan or Jazyge), Deva, East Gate, second half of the second century AD (*Tomatofarm reconstruction*).

The cavalryman is reconstructed from the famous Deva tombstone of the Sarmatian cavalryman at the Chester Museum. The tall, conical helmet has been copied from the Ostrov specimen of the Sarmatian type. The man has body red tattoos and has painted his face in red and black. The fringed rectangular woollen *sagum* has been copied from a specimen found in Mons Claudianus. The scale armour comes down nearly to his knees and has short scale sleeves to the elbows; the sleeves were attached separately. The iron scales were sewn on to a leather background and positioned so that they partially cover each other. The ankle boots are made of goatskin, tied with leather bands that passed around the ankle and under the sole.

The wind-sock tubular body of the Draco standard follows the descriptions of Arrian: 'sewing pieces of dyed material together'. The different pieces are silk covered. A dagger is attached to the thigh via two pairs of wings with leather straps, in the typical Sarmatian way. The horse straps show silver *phalerae* found in Chester The wearing of the 'Scythian whip'[i] was a prerogative of the nomad cavalryman, a custom also kept in the Roman army. The Sarmatians used to drink the blood of their horses if the necessity arose,[ii] a tradition still practised by the steppe nomads of the Middle Ages

i   Mart., *Ep.*, X, 62: '*cirrata Scytae loris horridis pellis*' (the Scythian whip made of straps of horrible skins).
ii   Mart., *Lib. Spect.*, 3.

279a **279b**

279 *Equites* in *lorica segmentata* on horseback, second century AD (*Museo Nazionale di Arte Sacra della Marsica, Sezione Archeologica,*

*Castello di Celano; **a)** author's photo, courtesy of the Soprintendenza per i Beni Archeologici per l'Abruzzo; **b)** detail drawing by Graham Sumner)*

280 Funerary relief with cavalryman from Apulum (Alba Julia), second century AD (*drawing by Graham Sumner*).

The cavalryman, probably an *eques vexillationis* of the *Legio XIII Gemina*, wears a helmet with an eagle metallic crest, like the specimen found in Hedderneim.[i] His scale armour has various parallels in scale armour fragments from the former territory of Dacia,[ii] and his carrying of two javelins corresponds perfectly to the Josephus passage in *Bellum Judaicum*, III, 5, 5, 96

---

i   Robinson, 1975, col. pl. IV; Garbsch, 1978, pl. 29.
ii   Popescu, 1998, fig. 118, scale bronze armour from Ulpia Traiana Sarmizegetusa.

but the only evidence for this is a relief from Alba Fucens, showing two cavalryman clad in *lorica segmentata* (**279**).[734] Horsemen in leather banded *lorica* are instead clearly visible on the Portonaccio Sarcophagus, together with horsemen clad in leather surcoats and doublets, or covered by long scale armours of the *plumata* type (**115**).

Scale armour was also widely employed. *Stelae* and monuments from all over the empire show cavalrymen clad in scale armour,[735] and from the Vize grave a complete suit of armour made of very small bronze scales has been recovered.[736] The Adamclisi monument (**264**), a terracotta figure from Alba Julia (**280**) and the figurative sources of Marcus Aurelius' time show cavalrymen clad in hip-length iron and bronze scale armour, sometimes with scalloped edges.

The use of linen, horn and leather armour by the Roman cavalrymen, alongside the metallic one, is explicity stated by Arrian.[737] Leather armour for the cavalry was worn the same way as metallic armour, so it was shorter and made of calf leather. A possible specimen can be seen on the stele of Niger,[738] today universally considered to be ring-mail armour. The *ala* horseman might instead be covered by a short rigid leather corselet, fitted with rigid shoulder guards, closed on the upper breast by hooks and laces. The degree of protection offered would have been very similar to that of the protecting coats of coarse leather worn by the European sixteenth- and seventeenth-century cavalry. Another possible leather armour is represented on the tombstone of Insus (**257**), where it is shaped like the leather corselet visible on many cavalrymen on Trajan's Column.

Leather muscled armour, with Attic-style helmet and round shield, seems to be part of the defensive equipment of the cavalrymen charged with the defence of the desert roads, represented on a pottery sherd from Mons Claudianus.[739] The Hellenistic traditions continued in the local garb in the lands that had been under strong Greek influence for centuries.

~ CAVALRY EQUIPMENT: THE HORSE ~

A good breed of horses was the Aemonian, a kind of Thessalian type, recorded in the campaigns against the Parthians.[740] In the early Imperial age we find the most complete equipment for the horse: bridle (*frenum, frena, freni*), reins (*habenae, lora*), hackamore noseband (*psalion, salivarium*), bit (*oreae, frenum*[741]), breast-harness (*antilena*), breeching (*postilena*), girth (*cingulum*) and metallic fittings (*phalerae*). The saddle (*scordiscus*)[742] was formed by the *stratum* or *ephippium*[743] (with a main body in wood or straw, covered by leather[744]) with four corners (*cornicula*) and a saddlecloth (*tapetum*),[745] that of the emperor being of red-purple dyed (*fucus*) cloth.

The metal stiffeners of these four-cornered saddles were made of bronze sheets, bent over in the upper part and widening gradually towards the lower part, losing its profile, sometimes with a semi-circular opening. These plates had a row of circular perforations within a raised border around the edge. Their function was to reinforce the four corners of the saddle, which helped to keep the rider on the horse and carrying out manoeuvres on horseback. The excavations of the military camps of Newstead, Rottweil, Boljetin[746] and many others have revealed such plates in great number, belonging to the time period of the first to second century AD.

The bits were mainly of two types: the less severe iron snaffle bit[747] and the very severe curb[748] bit. The first was of Celtic origin, designed to be used two handed; the second was derived from Thracian horsemanship, and allowed the cavalryman to control the horse with only one hand. A fragment of the second type has been recovered from the hoard of Ulpia Traiana Sarmizegetusa.[749] Lateral bronze *phalerae*, with three apertures, were sometimes used to attach the bridles to the bits.[750]

Nosebands (hackmores) were metallic fittings[751] consisting of a bar running above the nose and under the chin (**282**).[752] Their function was to prevent the horse from opening its mouth and losing the bit. A very important monument, the

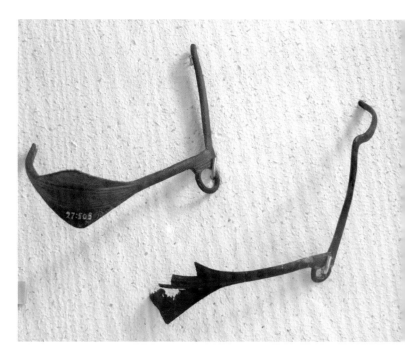

282 (Above and below) Roman huckamores first–second century AD (*photo Vindonissa Museum; courtesy of the museum*)

281 (Below) Horse harness elements and fittings from Vindonissa, first–second century AD (*photo Vindonissa museum; courtesy of the museum*)

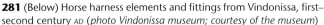

tombstone of Flavius Bassus of *Ala Noricorum*, shows that in the late first century AD *equites* used the huckamores in conjunction with the bits.[753]

From the *antilena* and *postilena* harness hung bronze, silver and gilded pendants of various shape and dimensions: trifid, double phallic, *pelta*-shaped, round, leaf-shaped, *lunulae*, and so on (**281**).[754] The equestrian statue of Marcus Aurelius in Rome shows *phalerae* ornamenting the junction of the brow and noseband with the frontal strap.[755] A horse's head found in Cartoceto near Ancona in 1946 shows the same system of harness, but this time the frontal strap is decorated with figures of gods (Quirinus and Venus).[756]

The harness was composed of many different elements at junctions, mostly in bronze, for the straps to pass through.

They were often circular with oblong fittings for joining straps.[757]

The monument of Niger shows a leather saddle covering with pillion, linked by the strap harness on the *antilina* and *postilina*. Much more splendid is the harness of the horse of Iulius Primus from Trier:[758] the saddle cover hangs down with long fringes and pendants on the borders. The oval shield – as described by Josephus – is attached, similar to many images on Trajan's Column, on the horse's left side. The cavalry fittings were very often gold, and these were not necessarily only those of the commanders.[759] Horseshoes (*soleae*) are frequently preserved at archaeological sites.[760] They were iron (*soleae ferreae*) or of organic material (*soleae spartae*).

~ THE *HIPPIKA GYMNASIA* ~

Arrian's text, written in about AD 136, gives a detailed description of the sporting games performed by the Roman cavalry, the *Hippika Gymnasia* (ιππικα γυμνασια). The cavalrymen, completely clad in special armour, took turns at charging and defending, throwing javelins with no iron heads, feigning assaults and attacks, so showing their ability and precision in front of senior officers and honoured guests.[761]

The equipment of the *Hippika* was the most decorative and rich of all the army. Luxurious equipment was conceived for use in parades or games, although this function did not exclude its employment also on battlefield. It would have been especially complete and protective: it comprised a gilded bronze or iron helmet, which covered the whole face like a mask, with eyeholes so that 'they can see while remaining protected'.[762] These helmets were though not commonly worn by all the cavalrymen performing the games, but only by those 'of distinguished station or superior in horsemanship'. The helmets have been found in various locations (**270**, **271**, **284**). They had Hellenistic origins, developed in local variants by the Thracians, easterners and Italics.[763] A common shape of the mask was that shown in the portrait of Alexander the Great, as demonstrated by many specimens of the last decades of the first century and through all the second century AD, from Silistra, Israel and Herzogenburg.[764] There is a helmet with oriental features from Emesa (Syria).[765]

Two-piece mask helmets, such as the iron specimen recently found in Germany,[766] had ears made together with the main mask and made with five holes that allowed the wearer to hear aural signals, an important element in games or battle. In some first-century AD types[767] the mask was hinged to the skull of the helmet by a clasp positioned at the height of the brow (**275**, **276**).

Other masks – with the same system of clasps – were simply visors attached to the skull of the helmet (**274**), such as the bronze and iron specimen from Volubilis, dated to about AD 60–80[768] and linked to the presence of an auxiliary force in Mauretania Tingitana. All masks and visors were internally lined with leather, so that the metallic material would have not chafed the face of the wearer[769].

The statement of Arrian that not all the helmets were masked is confirmed by the 'open-mask' specimens, i.e. helmets with the opening for the face, in which the mask was not inserted. A precious specimen of this category, dated to the Antonine period, comes from Ostrov, on the Black Sea (**273**).

In the accounts of Arrian[770] the yellow crests of the cavalry helmets are described as *xanthai* or bright blond. This is the most important reference to the crest colour of the Roman cavalry (**PLATE VII**). The Romans obtained a bright yellow colour from sulphur or saffron. The function was, hovever, merely decorative, for the purposes of the *Hippika Gymnasia*: '. . . in the charge, if there is a breeze, these float out to make a pleasant sight . . .' Some first- and second-century AD helmets, like the specimens from Ribchester, Newstead and Kostol (**271**) are furnished with plume loops above the brow or a plume tube riveted onto the left or the central part of the skull-piece.

No armour was used in the *Hippika Gymnasia*, according to Arrian, but only Cimmerian tunics, scarlet, purple or multi-coloured. These tunics are well known from Roman representations of Bosphoreans, Scythians, Amazons and Phrygians, where it is possible to see a long-sleeved loose multi-coloured shirt. The trousers were not of the baggy type of the Parthians (*sarabara*), but fitted to the legs (*anaxyrida*). Very interesting examples of this costume are shown on the frescoes of the Mithraeum from Santa Maria Capuavetere (**283**).

283 (Above and detail below) Mithra Tauroctonus and the Dadophori, frescoes from the Capua Mithraeum, second–third century AD (*author's photo courtesy of the Soprintendenza Speciale per i Beni Archaeologici di Napoli e Caserta*)

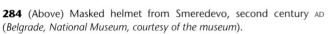

284 (Above) Masked helmet from Smeredevo, second century AD (*Belgrade, National Museum, courtesy of the museum*).

This masked helmet belongs to the category of cavalry 'sports' helmets with the form of idealised youthful faces with boldly embossed wavy hair across the brow. A very similar specimen is from Harsova (Romania)[i]

i   Petculescu, 2003, cat. 333.

286 Shield *umbo*, with representation of Minerva, second half of the second century to the first half of the third century AD (*ex Guttman collection, Christie's photo*).

The highly embossed *umbo*, decorated with the figure of Minerva, probably belonged to an officer. It is 21.5 cm in diameter, made in tinned copper alloy

285 Greave with representation of the god Mars, second–third century AD (*ex Guttman collection, Christie's photo*).

The greave is decorated in high relief, with an armed figure of the god Mars dressed as a high-ranking Roman officer. It shows four side-attachment holes, one with the riveted ring-tie still intact

287 (Opposite, top) Eye protector for horse, from unknown locality in Croatia, end of the first century AD (*Split, Archaeological Museum, no inv. H6066; T. Seser's photo, courtesy of the museum*)

288 (Opposite, bottom) Horse-hair *chamfron* crest from Noviomagus, first century AD, (*collection of Museum Het Valkhof, Nijmegen; courtesy of the conservator*)

Splendid specimens of greaves (**285**) and shields (**286**) were employed and have been confirmed by archaeological specimens. The shields were not '. . . of the standard fighting type, but lighter and profusely decorated to add to the beauty of the display . . .' The actual specimens appear to have been richly embossed with figures of gods, such as the specimen from Regensburg,[771] from the second century AD. The horses were also well protected with chamfrons (**288**), and eye guards sometimes directly attached to the chamfron sometimes directly to the bridle.

With the *Hippika Gymnasia* we have the first written reference to the Roman use of the 'wind-sock' standard, called a *draco,* and composed of a cloth multicoloured body to which the bronze head of a serpent (*draco* or oriental *senmurvu*) was attached, hissing in the wind when the air was blowing through it. The terrific image of such cavalrymen left a vivid impression on contemporaries. The first literary evidence is perhaps to be found in Saint John's Book of Revelation, describing the hordes of Apocalypse:

. . . like horses prepared for war. On their heads were something like golden crowns, and their faces were like men's faces. They had hair like women's hair, and their teeth were like those of lions. They had breastplates, like breastplates of iron. . . . the horses in the vision, and those who sat on them, having breastplates of fiery red, hyacinth blue, and sulphur yellow; and the heads of lions. Out of their mouths proceed fire, smoke and sulphur . . . By these three plagues were one third of mankind killed: by the fire, the smoke, and the sulphur, which proceeded out of their mouths. For the power of the horses is in their mouths, and in their tails. For their tails are like serpents, and have heads, and with them they harm . . .[772]

We have here a complete description of masked helmets (*ta prosôpa autôn hôs prosôpa anthrôpôn*) fitted with golden crowns (*stephanoi chrusôi*), like the helmets of Plovdiv (**270**),[773] Emesa[774] and Petronell–Carnuntum.[775] We have reference to masked helmets with women's hair, like the specimens in the Paul Getty Museum,[776] Eining[777] and Munich.[778] In the *Hippika Gymnasia* both male and female features were represented on the helmets, probably in order for some of the riders to take the role of Greeks and Amazons in the fictional battles.[779] The interesting mention of two different type of breastplates, one in iron and the other probably in leather or linen (*thôrakas hôs thôrakas sidêrous*), could confirm the hypothesis that, under or instead of the Cimmeric *chiton*, the cavalrymen also wore armour in the competitions; or maybe this was the costume in AD 100, later substituted by decorated *chitones*. The armour of the cavalrymen is described as being in three different colours: red, hyacinth blue and sulphur yellow. Could Saint John be describing linen or leather dyed armours? Or the Cimmeric *chitones?*

The wearing of the armour could also be referring to the horses. They could have coloured leather peytrals like those represented on the Flavius Bassus monument or on the Lancaster tombstone (**PLATE VII**, **257**), or peytrals of iron (blue) or bronze (yellow) or precious specimens with embossed figures of Romans and Barbarians in battle, as have been found in different localities.[780] The 'head of lions' of the horses were probably chamfrons of the type found in Novaesium, of Greek type.[781] The last part of Saint John's description, referring to mouths and tails like serpents, that he calls *ophis*, is obviously a reference to the *draco* standard.

The question of whether this kind of equipment was worn only in the games or also on the battlefield must surely be answered in the affirmative. We have a clear proof of it on the gravestone of S. Valerius Genialis of *Ala I Thracum* from Cirencester.[782] He is represented in full battle equipment, killing a Celtic opponent. With his right hand he wields the *hasta*, the oval shield is held with his left hand, together with a small *signum* ending in a medallion decorated with bands. On the head he wears a mask helmet of the Weiler type, which correspondes to an archaeological specimen from Ribchester.

A *gorgoneion* is attached to his armour, which could be linen or leather. His horse is clearly fitted with the *phalerae* and the chamfron typical of the *Hippika Gymnasia* equipment.

The helmet of Kostol (**271**) was probably lost during action in battle, or thrown into the river Danube as a votive offering to the gods. In any case, it was a battle helmet, because its direct prototype is visible on the Arc d'Orange, where, among the weapons of the trophy, are masked helmets with embossed hair and ears (**315m**, **315n**, **315o**, **315p**, **315v**).

~ THE HEAVY CAVALRY: THE FIRST *CATAFRACTARII* ~

Among the *numeri* particular relevance was given to the employment of units of cavalrymen called *kontarioi* (lancers). They are mentioned by Arrian as carrying a particularly heavy spear (*kontós*)[783] of Sarmatian origin and were probably created to counterbalance the heavy cavalry of the Sarmatian Rhoxolani and Jazyges during the Dacian Wars. Their bodies, and the bodies of many of their horses, were sometimes armoured and completely covered by a scale, lamellar or mail armour (*cataphractarii*).

A Thracian–Sarmatians elite force already strongly Hellenised, very quickly became the core of such *kontarii cataphractarii*, as the wonderful grave of the Chatalka tumulus I, grave 2,[784] has shown: here a Roman elite cavalryman of Thracian origin was buried with all his equipment, including that of the horse, in a period variably dated by the archaeologists to between the last quarter of the first century and the first half of the second century AD. In AD 45 the vassal kingdom of Thracia was transformed into a Roman province[785] and the aristocratic elite of the Thracian nobles supplied a number of the Roman cavalry auxiliaries, performing their military service as heavy armoured *contarii*.

The Chatalka defensive armament comprised a mask helmet, a metallic gorget, iron armoured trousers, three different armours (mail, scale, laminated) and two shields (**289**). Offensive equipment consisted of a couple of highly decorated swords, two spearpoints and fifty-five regular arrow points in their quiver. The helmet[786] is a bronze mask *kassis* that follows the Greco-Roman tradition, decorated by a gold laurel crown found in the same grave.[787] The metallic gorget[788] followed the Thracian–Macedonian tradition. Formed by a metallic (thick iron) cylindrical body[789] it was found with attached fragments of chain mail (**289c**, **289g**). The piece was made in two sections, connected by a belt or strap, and the outer surface was originally painted red. The mail fragments attached to the bottom of the collar were related to the chain-mail armour of the body, worn in combination with the scale armour in iron and bronze.[790]

The swords are characterised by a rich gold and silver decoration, showing a typical Sarmatian style 'similar to a wild beast': the hand guard of a sword is decorated with panther figures, the other one with branches of ivy (**289d**). These Sarmatian style swords are approximately 90 cm long. The gold flat pommel of one sword, 6 cm in diameter, is ornamented with Sarmatian tribal symbol *tamga*,[791] which are also visible on the gold, gilded bronze and silver scabbard plates, incised in the Sarmatian zoomorphic style.[792] The highly decorated scabbard slide in nephrite, which held the sword in a transversal position on the left side of the wearer is notable;[793] its origin is Chinese, and attests the very wide range of reciprocal influences that the Iranian peoples of the steppes had with western and eastern cultures.

Remains of cloth and shoes were found together with the armament. The armoured trousers[794] were about 1 m long and consisted of a padded coloured garment protected in the seams by scales (**289c**). Some metallic rivets positioned in regular way on their surface could be used for attaching further scales, and so making the trousers completely covered.

The horse, of Samatian breeding,[795] was protected by a complete suit of laminated rectangular scale armour, in iron.[796] The armour of both man and horse (**289a and 289b**) was made of scales with a central groove. The rounded *squamae* of the man's armour were essentially identical to the armour of the Rhoxolan cataphracts on the Sarmatian column (**223**, **225**).

This equipment, especially the fully armoured trousers, reveals strong similiarities with the Sarmatian weaponry, and it is an important indication of the relations among the Romanised Thracian military elite and the Sarmatian aristocracy, combining the use of the long spear with that of the reflex bow, as is visible on Trajan's Column (**223**).[797] Here some Sarmatians are very realistically represented in the 'Parthian shooting position'. This is not to exclude, though, the possibility that the cavalryman might have belonged to a newly formed Thraco-Sarmatian ethnic component serving in the Roman army like *cataphractarii*.

In the second century AD *cataphractarii* units were further composed by the same Sarmatians (Rhoxolans and Jazyges) shown on the column,[798] wearing a *lorica plumata* covering the whole body of the man, while the horse has a separate armour made of similar scales (**223**). Units of these heavy cavalrymen were enlisted in the army from the time of Trajan and Hadrian. The images on the column are often contested as fanciful artistic visions, with some element of reality. We should, however, bear in mind that scale armour covering the whole body and legs, have been found in Scythian barrows, and were a legacy of the Scythian costume passed on to the Rhoxolans.[799] The find of

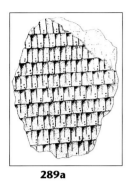

289a

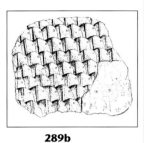

289b

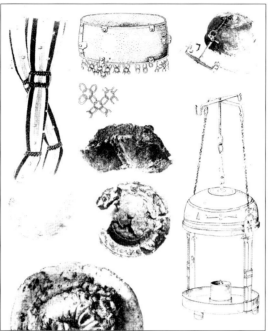

289c

289 Equipment of early Thraco-Roman *cataphractarius*, from Chatalka, first half of the second century AD (*ex Bujukliev, by kind permission of the Library of the Institute of Archaeology of Belgrade*)

289d

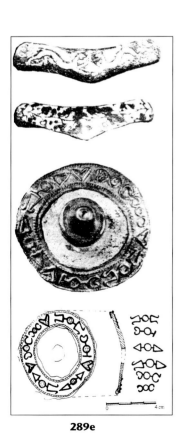

289e

289f

289g

Chatalka confirms moreover the wearing of such armoured trousers. So it is quite possible that the cataphracts on Trajan's Column have armour that completely covered the arms and legs, and that this was fitted to the body by a tight combination on the limbs of fastening strings and laces. This was a very old fastening system, already visible on some equipment from Iberian horsemen from the time of the Hannibalic Wars![800]

The national costume of the Sarmatians, with equipment that was partially Roman, is still visible on a fragmentary relief from Deva (Chester), dated to the time of Marcus Aurelius.[801] The armour of this man seems to be a long scale coat, with or without sleeves. Such Sarmatian armour is shown in a realistic manner on the pedestal of Trajan's Column (**200c**).

The main standard of these units was the wind-sock *draco* (**277**). Easterners (especially Bosphoreans) were widely used as heavy cavalrymen, armoured in iron (*cataphracti*).[802] The best example of this is the tombstone of Thyphon, from Panticapea (Kertch).[803]

Horse armour is explicity recorded by Virgil.[804] The horse's body was covered by heavy armour (*munitus equus*[805]) and eye protectors made of bronze and visible also on the horses of Trajan's Column and on the Chiusi frieze (**82**, **287**), and also confirmed by many archaeological specimens[806].

~ THE IMPERIAL GUARD AND *URBANICIANI* AND *VIGILES* EQUIPMENT ~

The *damnatio memoriae* to which the praetorians, *equites singulares* and the *urbaniciani* were condemned after their dissolution by Constantine the Great has deprived the scholars of much information about their equipment, since all the iconographical records were systematically erased together with the celebratory inscriptions on the public monuments.[807] However, many surviving images still allow us to have a good idea of the appearance of the best-equipped elite warriors of the Roman army. The main records of this age come from monumental reliefs, *stelae*, mosaics, frescoes, small objects linked to everyday life and little archaeological finds that have been made in the Italian cities and sometimes also in the provinces.

The *praitorianoi* – to use the Greek word used by Cassius Dio, writing about Trajan – are well represented on the Great Trajanic Frieze, showing that the *milites*, *equites*, musicians and standard-bearers of the guard were equipped with the best weapons (**291**). This circumstance came from their better allowance, which permitted them to purchase an expensive endowment. Most of the ancient texts explain then – against the widespread opinion of modern scholars – how this magnificent equipment was worn on the battlefield as well as in the parades.

Other relevant monuments representing Imperial guardsmen are the Cancelleria reliefs of the Flavian period, the Trajan and Marcus Aurelius columns, the pedestal of the Antonine Pius column and the decorative panels from Marcus Aurelius' time inserted on the Constantine Arch,[808] together with the funerary *stelae*. From the sources we in any case have confirmation that the praetorians wore a different outfit from the other *militia*, as recounted by Herodian,[809] describing the conspiracy of Maternus against the Emperor Commodus:

> This seemed to Maternus an ideal time to launch his plot undetected. By donning the uniform of a praetorian soldier

and outfitting his companions in the same way, he hoped to mingle with the true praetorians and, after watching part of the parade, to attack Commodus and kill him while no one was on guard . . .

But Maternus had no luck:

> . . . But the plan was betrayed when some of those who had accompanied him into the city revealed the plot. (Jealousy led them to disclose it, since they preferred to be ruled by the emperor rather than by a bandit chief.) Before he arrived at the scene of the festivities, Maternus was seized and beheaded, and his companions suffered the punishment they deserved.

Shafted Weapons and Swords, Daggers and Axes

On the figurative monuments the praetorians are armed with a *lancea*, *pilum* and *gladius*. *Equites* and *pedites* of the guard have a light spear (*lancea*) suitable for throwing or thrusting,[810] which the infantryman usually held at its centre of gravity and the cavalryman at the lower end (**291**). It was different from the longer *hasta*, this last mainly used for thrusting: on the Great Frieze the *hasta* or a *contus* is held by the Emperor Trajan in the same way as the *sarissa* of Alexander the Great in the Gaugamela mosaic, where he is piercing an enemy![811]

The *lancea* of one guardsman on the frieze has a triangular *cuspis*, similar to an actual specimen from the second century from Mogontiacum (Mainz), but with two rivets inserted into the socket to fix it to the wooden shaft. The wood was hazel (*corylus*) or ash (*fraxinus*), according to Pliny the Elder.[812]

The Cancelleria relief suggests that some praetorian *pila* was cord wrapped around the shaft to make a better handle;

290a

290b

290c

290d

290 (Above and following page) *Milites* and *signiferi* of the praetorian guard, Trajan's Column scenes XXXII and LXXIX (*cast, Roma, Museo della Civiltà Romana, author's photo, courtesy of the museum*).

Note the helmets of Weisenau typology, the shield's devices, the detail of the marching *aquilifer* in front of the other *signiferi* bearing *signa* with imperial portraits inscribed in *phalerae*

290e

290f

290g

290h

290i

290j

290k

290l

291 Details of Great Trajanic Frieze representing *praetoriani* and *equites singulares*, high relief from the Trajanic Forum, early second century AD (*cast of the Museo della civiltà Romana, Rome, author's photo, courtesy of the museum*).

The monument, which once decorated the podium of the Divine Trajan's Temple, was inserted in the fourth century AD in the Constantine Arch. It represents a very important source for the equipment of the praetorian guard. The represented warriors clad in Roman armour could be of Celtic or even Germanic origin, but Romans of the Rhenish or Danubian *milites* also enlisted in the guard. Many of the original colours visible on the Hottenroth drawings[i] have been recovered in the last restoration.[ii]

The cavalrymen have hexagonal shields (*scuta*), of Celto-Germanic origin, with a unique internal handgrip. The infantryman carries a slightly convex shield, oval in shape but truncated at the upper and lower rim like the typical rectangular infantry shield. The *scuta* seem to be plated in copper alloy with gold fittings. On their heads they wear helmets of the Attic type, embossed in gold and silver and similar to the imperial one,[iii] adorned with scorpions on the *bucculae* (cheek guards), the *insignia* of the praetorian guard; those of the *equites* have on top the *geminae pinnae* or side-feathers in white,[iv] flanking a round helmet metallic crest, representing the rose of life. The *pedites* wear high plumes dyed red-purple.

The guardsmen are protected by three different types of armour: the iron *lorica* segmentata, the iron and bronze *squama* and the iron or bronze *lorica gallica* or *lorica conserta hamis*, i.e. the mail armour. Their shields might have copper-alloy appliqués, usually a *digma* of golden engraved thunderbolts or four scorpions. The *umbo* shown on the Great Trajanic Frieze is very similar to a bronze specimen from Halmeag (Braşov, Romania), fixed by four rivets.[v]

The clothes represented are woollen tunics, a scarf round the neck *(focale)* and a pair of short *bracae* or *femoralia-feminalia*. The dress of the guardsmen of Celtic origin are probably decorated with Celtic-type patterns. The *focale* and the tunic perhaps represented one of the distinctive elements of the uniform. On their feet they wear the *caligae*, the typical Roman military leather footwear.

The horses have leather harness, originally painted in red. Three straps are represented as placed between the breast (*antilena*) and the neck and only one on the *postilena*. The embossed straps are decorated with volutes engraved on the leather, with pendants of different shapes: on the front, the strap around the neck showed ivy leaves alternating with *lunulae*; the breast belt has only one hanging *lunula*; the lower one, in the original fastened to the saddle and continuing as *postilina*, shows ivy leaves alternating with *lunulae*. The largest original specimens of bosses are of about 29 cm in diameter. The Roman saddle of this period – regardless of the accuracy of the Connolly wooden reconstructions – was also filled up with straw and lined with leather. It was further covered by a red scarlet saddle cover drape. The fastening system for the horse's bit seems be composed of two small rings attached to a main one, being part of an articulated kind of bit, here very similar to the actual specimen of the Trajanic period found on the Rhine *limes*, at Neuwied-Niederbieber

i   Hottenroth, 1888, I, pl. 50.

ii   Campisi, Melucco Vaccaro, Pinelli, 1987, p. 60 ff.

iii Touati, 1987, pl. 3; the Imperial helmet is worn by the *armiger* (shield-bearer, see Mart., *Ep..*, IX, 56) beside him.

iv Plin., *HN*, XI, 44, 2.

v   Of about 20.5 cm in diameter; see Various, 1998, p. 315, cat. N. 293.

the cord or metallic thread would have provided a better grip. On the same monument the *pilum* is furnished also with a pyramidal point, a long iron shank, a wooden shaft with a grooved handle[813] and a butt. It appears to be weighted by a spheroid that Antonucci suggested was made of metal[814] to give it additional thrusting and penetrative power. This bulbous weight, at least from the figurative monuments, seems to have been only used by the praetorian guard, at least at the beginning (**292**). The Adamclisi monument, however, shows *milites legionarii* with *pila* still of the old type, some with (**50, 51, 52**) and some without the spheroid. The progressive lightening of the tanged *pilum* had probably brought about the adoption of heavier specimens with the round lead weight inserted at the junction of the wood and iron.[815] On the spheroid of the Cancelleria *pilum* is engraved a decoration with an eagle, an imperial symbol, and small ovules. A small eagle identical to the Cancelleria eagle has been found in Augusta Raurica, and could be an appliqué from the same kind of spheroid.[816]

The *lanceae* were composed of a *hasta* (shaft) of ash (a yellowish wood) about 1.5 m long, showing a leaf-shaped point (*cuspis*). Specimens similar to the one on the Trajanic Frieze have been found at Ulpia Traiana in Dacia, and Newstead in Caledonia. It was fixed to the *hasta* by means of two rivets.

The sword, of Iberian type, was worn on the right side of the body by means of a *cingulum bullatum*, that is to say, bossed. It is well represented on the Great Trajanic Frieze, one of the few Roman monuments where the exact way in which the sword was suspended[817] is clearly visible, hung from the shoulder belt by means of small rings fixed to scabbard fittings (**291**). The rings were connected to metallic terminals closed by two rivets.[818] The presence of such suspension rings is easily seen on the authentic specimens, such as the swords from Pompeii[819] and the so-called sword of Tiberius from Mogontiacum (Mainz). The Tiberius sword shows the presence of a decorative fitting on the scabbard, constituted by a rivet with an imperial portrait. Such portrait fittings are perfectly visible on the sword worn by one of the praetorian cavalrymen on the Trajanic Frieze (**291**), and the presence of two similar rivets in the collection of Zagreb Museum,[820] made of bronze, are a possible confirmation of the realism of the Roman monumental art in the representation of military equipment. The sword's pommel was usually ivory. The scabbard (*vagina*)

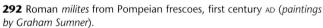

292 Roman *milites* from Pompeian frescoes, first century AD (*paintings by Graham Sumner*).

A yellow *Paenula* like that represented on the fresco has been found in Ballana, and the *miles* on the right is probably a member of the praetorian cohorts, due to his similarity with the Cancelleria relief *milites*. Note his weighted *pilum*. Martial recounts the marching of the praetorian cohorts armed with *pila* and the changing of the guard in the night.[i] The man on the left is usually described as a traveller, but he wears a yellow-brown *sagum* cloak and a white tunic.[ii] We should remember that sometimes the soldiers were dressed as civilians and armed with staves, as on the occasion of a Jewish insurrection in Jerusalem[iii]

i   Mart., *Ep..*, X, 48.
ii   Sumner, 2002, p. 21.
iii Josephus, *BJ* II, 9, 4.

hung from the *cingulum-balteus* through little rings fixed to its bands. The rings were linked to metallic fittings, blocked by two rivets on the *balteus*.

The daggers (*pugiones*) of the praetorian guards were identical in shape to those of the legionaries, although we might suppose that they were even more lavishly decorated on the scabbard. A marching *cohors* of praetorians is represented with their short *pugio* attached on the right side of the body (**293**). They carry no sword, and it is possible that when patrolling the Italian cities the equipment was relatively light; staff and *pugio* were enough to settle the riots of the mob!

The praetorian scabbard on the Trajanic Frieze is decorated with spirals and volutes,[821] probably incised on the leather. The same decoration of the scabbard can be seen on the Adamclisi *trophaeum* (**52**, **85**).

The *balteus* had edges of decorated reinforcement and plate decorated bosses; in particular the sources remind us that the praetorian *balteus* was 'made of leather, purple painted and with gold bosses'. A particularly ornamented *balteus* is represented on the armour of the *trophaeum* of Adamclisi, with bosses shaped like rosettes and *phalerae* ornamenting it (**85**).

The pick-axes or *dolabrae* (**249**, **250**) were the main weapon for the watchmen (*vigiles*), used to inflict crushing blows upon objects and also upon men if necessary. The blades had a cutting edge and a point. The blades were usually protected by ornamental scabbards with elegant pendants in copper alloy. The handle of the *dolabra* was around 50 cm long. The *vigiles* are mentioned in the *Satyricon*[822] as being armed with axes (*secures*) and, logically, equipped with water in case of fire. The *vigiles* also used *ferramenta*, pails, sickles, hooks and saws. During the night patrols, they were also equipped with staffs, whips and swords to arrest thieves, criminals and especially arsonists!

Shield and Helmets

Perhaps the first representation of the Augustan praetorian guard is the unique and famous mosaic from Praeneste (Palestrina), probably made in 30 BC, and possibly representing Augustus, Agrippa and their bodyguards on the borders of the Nile River.[823] The guardsmen are identified by the presence of the scorpion blazon on two rectangular shields, a symbol of the guard that is also visible on the coins representing the *adlocutio* of Galba and on the monuments of the Trajanic period. A further confirmation of it is an assemblage of praetorian arms and armour on a triumphal sculpture from Villa Albani, where a shield with the blazon of the scorpion is clearly visible.[824]

It is generally said that this blazon was used by praetorians from the time of Tiberius because that was his birth sign.[825] No sources mention this, though; instead it is much more probable that the scorpion, already a royal blazon in Ptolemaic armies

293 Relief with marching warriors, from Cuma (South Italy), probably praetorians, Flavian era, first century AD (*drawing by Graham Sumner*).
  Note the leather *loricae*, decorated at the centre of the breast with a Gorgon's head. These are very light armours and are worn over two garments, one fringed at the edges. The soldiers are *insigniti milites* as is shown by the *geminae pinnae* of their Attic and Weisenau helmets, and are armed only with *pugiones*

and linked with the old Egyptian tradition, was adopted by the praetorian guard of Caesar Augustus after the victory at Actium, to show a continuity from the pharaohs to the new rulers even in the symbols of the bodyguards. This can be confirmed by the Palestrina mosaic.

The Palestrina mosaic is also of extreme importance as a source for the colours of the praetorian *insignia*: the field of the shield is divided into two colours, three quarters in mauve and a quarter in red; the scorpions are outlined in white and black on the surface. These could also possibly be the colours kept for the shields in the Trajanic period.

Beside it, the *praetoriani* on the Palestrina mosaic are carrying oval and circular shields, typical of the Late Republican period. Such shields are still visible on the Cancelleria monument,[826] whereas a relief from Cuma representing marching guardsmen (**293**),[827] shows *scuta* with curved sides and a straight top edge. A monument of Aquileia,[828] related to C. Firmidius, warrior of the *VI Cohors Praetoriana*, shows an oval shield, together with the *pilum* and the *pugio*. In other sources of the first century AD the

294 *Speculator*, detail from the Marcus Aurelius column, in situ, (*Rome, ex Becatti, by kind courtesy of Editoriale Domus S.p.A.*).
On the Marcus column are first time visible imperial bodyguards, of probable Dacian origin, armed with scythed weapons, precursors of the Imperial Guardsmen of Byzantium armed with the *rhomphaiai*[i]

i   S. Coarelli, 2008, pl. IV.

praetorians show the use of the rectangular legionary shield.[829] We can therefore suppose a continuing use by the guard of both forms. If in the Trajanic monuments the praetorians carry only rectangular hexagonal or rectangular convex shields (**290, 291**), on the Antonine monuments they bear only oval flat shields.[830]

Besides the scorpions, the *praetoriani digma* of the shield was constituted by the usual metallic applications of lightning bolts. This is clearly visible on the Great Trajanic Frieze and on Trajan's Column (**PLATE VI, 290, 291**). As described by Virgil, the *fulmines* (lightning) shield appliqués were made of iron, because this metal was considered meteoric, so of divine origin.[831] In the text of Valerius Flaccus already mentioned, the reference to the fragments of embossed metals, such as those found in Mainz and related to iron lightning bolts, is clear. In particular, Flaccus' text refers to the *fulgur trifida* or *trisulca*, the triple-forked lightning, which is not only visible on the *stela* of C. Castricius,[832] but also on the shields of the *praetoriani equites* of the Great Trajanic Frieze (**291**).

These cavalrymen used hexagonal *scuta* of Celtic–German origin with a unique inner grip of iron or wood, lined with leather. The wooden *scutum* was painted, but sometimes the external side was completely metallic embossed with gilded iron showing *fulgures*. There were twelve different rays (*radii*) for the lightning: three for the wind, three of brilliant fire, three of hail and three of rain, following the ancient magic-religious belief.

The high degree of traditionalism visible in the helmets of the elite troops corresponds to real specimens. The Attic helmet is represented as the most used, in many variants, and provided with beautiful embossed skulls decorated with vegetal scrolls (**121, 259, 295, 296**) and *diadema* worked in relief. Cheekpieces were clasped under the helmet rim by hinges.

On the head of the praetorians the Great Trajanic Frieze shows a helmet (*cassis*) of an Attic shape, similar to the imperial one represented on the same monument; it was probably made of copper alloy engraved in gold and silver, with silvered rivets and gold and copper *fulgures* decorating the movable *bucculae* (cheek guards) with red[833] laces under the throat. Two white-silvered feathers, described by Pliny the Elder for the *milites gregarii*, were inserted from one side on its top, flanked a metallic round crest shaped like a rose or a wheel. This last was placed cross-wise on the top of the helmet, doubled and made of copper, like the shield ornaments. The feathers were inserted from one side in a square plume-holder.[834]

The Weisenau helmets were used by the praetorians as well; they are clearly visible on Trajan's Column (**290**). These helmets are variants of the Imperial-Gallic or Imperial-Italic style helmets: they are very similar to the actual specimens from Berzobis (Romania),[835] with a cross-bar reinforcement over the skull, and to the wonderful iron helmet (**PLATE VI**) with bronze decoration from Hebron (Judaea).[836] In the same scene on the

295 (Top left) Head of warrior, first–second century AD, Termae Museum, Rome; (Top right and bottom left) Head of praetorian or *eques singularis*, Trajanic period, Palazzo Poli, Rome (Bottom right) Head of praetorian *beneficiarius*, (see also 259), Museo Nazionale Romano, Rome (*Photos DAI*)

296 *Miles* from relief in Palazzo Ducale, Mantoua, late Flavian or Trajanic age (*drawing by Graham Sumner*).

The helmet was put on just before going into action. For this reason the soldier ready for the battle is said to be *galeatus*.[i] The elaborate helmet of Attic shape, with lightening bolts engraved on the cheek guards, could help to identify this man as a member of the praetorian guard. The guardsmen's helmets were often decorated with high plumes of ostrich or peacock feathers

297 Front and back of Phrygian helmet from Herculaneum, variously dated to the second century BC and the first century AD (*from Lipperheide collection, originally preserved in the Bibliothèque nationale de France in Paris, present location unknown, photo author's collection*)

---

i   Juv., *Sat.*, I, 165.

column, the praetorians are identified by the presence of crests on their helmets and their *digma* on the shield (**290**), or by the presence of *praetoriani signiferi* bearing *signa* with imperial portraits.[837]

Urbaniciani and *vigiles* also wore helmets linked to the ancient Italic tradition: a Montefortino type helmet with the inscription *AVRELIUS VICTORINUS MIL COH XII VRB*[838] shows that the city guards were still wearing the ancient traditional Roman panoply, a circumstance confirmed by the image of the dwarfs dressed as *urbaniciani* in the famous fresco from Pompeii.[839] They wear Montefortino helmets with red crests, muscled bronze and iron armour and round *clipei*. A Montefortino helmet completely identical to the helmet found in Cremona[840] is depicted on a painting of Fabius Rufus in Pompeii, surmounted by a red-pink plume. An Attic helmet, probably belonging to a *vigilis*, has been found in Herculaneum.[841] Also from Herculaneum comes a Phrygian shaped helmet of the Conversano type, decorated with a Roman eagle on the back (**297**). The helmet could be have been used by some *vigilis*, and worn as a family tradition until the destruction of the city in AD 79.

Splendid helmets reserved only for the imperial guard are confirmed from artistic monuments and archaeology: the most striking helmet is that from the Nemi ship, an Attic specimen with the crest shaped like a griffin's head (**298**). It was probably worn by a guardsman of Caligula; similar helmets, from the Julio-Claudian age, are visible on a military frieze from Turin (**106**).[842]

The presence of elements of traditionalism in the praetorian and *urbaniciani* equipment does not mean, as some scholars have stated, that helmets and other parts of the equipment represented on the figurative documents are just artistical conventions. Complete specimens of Attic-style helmets similar to the illustrated types have been found in Herculaneum[843] and Hamburg (**130**), this latter is also fitted with the traditional ring visible on most helmets represented on both columns. A browband or bronze decorated frontal from Lugdunum, from the Trajanic age, bears at the centre the embossed image of the emperor, together with ivy leaves;[844] there is also a bronze frontal from Noviomagus.[845] A cheek guard from such a helmet, with an embossed Victory carrying a trophy was formerly preserved in the collection of Mr Charles Ede, in London.[846] The old specimens of the Etrusco-Corinthian tradition are still visible on the Domus Aurea painting and on the carvings at Villa Albani, and a real specimen dated to the Flavian era, decorated with an embossed laurel crown, has been found in Lyon, and preserved in Autun Museum.

The different *equites* and *pedites* of the guard, including the *equites singulares*, wore various equipment, and of course those who fought beside the emperor, dressed like a new Alexander the Great, were equipped much more in the traditional Greco-Roman way, without loss of effectiveness. So the famous episode mentioned by Tacitus, where two *praetoriani* picked up

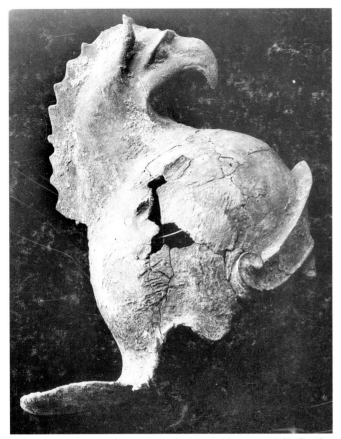

298 Helmet of a guardsman, from the Nemi ship, *c.* AD 40 (*Berlin Altes Museum; museum photo, courtesy of Antikensammlung SMB, Berlin*)

the shields of the *XVI Legio* and hid themselves amongst the Vitellian troops, succeeding in this way to cut the springs of a catapult, only signifies that these two soldiers were armed in a similar way to the enemies. But how were the *milites legionis* of Vitellius armed? We know very little about it. The episode is not an indicator that legionaries and praetorian were armed in the same way, but that the shield blazon was, as a general rule, the only distinctive element for the *milites*, who might also be dressed totally differently within the same *legio*.

Armour

The use of laminated armour by the praetorians *milites* is well attested by artworks. In the specimen sculpted on the fragment from the Templum Gentis Flaviae the decorative washers of the Corbridge type are even visible (**PLATE VI**, **259**). A statue from Villa Albani represent a similar armour, together with the use of an old-fashioned Etrusco-Corinthian helmet (**299**). The infantrymen on the Great Trajanic Frieze have a *lorica segmentata* that seems to be composed of smaller plates, and longer than the specimens visible on Trajan's Column (**291**). The praetorians represented on the column all have a metallic *lorica segmentata* of the best type (**290**).

A very little-known source representing a praetorian guard in Hellenistic fashion but with *lorica segmentata* is the fresco of

299 (Left and above) *Miles legionis* or praetorian in *lorica segmentata*, relief from Villa Albani, in situ, Rome, late Flavian era (*photo DAI; detail drawing by Graham Sumner*)

the Domus Aurea, where the Trojan hero Hector is dressed like a guardsman of the Neronian period (**86**). His helmet is of the pseudo-Corinthian type that in the early Imperial age is still used as helmet for elites, as shown by the original specimen from Autun.[847] The shield is oval and he carried a spear (*contus*). The body armour, painted yellow, seems to be a gilded and silvered *lorica segmentata* of a very expensive type. The colour yellow might also indicate bronze armour: fragments of a bronze *segmentata* armour of 'Corbridge A' type have been found in the military camp of Novae in Bulgaria (**301**). Among the artefacts from Novae were

> . . . numerous fragments of bronze sheet plates, clasps and hinges. The finds, of dark bronze sheet, with a thickness of 0.001 m are the most numerous. They are attached together by means of small rivets with flat heads. They are part of a plate armour. The pieces with the fastening points are the best preserved, because they are the thicker. Two clasps have been also discovered, made in fretwork, and small hinges in bronze[848] . . . The found relics match the *lorica segmentata* type Corbridge A . . . If all the discovered pieces were put together, it would in any case be impossible to reconstruct a complete specimen of an armour of this kind. Both the perforated clasps and the four small bronze hinges that still survive make it possible that we are in this case only looking at a shoulderpiece and, in all likelihood, of two parts of the breastplates . . .[849]

Apart from the unusualness of such a find and the confirmation of the existence of armour of this type made of bronze or copper alloy, the find is a further proof of the authenticity of the pictorial representation in Roman art. This kind of armour, in bronze sheets, was mainly reserved for the guardsmen, although the specimen from Novae should be ascribed to some *miles* of the *Legio I Italica*.[850] A guardsman of the Flavian period, in a Corinthian helmet and wearing a laminated *lorica*, is visible in the collections of Villa Albani in Rome (**299**).

A very intriguing banded armour is represented on the pedestal of Trajan's Column (**200**). It is a Sarmatian corselet that seems to be made of thick leather or metal bands butted together on a textile or leather backing, which continues like a shirt. The banded section would entirely cover the wearer's hips. The row of fastening buckles down the front, represented in great detail, are very similar to those used for the *lorica segmentata*.[851] This armour, reconstructed in the Hottenroth drawings in iron grey and yellow bronze,[852] reappears after some time, worn by the Roman praetorians of the Antonine period. It is in fact visible on the small statuette from the British Museum[853] and its shape is again represented in the laminated armour worn by legionaries and praetorians on the celebratory panels of the Aurelian age incorporated in the Constantine Arch.[854] The *segmentata* on the Antonine Pius column seems to represent well the *praetoriani* clad in such armours. On some

300 Hadrianic cavalryman (*Galleria Borghese, Rome; photo DAI*)

of these monuments and artworks this armour is worn over a padded *subarmale* furnished with fringed *pteryges*.

Possible evidence for the existence of this kind of armour in a double version (iron and leather) comes from a military report of a military workshop (*fabrica*), probably of the *Legio II Traiana*. It refers to '*lam{i}nae levisatares*' (light plates). In the description of the Sarmatian armour we see how Tacitus uses the same word *lamina* in combination with iron and with leather, presenting the possibility that the banded or scale armour of the Sarmatians could have been made of iron or in leather: '*tergimen ferreis laminis aut praeduro corio consertum*'. *Lamna* or *Lamina* means plate or sheet, and the quoted reference could also refer to the production of belt plates or metal fittings of the *balteus*. But we cannot put aside the possibility that we are in the presence of a reference to the production of a *lorica segmentata* made of iron or leather, like the Sarmatian prototype.

An important fragment of Roman chain mail comes from Mainz,[855] where it was recovered together with many Roman objects. Here the mail construction is completely identical to the armour worn by the praetorian on the Great Trajanic Frieze, showing the great degree of realism of the Roman artist. The interconnection of the rings could be achieved by a double or three-folded chain (*catena*), so forming a *bilix* and *trilix* chain mail. Describing a chain armour of an officer or a praetorian (referring to Aeneas), Virgil says '*loricam consertam hamis auroque trilicem*'.[856] The mail was certainly sewn on a leather backing, forming a short corselet, of muscled shape, coming down to the waist and dentilated at the extremities. The ivory artwork

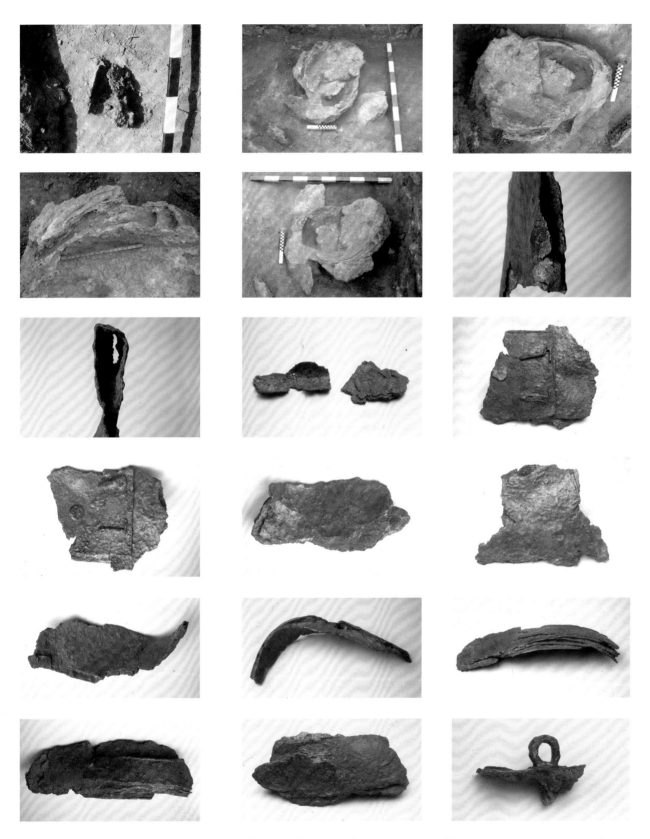

301 Fragments of *lorica segmentata*, from Novae, first half of first century AD, (*courtesy of the Professor Piotr Dyczek, University of Warsaw*)

Remains of bronze and iron specimens of *lorica segmentata* were found nearby in the *Scamnium Tribunorum* and in the *Valetudinarium*

(1-6). The remains of the bronze *lorica* are a very dark bronze, and formed part of the breast and shoulder defences.[i] The iron fragments formed a shoulder-guard of the late Newstead armour type, dated to the time of Alexander Severus

---

i   Gentshceva, 2002, pls. LV–LVI, pp. 54–5

from Ephesus (**121**) also shows, however, the employment of longer chain mail, still hinged on the front at the height of the *humeralia* by the old hook fastening system. Other guardsmen on the same ivory panel are just dressed in tunics and Attic helmets.

The scale armour was the most used by the guard. A relief of a possible *eques singularis* from Turin shows it clearly (**188**). On the Great Trajanic Frieze a *squama* is depicted with iron or bronze scales (**291**). The biggest scales, often of different dimensions,[857] had a central groove and were attached to a leather base. They were fixed from one side by means of two openings and sewn at the same time to the *substratum* by leather laces. Then they were placed one upon another so as to look like fish scales. A splendid example of it is visible on the sculpture of a guardsman of the Hadrianic period, whose *squama plumata* in leather or horn is highly decorated and shows the old system of fastening by means of *humeralia* (**300**).

The Marcus Aurelius column always shows the praetorians clad in scale armour, but their equipment is otherwise the same as the other *milites legionis*. In any case, Cassio Dio confirms that the praetorians were equipped with scale armour (*thorax lepidotòs*) until the empire of Macrinus.[858] The whole structure was worn on a short *subarmale* of sometimes slightly stressed muscular shape. This is the well-known smooth leather *subarmale* that we can often admire on Trajan's Column and that stands out from similar types of protection covered by iron rings.

Plain leather armour is visible on the praetorian officer on the base of the Antonine column.[859] Obviously it was given to the officers: a splendid specimen in leather is visible on the officer at the side of Marcus Aurelius in the relief of the imperial *clementia* at the Palazzo dei Conservatori.[860] It might represent the praetorian *praefectus* Tribonianus Gallus.

~ Clothing ~

Generally the stereotyped image of the Roman soldier has him with a scarlet tunic and bare arms and legs, even in northern regions like Britain or Germany. The reality was completely different: the soldiers adapted their dress to the local climates, and gradually mixed their original Mediterranean-designed equipment with regional variations. Moreover arms and armour were worn only in armed duties, in exercise and in battles, or when some danger arose; in daily life the Roman warrior wore only his clothes, and with them the symbol of the *militia armata*, the belt (*balteus* or *cingulum* or *zonì*). Weapons, such as daggers and swords, were elements that allowed a soldier to be recognised immediately.[861]

Representations of military clothing come from funerary art of the period, particularly from the portraits of el-Fayoum, in Egypt; some portraits are now identified to be those of soldiers. Not only do they give evidence that the hairstyle of the soldiers changed with the emperor,[862] but they are also a fundamental source for dress and equipment.

The distribution of clothing was now the responsibility of the government, but from Propertius[863] we learn that even in this period some soldiers' garments were woven by their wives. A certain Aretusa complains of the distance from her husband, who is engaged in the war against the Parthians, remembering the four *lacernae* she made for him, and the fact that she is always dealing with the camp clothes[864] (*pensa castrensa*) of the man! This document, together with other evidence from Vindolanda, confirms that the soldiers were able to receive items of clothing from home, and wear them on duty. Clothing (*vestimenta*)[865] might also be handed out as reward or pay for the soldiers, and much distinctive clothing, especially if it came

from notorious enemies, was considered an important war booty for the gods.

Many excavations, but especially those in Masada, the Bar Kochbà period cave of Nahal Hever in Israel, Vindolanda and Carlisle in England, Carnuntum in Austria and Mons Claudianus, Dydymoi, Antinoe and other Egyptian and Nubian localities have added new elements to the corpus and also provided further clues to the colour of military clothing and the related terminology. However, some important discoveries are still waiting for proper publication, as for example are the textiles of the Roman soldiers and their relatives found dead in cave 2001 near Masada.[866] Wool and linen were the main materials. The *vellera* (wool) of Tartessus, in Spain was famous, bright yellow in colour,[867] as was the wool of Altinus, Parma and Apulia.[868] The wool of Patavium (Padova) was instead very thick and three layers woven (*trilices vellera*).[869] The purple wool par excellence was the Thyrian one.[870] We should still remember that the Roman army in the east spoke Greek, so there were often two words for items of army clothing, in the two different languages: such as the Latin *tunica*, which was also called by the Greek words *imation*[871] or *chiton*.

Tunics and Cloaks

Tunics

We have, for the early Principate, the first evidence of remains of Roman tunics from many localities. The military *tunica* was very similar to the *tunica laticlavia*. It was made of two pieces of cloth and had no fastening. Although the Roman soldiers did not possess uniforms in the modern sense of the word, their clothing and especially their tunics were often indicative of their military status.

During this period the tunic was quite wide and always sleeveless, having a basic design with many variations. Two rectangular sheets of cloth were sewn together at the sides and under the arms, the neck and lower openings were selvedges and therefore had no need for hems. The average size for tunics is given by the papyrus BGU 1564: 1.55 × 1.40m wide.[872] Variations on this size are found in preserved examples, which range from the 0.65 × 0.90m of the Nahal Ever adult male tunic,[873] an example from Mons Claudianus which was 0.80 × 1.07m, to the Nubian specimen from Ballana, which was 1.27 × 1.40m. The tunic was usually made of wool or linen, and put on like a shirt through the head opening. The tunics were decorated, sometimes, by two vertical stripes from the shoulder to the lower edge (*clavi*). At Mons Claudianus many of the fragments of brownish wool could have been from the local garrison.[874]

In Israel *tunicae* with sewn *clavi* has been found in different localities, like Masada and Nahal Hever. The specimens of Nahal Hever are certainly amongst the most important Roman military tunics[875] found, not only because they were found in a very precise chronological context, dating it to about AD 135, but also because they correspond impressively with the Roman and Mishnaic sources.

The *tunicae* are of different colours, as are their decorating *clavi*, descending from the shoulders at the back and front. The *clavi* varied in sizes, and Yadin proposed the possibility that the width of the *clavi* designated the rank of the wearer.[876] Varro, in his encyclopaedic treatise on the origin of Latin words, said that 'if anyone were to sew together a tunic so that on one sheet of it the clavi were narrow and on the other wide, each part would have no analogy in its nature. . .',[877] thus confirming that tunics with *clavi* were two-piece (*plagulae*) tunics. A tunic woven in one piece is instead the type of tunic (*chitôn*) worn by Jesus Christ, which the Roman auxiliaries who crucified him drew lots for.[878]

So we are dealing with two kinds of *tunicae*, both used by the Romans. The tunics made of two pieces were the commonest, and are also recorded in the Mishnaic sources, where this kind of tunic is called *haluq* (divided) and the *clavi* are called *imrah*. In the Talmud[879] it says, '. . . the opening of a *haluq* which is made by two leaves'. The *clavi* were woven into the fabric during manufacture. At Mons Claudianus the majority of *clavi* on the textile fragments were between 1 and 4 cm wide, with decorated ones reaching 7 cm in width.[880] Some fragments also had two or three stripes.

These kinds of tunics were used by both soldiers and guardsmen. A relief of the Hadrianic age, in Chatsworth House, probably represents a group of praetorians clad in loose-fitting tunics tied behind the neck in a knot, with the edge of a second

tunic visible at the hem.[881] The guardsmen are not different in any way from their legionary counterparts; the bunched neck (*nodus*) is typical of many legionary tunics visible on Trajan's Column.[882] A similar bunched knot is also seen on a sculpture from Seville, probably representing a veteran picking olives. His short-sleeved tunic, of the type that can be let down off the shoulder, identifies him as a soldier in retirement (**102**).[883]

We have a good example of the *tunicae* of the auxiliary soldiers of the Rhine garrison with the *stela* of Annaius Daverzus, who is represented in a short sleeveless tunic, looped up at the sides to hang down in front in a series of folds.[884] This particular kind of strikingly curved drapery, visible on many tombstones, including some legionaries and officers' tombstones (**302**),[885] is not an artistical convention, as many scholars claim. Rather, it

302 Stele of Lucius Valerius Albinus, *centurio* of the *I Cohors Thracum* (first *cohors* of the Thracians), with the colour reconstruction alongside, first century AD (*Museum of Ritterhaus, Offenburg, courtesy of the museum*).

The *centurio* wears a folded tunic, a *paenula* fitted with a *cucullus* (cap), fastened at the neck and belt. The *gladius* is worn on the right side of the body, while the typical *vitis* is held in his right hand; his belt is fitted with the typical *baltea* or aprons of the early Imperial age, here ending with *lunulae*. The reconstruction of the colours was achieved by comparing the remaining traces of colour with other monuments such as the gravestone of Silius of the *Ala Piacentiana*[i]

i   Yupanqui, 2004, p. 47 ff.

was obtained by starching linen, following a procedure already known to the ancient Egyptians, or using other cloth that is still produced in Italy today and called *mussolina*. The pleats were folded while the cloth, probably starched, was still wet. These *tunicae* were usually short and used in summer time or in warm weather regions.[886]

Easterners wore fine linen clothes (*carbasa lina*) much appreciated by military commanders.[887] In winter the Emperor Augustus wore four tunics, a woollen corselet (*thorax laneus*) and a linen armour or jacket (the *linea*).[888] In his *Sermo* Augustus remembers that under all these garments was worn, against the skin, the *tunica interior*, made from linen.[889] These inner tunics, the '*camisiae*', are attested also from Dio, when he says that Trajan, after a long battle against the Dacians, made bandages for the wounded from strips of his clothing.[890]

The white toga, only worn by adult males, was worn by the soldiers off duty,[891] sometimes together with the Greek mantle or *pallium*.[892] This is attested by the many funerary sculptures showing the deceased at a banquet in their *triclinium* along with the servant or other members of the family.[893] It was usual, but not a rule, to dress in civilian garments only in Italy.[894] The pure white (*candidus*) of shining wool (*splendida lana*) was extremely important in social life.[895] That of the emperor (*toga praesidiaria*)[896] was embroidered in gold on the edge;[897] that of the *tribuni laticlavii* had a broad purple *clavus*.

Cloaks

A great range of military cloaks was used by the soldiers at this time.[898] The cloaks favoured by the soldiers were the *paenula* and the *sagum*, together with the *lacerna*, *abolla*, *armilausa*, *birrus*, *chlamys* or *paludamentum*, *ephaptis*, *ephestris*, *manduas*. The *paenula* was worn by all the soldiers – even centurions (**302**) and officers – apart from the emperor.[899] Suetonius[900] says that Nero '. . . was all but dead when a centurion rushed in, and as he placed a *paenula* to the wound, pretending that he had come to aid him . . .'. And Phaedrus speaking about two soldiers: '. . .The comrade drew his sword, and stripped the *paenula* back "Leave me alone with him! Stand back!" . . .'.[901] The way of fastening the *paenula* is well documented by the figurative monuments: there were small *fibulae*, arranged vertically on the breast (**304**) or a leather lace that was threaded through holes in a criss-cross pattern and fastened at the lower part of the garment (**303e**, **303f**).

A particular kind of cloak, the *lacerna*, is mentioned as part of cavalry equipment.[902] It was a cloak fastened on the breast or on the shoulders by a *fibula*, sometimes fringed, probably of Oriental origin;[903] sometimes it was very large. A passage from Martial says that a centre of production of these cloaks was Sagaris (Mantua),[904] but the *provincia* Baetica also supplied good-quality white wool for the *lacernae*.[905]

The *sagum* used by the *auxilia* was of the same type as that of the legionaries, as the Daverzus tombstone shows, as do many

scenes from Trajan's Column.[906] Some of the cloth found in many localities, such as Mons Claudianus, could be related to military blankets or cloaks from their shape and material, especially those that are of very fine and more standardised woollen twills.[907] *Fibulae* of many different shapes and sizes were used to fasten the cloaks, they were the personal property of the owner. Disc *fibulae* were used during the first and second centuries AD, as those found in the military *valetudinarium* of Novae.[908]

The *abolla* was a lighter version of the *sagum*, in double thickness cloth.[909] A interesting short military cloak is worn by the *signifer* of the Mainz *praetorium*:[910] on the original sculpture he is shown with a cloak edged with a broad band of tablet-weaving and a fringe. The thick fringe is held by two stitched strips. Although the significance of such a decoration is unknown, the cloak is certainly not a *sagum* or an *abolla* but looks very similar to a cloak discovered in Denmark, in Sogaard Mose.[911] Perhaps it is actually a representation of a *byrrus* cloak.

303 (Above and opposite page) Gravestone of S. Ennius Fuscus, *miles* of *Cohors VIII Voluntariorum*, and his wife, from Muć,[i] last quarter of first century AD (*Split, Archaeological Museum, T. Seser's photo, courtesy of the museum*)

i   Cambi, 2002, vol. I, p. 166; vol. II, fig. 36.

303a

303b

303c

303d

303e

303f

304 Gravestones of two soldiers and a woman, from the Porolissum region, end of the second century AD (*Zalau Museum; author's photo, courtesy of the museum*).

Although roughly sculpted, this gravestone represents the civilian and military dress of the Dacian legionaries of Rome: the *paenula*, fastened by two buckles, covers the whole body, and traces of red colour are still visible on the garments. The central man is of course the most interesting: under the *paenula* can be seen his *lorica segmentata*, of Sarmatian type

The *paludamentum* or *chlamys* was reserved for officers and the emperor, for whom it was the war garment (*paludati*).[912] It is often visible on the figurative monuments, reliefs and statues (**4**, **195**). Its general shape was similar to that of the *sagum*: a mid-length cloak, sometimes coming down to the calf. It was clasped on the right shoulder by a gold *fibula*,[913] usually of circular shape.[914] The right arm was free and passed through the hole in front of the cloak, and, to give to it more freedom, the cloak was rolled up around the cloth of the dress, or the finials of the cloak were held by the left hand.[915] A practical way of fighting while wearing the mantle (*pallium*) was that of wrapping the cloak round the arm, taking up a fighting posture.[916]

The word *cucullus* seems to indicate both a separate cap attached to the cloak, and a small cloak with a hood built in.[917] On his tombstone the *miles* Monimus is dressed in a *paenula*, to which the *cucullus* is attached and hanging down, on the back.[918] The *bardocucullus* was a *paenula* with a cap, of Gallic origin.[919] The *scortea* was the heavy coat for protection from rain and cold, together with the wide *laena*.[920]

Colour Evidence

A wide range of evidence for the colours of the soldier's garments comes from literary sources, the surviving traces of coloured pigments on the tombstones, artworks representing military scenes, warriors, soldiers, and the actual recovered specimens. These two latter sources are very important in helping us to understand the shade of the colours mentioned in the literary sources.

A standard uniform white colour for legionary tunics has been proposed by Fuentes,[921] but is probably far from the reality. Different colours and patterns of tunics and cloaks were employed even in the same unit and depending very often on the local availability of supplies. We cannot, however, exclude the possibility that some units wore distinctively coloured garments (**86**), and of course special colours and fabrics distinguished different orders of dress.[922]

The main colours documented chiefly for the army are the always-present red, the pure white (*candidus*) and the off-white (*albus*). James and Goldsworthy suggest that the soldiers, especially the praetorians, could perhaps afford to buy a purer woollen cloth than the civilians, who also wore white tunics. But on the Palestrina mosaic one of the praetorians wears a reddish[923] sleeveless tunic, knotted at the back of the neck. Moreover, the dress of the praetorians was strictly linked to the personal taste of the emperor. The guardsman dressed in Hellenistic style represented on the Domus Aurea (**86**) could well be representative of a elite guardsman: he reflected in his arms and dress not only the love of the Emperor Nero for Greek culture and civilisation, but also the Emperor's support for the green faction (*prasina factio*) of the Hippodrome. The dark-green crest of his helmet, together with the green tunic is

the sign of the support from Nero of the chariot's green team. The custom of the guardsmen following the colour of one of the four factions of the Circus (red, white, blue, green) was a Roman legacy that continued into the Byzantine age.[924]

White and red are the colours that are most documented in the artistic works, and according to Martial red (*rufus*) was the clothing colour expressly favoured by the soldiers.[925] Red[926] and white[927] *chitones* or tunics are visible in the el-Fayoum portraits from Egypt (**101**, **201**). The officers are distinctively represented with white *chiton*[928] with *clavi* in grey-violet. They wear red, dark-blue or dark olive-green cloaks, with silver *fibulae*; a crown is often worn on the head, still preserving the symbolism of the eight-pointed Macedonian royal star.

It is worth remembering at this point the passage from Tacitus relating to the triumphal march of the Vitellian army in Rome in AD 69, where the *praefecti*, *tribunes* and senior *centuriones* are described as dressed in dazzling *albae tunicae*.[929] The previously mentioned papyrus BGU 1564, a copy from Egypt of an order for clothing and a blanket to be provided for the army in Cappadocia by the weavers of Philadelphia, dated to AD 138, documents a unit ordering pure white belted tunics (*chiton*) for military use and specifies that all the garments should be made 'from fine soft white wool without dirt, well edged, pleasing and undamaged'.[930]

We could suppose that white was reserved for the officers and some members of the Imperial guards, red for junior centurions and officers, off-white and red for the *milites gregarii*. Considering that many soldiers would have had more than one tunic, we can even suppose that red, in its different hues, was the normal colour of the tunic during the military operations; white or off-white was the colour usually worn on parade or in peacetime, always with the *balteus* and *cingulum*. For the ordinary soldiers unable to afford the best dyed material, a red tunic – as the evidence shows – might mean anything in a wide range of shades from pink to brown and the same criteria would apply to their white tunics, which could be a yellowish or dirty brown shade.

Different shades of red *minium* and pink were used for the *clavi* of the tunics, bearing in mind that the pink and red shades were both referred to in the ancient ideology as red-purple. Propertius mentions, for instance, the Iberian red *minium*,[931] which should correspond to the colour already mentioned by Livy for the bands decorating the tunic of the Spanish soldiers.

The tunics from the Nahal Ever cave show three different colours: there is a red tunic with dark purple *clavi* (preserved in a single sheet); this echoed the tales of the Talmud about the red tunics of the Roman soldiers. This tunic is, in its preserved shape, 58 cm wide and 78 cm long. Then there is a mauve tunic with faded purple *clavi*, preserved with two of its sheets still sewn together, a slit for the head and the stitching at the selvedges. The third tunic is beige with dark red *clavi*.

The *chlamys*, like the *sagum*, was usually red or red-brown; the *clamys kokkinos*, which the soldiers put to mock Jesus was simply a military mantle.[932] Cloaks and military *paenulae* are often represented in a yellow-brown colour too, but the *paenula* of a soldier from the Pompeii painting is distinctively yellow-brown with dark reddish *clavi* (**292**) and a grey-green scarf. Apparently off-duty, he wears a white *tunica* under the *paenula*, just visible beneath the hem of the cloak and the soldier's left sleeve. He could be identified as a member of the praetorian guard by the weighted *pilum* held in his left hand. His appearance is in fact very similar to the praetorians of the Cancelleria relief.

Also from Pompeii a fresco shows a *taberna* scene with four men, perhaps a civilian and three soldiers (because their tunic hems are above the knee). However, they do not appear to have military belts or side arms, and many civilians also wore their tunics above the knee. The figure on the right wears a red tunic with thin dark *clavi*, and a narrow bluish-grey cloak (probably a *paenula*). A second one wears an unbelted off-white or yellowish tunic with narrow *clavi*. The others wear darker tunics than the right-hand figure, and *clavi* can be seen on one of them.[933]

Alternative colours for the *paenulae* exist. In a Greek illuminated papyrus of the Hadrianic period, the episode of a judicial litigation between a woman and a soldier shows the man clad in a medium blue *paenula*,[934] decorated by two running *clavi*. The Vindolanda tablets mention a white *paenula*, probably reserved for the commander of the garrison. This find corresponds to the mention by Martial of a *paenula gausapina*, i.e. made of very thin long animal hairs,[935] of pure white colour. *Lacernae* and *abollae* of red (*coccinus*), white (*albus*) and purple are also mentioned.[936]

Obviously, the *paludamentum* of the generals was strictly always red.[937] Purple was the colour reserved for the emperor, in its various shades.[938] Pliny the Elder[939] states that *paludamentum* cloaks were dyed with the *coccus*, the natural pigment that gave it a red brilliant colour. The *chlamis* of the probable praetorian guard on the Domus Aurea fresco is also red (**86**), wrapped around his armour and arm following the style of the Augustus from Prima Porta (**4**). Wool of purple and amethyst colours are also widely mentioned in the sources.[940]

Virgil, in the *Aeneid*, speaks of a type of cloak known as a *sagulum virgatum et lucens*. The descriptions in the Gaelic and Latin poems would lead us to believe that the Celtic tribal chiefs penetrating into Latium during the time of Camillus would have worn cloaks striped or fringed in deep red, purple or green, a fashion followed by the Romans.

The techniques of dyeing are now well known from the Nahal Hever specimens. The yellow (saffron) colour was obtained from the *crocus sativus*, the red or alizarin was produced from the so-called *rubia tinctorium*. Pliny the Elder also stressed the fact that this was the most important of the red dyes, because without it, leather and wool stuffs could not be dyed.[941] Blue was dyed with the indigo, which could, in various mixtures, imitate the so-called Tyrian purple (*murex brandaris*).

Caps and Other Clothes

It is known from the sources that a wide range of caps were worn by the soldiers.[942] The word for the cap was *pileus*[943] or *pilos*, indicating a kind of felt. Three unique hats of military use have been attested by the excavations of Mons Claudianus and Dydimoi, from Egypt. The first hat is, from the point of view of the study of the military hats of the Roman army, one of the most sensational discoveries of the last century. The Pannonian hat or '*pileus Pannonicus*' is the most recorded military cap for the late Roman Empire,[944] most often represented in the mosaics and other artwork from the late third century AD. Until now, however, it was known only from artistic iconography, which represented it as a pillbox hat of various sizes in height. In Mons Claudianus the specimen MC 922[945] is a cap entirely made of dark-green felt, which looks exactly like the low fez or pillbox hat shown in many sources. The wool, felted into this shape, measured approximately 2 mm in thickness (**309**). The crown, flat and oval, measured about 19.5 × 13.5 cm. The sides were more or less straight and reached a maximum height of 11 cm. The specimen could be dated to AD 100–20. This date is very important because it ascribes the use of such a cap in the Roman army – in the Roman garrisons of the Egyptian desert – 150 years earlier than the period in which it begins to be represented as the usual cap of the Roman *miles*. The flat-topped cap was clearly used by workmen and lightly armed soldiers, or worn by off-duty soldiers. It is believed to have been made of fur or leather, then its use became more widespread and it was finally adopted as the main military cap, until, at least, the sixth century AD. Its origins must perhaps be looked for in the similar caps worn by the *auxilia* Palmyrene and Osroene of the Eastern Provinces (**305**).

305 Palmyrene officer, third century AD (*Istanbul, Archaeological Museum; author's photo, courtesy of the museum*)

306 Tricoloured cap from Mons Claudianus, second century AD (*courtesy of Lise Bender Jørgensen*).

The cap is composed of alternating sections in red, yellow and green, meeting in a green triangle at the back, with two red triangles marking the forehead. It is perhaps this kind of cap that is represented as being worn by soldiers and legionaries, like those visible on the gravestone of Markos Aurelios Alexis

307 Under-helmet cap, from Didymoi (*textile D99. 2511.4., c. 96 AD, excavations funded by the French Ministery of Foreign Affairs and the French Institute for Oriental Archaeology (IFAO) in Cairo, under the direction of Dr. Hélène Cuvigny (CNRS); restored by Ms Danièle Nadal, Laboratory Materia Viva, Toulouse*).

A very exceptional model of cap, due to the way it was made. It is made of felt and wool; this kind of weaving is achieved by changing the direction of the weft, and it is ornamented by a tapestry band. This is one of the very rare specimens of undercap preserved, very similar in shape to that represented on the Pompeii painting of Aeneas wounded. Note the shape of the cheek guard lining

A second shape for the *pileus* was the conical one that could also be used as a helmet liner. In ancient Greece this kind of *pilos* was usually worn by miners, freedmen and light infantrymen (*psiloi*). It is obvious that in the Roman East its continued in the same way, so that a second multi-coloured conical *pileus* (MC 1110) from Mons Claudianus might be associated to the military garrison (**306**). It was found almost complete, with a round crown, earmuffs and neck protector. This could really be a cap for wearing under a helmet, it is made of fabric cut to shape and sewn together. The crown is divided into fifteen tri-coloured segments (green, red and yellow).

The third specimen, from Dydimoi,[946] is a unique piece in multi-coloured felt and wool, still with the shape of the helmet under which it was worn (**307**). This is a clear specimen of *Galericulum*, the underhelmet cap worn to cushion the weight of the helmet and to absorb the impact from blows and to protect the hair from sweat and dirt.[947]

A very unique specimen in leather, a *petasus* of the Greek type, has been recovered from the Vindonissa camp.[948] It was a typical headgear worn by fishermen, sailors, travellers, countrymen and soldiers, that the Romans adopted from *Italiotai* (Greeks from Magna Graecia). In the early Imperial age it was considered an exotic cap in Latin-speaking countries, but not in Greece or in the east. The fragments recovered from Vindonissa allowed the reconstruction of two *petasii* (**308**). Other kinds of caps were worn in the Eastern regions following the influence of the Parthians,[949] such as hats with Phrygian shapes or the typical Persian *tiara*. These were favoured by the Eastern auxiliaries.

The Vindolanda tablets mention other items of clothing: undertunics (*subuclae*), undercloaks (*subpaenulae*), overcoats (*superariae*) and cloaks made from bark (*sagacorticia*).[950] Obviously the soldiers, on or off duty, and especially in the far garrisons,

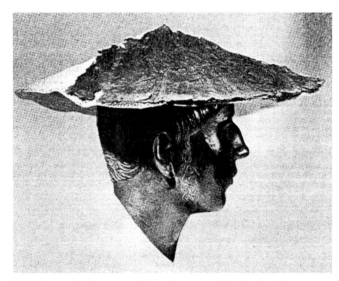

308 Roman leather *petasus* from the camp of Vindonissa, first quarter of first century AD (*photo Vindonissa Museum; courtesy of the museum*)

wore the same garments that were available to civilians. A particular garment of Gallic origin was the *sequanica*, probably originally used by the tribe of the Sequani, a Celtic people of the Saône Basin. It was a sort of heavy coat, very thick and ultraprotective against the cold weather.[951] It was shaped like a modern overall, with long sleeves, and its shape is visible on some Celtic statuettes of Gallo-Roman period. True overalls or *endromida* are mentioned in the sources.[952]

Around the neck was wrapped the *focale*, or *maphorion-maphortés*, the characteristic woollen[953] necklet or scarf, that, when the armour was worn, was pushed inside the neck opening (**PLATE III**, **97**, **111**, **157**, **290**). It protected the neck from the chafing of the armour and from the rough leather *vinculum*, the thongs of the *bucculae*. Its use is attested in many sculptures, some of them showing a very voluminous scarf, and attested as a visible part of the soldiers' uniform. On the columns of Trajan and Marcus Aurelius all the soldiers wear scarves either tucked beneath their armour (**214**) or worn outside the armour, tied in front (**57**, **59**). It is usually worn inside the armour with the laminated *lorica*, and outside with the mail and leather armour.

309 Pannonian cap from Mons Claudianus, second–third century AD, (*courtesy of Bender Lise Jørgensen*)
The lower edge is not as well preserved, but this exceptional specimen of *pileus* still measures 51 cm around the crown – bearing in mind that the sides possibly sloped slightly, the bottom circumference could have been slightly bigger. It was worn high on the head, so would have fitted an adult, especially a soldier. It is the oldest specimen of *pileus Pannonicus* preserved.

This is perhaps due to the possibility that the scarf helped to hold the position of the *segmentata* armour around the neck, so it needed to be tucked inside,[954] whereas with the other armour its protective function could be achieved just by wrapping it around the neck.

Very often it is worn in combination with the *paenula* (**304**)[955] or the cloak, or even the single tunic. Antonucci, by observing the scarf worn by the possible praetorian of the Domus Aurea, suggested that the scarf, much more than the tunic, could be used as a badge of the *cohors* to identify individual units through its colour. The same theory was proposed by Fuentes, who suggested for example that legions of naval origin might have traditionally retained a blue *focale*.[956] A white knotted scarf is visible on funerary el-Fayoum portraits and in a mosaic scene from Apamea.[957]

The scarf could also have a very practical purpose, considering that it was used by the paramilitary troops of provincial governors, the *diogmitai*. Saint Peonios, in Smyrna, was captured by a policeman who put his scarf or *maphorion* (or *maphórtés*) around the saint's neck and tightened it until he almost choked.[958] This implies that the scarf was rather long and could be used like a lasso to arrest prisoners and drag them '*obtorto collo*' (by the neck)! The *focale* or *maphorion* could be fastened around the neck by a *fibula*, sometimes ornamented with white pearls for the officers (**201**).

Some historians and re-enactors have suggested that worn around the waist beneath the military belts was a waistband or cummerbund that they have called, in a modern coinage, a *fascia ventralis*.[959] We can however just suppose that the word *ventralis* or *ventrale* indicates a waistband, wrapped one or more times around the belly.[960] V*entralis* is glossed as *ligatura ventris*, i.e. 'the ventralis which covers only the belly',[961] with a clear reference to the width of the clothing.

Pliny the Elder writes[962] that from his time the men had begun to wear *villosa ventralia*, made of *gausapae* and *amphimalia*, i.e. thick and double-lined clothing of wool. In a second passage he specifies that the *ventralis* was a bandage used for medical purpose, because absinthe was inserted in it as a prevention from testicular cancer.[963]

Nevertheless there was until recently no mention in ancient literary sources of these waistbands being worn specifically by military men. However, a newly discovered document from Vindolanda (1528C–E) records that a soldier called Taurinus bought *acia*, thread, to repair and re-stitch his *ventralis*. The purpose of these waistbands would be twofold. First they would act as a back support and second they would protect the tunic from any sharp edges on the back of the belt. The fact that Taurinus needed to repair his waistband could be seen as evidence for this. Furthermore, the band, like the scarf mentioned above, might have been used to identify individual units by different colours or simply another way of enhancing the military belt or showing off the soldiers' rank and status.

The best example of one of these waistbands appears to be the broken stele of a soldier found at Cassaco in northern Italy.[964] Although similar belts can be seen worn by civilian labourers (*fasciae interulae*) wrapped around the belly and this was the function of the *semicinctium*, a short waistcoat.[965]

An interesting juridical document[966] might explain a further function of this waistband. Ulpianus said that the Emperor Hadrian stated that it was possible to claim back the small coins (*nummuli*) from among the under garments (*pannicularia*) belonging to a man condemned to death '*victus sui causa in promptu habuerit*' ('the guilty should have had at his disposition'). So the *ventrale* could have also used as pocket (*funda*) by the wearer, a function that seems confirmed also by many *glossae* where the two words are assimilated.[967]

Trousers and Leg-coverings; Socks

Breeches and longer trousers (*bracae*) were now widely worn by the Romans, especially in the northern regions. The word *braca* is itself of Germanic origin. Breeches were worn, at first, only in the northern and eastern provinces, where breeches or leg-covering were a typical part of military costume. Then, in the early Imperial age, they became fashionable even in Italy. The Hellenised regions of the east adopted breeches from the Persians, Scythians and Iranians, while Parthian horse-archers were called[968] *milites bracati*.

Both the close-fitting type, of leather or linen, and the far looser and wider trousers made of wool, were used by the Roman army when the easterners became regular *auxilia* or irregular *numeri*. The horse-archer *numeri*, fighting in their own dress, began to spread the wide breeches of Persian fashion among the troops. Both these types could be tucked into short, soft leather riding boots, or worn over them in a loose way, keeping only the feet visible. So these clothes, of clear barbarian origin, penetrated into the Roman army long before the period of their wider use, in the third and fourth centuries AD.

Celtic breeches (*bracae*),[969] used by Gauls and Gallo-Roman *auxilia*, were often decorated with shining colours (*bracae virgatae*).[970] Usually the Gauls are represented with long breeches, but shorter versions were more commonly used by the soldiers. Two short types, one coming down to just above the knee, the other just under the knee, were used. They were fastened around the waist with a leather string or a rope.

The short breeches or *feminalia-femoralia* are seen on many monuments, first of all Trajan's Column (**112**, **148**, **214**) shows them as a familiar part of the legionary or auxiliary equipment, even being worn by the emperor. They could be of simple cloth but specimens in leather have been found in different locations, such as Bar Hill (**199**) and Vindonissa.[971] The stele of C. Valerius Crispus clearly shows his legs covered by short leather pants, with two rows of *pteryges* at the ends (**PLATE III**, **46**);[972] a large leather fragment from Vindonissa could be

a part of such breeches (**310**). A reinforcement was sewn on the edge of these shorts, fitted with five pairs of ring-shaped holes through which was threaded a binding, at the hip height. At the side were sewn further triangular reinforcements, where simple gussets were probably firmly sewn down. The average calculated by Gansser-Burckhardt for the width of the thigh was 45 cm.

The use of this kind of short trousers was not so common, considering that the military gravestones show them only worn in connection with corselets. Cavalrymen, on the other hand, are often represented clad in long trousers. So the *eques* Aurelius Saturninus, on his gravestone dating to the rule of Commodus, shows that long trousers were already established as part of the praetorian cavalry uniform.[973]

Leggings (*ocreae*)[974] were also used, and military versions would have been similar to the finds of complete examples from Britain and Denmark. Already mentioned from the age of Marcus Aurelius by Galen,[975] and confirmed by bandage-like textiles found in Vindolanda, these *fasciae* were the direct evolution of the *fasciae cretatae* cited in the Late Consulate age. The Emperor Augustus is remembered as wearing *fasciae feminalia* around the thighs and small boots (*tibiales*) on his feet.[976]

Underpants were used and called *subligares*. Documents from Vindolanda mention the gift of two pairs of *subligaria*. The *perizoma* was still widely employed, as confirmed by a hide specimen from Britain, variously dated between the second and

310 Fragments of possible leather trousers from Vindonissa, first half of the first century AD (*Vindonissa Museum, ex Gansser-Burckhardt, courtesy of Vindonissa Museum*).
The picture shows a fragment of the right front piece, with triangular reinforcement and the holes through which the fastening strings passed

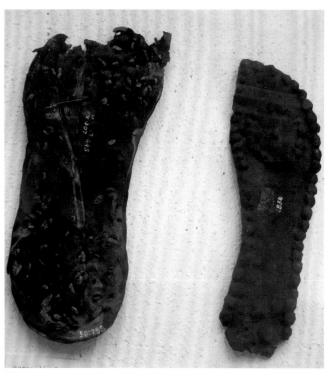

311 Military boots from Vindonissa, second century AD (*Vindonissa Museum; photo courtesy of the museum*)

the third centuries; this *perizoma* has six laces for closing.[977] This kind of garment was often designated as *campestris*.[978]

Socks (*udones*)[979] were often used, especially in combination with the open military boots called *caligae*. So on the Cancelleria relief in Rome praetorian guardsmen wear open-toed and open-heeled socks inside their *caligae*. They were made of wool and linen and especially goat hair.[980]

Shoes

The shoes in ancient times were a sign of social status, and this also was true for the military versions, Petronius mentions in the *Satyricon* a soldier who spotted a certain Encolpius impersonating a soldier because he was wearing white 'dandy' Hellenic shoes, called *phecasia*.[981]

The basic high Imperial age military boot was the *caliga*. Evolved from Etruscan forerunners, this military boot was of sturdy construction and studded under the sole (**311**), to allow a better grip upon the ground. Sometimes this created problems, as for the centurion Julian from Bithynia, whose shoes (Josephus calls them *hypodêmata*) 'were full of thick and sharp nails' so that, during the Jerusalem battle in AD 70, he slipped down during combat on the smooth surface of the Temple pavement, laid with marble of different colours, and was killed, in spite of gallant resistance, by the Jews.[982]

The *caliga* had an open appearance (**PLATE III**, **65**, **66**, **261**), and was made of three layers: a sole, insole and upper,

with the straps tightened to fit more closely. The insole was cut in one with the strapwork.[983] The sole was often fitted with nails (*clavi caligares*), destined to make marching easier.[984] The many different shoes of such a type often needed to have the nails renewed, as they tended to wear out. This has been noticed on some specimens from Vindonissa camp (**311**). The old Republican *calcei* were worn by the plebeians during the empire, and for this reason these shoes were 'cold-shouldered' by the contemporary highbrows such as Martial,[985] Petronius and so on. The colours, the quality of the leather and the sizes of the shoes were selected according to rank. White-yellow *calcei* are worn by the praetorians of the Palestrina mosaic. This kind of *calcei* is also depicted in Roman use on a number of Republican artworks.

The Roman senators, even with their military uniform wore their particular boots or *calcei* (**145**) with four thongs (*lora patricia*).[986] Valuable specimens of *calcei* and high boots (*cothurni* or *mullei*) were worn by the generals and emperors when they led their troops on the battlefield, although emperors such as Trajan preferred to wear simple military boots (**71**).[987] They are, at the moment, only attested from statues and other figurative monuments, because they were certainly made with soft leather uppers that do not survive very well.[988] Sculptures show them in any case as having a clearly defined separate sole, therefore many fragments of sewn boots soles found at Vindolanda and other localities have been classified as *calcei*.

During the empire, emperors and commanders lavishly decorated their boots. Isidorus speaks of bone or golden clasps called *malleoli*. A very detailed statue of a general, from the Forum of Nerva in Rome (**312**),[989] has *cothurni* that were once painted in soft red and gold leather, which would be used on the battlefield as well as on parade.[990] They are similar to those worn by the personification of Rome at the Museo Nazionale di Napoli (collezione Farnese). The small lion's heads could have been made from real cubs (maybe lion) or imitation heads that were clearly copies of real lions' heads.[991] We do not have written sources specifying the meaning of the small lion's heads: perhaps they derived from Hellenic and Thracian boots called *embadès* of suede leather or fawn lined in fur. Similar embroidered *cothurni*, with gilded heads of lions, are worn also by Trajan on the Great Frieze[992] and from numerous statues of emperors, governors and generals (**195**). They are also visible upon the *strator* of the Emperor Hadrian, on a exceptional monument from Villa Borghese (**300**).

From the second century AD other kinds of military footwear (*calciamenta*) begins to appear,[993] more tightly closed, which would gradually replace the old *caliga*, although over a very long period of time. These new shapes of military *calcei* have been recovered from Qasr Ibrim (Egypt).[994] Although the traditional style of *caligae* survives in some form until much later, there is no complete archaeological record of it at Vindolanda and elsewhere, but complete specimens of *karbatinai* that can be ascribed to some later specimens of *caligae* have been recovered

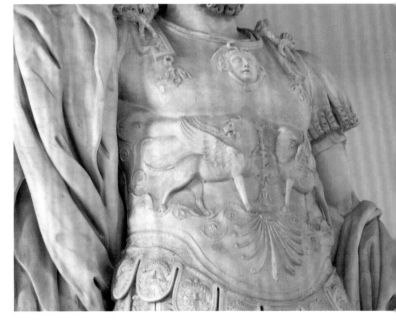

312 Statue of Roman general or Mars, from the Nerva Forum, end of the first century AD (*Rome, Musei Capitolini; author's photo, by kind permission of the Sovraintendenza per I Beni Culturali del Comune di Roma*).

The sculpture represents a specific set of armour, following the fine military traditions from the Greco-Roman world, entirely appropriate to the subject matter of the god of war. Note that the helmet is a combination of Corinthian and Chalcidian styles. The splendid muscled armour that the artist used as model for this statue was probably a unique piece, and probably a imperial one. The griffins, the *gorgoneion* and the *candelabrum* have exactly the same motifs as the imperial statues of the time. The detail shows as this was anything but a 'fantasy' piece. The skirt of the armour was made of metallic *pteryges*, embossed and linked by a clasp. The boots (*cothurni*) are extraordinarily ornate, and copied from originals made of soft leather and decorated with figures of small lions

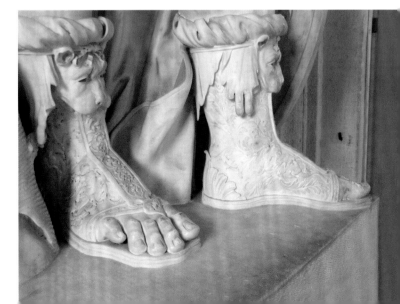

in Saalburg, Welzheim and Bar Hill.[995] The *karbatinai* were made from a single piece of leather from which were cut the sole and the borders that were pulled down on the foot.[996] If more soles and nails were added to it, they transformed it into a *caliga*. A fragment of a terracotta sculpture from the Vatican represents a soldier wearing this.[997]

Hobnailed soles were still applied to these shoes. In camp life sandals (*soleae*) or slippers were also used by soldiers. They were generally of raw leather and sometimes lined with wool (*soleae lanatae*).[998] An interesting document written on a ostrakon found in Krokodilô, in the Egyptian desert, attests the request from Ioulas, a slave of the soldier Lucretius, for a piece of leather for his sandals (σανδαλια = λανταλια in the Greek text!).[999] Shoe colour varied according to the rank of the owner; these regulations remain throughout the whole Imperial era. Another type of off-duty footwear worn by soldiers would have been the wooden-soled shoes that had to be worn when entering the baths because the floors were so hot! An example of one of these shoes was found at Vindolanda.

~ Naval Equipment ~

The general impression given by monuments relating to sailors (*classici milites*[1000]) and the fighting crew is that of lightly armed soldiers. The fighters were normally equipped with all type of weapons, but especially swords, spears and shields. The legionaries of the Mainz column attack the enemy under the protection of their rectangular convex shield,[1001] wearing a sculpted helmet of Imperial-Gallic type with a dolphin engraved on it: but their body is protected only by a double tunic. Hexagonal shields are depicted in the scene on Trajan's Column where *classiarii* are engaged in road-building.[1002]

Milites classiarii of the second century AD were armed with short swords and daggers, as attested in funerary reliefs. If the dagger follows the traditional form of the Imperial one, the sword seems to anticipate the *semispatha* of the later empire. But *pugio* and *gladius* were also worn, as by the *milites legionis*. The most spectacular find of equipment from a *faber navalis* of the Misenum fleet has been made in Herculaneum in 1982.[1003] The 37-year-old soldier was caught by the sudden eruption of Vesuvius of 25 August AD 79 and buried under the 20 cm of ash that covered the city. He was found with a scabbard and a single-edged sword of Pompeian type on the right side of the body, and a *pugio* attached to a plated *cingulum*. He had a leather purse attached to the belt, which contained coins of the Emperor Nero. The quality of the equipment shows that the marines of the Italian fleet were equipped with precious items; these were not reserved just for the officers. The silver *cingulum* was probably produced, like others found in Pompeii and also made of heavy silver,[1004] by local smiths working in the area around Misenum, who probably also made the *gladius* scabbard parts – such as the chapes with palmette-ends – and the single-edged short *gladius*. This marine bore tools on his shoulders, an adze and three chisels that appear to have been slung over the man's back,[1005] identifying him as a ship's carpenter, a *faber navalis* of the only possible fleet in this location, the *Classis Misenatis*.

The skeleton of the man tells us a lot about his life: three missing front teeth suggest a fight; an abnormal lump in the femur of his left leg could be the result of a stabbing wound; the rounded shaft of the femurs were signs of good nutrition and good muscular constitution; the adductor tubercle was slightly enlarged, probably because this man was used to holding lumber between his knees, as a marine soldier-carpenter usually did.

The axe (*dolabra*) was a favourite weapon of these sailors and marines (*dolatores*) for cutting the grapnels of the enemy. Oval and rectangular shields of the Celtic type, fitted with circular *umbones*, spears and heavy folded tunics similar to those of the Mainz monument are worn by the *nautae* represented in the famous pilaster of the Tiberian age built on the quay of the Ile de la Cité (Paris). They are wearing simple helmets of probable Coolus–Mannheim typology,[1006] or felt caps. The equipment is very similar to that of the Celtic auxiliaries of the Late Republican and Early Augustan period, and spears and swords loaded on a ship are visible on a fragment of the same pilaster, representing a ship on the Seine.

The relative lightness of the equipment does not exclude the possibility that bronze or metal armour was used. Proof of this is the exceptional piece recovered near Cueva del Jarro, at Almuñécar, coming from a Roman shipwreck and found together with *amphorae* of Dressel 20 and Dressel 38 type, i.e. dated around the beginning of the first and the end of the second centuries AD.[1007] It is a piece of armour, a muscled breastplate (*lorica*) in bronze, which reproduces a bare, markedly muscular torso. Its height is approximately 40 cm (**29**). This might have belonged to a senior officer on the ship.

The *classiarii* officers fighting against the Barbarians on the Danube, depicted on a sarcophagus variously dated between the first and the second centuries AD, are equipped with helmets of old Italic fashions, having *geminae pinnae* and a horsehair rigid crest. They are covered by muscled breastplates that seem to be made of leather, and one of them is armed with a knife (*culter*) with a slightly curved blade (**313**).

One of the most intriguing *stela* of *classiarii* has been recently found in Ravenna, in the excavations of the Classe

313 Fragment of sarcophagus related to a naval clash on the Danube, representing marines fighting Germans, Sora, in situ, first century–second century AD, present location unknown, (*photo reproduced by kind permission of Professor Tanzilli*).

This scene probably shows a successful episode in which the dead had participated. Professor Tanzilli is much more inclined to date it to the time of the Domitian or Trajanic wars along the Danube. Note the helmets, still linked to the old Italic tradition of the Buggenum–Montefortino typology, and the muscled leather armour. The wonderful sarcophagus was stolen many years ago and for the moment has still been not recovered by the Italian authorities

harbour. It is the *cippus* of a young roman officer in military dress, with armour, sword and sandals (**314**); in his right hand he holds a supposed javelin (*pilum*) and his left hand leans on the *gladius*. The soldier wears a muscled cuirass with *pteryges* on the shoulders and a fringed striped military skirt. A *pugio* is also visible and *caligae* are shown on his feet. A curiosity is the long transverse belt that is assumed not to hold a weapon, so was probably a military decoration. The incomplete inscription reports the soldier's name, MON(TAN)US[?] CAPITO, and his career status of *optio*, that he was in service on a *liburna* – a small ship used for reconnaissance and for fighting pirates – called *AURATA* (golden). The monument was commissioned by Cocneus, probably one of his colleagues.

Agrippa, if the identification of Fuentes is correct, wears a pale-blue tunic in the Palestrina mosaic[1008] and a muscled cuirass, in metal or even in leather or linen. The sky-blue colour was associated with the navy and especially with great admirals such as Agrippa.[1009]

If the scarf was used a means of identification, there is maybe the possibility that the sailors wore a blue *focale* around the neck. Some wore a simple cloth belt (*zona militaris*) around the waist, with fringes to which the sword appears to be fastened. The mid-blue/green colour (*venetus*) was the most widely used colour amongst the *nautae* and *classiarii* for their uniforms, but it was not exclusive, however.

Traces of red on the cloak and tunic are still visible on the tombstone of Statius Rufinus from Athens.[1010] The tombstone also shows a *sagum* cloak with a small tassel visible on one edge. This *stela* represents the dead man with a lamp in his hand, like those represented on Trajan's Column and that found on the Comacchio shipwreck in Italy.[1011] Lamps were an important means of signalling on military ships. Another possibility

314 *Stela* or *cippus* of Montanus Capito, *optio* of the *Classis Ravennatis*, first century AD (*Classe, Museo; author's photo, courtesy of the Soprintendenza Archeologica dell'Emilia Romagna, Sede di Ravenna*).

a) Detail of *balteus* and *pugio*. **b**) Detail of the hairstyle, of the *sagum* cloak fastened on the left shoulder and of the transversal *balteus* for the *gladius*. **c**) Detail of the *thorax stadios*. **d**) Detail of the first two rows of *kremasmata* coming out from the *lorica* shoulder and detail of the padded *subarmale* (sleeves). **e**) Detail of the *sagum*. **f**) Detail of the *hasta navalis*. **g**) Detail of the *gladius*. **h**) Detail of the protection of the neck and the *focale*. **i**) Detail of the padding of the lower *pteryges*. **j**) Detail of the *caligae*.

The tombstone is very rare due to the extremely detailed portrait that, even if relatively small, shows the real appearance of the deceased with his pudding basin haircut and the typical childlike appearance a common detail in the Julio-Claudian period. However, I would suggest a late Flavian date, due to the name of the *liburna* mentioned in the inscription, attested in other document of that age and probably linked with the new circus factions created by Domitianus. In a late Flavian stele from Constanza on the Black Sea, a T. Flavius Capito is mentioned, perhaps from the same family. The *cippus* of the *cornicen* C. Coponius Felicio, preserved in the Palazzo Ducale of Mantua (**198**) is virtually identical in the hairstyle, and in the quality of the details rendered in the sculpture. The letters – which preserve their original red colour in the Coponius monument – are practically of the same style as that employed in the *cippus* of the naval officer.

The archaeological context in which the Classis *cippus* was found is that of the fifth century. The *cippus* has been re-employed as support for some harbour structures when the Classis area began to expand at the beginning of the fifth century AD, as a result of the transformation of Classis as the harbour of the new capital of the empire, Ravenna. The *cippus* belongs without doubt to the necropolis of the first–third century excavated in Classis, just in the area around the warehouses. This is why the *cippus* was broken and the upper inscription not preserved.

It is possible that the armour worn by the man is a metal muscled cuirass. The *pteryges* and lappets are clearly separated by the main body of the muscled cuirass: on the shoulders you can see the line dividing the double rows of *kremasmata* (hanging strips) from the main body of the armour, and the *pteryges*, under the thick lappets of the lower part of the armour, are clearly separated from overlapping *cymation* by a thickness of approximately 5 mm on the original sculpture. The garment, without armour, would have been similar – with some differences – to the padded garment of the unknown military officer from Modena.

The padding of the sleeve protection is evident. The sculptor was so capable that not only did he show the muscled detail of the armour very well – look at the underlining of the signs at the breast level – but he also showed the thickness between the double rows on the shoulders by a line of approximately 2 mm. The *pteryges* then are evidently thicker than many other *pteryges* on other monuments, so the originals probably were made of different material, such as coarse silk mixed with felt

314a Detail of *balteus* and *pugio*

314b Detail of the hairstyle, of the *sagum* cloak fastened on the left shoulder and of the transversal *balteus* for the *gladius*

314c Detail of the *thorax stadios*

314d Detail of the first two rows of *kremasmata* coming out from the *lorica* shoulder and detail of the padded *subarmale* (sleeves)

314e Detail of the *sagum*

314f Detail of the *hasta navalis*

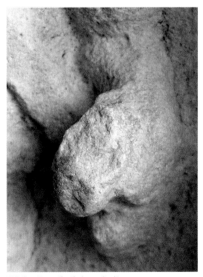

314g Detail of the *gladius*

314h Detail of the protection of the neck and the *focale*

314i Detail of the padding of the lower *pteryges*

314j Detail of the *caligae*

is that, in his hand, Rufinus is holding writing-tablets (*codex ansatus*), visible on other *classiarii* tombstones.[1012]

Very interesting details are also visible on the *stela* of C. Sabinianus, of the same fleet, always from Athens, preserved near the Church of Aghia Triada:[1013] he wears a short sleeveless tunic, a *paenula* cloak, apron belt, *caligae* on his feet and, besides the javelin, he carries a round shield. His dagger is not the usual type of *pugio*, but a more slender weapon, anticipating the *culter venatorius* of the later ages. On the tunic and on the *paenula* the original sculpture still shows traces of brown red.

A letter from the *classiarius* Claudius Terentianus of the *Classis Alexandrina*[1014] to his father sheds some light upon the uniform and the equipment of the sailors. He gives thanks for the *paenula*, a *tunica* and *fasciae* for the legs but he asks his father for a *byrrus castalinus*, i.e. a short mantle perhaps with a hood. Although the meaning of the adjective *castalinus* is obscure it might be an alternative spelling of *castorinus*, therefore meaning a *byrrus* made of beaver skin. This is perfectly conceivable for a garment worn at sea. Moreover he wears a *tunica bracilis* (i.e. with sleeves) with *bracae*, which correspond perfectly with the garments represented on the second-century monuments.

Surprisingly his letter also requests that his father send him more military items, including a battle sword (*gladius pugnatorius*), an axe (*dolabra*), a grapnel (*copula*) and two spears (*longae*)! His father evidently sent him a very good *dolabra* because in the next letter he asks his father for a new one,

because the previous one had been appropriated by his *optio*! (centurion's deputy). After reading the correspondence of Terentianus, one is tempted to ask what the army actually supplied to their soldiers!

In another letter Terentianus also asks for a pair of low-cut leather boots (*caligae*) and a pair of felt stockings (*udones*).[1015] The most ancient specimens of *caligae*, in leather, come from the Comacchio ship.[1016] They give a good idea of the military boots of the sea-fighters. They were strong boots, fastened high on the calf, low-cut, sometimes with nails in the soles, and lined internally with a small sock or a slipper of soft leather. This last detail is therefore confirmed by the tombstone of Rufinus and by the above-mentioned papyrus.

Other shoes used by the marines and shown on their *stelae* are the closed *calcei*, a practice further confirmed by the request addressed to the Emperor Vespasianus by the sailors of the Misenum Fleet to supply them with a higher *calciarium* (boot-money), because of the wear on their shoes caused by the march from Naples to Rome.[1017]

Variations in climate obviously led to differences in clothing between the different *classiarii*. For instance, the *nautae* of the pilaster in Paris are covered by heavy *paenulae* or *lacernae*; the sailors represented on the Danube fleet on Trajan's Column are just clad in the typical military tunic with the bunched neck.[1018]

CONCLUSION

The Roman army, the most efficient of the ancient world, was never an immutable organisation; it was able to adjust to the military and politico-social situations of the different periods of its history. This was a characteristic that allowed the Roman nation to conquer and to develop a dominant position in the Mediterranean world, to create the first European and Mediterranean empire and even to survive, at least in its eastern part, until the end of the Middle Ages. The syncretism of Rome, which allowed peoples of different nations to merge and to embrace a unitary political system, was also reflected in the huge composition of its army. The daily life of legionaries and *auxilia*, of the guardsmen and of the officers, was just the reflection of this complex society. Unity in diversity: this was the secret of Rome.

The weapons and clothing of the Roman soldier changed with the changes in the world that they, day by day, had helped to create. The material culture of the military man was also that of the *pater familias*, who lived in the terrible double dimension of peace and war. The changing and enlargement of the ethnic components of the empire were the main factors in the changing of military equipment and clothing.

The weaponry of the Romans was a symbol of the power of the *res publica*. They mirrored the divine and human symbols that created the myth of an invincible Rome. Their representation on the artistic works could not differ from the reality that the weapons themselves expressed when used on the battlefield. Weapons advanced technologically and, at the same time, were visual reminders of the imperial power and strength.

Changes in form and usage were the result not only of technological evolution, but also of the ever-growing number of people within the empire; they very soon made the Roman battle army look bright and varied. The huge number and variety of enemies and fighting techniques allowed a further development of the military equipment as well: all these phenomena were gradually changing the appearance of the Roman Latin soldier and were duly recorded in the artistic monuments all over the empire.

So the study of Roman military equipment cannot be limited to isolated finds or to single parallels: art, archaeology and literary sources must go in the same direction to allow us and the future generations of historians, archaeologists, re-enactors and lovers of history to understand fully, and with the logic of the men who created it, the fascinating and cruel culture that expressed the greatest military power of the ancient world.

APPENDIX

FURTHER DETAILS OF *MILITES*, *EQUITES* AND WEAPONS FROM
THE ARAUSIUS (ORANGE) ARCH

315a

315b

315c

315d

315e

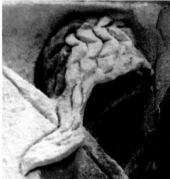

315f

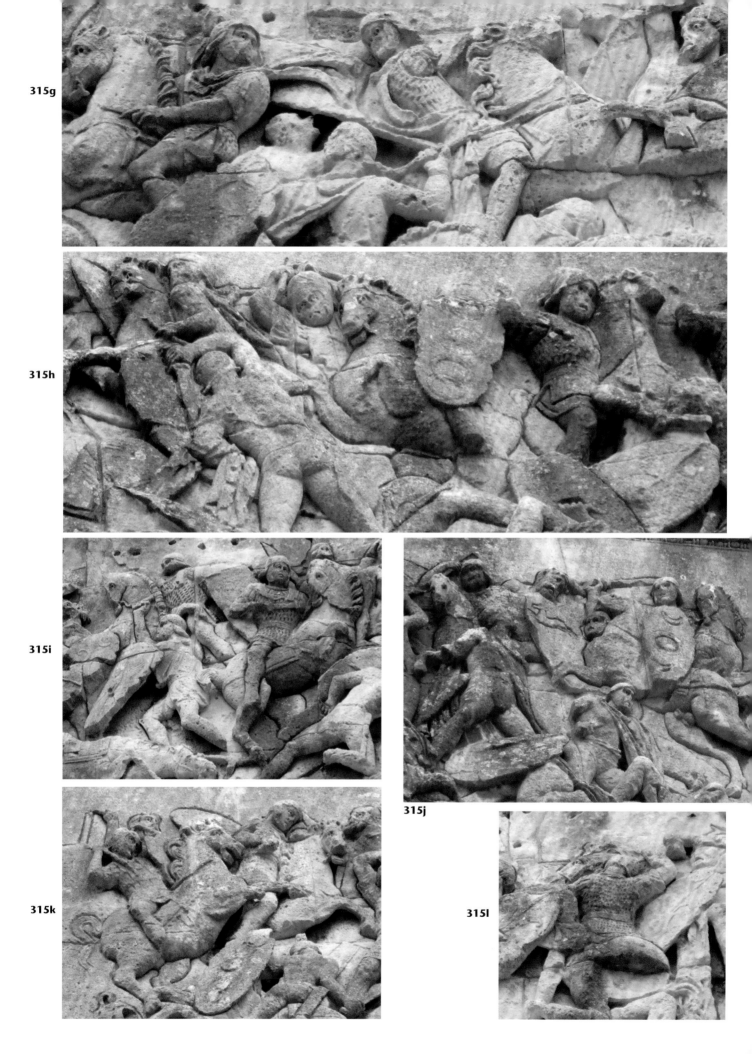

315g

315h

315i

315j

315k

315l

315m

315n

315o

315p

315q

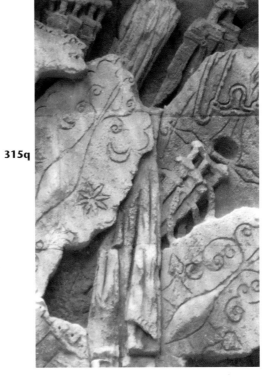

315r

315s

315t

315u

315v

315w

315x

315y

315z

315aa

Notes

~ Introduction ~

1 This assertion is open to the criticism that change was so great in the evolution of the Roman state that this is a meaningless continuity, certainly so after 1204, and arguably so long before. But if the bulk of Latin warriors on the Palatine Hill were of Indo-European origin and if the last defenders of Constantinople were Hellenised people proud to be 'Romans' with no or only very little ethnic connection to the original Latins, we are speaking of the evolution and development of a structure – the Roman army – inside the same state: the Roman Empire. Changes in organisation, structure and ethnic composition were strong from the time of Romulus to Caracalla's era, but there were no doubts among the Romans of Caracalla's time that they were the heirs and the uninterrupted continuation of Romulus' state. It is a undeniable historical truth that the Roman *res publica* (in its own meaning) was born in 753 BC and ended in AD 1453 at Constantinople (or Trebizond in AD 461).

~ Part I ~

1 The well-known expression 'First Triumvirate' is not correct because the *Triumviri* were a college of three magistrates, whereas Crassus, Pompeius and Caesar were just three citizens who concluded an unofficial pact among themselves. Cracco Ruggini and Cassola, 1982, p. 93.

2 It is noteworthy that the word '*legionarii*' was not used as technical term, but only as appellation; for all the Roman histories, the technical word to indicate the soldier was always *miles*. See Caes., *BC*, I, 78; *BA*, LXIX, 2.

3 '*Veni, vidi, vici . . .*'.

4 This was a real magistrature: *Triumviri Res Publicae constituendae*, i.e. charged to reform the Roman state.

5 Front., *Strat.*, I, 6, 1.

6 They were the ancient subdivisions and classifications of the Consular *legio*, introduced in the age of Camillus (fourth century BC): the *hastati* fought in the first line of the battle, responsible for launching the first attack against the wall of the enemy's battle array; the *principes* fought in the second line, ready to replace the *hastati*; the *triarii* were the more heavily armed legionaries, with more experience, fighting in the third line and ready to replace the *principes* or to form a defensive wall in case of a collapse of the first two lines, allowing so the reconstitution of the *legio*'s battle array. See Chiarucci, 2003, pp. 16–17.

7 Plut., *Pomp.*, LIX; App., Εμφ. Πολ., I, 82.

8 Plut., *Sull.*, IX; *Mar.*, XXXV; *Cic.*, XXXVI; Cic., *Ad Att.*, V, 15; App., *Mithr.*, LXXII.

9 But again it was not the rule; at the Battle of Pharsalus the Caesar's *cohortes* were composed of 275 men, and those of Pompeius of 409 men; see Caes., *BC*, III, 2, 87.

10 Caes., *BC*, III, 91.

11 Antonucci, 1996, p. 6.

12 The eleven legions of Caesar in the Gallic War were: the I, VII, VIII (Macedonica and Hispanica), IX, X, XI, XII, XIII, XIV, XV. Another eleven were added during the Civil Wars: the Gallic *Legio Alaudae*, especially trained in combat against elephants, the XXI, XXVI, XXVII, XXX, XXXVI, XXXVIII, the three legions of the client King Deiotarus and the so-called *Vernacula*. Another sixteen legions were levied in 44 BC for the war against the Parthians, although they were not employed. Gonzàlez, 2003, pp. 719—20.

13 Caes., *BG*, I, 52; II, 20; *BC*, III, 62; V, 1, 24–5.

14 Livy, VII, 5, 9; in 362 BC these *tribuni* were appointed through the elections of the people, when there were four legions, for a total of twenty-four *tribuni*.

15 Lindenschmit, 1882, p. 12; Coussin, 1926, p. 133ff.; Feugère, 2002, p. 30; following Bishop and Coulston, 1993, pp. 49–50; it was the final result of various throwing weapons used by the Italic populations.

16 Caes., *BG*, I, 25, battle against the Helvetii: '. . . It was a great hindrance to the Gauls in fighting, that, when several of their bucklers had been by one stroke of the [Roman] javelins [*pila*] pierced through and pinned fast together, as the point of the iron had bent itself, they could neither pluck it out, nor, with their left hand entangled, fight with sufficient ease . . .'.

17 Radman-Livaja, 2004, pp. 23ff.

18 Dautova Ruševljan – and Vujović, 2006, p. 51.

19 Antonucci, 1996, p. 6,

20 Plut., *Mar.*, XXV, 1–2.

21 Pol., *Prag.*, VI, 23, 8–11.

22 Caes., *BC*, III, 86.

23 Caes., *BG*, I, 25; App., *Kelt.*, I: 'what the Romans called *pila*, four-sided, part wood and part iron, and not hard except at the pointed end'.

24 Pomp. Porf., *Ad Horat. Sat.*, II, 1–3.

25 Caes., *BG*, II, 27.

26 Radman-Livaja, 2004, p. 25.

27 Vicente, Pilar Punter abd Ezquerra, 1997, p. 181.

28 Rovina, 2000, p. 102.

29 Antonucci, 1996, p. 7, from Alesia, inv. 24356 of the Musée de St Germaine en Laye; Brouquier-Reddé, 1997, p. 277.

30 Sievers, 1996, p. 74, fig. 14.

31 Connolly, 1997, p. 42, fig. 1, L.

32 Connolly, 1997, p. 42, fig. 1, P and Q; Antonucci, 1996, p. 10; Coussin, 1926, p. 286, fig. 80.

33 Caes., *BG*, V, 40.

34 Connolly, 1997, fig. 3, J and K.

35 Connolly, 1997, fig. 3, H.

36 Antonucci, 1996, p. 8; Coussin, 1926, p. 284, fig. 79.

37 Antonucci, 1996, p. 7, from Alesia, inv. 24364 and 24366 of the Musée de St Germaine en Laye.

38 Antonucci, 1996, p. 43.

39 Feugère, 2002, p. 83.

40 Feugère, 1990, p. 105, fig. 116.

41 Pol., *Prag.*, VI, 23; Livy, XXVIII, 24.

42 Radman-Livaja, 2004, p. 27.

43 Vicente, Pilar Punter and Ezquerra, 1997, pp. 181–7.

44 Antonucci, 1996, p. 14, fig. 2.

45 Antonucci, 1996, p. 7, from Alesia, inv. 10080–10081 of the Musée de St Germaine en Laye; Lindenschmit, 1882, pl. XI, no. 17, length 19 cm.

46 Vicente, Pilar Punter and Ezquerra, 1997, pp. 186–8, who also list the dimensions of all the found spear points,

47 Sievers, 1996, p. 74.

48 Brouquier-Reddé, 1997, p. 277; Lindenschmit, 1882, pl. XI, no. 20, length 41 cm.

49 Antonucci, 1996, p. 8.

50 Antonucci, 1996, p. 28; Plut., *Pomp.*, VII.

51 Daremberg and Saglio, 1871–1917, II, col. 1600ff.

52 Livy, XXVI,47; Pol., *Prag.*, VI, 23.

53 Suda Lexicon, under the heading '*machaira*' (mu 302 in Adler edition): '1. The Celtiberians differ greatly from others in the construction of their swords; for it has an effective point, and can deliver a powerful downward stroke with both hands. 2. Wherefore the Romans abandoned their ancestral swords after the [war] against Hannibal, and adopted those of the Iberians. But while they adopted the construction of the swords, they can by no means imitate the excellence of the iron or the other aspects of their careful manufacture.'

54 Iriarte, Gil, Filloy and Garcia, 1997, pp. 233–50, figs 15–16.

55 Radman-Livaja, 2004, p. 37; these swords were found in Šmihel (Slovenia) and dated to the first half of the second century BC (or in about 175 BC; Bishop and Coulston, 2006, p. 56, fig. 25, ns 2, 4.

56 Connolly, 1997, p. 54, fig. 11, E.

57 Connolly, 1997, fig. 8, E and F.

58 Sievers, 1996, p. 71, n. 1.

59 Connolly, 1997, fig. 9, E and F.

60 Feugère and Bonnamour, 1996, p. 100.

61 Radman-Livaja, 2004, p. 33ff., cat. 36/37; Hoffiler, 1911–12, fig. 36, n. 2, p. 102.

62 This does not make it impossible that these swords could be still in use in the first century AD. In all ages the weapons that offered guaranteed durability and efficiency were used for generations, as the Samurai world demonstrates.

63 Feugère, 2002, p. 64; various dates are proposed between 115 and 100 BC.

64 Coussin, 1926, p. 29,7 fig. 84; Antonucci, 1996, p. 9.

65 Like for example the swords from Sanzeno; see Various, 2004, p. 713ff.; however the sword represented in the Osuna relief also shows similarities, in its anthropomorphic hilt, with some swords of the Golasecca culture, also dated to the first century BC. See Various, 2004, p. 675.

66 Connolly, 1997, fig. 12, Y.

67 Antonucci, 1996, pl. A2.

68 Radman-Livaja, 2004, p. 38, cat. 38; Hoffiler, 1912, fig. 51, p. 120.

69 Front., *Strat.*, IV, 1, 27: 'Sulla ordered a cohort and its centurions, through whose defences the enemy had broken, to stand continuously at headquarters, wearing helmets and without belts [*discincti*]'; Plut., *Luc.*, XV.

70 Front., *Strat.*, IV, 1, 43.

71 Connolly, 1997, p. 56, fig. 12.

72 Allen, 2001, pl. J.

73 Quint., *Decl.* III, 5, 214: '. . . *vides munitum gladio latus . . .*' (. . . You see him with the sword at his side . . .).

74 Virg., *Aen.*, XII, 942.

75 Connolly, 1997, fig. 12, T.

76 *Caes.*, *BG*, V, 44.

77 Antonucci, 1996, p. 28; the brave Sestius Baculus, *centurio primus pilus* of the XII Legio, had his *balteus* pierced by an enemy javelin. *Caes.*, *BG*, V, 41.

78 Radman-Livaja, 2004, p. 47; Bishop and Coulston, 1993, pp. 54–5.

79 Connolly, 1997, fig. 13, H–L.

80 Radman-Livaja, 2004, p. 48.

81 Connolly, 1997, fig. 13, P.

82   Connolly, 1997, fig. 13, N–M.

83   *Caes.*, *BA*, LII, 2; *BH*, XVIII, 2; Front., *Strat.*, II, 7, 5.

84   Kovács, 2005, p. 963.; Val. Max, *Mem.*, 3, 5, 3: '*Possedit fauorem plebis Clodius Pulcher adhaerensque Fuluianae stolae pugio militare decus muliebri imperio subiectum habuit*' (Clodius Pulcher had the favour of the plebs and, allowing his military dagger to always be attached to the robes of Fulvia, he subjected his military honour to the will of a woman').

85   Cassius Dio, *Rom.*, LXV, 29, 2: 'He first dared, within the city walls, in the Forum, in the senate-house, on the Capitol, at one and the same time to array himself in the purple-bordered robe and to gird on a sword, to employ lictors and to have a bodyguard of soldiers.' The word *xiphos* can mean dagger or sword.

86   Florus, *Epit.*, II, 21: 'He wears a gold staff in his hand, a dagger on his side, a purple garment fastened with big precious gems; he wears even the crown . . .'

87   Hor., *Carm.*, I, 7,6;

88   Antonucci, 1996, p. 28.

89   Antonucci, 1996, p. 25.

90   Buzzi, 1976, pp. 4–5.

91   Livy, VIII, 8.

92   According to Clemens Alexandrinus this kind of Italic shield (*italon thureon*) was first used by the Samnites; *see* Clem. Alex., *Strom.*, I, 75, 7: 'and that Itanus (he was a Samnite) first fashioned the oblong shield [*thureos*]'. See also Hoffiler, 1912, p. 50.

93   Pol., *Prag.*, VI, 23, 2.

94   Sekunda, 1996, p. 3.

95   Many localities beginning with the word Kasr in Arabic are linked with Roman military camps: *kasr* from *castrum/kastron*.

96   Feugère, 2000, pp. 76–8 and fig. 84; Bishop and Coulston 2006, pp. 61–3, fig. 30; Sekunda, 1996, p. 6.

97   Bishop and Coulston, 2006, p. 61.

98   It could mean that the *spina* was painted or maybe that some specimens were of metal; see Liberati, 2002, p. 70.

99   Sekunda, 1996, p. 5.

100 Antonucci, 1996, p. 37; Robinson, 1975, p. 164; Olmos, 1997, p. 29.

101 Livy, IX, 40.

102 Sall., *Cat.*, LI, 38.

103 Antonucci, 1996, p. 45.

104 Festus, *De Verb. Sign.*, 316.

105 Garrucci, 1885, pl. CXXIV, 22.

106 Antonucci, 1996, p. 13.

107 Veg., *Epit.*, II, 18; Caes., *BG*, VII, 45, 7.

108 *Caes.*, *BA*, XVI, 3.

109 Quint., *Decl.* III, 216: '. . . *inscriptum in scuto C. Marii nomen* . . .'; the name could just be written or even incised, then the letters painted (**PLIb**).

110 *Caes.*, *BAL*, LVIII, 3.

111 Caes., *BH*, XXV, 7: '. . . *insignia scutorumque praefulgens opus caelatum* . . .'.

112 Suet., *Caes.*, LXVII.

113 Antonucci, 1996, p. 13; Robinson, 1975, p. 9.

114 Harmand, 1967, p. 67.

115 Cantilena, Cipriani and Sciarelli, 1999, cat. II, 33–4.

116 Antonucci, 1996, p. 40.

117 Antonucci, 1996, p. 15.

118 Plut., *Luc.*, XXVII: '. . . but when these men are merely on a march, they do not put on shining raiment, nor have they shields polished and their helmets uncovered, as now that they have stripped the leathern coverings from their armour . . .'

119 Caes., *BG*, II, 21.

120 Sil. It., *Pun.*, I, 53; Plaut., *MG*, I, vv. 1–2; the shield was highly polished: '. . . Take ye care that the lustre of my shield is more bright than the rays of the sun are wont to be at the time when the sky is clear . . .'

121 Sekunda, 1996, p. 5.

122 Robinson, 1975, p. 167.

123 Cantilena, Cipriani and Sciarelli, 1999, p. 10.

124 But against this dating see Polito, 1998, p. 88.

125 Antonucci, 1996, p. 30; Polito, 1998, p. 89;

126 Virg., *Aen.*, VIII, 626ff.

127 Polito, 1998, p. 121ff.

128 Polito, 1998, p. 122, fig. 49.

129 Polito, 1998, p. 124.

130 Polito, 1998, p. 126.

131 Buzzi, 1976, p. 4.

132 *Caes.*, *BG*, II, 21; *BA*, XII, 3; XVI, 3; in this last episode, relating to 47 BC, a veteran of the X Legion took off his helmet to allow Labienus to identify him.

133 Varro, *DLL*, V, 166.

134 Antonucci, 1996, p. 8.

135 Robinson, 1975, p. 17ff.; Feugère, 1994, p. 37ff.; the name is derived from the unnamed Celto-Etruscan necropolis near Ascoli Piceno (Italy), where many specimens of this category were found. See Feugère, 1994, p. 64; Robinson classified these helmets into six sub-categories (A–F) that try to follow a chronological development.

136 Bishop and Coulston, 2006, p. 65;

137 Radman-Livaja, 2004, p. 67

138 Cascarino, 2007, p. 105; Varro, *DLL*, V, 24.

139 Radman-Livaja, 2004, p. 65 and fig. 10, cat. 124.

140 Quesada Sanz, 1997, p. 157, fig. 6.

141 See also Various, 1997, cat. 52; it comes from the Sertorian wars.

142 Feugère, 1994, p. 78.

143 Caes., *BC*, III, 63.

144 So called by Coussin because the first specimen was found in the Netherlands (Buggenum, near Nijmegen); types C–D in the Robinson classification, dated to between the first century BC and the first century AD; see Cascarino, 2007, p. 107, fig. 4.9.

145 Feugère, 1994, p. 79; Bottini et al., 1988, p. 325, cat. 112.

146 Quesada Sanz, 1997, pp. 158–9; these helmets (Gruissan, Alcaracejos, Aljezur) could be linked to the expeditions against the Pompeians by Octavius, in 49–46 BC; see Feugère, 1994, p. 80.

147 Cascarino, 2007, p. 110, fig. 4.17.

148 Feugère, 1994, pp. 47–9.

149 Bottini et al., 1988, p. 323, fig. 7.

150 Sievers, 1996, p. 80.

151 The name is from the locality of Coole, near the river Marne, and Mannheim near Straubing, type A in the Robinson classification of such helmets; see Cascarino, 2007, p. 111.

152 Feugère, 1994, pp. 42–3; Cascarino, 2007, pp. 111–12, fig. 4.18–21.
153 Dautova Ruševljan andVujović, 2007, pp. 32–3.
154 Feugère, 1994, p. 47.
155 Feugère, 1994, pp. 45–6; Cascarino, 2007, p. 112, fig. 4.20.
156 So called from the localities (Agen and Port bei Nidau) in which they were first found, see Cascarino, 2007, p. 117.
157 Antonucci, 1996, p. 8; Val. Fl., *Arg.*, VII, 626.
158 Cascarino, 2007, p. 117, fig. 4.29.
159 Antonucci, 1996, p. 11; Cascarino, 2007, p. 117.
160 Cascarino, 2007, p. 118, fig. 4.30.
161 Antonucci, 1996, p. 12.
162 'Jockey-cap' helmet in the terminology of Robinson, as he also calls both the Montefortino and Coolus types; following Robinson, this helmet is a evolution of the Coolus–Mannheim type; see Robinson, 1975, pp. 13ff. and 26ff. The name Haguenau is derived from Coussin, from a specimen found in Drusenheim; see Coussin, 1926, p. 329.
163 Cascarino, 2007, p. 112, fig. 4.22.
164 Feugère, 1994, p. 84.
165 Cascarino, 2007, pp. 103–4.
166 Antonucci, 1996, p. 43, nos. 5, 7.
167 Sekunda, 1994, fig. 13.
168 Cantilena, Cipriani and Sciarelli, 1999, cat. I.14–15; Cascarino, 2007, pp. 121–2, figs 4.37–9.
169 Virg., *Aen.*, VIII, 681–2 '. . . His beamy temples shoot their flames afar, And over his head is hung the Julian star . . .'; A similar contemporary helmet is shown on the head of a painted statue preserved in the Museum of Ashkhabad; see Curtis, 2000, col. pl. I; a very clear image of the *sidus Iulium* in Cantilena, Cipriani and Sciarelli, 1999, cat. II.38–9.
170 Cascarino, 2007, p. 103.
171 Quint., *Decl.* III, 215: '. . . *clausam galea faciem* . . .'.
172 Rizzello, 1979, p. 21, photo 1; Tanzilli, 1982, p. 124, ns 7, 10.
173 Treviño, 1986, p. 45, pls A–E, G.
174 Coarelli – Lucignani – Tamassia – Torelli, 1975, p. 1417; Buzzi, 1976, p.5;
175 Caes., *BA*, 12.
176 Caes., *BG*, II, 21.
177 Antonucci, 1996, p. 10.
178 Buzzi, 1976, p. 4.
179 Vicente, Pilar Punter and Ezquerra, 1997, p. 190, fig. 43; the dimensions of the fragment are 4.7 x 2.7 cm.
180 Cascarino, 2007, p. 105.
181 Luc., *Phars.*, VII, 586–7, mentions a *cassis plebeia*, i.e. a simple helmet, like that of Brutus at the Battle of Pharsalus.
182 Plut., *Luc.*, XXVII.
183 Buzzi, 1976, p. 4.
184 Daremberg and Saglio, 1873–1917, s.v. *lorica*, III, 2, col. 1302ff.
185 Antonucci, 1996, p. 44.
186 Sil. It., *Pun.*, X, 400–1.
187 Varro, *DLL*, V, XXIV: '. . . *ex anulis ferrea tunica* . . .' (an iron tunic of rings); here the origin of the mail shirt and its adoption from the Celts by the Romans is strongly supported, see Robinson, 1975, p. 164; Daremberg and Saglio, 1873–1917, col. 1315, s.v. *lorica*; in any case we cannot exclude other theories that attribute the origin of the mail armour to easterners, then spreading widely to the Greek world, but as far as the spread of this armour near Etruscans and Romans is concerned, the Celts played a dominant role. For the eastern origin see Polito, 1998, p. 48.
188 Luc. *Phars.*, VII, 498–9: '. . . *qua torta graves lorica catenas opponit tutoque latet sub tegmine pectus* . . .'. One of the words used by the Romans to designate such armour was effectively 'armour of chain mail'.
189 Quint. *Decl*. III, 214: '. . . with the hard iron armour . . .'.
190 Antonucci, 1996, p. 15, no. 1; Polito, 1998, p. 173 fig. 120.
191 Baldassarre and Pugliese Caratelli, 1993, cat. 141a–c, vol. VI (Regio VII of Pompeii); this reproduces a painting that is lost today, showing a trophy of gladiatorial weapons but with a very detailed image of a mail armour: the chain mail is hip length and here represented with *humeralia* of trapezoidal shape.
192 Antonucci, 1996, p. 45.
193 Radman-Luvaja, 2004, p. 76.
194 Cascarino, 2007, pp. 128–9 and fig. 4.53.
195 Robinson, 1975, pls 463, 464, 467.
196 Robinson, 1975, pl. 461.
197 Antonucci, 1996, p. 12 and pl. A1.
198 Cantilena, Cipriani and Sciarelli, 1999, p. 29, cat. I.29–31, *denarius* of Manlius Aquilius.
199 Caes., *BC*, III, 44.
200 Val. Max, *Mem.*, III, 2, 23.
201 Cic., *In Pis.*, 36.87.
202 Coarelli et al., 1975, p. 1417; Buzzi, 1976, p.5; the brown-yellow colour of the corslet makes it impossible to tell if the artist meant to represent a leather or metallic one, although the cut of the armpit seems to suggest that the intention was to represent a leather corselet of muscled shape, very stylised.
203 Antonucci, 1996, p. 15, no. 2.
204 See the coin of Octavianus of 32–29 bc, where he is represented in such an armour, with the *hasta summa imperii* resting on the shoulders, in the gesture of the *adlocutio*; see Cantilena, Cipriani and Sciarelli, 1999, cat. II.33–4.
205 A tribe from what is today Georgia.
206 Plut., *Pomp.*, XXXV, 3.
207 Antonucci, 1996, p. 16, explains that the statue was the Trajanian copy of the original erected by Augustus for the Temple of Mars Ultor; Buzzi, 1976, p. 39.
208 Antonucci, 1996, p. 25.
209 Maiuri, Jacono and Della Corte, 1928, pp. 20–1; Pompeii, REG. I., Ins. VII, House no. 7.
210 Settis et al., 1991, p. 180; Antonucci, 1996, p. 25.
211 Cantilena, Cipriani and Sciarelli, 1999, p. 67.
212 Radman-Luvaja, 2004, p. 79.
213 Plut., *Luc.*, XXVIII, 1.
214 Buzzi, 1976, p. 39.
215 Caes., *BC*, III, 44: '. . . all the soldiers made coats or coverings for themselves of hair cloths, tarpaulins, or raw hides to defend themselves against the weapons . . .'
216 Antonucci, 1996, p. 37; Robinson, 1975, p. 164, fig. 175.
217 Plut., *Crass.*, XXIV, 4.
218 Antonucci, 1996, p. 29.
219 Antonucci, 1996, p. 37; they are not worn only on the left leg, as mentioned in Bishop and Coulston, 2006, p. 64, (**8**).
220 Maiuri, Jacono and Della Corte, 1928, fig. 22.

221 Lydus, *De Mag.*, I, 12; examples from south Italian paintings show an extra reinforcement strip on the instep

222 Schlette, 1971, p. 199; finds from Kowel (Ukraine) and Müncheberg-Dahmsdorf (Germany). The spear was the national weapon of the Germans, from which their name is derived: *Ger-mannen* = the men who carry the javelins or spear called *gêre*. This *ger* was very heavy and, according to the hypothesis of Gustav Kleimm, it would have been a spear with a barbed blade. The original meaning of the word '*ger*' indicates that this is not a sharp notched blade; *ger* is a triangular dowel. See D'Amato, 1999, p. 12.

223 Tac., *Germania*, XLIV: '. . . *breves gladii et rotunda scuta . . .*'.

224 Caes., *BG*, I, 52; Hoffiler, 1912, p. 51, fig. 22. For the Mondragon warrior reconstruction see Antonucci, 1996, pl. E1.

225 Tac., *Germania*, VI.

226 Tac., *Germania*, XVII: '. . . *Eligunt feras et detracta velamina spargunt maculis pellibusque beluarum, quas exterior Oceanus atque ignotum mare gigni*t . . .' (. . . They choose certain wild beasts, and, having flayed them, diversify their hides with many spots, as also with the scales of monsters from the deep, such as are engendered in the distant ocean and in seas unknown . . .). See also Varro, *DLL*, V, 167.

227 Caes., *BG*, I, 26; *matara* used by the Helvetii; specimens of *matara* were found on the Alesia battlefield, see Antonucci, 1996, p. 7.

228 Caes., *BG*, V, 48; the *tragula* is used by a Gallic warrior to throw a message attached to the *amentum* inside the besieged Roman camp.

229 Antonucci, 1996, pp. 38–9.

230 Caes., *BG*, VIII, 23, for instance, uses the same denomination for the Celtic swords.

231 Robinson, 1975, p. 165 pl. 461.

232 Plut., *Caes.*, XXVII.

233 Racinet, 1883, vol. I, fig. 35; Racinet, 2003, pls 56–7, n. 35.

234 Wilcox, 1985, pl. B3; Condurachi and Daicoviciu, 1975, fig. 83.

235 Antonucci, 1996, p. 46.

236 Antonucci, 1996, p. 42,

237 Maiuri, Jacono and Della Corte, 1928, p. 69, fig. 31.

238 Antonucci, 1996, p. 42.

239 Prop., *El.*, IV, 6, 55.

240 Feugère, 1996, p. 173; Feugère, 1994, p. 41ff.

241 Caes., *BG*, II, 7.

242 Sievers, 1996, p. 76.

243 Caes., *BG*, VIII, 48; Volusenus, the *praefectus equitum* of Antonius, is wounded on the femor by the *lancea* of a Gallic cavalryman.

244 Vicente, Punter and Ezquerra, 1997, pp. 193–4 and fig. 32.

245 Maiuri, Jacono and Della Corte, 1928, pp. 48, 50; Baldassarre and Pugliese Caratelli, 1993, cat. 24 (painting in REG. I of Pompeii), showing the fight for the body of Patroclus; cat. 141a–c, vol. VI (painting of REG. VII of Pompeii), representation of helmets, swords and shields of Greek typology together with mail armour in the context of gladiatorial trophies; this equipment was also used by the Roman officers, as attested in the *Gemma Augustea*; there is no reason to consider the equipment represented on it is 'heroic or historical weaponry' just borrowed by artistic conventions of the Greek world in the representation of the warriors; Waurick, 1983, has considered this possibility, by saying that the armament of the *Gemma Augustea* officers is a pastiche of old Greek weaponry not worn by the actual Roman of the Augustan age, but all the equipment shown (helmets of Attic type, of Beotian or other Greek fashion, breastplates of muscled shape and Greek sword of *Parazonia* typology) is still found in archaeological material of the first century BC and first century AD, and confirmed by literary sources of the Imperial age as being equipment used by Roman officers. We should remember that, after the victory of Octavian, a huge amount of Greek weaponry was available to the Roman army. The Greek style of armament was anyway used by the Roman officers from the Punic Wars until the first century AD. See Connolly, 2006, pp. 214, 227; Waurick, 1983, p. 268, says, after the list of the places where Attic helmets of the fourth to second centuries BC have been found, that '. . . these finds show very clearly to which prototypes the Attic helmets of the *Gemma Augustea* are to be brought back . . .' This is true, but not because the production of these helmets – as of that of the other helmets of Greek type represented on the *Gemma Augustea* – stopped in the second century BC and survived only in the artistic works, but because they still existed, in various types, at the time of Augustus and later. Apart from the helmet from Hamburg (**2**) of Beotian typology and now dated to the end of the fist century BC (see Köhne and Ewigleben, 2001, fig. 19), helmets of the type shown on the *Gemma Augustea* have been found in Herculaneum in a first-century AD context (see Connolly, 1975, p. 53; Antonucci, 1996, p. 28) and also in Sarmatian graves of the first century BC to the first century AD (see Aleksinskii et al., 2005, pp. 111–14). Muscled bronze breastplates in the Greco-Italic tradition were used by Roman officers until the end of the Western Empire and in Byzantium. See for instance Christies, 2004, p.159, n. 163, and Chapter 2 below.

246 Plut., *Mar.*, XIII, 1: '. . . he laboured to perfect his army as it went along, practising the men in all kinds of running and in long marches, and compelling them to carry their own baggage and to prepare their own food . . .'

247 Daremberg and Saglio 1873–1917, IV, 2, col. 1063,

248 Luc., *Phars.*, IV, 294.

249 Luc., *Phars.*, III, 433.

250 Plin., *HN*, XVIII, 75; Lydus, *De Mag.*, I, 32; Antonucci, 1996, p. 48; for an image of *lictores* in 54 BC see a coin of Marcus Junius Brutus, in Cantilena, Cipriani and Sciannella, 1999, cat. I.39–40.

251 Cassius Dio, *Rom.*, XLIII, 43, 2; Is., *Et.*, IX, 24; Mart., *Ep.*, II, 29; these boots were ascribed in legend to the kings of Alba; since that city was founded by Iulus – the son of Aeneas – Julius Caesar thus marked his divine investiture and mythological ancestry. The boots are clearly visible on his statue in Palazzo dei Conservatori; see Buzzi, 1976, p. 39.

252 Prop., *El.*, IV, 6, 56.

253 Plin., *HN*, X, 5, 16.

254 Cic., *In Cat.*, I, 9, 24,

255 Plin., *HN*, XXXIII, 58; Caes., *BA*, LXXV, 5.

256 The recovery of the *signa Crassi* from Augustus were a constant argument in the literature of the period; see Prop., *El.*, III, 5, 48.

257 Glyptotek Munchen., 2004, p. 186ff.
258 I would like to thank Claudio Antonucci for Amelung's original text concerning the colouring of the Augustan statue of Prima Porta.
259 Cantilena, Cipriani and Sciarelli, 1999, p. 55 and cat. III.33; reconstruction in Antonucci, 1996, p. 36.
260 Antonucci, 1996, p. 34 and reconstruction in p. 35.
261 Cantilena, Cipriani and Sciarelli, 1999, p. 29 and cat. I.23–4.
262 Cantilena, Cipriani and Sciarelli, 1999, p. 49 cat. II.27–8.
263 Quint., *Decl.*, III, 34–5; '. . . *Signa militaria aquilaeque . . .*'.
264 Antonucci, 1996, p. 25 and pl. B2.
265 Cassius Dio, *Rom..*, XL, 18.
266 Such a *vexillum* is visible on coins of L. Caninius Gallus of 12 BC; the *vexillum* is fringed at the borders and furnished with *phalerae*; Cantilena, Cipriani and Sciarelli, 1999, p. 13.
267 Plut. *Pomp.*, LXVIII; *Fab. Max.*, XV.
268 Virg., *Aen.* VIII, 1.
269 Caes., *BG*, II, 25; VI, 34.
270 Cantilena, Cipriani and Sciarelli, 1999, p. 55 and cat. III.34–6; this shows the *signa* of Crassus recovered from Augustus in 20 BC; the number X on the *vexillum* probably referrs to the *cohors*.
271 Of the Augustan period, celebrating the restitution of the Crassus *signa* by the Parthians; see Antonucci, 1996, p. 36.
272 Suet., *Caes..*, LXII.
273 Caes., *BG*, V, 37; *BC*, III, 64.
274 Antonucci, 1987, p. 34; Bishop and Coulston, 2006, p. 68.
275 Varro, *DLL*, V, 24, 117; the Etruscan origin of the *cornu* is confirmed by Ath., *Deipn.*, IV, P. 184 A.
276 Luc., *Phars.* I, 237–8;
277 Caes., *BG*, VII, 47; *BC*, III, 46; the playing was that of the *classicum*, see Quint., *Decl.*, III Pro Mil., 211;
278 Luc., *Phars.* X, 400–1; Quint. *Decl.* III; Cic., *Pro Mil.*, 211.
279 Caes., *BC*, II, 35.
280 Varro, *DLL*, VI, 75.
281 Feugère, 2002, p. 52.
282 Graham, 1981, pp. 12–13.
283 Grueber, 1970, n. 4209, pl. LV, 17.
284 Franzoni, 1987, p. 103, n. 13.
285 Sall., *Jug.*, LXXXV, 29: '. . . *hastas, vexillum, phaleras, alia dona militaria . . .*'.
286 Payne, 1962, p. 101.
287 Suet, *Caes.*, LXXIX.
288 Strabo, *Geogr.*, IV, 2–3.
289 Cascarino, 2007, p. 146. In spite of the bravery of the Celtic cavalrymen led by his son Publius, Crassus could not avoid the disaster at Carrhae.
290 Sekunda, 1996, p. 45.
291 Luc, *Phars.*, VI, 221.
292 Luc., *Phars.*, I, 210.
293 Strabo, *Geogr.* XVII, 7: '. . . But nevertheless they beautify their appearance by braiding their hair, growing beards, wearing golden ornaments, and also by cleaning their teeth and paring their nails. And only rarely can you see them touch one another in walking, for fear that the adornment of their hair may not remain intact. Their horsemen anyway [are armed] mostly with a javelin, using bridles made of rush, and riding bareback; but they also carry daggers. The foot-soldiers hold before them as shields the skins of elephants, and clothe themselves with the skins of lions, leopards and bears, and sleep in them. I might almost say that these people, and the Masaesylians, who live next to them, and the Libyans in general, dress alike and are similar in all other respects, using horses that are small but swift, and so ready to obey that they are governed with a small rod. The horses wear collars made of wood or of hair, to which the rein is fastened, though some follow even without being led, like dogs. These people have small shields made of rawhide, small spears with broad heads, wear ungirded tunics with wide borders, and, as I have said, use skins as mantles and shields . . .'
294 Cascarino, 2007, p. 146.
295 Lindenschmit, 1882, pl. XI, no. 3.
296 Livy, XXI, 4–5.
297 Sall., *Hist.*, IV,4.
298 Hor., *Carm.*, II, 7, 10.
299 Hoffiler, 1912, p. 55,
300 Junkelmann, 1991, pp. 34–5 and fig. 17; the monument is preserved at Hever Castle, England.
301 The image of the Barbarians on the grave is much too poor to represent Celtic cavalrymen, but fits very well with the descriptions of the Germans from Tacitus and Caesar.
302 Payne, 1962, p. 101.
303 Antonucci, 1996, p. 31 and pl D2.
304 Caes., *BG*, II, 25; infantry *scutum* used by Caesar in the battle against the Nervii; *BC*, II, 35, *scutum* used by the Pompeian *legatus* Publius Attius Varus, against the blow of a Caesarian *miles*.
305 It probably represents a battle scene relating to the occupation of the territory around the mid Liger (Loire) carried out by Publius Crassus in September 57 BC. We know he was still using Celtic cavalrymen as bodyguards and elite troops in the Battle of Carrhae. The man of the stele was probably one of these cavalrymen.
306 Caecilia Metella was the daughter of Quintus Metellus – the conqueror of Crete – and wife to Publius Crassus.
307 Caes., *BG*, VII, 45; with the word *cassis* Caesar probably has in mind a helmet heavier than the *galea*.
308 Polito, 1998, figs 27–32.
309 Antonucci, 1996, p. 33; Robinson, 1975, pl. 464.
310 Settis et al., 1991, p. 156; it is the funerary monument of G. Pompullius.
311 Following Antonucci this man should be also a *evocatus*; see Antonucci, 1996, p. 31.
312 Franzoni, 1987, pl. VII, 3.
313 Sekunda, 1984, pl. A2.
314 Lydus, *De Mag.* II.13.
315 Buzzi, 1976, p. 5.
316 Plut., *Pomp.*, XXX; for an armour similar to that of Sulla see Antonucci, 1996, p. 27.
317 Junkelmann, 1992, pp. 186–7, fig. 164.
318 Sekunda, 1994, figs 32–3, 54.
319 Xen., *Perì Hipp.*, XII, 5 and see Bishop, 2002, p. 22, n. 6.
320 Bishop, 2002, p. 18 and fig. 3.3.
321 Plut., *Pomp.* XIX, 3.
322 Cic., *De Fin. Bon. Et Mal.*, III, 15.
323 Antonucci, 1996, p. 36,

324 Sekunda, 1984, pl. A1; the mosaic is so called but it is more proable that it represents the Battle of Gaugamela.

325 Antonucci, 1996, p. 40 and pl. E3.

326 Caes., *BG*, VII, 70.

327 Caes., *BG*, IV, 2.

328 Caes., *BG*, VII, 65.

329 Caes., *BG*, VII, 55.

330 Suet., *Caes*.., LXVIII.

331 Caes., *BG*, I, 62.

332 Caes., *BG*, VII, 45.

333 Bianchi-Bandinelli, 1977, fig. 121.

334 Baldassarre and Pugliese, 1993, cat. 3.

335 Moreno, 1998, pp. 92–3.

336 Quint., *Decl.*, III: '. . . *Martio habitu horrentem* . . .'; Sumner, 2002, p. 23.

337 Baldassarre and Pugliese, 1993, cat. 141a–c, vol. VI (painting of REG. VII of Pompeii): representation of a red tunic together with mail armour in the context of gladiatorial trophies.

338 Plut. *Pomp.*, LXVIII.

339 Confirming the propensity of the soldiers to keep to their traditions, refusing the Hellenic and eastern long-sleeved tunics; Caesar was also criticised for wearing a tunic with long fringed sleeves, see Suet., *Caes.*, XLV ('*usum enim lato clauo ad manus fimbriato nec umquam aliter quam {ut} super eum cingeretur, et quidem fluxiore cincture*' (that he wore a senator's tunic with fringed sleeves reaching to the wrist, and always had a girdle over it). See also Virg., *Aen.*, IX, 615.

340 Sumner, 2002, p.4.

341 Quint., *Inst. Or.*., XI, 138; but from the tombstones this also seems to be the rule for the *milites gregarii*.

342 Luzzatto and Pompas, 1988, pp. 130–45.

343 Buzzi, 1976, p. 5.

344 Buzzi, 1976, p. 44; the scene shows King Agamemnon at the sacrifice of his daughter Ifigenia.

345 Buzzi, 1976, p. 43.

346 Quint., *Decl.*, III, 212–13.

347 Plin., *HN*, XXII, 6,11.

348 Cic., *De Or.*, III, 42 ; '*Toga pro pace*'; also *In Pis.*, XXX, 73 : For Cicero toga was the dress of peace and so more fitted to civilians.

349 Front., *Strat.*, IV, I; 26; this punishment was inflicted to G.Titius by L. C. Piso, father-in-law of Caesar.

350 Caes., *BC*, I, 6.

351 Plin., *HN*, XXXIII, 12; Buzzi, 1976, p. 39.

352 Caes., *BA*, LVII, 54–6; to avoid problems with the allied King Juba I, who was accustomed to dress in red, Scipio changed the colours of his clothes to white.

353 Antonucci, 1996, p. 34; Bianchi-Bandinelli, 1969, p. 86, fig. 93; see a cloak of the same colour in a Pompeian painting representing Mars and Venus, in Buzzi, 1976, p. 4.

354 Plut., *Sert.*, XIV, 3.

355 Varro, *DLL*, XIX, 24; Livy, VII, 34.

356 Cic., *Pro Mil.*, XX; Quint., *Decl.*, VI, 3 and 66.

357 Cic., *Ad Att.*, XIII,33.

358 This figure helps to explains Cicero's expression: '*paenula irretitus*' (wrapped in the cloak).

359 Cic., *Ad Fam.*, IX, 15, 2–6: '. . . *bracatae nationes* . . .' (trouser-clad people).

360 Generally used as garments, in Caes, *BG*, VI; *BC*, III; in some original manuscripts '*tegumenta*' is used.

361 Suet., *Caes.*, LVIII.

362 Connolly, 2006, p. 114.

363 Antonucci, 1996, p. 13; '*campestri sub toga cinctus*', Ascon., *Ad Cic.*; *Pro Scauro*; Hor., *Ep.*, I, 11, 18; *SHA*, Avid. Cass., IV.

364 Val. Max., *Mem.*, IX, 12, 7.

365 Cic., *Ad Att.*, II, 3; Quint., *Decl.*, III, 304, 376: '*caligatum*', '*caligati militis*'.

366 Seneca, *De Benef.*, v. 16.

367 Plin., *HN.*, XXXIV, 41; IX, 18; Juv. *Sat.* III, 232; XVI, 25.

368 Buzzi, 1976, p. 5.

369 But Horace recounts how in the first century BC Cato was barefoot and dressed in the short toga or *exigua*, according to the early fashion; see Hor., *Ep.*, I, 19, 12–14.

370 Is., *Et.*, IX, 24; Antonucci, 1996, p.25.

371 Juv., *Sat.*, VII, 192: '. . . he sews on to his black shoe the crescent of the senator . . .'

372 Carro, 1997, p. 24.

373 Carro, 1997, p. 68.

374 Carro, 1997, p. 55.

375 Liberati, 2003, p. 138.

376 Plut., *Sert.*, VII, 3: '. . . After a short time, however, Annius came with numerous ships and five thousand men-at-arms . . .'

377 Buzzi, 1976, p. 17.

378 I could not see on the original, though, the pair of greaves that all the previous scholars have represented in the reconstruction of the *miles classiarius* wearing the Etrusco-Corinthian helmet. His legs are naked on the sculpture.

379 Cantilena, Cipriani and Sciarelli, 1999, cat. II.8–9; on the verso of the coin is shown a helmeted Rome with a plumed helmet of Montefortino type with a *insignia* (double) crest.

380 Saxtorph, 1972, pp. 164–5.

381 Cassius Dio, *Rom.*, L, 32.

382 Sekunda, 1996, p. 14.

383 Prop., *El.*, IV, 6, 22.

384 Cassius Dio, *Rom.*, L, 18.

385 Cassius Dio, *Rom.*, L, 33, 7.

386 App., Εμφ. Пол., V, 100.

387 Cassius Dio, *Rom.*, XLVIII, 48; Sumner, 2002, p. 44 and pl. A3.

388 Cantilena, Cipriani and Sciarelli, 1999, p. 43.

389 Plaut., *MG*, IV, 1178ff.

390 Carro, 1992, p. 13.

391 Prop., *El.*, IV, 24.

~ PART II ~

1   I.e. Caesar the victorious general.

2   In 27 BC.

3   I.e. first among the citizens.

4   Palestine, Armenia and Pontus; see Cracco Ruggini and Cassola, 1982, pp. 146–7.

5   Like Galatia in 25 BC.

6   Switzerland, Austria, north-east Italy.

7   Upper Danube.

8   Austria.

9   Respectively Hungary, parts of the Balkans and Bulgaria.

10   Simon Bar Kosiba was the leader of the revolt; his name was transformed into Bar Kochbà, the 'son of the star'.

11   The stele of Trenčin, in modern Slovakia, indicates the penetration of the Roman army deep into the enemy territory; see Cracco Ruggini and Cassola, 1982, p. 224.

12   The best sources for the organisation of the army in this period are Josephus, Pseudo-Hyginus, Frontinus and Cassius Dio.

13   Josephus, *BJ*, I, 4, 3; it was not always a rule; Martial remembers a *centurio* who died in Egypt, mourned by his 100 men; see Mart., *Ep.*, X, 26.

14   Josephus., *BJ*, VI, I, 8.

15   Mart., *Ep.*, I, 31; 93.

16   Sometimes, as in the desert *praesidium* of Pselchis in Egypt, they acted as *paralèmptès*, i.e. officers in charge of the distribution of the straw to the soldiers; see Cuvigny, 2005, p. 16.

17   Pinterović, 1968, p. 64; Ciobanu, 2006, p. 372.

18   Dyczek, 2007, p. 18.

19   Six *centuriae*, according to Pseudo-Hyg., *De Mun. Castr.*, I, 7, 8, 30; see Cowan, 2003a, p. 7.

20   Josephus, *BJ*, I, 15, 6; Pseudo-Hyginus remembers 480 men to a *cohors* in the Trajanic era, *De Mun. Castr.*, I, 2.

21   Pseudo-Hyg., *De Mun. Castr.*, III.

22   Aul. Gell., *Noct. Att.*, XVI, 4, 6.

23   Bohec, 1997, p. 16. It was a technical term to indicate the picked man of each *cohors*, fighting in front or behind the standards.

24   Vujović, 2001, p. 125; CIL X, 3044; 4868; 6098; for example the CIL X, 3044 mentions Sextus Pedius, *praefectus* of Raetii and Vindolicii, of Poeninae Vallis (the three regions forming the *provincia* of Raetia) and of the lightly armoured soldiers (*levis armaturae*).

25   Josephus., *Contra Ap.*, 21, 38.

26   *SHA*, Comm., VI, 1.

27   An example of this is the case of unfortunate Poenius Postumus, *praefectus castrorum* of *Legio II Augusta* during the Boudiccan revolt.

28   Josephus, *BJ*, III, 69.

29   Cowan, 2003a p. 7. In 6 BC the military *erarium*, was also created, a branch of the public treasury designated to the veterans' leave. See Cracco Ruggini and Cassola, 1982, p. 118.

30   Such as the veterans sent to Raetia to defend the region against the Suebi, Tac. *Ann.*, I, 44; or the victors over the Numidian rebel Tacfarinas in AD 20, see Tac., *Ann.*, III, 21.

31   But in any case the *legio* was distinguished by the name, e.g. *Legio I Italica, Legio I Minervia, Legio I Adiutrix*, etc. The single appellatives were given for different reasons: a) a province name (e.g. *Legio IV Macedonica*); b) an emperor's name (e.g. *Legio XXX Ulpia Victrix*); c) a god's name (e.g. *Legio XIV Gemina Martia Victrix*); d) a simple attribute of good luck (e.g. *Legio VI Victrix*); e) an element of the *legio* equipment (e.g. *Legio V Alaudae*); f) the duplication of the original unit (e.g. the creation of a *Gemina Legio* (a twin) such as the *Legio XIII Gemina Pia Fidelis*; or the combination of any of these elements. But the numbers of the lost legions of Varus was never restored. See Rossi, 1991, p. 256.

32   Segenni, 1991, p. 247; AD 60: Cowan, 2003a, p. 7.

33   Later increased to ten.

34   From which they were mainly recruited until the age of Septimius Severus, see for example the *Tabula Clesiana*, in Ciurletti and Tozzi, 1989, p. 12.

35   Called *armigeri* in Prop., *El.*, III, 4, 8.

36   They received, if they did not already hold it, Roman citizenship at the act of the enlistment in the Imperial Guard.

37   Suet., *Galba*, 12.

38   CIL VI, 2789;

39   Cassius Dio, *Rom.*, LV, 24: '. . . his is at present the number of the legions of regularly enrolled troops, exclusive of the city cohorts and the pretorian guard; but at that time, in the days of Augustus, those I have mentioned were being maintained, whether the number is twenty-three or twenty-five, and there were also allied forces of infantry, cavalry, and sailors, whatever their numbers may have been (for I can not state the exact figures). Then there were the body-guards, ten thousand in number and organized in ten divisions, and the watchmen of the city, six thousand in number and organized in four divisions; and there were also picked foreign horsemen, who were given the name of Batavians, after the island of Batavia in the Rhine, inasmuch as the Batavians are excellent horsemen. I can not, however, give their exact number any more than I can that of the Evocati. These last-named Augustus began to make a practice of employing from the time when he called again into service against Antony the troops who had served with his father, and he maintained them afterwards; they constitute even now a special corps, and carry rods, like the centurions . . .'

40   CIL VI, 2384, 2803, 2870.

41   CIL X, 3417.

42   CIL VI, 2009.

43   Pseudo-Hyg., *De Mun. Castr.*, VI.

44   CIL III, 586; VI, 2725, 2733, 5839, 5840; VII, 257; X, 3732; XI, 19,

45 Josephus, *BJ*, II, 11, 1, 4.

46 Bohec, 1989, p. 22.

47 In Judaea, for instance, the garrison troops were first recruited from the locals, and so a good percentage of the auxiliaries were of Syrian (i.e. Hellenistic) origin, Greek speaking and of Greek origin. Arab auxiliaries infantry and cavalry under Areta assisted Varus in AD 4, the Arabs being recorded as terrible raiders, see Josephus, *BJ*, II, 13, 7; *BJ*, II, 5, 1; *BJ*, l, I, 6, 2. In the army of Caestius Gallus in AD 66 there were auxiliary troops from Commagene (infantry and cavalry archers), cavalrymen from Batania and Traconitidis, and infantrymen and cavalrymen from Edessa; see Josephus, *BJ*, II, 18, 9; their name could not be considered as indicative of their ethnic background, since from at least Hadrian's age – but perhaps also before – the manpower was recruited from the *provincia* in which they were stationed; see Condurachi and Daicoviciu, 1975, p. 133.

48 They received citizenship after twenty-five years of service.

49 Rossi, 1980, p. 289; Rossi, 1991, p. 256.

50 It is interesting to list the *cursus honorum* of the Emperor Pertinax: centurion, *praefectus cohortis*, *praefectus alae*, *legatus legionis* (*I Adiutrix*), *praeses Daciae* and *Moesiae*, *praeses Syriae*; see *SHA*, Pert., II–III.

51 *SHA*, Clod. Alb., VI, 2.

52 *SHA*, Clod. Alb., X, 6.

53 The number was created with reference to the number of units created in the same *provincia*, with the indication of the civic and ethnic provenence: e.g. *XX Cohors Palmyrenonrum*; sometimes the name of the first commander was added (e.g. *Ala Petriana*) and/or of their armament speciality (e.g. *Numerus Sagittariorum*); sometimes the criteria were the composition (e.g. *Cohors Equitata*) or the decoration (*Cohors Torquata*); they also sometimes earned the appellative *Pia Fidelis* (also used for some *legio*) for the attachment to the emperor and the dynasty. Some of them received the appellative *Auxilia Civium Romanorum* (auxiliaries of Roman citizens). A few *cohortes* had Latin citizenship (*Civium Latinorum*) and others were composed of citizens of Latin law (*Civium Campanorum, Ingenuorum*).

54 Prop., *El.*, II, 10, 3.

55 *SHA*, Niger, IV, 2.

56 Josephus., *BJ*, I, 20, 2.

57 *SHA*, Div. Marc., XXI, 7.

58 Josephus, *BJ*, II, 3,1.

59 Josephus, *BJ*, II, 5,1.

60 Bishop and Coulston, 1993, ch. 1.

61 *SHA*, Hadr., XXVI, 2.

62 Cowan, 2003a, p. 25; Radman-Livaja, 2004, p. 24; six of the specimens of *pila* from Sisak and preserved in Zagreb Museum present a pyramidal head, see idem cat. 1–6; they are dated to the time of the Augustan conquest of Pannonia.

63 However, some specimens from Siscia (Sisak), Oberaden, Haltern and Vrhnica had only one hole; see Hoffiler, 1912, pp. 84–5; Radman-Livaja, 2004, p. 26.

64 Radman-Livaja, 2004, p. 25, fig. 1.

65 Cowan, 2003a, pp. 25–6; Nationalmuseet, 2003, p. 156, fig. 12.

66 Bishop and Coulston, 2006, pp. 73–5 and fig. 36; Connolly, 1988b, p. 25.

67 Lindenschmit, 1882, pl. IV, 1; Bishop and Coulston, 2006, p. 11, fig. 3, no. 1; from Wiesbaden.

68 Connolly, 1988b, p. 25, nos 2, 3, from Saalburg, Germany; Dautova, Ruševljan and Vujović, 2007, p. 51, fig. 25, from Nikinci (Serbia), first century AD; for other specimens see Hoffiler, 1912, p. 82ff., fig 30, from various localities of Croatia.

69 Lindenschmit, 1882, pl. XI, no. 14 and reconstruction in no. 15.

70 Bishop and Coulston, 2006, p. 75, no. 4.

71 Lindenschmit 1882, pl. XI, no. 12, and reconstruction in no. 13.

72 Lindenschmit, 1882, pl. IV, np.2.

73 Arrian., *Tact.*, 17.

74 Curle, 1911, pl. XXXVIII, no. 11.

75 Bishop and Coulston, 2006, p. 129; Matthews and Stewart, 1987, p. 173.

76 Gonzalez, 2003, p. 703; they were usually stationed in *Isca Silurum* (today Caerleon), but in AD 122 they helped to build Hadrian's Wall; see Graham, 1984, p. 159; Gonzalez, 2003, p. 91; in 139–42 the III and IV *Cohortes* of the *legio* were in Corstopitum, and under the command of the *legatus* A. Claudius Charax they were engaged in operations against bandits. All three legionaries carry heavy flat-tanged *pila* and their cylindrical shields (*scuta*) are decorated with rosettes and Capricorn emblems derived from distance slabs set up on the Antonine Walls by *Legio II Augusta* to commemorate the completed sectors of rampart. These detachments subsequently helped the Governor G. Julius Verus to reject the new raids of the Caledonians. On this occasion (AD 155) the legion's contingents were united with others from different legions and concentrated at Pons Aelius (Newcastle upon Tyne).

77 Bishop and Coulston, 2006, p. 129.

78 Coussin, 1926, p. 364, figs 414–15.

79 App., *Kelt.*, I.

80 Particularly recommended was the steel of the Hispanica Bilbili; see Mart., *Ep.*, IV, 55.

81 Etienne, Piso and Diaconescu, 2002–3, pl. XIV, nos 10–13.

82 Josephus, *BJ*, III, 5, 95.

83 Arr., *Acies*, XII.

84 Arr., *Tact.*, XXI, 31.

85 Prop., *El.*, IV, 24; Mart., *Ep.*, V, 65; VII, 63; IX, 56; *Apoph.*, 179.

86 Prop., *El.*, II, 1, 64; Mart., *Ep.*, VII, 27.

87 See for instance the spear-butt from Vindonissa with remains of ash still preserved inside, see Unz and Deschler-Erb, 1997, p. 21, cat. 304, inv. 6977.

88 Dautova, Ruševljan and Vujović, 2007, p. 52 and cat. 18, spearhead from Jarak.

89 Lindenschmit, 1882, pl. XI, no. 18, length 36 cm; Pekovic, 2006, p. 101 inv. 16830 Belgrade War Museum, length 33.7 cm; Radman-Livaja, 2004, p. 27.

90 Pekovic, 2006, p. 101, inv. 16827, Belgrade War Museum, length 39.8 cm; Ilies, 1981, pl. I, nos 4–6.

91 Etienne, Piso and Diaconescu, 2002–3, pl. XVII, nos 1–3 for similar specimens found in the hoard of Ulpia Traiana Sarmizegetusa.

92 Goldsworthy, 2002, p. 120.

93 Dautova, Ruševljan and Vujović, 2007, p. 51.
94 Dautova, Ruševljan and Vujović, 2007, fig. 56.
95 Siscia (Sisak), see Radman-Livaja, 2004, p. 27, cat. 8; Augst, see Deschler-Erb, 1999, p. 21, cat. 61.
96 Siscia (Sisak), see Radman-Livaja, 2004, pp. 27–8, cat. 10; Vindonissa, see Unz and Deschler-Erb, 1997, pp. 20–1, cat. 250, 274.
97 Siscia (Sisak), see Radman-Livaja, 2004, p. 28, cat. 9; Vindonissa, see Unz and Deschler-Erb, 1997, p. 20, cat. 264; Feugère, 2002, p. 131.
98 Siscia (Sisak), see Radman-Livaja, 2004, p. 28, cat. 11–14; Augst, see Deschler-Erb, 1999, p. 20, cat. 65–8; Vindonissa, see Unz and Deschler-Erb, 1997, p. 20, cat. 247; Bishop and Coulston, 1993, p. 68, fig. 35, no. 12.
99 Radman-Livaja, 2004, cat. 15, 16, 17.
100 Cowan, 2003a, p. 26.
101 Ilies, 1981, pl. I,1; the spearheads, from Ulpia Traiana Sarmigezetusa, measure 40.3 cm in length. See also Coussin, 1926, p. 361, fig. 111.
102 Various, 1998, cat. 216.2, spearhead in iron, 44.3 cm long.
103 Dautova, Ruševljan and Vujović, 2007, fig. 26, 58a–b.
104 Ov., Met.., VIII, 375.
105 S., for instance, Becatti, 1957, pls 5, 61, 62: without butt; but a specimen with butt is visible in pl. 4.
106 Radman-Livaja, 2004, p. 29; Coulston and Bishop, 1993, p. 52.
107 Etienne, Piso and Diaconescu, 2002–3, pl. XVII, nos 6–9; specimen no. 9 is very interesting because it ends with a spherical button.
108 Radman-Livaja, 2004, cat. 26–7.
109 Josephus, BJ, III, 5, 5, 93–4.
110 Florescu, 1961, p. 440, fig. 207.
111 Prop., El., XXI, 7; generically called ensis; more commonly gladius, see Mart., Ep., V, 69; IX, 56; SHA, Comm., IV, 1.
112 Like the sword of Magdalensburg and the finds from Sisak, see Radman-Livaja, 2004, pp. 39-40 and cat. 47-8.
113 Mihaljević and Dizdar, 2007, p. 128; Miks, 2007, p. 670, nos A494, 495, 496, pls 9, 16, 26.
114 Bishop and Coulston, 1993, p. 73 (scabbard); Various, 2007, p. 15 (col. photo).
115 Analysis of Bishop and Coulston, 2006, p. 78; they indicate the length of the point to be between 2 and 9.6 cm; following Radman-Livaja, 2004, p. 33 the majority range from 48 to 53 cm.
116 Pekovic, 2006, cover and p. 19, 100, col. pl. 4; Vujović, 2001, pls 2, 3, 5, 9, 11, 12; Vujović, 2000–1, fig. 2.
117 Vujović, 2001, p. 119; the dimensions of the sword are: total length 68 cm, blade lenth 55 cm, blade width 6 cm and tang 13 cm. The blade is widest at the base from which it tapers towards a long point ; a second sword of Mainz type is preserved in the medieval collection of the archaeological department of Belgrade City Museum, with a preserved blade of 31.5 cm and a tang of 15.3 cm. See Vujović, 2000–1, fig. 1.
118 Oral communication from Dr Vujović, to whom I am debted for this; see Vujović, 2000–1, fig. 4, gladius from Stara Gradiška, found in Sava River; Hoffiler, 1912, p. 103, fig. 37.
119 Various, 1998, cat. 103; Bishop and Coulston, 1993, p. 70, fig. 36, 1.
120 S. MacMullen, 1960, p. 38, CIL XIII, 10026, 17: L.VALERIUS FEC(IT) P(OND)O (SEMUNCIA) (SICILICUS or SCRIPULA?) VII = L. Valerius made this of the weight of 21.6 g.
121 Sumner, 2002, p. 8, fig. B.
122 Bishop and Coulston, 2006, p. 78; from the place of the find.
123 Antonucci, 1994, p. 6, figs 10a, b; Avvisati, 2003, fig. 11.
124 Curle, 1911, pls XXXIV and XXXV.
125 Bishop and Coulston, 1993, fig. 36/2 and p. 71.
126 For instance Vindonissa, see Feugère, 2002, p. 114; Unz and Deschleer-Erb, 1997, cat. 3, 10–12, 25–44, 60–2, 111–14; 149–64, 174–5, pls 1, 2, 3, 5, 8, 9, 81.
127 Vujović, 2001, pp. 126–7.
128 Various, 1998, cat. 289, p. 313; total length 64.5 cm; the handle was bone, 10 × 3.5 × 2.4 cm, Various, 1998, cat. 290.
129 Dautova, Ruševljan and Vujović, 2007, pp. 49 and 91, cat. 7–8.
130 Radman-Livaja, 2004, p. 33.
131 Pekovic, 2006, p. 19, 100, col. pl. 4; Vujović, 2001, pls 14–15; total length 65 cm, blade length 51.5 cm, blade width 5.8 cm and tang length 13.5 cm.
132 Various, 1983, p. 413 and fig. 21.
133 Bishop and Coulston, 2006, p. 131.
134 Feugère, 2002, pp. 122–5.
135 Kovács, 2005, p. 960ff.
136 Kovács, 2005, fig. 6; the sword is 57 cm long; the longer specimens, at least in Pannonia, measured between 55 and 70 cm in length.
137 Kovács, 2005, p. 963ff.
138 Kovács, 2005, fig. 8.
139 See the later discussion of symbols of rank for further details.
140 In the Rheingönheim specimen the rivet has a small ring for attaching it to a bronze chain, see Bishop and Coulston, 2006, p. 78.
141 Feugère, 2002, p. 108.
142 Vindonissa (first century), see Coulston, 2007, p. 78;
143 Rheingönheim (first century) s. Coulston, 2007, p. 79, no. 1; Cowan, 2003a, p. 28.
144 SHA, Hadr., X, 5; Various, 2007, p. 86, cat. 1b.
145 Dyczek 2007, p. 20, fig. 21; generally the bones employed are metapodia from horses or calfsee Miks, 2007, p. 202.
146 Miks, 2007, p. 199.
147 Kovács, 2005, p. 962.
148 Feugère and Bonnamour, 1996, pp. 101–2.
149 Radman-Livaja, 2004, p. 39, cat. 39–42, belonging to specimens of the Mainz and Pompeii types.
150 This is widely discussed among scholars; some scenes on Trajan's Column show the employment of the two upper rings only (223).
151 Tanzilli, 1983, p. 37; the frieze shows a muscled armour worn over a thick subarmale, the sword in the scabbard, a Coolus helmet with cheek guards, an oblong shield and a pilum; a second oval shield is visible under the weapons.
152 They are 1 cm on each side in the Dubravica sword; see Vujović, 2001, p. 119.
153 Vujović, 2001, p. 121; ten specimens of swords with openwork scabbard decoration came from the Rhine regions, chiefly dated between 31 BC and AD 41.
154 Bishop and Coulston, 1993, p. 71; Various, 2007, p. 22.

155 Cowan, 2003a, pp. 29–30.
156 Cowan, 2003a, p. 28 (AD 40–60) of Mainz type, found in the Thames; Various, 2007, p. 86.
157 Cowan, 2003a, p. 29. Vujović, 2001, pls 16 (tin scabbard mouth in copper-alloy from Novae near Cezava).
158 Vujović, 2001, p. 120, pl. 9; Ulbert, 1969, pls 127/4–128/13; Radman-Livaja, 2004, cat. 43–6.
159 Radman-Livaja, 2004, p. 39, cat. 43–6 for some specimens from the first half of the first century AD.
160 Radman-Livaja, 2004, p. 40 and cat. 49, from Siscia dated from the Claudian to Flavian period; Deschler-Erb, 1999, p. 27, from Augst; Unz and Deschler-Erb, 1997, cat. 149–64 from Vindonissa.
161 Vujović, 2001, p. 128, pl. 17 (from Ljubicevac) and 18 (from Saldum); Ulbert, 1969, pls 19/1b, 2, 3, 26/a, b, 27/1a, b.
162 Unz and Deschler-Erb, 1997, pl. 5, cat. 62.
163 Feugère, 2002, p. 125.
164 Feugère, 2002, p. 109, fig. 135.
165 Feugère, 2002, fig. 168; the blade of the sword is of iron, so proving that it is not a part of a statue.
166 Feugère, 2002, p. 127.
167 Mart., Apoph., 33: 'This pugio, marked with serpentine veins, Salo [a Spanish river], while it was hissing with heat, was tempered with ice-cold water.. . .'; SHA, Comm., VI, 13;
168 See for example the gravestones of Flavoleius Cordus, Miles Legionis XIIII Geminae, in Lindenschmit, 1882, V, 1; Quintus Petilius, Miles Legionis XV Primigeniae, Lindenschmit, 1882, IV, 2; see the reconstruction of the Velsen pugio, with decoration in enamel inlay, in Bishop and Coulston, 2006, fig. 45; Ross Cowan, however, provides an alternative position at an angle, with the employment of three rings, following the Spanish antecedents of the dagger, see Cowan, 2003a, pl. H7.
169 Radman-Livaja, 2004, p.47,
170 Radman-Livaja, p. 48.
171 The scholars use this means to divide the typology of the first century AD in to Mainz (group A) and Vindonissa (group B) types; see Bishop and Coulston, 2006, p. 83.
172 Dautova Ruševljan and Vujović, 2007, p. 54; Hoffiler, 1912, pp. 115–20, figs 46–9; Radman-Livaja, 2004, p. 47ff., figs 8–9, cat. 57–60.
173 Obmann, 1992, pp. 37–8.
174 Unz and Deschler-Erb, 1997, pl. 11, cat. 202, from Vindonissa, 10.4 cm long; a hilt from a very well-preserved pugio found in the military camp of Haltern, abandoned after AD 9, shows an inlaid decoration, with red enamel and a crux gammata (swastika) on the top, as in the Vindonissa specimen; the find is 32.3 cm long; see Katalog Berlin, 1988, p. 587, cat. 418.
175 As in the first-century specimen found in Danube near Belgrade, Serbia, with decoration on the hilt of silver inlay and niello; see Nationalmuseet, 2003, fig. 10, p. 157; two functional iron rivets usually pass through the top of the blade, connecting the front and back part of the fitting.
176 Various, 2007, p. 86, cat. 1a; the incisions with floral motifs on the handle could lead us to ascribe such specimen to a praetorian guardsman.
177 Dated to the last two decades of the first century BC and the first two decades of the first century AD; see Radman-Livaja, 2004, pp. 50–3, cat. 57; in these specimens there are seven

rivets for the scabbard fittings: two iron rivets connecting the front and the back part of the fitting, two decorative rivets with oval bronze heads on the outer side of the fitting and three rivets on the hilt, connecting the outer fitting with the bone plates and with the tang; for an other specimen, with only the hilt preserved and today lost, see Hoffiler, 1912, p. 118, fig. 49.
178 Bishop and Coulston, 2006, p. 83 and fig. 44, 1.
179 Radman-Livaja, 2004, p. 53, cat. 58.
180 Like the specimens from Allériot, Hod Hill, Auerberg, Oberammergau (23.5 cm), see Bishop and Coulston, 2006, fig. 44, nos 4–5, pl. 1; a unique find comes from the grave of a Germanic chieftain in Hedegard, in central Jutland, see Nationalmuseet, 2003, p. 185, fig. 6; their use probably begins in the Augustan age; under the hilt, the sheath from Oberammergau has the name of the Italic workshop that produced it: C(aius) ANTONIUS FECIT.
181 See for instance the specimens from Vindonissa, Unz and Deschler-Erb, 1997, pls 12–14, cat. 206–18; this decoration was probably linked with the old function of the pugio as status symbol, mentioned in the sources; see Radman-Livaja, 2004, p. 47; they were in use, at least, from the Tiberian age.
182 Radman-Livaja, 2004, p. 49 cat. 59–60.
183 As in the Allériot specimen, see Feugère and Bonnamour, 1996, p. 143; all the specimens from Vindonissa are plated with silver inlays, see Unz and Deschler-Erb, 1997, cat. 208–18; one of them has red inlays, see cat. 215 .
184 As in the mentioned specimen from Vindonissa; see above.
185 Aquincum Museum, 1995, fig. 47; the specimen, from Aquincum, still has remains of wood on its reverse side; its size is 39 × 9 cm.
186 Like one specimen from Siscia, see Radman-Livaja, 2004, p. 53, cat. 60.
187 Specimen from Mainz, (39 cm), see Various, 1997, pp. 132, 134, no 234; from Allériot, see above.
188 Specimens from Mainz, (38 and 22.5 cm), see Various, 1997a, pp. 132–3, nos 232–3; from the second half of first century AD and AD 70; see also Various, 1998, cat. 98.
189 The one field decoration is visible in some specimens of the Claudian age, see the finds of Moers-Aberg, Radman-Livaja, 2004, p. 49, no 260.
190 The above-mentioned specimen from Mainz shows the name of the LEGIO XXII PRIMIGENIA; see Various, 1998, cat. 99.
191 Feugère, 2002, p. 127.
192 Radman-Livaja, 2004, p. 50; enamel fixing rivets are still attested in the Trajanic wars, see Etienne, Piso and Diaconescu, 2002–3, pl. X, no. 29.
193 Bishop and Coulston, 2006, p. 135; Kolnìk, 1984, cat. 106.
194 Petru, 1958, fig. 1 and pl. I, pp. 264–5.
195 They were certainly used as weapons, although it is not said that their owners were soldiers. Varro (De Re Rust., II, 10), says, 'For herds of larger cattle older men, for the smaller even boys; but in both cases those who range the trails should be sturdier than those on the farm who go back to the steading every day. Thus on the range you may see young men, usually armed, while on the farm not only boys but even girls tend the flocks . . .'
196 Bishop and Coulston, 2006, p. 87, fig. 42, 8.

197   Another blade of the same type is preserved in the same museum; in the Museum of Ulpia Traiana Sarmizegetusa there is also an identical dagger with a copper-alloy hand guard (personal observation of the author).

198   Pio Franchi de Cavalieri, 1928, p. 221.

199   Suet, *Aug.*, XXIV.

200   Mart., *Apoph.*, 32: 'Honour of the militia, good omen of a grateful appointment, worthy of surrounding the hips of a *tribunus*'.

201   SHA, *Av. Cas.*, VI, 1.

202   Greek was generally spoken, but was not the official language of the army in the Eastern Hellenised *provinciae*.

203   Bishop and Coulston, 2006, p. 106.

204   Statius, *Theb.*, VI, 225: 'and each throws some offering snatched from his own armour, be it rein or belt, he is pleased to plunge into the flames, or javelin or helmet's shady crest'; VIII, 405: '. . . plumes stand erect, horsemen bestride their steeds, no chariot is without its chief; weapons are in their place, shields glitter, quivers and belts are comely . . .'; VIII, 567: '. . . she had plated with gold his harness and with gold his arrows and his belt and armlets, and had encrusted his helm with inlay of gold . . .', XII,440: '. . . I recognise the broken buckler and the charred sword-belt, ay, it was his brother! . . .'; XII, 528: '. . . light quivers too are borne and baldrics fiery with gems and targes stained with the blood of the warrior-maids . . .'

205   Varro, *DLL*: '. . . The *balteum*, i.e the *cingulum* that they had in embossed leather, called *balteum* . . .'. See Lindenschmit, 1882, p. 8.

206   SHA, *Hadr.*, X, 5, where the Emperor Hadrian is described as having no gold ornaments on his sword belt or jewels on the clasp, and his sword just furnished with an ivory hilt.

207   Often inlaid with niello, like the specimens from Vindonissa: see Unz and Deschler-Erb, 1997, cat. 876–1137; or decorated with red enamel, like the specimen from Rheingönheim, see Popescu and Various, 1998, fig. 104 p. 234.

208   Specimens from Augusta Raurica (Augst): see Deschler-Erb, 1999, cat. 318–65.

209   Künzl, 1977, pp. 183, 185, plates from Pompeii and Tekjia (Serbia); Radman-Livaja, 2004, p. 87; the height of the plates is more or less attested to be over 4 cm.

210   Künzl, 1977, p. 178.

211   Deschler-Erb, 1999, p. 43; Kemkes, Scheuerbrand and Willburger, 2005, p. 83; Künzl, 1977, p. 177, figs 7–8; the author suggests that they could be a special series made for the *Legio XIII*.

212   Künzl, 1977, pp. 188–91 and fig. 14 (dagger from Risstissen).

213   Künzl, 1977, figs 1–6; the author's supposition that these highly decorated parts of massive silver *cingula* belonged to *classiarii* of the *Misenatis* fleet have now been confirmed by the similar *cingulum* found in Herculaneum on the body of a dead *Faber Navalis*, see Miks, 2007, pp. 577–8.

214   Radman-Livaja, 2004, cat. 207, typical of the first century AD; Etienne, Piso and Diaconescu, 2002–3, pl. X, nos 19–20.

215   Radman-Livaja, 2004, cat. 208; for the specimens from Tekjia from the Domitian period, see Connolly, 1988b, p. 25, nos 8–12; Künzl, 1977, p. 189, fig. 12.

216   Künzl, 1997, fig. 11.

217   Franzoni, 1987, pl. IX, 1–2; in these kinds of belt plates four corner rivets fixed each plate to the belt, as did a central rivet, often shaped in a floral motif, see Radman-Livaja, 2004, cat. 207.

218   Radman-Livaja, 2004, cat. 205; this specimen, from Siscia, represents the typical buckle used for the whole of the first century AD, with twisted projections at the terminals forming triangular holes. The lack of decorative volutes within the buckle frames could be the proof, following Radman-Livaja, of a later date, i.e. early second-century AD (Radman-Livaja, 2004, cat. 203–4). As in this example, many buckles were silvered and had inlaid silver wires on the hinge.

219   For instance the wreath of laurel leaves is typical of the periods of Tiberius and Nero; see Radman-Livaja, 2004, p. 88, cat. 206.

220   Cowan, 2003a, p. 31; Lindenschmit, 1882, pl. V,1; Vujović, 2001, pls 6–8.

221   Radman-Livaja, 2004, cat. 255–69.

222   Plin., *HN*, XXXIII, 54, 152: '. . . *cum capuli militum ebore etiam fastidito caelentur argento, vaginae catellis, baltea lamnis crepitent . . .*' (when our very soldiers, holding even ivory in contempt, have the hilts of their swords made of chased silver, when, too, their scabbards are heard to jingle with their silver chains, and their belts with the plates of silver with which they are inlaid . . .).

223   These studs were often decorated with portraits (generally typical of the period from Nero to Trajan), *quadrigae*, or stylised vegetal motifs (laurel wreaths, a cross interlaced with a star), in niello; see Radman-Livaja, 2004, cat. 209–36; the same author has put forward the possibility that small rivets with figures of various divinities could be apron studs, see pp. 90–1 and cat. 237–46; Professor Radman does not discount the fact that they could be also parts of caskets or horse harness fittings. My personal opinion is that these rivets could also be the terminal studs of some muscled leather armour border or *cymation*, which was often decorated by rivets with images of divinities, as can be seen in some statues of *loricati*.

224   Radman-Livaja, 2004, cat. 249, second half of the first century AD; Unz and Deschler-Erb, 1997, p. 38, cat. 1275, 1277–83; Etienne, Piso and Diaconescu, 2002–3, pl. X, nos 21–8.

225   Radman-Livaja, 2004, cat. 250–4, pp. 91–2; the author interestingly underlines that a rhomboidal pendant from Siscia (cat. 251) is substantially identical to a belt pendant from Aldborough, England, and links it with the fact that in both localities were stationed, only three decades apart, the *Legio IX Hispana*. Moreover, a similar apron pendant comes from the camp of Herrera de Pisuerga, Spain.

226   Is., *Et.*, XIX, 33, 2: '. . . *Balteum cingulum militare est, dictum pro quod ex eo signa dependant ad demonstrandam legionis militaris summam, id est sex milium sescentorum, ex quo numero et ipsi consistunt. Unde et balteus dicitur non tantum quod cingitur, sed etiam a quo arma dependant. . .*' (. . . the *balteum* is the military belt, so called for the reason that from it hang the *signa* indicating the amount of the military legion, i.e. 6600, number of which themselves are formed. Whence *balteus* is called not only what it is girdled, but also what from which the weapons hang . . .'

227   Varro, *DLL*, V, 24.

228 It was not always the rule: the Trophaeum of Adamclisi, showing the armour of a centurion – if not of a superior officer – probably of the praetorian *cohortes*, attests a baldric resting on the left shoulder (**85**).

229 Virg., *Aen.*, V, 313.

230 Prop., *El.*, IV, 3, 34: *vellera tyria*, i.e., literally, leather strips of Tyrian purple.

231 Antonucci, 1994, fig. 11; Doxiadis, 1995, cat. 15–16, portrait of soldiers, late Trajanic–early Hadrianic; p. 34, fig. 2; cat.18–19, *c.* AD 125–92.

232 Bishop and Coulston, 2006, p. 144 and fig. 88; Petculescu, 2003, cat. 342; Radman-Livaja, 2004, cat. 271–8.

233 Radman-Livaja, 2004, fig. 21.

234 Popescu, 1998, cat. 259.

235 Josephus, *BJ*, V, 5, 95.

236 Tac., *Ann.*, II, 21.

237 Fogliato, 1984–5, p. 76.

238 Etienne, Piso and Diaconescu, 2002–3, pl. XIII, no 50.

239 *Umbo* from Njimegen, see Bishop and Coulston, 2006, p.93, fig. 7; from Halmeag, see Petculescu, 2003, cat. 330.

240 *Umbo* of *Legio II Augusta*, recovered by the River Tyne, see Bishop and Coulston, 2006, p. 93, fig. 49, no. 8; Trustees of the British Museum, 1971, pp. 67, 69, fig. 35

241 Bronze *umbo* from Zugmantel: 19–23 cm in diameter, see Hoffiler, 1912, p. 65.

242 For shield bosses in bronze or iron found in the territory of former Yugoslavia, see Dautova-Ruševljan and Vujović, 2006, p. 41.

243 Curle, 1911, pl. XXXIV, Newstead, second century.

244 Bishop and Coulston, 2006, pp. 92–3.

245 Petculescu, 2003, cat. 331;

246 Etienne, Piso and Diaconescu, 2002–3, pl. XIII, nos 50–4.

247 Gansser-Burckhardt, 1942, p. 74, of curved shape.

248 Of semicircular shape.

249 Castricius Victor of *Legio II Adiutrix*, in Aquincum Museum; see Szylàgyi, 1956, p. 62 and pl. XXXVI.

250 Bishop and Coulston, 2006, p. 256, fig. 150, no. 1.

251 But the polygonal rectangular shield is still represented, as in scene 62, where the legionaries attack an enemy fortress with the *testudo*, see Hoffiler, 1912, p. 59,

252 Hoffiler, 1912, pp. 62–3.

253 Mart., *Ep.*, IX, 56,

254 Polito, 1997, p. 157, fig. 90; from San Vittorino dell'Aquila, località Torricella (Amiternum).

255 I.e. the face of a Gorgon, the monstrous woman with snake hair who turned to stone the men who looked at her. The legionary oval shield of C. Castricius shows a similar embossed *umbo*; an *umbo* with an embossed Gorgon's head (Medusa), with a diameter of 26 cm., has been found in Blariacum (Blerich), see Hoffiler, 1912, p. 65.

256 Polito, 1997, p. 162, fig. 99; I suggest linking the monument, dated to the first half of the first century AD, with some commander of the war against Sacrovir, bearing in mind the presence of Celtic weapons (shields, *carnyx*) and of a gladiator's *manica* among the trophy. The *cruppellarii* (gladiators completely covered by segmented armour) fought for Sacrovir in the rebellion of AD 21.

257 Tac., *Hist.*, I, 38.

258 Caes., *BG*, II,21.

259 Veg., *Epit.*, II, 18.

260 Tac., *Hist.*, III, 23.

261 Bishop and Coulston, 2006, p. 92.

262 Hoffiler, 1912, p. 63 and no 7 (CIL VII 570).

263 CIL VII 495: LEG(IO) VIII AUGUSTA, (CENTURIA) IUL(I) MAGNI, IUNI DUBITATI (of Iunius Dubitatus, of the *centuria* of Iulius Magnus, in the *Legio VIII Augusta*); see Graham, 1981, p. 31.

264 And afterwards, in the Antonine period, by the Christian symbol of the cross painted or engraved on their shields, together with some vegetal ornaments (**57, 63**).

265 Val. Flac., *Arg.*., VI, 54–6: '. . . *cuncta phalanx insigne Iovis caelataque gestat tegmina dispersos trifidis ardoribus ignes; nec primus radios, miles Romane, corusci fulminis et rutilas scutis diffuderis alas* . . .'. Interestingly, the Romans linked the flamboyant character of the *fulmen* (lightning bolt) with the *phalarica*, the flaming spear used by the Iberian warriors, see Virg., *Aen.*, IX, 705–6. The *malleolus* – the double wooden *hasta* – was also linked to the *bifida fulgur*, the double light of the lightning bolt.

266 Virg, *Aen.*, VIII, 424–30:

'. . . The Cyclops here their heavy hammers deal; Loud strokes, and hissings of tormented steel, Are heard around; the boiling waters roar, And smoky flames thro' fuming tunnels soar. Hither the Father of the Fire, by night, Thro' the brown air precipitates his flight. On their eternal anvils here he found The brethren beating, and the blows go round. A load of pointless thunder now there lies Before their hands, to ripen for the skies: These darts, for angry Jove, they daily cast; Consum'd on mortals with prodigious waste. Three rays of writhen rain, of fire three more, Of winged southern winds and cloudy store As many parts, the dreadful mixture frame; And fears are added, and avenging flame . . .'

267 Val. Fl., *Arg.*, VIII, 354–5.

268 Gansser-Burckhardt, 1942, p. 79, fig. 70; those of the *Legio XI Pia Fidelis* have been found in Vindonissa.

269 Gansser-Burckhardt, 1942, p. 72.

270 The effective height of the fragment is 45 cm; Gansser-Burckhardt, 1942, p. 75.

271 Siege of a Dacian fortress.

272 Mart., *Ep.*, IX, 56; *Apoph.*, 179; SHA, *Comm.*, XVI, 7.

273 For example, two bronze specimens from Serbia, one of Buggenum and the other of Coolus type, see Dautova Ruševljan and Vujović, 2007, p. 31; they were recovered from the Sava River, and dated to the end of the first century BC–beginning of the second century AD (Buggenum–Montefortino) or to the first century AD (*Coolus*).

274 Feugère, 1994, pp. 78–81 and map of the finds at p. 81.

275 The original specimen came from Drusenheim, Alsace, and was preserved in Haguenau Museum which gave it its name, see Coussin, 1926, p. 329/

276 Bottini et al., 1988, pp. 327–33 and 354–6.

277 Radman-Livaja, 2004, p. 67; welded laths are visible, for instance, on the specimen found in the Sava at Bok near Sisak, used to attach the decorative crests; see cat. 125.

278 Such as the specimen preserved in Njimegen, see Feugère, 1994, p. 81.

279 Such as the specimen from Mainz, found in the Rhine, see Feugère, 1994, p. 83.

280 See the specimen in Njimegen Museum, the cheek guards are round at the base and furnished with a small prominence to protect eyes and mouth; see Feugère, 1994, p. 83.

281 Köhne and Ewigleben, 2001, fig. 19; (**223**).

282 The very famous Louvre relief from the lost arch of Claudius and often interpreted as representing praetorians of the second century AD, should in all probability really be linked with the celebration of the conquest of Britannia. So the warriors wearing Attic helmets with frontal *diadema* and high plumes (some of them the object of restoration in modern times) are probably *milites ostensionales* of the *Legio XI Claudia Pia Fidelis*, as shown by the *aquilifer* in the background who is not carrying a praetorian but a legionary eagle. See Robinson, 1975, p. 147.

283 Some analysis conducted by Oxford University gave rise to doubts about the metallic silvered patina of the helmet and found traces of restoration work conducted in the nineteenth century. The Toledo helmet should also have a low gold content, whereas in fact the silver content is too high, and there is evidence of some of the corrosion having been chiselled out in the nineteenth century.

284 Kondoleon, 2001, p. 157, no. 42; reportedly found at Tell Abou Saboun, in a group of tombs in the necropolis of Emesa (modern Homs).

285 See McDowell and Embleton, 1994, pls E and L and p. 53; McDowell, 1995, pl. L and p. 59.

286 Mendel, 1966, I, no. 20, pp. 6–7; a similar fragment, showing the same helmet and perhaps dated to the rule of Commodus is at the Louvre Museum, see Bianchi-Bandinelli, 1970, fig. 48.

287 Robinson, 1975, pls 413–16.

288 Robinson, 1975, p. 26, fig. 31.

289 Feugère, 1994, p. 91.

290 Mihaljević and Dizdar, 2007, p. 125; Jàżdżewska, 1985, pp. 112–16 and 129; fig. 4 and cover.

291 Radman-Livaja, 2004, p. 73.

292 Radman-Livaja, 2004, p. 71; Junkelmann, 2000, p. 69.

293 A bronze cheekpiece similar to those of the helmet of Brigetio, classified as Imperial-Gallic I from Robinson, has been recently found in Ulpia Traiana Sarmizegetusa, see Etienne, Piso and Diaconescu, 2002–3, pl. IX, no. 15; compare Robinson, 1975, pl. 219.

294 Various, 1997, no. 74; Various, 1998, no. 291.

295 Feugère, 1994, p. 93; Robinson, 1975, pls 175–8.

296 Feugère, 1994, p. 96; Robinson, 1975, pls 166–9.

297 Bishop and Coulston, 2006, p. 142 and fig. 1, p. 143.

298 Radman-Livaja, 2004, pp. 71–2 and figs 14–15, cat. 127.

299 Boss, 1994, p. 22 and col. pl. C.

300 Radman-Livaja, 2004, cat. 126, Coolus–Haguenau specimen from Martinska Ves near Sisak.

301 Such as the helmet of Xanten-Wardt, of Coolus–Haguenau typology, see Feugère, 1994, p. 83; the same shows the helmet of Drusenheim–Haguenau, the helmet of Mainz and the helmet of Xanten-Wardt, belonging to the same category.

302 Radman-Livaja, 2004, p. 68.

303 Radman-Livaja, 2004, cat. 128, fig. 16.

304 The Eich helmet, for example, see Feugère, 1994, p. 84; see also Radman-Livaja, 2004, cat. 126.

305 MacMullen, 1960, p. 23; Dautova Ruševljan and Vujović, 2007, p. 38; Radman-Livaja, 2004, cat. 126 (helmet from Martinska Ves: (CENTURIA) LUCC(I), VARRONIS (of Varro, of the *centuria* of Lucius).

306 Mart., *Ep.*, IX, 56.

307 Josephus, *BJ*, III, 5, 5, 93.

308 Paus., *Per.*, X, 27, 2.

309 Paus., *Per.*, X, 26, 2.

310 Mart., *Ep.*, VII, 1, 1–4: '*Accipe belligerae crudum thoraca Mineruae, ipsa Medusaeae quem timet ira comae. Dum uacat, haec, Caesar, poterit lorica uocari: pectore cum sacro sederit, aegis erit . . .*' (Receive the hard *thorax* of the warlike Minerva, which frightens even the furious hair of Medusa. Until that it will not worn, we could not, Caesar, call it armour; when it will be posed upon your sacred breast, then it will be the Aegis . . .' The Domitian armour described by Martial is visible on his *loricata* statue in the theatre of Vaison la Romaine, see Guitteny, 2002, p. 16; the armour has a metallic body with two ranges of leather lappets attached, with metallic appliqués and it is worn over a doublet with one row of fringed *pteryges*; see also Mart., *Apoph.*, 179.

311 Statue from Susa, first half of the first century AD, see Brecciaroli Taborelli, 2004, p. 39.

312 Statue from Susa, second century AD, see Brecciaroli Taborelli, 2004, p. 39.

313 Robinson, 1975, pl. 430.

314 Florescu, 1961, fig. 189b, p. 419.

315 See also *metopa* XXXII, where a very similar armour is worn over the same doublet, probably with the addition of shoulder pieces or with a cloak over the left shoulder, in the same position of that of Favonius Facilis in Colchester Museum. See Florescu, 1961, p. 444, fig. 211.

316 Cahn, 1989, p. 96, fragment of first-century BC–first-century AD armour from Lanuvium, showing a part of the abdomen muscle with the lower side hinges of the breastplate and a ring attached to a staple through which the hinge joint pin passed.

317 Observation of Dr Travis Lee Clark, on his website.

318 Statue from Susa, second century AD, see Brecciaroli Taborelli, 2004, p. 39.

319 Buora and Jobst, 2002, p. 232, no. IVa.21; diameter 4.3 cm. Inv. 11904 Museum of Carnuntum; also a small *phalera* preserved in the same museum, which was probably part of the decoration of a *cymation*, although it could be used for a leather or metallic armour as well; inv. 18/88.

320 Potter and Johns, 2002, p. 56; large *cymation* plates are, however, visible on the statues of *loricati* (**312**).

321 Brecciaroli Taborelli, 2004, p. 40; this specimen is also decorated with a Medusa head in the centre of the breast.

322 Lindenschmit, 1882, pl. I, no. 7.

323 Coussin, 1926, p. 442, no. 4.

324 Xen., *Perì Hipp.*, XII. 6.

325 *SHA, Al. Sev.*, XXXIII, 3.

326 Robinson, 1975, p. 157 and pl. 450.

327 Virg., *Aen.*, XI, 487: '. . . *thorax* covered by bronze scales (*thoraca indutus aenis squamis*) . . .'.

328 See the finds of Novae in Dyczek, 2007, p. 20.

329 Daremberg and Saglio, 1873–1917, col. 1316, fig. 4554.

330 Arr., *Tact.*, 13, 14.

331 Robinson, 1975, p. 156, pls 442 and 444; Lindenschmit, 1882, pl. I, no. 6; middle first century AD.

332 Negin, 1998, p. 70, no. 11; they are of different sizes, from 2 cm to 6–8 cm in length and 2 cm wide. They were fixed to the backing by leather thongs.

333 Robinson, 1975, p. 156.

334 Bishop and Coulston, 2006, p. 95.

335 Robinson, 1975, pls 446–8/

336 *Metopa* XVI, XXIX, XXXIII, see Florescu, 1961, figs 195b, 208, 212.

337 *Metopa* XVII, see Florescu, 1961, fig. 196.

338 Florescu, 1961, p. 427, fig. 195b.

339 Gansser-Burckhardt, 1942, p. 47, fig. 29c; Unz and Deschler-Erb, 1997, nos 844–57.

340 Compare with Robinson, 1975, pl. 436.

341 Florescu, 1961, p. 441, fig. 208.

342 Robinson, 1975, pl. 446.

343 Robinson considered the reproduction not accurate because the cut-outs of the shoulder guard were drawn at the lower corners on the inside edges instead of outside. But, in spite of the very bad condition of the sculpture, which does not even allow us to see whether the left *humeralis* is present, I do not see why there is a problem in accepting a reinforcement system shaped in this way. Personal taste and practical exigencies unknown to us could have been the reason for positioning the shoulderpiece in that way. If the shoulder plate was a part of a laminated protection worn only on the right side, the shape is perfectly credible, creating a further extra protection only on the exposed arm. Of course the Roman provincial artist knew the Roman military equipment better than we do.

344 Becatti, 1957, see for instance pls 4, 6, 8, 10, 11, 14, 15, 16, 51, 62; this is a clear demonstration of how the demands of visual art can combine with the representation of reality. The incidence and specific use of different types of body armour must be joined to the demonstrably decorative 'rhythm' or symmetry of cuirasses. The sculptors chose to depict plate, mail and scale armour on adjacent figures (e.g. plate–mail–scale–plate–mail–scale in the same scene), both for visual effect – probably enhanced by paint – and because it was a way to represent different kind of armour used by soldiers in the same *legio* or *cohors*.

345 Buora and Jobst, 2002, p. 233, no. 4a.

346 Becatti, 1957, pl. 16.

347 Giuliano, 1955, pl. 18.

348 Giuliano, 1955, pl. 20.

349 Robinson, 1975, p. 156.

350 Bishop and Coulston, 2006, p. 139, who correctly impute such scale-armours parts to the infantrymen, not just the cavalry.

351 Bishop and Coulston, 2006, p. 140.

352 This is the general word to indicate the soldier in this period. Sometimes the soldiers were just called '*viri*' (men). Prop., *El.*, I, 21, 2; II, 1, 44; II, 25, 5; III,4,3; III, 11, 6.

353 Prop., *El.*, IV, 1, 27.

354 Prop., *El.*, IV, 3, 23.

355 Coussin, 1926, p. 339; Robinson, 1975, p. 26, fig. 31.

356 Feugère, 2002, p. 75.

357 Cowan, 2003a, p. 41.

358 Statius, *Theb.*, XII, 775: '. . . *tunc, qua subtemine duro multiplicem teneces iterant loricam catenae . . .*'. See also Robinson, 1974, p. 173.

359 Robinson, 1975, p. 171 and pl. 481.

360 Cowan, 2003a, p. 32;

361 Kemkes, Scheuerbrand and Willburger, 2005, p. 86.

362 Daremberg and Saglio, 1873–1917, col. 1415, no. 6.

363 Robinson, 1975, p. 169, pl. 473.

364 Robinson, 1975, pl. 479, where the soldiers are identified as *auxilia*, but legionary units are also represented on Trajan's Column armed with mail shirt and oval shield.

365 Robinson, 1975, pls 476–7.

366 Becatti, 1957, pls 11–12.

367 Becatti, 1957, pls 4, 5, 6, 8.

368 Marc. Aur., *Ad se Ipsum*, VII, 7, writing in Greek, he naturally uses the word *stratiothes* to indicate the *miles gregarius*. Greek and Latin were now the main languages of the empire. In the eastern part of the empire the vernacular of the soldiers was principally Greek, although the orders were given in Latin; this continued after the fall of the western part.

369 Becatti, 1957, pls 66, 67, 68.

370 Becatti, 1957, pls 22, 24, 34.

371 Sumner, 1997, p. 52.

372 Sumner, 1997, p. 49.

373 Radman-Livaja, 2004, p. 81.

374 Bishop, 2002, p. 23ff., figs 4.1, 4.2.

375 Carnuntum – Bad Deutsch Altenberg, Iža, Siscia – Sisak (Pannonia Superior), see Bishop, 2002, figs 6.1 and 6.7, pp. 47, 58; Thomas, 2003, pp. 6, 10, no. 46; Banasa, Volubilis (Mauretania Tingitana), see Boube-Piccot, 1994, pp. 11–12 and 56ff., pls 3, 4, 58; Ehingen-Risstissen (Raetia) see Kemkes, Scheuerbrand and Willburger, 2005, pp. 86–7; Favianis – Mautern (Noricum), see Thomas, 2002, p. 33; Corbridge, Newstead, London, Chichester, Caernarfon, Usk (Britannia), see Robinson, 1975, p. 174ff., Bishop, 2002, p. 27, Thomas, 2002 p. 121ff.; Gamala (Judaea), see Peterson, 1992b, p. 39, Bishop, 2002, p. 31; Vindonissa – Windisch (Germania Superior), see Gansser-Burckhardt 1942, pp. 47–8; Novaesium – Neuss (Germania Inferior), see Simpson, 2000, pl. 25 and p. 74ff.; Teutoburgensis Saltus (Ultra Limes), see Cowan, 2003a, p. 32; Iruna (Hispania Citerior Tarraconensis), see Bishop, 2002 p. 26, fig. 4.3, no. 1; Conimbriga (Lusitania), see Luik, 2002, p. 101; Audennacum – Aulnay de Santonge (Aquitania), see Thomas, 2002, p. 6 and fig. 3, p. 9, Tronche, 1996, pp. 177–88; Vaison la Romaine (Narbonensis), see Thomas, 2003, p. 61; Lutetia Parisiorum – Paris (Lugdunensis), see Feugère and Poux, 2001, p. 89, fig. 10; Buciumi (Dacia Porolissensis), see Chirila et al., 1972, pls LXXI, no. 48, CXVIIIa, no. 5, CXIII, nos 38, 42, 47, CXV, no. 2; Tekija (Dacia Ripensis), see Cermanovic Kuzmanovic and Jovanovic, 2004, p. 218, cat. 3, 6, 16, 25; Novae – Svistov, Oescus – Gigen (Moesia Inferior), see Gentscheva, 1999, pp. 28–9, figs 7, 12, Thomas, 2002, p. 40, Dyczek, 2007, p. 20, fig. 19; Bedriacum – Cremona (Italia), see Passi Pitcher, 1996, p. 124; Tilurium – Gardun – Trilj (Dalmatia), see Ivcevic, 2004, pl. I, nos 13–15, p. 170; fragment of unknown provenance in Axel Guttmann collection, see Christie's, 2004, no. 130.

376 Kemkes, Scheuerbrand and Willburger, 2005, p. 87.

377 Rome: Trajan's Column (Bishop, 2002, p. 10); the Marcus Aurelius column (Becatti, 1957, pls 3, 4, 5, 8, 10, 17, 18, 40, 41, 47, 48, 51, 52, 54, 55, 61, 69; Bishop, 2002, p. 11), the Templum Gentis Flaviae fragments (**259**). Susa (Augusta Seguvina): the Arch of Augustus (Fogliato, 1984–5, p. 78); Alba Fucens reliefs (**279**) see Various, 2003, pp. 72–5 and fig. 63. Mainz: the column pedestal reliefs (Bishop, 2002, p. 13). Saintes: the relief (Maurin and Thauré, 1988 p. 13, fig. 62). Madrid: collection of the Duke of Medina, trustees of Madrid Museum, see *DAI* arch. Ph. R 1050/1 381 (probably heavily restored in modern times).

378 Domitian, *Concordia* (in Brentchaloff, 1996, fig. 91); Galba, *Adlocutio*; Marcus Aurelius, *Profectio*.

379 Domus Aurea, (**3**) see Sumner, 2002, pp. 22, 46 and pl. F1.

380 Buzzi, 1976, p. 24; second-century AD Roman mosaic from Spain representing a legionary in iron *lorica segmentata* and iron helmet of the Attic type with yellow-orange crest; Isenburg, 1965, p. 60. In this last the picture credit is 'collection of Dr Joseph W. Owen, New York'.

381 Statuette of the Antonine period from the British Museum, see Robinson, 1975, p. 184, pl. 501.

382 The types have been named from the place of the finds.

383 Radman-Livaja, 2004, p. 83, cat. 175, 171–2, fig. 20; new elements of such a *Lorica* have been recovered from Banovci–Burgenae, in Croatia, see the forthcoming work by Radman-Livaja.

384 Bishop, 2002, p.26.

385 Bishop, 2002, p. 31 ff.,

386 Robinson, 1975, p. 177 and fig. 178.

387 Coussin, 1926, p. 453; Buora and Jobst, 2002, pp. 234–6.

388 Bishop, 2002, p. 31;

389 Bishop 2002, p. 46 ff.

390 Humer, 2004, cover.

391 Bishop, 2002, p. 56, discussing the method proposed by Poulter.

392 Bishop, 2002, p. 57.

393 Humer, 2004, pp. 114–15; the armour was found in a circular cavity about 70 cm in diameter, together with a Roman oil lamp, a wine vessel and other offering goods, dated to about the second half of the second century AD; the armour was so well preserved because it was abandoned on a Roman road that was successively covered, leaving the objects under a layer 10 m thick.

394 Becatti, 1957, pl. 69.

395 Bishop, 2002, p. 57 and note 42.

396 Bishop, 2002, fig. 6.12, no. 2.

397 Bishop, 2002, pl. 9.

398 Bishop, 2002, fig. 6.11.

399 Tac., *Ann.*, I, 64; describing the massacre of Varus' *milites*, the phrase 'the bodies weighted by the *loricae*' seems more likely to refer to the first type of segmented armour, attested by the Kalkriese finds.

400 Bishop, 2002, p. 80.

401 Becatti, 1957, pl. 69.

402 Coussin, 1926, p. 337; Polito, 1998, p. 46.

403 Robinson, 1975, pls 430 (Augustus from Berlin), 432 (Augustus from Chercel) and 433 (armour of Augustus Prima Porta, see also (**4**)).

404 Pace, 2003, p. 22.

405 Unz and Deschler-Erb, 1997, fig. 1650, pl. 59. These kinds of attachments are sometimes very difficult to distinguish from the harness pendants of various shape and dimensions, probably because they were produced by the same craftsmen although destined for different purposes. So it is not unusual to find many of these pieces in the archaeological texts classified as horse harness: apart from the context, only comparative study with sculpture representing muscled armour could help to understand the exact derivation of the pieces.

406 Observations of Dr Travis Lee Clark, to whom I am indebted, on his website.

407 Nationalmuseet, 2003, p. 150; Lindenschmit, 1882, pl. 1, no. 1; this is one of the most complete models of classic epigraphy, having the *praenomen* (Marcus), the *nomen* (Caelius, of Etruscan origin), the *origo* (Bononia), the tribe (Lemonia).

408 Barbagli, Becattini and Pruneti, 2001, p. 52; here a man dressed as a *centurio* is performing a dance in a context of an Isiac scene. The muscled armour and the attached *pteryges* are rendered in a brown colour.

409 Lindenschmit, 1882, pl. 1, no. 7; the distinctive signs of the *evocati* were identical to those of the centurions, with whom they held equal rank, see Lindenschmit, 1882, p. 17, n. 1.

410 Bianchi-Bandinelli, 1969, fig. 209; Waurick, 1983, fig. 6.

411 Liberati and Silverio, 1989, p. 28.

412 Robinson, 1975, p. 169.

413 Polito, 1998, pp. 155–6.

414 The *pteryges* are clearly made of double-thickness material, shown by the horizontal rows depicted upon each of them: perhaps it was coarse linen with felt, the same kind of material as used in the later Roman army of Byzantium.

415 Travis Lee Clark, on his website; the cuirass has all the details of a typical *lorica* of his category: the anatomical waistline, the tongue *cymation*, the shoulder copings and harness, which are always on the outside of the *lorica*.

416 Rossi, 1980, fig. 73,

417 Rossi, 1980, fig. 74,

418 Polito, 1997, p. 46.

419 Polito, 1997, p. 202, fig. 142, monument from Sorrento (Trajanic/Adrianic age).

420 Polito, 1997, p. 203, fig. 144, monument from Tusculum (Trajanic/Hadrianic period); p. 206, fig. 150, panel from Merida (Trajanic period).

421 Polito, 1997, p. 221, fig. 170.

422 The Antonine period: see Polito, 1997, p. 47.

423 Even the re-enactors' experiments have shown the capacity of protection of leather armour.

424 But not boiled inside, because it would destroy the leather. See Nicolle, 2002, p. 180.

425 Lindenschmit, 1882, pl. II, no. 1; Gansser-Burckhardt, 1942, fig. 28b.

426 Gansser-Burckhardt also expressed many doubts on the certain designation of some leather pieces as parts of leather armour or doublets. However, we cannot exclude, on the analysis of the figurative monuments, that many fragments are exactly this. Strangely it seems that there is a general reluctance to accept the fact that the Roman soldier was clad in leather, when this was perhaps the easiest and most widespread material to be used

for military equipment. This reluctance is only modern, if we consider the astonishing result achieved by the famous painter Alma-Tadema in reconstructing the armour of Crispus in his *A Silent Greeting* of 1889 (**181**), see Barrow, 2001, p. 177.

427 I.e. on smooth corselets. Of course yellow and iron colour traces have been found on the monuments, where scale armour or mail armour is at the same time clearly represented, or when the intention of the artist was to depict the smooth surface of plate armour.

428 Junkelmann, 1992, fig. 46, gravestone of Silius of the *Ala Picentiana*.

429 Robinson, 1975, pl. 197.

430 Daremberg and Saglio, 1873–1917, col. 1310, sub v. *lorica*.

431 Xen., *Anabasis*, III, 3, 20.

432 Tincey, 1990, p. 45; the author shows the buff coat of a Royalist officer, where the edge of the upper sleeve clearly shows the thickness of the leather used for the main part of the coat, and the lower edge of the sleeve made of thinner leather to enable the wearer to move his arms freely. See also p. 15ff.

433 Beabey and Richardson, 1997, p. 64ff. on the capacity of the hardened leather armour.

434 This is the only way to understand details that a photo cannot reveal.

435 This garment was in fact made of chamois leather, see Gansser-Burckhardt, 1942, p. 41.

436 Gansser-Burckhardt, 1942, p. 42; Leguilloux, 2004, p. 152.

437 Gansser-Burckhardt, 1942, p. 46.

438 Coussin, 1926, p. 444.

439 Coussin, 1926, p. 443.

440 Veg., *Epit.*, I, 16: '. . . Soldiers, notwithstanding being covered with helmets, heavy armours [*cataphractis*] and light armours [*loricis*], are often more annoyed by the round stones from the sling than by all the arrows of the enemy . . .'

441 Lindenschmit, 1882, p. 6.

442 Suet., *Galba*, 19; Arr., *Tact.* p. 14.

443 Paus., *Per.*, I, 21 and 8.

444 Ael., *DNA*, IX, 17: '. . . *neque si percutias saxo rumpi, neque ferro discindi possunt, non magis quam lineus ille thorax, quem Minervae Lindiae consecrasse Amasis dicitur. . .*' (neither could it be damaged by hits of stone or iron, no more than the linen armour that it is said has been consecrated by Amasis to Minerva Lindia)

445 Polito, 1997, p. 158, fig. 91.

446 Tanzilli, 1982, p. 81; the author explains that most of these funerary monuments were commissioned by veterans or ex-servicemen settled in the colonies of central Italy after the Battle of Philippi.

447 Connolly, 1988, p. 221.

448 Robinson, 1975, pls 446–9.

449 A very good and clear photo appears in Antonucci, 1996, p. 47.

450 Chiarucci, 2003, p. 94.

451 Coussin, 1926, figs 158–9, with details of the two different kinds of armour represented on the same monument.

452 Coussin, 1926, p. 451, no. 2.

453 Plin., *HN.*, VIII, 192; '*lanae et per se coactae vestem faciunt et, si addatur acetum, etiam ferrum resistunt*'.

454 CIL V, 4504–5 and CIL VI, 9494 (*lanarius coactiliarius*).

455 Angelone, 1986, p. 55.

456 Giordani, 2001, pp. 11–12.

457 Graham, 1984, p. 292; today High Rochester.

458 Suet., *Aug.*, LXXXII.

459 Tac., *Ann.*, I, 79; see Brzezinsky and Mileczarek, 2002, p. 21; Lebedynsky, 2002, pp. 163–4.

460 Paus., *Per.*, 1, 21, 8.

461 Amm. Marc., *Res Gestae*, XVII, 12, 2.

462 Daremberg and Saglio, 1873–1917, col. 1315, fig. 4553.

463 Avvisati, 2003, fig. 11.

464 Real Museo Nazionale di Napoli, 1858, vol. V pl. XXIX.

465 Mart., *Ep.*, VII, 2; this armour is described as being composed of 'slick boar toes' (or maybe boar tusks), 'not penetrable by the arrows of the Sarmatians' and able to withstand spear strikes.

466 Armoured horse with the head covered by scales and eye guards are perfectly represented.

467 Welkov, 1937, p. 160.

468 Lindenschmit, 1882, pp. 7–8.

469 Varro, *DLL*, V, 116.

470 Arr., *Tact.*, III, 1.

471 Inv. 80.1.21.75; we are deeply indebted to the British Museum for allowing the publication of this important fragment of armour, otherwise unpublished, to my knowledge.

472 Doxiadis, 1997, p. 54.

473 Gansser-Burckhardt, 1942, p. 38.

474 Robinson, 1967, pp. 54–5.

475 Coussin, 1926, p. 444.

476 Josephus, *BJ*, II, 12, 1.

477 Bishop, 2002, p. 71, fig. 8.3. The other complete specimen of *manica*, found in Ulpia Traiana Sarmizegetusa, still awaits proper publication. The specimen was found in the debris of the Forum Augustalis and was sent for restoration to Timişoara, where it probably remains. A small possible fragment of a second *manica* has been shown to me by the director of the museum, to whom I am indebted.

478 Polito, 2002, fig. 99.

479 Polito, 2002, fig. 153 and p. 53.

480 Robinson, 1975, p. 185, pls 502–4, at that time interpreted as thigh defences; Bishop, 2002, pp. 68–71, 70 and fig. 8.2.

481 Robinson, 1975, pl. 508.

482 Polito, 2002, p. 157, fig. 90.

483 Robinson, 1975, pl. 411.

484 Polito, 2002, fig. 110.

485 Robinson, 1975, fig. 192.

486 Robinson, 1975, pl. 445.

487 Robinson, 1975, pl. 442; p. 187, also recalls the greaves of M. Petronius Classicus at St Veit in Carinthia as embossed or decorated.

488 Arr., *Tact*. III, 5: '. . .in the Roman style one greave to protect the leg which was thrust forward in fighting . . .'; Arrian was of Bythinian origin and received important military and civilian appointments under Hadrian.

489 Plin., *HN*, XIX, 7; Pall., *Op. Agr.*, I. 43.

490 Hor., *Sat.*, II, 3, 234: the hunter sleeps '*ocreatus*' i.e furnished with *ocreae* in the snow of Lucania.

491 The restoration works conducted by Gansser-Burckhardt on this piece could, however, have altered its original structure. But in any case the general shape is that of a greave.

492 Robinson, 1975, pl. 510, pp. 188–9.

493 A *diploma* or *tabulae honestae missionis* was given to each auxiliary at his discharge, after twenty-five years of service. See Embleton, 1979, p. 3.

494 Tac., *Ann.*, XII, 16: 'Then the army advanced in regular formation, the Adorsi in the van and the rear, while the centre was strengthened by the cohorts, and native troops of Bosporus with Roman arms . . .'

495 Cermanovic Kuzmanovic and Jovanovic, 2004, p. 220ff., cat. 1–9; nos 6, 7, 8, 9 are dated to the third century AD.

496 Cermanovic Kuzmanovic and Jovanovic, 2004, p. 218, cat. 22–3, probably parts of hanging studded straps (*baltea*); cat. 4 (bronze heart-shaped appliqué of a possible officer belt, but also a possible piece of horse harness), 9.

497 Cermanovic Kuzmanovic and Jovanovic, 2004, pp. 218–19, cat. 8 (scabbard chape); 5, 11, 12 (scabbard appliqués); 1 (hoop for the scabbard stretcher).

498 Cermanovic Kuzmanovic and Jovanovic, 2004, p. 219, cat. 24 (shield).

499 Cermanovic Kuzmanovic-Jovanovic, 2004, p. 219, cat. 2, 4 (pendants).

500 Cermanovic Kuzmanovic and Jovanovic, 2004, p. 33.

501 Maurin and Thauré, 1988, p. 8.

502 Feugère, 1994, pp. 106–9.

503 Lindenschmidt, 1882, p. 22, pl. VI, no. 1.

504 Lindenschmit, 1882, p. 14 and pl. XI, nos 17, 18, 19.

505 Lindenschmit, 1882, p. 22, pl. VI, no. 2.

506 Josephus, *BJ*, III, 5, 96.

507 Radman-Livaja, 2004, p. 29.

508 Aul. Gell., *Noct. Att.* X, 25; *hasta, pilum, phalarica, semiphalarica, soliferrea, gaesa, lancea, spari, rumices, trifaces, tragulae, frameae, mesanculae, cateiae, rumpiae, scorpii, sibones, siciles, veruta.*

509 Bishop and Coulston, 2006, pp. 78–80.

510 Mart., *Ep.*, IV, 55.

511 Bishop and Coulston, 2006, p. 78.

512 Lindenschmit, 1882, pl. XI, no. 21; Veg., *De Re Militari*, II, 15: '. . . and other smaller missile, with a triangular iron of five ounces, which is called now *vericulum*, now *verutum* . . .'

513 Mart., *Ep..*, VIII, 53; *Apoph.*, 30–1.

514 Radman-Livaja, 2004, p. 29.

515 Kliškić, 2002, pp. 547–8, pls I, VI, no. 1.

516 Cermanovic Kuzmanovic and Jovanovic, 2004, p. 239, cat. 2–5 (long battle spears), 7–9 (throwing spears). 14–15 (spears butt).

517 Connolly, 1997, p. 50, fig. 7, nos C and D.

518 Suggested by monuments such as the Augustan Arch in Augusta Seguvina (Susa) in 14 BC, see Fogliato, 1984–5, p. 65ff.

519 Connolly, 1997, figs 7–8; Various, 2004, p. 337.

520 Prop., *El.*, II, 25, 15.

521 Connolly, 1997, p. 50 suggested the presence of a Roman sword factory situated in the Po Valley. Maybe the weapons could be associated with the Raeti Gaesati, important allies of the Romans in the conquest of the Alpine territories at the end of the first century BC; see CIL XIII, 1041, preserved in Saintes Museum, inv. 949.564, *epitaphium* of Julius Macer, *duplicarius dell'Ala Atectorigiana* and *evocatus* of the Raeti Gaesati, first half of the first century AD.

522 Coussin, 1926, p. 371; Tacit., *Ann.* XII, 35, battle against Caractacus: '*postquam facta testudine rudes et informes saxorum compages distractae parque comminus acies, decedere barbari in iuga montium. sed eo quoque inrupere ferentarius gravisque miles, illi telis adsultantes, hi conferto gradu, turbatis contra Britannorum ordinibus, apud quos nulla loricarum galearumve tegmina; et si auxiliaribus resisterent, gladiis ac pilis legionariorum, si huc verterent, spathis et hastis auxiliarium sternebantur*' (but when we had formed the military *testudo*, and the rude, ill-compacted fence of stones was torn down, and it was an equal hand-to-hand engagement, the barbarians retired to the heights. Yet even there, both light- and heavy-armed soldiers rushed to the attack; the first harassed the foe with missiles, while the latter closed with them, and the opposing ranks of the Britons were broken, destitute as they were of the defence of breastplates or helmets. When they faced the auxiliaries, they were felled by the swords and javelins of our legionaries; if they wheeled round, they were again met by the sabres and spears of the auxiliaries).

523 Lindenschmidt, 1882, pl. 17, 1.

524 Künzl, 1977, fig. 13.

525 Nationalmuseet, 2003, p. 189, fig. 11.

526 Nationalmuseet, 2003, p. 187, fig. 10 (Møllerup in Djursland).

527 *SHA*, Hadr., 10.

528 Cermanovic Kuzmanovic and Jovanovic, 2004, p. 239, cat. 10–13.

529 Junkelmann, 1992, p. 185.

530 Feugère, 2002, p. 89, fig. 102; Junkelmann, 1992, p. 183, considers the possibility that this shield could be a cavalry shield belonging to a *cohors equitata*. It could be, considering its analogy with the shields on the monuments of Silius Attonis on the *Ala Picentiana* (Junkelmann, 1992, fig. 46) and Flavius Bassus from Cologne (Junkelmann, 1992, fig. 84), but the same Dr Junkelmann does not exclude the possibility of it being an infantry shield, considering the perpendicular position of the handgrip.

531 Feugère, 2002, p. 93.

532 Feugère, 2002, p. 91, fig. 105 .

533 Etienne, Piso and Diaconescu, 2002–3, pl. IX, no. 18.

534 Junkelmann, 1992, p. 184 and fig. 162. The specimen measures 100 × 53–4cm. It is a compact shape with straight sides and rounded corners.

535 See *metopa* XXXIV, in Florescu, 1961, fig. 213; Sumner, 1997, p. 63.

536 Pissarova, 1995, p. 18ff.

537 In Valerius Flaccus' *Argonautica*, VI, 100–4, Alazonii appear as neighbors with Ba[s]ternii, and bear shining white shields (*albentes parmas*), considered by some authors to be an allusion to their silver mines at Alybe; we should remember that Basternii and Alazonii were the names of Geto-Thracian tribes; so the white colour of the shield in the grave could be linked to his Thracian origins;

538 Pissarova, 1995, pp. 23 and 28.

539 Pissarova, 1995, figs 5 (plan of the grave with all the finds), 9–10 (shield still in place, where the oval shape is clearly visible), 11, 16 (*umbo*), 12 (sword and spears at the moment of the discovery).

540 In the grave were also found clay pots, a cup, a *balsamarium*, a glass bottle and a copper-alloy vessel; the only parts of the auxiliary dress that were preserved were iron elements of the belt (in a very bad condition), a typical *fibula* of the second half of the second century AD and some nails from military boots. The Thracian origin of the soldier and the fact that the weapons were buried inside the grave was very fortunate for Roman military archaeology, as soldier graves are usually only identifiable by the presence of the belt, at least until the end of the second century AD. See Pissarova, 1995, figs 8 (*fibula*), 14–15 (pottery), 16 (copper-alloy vessel and *umbo*), 17–18 (pottery), 19 (*balsamarium*, cup and glass bottle).

541 Robinson, 1975, p. 82 and pl. 199.

542 Robinson, 1975, p. 84 and pls 234–6.

543 See the surviving cheekpiece from Ulpia Traiana Sarmizegetusa, in Etienne, Piso and Diaconescu, 2002–3, pl. IX, no. 14; compare with Robinson, 1975, fig. 107.

544 Robinson, 1975, p. 85 and figs 103–7

545 The first hypothesis was that of a ring for the helmet suspension; but this theory was refuted by Coussin, considering that many *milites legionis* in march order travel with their helmet hung from the breast (**247**).

546 Etienne, Piso and Diaconescu, 2002–3, pl. X, nos 16–17,

547 Tac., *Ann.*, I, 51.

548 Robinson, 1975, pl. 243: gravestone of Firmus, Landesmuseum Bonn.

549 Robinson, 1975, pl. 244: grave *stela* of anonymous infantryman from Andernach, Landesmuseum Bonn.

550 Robinson, 1975, pl. 245.

551 Junkelmann, 1992, fig. 46, p. 48.

552 Sumner, 1997, p. 51.

553 Florescu, 1964, fig. 194b, p. 425, *metopa* XV; fig. 211, p. 444, *metopa* XXXII; fig. 213, p. 446, *metopa* XXXIV; figs 215a–b, pp. 448–9, *metopa* XXXVI.

554 An identical complete helmet was found in tumulus 2 of Cugir, and represents an interesting specimen of transition between the Agen–Port and proto-Weisenau typology, see Sîrbu and Arsenascu, 2006, p. 181, and compare with Bottini et al., 1988, cat. 115, p. 531; the helmet of tumulus 2 of Cugir is a one-piece helmet, its rounded cheekpieces, with one large and three small rivets, are similar to some cheekpieces of Novo Mesto/Agen–Port typology. See Mihaljević and Dizdar, 2007, p. 125.

555 Feugère, 1994, pp. 108–9; Maurin and Thauré, 1988, p. 13, no. 62; Feugère supposes that the represented soldiers are more probably cavalrymen, but it seems unusual that cavalrymen are represented in a group, on foot, and moreover looking at each other face to face .

556 Ceramanovic-Kuzmanovic and Jovanovic, 2004, p. 218, kat. 3 (tie loop), 6,16 (buckle), 25; the no. 6 seems to belong to the category FVI of Thomas (see Thomas, 2003, p. 75 ff.), but the shape is very unusual and the armour seems more likely to belong to a later context (beginning of the third century); no. 25 fits more with the usual Corbridge types.

557 Sumner, 1997, p. 60.

558 *SHA*, Av. Cas., VI, 3.

559 Herodian, *Hist. Rom.*, I, XV, 2.

560 See especially Coulston, 2007.

561 Prop., *El.*, IV, 3, 67.

562 Rossi, 1980, p. 149.

563 Cheesman, 1968, p. 12, no. 2.

564 Sumner, 1997, p. 113.

565 Lindenschmit, 1882, pl. V, 2–3: monuments of Hyperanor, of the *Cohors II Sagittariorum*, and Monimus, *Cohors I Ituraerorum*.

566 Cermanovic Kuzmanovic and Jovanovic, 2004, pp. 239–40, kat. 17 (14.5 × 1.6 cm).

567 Prop., *El.*, II, 12, 9–10.

568 Etienne, Piso and Diaconescu, 2002–3, pl. XV, nos 19–39; they are of pyramidal or triangular shape, and they belong to the category of heavy (nos 21–31) and light (32–9) arrowheads; considering the context of the discovery (a hoard from the Trajanic period, where a hard battle was fought between Romans and Dacians) we should not discount the possibility that some of them were used by the attacking Dacians, see Etienne, Piso and Diaconescu, 2002, p. 74.

569 Prop., *El.*, IV, 2, 33; Mart., *Epigr.*, X, 16.

570 Rossi, 1981, p. 51 and pls V–VI, j, m, n, o.

571 Long Syrian tunics are visible on ancient Egyptian paintings of the second millennium BC and on polychrome pottery in the Louvre, dated to at the time of Ramesses III (1180 BC), representing Syro-Phoenician prisoners.

572 Sumner, 1997, p. 113.

573 Modern Bulgaria; see Fol, 1989, p. 31; reconstruction in Connolly, 1988, p. 309, no. 12; Welkow, 1929, p. 54 and pls III–V.

574 Hottenroth, 1888, pl. 62, no. 20; Welkow, 1929, fig. 9.

575 Welkow, 1929, fig. 24.

576 Welkow, 1929, p. 54.

577 CIL III, 3676.

578 The Housesteads archer gravestone has no accompanying inscription, but could be a sufficient evidence that the *Cohors I Hamiorum* was stationed at Housesteads. It is true that it was not a *cohors milliaria*, whereas Housesteads fort was most probably built for this size of unit, but there is no evidence to the contrary, instead the presence of this *stela* there leads us to consider the possibility of the presence of this unit; the presence of a *cohors milliaria* beside it would not exclude such a possibility.

579 Graham, 1978, p. 17.

580 The helmet comes from the territory around Sarajevo, and it is preserved in the archaeological collection of Zagreb Museum. I would like to express all my gratitude to Professor Radman-Livaja, who allowed me to see the helmet and take the related pictures published in this book.

581 See, for example, the relief of the cavalryman of the *Ala I Ituraeorum*, representing the shooting to a target.

582 CIL VIIII, 18042.

583 Prop., *El.*, IV, 65–6.

584 Sumner, 1997, pp. 108–9.

585 Tac., *Hist.*, II, 88.

586 Trustees of the British Museum, 1971, p. 62, pl. XXV. The famous Wilton crown was found together with other crowns and diadems, and is considered to be a priest's regalia. But we cannot discount that it might be an original auxiliary helmet transformed into a religious device. The similarity with the helmets worn on Trajan's Column is striking.

587 They are represented on scenes XXIV, XXXVI, XXXVIII and LXX of Trajan's Column.

588 Tac., *Germania*, XLV.

589 Sumner, 1997, p. 40; Bianchi-Bandinelli, 1969, fig. 268.

590 Aleksinskii et al., 2005, p. 94.

591 Mart., *Ep.*, X, 6.

592 Bèjaoui et al., 1994, cover; this suit is composed of a long-sleeved dress with a central embroidered square *tabula* and long trousers with yellow boots; the shape of the tunic is that of a military corselet with lappets, and we cannot exclude that some parts of the dress were made of red leather;

593 Foucher, 1968, pl. 5 and p. 188ff.; one of the warriors wears on the breast a round protection in leather sewn upon his green garment, inside which is painted a lion; the garment seems to be a leather protection reinforced by bossed scales.

594 Pl., *HN*, VIII, 9, 5.

595 Cuvigny, 2005, pp. 1–5: Maximianon, Dydimoi, Krokodilô, Mons Claudianus, Persiou, Simiou; following Maxfield the garrisons were composed of no more than fifteen to eighteen horsemen and twenty-eight to thirty-six infantrymen; however, the *ostraka* attest that some garrisons were composed of regular *equites alares* and not *numeri*, as in the case of Krokodilô, defended by troopers of the *Ala Vocontiorum*, stationed at Koptos. These cavalrymen often acted as *dispositi*, relay riders charged with the exchange of military information and related correspondence, or as *prosecutores*, escorts to travellers, animal trains destined for military supply, and *dromedarii* against the desert raiders; two Roman cavalrymen were considered enough for bands of sixty Bedouins! See Lavigny, 2005, p. 7.

596 Moukatralis, Krinolaos and Ditouzanis, are some examples of local soldiers' names from Krokodilô; but Dacians are also mentioned, such as a certain Dida, who engraved a graffito of a crocodile on the rocks and is mentioned on some *ostraka* in Krokodilô. See Cuvigny, 2005, p. 4.

597 Sumner, 1997, p. 61.

598 Various, 2002, p. 118, fig. 144.

599 Prop., *El.*, III, 17, 30.

600 Prop., *El.*, IV, 95–6.

601 A specimen in bronze of the first to second centuries AD is visible in the ex-Guttman Collection, see Christie's, 2002, no. 98, p. 125; another bronze specimen has been found in Bulgaria, 12 cm high. See *Bulletin de l'Institut Archéologique bulgare*, 11 (1929), pp. 377–8, fig. 253.

602 Such as the legionary eagle on the Hutcheson Hill milestone from the Antonine period; see Bishop and Coulston, 2006, pp. 144 and 146, fig. 1.

603 Domaszewski, 1885, fig. 3; L. Sertorius Firmus, of the *Legio XI Claudia Pia Fidelis*, from Verona; see Lindenschmit, 1882, pl. II, no. 2.

604 Lindenschmit, 1882, p. 19.

605 Prop., *El.*, III, 12, 2; Mart., *Ep.*., XI, 3.

606 Such as the *stela* of Genialis, from Mainz, *imaginifer* of the *Cohors VII Raetorum*, and that of Aurelius Diogenes, from Chester (Deva); see Alexandrescu, 2005, p. 148 and figs 1–3.

607 Künzl, 1983, pls 81, no. 1 (Marcus Aurelius from Avenches); 85, no. 3 (Galba from Herculaneum); no. 4 (Lucius Verus from Marengo).

608 Alexandrescu, 2005, figs 3.3; 5/a; 2.4; 4.1.

609 Strobel, 1998, p. 17, scene LXXV.

610 Chiarucci, 2003, fig. 10.

611 Etienne, Piso and Diaconescu, 2002–3, pl. XVI, no. 55.

612 Pintaius from Bonn; Lindenschmit, 1882, pl. III, no. 2: Pintaius was a *signifer* of the *Cohors V Asturum*.

613 Lindenschmit,1882, pl III, no. 1.

614 Quintus Luccius of the *Legio XIII Gemina Martia Victrix*, see Domazsweski, 1885, fig. 12.

615 Veg. *Ep.*, II, XVI; '. . . Instead all the *signarii* and *signiferi*, although infantrymen, did receive the light armour and helmets covered in wild animal skins, to frighten the enemies . . .'

616 Lindenschmit, 1882, pl.III,1;

617 Cowan, 2003a, p. 63; Junkelmann, 1996, fig. 28.

618 Christies, 2002, no. 96; the mask is 18.5 cm high, the helmet 23 cm. The helmet is made of iron, decorated with a copper-alloy layer in repoussé work, representing vegetal elements and a central victory wreath on the central *diadema*. Remains of a flanged browband, like that shown on the Luccius monument, are visible above the right ear.

619 Kolias, 1988, p. 117.

620 Robinson, 1975, pl. 242, p. 88; Gansser-Burckhardt, 1942, p. 45, fig. 28a.

621 Robinson, 1975, pl. 471; Lindenschmit, 1882, pl. III,2.

622 Lindenschmit, 1882, pl. II, no.1; this tombstone is very important because it is the only one that shows the shape of the padding on the shoulders of a *subarmale*, made in concentric circles to which the *pteryges* are attached. For the colour reconstruction of the gravestone see Von Hase Salto, 2005, p.75.

623 Domaszewski, 1885, fig. 4.

624 Robinson, 1975, pl. 443.

625 Robinson, 1975, pl. 442,444;

626 Junkelmann, 1996, p. 20, fig. 29.

627 Fol, 1989, p. 29, for a set of medical instruments found in a Thracian tumulus of the Trajanic age; the archaeological expedition of Warsaw University discovered a whole military hospital (*valetudinarium*), one of the largest and best preserved of the Roman world; it was erected in about AD 100 during the Dacian Wars and perhaps is the base of the *Legio I Italica* depicted in scenes XXXIV and XXXV of Trajan's Column; see Dyczek, 1992, p. 365.

628 Cermanovic Kuzmanovic and Jovanovic, 2004, p. 215, cat. 1–4; Féugere, Künzl and Weisser, 1985, pl. 62, 3 (from Reims).

629 Féugere, Künzl and Weisser, 1985, pl. 57, from Vermand; pls 61, 63, 8 (from Reims).

630 Féugere, Künzl and Weisser, 1985, pl. 63, 1–7 (from Reims).

631 Cermanovic Kuzmanovic and Jovanovic, 2004, p. 215, cat. 5–6.

632 Féugere, Künzl and Weisser, 1985, pl. 65, 1–2 (from Reims).

633 Feugère, Künzl and Weisser, 1985, pls 53–5 (from Montbellet); these needles used for eyes were kept in a cylindrical box; pl. 59 (Italian and Spanish specimens); pl. 62, 3a (from Kolophon, Turkey); pl. 62, 1 (from Reims).

634 Féugere, Künzl and Weisser, 1985, pl. 56 (from Pompeii); pl. 57 (from Balcik, Bulgaria), Sirmium (Serbia); pl. 58 (Cologne); pl. 61 (Kos).

635 Idem, pl. 65, 3-4, from Reims.

636 Krunic, 2001, figs 6–7, from Viminacium.

637 Féugere, Künzl and Weisser, 1985, pl. 65, 5.

638 *SHA, Hadr.*, XVII, 2.

639 Ap., *Met.*, X,1: '*Die sequenti meus quidem dominus hortulanus quid egerit nescio, me tamen miles ille, qui propter eximiam impotentiam pulcherrime vapularat, ab illo praesepio nullo equidem contradicente dictum abducit atque a suo contubernio – hoc enim mihi videbatur sarcinis propriis onustum et prorsum exornatum armatumque militariter producit ad viam. Nam et galeam nitore praedicantem et scutum gerebam longius relucens, sed etiam lanceam longissimo hastili conspicuam, quae scilicet non disciplinae tunc quidem causa, sed propter sarcinarum cumulo ad instar exercitus sedulo composuerat. Confecta campestri nec adeo difficili via quandam civitatulam pervenimus nec in stabulo, sed in domo cuiusdam decurionis devertimus. Statimque me commendato cuidam servulo ipse ad praepositum suum, qui mille armatorum ducatum sustinebat, sollicite proficiscitur.*'

640 Prop., *El.*, IV, 3, 46.

641 Scene IV, see Bohec, 1989, pl. XI.

642 *SHA, Hadr.*, X, 2.

643 Etienne, Piso and Diaconescu, 2002–3, p. 74; pl. XVI, nos 56–7; XVIII, nos 58–64.

644 Rhamani, 1981, fig. 4; a similar *patera* was also found in the Karagaatch tomb, but decorated with a ram's head; see Welkow, 1929, figs 22–3.

645 Mart., *Apoph.*, 34/

646 See the specimens from Tekjia in Cermanovic Kuzmanovic and Jovanovic, 2004, pp. 216–17, cat. 2-6-7, in bronze; the bushel has the very interesting inscription CO(HORS) V GALL(ORUM) (HEMINA) EXACTA AT LEG(IONEM) VII C(LAUDIAM) R(EGINAM COGNITA) (Bushel purchased by the *Cohors V Gallorum* from the well-known *Legio VII Claudia Regina*).

647 Etienne, Piso and Diaconescu, 2002–3, pp. 74 and 86; pl. X, 58–9 (*dolabra* case fragments); the dating has been possible thanks to the recovered coins, some of which were kept in a burned leather bag.

648 Prop., *El.*, XVI, 3.

649 Prop., *El.*, III, 9, 53.

650 Mart., *Ep..*, VII, 8; Ov., *Tristia*, II, 184.

651 Fol, 1989, pp. 23 and 28.

652 Virg., *Aen.*, VIII, 506.

653 Mart., *Ep.*, XI, 98.

654 *SHA*, Hadr., X, .

655 Maier and Karageorghis, 1984, p. 272.

656 Prop., *El.*, II, 7, 12; III, 11, 43; IV, 3, 20; Mart., *Ep.*, VII, 80; VIII, 55; X, 64.

657 Prop., *El.*, IV, 10, 29,

658 Prop., *El.*, III, 3, 40–1.

659 Aquincum Museum, 1994, pp. 38–40.

660 Sumner, 1997, p. 36.

661 Bishop and Coulston, 2006, fig. 66 no. 1.

662 Popescu,1998, p.206, dates it to the first half of the second century AD.

663 Fontana, 2000, pp. 42–3 dates it to the second half the of second century AD.

664 Bishop and Coulston, 2006, p. 115, fig. 66.

665 Bishop and Coulston, 2006, p. 146 fig. 89.

666 Deschler-Erb, 1999, pp. 71–3.

667 Feugère, 2002, pp. 58–9.

668 *SHA*, Div. Marc., XII, 7.

669 Dyczek, 2007, p. 8: *phalera* of glass representing Drusus the younger, probably from the *Legio VIII Augusta*.

670 After being in service for about thirty years in a local body of *auxilia* in Mediolanum (Saintes), he received Roman citizenship and the rank of *tribunus* of a *cohors* of Raeti stationed on the high Danube, at Castellum Ircavium. See Maurin and Thauré, 1988, p. 7.

671 Mart., *Ep.*, VII, 6.

672 Mart., *Ep.*, VII, 8.

673 Plin., *HN*, XXXIII, 37; '*Sunt adhuc aliquae non omittendae in auro differentiae. Auxilia quippe et externos torquibus aureis donavere, at cives non nisi argenteis, praeterque armillas civibus dedere, quas non dabant externis.*'

674 Mendel, 1966, no. 1155.

675 Alföldi, 1959, p. 11.

676 Kovàcs, 2005, p. 956, lists *frumentarii, speculatores, immunes*, centurions.

677 Kovàcs, 2005, p. 955ff.

678 Such as the spears found in the shrine of Mars Leucetius and Nemetona in Kleinwinterheim, see Klein, 1999, pp. 87–94.

679 Bishop and Coulston, 1993, p. 21; Settis, 1991, p. 186, fig. 211.

680 Klein, 1999, figs 1, 3.

681 Klein, 1999, p. 87, describes one of the spearheads from Kleinwinterheim as 72 cm long, with a blade 2.5 cm wide!

682 Originally *pila* referred to the spears used for training, without tips, and called *hastae prepilatae*, see Plin., *HN*, VIII, 17.

683 Such as the specimen from Sarszentimiklos, Hungary, dated to the second half of the second century AD; see Klein, 1999, pp. 89–90.

684 Klein, 1999, fig. 3.

685 Klein, 1999, fig. 9 and p. 92.

686 Feugère, 1990, pp. 110–11, cat. 129–30.

687 Dated to the middle of the second century, see Feugère, 1990, p. 92, fig. 10.

688 Kovàcs, 2005, p. 960ff.

689 Josephus, *BJ*, III, 5, 5, 96.

690 Junkelmann, 1992, p. 135.

691 Pliny the Younger, *Ep.*, I, 6.1.

692 The combination of the javelins called *iacula* and the cavalry *parma* shield is mentioned in Mart., *Ep.*, IX, 20.

693 Radman-Livaja, 2004, p. 29.

694 Junkelmann 1992, p. 137, figs 120–2.

695 Junkelmann 1992, p. 146, fig. 126.

696 Lindenschmit, 1882, pl. XI, no. 2.

697 Bishop and Coulston, 2006, p. 79.

698 Junkelmann, 1992, p. 148.

699 Prop., *El.*, II, 25, 8; Mart., *Ep..*, IX, 38; Mart., *Apoph.*, 213.

700 Augustus, *Res Gestae*, 52.

701 Hoffiler, 1912, pp. 54–5.

702 Josephus, *BJ*, III, 5, 5.

703 See two *stelae* from the Museum of Cherchel, probably two *equites* of the *Cohors VI Delmatarum* of the late first century and beginning of the second century See Musée de l'Arles Antique, 2003, figs 35 and 38.

704 Josephus correctly calls it *thyréos*, *BJ*, 5, 5, 97. See the description of an oval shield together with a *parma* and a Coolus helmet carved on a frieze from Sora, in Tanzilli, 1983, p. 38.

705 Junkelmann, 1992, p. 183; they were typical of the first half of the first century AD, because later the monuments show mainly oval shields.

706 Joseph., *BJ*, III, 5, 5.

707 *Stela* of Romanus of the *Ala Afrorum*, from Colonia Agrippina (Cologne), late first century AD; *stela* of Cusides, of the *Ala I Tungrorum Frontoniana*, from Campana (Intercisa), AD 100; see Junkelmann, 1992, figs 35, 165.

708 Junkelmann, 1992, pp. 183–4 and fig. 162. The specimen measures 128 × 65 cm. From it Dr Junkelmann has calculated a shield size of approximately 120 × 57 cm. The specimen corresponds to that worn by an unknown cavalryman from Cologne, maybe a guardsman of the provincial governor (Junkelmann, 1992, fig. 117; Feugère, 1994, p. 102).

709 Robinson, 1975, fig. P.

710 Robinson, 1975, pls 297–304.

711 This name derives from a Luxembourg locality, where a grave of AD 30/40 containing the helmet has been found. See Feugère, 1994, p. 104.

712 Feugère, 1994, p. 104.

713 As on the Flavius Bassus, Romanius and Annausus monuments, see Feugère, 1994, p. 103.

714 Robinson, 1975, pls 399–400, from Waal near Yrendoorn and Newstead; a bronze helmet's cheekpiece of this typology, probably belonging to a legionary cavalryman, has been found in Grădiştea Muncelului (Romania) and it is dated to the first two decades of the second century AD, see Petculescu, 1982, fig. 1; in the same territory, a similar iron cheekpiece has been found in the hoard of Roman weaponry lost in the couch 9 of the Forum Vetus of Sarmizegetusa, probably during a sudden attack of the Dacians, see Etienne, Piso and Diaconescu, 2002–3, pl. XIII, no. 14.

715 Feugère, 1994, pp. 106–7; this helmet was produced for a single individual, an officer who had a physical deformity on the skull, maybe following a blow received in battle.

716 Probably a distinction granted to the cavalrymen for a particular event, such as a military triumph, an *ovatio*, or a single deed. See Feugère, 1994, p. 107.

717 The intriguing hypothesis of the archaeologists is that this helmet, found in a pre-invasion context, could belong to a Celtic mercenary of the Corieltauvi tribe in the Roman army This hypothesis may be confirmed by the coin of King Cunobelinus, minted around AD 10–41 and representing the king with a Roman cavalry helmet of this type. See Rudd, 2003, pp. 10–11; a further specimen has been found in Rennes, see Feugère, 1994, p. 107.

718 From the locality where one of the first specimens was found, but the true helmet of the Guisborough type could be dated to the end of the second and the beginning of the third century AD.

719 Petculescu, 2003, cat. 326 (from Sarmizegetusa Regia, early second century); Dautova Ruševljan and Vujović, 2007, p. 31, from Petrovaradin, embossed with the image of a eagle, first to second century AD.

720 I would like to thank Dr Jelena Kondic, head of the Iron Gate Museum, for permission to take pictures of the helmet.

721 Junkelmann, 1992, fig. 84.

722 Robinson, 1975, pl. 254.

723 Feugère, 1994, p. 114–15; the first owner was Attonis, of the *Turma Patercliana*; then Flavius Flavianus, of the *Turma Ataluans*; and then to two different troopers of the *Cohors III Bracara Augustanorum*.

724 Robinson, 1975, pls 250–3, dated to the first century AD.

725 Josephus, *BJ*, V, 9, 350ff.

726 This is the case of the Chassenard helmet, found together with a complete war panoply, or of the Vize helmet, of Weiler type but with an incorporated mask allowing only the eyes of the wearer to be seen. For Chassebard see Feugère, 1996, p. 169; for Vize see Mansel Arif Mufid, 1941, figs 201–2.

727 Lebedinsky, 2002, p. 141.

728 As Roman cavalrymen were called in the Eastern army: see Cuvigny, 2005, p. 17.

729 Specimens from Chassenard, AD 37–41, see Robinson, 1975, p. 172, pl. 480.

730 See also the monument of Romanius Capito, in Popescu, 1998, p. 197, cat. 7.

731 Robinson, 1975, fig. 176, p. 169.

732 All the scholars agree on mail armour, but the coat emerging from under the plates has scalloped edges on the rims; moreover no traces of mail are visible on the surface of the armour; nor are all the armours similar, because the *pteryges* of the *subarmale* on one occasion springs out directly from the plates, in a second man they emerge from a straight-cut coat and in the third specimen they are like a continuation of the leather support for the shoulder-guards; so perhaps these represent mail and leather armour used in the same context; the helmets are of the Weiler type.

733 Junkelmann, 1992, fig. 163.

734 Various, 2003, fig. 63; the relief is in a very bad condition, and we cannot exclude that the soldiers were represented marching in front of a horse parade on the background, or that they are escorting the emperor's horse. In any case this is, to my knowledge, the only associated evidence of this kind of armour with cavalrymen.

735 *Stelae* of unknown cavalryman with his *calo* (servant) and of Daza, *Cohors III Delmatarum*) see Musée d'Arles, 2003, figs 36, 38; *stela* of Vonatrix, showing *squama* with shoulder straps, s. Robinson, 1975, pl. 452.

736 Mansel Arif Mufid, 1941, fig. 203.

737 Arrian, *Tact.*, IV, 1: 'But the equestrian army is either equipped with armour, or it lacks armour. The part that is armoured has both men and horses covered by armour; the men have scale armour or linen or horn protections, and groin coverings (*perimeridia*), the horses instead protections for the brown (*prometopidia*) and the sides (*parapleuridia*) . . .'

738 Gansser-Burckhardt, 1942, fig. 28.

739 Breeze, Jilek and Thiel, 2005, p. 38.

740 Prop., *El.*, II, 10, 2: '. . . *equo aurato*. . .' (horse covered in gold harness).

741 Mart., *Ep.*, VIII, 21.

742 Feugère, 2002, p. 136.

743 Mart., *Apoph.*, 86.

744 Groeman van Waateringe, 1967, fig. 4; Connolly, 1988, p. 31.

745 Junkelmann, 1992, p. 12,

746 Vujović, 1995, p. 119, fig. 1; it was part of a plate from the front section of the saddle (20 × 11 cm), from Castrum Smorna, from to one small equestrian unit situated in the region for the control of the Danube Limes in the first–second centuries AD.

747 Junkelmann, 1992, p. 18ff., figs 6 (from Aalen), 7 (from Newstead), 14 (from Niederbieber, furnished with chin and mouthpieces); all dated to first and second centuries AD; Dixon and Southern, 1992, p. 63, fig. 31 (from Hod Hill, Dorset), second century AD.

748 Junkelmann, 1992, p. 20ff., figs 10 (from Ausgburg, c. AD 9), 11 (from Newstead, first–second century AD), 12 (unknown provenance); Dixon and Southern, 1992, p. 64, fig. 32 (from Newstead).

749 Etienne, Piso and Diaconescu, 2002–3, pl. XI, no. 31.

750 Etienne, Piso and Diaconescu, 2002–3, pl. XII, no. 34.

751 In bronze and iron: see Dixon and Southern, 1992, pp. 64–5 and fig. 33 (from Wiesbaden, first century AD); Junkelmann, 1992, p. 21, figs 18 (iron, from a legionary camp in Westfalen, beginning of the first century AD), 21 (bronze, from Newstead, first–second century AD) 22–6 and 28 for the reconstruction of the method of carrying.

752 Fragments and specimens from many different localities: see Etienne, Piso and Diaconescu, 2002–3, pl. XI, nos 32–3.

753 Dixon and Southern, 1992, pp. 39, 65.

754 Etienne, Piso and Diaconescu, 2002–3, pl. XI, nos 50–3.

755 Junkelmann, 1990, fig. 214.

756 Bendall and Morrison, 2003, p. 39, no. 34.

757 Bendall and Morrison, pl. XII, nos 36–48.

758 Gansser-Burckardt, 1942, fig. 28d.

759 Prop., El., III, 12, 12.

760 Junkelmann, 1992, pp. 90–1, figs 100–2.

761 Feugère, 2002, p. 146.

762 Arr., Tact. XXXIV; in saying this Arrian specifies that they '. . . are made to fit all around the faces of the riders with apertures for the eyes, so to give protection to the eyes without interfering with vision . . .' So if he seems to distinguish such helmets from those worn in active service, he also gives an important reference to the practicality of these helmets. It was probably up to the wearer to decide whether use it only in display games or on the battlefield too.

763 Junkelmann, 1996, p. 32ff.

764 Junkelmann, 1996, figs 54–8.

765 Dixon and Southern, 1992, pl. 22.

766 JRGZM, 2002, fig. 28; it is 17 cm high.

767 Type O of Garbsch classification, with similar specimens from Rome, Nijmegen, Vechten, Mainz, see Garbsch, 1978, p. 62ff., pl. 18.

768 Various, 1997, p. 110, cat. 35.

769 I have to thank Professor Radman-Livaja for such information, based upon the traces of leather remaining inside some specimens.

770 Arr., Tact. XXXIV, 4.

771 Junkelmann, 1996, fig. 152.

772 John, Ap., IX, 7ff.

773 Junkelmann, 1996, fig. 50 (first quarter of first century AD).

774 Junkelmann, 1996, figs 35–7, first quarter of first century AD.

775 Junkelmann, 1996, figs 39–41 and reconstruction in figs 77–86, second half of second century AD.

776 Junkelmann, 1996, fig. 87, second half of second century AD.

777 Junkelmann, 1996, fig. 88, late second century AD.

778 Junkelmann, 1996, fig. 90, second century AD.

779 Dixon and Southern, 1992, p. 128ff.; Robinson, 1975, p. 124; the female heads can be recognised by the use of diadems, ribbons and jewels (Dobrosloveni, Romania, see Dixon and Southern, 1992, pl. 20); for male heads see Various, 1997, no. 142 and Various, 1998, no. 292 (from Carsium).

780 Various, 2005, p. 688ff.

781 Junkelmann, 1992, pp. 202–3, fig. 181; probably belonged to the Ala Afrorum.

782 Junkelmann, 1996, fig. 31.

783 Arr., Tact. IV; the contarii were a special class of regiments, see Cheesman, 1968, p. 128.

784 Bujukliev, 1986, p. 148ff.

785 Augusta Trajana later became the main colony.

786 Fol, 1989, p. 27; Bujukliev, 1986, pls 8, 91.

787 Bujukliev, 1991, fig. 1.

788 Bujukliev, 1991, fig. 10.

789 Bujukliev, 1991, p. 15, mentions 16.2 cm in diameter and 7 cm high.

790 Bujukliev, 1991, fig. 12.

791 Bujukliev, 1991, figs 2–4.

792 Bujukliev, 1991, figs 7–9; one of these Tamga has been identified as bearing the name of the Sarmatian King Inismei.

793 Bujukliev, 1991, fig. 6 and p. 13; on the scabbard slide are engraved stylized figures of a griffin and a fox; it measures 11 cm in length and 0.25 cm in width.

794 Bujukliev, 1991, fig. 11.

795 Mart., Ep., VII, 30.

796 Bujukliev, 1991, fig. 13.

797 Bujukliev, 1991, p. 19.

798 Scene XXVII.

799 Negin, 2000, pp. 68–9 and pl. 5, figs 4–5.

800 Trevigno, 1986, pl. B3.

801 Cheesman, 1968, p. 129.

802 Prop., El., III, 12, 11: 'ferreus cataphractus'.

803 Negin, 2000, pl. I, 1.

804 Virg., Aen, XI, 770: '. . . Forte sacer Cybelo Chloreus olimque sacerdos insignis longe Phrygiis fulgebat in armis spumantemque agitabat equum, quem pellis aënisin plumam squamis auro conserta tegebat . . .'

805 Prop., El., IV, 3, 8.

806 Garbsch, 1978, pls 45–8.

807 Antonucci, 1994, p. 3.

808 Settis et al., 1991, pp. 162, 186, 265; Bohec, 1989, fig. 9; Giuliano, 1955, pls 17–28.

809 Herodian., Rom. Hist., I, 10, 6.

810 Antonucci, 1994, fig. 2, 14; Touati, 1987, pls 1, 2, 4, 5, 6, nos 1–2; 14; 15, no. 1; 16; 17, no. 3; 36, nos 2, 7; 44, no. 3; 45.

811 Touati, 1987, pl. 7.

812 Plin., HN, XVI, 186–219; 223–33: '. . . The ash is found to be most pliable wood of all for working; and, indeed, for making spears it is even better than hazel, being lighter than the cornel, and more pliable than the wood of the service-tree . . .'

813 Antonucci, 1994, pp. 6–7, fig. 3.

814 Probably lead, see Radman-Luvaja, 2004, p. 25.

815 Connolly, 2006, p. 233.

816 Deschler-Erb, 1999, p. 62 figs 65–6 and cat. 695; the small specimen presents niello decoration on the wings and two rivets for fastening the spheroid; it has been dated to the time of Vespasianus by coins found in the same context, see Deschler-Erb, 1999, p. 177.

817 Antonucci, 1994, p. 9.

818 Antonucci, 1994, figs 8b, 9,12; Touati, 1987, pls 13, 14, 22, nos 1, 2.

819 Antonucci, 1994, figs 10a, 10b; Bishop and Coulston, 1993, fig. 38, 2; Popescu et al., 1998, p. 69; Rankov, 1994, p. 30.

820 Radman-Livaja, 2004, p. 40, cat. 212 (Vespasianus) and p. 248 (Tiberius?); their size is respectively 4.5 cm and 3.5 cm in diameter.

821 Antonucci, 1994, fig. 8b p. 6.

822 Petr., *Sat.*, XI, 78.

823 Rankov, 1994, p. 19; Sumner, 2002, p. 19; the Meybon theory that the mosaic was a copy of an earlier work does not fit with the insertion of the group of the soldiers, whose rectangular shields and Montefortino helmets could only designate them as Romans.

824 Menéndez Argüin, 2006, p. 92, dated at the second century AD.

825 Rankov, 1994, p. 4.

826 Rankov, 1994, p. 46; on this relief a single guardsman, perhaps a *signifer*, is carrying a circular shield decorated with embossed *plumae*.

827 Rankov, 1994, p. 21.

828 Hoffiler, 1912, p. 59,

829 As on the Caligula coins, see Rankov, 1994, p. 21.

830 Hoffiler, 1912, p. 59.

831 In Italy still today the expression '*toccare ferro*' (touch iron) is used in a talismanic way; the Romans shared curious beliefs with the Native Americans about the weather elements; the Dakota Sioux also painted rain, wind and hail on their shields.

832 Robinson, 1975, pl. 470.

833 The colour of the Great Trajanic Frieze was still probably recorded in the Hottenroth reconstructions of 1888.

834 See the details in Touati, 1987, pls 26–30.

835 Popescu et al., 1998, p. 314, no. 291, Trajanic age. The helmet, of Weisenau typology, has the innovation of the tranverse cross-bars over the bowl; the dimensions are 29.5 × 11.5 × 19 cm.

836 Robinson, 1975, pls 175–8; see pp. 71–3 for technical details.

837 Scenes XXXII and XCVIII. On the monuments of the Antonine period the praetorians wear a crest on their helmets.

838 Connolly, 1988, p. 225: 'Aurelius Victorinus soldier of the XII Urban Cohort'.

839 Sumner, 2002, p. 20.

840 For the Cremona helmet, probably belonging to a Vitellian soldier, see Robinson, 1975, pls 34–6; the plume of the helmet in the Pompeii painting is similar to that of the officer from the House of Vettii (**86**).

841 Antonucci, 1996, p. 28.

842 Polito, 1998, fig. 109.

843 Robinson, 1975, pls 150–1; Buzzi, 1976, pp. 18–19; the bronze helmet is in good condition, and still has the check guards intact, as is a hinge on the *diadema* brow for attaching the crest.

844 Robinson, 1975, pls 417–20, early second century AD, Rijksmuseum van Oudheden, Leiden, Netherlands.

845 Robinson, 1975, fig. 112; first century AD, Rjiksmuseum G.M. Kam, Nijmegen, Netherlands.

846 Robinson, 1975, fig. 140.

847 Robinson, 1975, pls 413–16.

848 The probable two corselets of this age were found in the north-western corner of the *valetudinarium*, near the *scamnum tribunorum*; see Dyczek, 1996, p. 57; Gentscheva, 2000, p. 74; there were in fact other things found there: two decorated copper-alloy lobate hinges, four tie-loops, two hinged fittings and a lot of small fastening of different shapes; although all the fragments were found in a posthole of the same barracks, related to the first period of the camp, they do not belong to the same armour. The barracks, destroyed through a fire, covered the debris, whereas the parts of the armour were dispersed in a regular way. Some parts of the armours, probably two, melted. In any case the buckles belong to the Corbridge B type, where they fastened the shoulder guards to the breastplates; the single buckles belong to an armour of the same but different type that is difficult to identify; see Gentscheva, 2000, pls VIII, IX–X.

849 Gentscheva, 1999, p. 28, figs 6–7; translation from the German.

850 Dyczek, 1996, pp. 54–5.

851 Brzezinsky-Mileczarek, 2002, p. 17.

852 Hottenroth, 1888, pl. 62, nos 2, 10.

853 Robinson, 1975, pl. 501; Buzzi, 1976, p. 53.

854 Giuliano, 1955, pls 18–20.

855 Daremberg and Saglio, 1873–1917, col. 1415, no. 4550.

856 Virg. *Aen.* III, 467: '. . . A trusty coat of mail to me he sent, thrice chain'd with gold, for use and ornament . . .' See also V, 231: '. . . their chains of burnish'd gold hung down before . . .'; XII, 375: '. . . Nor aught, beneath his arms, the coat of mail . . .'.

857 Identical examples to the Great Trajanic Frieze type come from Vozdizhenskaya Stanitsa and from Chatalka, usually from 3.6 × 2.3 cm to 4.5 × 3.2 cm.

858 Cassius Dio, *Rom..*, LXXVIII, 37.

859 Robinson, 1975, pl. 497.

860 Settis et al., 1991, p. 162.

861 *Lex Iulia de vi publica*, in Just., *Dig.*, XLVIII, VI, I.

862 This is a fashion that can still be seen today: Iraqi officers had the same hairstyle as their leader Saddam Hussein.

863 Prop., *El.*, IV, 3, 18.

864 Prop., *El.*, IV, 3, 33.

865 Petr., *Sat.*, 9, LXII; SHA, *Av. Cass..*, VI,2.

866 The presence of pigs among the dead exclude the possibility that they could be Jews, particularly that they could be some of the last defenders of Masada. Considering that Romans sacrificed pigs at burials, we are perhaps in front of a unique discovery that still waits to be published in an appropriate way. Some scholars are against the theory that these are Roman bodies; it is in fact possible that the Romans desecrated Jewish remains by throwing in dead pigs.

867 Mart., *Ep..*, IX, 61.

868 Mart., *Apoph.*, 155.

869 Mart., *Apoph.*, 143.

870 Mart., *Apoph.*, 156.

871 See papyrus Ryl. 189 (128p), receipt for the clothing released partially by the officer in charge, the '*paralèmptès*' of the common custody of the tunics'.

872 'One white, belted tunic, three and half cubits long and three cubits, four fingers wide, weighing three and three quarters *minae* ...'; see Sheridan, 1998, p. 75, no. 15.

873 Yadin, 1971, p. 66ff.; a second man's tunic was 0.80 m long by 1.07 m wide.

874 Personal comment by L. Bender Jorgenson.

875 The tunics were found together with the bodies of Jewish warriors, so it might be supposed that they belonged to regular units of the Roman army after being taken as war booty; it is true that the tunics have not been found in a Roman military context, but they have been found in a place of military operations. Bishop and Coulston have said they are possibly not Roman and certainly not military. While we cannot be certain that all of them are military, even if they are not Roman they do follow Roman designs and methods of manufacture. So the present authors would not dismiss them as easily as Bishop and Coulston do, nor the possibility that they were Roman and that some of them could be looted war booty! The colours found, red, green and yellow, all correspond too with the colours worn by men, women and girls shown in the el-Fayoum paintings, and also with the later paintings of the Dura-Europos Synagogue.

876 Yadin, 1971, p. 69.

877 Varro, *DLL*, XLVII, IX.

878 John, *Gosp.*, XIX, 23, 4: 'The soldiers, having crucified Jesus, took possession of his clothes, and divided them into four parts, one for each soldier, leaving out the tunic. The tunic was seamless, woven in one piece throughout . . .'.

879 Palestinian Talmud, Shabbath 15a; Mo'ed Qatan 8od.

880 Sumner, 2002, p. 10.

881 Sumner, 2002, p. 46.

882 Sumner, 2002, p. 11.

883 Sumner, 2002, p. 12; the use of the bunched knot is, however, also represented in the sources on many blacksmiths and shepherds.

884 Sumner, 2002, p. 3.

885 Pintaius, Bonn, see Lindenschmidt, 1882, pl. III, no. 2.

886 Similar tunics are worn by other *milites* on the Rhine monuments, such as Caius Valerius Crispus of *Legio VIII Augusta*; Hyperanor of *Cohors II Sagittariorum*; Licaius of *Cohors I Pannoniorum*; see Lindenschmit, 1882, pls IV, 2; V, 2; VI, 2; their dress on the *stelae* is not that of the winter, considering that in the northern regions the Romans widely used *bracae* and heavy cloaks.

887 Prop., *El.*, IV, 3, 64.

888 Suet., *Aug..*, LXXXII.

889 Aug., *Sermo*, 37, 5 in Migne, *PL*, XXII, col. 492.

890 Cassius Dio, *Rom.*, LXVIII, I, 28.

891 Prop., *El.*, III, 15, 3.

892 SHA, *Hadr.*, XXII, 4.

893 Sumner, 2002, p. 43: *stela* of M. Aemilius Durises from Colonia Agrippina (Cologne); see also the *stela* of Titus Aurelius Avitus of *Legio II Adiutrix*, from Mursa, in Pinterović, 1978, p. 64, pl. II, 3.

894 SHA, *Div. Marc.*, XXVII, 3,

895 Mart., *Ep..*, VIII, 28; IX, 49.

896 SHA, *Sev.*, I, 7.

897 Mart., *Ep.*, VII, 2.

898 Daremberg and Saglio, 1873–1917, col. 901.

899 SHA, *Hadr.*, III, 5.

900 Suet, *Nero*, LXIX; '. . . *irrumpenti centurioni et paenulas ad vulnus adposita in auxilium se venisse similanti . . .*''

901 Phaedr., *Fab.* V, 2, 4ff.: '. . . *accurrit comes stringitque gladium, dein reiecta paenula: cedo inquit, illum . . .*'

902 Prop., *El.*, III, 12, 7.

903 Levi Pisetzky, 1964–5, I, p. 33.

904 Mart., *Ep.*, VIII, 58; see also IX, 57.

905 Mart., *Apoph.*, 133.

906 Burrell, 1997, p. 255.

907 Mannering, 2006, p. 153.

908 Dyczek, 1992, p. 368.

909 Virg., *Aen.*, V, 421.

910 Sumner, 2003, p. 3; Buzzi, 1976, p. 52; the cloak is fastened by a shell-shaped *fibula*, perhaps an element linked with the marine origin of the *Legio I Adiutrix*, whose *milites* are represented on the pilasters of the *praetorium*.

911 Sumner, 2003, p.11.

912 SHA, *Div. Marc.*, XIV, 1.

913 Mart., *Ep.*, V, 41.

914 Chiarucci and Gizzi,1996, p. 93, portrait of Commodus in *paludamentum*.

915 Daremberg and Saglio, 1873–1917, col. 295 and figs 5486–7.

916 Petr., *Sat.*, XII, 80.

917 Mart., *Ep.*, X, 76; Mart., *Apoph.*, 140, where it mentions Illyrian (Liburnici) caps of colours other than the white *lacerna* to which they are attached.

918 Lindenschmit, 1882, pl. V, 3.

919 Mart., *Apoph.*, 128.

920 Mart., *Apoph.*, 130, 138.

921 Fuentes, 1987, p. 60ff.

922 Goldsworthy, 2002, p. 121,

923 Brownish-yellow according to Meyboom. See Sumner, 2002, p. 19; this warrior has been interpreted as a centurion by Fuentes, but no signs of this rank are visible on the mosaic;

924 It is not widely accepted that the Palestrina mosaic or the Domus Aurea fresco shows praetorians, although the evidence of the shield should confirm this identification. The dating of the mosaic ranges from the late Republic to the middle Empire; Meyboom thought they were Ptolemaic troops, he even says they had rectangular shields with scorpion motifs. The idea that the fresco from the Domus Aurea shows a praetorian is attractive and also correspondeswith the sculpture from Villa Albani (**299**), where a *lorica segmentata* is worn by a praetorian wearing the same Corinthian helmet. Some people might wonder why Hector, if indeed that is who he is, would be dressed as an ordinary praetorian and not as at least the praetorian prefect in the Domus Aurea fresco. This is probably because it represents a well-known guardsman favoured by the emperor. His *lorica segmentata* could be evidence of an early Hellenistic version of this armour.

925 Mart., *Apoph.*, 129: 'Rome is more dressed by brown, the Gallia of red, the favourite colour of children and soldiers'; This reference is not necessarily only to the tunics, but it is a confirmation of the red colour in military context.

926 Parlasca, 2001, II, no. 354; but it is not clear in this specimen if red is the colour of the cloak or of the tunic.

927 Parlasca, 2001, II, no. 366, Hadrianic era; that this man belonged to the *ordo militaris* could be attested by the white

colour of his *chiton* and *chlamys*, fastened by a round gold *fibula*; on the tunic is also visible a dark purple *clavus*, as in the Dura-Europos frescoes.

928   Parlasca, 2001, II, no. 180.

929   Tac., *Hist.*, II, 89; white-dressed soldiers are often mentioned in the parades, where they were unarmoured. So in Tacitus the '*Praefecti castrorum tribunique et primi centurionum*' who at the entrance of Vitellius in Rome went before the eagles in '*candida veste*' should be interpreted as being in parade dress, like the emperor, because the historian compares them to the armed troops '. . . *ceteri armis donisque fulgentes* . . .' (the others shining in gifts and weapons).

930   Sumner, 2002, p. 5; Sheridan, 1998, p.75.

931   Prop., *El.*, II, 3a, 11.

932   In this way see also Virg., *Aen*, IX, 582 : '. . . *pictus. . . chlamidem et ferrugine claro hibera* . . .' (in an embroidered *clamys* of Hiberian purple colour); SHA, *Pert.*, VIII, 8 '*vestis subtegmine serico aureis filiis insignior praeter tunicas paenulasque lacernas et chrodytas dalmatarum et cirratas militares purpureasque clamydes graecanicas atque castrenses et cuculli bardaici et saga armaque gladiatoria gemmis auroque composita* (inventory of the objects and dresses belonging to Commodus: 'a silk interwoven dress decorated with gold, trip tunics and mantles, loose garments and Dalmatian tunics, military fringed tunics, war mantles in the Greek manner, Bardaic hoods, gladiatoral mantles and arms decorated by golden gems').

933   Maiuri, 1953, title page and p. 144.

934   Settis and Gallazzi, 2006, no. 280; the soldier, a certain Demetrios, is quarrelling with a woman before a local *strategos* (general) for a large amount of money.

935   Mart., *Apoph.*, 145.

936   Mart., *Ep.*, VIII, 10; 48; *Apoph.*, 131, 136.

937   SHA, *Clod. Alb.*, II, 5.

938   Tyrian purple, see Prop., *El.*, III, 13, 7.

939   Plin., *HN*, XXII, 3.

940   Mart., *Apoph.*, 154.

941   Yadin, 1971, p. 66.

942   Daremberg and Saglio, 1873–1917, IV, 1, col. 481, see *pileus, pilos*.

943   Also *pilleum*, see Mart., *Apoph.*, 132.

944   Veg., *Ep.*, I, 20.

945   Mannering, 2006, p. 153ff., fig. 3.

946   Cardon, 2002, pp. 42–3, fig. 2; this important piece of military equipment is still waiting proper publication!

947   Mart., *Apoph.*, 50.

948   Gansser-Burckhardt, 1948/9, p. 44.

949   Mart., *Ep.*, X, 73.

950   Sumner, 2002, p. 42.

951   Mart., *Ep.*, IV, 19.

952   Mart., *Apoph.*, 126.

953   Mart., *Ep..*, VI, 41; *Apoph.*, 137.

954   The scarf could also have been tucked inside the armour for another practical function, as it would provide extra padding.

955   Adamclisi monument, Sumner, 2002, p. 16; stele of *miles* of *Legio VIII Augusta* from Corinth, Sumner, 2002, p. 15; praetorians on the Puteoli monument and Cancelleria relief, Sumner 2002, p. 13, A; tombstone, Belgioioso, Sumner, 2002, p. 116, C.

956   Fuentes, 1987, p. 62.

957   Sumner, 2002, p. 37.

958   *Acta Martyria Peoni*, XV, 5.

959   Sumner, 2002, pp. 38–9.

960   *Corpus Glossae Latinarium*, II, 351, 44 (*koiliodesmos*); II, 402, 44 (*perizoma, cinctum lombare, ventrale*); II, 495, 61 (*ventralis*); IV, 400, 31 (*ventrale*); V, 631, 68 (*fascia*).

961   *Corpus Glossae Latinarium*, IV, 190, 30; 577, 38 (*ventrale*).

962   Plin., *HN*, VIII, 193.

963   Plin., *HN*, XXVII, 52.

964   Franzoni, 1987, pl. XI, fig. 1, no. 24, p. 41.

965   Mart., *Apoph.*, 153.

966   Ulpianus., *Dig.*, XLVIII, 20, 6: '*Divus hadrianus aquilio braduae ita rescripsit: "panniculariae causa quemadmodum intellegi debeat, ex ipso nomine apparet. non enim bona damnatorum pannicularia significari quis probe dixerit, nec, si zonam circa se habuerit, protinus aliquis sibi vindicare debebit: sed vestem qua is fuerit indutus, aut nummulos in ventralem, quos victus sui causa in promptu habuerit, aut leves anulos, id est quae rem non excedit aureorum quinque. alioquin si quis damnatus digito habuerit aut sardonychica aut aliam gemmam magni pretii vel si quod chirographum magnae pecuniae in sinu habuerit, nullo iure illud in panniculaira ratione retinebitur". pannicularia sunt ea, quae in custodiam receptus secum attulit: spolia, quibus indutus est, cum quis ad supplicium ducitur, ut et ipsa appellatio ostendit. ita neque speculatores ultro sibi vindicent neque optiones ea desiderent, quibus spoliatur, quo momento quis punitus est, hanc rationem non compendio suo debent praesides vertere, sed nec pati optiones sive commentarienses ea pecunia abuti, sed debent ad ea servari, quae iure praesidum solent erogari, ut puta chartiaticum quibusdam officialibus inde subscribere, vel si qui fortiter fecerint milites, inde eis donare: barbaros etiam inde munerari venientes ad se vel legationis vel alterius rei causa. plerumque etiam inde conrasas pecunias praesides ad fiscum transmiserunt: quod perquam nimiae diligentiae est, cum sufficiat, si quis non in usus proprios verterit, sed ad utilitatem officii patiatur deservire*' ('The Divine Hadrian stated in a Rescript to Aquilius Bradua: 'It is evident that, by the name itself, one ought to understand what is meant by clothing. For no one can reasonably say that under this term is included the property of persons who have been condemned, for if anyone is wearing a girdle, no one should claim it on this ground; but any clothing which he wears, or any small sums of money which he may have in his possession for the purpose of living, or any light rings, that is to say, any which are not worth more than five *aurei*, can be demanded. "Otherwise, if the convicted person should have on his finger a sardonyx, or any other precious stone of great value, or have in his possession any note calling for a large sum of money, this can, by no right, be retained as part of his clothing." Clothing of which a man can be stripped are those things which he brought with him when he was placed in prison, and with which he is attired when he is conducted to punishment, as the name itself indicates. Hence, neither the executioners nor their assistants can claim these things as spoils at the moment when the culprit is executed. Governors should not appropriate these articles for their own benefit, or suffer assistants or jailors to profit by this money, but they ought to preserve it for expenditures which Governors have the right to make; as, for instance, for paper for the use of certain officials; or as donations for soldiers who have distinguished themselves by their courage; or to be

967 *Corpus Glossae Latinarum*, II, 206, 3; II, 548, 65; III, 370, 9.

968 Prop., *El.*, III, 4, 17.

969 Mart., *Ep.*, XI, 21.

970 Prop, *El.* IV, 10, 43

971 Gansser-Burckhardt, 1942, p. 50, fig. 31; the new interpretation of Volken, who considers this piece a seat leather part of a *sella curulis* does not present any evidence to discount the truth of the first interpretation of Gansser-Burckhardt. See Volken and Volken, 2006, p. 35ff.

972 Lindenschmidt, 1882, pl. IV, 1.

973 Daremberg and Saglio, 1873–1917, fig. 2743, p. 787; Aurelius was an *eques* of the *Cohors II Praetoria*, then *tesserarius* of the *Legio II Italica*.

974 SHA, *Av. Cass.*, VI, 2.

975 Sumner, 2003, p. 35.

976 Suet,. *Aug.*, LXXXII, 1.

977 From Queen Street, London; see Leguilloux, 2004, p. 93.

978 *SHA*, Av. Cas., IV, 7; the emperor in front of the soldier wears only a wrestler's loin-cloth.

979 Sumner, 2001, p. 38.

980 Mart., *Apoph.*, 141.

981 Petr., *Sat.*, XI, 82: '. . . do the men of your division go about the streets in Greek pumps [*phecasiati milites*]?'

982 Josephus, *BJ*, VI, 1, 8, 85.

983 Van Driel-Murray, 2001, p. 362.

984 Leguilloux, 2004, p. 121.

985 Mart., *Ep.*, IX, 73.

986 Seneca, *De Tranq.*, X, 9.

987 Mart., *Ep.*, VIII, 3.

988 Sumner, 2002, p. 39.

989 Hottenroth, 1888, I, pl. 46, no. 17, where the original colours are reconstructed.

990 Goldman, 2001, pp. 124–5, figs 6, 28–9.

991 Hottenroth, 1888, I, pl. 50, nos 6–7.

992 Touati, 1987, pl. XXV, figs 1–4; Hottenroth, 1888, I, no. 51.

993 SHA, *Av. Cas.*, VI, 2.

994 Sumner, 2002, p. 39, dated to the second century AD; as with the banded leather armour found in the same locality, they correspond to the shoes worn by some soldiers of the Portonaccio sarcophagus.

995 Leguilloux, 2004, pp. 123–4.

996 Catullus, *Carm.* XCVIII, 4; Luci., *Phil.*, XXXIX; Hesychios of Alexandia, *Lex.*, (καρβατινη μονηπελμον = with the sole made of a single piece of leather).

997 Daremberg and Saglio, 1873–1917, I, 2, fig. 1180.

998 Mart., *Apoph.*, 65.

999 Ostrakon B3 – US 61; K224, dated to AD 109; see Cuvigny, 2005, pp. 121–3.

1000 CIL V, 938.

1001 Liberati and Silverio, 1989, p. 31; this is a very important image of the way in which the Romans marched against the enemy.

1002 Scene LXVIII.

1003 Judge, 1982, pp. 687, 690–1; Gore, 1984, pp. 572–3.

1004 Künzl, 1977, pp. 196–7, had already assigned to the *classiarii* of the Misenatis fleet the precious *cingula* found in Pompeii.

1005 Gore, 1984, p. 572.

1006 Feugère and Poux, 2002, p. 91, figs 13–14.

1007 Parker, 1992, p. 118, fig. 12; the armour is now exhibited in the Archaeological Museum of Granada, where, notwistanding the dating made possible by the presence of the pottery, it is still classified as a Greek bronze armour of the fourth century BC!

1008 White, according to Meyboom.

1009 Suet., *Aug.*, XXV, Octavian presented to Agrippa a *caeruleum vexillum* (sky-blue flag) for his victory at Actium.

1010 *Stela* of Statius Rufinus (literally 'the little red-one'), see Sumner, 2002, p. 47, mid-second century AD; this man was probably of Greek origin.

1011 Fede Berti, 1990, pp. 240–1, n. 188.

1012 Franzoni, 1987, p. 64, stele of the *classiarius* M. Titius Honoratus, in the Museo Civico of Padua.

1013 Liberati, 1997, p. 72; end of first century AD–early second century AD.

1014 Papyrus. Michigan. VIII 467, P. Mich. inventory Code 5391; Michigan APIS record 2445; from Karanis, dated to the first half of the second century AD.

1015 Mason, 2003, p. 34.

1016 Fede, Berti 1990, nos 140–4, pp. 210–19.

1017 The sailors of the Misenum fleet were charged with moving the great *velarium* in the Colosseum during the spectacles. In response the emperor ordered them to match barefoot!

1018 Scene LXIX.

BIBLIOGRAPHY

~ ANCIENT TEXTS AND ABBREVIATIONS USED IN TEXT AND NOTES ~

Aelianus (Ael.)	*On the Characteristics of Animals – De Natura Animalium – Περί Ζώων Ιδιότητος* (DNA)	Greek Text in Hercher, *R. Claudii Aeliani, De Natura Animalium libri XVII*, Leipzig, 1864
Ammianus Marcellinus (Amm. Marc.)	*Res Gestae*	Latin text and English translation by J.C. Rolfe, Loeb Classical Library, 3 vols, London, 1939–1950
Appian (App.)	*Roman History – Ρωμαϊκά* (Civil Wars – Εμφύλιος πόλεμος (Εμφ. Πολ.); *Mithridatic Wars – Mithridateios* (*Mithr.*); *Gallic Wars – Keltikê* (*Kelt.*)	Greek text in Appian, *The Foreign Wars*, ed. L. Mendelssohn, Leipzig, 1879; English translation in Appian, *The Foreign Wars*, ed. H. White, New York, 1899
Apuleius (Ap.)	*Metamorphoses – Aureus Asinus* (*Met.*)	Latin text available online at <http://www.thelatinlibrary.com/apuleius.html>; English translation by William Adlington, 1566, available online at <http://www.gutenberg.org/etext/1666>
Arrian (Arr.)	*Essay on Tactics – Techne Taktika* (*Tact.*); *Order of Battle Against the Alans – Ektaxis* (*Acies*)	Greek and Latin text in *Arriani Ars Tactica, Acies Contra Alanos, Periplus Ponti Euxini, Periplus Maris Erythraei, Liber De Venatione, Epicteti Enchiridion, Ejusdem Apopthegmata et Fragmenta, Quae in Joannis Stobaei Florilegio, et in Agellii Noctibus Atticis Supersunt*, Janssonio – Waesbergios, Amstelodami 1683 – Amsterdam, 1683
Asconius (Ascon.)	*Commentaries on Five Speeches to Cicero – Ad Cicero* (*Ad Cic.*) – *In Pisonem; Pro Scauro; Pro Milone; Pro Cornelio; In Toga Candida*	Latin and English text in *Asconius, Commentaries on Speeches of Cicero of Quintus Asconius Pedianus*, ed./trans. R.G. Lewis, Jill Harries and A.C. Clark, Oxford, 2006
Atheneus (Ath.)	*The Deipnosophists – Deipnosophistae* (*Deipn.*)	Greek and English text in *Athenaeus, The Learned Banqueters, Deipnosophists II*, ed./trans. S.D. Olson, Loeb Classical Library, Cambridge, MA, 2006
Augustus (Aug.)	*Sermo*; *The Deeds of Augustus – Res Gestae Divi Augusti* or *Monumentum Ancyranum* (*Res Gestae*)	Greek, Latin and English text in *Res Gestae Divi Augusti*, ed./trans. F.W. Shipley, Loeb Classical Library, London, 1924

Aulus Gellius (Aul. Gell.)	*Attic Nights – Noctes Atticae (Noct. Att.)*	Latin text and English translation by J.C. Rolfe in Aulus Gellius: *Attic Nights*, Volume II, Books 6–13, Loeb Classical Library, London, 1927
Caesar (Caes.)	*The Wars (Commentaries on the Gallic War – De Bello Gallico (BG); Commentaries on the Civil War – De Bello Civile (BC); On the African War – De Bello Africano (BA); On the Hispanic War – De Bello Hispaniensi (BH); On the Alexandrine War – De Bello Alexandrino (BAL)*	Latin Text in *Commentarii de Bello Gallico*, ed. Otto Seel, Leipzig, 1961; *Commentarii belli civilis*, ed. A. Klotz, Leipzig, 1927; *De Bello Africo, De Bello Hispaniensi* and *De Bello Alexandrino* available at <http://www.thelatinlibrary.com/caes.html>. English text in *De Bello Gallico & Other Commentaries*, translation by W.A. MacDevitt, Introduction by Thomas De Quincey, London & Toronto, 1940
Cassius Dio	*Roman History – Romaika (Rom.)*	Greek and English text in Loeb Classical Library, 9 vols, Harvard University Press, 1914–1927, translation by Earnest Cary
Catullus	*Poems – Carmina (Carm.)*	Latin and English text in *Catullus, Tibullus, Pervigilium Veneris*, Loeb Classical Library, 6 vols, Harvard University Press, 1913, translation by F.W. Cornish
Cicero (Cic.)	*Against Piso – In Pisonem (In Pis.)*	Cicero. *Pro Milone, In Pisonem, Pro Scauro, Pro Fonteio*, trans. Loeb Classical Library, Cambridge, Harvard University Press, 1992, translation by N.H. Watts
	Against Catiline – In Catilinam I-IV (In Cat.)	Cicero, *In Catilinam I–IV, Pro Murena, Pro Sulla, Pro Flacco*, Loeb Classical Library, Cambridge, MA, Harvard University Press, 1996, translation by C. Macdonald
	On Behalf of Titus Annius Milo – Pro Milone (Pro Mil.)	Cicero. *Pro Milone, In Pisonem, Pro Scauro, Pro Fonteio*, Loeb Classical Library, Cambridge, Harvard University Press, 1992, translation by N.H. Watts
	On Ends – De Finibus Bonorum et Malorum (De Fin. Bon. et Mal.);	Cicero, *On Ends,* Loeb Classical Library, Cambridge, MA, Harvard University Press, 1999, translation by H. Rackham
	About Oratory – De Oratore (De Or.);	Cicero *De Oratore Book III, De Fato, Paradoxa Stoicorum, De Partitione Oratoria*, Loeb Classical Library, Cambridge, MA, Harvard University Press, 1942, translation by H. Rackham
	On Divination – De Divinatione (Divin.);	Cicero, *On Old Age – On Friendship – On Divination*, Loeb Classical Library, Cambridge, MA, Harvard University Press, 1923, translation by W.A. Falconer
	On the Nature of the Gods – De Natura Deorum (De Nat.);	Cicero, *On the Nature of the Gods – Academics* in Loeb Classical Library, Cambridge, Harvard University Press, 1933, translation by H. Rackham
	Letters – Epistulae (To Atticus – Ad Atticum (Ad Att.); To his Friends – Ad Familiares (Ad Fam.))	Cicero. *The Letters to his Friends III, books XIII–XVI*, Loeb Classical Library, Cambridge, Harvard University Press, 1979, translation by W.G.Williams; Cicero. *The Letters to his Friends I, books I–VI,* Loeb Classical Library, Cambridge, MA, Harvard University Press, 1990, translation by W.G.Williams; Cicero. *The Letters to his Friends II, books,* Loeb Classical Library, Cambridge, MA, Harvard University Press, 1979, translation by W.G. Williams; Cicero. *Letters to Atticus I*, Loeb Classical Library, Cambridge, MA, Harvard University Press, 1980, translation by E.O. Winstedt; Cicero. *Letters to Atticus II,* Loeb Classical Library, Cambridge, MA, Harvard University Press, 1984, translation by E.O. Winstedt; Cicero. *Letters to Atticus III*, Loeb Classical Library, Cambridge, MA, Harvard University Press, 1967, translation by E.O. Winstedt
Clemens Alexandrinus (Clem. Alex.)	*Miscellanies – Stromata (Strom.)*	Greek Text in *Migne Patrologia Graeca* Volume 8, col. 685–1384
Corpus Glossariorum Latinarum		Latin Text in *Corpus glossariorum Latinorum a Gustavo Loewe incohatum auspiciis Societatis litterarum regiae Saxonicae; composuit, recensuit*, ed. Georgius Goetz, Leipzig, 1888–1923, Amsterdam, 1965
Dionysius of Halicarnassus (Dionys.)	*Roman Antiquities – Rhōmaikē Archaiologia (Rom.)*	Greek and English text in Loeb Classical Library, Dionysius of Halicarnassus, 7 vols, Harvard University Press, 1913–1937, translation by E. Cary
Eusebius of Caesarea (Euseb.)	*History of the Church – Historia Ecclesiastica (HE)*	Greek and English text in Loeb Classical Library, *Eusebius, Ecclesiastical History, Books I–V*, Harvard University Press, 1949 (1998), translation by K. Lake
Festus	*Lexicon – De Verborum Significatu (De Verb. Sign.)*	Latin text and French translation at <http://remacle.org/bloodwolf/erudits/Festus/index.htm>

Florus	*Epitome – Epitome de T. Livio Bellorum Omnium Annorum DCC Libri Duo (Epit.)*	Latin and English text in Loeb Classical Library, *Florus, Epitome of Roman History*, Harvard University Press, 1984, translation by E.S. Forster
Frontinus (Front.)	*Stratagems – Strategemata (Strat.)*	Latin and English text in Loeb Classical Library, *Frontinus, Strategems – Aqueducts of Rome*, Harvard University Press, 1950 (1997), translation by C.E. Bennett
Herodian	*History of the Empire from the Time of Marcus Aurelius – Herodiani Historiae a Marci Principatu – Ηρωδιανου μετα της Μαρκον Βασιλειας ιστορι ας (Rom. Hist.)*	Greek and English text in Loeb Classical Library, *Herodian, History of the Empire, Books I–IV*, Harvard University Press, 1961; English translation by E.C. Echols at <http://www.tertullian.org/fathers/herodian_00_intro.htm>
Hesychios of Alexandria	*Lexicon (Lex.)*	Greek text in *Hesychii Alexandrini Lexicon*, ed. K. Latte I–II (= A–0), Kopenhagen, 1953–1966
Horace (Hor.)	*Odes – Carmina (Carm.)*	Latin and English text in Loeb Classical Library, *Horace, Odes and epodes*, Harvard University Press, 2004, translation by N. Rudd
	Letters – Epistulae (Ep.); Satires – Satirae (Sat.)	*Horace, Satires – Epistles – Ars Poetica*, Harvard University Press, 1926, translation by H.R. Fairclough
Isidorus of Seville (Is.)	*Etymologiae (Et.).*	Latin text in *Isidori Hispanensis Episcopi Etymologiarum sive Originum Libri XX*, ed. W.M. Lindsay I-II, Oxford, 1911, available online at <http://en.wikipedia.org/wiki/Etymologiae>
Josephus	*The Jewish War – Bellum Judaicum (BJ); Against Apio – Contra Apionem (Contra Ap.)*	Greek texts in B. Niese, *Flavii Iosephi opera*, Berlin, Weidmann, 1895; English texts in *The Works of Josephus*, Peabody, 1987, translation by William Whiston
Justinian (Just.)	*Digest or Pandects Digestum Novum seu Pandectarum Juris Civilis (Dig.)*	Latin text in *Iustiniani Digesta, Corpus Iuris Civilis* I, ed. T. Mommsen and P. Krueger, Berlin, 1954; English text in *The Digest or Pandects of Justinian*, Cincinnati, 1932, translation by S.P. Scott
Juvenal (Juv.)	*The Satires – Satirae (Sat.)*	Latin and English text in Loeb Classical Library, *Juvenal and Persius, Satires*, Harvard University Press, 1918 (1999), translation by G.G. Ramsay
Livy	*History of Rome from the Founding of the City – Ab Urbe Condita*	Latin and English text in Loeb Classical Library, *Livy, (Ab Urbe Condita), History of Rome, Volume III, Books 5–7*, Harvard University Press, 1924, translation by B.O. Foster; Loeb Classical Library, *Livy, (Ab Urbe Condita), History of Rome, Volume IV, Books 8–10*, Harvard University Press, 1926, translation by B.O. Foster; Loeb Classical Library, *Livy, (Ab Urbe Condita), History of Rome, Volume V, Books 21–22*, Harvard University Press, 1929, translation by B.O. Foster; Loeb Classical Library, *Livy, (Ab Urbe Condita), History of Rome, Volume VII, Books 26–27*, Harvard University Press, 1943, translation by F.G. Moore; Loeb Classical Library, *Livy, (Ab Urbe Condita), History of Rome, Volume VIII, Books 28–30*, Harvard University Press,1949, translation by F.G. Moore
Lucanus (Luc.)	*Civil War – Pharsalia (Phars.)*	Latin and English text in Loeb Classical Library, *Lucan, The Civil War*, Harvard University Press, 1928, translation by J.D. Duff
Lucianus (Luci.)	*Lover of Lies – Philopseudes (Phil.)*	Greek and English text in Loeb Classical Library, *Lucian, Volume 3, Dead come to Life or Fisherman; Double indictment or Trials by Jury; On sacrifices; Ignorant Book-Collector; Dream or Lucian's Career; Parasite; Lover of Lies; Judgement of the Goddesses; On Salaried Posts in Great Houses*, Harvard University Press, 1921, translation by A.M. Harmon
Lydus	*On the Magistrates – De Magistratibus Reipublicae Romanae – Περί αρχών της Ρωμαίων πολιτείας (De Mag.)*	Greek and Latin text in *Joannis Laurentii Lydi Philadelpheni, De Magistratibus Reipublicae Romanae, Libri tres*, ed. Fuss, Paris, 1812
Marcus Aurelius Antoninus	*Meditations – Ad se Ipsum*	Greek and English text in Loeb Classical Library, *Marcus Aurelius*, Harvard University Press, 1916 (1999), translation by C.R. Haines
Martial (Mart.)	*Epigrams – Epigrammata (Ep.); Apophoreta (Apoph.); The Book of the Spectacles – Liber Spectaculorum (Lib. Spect.)*	Latin and English texts in Loeb Classical Library, *Martial, Epigrams, Volume I, Books 1–5*, Harvard University Press, 1993, translation by D.R. Shackleton Bailey; Loeb Classical Library, *Martial, Epigrams, Volume II, Books 6–10*, Harvard University Press, 1993, translation by D.R. Shackleton Bailey; Loeb Classical Library, *Martial, Epigrams, Volume III, Books 11–14*, Harvard University Press, 1993, translation by D.R. Shacketon Bailey

	Martyrium Peoni	Greek Text in Pio Franchi de Cavalieri, 'Come andavano vestiti ed armati i militi dell'adparitio', *Note Agiografiche*, 7 (1928), p. 207, n. 5 and in Gebhardt, O. von, Adolfus Harnack and Theodor Zahn, *Patrum Apostolicorum opera, textum ad fidem codicum et graecorum et latinorum adhibitis praestantissimis editionibus, recensuerunt commentario exegetico et historico illustraverunt, apparatu critico versione latina passim correcta prolegomenis indicibus i*, Leipzig, 1876–1978
Ovid (Ov.)	*The Festivals – Fasti*	Loeb Classical Library, *Ovid, Fasti*, Harvard University Press, 1989, translation by J.G. Frazer
	Metamorphoses (Met.)	Latin and English texts in Loeb Classical Library, *Ovid, Metamorphoses, Books I–VIII*, Harvard University Press, 1916 (1999), translation by F.J. Miller; Loeb Classical Library, *Ovid, Metamorphoses, Books IX–XV*, Harvard University Press, 1916, translation by F.J. Miller
	Sorrows – Tristia	Loeb Classical Library, *Ovid, Tristia, Ex Ponto*, Harvard University Press, 1968, translation by A.I. Wheeler
Palladius (Pall.)	*On Husbandry – Opus Agriculturae (Op. Agr.)*	*Palladius, Opus Agriculturae. In Palladii Rutilii Tauri Aemilian Vri Inlustris. Opus Agriculturae, De Veterinaria Medicina, De Insitione*, Bibliotheca Scriptorum Graecorum et Romanorum Teubneriana, Leipzig, B.G. Teubner Verlagsgesellschaft, 1975
Patrologia Latina (PL)		(*Patrologiae cursus completus. Series latina*), ed. J.P. Migne, Paris, 1841–64
Pausanias (Paus.)	*Description of Greece – Hellàdos Perièghesis (Per.)*	Greek and English texts in Loeb Classical Library, *Pausanias, Description of Greece, Volumes I–II*, Harvard University Press, 1918, translation by W.H. Jones; Loeb Classical Library, *Pausanias, Description of Greece, Volumes III–V*, Harvard University Press, 1926, translation by W.H. Jones; Loeb Classical Library, *Pausanias, Description of Greece, Volumes VI–VII–VIII, Chapters 1–21*, Harvard University Press, 1933, translation by W.H. Jones; Loeb Classical Library, *Pausanias, Description of Greece, Volumes VIII.22–X*, Harvard University Press, 1935, translation by W.H. Jones; Loeb Classical Library, *Pausanias, Description of Greece, Illustrations and Index*, Harvard University Press, 1935 (1995), edited by R.E. Wicherley.
Petronius Arbiter (Petr.)	*Satyricon (Sat.)*	Latin and English text in Loeb Classical Library, *Satyricon – Apocolocyntosis, Petronius – Seneca*, Harvard University Press, 1913, translation by M. Heseltine and W.H.D. Rouse
Phaedrus (Phaedr.)	*Fables (Fab.)*	Latin and English text in Loeb Classical Library, *Fables, Babrius and Phaedrus*, Harvard University Press, 1965, translation by B.E. Perry
Plautus (Plaut.)	*Boastful Soldier – Miles Gloriosus (MG)*	Latin and English text in Loeb Classical Library, *Plautus III, The Merchant. The Braggart Warrior. The Haunted House. The Persian*, translation by P. Nixon
Pliny the Elder (Plin.)	*Natural History – Historia Naturalis (HN)*	Latin and English text in Loeb Classical Library, *Pliny (the Elder). Natural History,* 10 vols, Harvard University Press, 1938–1962, translation by H. Rackham
Pliny the Younger	*Letters – Epistulae (Ep.)*	Latin and English text in Loeb Classical Library, *Pliny (the Younger). Letters 1*, Harvard University Press, 1969, translation by B. Radice
Plutarch (Plut.)	*Parallel Lives – Paralleloi Bioi (Caesar (Caes); Cicero (Cic.); Crassus (Crass.); Caius Marius (Mar.); Fabius Maximus (Fab. Max.); Lucullus (Luc); Pompey (Pomp.); Sertorius (Sert.); Sulla (Sull.)*	Greek and English text in Loeb Classical Library, *Parallel Lives, Plutarch*, 11 vols, Harvard University Press, 1914–1926, translation by B. Perrin
Polybius (Pol.)	*Histories – Pragmateia (Prag.)*	Greek and English text in Loeb Classical Library, *Histories III, Books 5–8, Polybius*, Harvard University Press, 1923, translation by W.R. Paton
Pomponius Porphyrio (Pomp. Porf.)	*Commentary on Horace – Scholia ad Horatium (Ad Horat. Sat.)*	Latin text in *Pomponi Porphyrionis Commentum in Horatium Flaccum*, recensuit A. Holder, Hildesheim 1967
Propertius (Prop.)	*The Elegies – Elegiae (El.)*	Latin and English text in Loeb Classical Library, *Propertius, Elegies*, Harvard University Press, 1990, translation by G.P. Goold

Pseudo-Hyginus (Pseudo-Hyg.)	*The Fortifications of the Camp – De Munitionibus Castrorum (De Mun. Castr.)*	Latin and English text in C. M. Gilliver, 'The *de munitionibus castrorum*: Text and Translation', *Journal of Roman Military Equipment Studies*, Volume 4, 1993, pp. 33–48
Quintilianus (Quint.)	*Declamations – Declamationes (Decl.); Of the Education of an orator - Institutio Oratoria (Inst. Or.)*	Latin Text in *Mar. Fabii Quintiliani Declamationes, apud Seb. Gryphius*, Lugduni (Lyon), 1540; Latin and English text in *The Orator's Education, V, Books 11–12, Quintilian*, in Loeb Classical Library, Harvard University Press, 2002, translation by D.A. Russell
Sallust (Sall.)	*Catiline's War – Bellum Catilinae (Cat.); Jugurthine War – Bellum Jugurthinum (Jug.); The Histories – Fragmenta Historiarum (Hist.)*	Latin and English text in *War with Catiline. War with Jugurtha. Selections from histories. Doubtful works. Sallust*, in Loeb Classical Library, Harvard University Press, 1921, translation by J.C. Rolfe
Scriptores Historiae Augustae (SHA)	*Alexander Severus (Al. Sev.); Avidius Cassius (Avid. Cass.); Clodius Albinus (Clod. Alb.); Commodus (Comm.); Hadrian (Hadr.); Macrinus (Macr.); Marcus Aurelius Antoninus (Div. Marc.); Pertinax (Pert.); Pescennius Niger (Niger); Septimius Severus (Sev.)*	Latin and English text in *Historia Augusta*, 3 vols, Loeb Classical Library, Harvard University Press, 1921–1932, translation by D. Magie
Silius Italicus (Sil. It.)	*Carthaginian War – Punica (Pun.)*	Latin and English text in *Punica, Books 1–8, Silius Italicus*, Loeb Classical Library, Harvard University Press, 1934, translation by J.D. Duff
Statius	*The Theban War – Thebais (Theb.)*	Latin and English text in Statius, II, *Thebaid,* 2 vols, Loeb Classical Library, Harvard University Press, 2004, translation by D.R. Shackleton Bailey
Strabo	*Geography – Geographica (Geogr.)*	Latin and English text in *Geography, II, Books 3–5, Strabo*, Loeb Classical Library, Harvard University Press, 1923, translation by H.L. Jones; *Geography, II, Books 17 and general Index, Strabo*, Loeb Classical Library, Harvard University Press, 1932, translation by H.L. Jones
Seneca	*On Benefits – De Beneficiis (De Benef.)*	Latin and English text in *Seneca, III, Moral Essays, De Beneficiis*, Loeb Classical Library, Harvard University Press, 1935, translation by J.W. Basore
	On Tranquillity of Mind – De Tranquillitate Animi (De Tranq.)	*Seneca, II, Moral Essays, De Consolatione ad Marciam. De Vita Beata. De Otio. De Tranquillitate Animi. De Brevitate Vitae. De Consolatione ad Polybium. De Consolatione ad Helviam.* Loeb Classical Library, Harvard University Press, 1932, translation by J.W. Basore
Suda	*Lexicon*	in A. Adler (ed.), *Suidae Lexicon*, 5 vols, Stuttgart, 1928-1938; English translation available online at <http://www.stoa.org/sol/about.shtml>
Suetonius (Suet.)	*The Twelve Caesars – De Vita Caesarum Augustus (Aug.); Caesar (Caes.); Galba; Nero*	Latin and English text in *The lives of the Caesars, Suetonius*, 2 vols, Loeb Classical Library, Harvard University Press, 1914, translation by J.C. Rolfe
Saint John the Evangelist (John)	*The Gospel (Gosp.); The Apocalypse/Revelations (Ap.)*	Greek Text in *The Text of the New Testament in the original Greek*, revised by B. F. Westcott, D.D. and Fenton J. A. Hort, D.D., New York, 1885; English Text in *World English Bible*, ed. Rainbow Missions, Inc., 1901
Tacitus (Tac.)	*Annals – Annales (Ann.)*	Latin and English text in *Tacitus IV, Annals 4–6, 11–12*, Loeb Classical Library, Harvard University Press, 1937, translation by J. Jackson; *Tacitus V, Annals 4–6, 13–16*, Loeb Classical Library, Harvard University Press, 1937, translation by J. Jackson
	The Histories – Historiae (Hist.)	*Tacitus II, Histories 1–3*, Loeb Classical Library, Harvard University Press, 1925, translation by C.H. Moore; *Tacitus III, Histories 4–5, Annals 1–3*, Loeb Classical Library, Harvard University Press, 1931, translation by C.H. Moore and J. Jackson
	Germania – De origine et situ Germanorum (Germania)	*Tacitus I, Agricola. Germania. Dialogue on Oratory*, Loeb Classical Library, Harvard University Press, 1914, translation by M. Hutton and W. Peterson
Talmud		*The Steinsaltz Edition of the Talmud*, New York, 1989, translation by I.V. Berman
Valerius Flaccus (Val. Fl.)	*Argonautica (Arg.)*	Latin and English text in *Argonautica, Valerius Flaccus*, Loeb Classical Library, Harvard University Press, 1934, translation by J.H. Mozley

Valerius Maximus (Val. Max.)	*Nine Books of Memorable Deeds and Sayings – Memorabilia, Factorum et Dictorum Memorabilium Libri Novem (Mem.)*	Latin and English text in *Memorable Doings and Sayings*, 2 vols, Loeb Classical Library, Harvard University Press, 2000, translation by D.R. Shackleton Bailey
Varro	*On the Latin Language – De Lingua Latina (DLL)*	Latin and English text in *On the Latin language, Varro*, 2 vols, Loeb Classical Library, Harvard University Press, 1938, translation by R.G. Kant
	Agricultural Topics – De Re Rustica (De Re Rust.)	*On Agriculture, Cato – Varro*, Loeb Classical Library, Harvard University Press 1934, translation by W.D. Hooper and H.B. Ash
Vegetius (Veg.)	*Military Art – Epitoma Rei Militaris/De Re Militari (Epit.)*	Latin text in *Vegetius Epitoma Rei Militaris*, ed. M.D. Reeve, Oxford, 2004; English translation by Lieutnant J. Clarke, 1767 available online at <http://www.pvv.ntnu.no/~madsb/ home/war/vegetius/>
Virgil (Virg.)	*Aeneid – Aeneis (Aen.)*	Latin and English text in *Virgil, 1, Eclogues.Georgics. Aeneid*, Loeb Classical Library, Harvard University Press, 1916, translation by H. Rushton Fairclough; *Virgil, II, Aeneid – Appendix Vergiliana*, Loeb Classical Library, Harvard University Press, 1918, translation by H. Rushton Fairclough
Xenophon (Xen.)	*On Horsemanship – Perì Ippikès (Perì Hipp.)*; *Anabasis*	Greek and English text in *Xenophon, VII, Hiero. Agelasilaus. Constitution of the Lacedaemonians. Ways and means. Cavalry Commander. Art of horsemanship. On Hunting. Constitution of the Athenians. Xenophon.* Loeb Classical Library, Harvard University Press, 1925, translation by E.C. Marchant and G.W. Bowersock

~ MODERN TEXTS ~

Abdul-Hak, S., 'Rapport préliminaire sur des objets provenant de la nécropole romaine située a proximité de Nawa (Hauran)', *Les Annales Archéologiques de Syrie*, 4–5 (1954–55), pp. 163–88

Aleksinskii, D.P., K.A. Jukov, A.M. Butiàgin and D.C. Korovkin, *Warriors Horsemen, European Cavalry* (in Russian), Minsk, 2005

Alexandrescu, C.G., 'A Contribution on the Standards of the Roman Army', *Limes XIX*, *Procedings of the XIXth International Congress of Roman Frontier Studies*, Pécs, 2005, pp. 147–51

Allen, S., *Celtic Warrior 300 BC–AD 100*, Oxford, 2001

Alföldi, A., 'Hasta-Summa Imperii: The Spear as Embodiment of Sovereignty in Rome', *AJA*, 63:1 (January 1959), pp. 1–27

Angelone, R., *L'Officina coactiliaria di M. Vecilio Verecundo a Pompei*, Naples, 1986

Antonucci, C., 'The Praetorians, the Bodyguard of the Emperor Trajan, 2nd cent. AD', *Ancient Warrior*, 1 (1994), pp. 3–11

Antonucci, C., *L'esercito di Cesare 54–44 a.C.*, Concorezzo, 1996

Antonucci, C., 'The Roman Army During the Republican Age, 506 to 272 BC', unpublished manuscript

Aquincum Museum, *Aquincum, the Roman Town in Budapest*, Budapest, 1994

Aquincum Museum, *Gods, Soldiers, Citizens in Aquincum*, Budapest, 1995

Avvisati, C., *Pompei, mestieri e botteghe 2000 anni fa*, Rome, 2003

Baldassarre, I. and G. Pugliese Caratelli, *Pitture e mosaici*, Rome, 1993

Barbagli, D., M. Becattini and P. Pruneti, 'Cleopatra, una donna nell'oceano della storia', *AV*, 10:85 (2001), pp. 38–53

Barker, P., *The Armies and the Enemies of the Imperial Rome*, Worthing, 1981

Barrow, R.J., *Lawrence Alma-Tadema*, New York, 2001

Baur, P.V.C., M.I. Rostovtzeff and A.R. Bellinger (eds) *The Excavations at Dura-Europos, Preliminary Report of the Fourth Season of Work, October 1930–March 1931*, London and New Haven, CT, 1933

Becatti, G., *La colonna di Marco Aurelio*. Milan, 1957

Beabey, M. and T. Richardson, 'Hardened Leather Armour', *Royal Armouries Yearbook*, 2 (1997), pp. 64–71

Bèjaoui, F., S. Ben Mansour, M.H. Fantar, L. Foucher, F. Ghedini, N. Jeddi, M. Khanoussi, G.C. Picard H. Slim and M. Yakoub, *I mosaici Romani di Tunisia*, Paris, 1994

Bendall, S. and C. Morrison, 'Protecting Horses in Byzantium. A Bronze Plaque from the Armamenton, a Branding Iron and a Horse Brass', Βυζαντιο Κρατος Και Κοινωνια, μνηνη Νικου Οικονομιδη, Αθηνα (2003), pp. 31–48

Berti, F., *Fortuna Maris, la nave romana di Comacchio*, Bologna, 1990

Bianchi-Bandinelli, R., *L'arte Romana al centro del potere*, Milan, 1969–77

Bianchi-Bandinelli, R., *Roma, la fine dell'arte antica*, Milan, 1970

Bishop, M., 'The Early Imperial Apron', *JRMES*, 3 (1992), pp. 81–104

Bishop, M.C., *Lorica Segmentata volume I*, Chirnside, 2002

Bishop, M.C. and J.C.N. Coulston, *Roman Military Equipment, From the Punic Wars to the Fall of Rome*, London, 1993

Bishop, M.C. and J.C.N. Coulston, *Roman Military Equipment, From the Punic Wars to the Fall of Rome*, Oxford, 2006

Bohec, Y. Le, *L'armée Romaine*, Paris, 1989

Bosi, R., *Il libro della storia*, Milan, 1984

Boss, R., 'The Sarmatians and the Development of Early German Mounted Warfare', *Ancient Warrior*, 1 (1994), pp. 18–25

Bottini, A., M. Egg, F.W. Von Hase, H. Pflug, U. Schaaff, P. Schauer and G. Waurick, *Antike Helme*, Mainz, 1988

Boube-Piccot, C., *Les bronzes antiques du Maroc, IV, L'équipement militaire et l'armement*, Paris, 1994

Brecciaroli Taborelli, L., *Alla moda del tempo, costume, ornamento, bellezza nel Piemonte Antico*, Turin, 2004

Breeze, J.D., S. Jilek and A. Thiel, *Frontiers of the Roman Empire*, Edinburgh, Esslingen and Vienna, 2005

Brentchaloff, D., *Monnaies et bijoux antiques des fouilles de Fréjus*, Fréjus, 1996

Brouquier-Reddé, V., 'L'équipement militaire d'Alésia d'après les nouvelles recherches (prospections et fouilles)', *JRMES*, 8 (1997), pp. 277–88

Brzezinski, R., M. Mileczarek, *The Sarmatians 600 BC–AD 450*, Oxford, 2002

Bruhn, J.A., *Coins and Costume in Late Antiquity*, Washington, DC, 1993

Bujukliev, H., *La necropole tumulaire Thrace près de Catalka, region de Stara Zagora, Razkopki i prouchvaniya*, Vol. XVI, Sofia, 1986

Bujukliev, H., 'Au sujet des relations thraco-sarmates pendant le premier et le début du deuxième siècle (d'après des données archéologiques)', *Archeologjia*, 2 (1991), pp. 11–20

Bull, S., *Triumphant Rider, the Lancaster Roman Cavalry Tombstone*. Lancaster, 2007

Buora, M., and W. Jobst, *Roma sul Danubio, da Aquileia a Carnuntum lungo la via dell'ambra*, Rome, 2002

Burrell, R., *Children's Ancient History*. Oxford: 1997

Buzzi, G., *Giulio Cesare*, Milan, 1976

Cahn, D., *Waffen und Zaumzeug, Antiken Museum Basel und Sammlung Ludwig*, Basel, 1989

Cambi, N., 'Kiparstvo (sculpture)', in Various, *Longae Salonae*, Vol. II, Split, 2002

Campisi, M., A. Melucco Vaccaio and A. Pinelli, *I colori perduti e la policromia nell'architettura e nella scultura classica*, *Archeo* dossier, 29 (July 1987)

Cantilena, R., M. Cipriani and G.T. Sciarelli, *Accumulare denari, in un tesoro da Paestum due secoli di Storia*, Rome, 1999

Cardon, D., 'Chiffons dans le desert: textiles de Maximianon et Krokodilô', in H. Cuvigny et al., *La trame de l'histoire, textiles pharaoniques, coptes et islamiques*, Paris, 2002

Carro, D., 'Le origini', in *Classica, Storia della marina di Roma, Testimonianze dell'antichità*, Vol. I, Rome, 1992

Carro, D., 'Pompeo Magno e il dominio del mare', in *Classica, Storia della marina di Roma, Testimonianze dell'antichità*, Vol. VI, Rome, 1997

Cascarino, G., *L'esercito Romano, armamento ed organizzazione. Vol. I: dalle orgini alla fine della Repubblica*, Rimini, 2007

Cermanovic Kuzmanovic, A. and A., Jovanovic, *Tekija*, Belgrade, 2004

Cheesman, G.L., *The Auxilia of the Roman Imperial Army*, Rome, 1968

Chiarucci, P., T. Gizzi, *Guida al museo civico Albano*, Albano, 1996

Chiarucci, P., *L'esercito Romano*, Albano, 2003

Chirila, E., N. Gudea, V. Lucatel and C. Pop, *Castrum Roman de la Buciumi*, Cluj, 1972

Christie's, *The Axel Guttmann Collection of Ancient Arms and Armour, Part 1*, London, 2002

Christie's, *The Axel Guttmann Collection of Ancient Arms and Armour, Part 2*, London, 2004

Ciobanu, R., 'Les grands espaces publics dans l'architecture civile et militaire de la Dacie Romaine', *Caesarodunum*, 40 (2006), pp. 352–96

Ciurletti, G. and P. Tozzi, 'Il Trentino in età Romana', *Archeologia Viva*, 8:3 (1989), pp. 10–17

Clark, Travis Lee, *The Lorica Musculata in Roman Statuary*, forthcoming

Coarelli, F., L. Lucignani, R. Tamassia and M. Torelli, *Le grandi avventure dell'archeologia, I misteri delle civiltà scomparse*, Vol. IV, Rome, 1975

——, *La colonna di Marco Aurelio*, Rome, 2008

Condurachi, E. and C. Daicoviciu, *Romania*, Geneva, 1975

Connolly, P., *Greece and Rome at War*. London, 1988a

Connolly, P., *Tiberius Claudius Maximus, the Legionary*, Oxford, 1988b

Connolly, P., *Tiberius Claudius Maximus, the Cavalryman*, Oxford, 1988c

Connolly, P., 'Pilum, Gladius and Pugio in the Late Republic', *JRMES*, 8 (1997), pp. 41–57

Connolly, P., 'The Pilum from Marius to Nero', *Exercitus*, 3: 5 (2005), pp. 103–12

Connolly, P., *Greece and Rome at War*, London, 2006

Coussin, P., *Les Armes Romaines*, Paris, 1926

Coulston, J.C.N., 'The Draco Standard', *JRMES*, 2 (1991), pp. 101–14

Coulston, J.C.N., *All the Emperor's Men: Roman Soldiers and Barbarians on Trajan's Column*, Oxford, 2007

Cowan, R., *Roman Legionary, 58 BC–AD 69*, Oxford, 2003a

Cowan, R., *Imperial Roman Legionary AD 161–284*, Oxford, 2003b

Cowan, R., *Roman Battle Tactics 109 BC–313 AD*, Oxford, 2007

Cracco Ruggini, L. and F. Cassola, *Storia antica delle Grandi civiltà*, Vol. II, Florence, 1982

Cumont, F., *Fouilles de Doura-Europos 1922–1923*, Paris, 1926

Curle, J., *A Roman Frontier Post and its People, the Fort of Newstead in the Parish of Melrose*, Glasgow, 1911

Curtis, J., *Mesopotamia and Iran in the Parthian and Sasanian Periods: Rejection and Revival c. 238 BC–642 AD*, London, 2000

Cuvigny, H., *Ostraka de Krokodilô, La correspondance militaire et sa circulation*, IFAO, 51, Cairo, 2005

D'Amato, R., *Siegfried*, Sondrio, 1999

Daremberg, C., E. Saglio, *Dictionnaire des Antiquités Grecques et Romaines*, Paris, 1873–1917

Dautova Ruševljan, V. and M. Vujović, *Roman Army in Srem*, Novi Sad, 2006

Deschler-Erb, E., *Ad Arma! Römisches Militär des 1. Jahrhunderts n. Chr. In Augusta Raurica*, Augst, 1999

Dixon, K.R. and P. Southern, *The Roman Cavalry*, London, 1992

Domaszevski, A. von, *Die Fahnen in Römischen Heere*, Vienna, 1885

Doxiadis, E., 'Misteriosi ritratti del Fayyum', *Archeo*, 10: 152 (1997), pp. 49–89

Doxiadis, E., *The Mysterious Fayum Portraits, Faces from Ancient Egypt*, Cairo, 1995

Dyczek, P., 'Bronze Finds from the Site of the Valetudinarium at Novae (Moesia Inferior)', in *Acta of the 12th Congress on Ancient Bronzes*, Nijmegen, 1992

Dyczek, P., 'Novae – Western Sector, 1992–1995', *Archeologia*, 47 (1996), pp. 51–64

Dyczek, P., *Everyday Life in the Fortress of the First Italic Legion at Novae*, Warsaw, 2007

Embleton, R., *Chesters and Carrawburgh in the Days of the Romans*, Newcastle upon Tyne, 1979

Etienne, R., I. Piso and A. Diaconescu, 'Le fouilles du Forum Vetus de Sarmizegetusa', *AMN*, 39–40:1 (2002–3), pp. 59–86

Féugere, M., E. Künzl and U. Weisser, 'Les aiguilles à cataracte de Montbellet (Saône-et-Loire). Contribution à l'étude de l'ophtalmologie antique et islamique. Die Starnadeln von Montbellet (Saône-et-Loire). Ein Beitrag zur antiken und islamischen Augenheilkunde', *JRGZM*, 32 (1985), pp. 436–508

Feugère, M., 'Les armes romaines', in L. Bonnamour (ed.), *Du silex à la poudre . . . 4000 ans d'armement en Val de Saône, catalogue d'exposition*. Chalon-sur-Saône, 1990, pp. 93–118

Feugère, M., *Casques antiques, les visages de la guerre de Mycènes à la fin de l'Empire Romaine*, Paris, 1994

Feugère, M., 'Le tombes à armes et l'aristocratie Gauloise sous la paix Romaine', in M. Reddè, *L'armée Romaine en Gaule*, Paris, 1996, pp. 165–76

Feugère, M., L. Bonnamour, 'Les armes Romaines de la Saône', in M. Reddè, *L'armée Romaine en Gaule*, Paris, 1996, pp. 133–46

Feugère, M. and M. Poux, 'Gaule pacifiée, Gaule liberée? Enquête sur les militaria en Gaule civile', *Jahresbericht* (2001), pp. 79–95

Feugère, M., *Weapons of the Romans*, Stroud, 2002

Florescu, F.B., *Monumentul de la Adamklissi, Trophaeum Traiani*, Bucharest, 1961

Fogliato, D., 'Ceivitates Cottianane, Note preliminari per uno studio del processo di romanizzazione della Valle di Susa', *Ad Quintum, archeologia del Nord-Ovest*, 7 (1984–5), pp. 65–87

Fol, A., 'Dalla parte dei Traci, arte e cultura nelle terre di Bulgaria', *Archeologia Viva*, 8:6 (1989), pp. 22–31

Fontana, E., 'Die Tuba aus Zsámbek', in Limesmuseum Aalen, *Von Augustus bis Attila: Leben am ungarischen Donaulimes, Zweigmuseum des Wurttembergischen Landesmuseums Stuttgart*, Schriften des Limesmuseums Aalen, Aalen, 2000, pp. 41–44

Forestier, A., *The Roman Soldier*. London, 1928

Foucher, L., 'Découvertes fortuites à Sousse', *Africa*, 2 (1968), pp. 183–204

Franzoni, C., *Habitus atque habitude militis, monumenti funerari di militari nella Cisalpina Romana*, Rome, 1987

Fuentes, N., 'The Roman Military Tunic', in *Roman Military Equipment: The Accoutrements of the War, Proceedings of the Third Military Equipment Research Seminar*, British Archaeological Report 336, Oxford, 1987, pp. 41–75

Gansser-Burckhardt, A., *Das Leder und seine Verarbeitung im Romische Legionslager Vindonissa*, Basel, 1942

Gansser-Burchardt, A., 'Neue Lederfunde Von Vindonissa', *Jber GpV* (1948/9), pp. 29–52

Garbsch, J., *Römische Paraderüstungen*, Munich, 1978

Garrucci, R., *Monete dell'Italia Antica*, Rome, 1885

Gentscheva, E., 'Neuen Angeben Bezuglich des Militarlagers von Novae im Unterdonaubecken aus der fruheren Kaiserzeit', *AB*, 3 (1999), pp. 21–33

Gentscheva, E., *Pierwszy obòz woiskowy w Novae, prowincja Mezja (Pòlnoczna Bulgaria)*, Sofia and Warsaw, 2000

Gichon, M., 'Aspects of a Roman Army in War According to the *Bellum Judaicum* of Josephus', in D. Kennedy and P. Freeman (eds), *The Defence of the Roman and Byzantine East, Vol. 1*, British Archaeological Report 297i, Oxford, 1986, pp. 287–310

Giordani, N., 'Allevamento, lana, tessuti: aspetti dell'economia nella colonia di Mutina', in C. Corti and N. Giordani, *Tessuti, colori e vestiti del Mondo Antico, momenti di archeologia sperimentale*, Finale Emilia, 2001

Giuliano, A., *Arco di Costantino*, Milan, 1955

Glyptothek Munchen, *Bunte Gotter, Die Farbigkeit Antiker Skulptur*, Munich, 2004

Goldman, B., 'Roman Footwear', in J.L. Sebesta and L. Bonfante, *The World of Roman Costume*, Madison, 2001

Goldsworthy, A., *The Complete Roman Army*, London, 2002

Gonzàlez, J.R., *Historia de las Legiones Romanas*, 2 vols, Madrid, 2003

Gore, R., 'The Dead Do Tell Tales at Vesuvius', *NG*, 165 (May 1984), pp. 556–625

Gorelik, M.V., *Warriors of Eurasia*, Stockport, 1995

Graham, F., *Housesteads in the Days of the Romans*, Newcastle upon Tyne, 1978

Graham, F., *Dictionary of Roman Military Terms*, Newcastle upon Tyne, 1981

Graham, F., *Hadrian's Wall in the Days of the Romans*, Newcastle upon Tyne, 1984

Groeman-Van Waateringe, W., *Romeins lederwerk uit Valkenburg Z.H.*, Nederlanse Oudheden 2, Groningen, 1967

Grueber, H.A., *Coins of the Roman Republic in the British Museum*, Oxford, 1970

Guitteny, M., *La Provence Romaine*, Monaco, 2002

Harmand, J., *L'armée et le soldat à Rome de 107 à 50 avant Notre Ere*, Paris, 1967

Hoffiler, V., 'Oprema rimskoga vojnika u prvo doba carstva [The Roman Soldier's Equipment in the First Period of the Empire]', *Vjesnik Hrvatskoga Arheoloskoga drustva*, 11–12 (1911–12), pp. 10–240 and 16–123

Horn, H.G. and Rüger, C.B., *Die Numider, Reiter und Könige nordlichen der Sahara*, Cologne, 1979

Hottenroth, F., *Il Costume, Le Armi, Gli Utensili dei Popoli Antichi e Moderni*, Vols I–II, Rome, 1887–92

Humer, F., *Marc Aurel und Carnuntum*, Horn, 2004

Ilies, C., 'Arme Romane descoperite La Ulpia Traiana Sarmizegetusa', *AMN*, 18 (1981), pp. 413–24

Iriarte, A., Gil. E., Filloy I., Garcia M.L., 'A Votive Deposit of Republican Weapons at Gracurris' *JRMES*, 8 (1997), pp. 233–50

Isenburg I, *Caesar*, London, 1965

Ivcevic, S., 'Components of Roman Military Equipment from Gardun', *Opuscula Archaeologica*, 28 (2004), pp. 159–76

Jażdżewska, M., 'Selected Features from the Przeworsk Culture Site at Siemiechów on the Upper Warta', *Prace i Materiali Museum Archeologiznego i Etnograficznego w Łodzi*, 32, 1985 (1988), pp. 109–42

JRGZM, 'Maskenteil eines Römischen Paradehelms aus Reinheim, Saar-Pfalz-Kreis, Saarland', *JRGMZ*, 49 (2002), pp. 433–4

Judge, J., 'A Buried Roman Town Gives Up its Dead', *NG*, 162 (December 1982), pp. 686–93

Junkelmann, M., *Die Reiter Roms, Teil I, Reise, Jagd, Triumph und Circusrennen*, Mainz, 1990

Junkelmann, M., *Die Reiter Roms, Teil II, Der militärische Einsatz*, Mainz, 1991

Junkelmann, M., *Die Reiter Roms, Teil III, Zubehör, Reitweise, Bewaffnung*, Mainz, 1992

Junkelmann, M., *Reiter wie Statuen aus Erz*, Mainz, 1996

Junkelmann, M., *Romische Helme*, Mainz, 2000

Katalog Berlin, *Kaiser Augustus und die Verlorene Republik*, Berlin, 1988

Kemkes, M., J. Scheuerbrand and N. Willburger, *Der Limes, Grenze Roms zu den Barbaren*, Ostfildern, 2005

Klein M. J., 'Votivwaffen aus einem Mars-Heiligtum bei. Mainz', *JRMES*, 10 (1999), pp. 87–94

Kliškić, D., 'Tools and Weapons', in Various, *Longae Salonae*, 2 vols, Split, 2002

Köhne E. and C. Ewigleben, *Caesaren und Gladiatoren. Die Macht der Unterhaltung im antiken Rom*, Mainz, 2001

Kolias, T., *Byzantinische Waffen*, Vienna, 1988

Kolnik, T., *Rimske a Germanske Umenie na Slowensku*, Bratislava, 1984

Kondoleon, C., *Antioch, The Lost Ancient City*, Princeton, NJ, 2001

Kovács, P., 'Beneficiarius Lances and Ring-Pommel Swords in Pannonia', in *Limes XIX, Proceedings of the XIXth International Congress of Roman Frontier Studies*, Pécs, 2005, pp. 955–70

Krunic, S., 'Antique Doctors' Boxes of the Loculamentum Type', *Recueil du Musée National de Belgrade*, 17:1 (2001), pp. 121–34

Künzl, E., 'Cingula di Ercolano e Pompei', *Cronache Pompeiane*, 3 (1977), pp. 177–97

Künzl, E., 'Zwei slberne Tetrarcheportrats im RGZM und die Romischen Kaiserbldnisse aus Gold und Silber', *JRGZM*, 30 (1983), pp. 381–402

Lange, J., 'Rovine a Sud', *Archeologia Viva*, 7:1 (1988), pp. 42–51

Lebedynsky, I., *Les sarmates, amazons et lanciers cuirassés entre Oural et Danube, VII siècle av. J.C.–VI siècle apr. J.C.*, Saint Germain du Puy, 2002

Leguilloux, M., *Le cuir et la pelleterie à l'époque romaine*, Paris, 2004

Leguilloux, M., *Les objets en cuir de Dydimoi, praesidium de la route caravanière Coptos-Bérénice*, Cairo, 2006

Lee, A.D., *War in Late Antiquity, A Social History*, Singapore, 2007

Levi Pisetzky, R., *Storia del costume in Italia*, 5 vols, Milan, 1964 – 1969

Liberati, A.M. and F. Silverio, 'Con la forza dell'artiglieria', *AV*, 8:8 (1989), pp. 28–33

Liberati, A.M., 'L'esercito di Roma nell'età delle guerre puniche, Ricostruzioni e plastici del Museo della civiltà Romana di Roma', *JRMES*, 8 (1997), pp. 25–40

Liberati, A.M., 'Navigare con gli antichi', *Archeo* 8 (1997), pp. 45–93

Liberati, A.M., 'L'esercito Romano nell'età delle guerre puniche, in M. Luni, *La battaglia del Metauro, traduzione e studi*. Quaderni di Archeologia nelle Marche 11 (2002), pp. 69–74

Liberati, A.M., 'La marina militare', in *Sotto il segno dell'aquila, l'esercito e la marina militare dell'antica Roma*, *Roma Archeologica*, 18–19, (July 2003), pp. 109–21

Lindenschmit, F., *Tracht und Bewaffnung des Römischen Heeres während der Kaiserzeit*, Braunschweig, 1882

Luik, M., 'Militaria in stadtischen Siedlungen der Iberischen Halbinsel', *Jahresbericht 2001* (2002), pp. 97–101

Luzzatto L. and R. Pompas, *Il Significato dei Colori nelle Civiltà Antiche*, Milan,1988

MacDowell, S. and G. Embleton, *Late Roman Infantryman 236–565 AD*, London, 1994

MacDowell, S., *Late Roman Cavalryman 236–565 AD*, London, 1995

MacMullen, R., 'Inscriptions on Armour and Supply of Arms in the Roman Empire', *AJA*, 64 (1960), pp. 23–40

Maier, F.G. and V. Karageorghis, *Paphos, History and Archaeology*, Nicosia, 1984

Maiuri, A., L. Jacono and M. Della Corte, *Pompei, nuovi scavi in Via dell'Abbondanza*, Milan, 1928

Maiuri, A., *The Great Centuries of Painting: Roman Painting*, Cleveland, 1953

Mannering, U., 'Questions and Answers on Textiles and their Find Spots. The Mons Claudianus Textile Project', in S. Schrenk (ed.), *Textiles In Situ. Their findspots in Egypt and Neighbouring Countries in the* first *millennium CE*, Riggisberger Berichte 13, Riggisberg, 2006, pp. 149–59

Mansel, A.M., 'Grabhugelforschung in Ostthrakien', *Bulletin de l'Institut archèologique bulgare*, 13 (1939), pp. 154–89

Mason, D.J.P., *Roman Chester, City of the Eagles*, Stroud, 2001

Mason, D.J.P., *Roman Britain and the Roman Navy*, Stroud, 2003

Mattesini, S., *Gli elmi delle legioni romane*, Rome, 2004

Mattesini, S., *Storia dell'armamento delle legioni romane*, Rome, 2005

Matthews, J.and B. Stewart, *Warriors of Arthur*, London, 1987

Maurin, L. and M. Thauré, *Guide du Musée Archéologique de Saintes*, Saint-Jean d'Angely, 1988

Menéndez Argüin, A.R., *Pretorianos: la Guardia Imperial de la Antigua Roma*, Madrid, 2006

Mendel, G., *Catalogue des sculptures grecques, romaines et byzantines*, 3 vols, Rome, 1966

Mihaljević, M. and M. Dizdar, 'Late La Tène Bronze Helmet', *VAMZ*, 3:40 (2007), pp. 117–46

Miks, C., *Studien zur Römischen Schwertbewaffnung in der Kaiserzeit*, Vols I–II, Rahden, 2007

Millar, F., *Rome, the Greek World and the East. Vol. 2: Government, Society and Culture in the Roman Empire*, Bembo, 2004

Millar, F., *Rome, the Greek World and the East. Vol. 3: The Greek World, the Jews and the East*, Bembo, 2006

Ministero per i beni culturali ed ambientali, *Il tesoro dei Kurgani del Caucaso Settentrionale*, Rome, 1990

Moreno, P., 'Il museo dimenticato: la collezione Borghese di Antichità', *Archeo*, 12 (1998), pp. 47–94

Musée de l'Arles Antique, *Algérie antique*, Arles, 2003

Nationalmuseet, *The Spoils of the Victory, Catalogue of the Exhibition*, Gylling, 2003

Negin, A,E., 'Sarmatian Cataphracts as Prototypes for Roman Equites Cataphractarii', *JRMES*, 9 (1998), 65–76

Nicolle, D., 'Jawshan, Cuirie and Coats-of-Plates: An Alternative Line of Development for Hardened Leather Armour', in *Companion to Medieval Arms and Armour*, Woodbridge, 2002

Obmann, J., 'Zu einer elfenbeinernen Dolchgriffplatte aus Nida/Heddernheim Frankfurt am Main', *JRMES*, 3 (1992), pp. 37–8

Olmos, R., 'Forme e pratiche dell'Ellenizzazione nell'Iberia d'età Ellenistica', in Various, *Hispania Romana, da terra di conquista a Provincia dell'Impero*, Martellago, 1997, pp. 20–30

Pace, R., 'Edifici monumentali sulle monete provinciali di Obla-Diocesarea in Cilicia', *Monete Antiche*, 2:10 (July/August 2003), pp. 16–25

Parker, A.J., *Ancient Shipwrecks of the Mediterranean & the Roman Provinces*, BAR International Series 580, Oxford, 1992

Parlasca, K., *Ritratti di mummie, Repertorio d'Arte dell'Egitto Greco-Romano*, Vol. II, Rome, 2001

Passi Pitcher, L., *Bedriacum, ricerche archeologiche a Calvatone, studi sul vicus e sull'ager il campo del generale: lo scavo del saggio 6*. Milan, 1996

Payne, R., *The Roman Triumph*, Toronto, 1962

Peeva, E. and M. Sharankov, 'A 1st cent. AD Roman helmet with inscriptions', *AB*, 1 (2006), pp. 25–34

Pekovic, M., *Archaeological Collection of the Military Museum in Belgrade*, Belgrade, 2006

Petculescu, L., 'Obrazare de Coifuri Romane din Dacia', *AMN*, 19 (1982), pp. 291–300

Petculescu, L., 'Armamentul roman în Dacia în secolele I–III', PhD thesis, Institutul de Arheologie Vasile Pârvan al Academiei Române, Bucharest, 1999

Petculescu, L., *Antique Bronzes in Romania*, Bucharest, 2003

Peterson, D., *I Legionari Romani, nelle fotoricostruzioni di Daniel Peterson*, Singapore, 1992a

Peterson, D., 'Legio XIIII GMV: Roman Legionaries Recreated', *Military Illustrated*, 47 (1992b), pp. 36–42

Petru, P., 'Latenoidni enorezni noži iz rimske nekropole v bobovku pri Kranju [Archaic Shapes of Slashers in the Roman Necropolis in Bodovk near Kranj]', *Vesnik Vojnog Muzeja Jugoslovenske Narodne Armjie*, 5 (1958), pp. 263–6 (in Serbian with German summary)

Phillips, E.J., 'The Gravestone of M. Favonius Facilis at Colchester', *Britannia*, 6 (1975), pp. 102–5

Piletić, D., 'O rimskim mačevima', in *Vesnik Vojnog Muzeja* 1, Beograd, 1954, pp. 9–17

——, 'Rimsko oružje na teritoriji Gornje Mezije', in *Vesnik Vojnog Muzeja* 17, Beograd, 1971, pp. 7–24

Pinterović, D., 'Limesstudien in der Baranja und in Slawonien', *Archaeologia Iugoslavica*, 9 (1978), pp. 55–82

Pio Franchi de Cavalieri, 'Come andavano vestiti ed armati i milites dell'adparitio', *Note Agiografiche*, 7 (1928), pp. 203–38

Pissarova, V., 'Tombe tumulaire de soldat des environs de la Serdica Romaine', *Archeologjia*, 3 (1995), pp. 18–28

Polito, E., *Fulgentibus Armis*, Rome, 1998

Popescu, G.A. and Various, *Traiano, ai confini dell'Impero, catalogo della mostra*, Rome, 1998

Potter T.W. and Johns, C. *Roman Britain*, London, 2002

Quesada Sanz, F., 'Montefortino-type and Related Helmets in the Iberian Peninsula: A Study in Archaeological Context', *JRMES*, 8 (1997), pp. 151–66

Racinet, A., *Le Costume Historique*, 6 vols, Paris, 1883

Racinet, A., *The Complete Costume History*, Cologne, 2003

Radman-Livaja, I., *Militaria Sisciensia, Finds of the Roman Military Equipment in Sisak in the Holdings of the Archaeological Museum in Zagreb*, Zagreb, 2004

Radman-Livaja, I., 'Lorica Segmentata Fittings from Burgenae', forthcoming

Radulescu, A., 'Elmi bronzei di Ostrov', *Dacia*, 7 (1963), pp. 543–51

Rahmani, L.Y. 'A Roman Patera from Lajjun', *Israel Exploration Journal*, 31:3–4 (1981), pp. 190–6

Rankov, B., *The Praetorian Guard*, London, 1994

Real Museo Nazionale di Napoli, vols I–XVI, Naples, 1858

Rizzello, M., *Monumenti funerari Romani con fregi dorici nella media Valle dell'Iri*, Sora, 1979

Robertson, A.S., M. Scott and L.J.F. Keppie, *Bar Hill: A Roman Fort and its Finds*, Oxford, 1975

Robinson, H.R., *Oriental Armour*, London, 1967

Robinson, H.R., *The Armour of Imperial Rome*, London, 1975

Robinson, H.R., *What the Soldiers Wore on Hadrian's Wall*, Newcastle upon Tyne, 1976

Rossi, L., *Rotocalchi di pietra*, Milan, 1980

Rossi, L, 'L'esercito e l'arte della Guerra', in S. Settis et al., *Civiltà dei Romani, il potere e l'esercito*, Milan, 1991, pp. 253–72

Roth, J.P., *The Logistic of the Roman Army at War, 264 BC–AD 235*, Leiden, Boston and Cologne, 1999

Rovina, D., *La sezione Medievale del Museo G.A. Sanna' di Sassari*, Piedimonte Matese, 2000

Rudd, C., 'Un enorme tesoro Druido dal Leichestershire', *Monete Antiche*, 2:10 (July/August 2003), pp. 9–15

Saxtorph, N.M., *Warriors and Weapons, 3000 B.C. to A.D. 1700*, London, 1972

Schlette, F., *Germanen, zwischen Thorsberg und Ravenna*, Leipzig, 1971

Scrinari, V.S.M., *Sculture Romane di Aquileia*, Rome, 1972

Segenni, S., 'Esercito: organizzazione e carriere', in S. Settis et al., *Civiltà dei Romani, il potere e l'esercito*, Milan, 1991, pp. 241–52

Sekunda, N., *The Ancient Greeks*, London, 1986

Sekunda, N., 'The Roman Army and the Samnite Wars', *Ancient Warrior*, 1 (1994), pp. 12–17

Sekunda, N., *Seleucid and Ptolemaic Reformed Armies 168–145 BC. Vol. I: The Seleucid Army*, Stockport, 1994

Sekunda, N., *Seleucid and Ptolemaic reformed armies 168–145 BC. Vol. II: The Ptolemaic Army*, Stockport, 1995

Sekunda, N., *Republican Roman Army, 200–104 BC*, London, 1996

Settis, S. et al., *Civiltà dei Romani, il potere e l'esercito*, Milano, 1991

Settis, S. and C. Gallazzi, *Le tre vite del papiro di Artemidoro, voci e sguardi dall'Egitto greco-romano*, Milan, 2006

Sheridan, J.A., *Columbia Papyri IX, The Vestis militaris codex*, Atlanta, 1998

Sievers, S., 'Armes celtiques, germaniques et Romaines: ce que nous apprennent les fouilles d'Alesia', in M. Reddè, *L'armée Romaine en Gaule*, Paris, 1996, pp. 67–81

Sîrbu, V. and M. Arsenascu, 'Dacian Settlements and Necropolises in Southwestern Romania (2nd c. B.C.–1st c. A.D.)', *Acta Terrae Septemcastrensis*, 5:1 (2006), pp. 163–86

Simkins, M., *The Roman Army from Caesar to Trajan*, London, 1974

Simkins, M., *The Roman Army from Caesar to Trajan*, revised edition, London, 1984

Simkins, M., *Warriors of Rome*, London, 1988

Simpson, G., *Roman Weapons, Tools, Bronze Equipment and Brooches from Neuss-Novaesium Excavations 1955–1972*, Oxford, 2000

Smith, W., *A Dictionary of Greek and Roman Antiquities*, London, 1875

Strobel, K., 'L'età Trajanea e la storiografia moderna', in G.A. Popescu et al., *Traiano, ai confini dell'Impero, catalogo della mostra*, Rome, 1998, pp. 13–29

Stuart Jones, H. *A Catalogue of the Ancient Sculptures Preserved in the Municipal Collections of Rome. The Sculptures of the Palazzo dei Conservatori*, Oxford, 1926

Sumner, G., *Roman Army Wars of the Empire*, London, 1997

Sumner, G., *Roman Military Clothing. Vol. I: 100 BC–AD 200*, Oxford, 2002

Sumner, G., *Roman Military Clothing. Vol. II: AD 200–400*, Oxford, 2003

Szylàgyi, J., *Aquincum*, Budapest, 1956

Tanzilli, A., *Antica Topografia di Sora e del suo territorio*, Isola del Liri, 1982

Tanzilli, A., 'Due fregi inediti del territorio Sorano', *Antiqua*, 2 (March–April 1983), pp. 37–8

Thomas, M.D., *Lorica Segmentata. Vol. II: A Catalogue of Finds*, Chirnside, 2003

Tincey, J., *Soldiers of the English Civil War, Vol. II*, London, 1990

Torbatov, S., 'Diplôme militaire romain de l'an 145 de Nigrinianis, Mésie inferieure', *Archeologjia*, 1 (1991), pp. 23–7

Torelli, M., 'Il fregio d'armi nel museo di antichità di Torino. Ipotesi per un monumento di un Senatore di epoca Claudia', in L. Mercando, *Archeologia a Torino. Dall'età preromana all'Alto Medioevo*, Turin, 2003, pp. 151–70

Touati, A.M.L., *The Great Trajanic Frieze*, Stockholm, 1987

Treviño R., *Rome Enemies. Vol. IV: Spanish Armies 218–19 BC*, London, 1986

Tronche, P., 'Le camp d'Aulnay de Santonge', in M. Reddè, *L'armée Romaine en Gaule*, Paris, 1996, pp. 177–88

Trustees of the British Museum, *Guide to the Antiquities of Roman Britain*, London, 1971

Ulbert, G., 'Gladii aus Pompeji', *Germania*, 47:1–2 (1969), pp. 97–128

Unz, C., E. Deschler-Erb, *Katalog der Militaria aus Vindonissa*, Brugg, 1997

van Driel-Murray, C., 'Footwear in the North-Western Provinces of the Roman Empire', in *Stepping through time. Archaeological footwear from prehistoric times until 1800*, Zolle, 2001, pp. 337–76

Various, 'Tibiscum, Cercetari Arheologice II, 1976–1979', *AMN*, 20 (1983), pp. 405–32

Various, *Tesori d'Eurasia, 2000 anni di Storia in 70 anni di archeologia Sovietica*, Milan, 1987

Various, *Il Marocco e Roma, i grandi bronzi dal Museo di Rabat*, Rome, 1991

Various, *Riflessi di Roma: Impero Romano e Barbari del Baltico*, Rome, 1997a

Various, *Miles Romanus in Provincia Dacia*, Cluj Napoca, 1997b

Various, *Antinoe, 100 anni dopo*, Florence, 1998

Various, *Zenobia, il sogno di una regina d'Oriente*, Milan, 2002

Various, *La collezione Torlonia di Antichità del Fucino*, Pescara, 2003

Various, *Guerrieri Principi ed Eroi, fra il Danubio ed il Po, dalla Preistoria all'Alto Medioevo*, Trento, 2004

Various, *Costantino il Grande, la civiltà antica al bivio tra Occidente ed Oriente*, Cinisello Balsamo, 2005

Various, *A bon droyt, spade di uomini liberi, cavalieri e Santi*, Milan, 2007

Vicente, J.D., M. Pilar Punter and B. Ezquerra, 'La catapulta tardo-republicana y otro equipamiento militar de 'La Caridad' (Caminreal, Teruel)', *JRMES*, 8 (1997), pp. 167–99

Volken, M. and S. Volken, 'Drei neue interpretierte Lederfunde aus Vindonissa: Kopfstuck einer Pferdedecke, Sitzflache eines Klappstuhls und Schreibtafeletui', *Gesellschaft Pro Vindonissa 2005*, (2006), pp. 33–40

Von Hase Salto, M.A., 'Il limes dell'Impero Romano, 2: di là dal Reno e tra gli alberi', in *Archeo*, n.12 (250), December 2005, p. 72–83

Vujović, M., 'The Fragment of the Roman Saddle Shackle from Boljetin', *Glasnik*, 10 (1995), pp. 118–23

Vujović, M., 'Two Swords in the Museum of the City of Beograd', *Annual of the City of Beograd*, 47–8 (2000/1), pp. 45–50

Vujović, M., 'Gladii from Dubravica. A Contribution to the Study of the Roman Swords on the Territory of the Serbia', *Vestigatio Vetvstatis* (2001), pp. 119–33

Warry, J., *Warfare in Classical World*, London, 1980

Waurick, G., 'Untersuchungen zur historisierenden Rüstung in der römischen Kunst', *JRGZM*, **30** (1983), pp. 265–301

Welkov, I., 'Die Ausgrabungen bei Mezek und Svilengrad', *Bulletin de l'Institut Archéologique bulgare*, 11 (1937), pp. 147–70

Widawnictwa Uniwersytetu Warszawskiego, *Novensia, Badania Ekspedycji archeologicznej Uniwersytetu Warszawskiego w Novae 5, Studia i materialy pod redakcja naukowa*, Warsaw, 1993

Wilcox, P., *Rome's Enemies. Vol. 2: Gallic and British Celts*, London, 1985

Windrow, M. and A. McBride, *Imperial Rome at War*, London, 1997

Yadin, Y., *The Finds from the Bar Kokhba Period in the Cave of Letters*, Jerusalem, 1963

Yadin, Y., *Bar Kokhba, the Rediscovery of the Legendary Hero of the Second Jewish Revolt Against Rome*, New York, 1971

Yupanqui, M., 'Auge in Auge mit einem römischen Offizier. Anmerkungen zur Rekonstruktion eines römischen Militärgrabsteines aus Offenburg', in C. Bücker, M. Hoeper, N. Krohn and J. Trumm, *Archäologie und Geschichte an Ober- und Hochrhein. Festschrift für Gerhard Fingerlin zum 65. Geburtstag*, Rhaden, 2004, pp. 45–9

Other Works

The Glory of Rome, 12 colour plates, reconstruction of Roman warriors, R&K Productions, Westlake Village, 1997

Biblioteca Apostolica Vaticana, *Vergilius Vaticanus – Codex Vaticanus Latinus 3225*, special postcard colour edition, Graz, 1980

Website of Dr Travis Lee Clark, <http: //astro.temple.edu/~tlclark/ lorica/origins.htm>, about the *lorica musculata*. In particular: art historical problems in reconstructing the *lorica musculata*; whether it is bronze or leather; the origins of the *lorica musculata*

Abbreviations

AB	*Archaeologia Bulgarica* (Bulgaria)
AJA	*American Journal of Archeology* (USA);
AMN	*Acta Musei Napocensis* (Romania)
AV	*Archeolologia Viva* (Italy);
CIL	*Corpus Inscriptionum Latinarum*
DAI	*Deutsches Archäologisches Institut, Roma* (Italy)
GpV	*Gesellschaft pro Vindonissa. Jahresbericht* (Switzerland)
JRMES	*Journal of Roman Military Equipment Studies* (England);
JRGZM	*Jahrbuch des Romisch-Germanischen Zentralmuseums Mainz* (Germany);
IFAO	*Institut Français d'archéologie orientale* (Egypt)
NG	*National Geographic* (USA)
VAMZ	*Vjesnik Arheološkog Muzeja u Zagrebu*

Glossary

Acies: line of battle, battleline formation (double – *duplex*; triple – *triplex*)

Agmen: the marching column or a particular line of battle

Ala: cavalry regiment

Albus: off-white colour

Akinakes, medus acinaces: Persian dagger, straight-shaped, usually worn upon the right thigh on a leather belt

Aquila: eagle standard symbol of each legion, made of silver and later in bronze and gold

Aquilifer: the senior-standard bearer who carried the eagle

Antesignani: in the Marian age, light infantrymen equipped with *parma bruttiana* and acting as skirmishers; in general, and especially in the sources of the Imperial age, soldiers fighting in front of the standards

Armilla: military decoration in the form of an armband

Auxilia: troops recruited from among provincials and allies, not legionaries

Baculum: staff

Balista, ballista: a military machine for throwing projectiles

Ballistarii: soldiers operating the ballista

Balteus: military belt, and also baldric (sword-belt passing over the shoulders); symbol of military service

Beneficiarius: soldiers exempted from menial duties and acting as orderlies of senior officers; they were also charged with particular duties, such as custom officers etc., by governors and generals

Bipennis: double-bladed axe

Bracae: trousers or breeches worn by soldiers, in leather or in cloth; they usually were skin tight and reached below the knees (see *feminalia/femoralia*)

Byrrus: travelling garment, probably a shaggy hooded cloak

Bucina: military crooked horn or trumpet for the signalling the army

Bucinator: junior officer responsible for blowing the *bucina*

Caetrati: soldiers equipped with a round leather shield of Iberian origin

Calcar, calcares: spurs

Calceus: low military boot

Caliga, caligae: military shoe or boot

Caligati: those serving in military boots, i.e. the soldiers

Calo, calones: servant (usually slave) acting as an assistant to the miles

Candidus: pure white colour

Capulus: pommel, hilt of the sword

Cassis: helmet of bronze, iron, silver or other metallic material

Castrum: legionary or auxiliary camp

Cataphractarii: full-armoured cavalrymen of Sarmatian or eastern origin; enlisted as regiments (*numeri*) in the army from the second century AD

Cataphractus, cataphractarius, kataphraktos: armoured cavalryman or infantryman

Catapulta: arrow-shooting machine

Centuria: sub-unit of a *legio* of around eighty to one hundred men; usually there were sixty *centuria* to a legion

Centurio: commander of a *centuria*

Chiton: tunic

Chlamys: military cloak

Cingulum militiae: the military belt (see balteus)

Cippus: a tombstone sometimes with the image of the dead engraved on it; sometimes used as boundary mark

Classiarii: milites fighting on sea, marines

Classicum: a fanfare played on the *cornu* for military drills

Clavus, clavi: vertical decorative stripes on clothing

Clipeus: round shield

Cohors: military unit of infantry usually consisting of 250/500 men; there were about ten cohorts in a legion, each *cohors* comprising six *centuriae* and three maniples; according to Vegetius the cohors was divided into ten (miliaria) or five (*quingenaria*) *centuriae*

Cohors equitata: unity of mixed cavalry and infantry of 500–1,000 men

Contus: long spear for cavalry

Contarii: cavalrymen armed with the long spear called *contus*

Cornicen: the junior officer charged with playing the *cornu*

Cornicularius: soldier who received for his bravery the right to wear two small *cornicula* (horns) on his helmet; later camp adjutant;

Cornu: large curved horn, a military musical instrument made of brass

Corona: military decoration

Cothurni: calf-length boots with open lacing, usually reserved for the officers

Crista: the crest or plume of the helmet

Crista transversa: the crest or plume *insignia* on the centurion's helmet, silver or ornamented with silver

Cucullus: hooded cloak or cap attached to the cloak

Custos armorum: senior officer in charge of the armoury, armourer

Decurio: cavalry officer

Decursio: military march, and military marching procession around the body of the dead commander; also military manoeuvre performed by the cavalrymen (*decursio equestris*) following a *vexillifer* or a warrior holding a *hasta*

Dictator: emergency magistrate of Rome, placing power (*imperium*) in the hands of one man

Diploma: small booklet composed of two bronze plates and inscribed with the abstracts of an edict through which the emperor gave privileges to the soldiers who had obtained their discharge in honourable conditions (*honesta missio*); for the *auxilia* it contained a certificate of Roman citizenship given to the dismissed soldier

Dolabra: pick-axe with one cutting edge and projecting point

Draco: standard with a bronze head in the form of a dragon, with the body made of cloth

Duplicarius: troop commander, who received double pay as reward, sometimes a junior officer such as an *optio*, *signifer* etc.

Eques, equites: horsemen, cavalry

Equites singulares: governor's or general's mounted bodyguards

Equites singulares Augusti: emperor's mounted bodyguards

Explorator: scout of the army

Evocatus (Revocatus): soldier (*dilectus*) called to military service by means of a personal invitation of a military commander, usually linked by a fiduciary connection; normally a veteran recalled to service, usually with the same rank as the centurio

Exercitus: the army

Fabrica: a workshop or factory

Falx: long Thracian sword with curved blade, called *rhomphaia* in Greek, and especially used by the Geto-Dacian warriors and by the Dacian auxiliaries in Roman army

Fasciae: cloth leg-bindings, puttees

Fibula: pin used to fasten cloaks and military garments

Femoralia, feminalia: short trousers or short leg coverings

Forum: public place of the *colonia*

Framea: a spear or javelin of Germanic origin

Frumentarius, frumentarii: soldiers responsible for the grain supply for the troops, especially those who composed and escorted the convoys. Or special body of soldiers, called *milites frumentarii*, stationed in Rome and acting as special policemen, or charged by the emperor with police duty

Furca: T-shaped carrying pole on which the Roman *miles* carried his equipment

Galea: helmet, originally of leather, then also metallic, but lighter than the *cassis*

Gaesum: large javelin of Celtic origin

Gladius: sword

Gladius hispaniensis: the main legionary double-edged sword

Glans: ball of lead or clay of acorn-shape used in a sling

Graffito: picture scratched on stone

Genius: guardian spirit of the *legio*

Hasta: spear

Hasta pura: silver blunt spears awarded to officers for distinguished service

Hastati: the front-rank men of the *legio*

Hippika Gymnasia: cavalry display and games

Imaginifer: junior officer standard-bearer of the imperial *imago*

Imago: standard with the bust or the portrait of the emperor

Immunes: soldiers exempt from menial duties

Impedimenta: heavy baggage containing the legionary's equipment and carried by the *furca* or the in baggage train, by mules

Insignia: rank badges, often distinctive signs attached to armour or uniform, or crest on the helmet

Legatus legionis: *legio*'s commander, of senatorial rank

Legio: main unit of the Roman army, usually comprised of sixty *centuriae* divided in ten cohorts

Legionarius: man of the *legio*

Lictor, lictores: imperial or consular escort carrying the *fascii* with the *secures*, symbol of the Roman command (*imperium*)

Linea: linen short jacket or undertunic, or light tunic

Lorica: body armour

Machaira: Greek equivalent of *gladius*, double-edged sword; sometimes it also means the single-edged sword known as *falcata*

Manipulus: division of the *legio*, usually the third of a cohors and composed of two centuries, *prior* and *posterior*

Miles: soldier

Miles gregarius: simple legionary

Miles legionis: legionary

Nautae: sailors, sometimes fighters on the sea

Numerus, numeri: units of cavalry and infantry recruited by border peoples (*nationes*) who fought under the command of tribal leaders

Ocreae: greaves, armour for the protection of the legs

Officium: staff of a governor

Oppidum: Celtic fortress, usually on a hill top

Optio: junior officer, under the centurion, his understudy, one for each *centuria*

Ordo: early division of the *legio*, hierarchy in the legion, battle-order of the marching legion, row of oarsmen

Ordo equestris: originally those wealthy enough to equip themselves as cavalrymen; Late Consular and early Imperial middle class, having in the army a rank superior to those of the ordinary soldiers, hence they could be promoted to the rank of *centuriones* or *tribuni* without prior war experience

Ordo senatorius: members of the Senate, the ruling class and council of Rome

Origo: place of origin

Ostensionales: milites dressed for parade or in parade uniforms

Paenula: travelling cloak of soldiers and civilians, of Etruscan or Celtic origin, often hooded, fastened in front by laces or small buckles and *fibulae*

Pallium: cloak of Greek origin, probably similar to the *paludamentum*, worn preferentially by senior officers and other elites

Paludamentum: the purple military cloak of generals and emperors

Parma equestris: round cavalry shield, used especially during the Consular age

Patera: mess tin or skillet cast in bronze

Pelta: small light shield shaped as half-moon, of Thracian or Anatolian origin

Peregrini: the auxiliary troops, not citizens

Perizoma: cloth wrapped around the groin; sometimes the belt of underpants

Pero, perones: closed boot of buckskin, or sometimes over-boots, worn by the soldiers in cold climates

Phalera: medallion or disc of silver, gold or glass, usually embossed, used in horse harness or as a military decoration, attached to the armour by means of a leather strap worn on the chest

Pila muralia: short-range weapons thrown downwards from the ramparts

Pileus pannonicus: pillbox shaped military cap

Pilos: felt cap of cylindrical or conical shape

Pilum: the javelin of the *milites*

Pilus: equipped with spear or javelin, with special reference to the centurion

Posterior: 'rear', especially referring to a *centurio*

Postsignani: those who fought behind the standards

Praefectus: commander of an auxiliary or allied army; commander of legions in Egypt of equestrian order, from the Augustan period

Praefectus castrorum: camp prefect and third-in-command of a *legio*

Praesidia: guard points, often fortified

Praetoriani: imperial bodyguard

Primi ordines: centurions of the first cohort, or simply front rankers

Primus pilus: leading centurion of the first *cohors* and most senior in the *legio*; or, simply, first spear (*pilum*)

Princeps: centurian title – the second and the fifth centurion of each *cohors* (*centurio princeps prior* and *centurio princeps posterior*); officer responsible for headquarters staff of a legion and for training (*princeps praetorii*, usually the *centurio princeps prior*); or simply 'the foremost' soldier

Principales: under and junior officers

Principia: headquarters

Pteryges: protective strips for waist and shoulders hanging from the borders of the armour or from the padded garment under it, often made of silk, linen, leather

Pugio: short dagger

Quaestor: quartermaster; also senior officer sometimes with the command of a *legio* in late Consular age

Sacellum: shrine of the standards

Sagittarius: archer

Sagulum: miles' simple cloak

Sagum, saga: rectangular military cloak

Sarabara: wide trousers of eastern origin

Scutati: Iberian troops equipped with a big *scutum* and recruited in Hiberia Citerior; then the word grew to include troops protected by big shields

Scutum: shield, usually the polygonal curved shield of the *milites legionis*

Signifer: standard-bearer, one for each *centuria*

Signum: military standard

Spatha: long sword, usually assigned to cavalry or auxiliary troops

Speculator: originally a scout or spy, a messenger and then a bodyguard with the function of executioner

Squama: scale or lamellar armour

Stele, στηλη: a carved pillar used as a tombstone

Subligaculum: underpants or short pants, wrapped around the groin and worn as underwear

Taberna: tavern

Tabula: square embroidered panels stitched onto clothes

Tabula ansata: decoration with the name of the *legio* inscribed, worn over the leather *tegimen* of the shield, painted on the shield or incised onto the neck guard of a helmet with a carrying handle

Tessera: small wooden plaque with the password written on it

Tesserarius: officer of the watch, sometimes commander of the guard of the *castra*, one per *centuria*

Testudo: tortoise formation, with the shields put together to form a wall and roof

Thoracomachus: padded garment, made of leather and other organic material, used as protective armour or as underarmour corselet, see *subarmale*

Thorax stadios: plate armour of bronze or iron, shaped as a muscular torso.

Tibialia: leggings

Torques: neckband given as military decoration

Triarii: maniples of the *legio*, usually formed by sixty veteran spearmen

Tribunus: senior officer of the *legio*, under the *legatus*, six to each *legio*

Tribunus angusticlavius: tribunus of equestrian rank, junior tribune

Tribunus laticlavius: tribune of senatorial rank, senior tribune

Trophaeum: trophy, memorial of a victory, and also a standard formed by a pole from which were hung the spoils of the defeated enemies or reproductions of armour

Tuba: bronze trumpet, usually straight

Tubicen: the junior officer charged to play the tuba

Tunica militaris: the military tunic

Turma: cavalry unity of thirty horsemen

Umbo: central boss of the shield, of bronze or iron

Vagina: scabbard sheath

Valetudinarium: military hospital

Velites: lightly armed *milites*

Venatores: hunters or special fighters of wild beasts

Verutum: type of javelin

Vestis militaris: military clothing, or taxation to pay for it

Veteranus: soldier who has completed his service, or has been re-enlisted

Vexillatio: detachment from one or more *legiones* or *cohortes* composed of *milites legionis* and *auxilia*

Vexillarius: the junior officer who carried the *vexillum*

Vexillum: square cloth flag, used as a standard by the cavalry and infantry

Vexillum veteranorum: units of veterans attached to a legion, about 500 men

Via: road

Vicus: settlement of civilians living near the military camp

Vitis: twisted vine wood staff, symbol of the centurio's rank

Zona militaris: sash knotted at the breast, the mark of a senior officer or emperor

ACKNOWLEDGEMENTS

A great number of people, museums, institutions and libraries have participated in the realisation of this book. It is therefore very difficult to remember all of them and we apologise for any unintentional omissions. Material has come from just about all the 'provinces of the Roman Empire'; I will therefore proceed to give acknowledgements by region.

Italy (Rome and Italia)

Very special thanks must be given to Professor Annamaria Liberati, Director of the Museo della Civiltà Romana, in Rome, first of all for her assistance and allowing me to spend the necessary days in the museum in order to analyse the copies of Roman monuments and artworks preserved there; secondly for the kind permission to publish the author's photos and related documentation.

For the same reason it is my duty and pleasure to thank the Soprintendente Professor Umberto Broccoli who has kindly given his permission for the publication of such important items.

The archaeological material from Sora has been obtained thanks to Professor Alessandra Tanzilli, Director of the Archaeological Museum of Sora, who kindly accompanied me to the sites, and with the help of Bruno La Pietra, Assessore alla cultura.

Of great assistance and help has been Dr Giuseppe Chiarucci, Director of the Musei Civici in Albano, who has kindly furnished me with precious and important material and documentation.

A very special thank you must also be given to the late Dr Gabriele Cateni, Director of the Guarnacci Museum of Volterra, for his kind help and assistance in allowing me to collect the photographic material and permission to publish.

Deep thanks also go to Dr Francesco Petrianni and Dr Giuseppe Anelli of the Archaeological Museum of Sezze Romano, for the very kind permission to publish the material and for assistance in the field.

The Turin finds have been published with the kind permission of the Ministero per i beni e le attività culturali – Soprintendenza per i beni archeologici del Piemonte e del Museo Antichità Egizie. Special thanks are extended to the Soprintendente Dr Marina Sapelli Ragni.

For the publication of the Catavignus stele I should express my thanks to the Director of the Civico Museo in Cuneo, Dr Sandra Viada.

The important stele of the Ravenna *classiarius* has been published thanks to Dr Maria Grazia Maioli, of the Soprintendenza Archeologica dell'Emilia Romagna, sede di Ravenna. Incomparable assistance in the field was also provided by Dr.ssa Fede Berti, of the Archeological museum of Ferrara, and by Professor Andrea Augenti and Dr Enrico Cirelli of the Dipartimento di Archeologia of Ravenna.

Furthermore, for permission to use the author's photos, I would like to thank Professor Pietro Giovanni Guzzo and Dr.ssa Grete Stefani of the Soprintendenza per i Beni Archeologici delle Province di Napoli e Caserta, Museo Archeologico Nazionale di Napoli and Museo Archeologico dell'Antica Capua; Dr Rosanna Friggeri of the Ministero per i Beni e le Attività Culturali Soprintendenza Speciale per i Beni Archeologici di Roma, Museo Nazionale Romano, Rome; Soverintendente Professor Umberto Broccoli and Dr Claudio Parisi Presicce of the Sovraintendenza per i Beni Culturali del Comune di Roma, Musei Capitolini, Rome; and Soprintendente Dr Giuseppe Andreassi of the Soprintendenza per i Beni Archeologici dell'Abruzzo.

Spain (Baetica)

A special thank you is due to the Junta de Andalucia, to the Director of the Museo Arqueologico y etnologico de Cordoba

Dr Manuel Osuna Ruíz for the material kindly given for the publication.

Furthermore, for permission to use the author's pictures, I am grateful to the Director of the Archaeological Museum of Granada, Dr Isidro Toro, to the Museo Arqueologico Provincial de Sevilla and to Dr Juan Paz Peralta, conservator of the Museo Arqueologico de Zaragoza.

France (Gallia Narbonensis)

For permission for the author's pictures, I would like to thank Dr Michel Marti of the Musée de l'Arles et de la Provence Antiques and Dr Odile Cavalier, Conservateur en chef du patrimoine at the Musée Calvet d'Avignon.

Switzerland (Germania Superior)

To the Vindonissa Museum and particularly to Dr Renée Hengii, Director of the Museum, must be given all my thanks for their precious help in supplying the location of the photographic documentation of the leather finds in Vindonissa and for the permission to reproduce the photos taken *in loco*.

Germany (Germania Superior-Inferior)

I would like to thank the Stadt Offenburg Museum in Ritterhaus, LandesMuseum of Bonn for material and permissions.

The Netherlands (Belgica)

I would like to thank Dr Louis Swinkels, Curator of the archaeological collections, Museum Het Valkhof, Nijmegen, and the Rijksmuseum van Oudheden, Leiden, for permission to publish the author's photos.

Austria (Pannonia Superior)

For information and kind permission to reproduce the photos of the armour from Stiellfried, I am deeply indebted to Professor Clemens Eibner of the University of Heidelberg as well as Dr Ernst Lauermann, Dr Franz Humer and Dr Mag Humer of the Archäologischer Park Carnuntum.

Poland (Barbaricum)

It is not only the Roman provinces that have contributed to the material for the book but also the territories beyond the borders of the Roman Empire:

Inestimable help has come from Professor Piotr Dyczek of Warsaw University, who has given me precious information and unknown material from the military camp of Novae, allowing me also to reproduce the related pictures and assisting me with his kind revision of the related text in the book.

United Kingdom (Britannia)

The tombstone of the Lancaster cavalryman has been reproduced by the kind permission of the Lancashire Museums/ Museum of Lancaster, Dr Stephen Bull. The banded armour from Qasr Ibrahim has been reproduced by the kind permission of Dr Alan Jeffrey Spencer of the British Museum, London.

I am also grateful to Theresa Calver, Administration Assistant, Colchester Museums, Museum Resource Centre, Colchester, for permission for the author's pictures relating to the tombstone of Favonius Facilis.

Croatia (Dalmatia)

First I would like to express my great thanks to Professor Ivan Radman-Livaja, of the Archaeological Museum of Zagreb for supplying material and for kind permission to reproduce the necessary illustrations from his valuable book *Militaria Sisciensia*. Further, I have to thank him for his helpful assistance in the collection of photographic material in the Archaeological Museum in Zagreb. My acknowledgements are also owed to the talented Dr Miljenka Galić for the excellent drawings of the Zagreb finds.

It is also my duty to express my deepest thanks to Dr Ante Rendic-Miocevic, Director of the Archaeological Museum in Zagreb, for the kind permission to publish material exhibited in their collections.

I also thank the Director of the Museum of Split, Dr Zrinka Buljevic, and Dr Sanja Ivčević for supplying illustrative material and for assistance in collecting photographic material in the Split Museum.

Serbia (Moesia Superior – Pannonia Inferior)

I wish to thank particularly first of all Dr Aleksandra Sojic, former public relations manager of the National Museum of Belgrade for her precious help and assistance with contacts and travel in the Balkan countries.

For the supplied material it is my duty to give a big acknowledgement to the Director of the National Museum in Belgrade, Dr Tatjana Cvjeticanin; to Dr Jelena Kondic, Director of Statio Cataractarum Diana/Zanes Project and the Iron Gates Museum; to Dr Deana Ratkovic, MA, Senior Curator of the Roman collection of the National Museum Belgrade; to Dr Bora Dimitrijevic of the National Museum in Zajecar; to the pukovnik Colonel Miroslav Knezevic, Director of the War Museum in Belgrade; to Mirko Pekovic, Curator of the Ancient and Medieval artefacts in the War Museum in Belgrade; to Dr Miroslav Vujović, Assistant Professor of Classical Archaeology in Belgrade; to Dr Ivan Bugarski and Gordana Milosevic, of the Institute of Archaeology in Belgrade; to Milorad Djorvjevic, Director of the National Museum of Požarevac; to Professor Velika Dautova Ruševljan, Director of the Museum of Vojvodina, Novi Sad; to Nikola Stovanović, Director of the Museum of Srem, Sremska Mitrovica; and to Miss Jasmina Davidovic, conservator of the Roman collection.

Special thanks must be given to Professor Vujadin Ivanisevic of the Institute of Archaeology in Belgrade, not only for supplying material but also for the kind access to the library of the Institute.

Bosnia-Herzegovina (Dalmatia)

The Director of Zemaljski Museum, Dr Aiša Softić, and Dr Adnan Busuladžić, Curator of Antiquities, have been of great help in supplying me with photographic material and assisting in taking pictures of the finds preserved in the museum.

Macedonia (Moesia Superior)

Due acknowledgement must be given to Professor Kiril Trajkovski of the Archaeological Museum of Skopje for his invaluable assistance and help in the territory of the ancient Moesia Superior and for the kind permission to take the necessary pictures in the Skopje Museum.

Greece (Thracia, Achaia)

I am very much indebted to Professor Taxiarchis Kolias, Director of the Institute for Byzantine Research, National Hellenic Research Foundation, for his assistance in the search for material and for introducing me to the various museums and institutes in the Balkans. Very important also was the help of Professor Andrea Babuin, of the University of Ioannina, for his effort in searching material *in loco*.

For permission for the author's pictures, I would like to thank Dr Michalis Petropoulos, Director of the Archaeological Museum of Patrassos.

Bulgaria (Thracia)

Professor Lyudmil F. Vagaliski of the Archaeological Institute of Sofia has been of great support and help in collecting precious photos of Roman military artefacts and allowing me to reproduce them. I should also thank him for the contacts he kindly furnished me with in the Balkans.

Romania (Moesia Inferior, Dacia)

The attainment of material in the Provincia Dacica was possible only thanks to the inestimable and precious help of Dr Radu Ciobanu, Associate Professor at the Ecole Normal Superieure de Paris (Departement des Sciences de l'Antiquité) from 1997–2001, and scientific researcher in archaeology at the National Museum of Alba Iulia. A special thank you must be given also to Dr Constantin Chera, Director of the Museum of Natural History and Archaeology of Costanta, who not only has allowed me to make a deep analysis of the Ostrov helmets but has accompanied me to all the relevant archaeological sites of Dobrugia. Essential also was the assistance of Dr Gica Baestean, Director of the Archaeological Museum of Sarmizegetusa, who has kindly helped me directly on the site. Special thanks also go to Dr Gabriel Rustoiu, General Director of Alba Iulia National Museum, Dr Alexandru Matei, Director of Excavations on the site of Porolissum, and to Dr Helena Musca, Director of the Historical Museum of Zalau.

Turkey ('Asia')

I would like to give deep thanks to my dear friend Dr Ayca Dost in Istanbul for her valuable help in obtaining permissions from Turkish authorities relating to various archaeological finds and photos.

Professor Metin Gökçay of the Archaeological Museum of Istanbul has also been of inestimable help in obtaining permissions for the photos of important items preserved in the same museum, and from the Ephesus Museum. For the same reason I am deeply indebted to the Director of the Archaeological Museum in Istanbul, Dr Ismail Karamut, and to the Director of the Archaeological Museum of Ephesus, Dr Cengiz Topal.

Egypt (Aegyptus)

In the lands of the pharaohs I am deeply indebted to my dear friend Dr Ashraf Nageh, Consultant of the Coptic Museum – Office of the General Secretary of the Supreme Council of Antiquities, for the patient assistance shown during my travel, in research and in collecting the photographic material.

Further, I would like to thank Dr Philip Halim, Director of the Coptic Museum of Cairo; Dr Wafaa Sadik, Director of the Egyptian Museum; May Trade, 'Soul' of the Egyptian Museum; Dr Laure Pantalacci, Director of IFAO; and Dr Vanessa Desclau and Dr Mervet Doss, Directors of IFAO Library.

Special thanks

I would like further to express my deep gratitude to Professor Hesberg Von Henner, Director of Deutsches Archeologiches Institut in Rome and to Dr Luisa Veneziani of the Photographic Archive of the DAI, for access to the inestimable Library of the Institute and for kind permission to reproduce the photos from the DAI Archive.

Special thanks must be given also to Dr Martin Maischberger of the Antikensammlung SMB Berlin, for permission to reproduce the photo of the helmet of Nemi, formerly from the Lipperheide collection.

Further illustrative material has been used with the kind permission of the following museums, institutes and libraries: Staatliche Antikensammlung und Glyptothek, Anschrift, Munich; the Museum für Kunst und Gewerbe, Hamburg; the Library of the Institute of Archaeology of Belgrade; the Toledo Museum of Art; the Oriental Institute of Chicago (USA); the Tate Gallery of London; Christie's; and Editoriale Domus S.p.A.

Further special thanks must be given to all scholars, friends and people who have given support and guidance during discussion, research and fieldwork.

First of all, I am deeply grateful to Dr Lise Bender Jørgensen, Docent of the Institute of Archaeology and Antique Culture of the Humanistic Faculty of the University of Gothenburg, for the kind permission to reproduce the splendid specimen of a Roman military cap from Mons Claudianus.

The precious under-helmet specimen from Dydimoi has been published thanks entirely to the help of Dr Dominique Cardon, Directeur de Recherche in the CNRS of France. To her I would like to express my deepest gratitude.

For the discussions about the Roman muscled armour and permission to use it in this book I am grateful for the assistance of Dr Travis Lee Clark, Assistant Professor of Art History in the Department of Fine Arts and Communications at the Sul Ross State University, Texas, USA.

Three friends have given me precious assistance and inestimable help in collecting photographic material, in the search for sources, in the preparation of the drawings, in patient assistance in my various travels and in many other numerous activities that cannot be listed: Dr Andrea Salimbeti, Dr Massimo Bizzarri, Dr Vito Silvestro. To them are due respectful and special thanks.

I am deeply grateful to Dr Monia Baldi, to my beloved wife Dr Ilenia Lombardo and to Graham Sumner for the translation and correction of the English text; and I would like to thank my lovely friend Miss Monika Szamocka for her invaluable help in the preparation of the book's index.

I am also grateful to: Professor Giorgio Ravegnani, of the Library of the Historic Institute of Venezia; Dr Elena Borgi of the Biblioteca dell'Accademia delle Scienze of Turin; Gianbaldo Baldi; Dr Stefano Izzo; Agostino Carcione; Claudio Antonucci; and Dr Andrea Corona, for their help in collecting and supplying books and photographic material.

The Studio Tomato Farm of Tommaso D'Alessandro, Elaine Norbury and Dr Andrea Salimbeti have provided beautiful colour and black-and-white drawings for the book.

A special acknowledgement must be given to my dear friend and illustrator Graham Sumner who has so painstakingly carried out my instructions to provide the splendid colour illustrations that have brought to life the real warriors in their magnificent equipment.

We also cannot omit to thank the models and the group of re-enactors who have posed for the pictures that were taken as the basis for the creation of the colour pictures: Roberto Prina, Fabrizio Merlo, Capitano of Carabinieri Giuseppe Marseglia and Davide Grassi, Martino Cervellera and Luca Bonacina of the Associazione culturale cisalpina, re-enactors of the *Cohors III Praetoria*.

Finally, special debts of gratitude are again owed to my beloved wife Dr Ilenia Lombardo, without whose constant support and very valuable help this project would not have been completed.

Raffaele D'Amato

INDEX

Italicised numbers refer to illustrations on a page

A

Aalen 257, 270
Abruzzo *192*, 279
Acarnanian slingers 6
acies 243, 252, 263, 275
Actium 5, 15, 46, 58, 59, *112*, 115
aci 173
Adamclisi 66, 67, 70, *71*, 72, *72*, 76,
    77, *79*, *80*, 81, *81*, 85, *85*, 87, *93*,
    96, 105, *105*, 121, *121*, 122, 125,
    126, 129
Adana 135
adlocutiones 128, 205, 238, 250
aediculae 97, 169
Aedui 4, 6, 43
aegis 248
Aelius Herodianus 63
Aemonian, breed of horse 193
Aeneas 8, 32, 37, 39, 43, 46, 51, 54, 210,
    219, 239
Aeneid 8, 218, 268
Aestii 167
Africa 3, 4, 54, 137, 270
African 3, 29, 36, 164, 167, 264
Agen-Port helmet 8, *23*, 27, *30*, *35*, *46*,
    49, 114, 120, *180*, *253*
agmen 275
Agrippa 5, *15*, 59, 205, 225, 261
Ahenobarbus monument 8, *11*, 15, 22,
    24, 25, *27*, 32, 33, 38, 49, 51, 54,
    95, *129*
akinakes 24, 275
akontia 43, 48
ala 6, 58, 66, 192, 243, 275
    Afrorum 256, 257
    Atectorigiana 252
    Augusta 178, *180*
    Milliaria 67
    Noricum 194
    Piacentiana 213
    Prima Ituraeorum 253
    Prima Thracum 197
    Prima Tungrorum Frontoniana 256
    Petriana *180*, 243
    Picentiana 159, *180*, 251, 252
    Vocontiorum 254

Alans 64, 73, 263
Alazonii 252
Alba Fucens 192, 250
Alba Julia *25*, 85, 87, *130*, *145*, *159*, *160*,
    185, *192*, 192
Albania 114
Albanians 39
Albano 269, 279
albus 53, 218, 275
Aldborough 246
alder *13*, 92, 157
Alesia 4, 7, 12, 13, 24, 29, 32, 35, 44,
    49, 53, 183, 236, 239, 268, 272
Alexander the Great 5, 52, 194, 200, 208
Alexandria 4, 265
Alybe 252
AlLériot 245
Alma Tadema *137*, 251, 268
Almuñécar armour *42*
Amazons 197, 270
amenta 44, *71*, 74, 239
Amiternum 107, 151, 247
Ammianus Marcellinus 63, 142, 263
Anabasis 251, 268
Anchialus 164
Andalucia *29*, 279
animal skins 43, 176, 254
Annaius Daverzus 152, 153, 213
antesignani 5, 65, 275
antitupos, 43
Antioch 114, 270
Antiochus 43
Antonine Column 200, 210, 212
Antoninus Pius 64, 66, 97, 122
Antonius, C. 245
Antonius, M. 4, 5, *15*, 24, 46, 48, 52,
    58, 66, 140, 239
anvils 247
Apamea 220
apex 33, 34, 35, 37, 77, 121, 162, 187,
    188
Appianus 3, 59, 63
Apollo 139, *164*
Apollodorus 66, 67
aprons 54, 68, 70, *89*, *98*, 142, 153, 171,
    213, 228, 246, 268
Apuleius 63, 82, 175, 263

Apulum 85, 87, 101, *130*, 146, 192
aquilae 46, 169, 240, 271, 275
Aquileia 43, 64, *8*, *30*, 32, 36, 39, 41,
    205, 269, 272
Aquilifer 5, 64, 71, 169, 171, *172*, 173,
    201, 248, 275
Aquilius 32, 238
Aquilius Bradua 260
Aquincum 128, 136, 176, 245, 247–8,
    255, 268, 272
Aquitania 249
Arabia Petraea 64
Arausius Arch *see* Arch of Orange
Arbulai 43
Arch of Augustus at Susa *40–1*, 250
Arch of Claudius 248
Arch of Constantine 66, *106*, 128, 140,
    200, *203*, 210
Arch of Orange 14, *15–21*, 24, 29, 38,
    84, 92, 114, *127*, 128–9, 140, 151,
    180, 184–5, 198, *230–4*
archers 4, 6, 34, 43–4, 58, 66, *121*,
    160–4, 169, 221, 243
arci 160, 164
Arelatum *102*
argentum 246
Argonautica 108, 252, 267
Arlon 191
armamentaria 107
Armenian 4, 66
armillae 178, *180*, 275
Arminius 63
armour 38–43, 49–52, 57–8, 122–52,
    159–60, 168–74, 191–3, 198–200,
    209–11; *see also* graves, helmets,
    loricae
    arm protections 52, 149–50, 198–200
    backplates 118, 130–1, *131*, 133
    body armour 38–43, 122–52, 164,
        180, 210, 249, 276
    breastplates *13*, 39, 41, 49, 52, *90*,
        122–3, 128–32, 133, 139, 141,
        143, 159, 182, 187, 197, 210,
        224, 239, 248, 252, 258
    coifs 37
    fasteners 38, 122, 128, *128*, 133, 135,
        159

felt *18*, 38–9, 41, *106*, 123, 135,
    139–41
gauntlets *127*, 149, *149*
gorgets 39, 198, *199*
horse armour 52, 200
lamellar 124, *168*, 169, 198, 277
laminated 52, 67, 81, *118*, 125, 128,
    129, 130–4, 136, 145, 146, *146*,
    149, 150, 160, 191, 198, 209, 210,
    220
leather 8, 9, *30*, *31*, 39, 58, 67, 68,
    81, *82–4*, *88–91*, *93*, *94*, 99, *102*,
    103, *115*, 122, 123, 128, 135–49,
    161–3, *166*, *168*, 169, 171, 173,
    177, *180*, *181*, 191–2, 197, 198,
    205, 210, 220, 224, 225, 238, 246,
    248, 250, 251, 254, 256, 261, 268,
    271, 273, 277
limb 41, 51, 140, 149–51, 200
linen *27*, *30*, *31*, 38, 39, 49, *82*, 123,
    124, 135, 139–49, 197, 225, 251
mail 8, 9, *15–17*, *18–19*, 22, *25*, 38,
    38, 43, 44, 51, 67, 68, 76, 77, *81*,
    106, *110*, 123, 124, 125, 128–9,
    130, 139, 145, 146, 147, 148, 149,
    159, 164, *165*, 171, 173, 176, *180*,
    185, 191, 192, 198, *203*, 210, 212,
    220, 238, 239, 241, 249, 251, 254,
    256, 258
muscled cuirasses 8, 9, *10*, 37, 38,
    39, *42*, 44, 45, 49, 58, 81, *102*,
    122–4, 145–7, *145*, *146*, 146,
    168, 192, 208, 210, *223*, 224,
    225, *225*, *226*, *227*, 238, 239,
    244, 246, 250, 281
'parade' xiv, 159
plate 8, 39, 122, 145, 176, 210, 251,
    277
scale 38, 41, 43, 58, 70, 76, 88, 96,
    102, 121, 123–6, *127*, 128, 129,
    133, 137, 140, 141, *141*, *142*, 145,
    146, 152, 160, 169, 162, *164*, *165*,
    169, 171, 173, *191*, 192, *192*, 198,
    200, 210, 212, 239, 248, 251, 254,
    256, 277
segmentatae xiv 11, *41*, 67, 76, 78, *80*,
    89, 94, 99, *105*, *106*, *114*, 130,

131, 134, *143*, *144*, 145, 160, *179*, 191, 192, 203, 209, 210, *211*, *216*, 220, 250, 259, 268, 272
shoulder doublings 128
washers 131, *132*, 209
Arrian 63, 71, 72, 73, 74, 143, 151, *159*, 194, 198, 243, 251, 256, 257, 263
arrows 43, *53*, 74, 129, 130, 143, *152*, 160, 162, 164, *166*, 198, 246, 251
flights 162
heads 44, 162, 253
incendiary 162
plumes 162
Asia 3, 4, 36, 44, 66, 139, 144, 148, 281
Asconius 3, 263
Athena 139, *164*
Atheneus 3, 263
Athens 141, 225, 228
Aucissa *30*
Audennacum 249
Augusta Raurica *73*, 98, 176, 204, 246, 269
Augusta Seguvina *41*, 250, 252
Augustus 5, 7, *13*, 32, 36, *41*, 43, 46, 49, *145*, 184, 205, 214, 218, 221, 238, 239, 240, 242, 250, 255, 263, 267, 270
Augustus Prima Porta statue *13*, 46, 135, 218, 240, 250
Auerberg 245
Aulnay de Santonge 249, 272
Aulus Gellius 63, 152, 264
aurei 260
auriscalpii 173
Austria 280, 212
auxilia 5, 6, 21, 43–5, 46, 48, 64, 66, 67, 87, *104*, *105*, 107, *121*, 121, *139* 141, 149, 152–69, 175, 218, 221, 229, 243, 249, 255, 269, 275, 276, 277
auxiliaries 11, 35, 49, 53, 79, 107, 138, 152, 153, 156, 157, 158, 159, 162, 167, 169, 198, 213, 219, 224, 243, 252
Avenches 129, 254
Avignon 22, 43, 151, *180*, 280
axes vi, *37*, 45, 46, 58, 164, 175, 182, 200, 205, 224, 228, 275, 276

B

bacula 24, 275
bags *148*
baldrics 22, *23*, 24, 39, 44, 45, 58, 92, 98, 100, 101, 156, *179*, *180*, 246, 247, 275
fasteners 100
fastening 22, 100, *143*, 143
fittings 20, 98, 100, *100*, 101, 153, 171, 205, 210
leather 20, 98, 101, 205
terminals 100
Balearic slingers 6, 43, 44, 164
Balkans 64, 179, 242, 281
ballistae 152, 275
ballistarii 65, 275
baltea 22, 24, *30*, 68, *92*, 98, *98*, 100, *112*, 171, 205, 210, 212, *213*, 217, *226*, *227*, 236 246, 252, 275
baltiones 98, 280
Banasa 249
Barbaricum 280
Bar Hill 72, 97, *147*, 149, 221, 224, 272
Bar Kochbà 64, *90*, *118*, 129, 212, 242
barracks 72, 175, 258
Basel 109, 269, 270
Βασιλεια 275
Basilica
Aemilia 32
Saint Agnese *154*
Saint Paolo Fuori le mura *177*
Bassus, T.F. 146, *180*, 185, 194, 197, 252, 256

Batavians 64, 242
battles xiv, 4, 5, 13, 14, 22, 37, 39, 46, 48, 49, 51, 53, 57, 58, 73, 74, 87, *88*, 107, 108, 122, 129, 135, 142, 152, 158, 160, 178, 184, 194, 197, 198, 208, 212, 214, 228, 229, 245, 246, 240, 252, 253, 256, 263, 269, 275
Acquae Sextiae 3
Bedriacum 63, *90*
Campi Raudii 3
Carrhae 4, *8*, 41, 46
Cremona 63
Gaugamela 241
Jerusalem 222
Pharsalus 4, 6, 43, 235, 238
Philippi 8, 49, 112, 251
Teutoburgus 67
Thapsus 4, *8*
Tigranocerta 441
Zama 167
battlefields xiv, *30*, 36, 48, 90, 96, 121, 158, 159, 171, 194, 200, 222, 229, 257
Alesia 7, 35, 44
Kalkriese 128, 130, 171
Mancetter 63
Munda 4
Belgica 280
Belgrade 85, *86*, 112, *123*, *187*, *195*, *199*, 243, 244, 245, 269, 270, 271, 280, 281
Bellum
Africanum 36, 264
Catilinae 267
Civile 264
Gallicum 264
Judaicum 192, 265, 270
Jugurthinum 267
belts 8, 12, *15*, 20–2, 24, *30*, 38, 44, 54, 58, 70, 80, *82*, 97, *98*, 98, 100–1, *102*, 104, 129, 136, 140, 142, 143, *147*, 152, 153, 160, 164, 166, 175, 179, *179*, 198, *203*, 204, 210, 212, *213*, 218, 220, 221, 224, 225, 228, 236, 246, 252, 253, 275, 276
buckles 22, 24, 100, 101, 143, *143*, 246
Celtic 22, 101
fittings 20, 98, 100, *100*, 101, 153, 171, 205, 210
niello inlaid 100
plates 22, 98, 153, 171, 210, 246
beneficiarii 5, 48, 64, 118, 179, *179*, 270, 275
beneficiarii hastae 48, 118, 179, *179*, 270
Bergama 136
Berlin 149, *209*, 245, 250, 265, 270, 281
Berry-Bouy 14, 81
Berzovia 120
Bingen 152
bipennes 45, 275
bireme of Praeneste 52, 58, *115*
bits *82*, 193, 194, 203
snaffles 52, 193
Bithynia 4, 43, 109, 222
byrri 214, 228, 275
castalini 228
Black Sea Region 101
Blanchs Hotel 156
blankets 214
Blümlein 105
Bocchus 32, *33*
bogs *88*, 137, 166
bolts 74, 107, 108, 123, 135, 150, *152*, 157, 169, 206, *208*
bone 15, 24, 38, *86*, 92, 97, 98, 114, 141, 142, 153, *156*, 160, 183, 222, 244, 245
Bonn 70, 90, *111*, 139, 158, 171, *172*, 253, 254, 259, 280
Bonn-Bad Godesberg 159
Bonner Berg 108

Bononia 250
Book of Revelation of Saint John 197
boots 13, 46, 56, 166, *168*, *180*, *191*, *221*, 221, 222, *222*, *223*, 228, 239, 253, 254, 275, 276
Bornholm 156
Bosnia-Herzegovina 88, 183, 280
Boudicca 63, 242
Bourges 14
bows 43–4, 160, *160–2*, 162, *163*, 164, *164*, 198
cases 44
Boyer 14
bracae 54, *90*, 166, *180*, *203*, 221, 228, 259, 275
brachialia 138
Bratislava 270
breeches 68, 166, 221, 275
Bremenium 140
Brescia 140
bridles *184*, 193, 240
Brigetio 120, 248
Britain 4, *39*, 63, 97, *107*, 166, *180*, *212*, *221*, 271, 272
Britannia 63, 64, 67, *67*, *167*, 248, 249, 271, 280
British Museum 84, *144*, 144, 150, 210, 247, 250, 251, 253, 270, 272, 280
Britons 4, 252
brooches 180, 272
Brixia 140
Bruttium 29, 144
Brutus, M.I. 4, *8*, 238, 239
bucculae 35, 37, *156*, *203*, 206, 220
bucinae 176, 275
bucinatores 275
bucklers *168*, 236
Budapest 268, 272
Buggenum 8, 15, 34, 57, 58, *81*, 109, *111*, *225*, 237, 247
Bulgaria 94, 210, 242, 253, 254, 270, 273, 281
bulls 29, 46, 68, *178*, 268, 280
burials 258
Byzantine ix, 136, 156, 217, 270, 271
Byzantium 147, 171, 239, 250, 268

C

Cáceres el Viejo 7, 24
Caecilius Metellus 240
Caelius *127*, 135, 176, 177, 250
Caerleon 123, 133, 243
Caesar xii, 3–8, *8*, *10*, 14, 20, *23*, 24, 29, *30*, 32, 34–5, 36, 37–9, 41, 43–4, 46, 48, 49, 52–4, 56, 58, 63, 107, *124*, 130, 235, 239–42, 264, 266–7, 270, 272
Caesarea 264
caetrati 45, 275
calcares 52, 275
calcei 56, *90*, 275
Calidius Severus 140, 151
caligae 8, 56, *5*, *70–71*, 222, 225, *226–227*, *178*, *203*, 228, 275
clavi caligarii 56
caligati 241, 275
calones 65, *65*, 275
Calpurnius Piso 39, 241
Camelon 183
Caminreal 7, 12, 37, 45, 272
Campania 109, *186*
campestres 54; see also *subligaculi*
Campi Decumani 64
Campidoglio 32, *33*, 36, 39, 92, 96, 100
Campus Martius 54
Camulodunum 63; see also Colchester
Cancelleria relief 71, 118, 179, 200, 204–5, 218, 222, 260
candelabra 223
candidus 214, 217, 275
Capito, M. 225, *226*
Capito Romanius 256

Capito, T.F. *226*
Capricorn *15*, 108, 243
capuli 12, 15, 275
Caracalla 235
Caratacus 63
carbatinae 56
cardiophylaces 54
Carlisle 128, 149, 212
carminium 25, 51
Carnuntum 72, 76, 107, 123, 128, 131, 149–50, 197, 212, 248–9, 269–70, 280
carnyx 247
Carrawburgh 269
Carthage 3
Cassaco 98, 221
cassisedes xiv, 32, 109, 206, 238, 240, 275–6
Cassius Dio, 3, 59, 63, 75, 200, 237, 239–42, 258–9, 264
castra 65, 237, 257, 269, 275
Caecilia 24, 49
Castricius Victor 105, 206, 247
cataphractarii 198–200, 257, 271, 275
catapulta 272, 275
Catalka 269; see also Chatalka
Catavignus *167*, *167*, 279
catellae 100
Cato 241, 268
cavalry 4, 65–6, 73, 88, *111*, *127*, *128*, 137, 138, *138*, 142, 171, 214, 221, 242, 243, 249, 252, 255–6, 268–9, 275–7
equipment 48–53, 152–69, *180–200*
lancers 198
regiments *see ala*
Cave of Letters 273
Cecilia Metella 49, *51*, 240
Celtiberian 34, 45, 49, 236
Celtic peoples 3, 4, 35, 43–5, 49, 53, 63, 138, 140, 153, *154–5*, 156, *167*, *180*, 197, *203*, 218, 220–1, 240, 256, 268
Celsus 166
Celsus, Q.S. *95*
centones 41, 140
centuriae 5, 64–6, 107, *111*, 158, *167*, 242, 247–8, 275–7
centuriones (centurions) 5, 14, *15*, *22*, 24, *30*, *33*, 37, *39*, 48, 53–4, 64, *65*, 65, 81, *82*, 89, 90, 93, 98, 105, 109, *112*, 114, *116*, 121, 123–4, 128, 135–6, *136*, 137, *139*, 140, 143, 150–1, 158, 173, 176, 177, 179, *213*, 214, 217, 222, 228, 236, 242–3, 247, 250, 255, 259–60, 275–7
Chalon *14*, 269
chamfrons 52, *196*, 197–8
Charax, A.C. 243
Chassenard 256
Chatalka 198, *199*, 200
Chatsworth House relief 213
Chester 191, *191*, 200, 254, 271
Chichester 92, 249
chitones 46, 162, 197, 212–13, 217, 260, 275
Chiusi Frieze *88*, 138, 142, 200
chlamydes 214, 217, 260
Cicero 3, *8*, 46, 56, 241, 263–4, 266
Cimbrians 54
cinctus 241
cingula 20, 22, 38, 68, *92*, 96, 98, 100–1, 129, 136, 143, 163, 171, 193, 204–5, 212, 217, 224, 246
cippi, 36, 225, *226*, 275
Cirencester *180*, 197
civilians 166, 204, *217*, 218, 220, 241, 276–7
Civilis 63
Classe 224, *226*
classiarii 15, 57–9, 224–8, 246, 261, 275

classicum 176, 240, 275
classis
   Alexandrina 228
   Misenatis 65, 224
   Ravennatis 226
clavi 90, 118, 213, 214, 217–18, 260, 275
Claudius 63, 97, 123, 152, 248
Claudius Terentianus 228
clay 253, 276
clipei, 49, 90, 107, 275
cloaks 8, *30*, 44, 48, 54, 59, *145*, 164, 167, *167*, *168*, 176, *180*, *204*, 212–20, 225, *226–7*, 228, 241, 248, 259, 275–6
clothing 9, 11, 13, 53–7, 107, 175, 212–25, 228–229, 258, 260, 272, 275, 277
Cluj 269, 272
coactile 18, 76, 140
cohortes 5, 46, 64–5, 108, 158, 220, 240, 242, 249, 252, 275–7
   V Asturum 254
   Bracara Augustanorum 256
   III Britannorum 167
   VI Commagenorum 164
   III Delmatorum 256
   IV Dalmatorum 152
   VI Delmatarum 255
   Equitata 53, 275
   V Gallorum 255
   I Hamiorum Sagittariorum 164, 253
   I Ituraeorum 253
   VIII Lusitanorum 95
   Milliaria 253
   XX Palmyrenorum 243
   I Pan(n)oniorum 152, 259
   Praetorian *118*, 205, 261
   Raeti 255
   II Raetorum 159
   VII Raetorum 254
   II Sagittariorum 253, 259
   I Thracum 213
   Torquata 53
   Volontariorum 89
   VIII Voluntariorum 214
coins 8, 29, 32, 36–7, *37*, 39, 41, 44, 46, 48–9, 59, 100, 130, 185, 205, 221, 240, 255, 258, 269–70
Colchester 63, *82*, 92, 136, 248, 271, 280
collegium of *liticines* and *cornicines* 176
Comacchio 20, 225, 228, 268
Commentarii 38, 264
Commodus 64, 87, 160, 200, 221, 248, 259, 260, 267
Concordia 250
congeries armorum 96
Constanta *100*, 100, *188*
Constantine 66, *106*, 128, 140, 200, *203*, 210
Constantinople 11, 235
contarii 198, 257, 275
conti 182, 200, 210, 275
conum 34
copper 32, 156, 173, 206
copper alloy 8, *14*, 85, *8*, 88, 90, 92, 97, *97*, 98, 100, 105, *112*, 120, 124, 130, 131, *132*, 133, 158, 162, 171, *175*, *196*, *203*, 205–6, 210, 245–6, *179*
Corbridge xiv, 131, *131*, *132*, 133, 169, *179*, 209, 210, 249, 253, 258
   hoard 11
Cordoba *18*, *43*, *45*, 98, 279
Corinth 260
coria 30, 39, *84*, 135, 138, 140
Cornelius Sulla 3, 4, *8*, *33*, 34, *35*, 36, 39, 49, 51, 57, 236, 240, 264, 266
cornicenes 6, 64, 176, *176*, 226, 275
cornicularii 10, 51, 275
cornicula 8, 48
cornua 46, 48, 176, 240, 275

corona 177, 275
   aurea 48, 108, 178–9
   civica 48, *95*, 108, 177, *188*
   classica 48
   muralis 48, 177
   navalis 59
   obsidionalis 48
   rostrata 48
   vallaris 48, *95*, 178–9
Corstopitum 179, 243; *see also* Corbridge
cothurni 13, 54, 56, 222, *223*, 275
Crassus 4, *8*, *13*, 41, 46, 49, 51, 235, 240, 266
Cremona 208, 249, 258
Croatia 20, 34, 85, *102*, 136, 149, *196*, 243, 250, 280
Croy Hill 72
cruppellarii 247
cuculli 57, *213*, 217, 275
Cugir 25, 159, *159–60*, 253
custodes armorum 64, 80, 275
cymationes 39, 51, 123, *123*, 135, *135*, 142, 145, *226*, 246, 248, 250

D

Dacia 64, 66, 87, *126*, 173, 204, 271–2, 281
   Porolissensis 249
   Ripensis 249
Dacian Wars 64, 66, 67, 121, 125, 142, 149, 160, 178, 198
Dacians 64, 67, 70, 76, 77, 79, *80*, *81*, 85, 87, 121, 138, 142, *156*, *158*, 159, 175, *178*, *183*, *192*, 214, *216*, 253, 254, 256, 276
Dacurdo 15
Dadophori *195*
daggers 12, 24, *30*, 44, 80, *84*, 96–7, *96–7*, 98, 100, 153, 160, *191*, 200, 205, 212, 224, 228, 237, 240, 245–6, 275, 277; *see also pugio*
   Augustan 97
   blades 24, 96–7, 246
   frogs 98
   handles 24, 97–8, 245
   Iberian 24
   pommels 97
   sheaths 97, 245
   tang 24, 97, 245
   use 24, 96
Dakota Sioux 258
Dalmatae 66
Dalmatia 16, 249, 280
Damascus 66, *168*
Dangstetten 131
Danish bogs 88, 137, 166
Danube 63, 64, 66, 92, *146*, 156, 160, *161*, 164, 198, 224, *225*, 228, 242, 245, 255, 257, 270
Danubian *limes* 80
Danubian wars 64
Dardani 22
darts 182, 247
Daza 256
Decebalus 64
decora militiae 98
decuriones 6, 255, 276
decursio 41, 276
Deiotarus 43–4, 235
Delos 8, 14, 20, 22
Delphi 122
denarii 46, 184, 238
Denmark 214, 221
deposition of finds
   burials 258
   in water 198
Deva 191, *191*, 200, 254; *see also* Chester
diadema 177
Diana 32
dictators 4, 46, 276
Digestum 63, 265

digmata 15, 29, *75*, 107–8, 129, 157, 167, *174*, *203*, 206, 208
Diodorus, M. Aurelius 144, *148*
diogmitai 66, 143–4, *148*, 220
Dioscuri 32–3, *188*, 191
diplomae 252, 276
Divico 4
dolabrae 45, 175, *175*, 205, 224, 228, 255, 276
   cases 175
dolatores 224
Dolope 43
dolphin on helmet 224
Domitian 64, 92, 96, 142, 149, 179, *179*, *225–6*, 246, 248, 250
Domitian's monument on Campidoglio 92, 96, 100, 124, 142, 145
Domus Aurea *94*, 208, 210, 217–18, 220, 250, 259
Domus Divina 179
dona militaria *30*, 48, *178*, 240
Doncaster 105, 157
dorua 12, 48, 51
dracones 191, 197, 200, 269, 276
dragons 32, 276
Dressel *amphorae* 224
Drnovo 97
Drusenheim 238, 247–8
Drusus 63, 200
Dubravica 84–5, 244, 273
duplicarii 252, 276
Dura-Europos 64, 105, 259–60, 268
Dydimoi *90*, 218, *219*, 219, 254, 270
Dyrrachium 34

E

eagles 5, *15*, 24, 32, 46, 58, 64, *71*, 92, *95*, 107, *127*, 157, 169, 171, 176, 248, 254, 260, 271, 275
   motif on weapons 122, 135, 187, *188*, *192*, 204, 208, 256
Edessa 243
Egypt 4, *26*, 36, 66, 89, 90, 137, 139, 143, *144*, *148*, 149, *168*, 212, 217, 218, 222, 242, 269, 271, 273, 277, 281
Eich 248
Eining *146*, 197
Ektaxis kat'Alanon 263
elephants 8, *166*, 235, 240
embadès 222
embossing *104*, 135, 139
Emesa 112, 194, 197, 248
enamel 8, *96*, 97, *112*, 120, *180*, 245–6
endromida 220
England 212, 240, 246, 273
entrenching tools 45
ephaptis 214
ephestris 54, 214
Ephesus 110, 138, 191, 212, 281
ephippia 52, 193
epigraphy 250
Epitoma Rei Militaris 268
equites 3, 5, *10*, *15*, 41, 45, 49, *51*, 52, 52, 53, *138*, *156*, 164, 167, 175, *178*, *180*, *182*, *183*, 184, *184*, *185*, 191, *191*, 194, 221, *230*, 254–5, 276
   mauri 167
   praetoriani 206, 208, 261
   singulares 276
   singulares Augusti 65, 67, 77, *110*, 200, *203*, *207*, 208, 212, 276
   vexillationis 192
equus 200, 256–7
Esquiline Fresco 25, *28*, *30*, 39, 53
Etolia 43
Etruria 109
Etruscans 8, *15*, 22, *35*, 36, *36*, 37–9, *42*, 43, *46*, 46, 48, *51*, 51, 52, 54, *55*, 56, 56, 57, *58*, 129–30, 141–2, 151, 169, 222, 237–8, 240, 250, 276

Eusebius 264
evocati 6, *30*, 52–3, 135, 240, 242, 250, 252, 276
   Augusti 65, 67
exempla virtutes 184
exerciti 5, 255, 269, 276
Exeter 97
exploratores 276
eye-guards 197, 251

F

Fabius Rufus 49, 145, 208
fabricae 210, 277
falcatae 45, 102, 276
falces 80, 121, 150, 175, *178*, 276
fasciae 8, *43*, 221, 228, 276
   cretatae 8, 56, 221
   crurales 8
   interulae 221
   ventralis 220
Favonius Facilis *82–4*, *94*, *102*, 136, 248, 271, 280
Fayoum *13*, *26*, 100, *101*, 105, *148*, 149, 212, 217, 220, 259
'Felicitas Tiberii' *gladius* 84
Felix Pompeianus 48
felt 11, 13, *18*, 25, 37, 38, 39, 41, 57, *68*, *106*, 123, 135, 139–41, 145, 162, 169, 218, 219, *219*, 224, *226*, 228, 250, 276
femoralia *178*, *203*, 221, 275, 276
feminalia 68, 140, *203*, 221, 275, 276
ferrum 251
Festus 3, 237, 264
Festus, S. 124, 125, *127*, 151, 173
fibulae 8, *30*, 54, 98, 100, 152, 179, 214, 217, 220, 253, 259–60, 276
Firmus (Bonn) 172, 253
Firth of Forth 64
Flaccus, H.F. 3
Flaccus, Q.H. 108, 206, 252, 267
Flaccus, V.F. 63
Flaccus Valerius 46
flask 173
Flavinus *180*
Flavius Bassus 146, *180*, 185, 194, 197, 252, 256
Flavius Mikkales 109
Flavoleius Cordus 74, 245
Florence 159, 269, 272
Florus 3, 24, 237, 265
flutes 48
focales 8, 54, 68, 70, *203*, 220, 225, *226*, 227
footwear 43, 56, *203*, 222–4, 270, 272
fora 237, 276
   Nerva 114, 222, *223*
   Trajan 66, *203*
   Vetus Sarmizegetusa 256, 269
forts 129, 157, 160, 185, 253, 269, 272
Fortuna Primigenia Sanctuary in Palestrina 52
framea 43, 252, 276
France 6, 34, 114, *118*, *208*, 280
Frankfurt-Heddernheim 271
frena 52, 193
Frontinus 3, 63, 242, 265
frumentarii 179, 255, 276
fucatus 100
fulgures 107, 206, 247
Fulham 92
fulmines 115, 247
fundae 164, 221
funditores 164, 166
funerary monuments 8, 23, 29, 30, 36, 37, 48, 49, 51, 52, 52, 58, *101*, *112*, 140, 144, *148*, 149, *149*, 151, 176, 178, 184, *192*, 200, 212, 214, 224, 240, 251
furcae 175, 276
fustis 167

G

gaesa 6, 7, 8, 152, 276
Gaeta 8, *23*, 24, 39, 49, 51
Gaius Caligula 63, *104*, 185, 208, 258
Galatians 6, 25, 43–4
Galba 63, 65, 139, 242, 250, 251, 254, 267
galeae 32, 33, 44, 109, 111, 175, 208, 238, 240, 252, 255, 276
galeatus 68
Gallic 4, 7, 10, 35, 48, 53, 63, 102, 107, 180, 203, 217, 220, 235, 239, 248, 263–4, 273
gallica 8, 38, 41, 44, 51
Gallo-Romans 152
Gallus Caestius 243
Gallus Cornelius 63
Gallus, L. Caninius 140
Gallus Sextus Vibius 178, *178*
Gallus Tribonianus 212
Gamala 131, 249
gardeners 82, 175
Gardun 102, 136, 249, 270
Gaul 3, 4, 6, 15, 20, 35, 44, 54
Gauls 5, 7, 43–4, 48, 52, 64, 221, 236
Gellius, A. 63, 152, 264
geminae pinnae 8, 120, 121, 180, 203, 205, 224
Gemini 157
Geneva 4, 88, 269
Genialis Clusio 171, 254
Genialis, Valerius S. 197
genii 108, 169, 276
Germania 29, 54, 63–4, 239, 254, 267, 272
    Inferior 64, 167, 280
    Superior 64, 249, 280
Germanic 3, 4, 6, 43, 49, 52, 54, 64, 66, 85, 136, 156–7, *157*, 166, 167, 178, 203, 221, 245, 276
Germans 3, 4, 6, 43, 52–3, 64, 87–88, 130, 167, 225, 239–40
Germany 54, 63, 97, 114, 185, 194, 212, 239, 243, 273, 280
Geographica 48, 267
Geto-Dacian 150, 276
Giubiasco 14, 153
gladiatores 4, 66, 144, *144*, 149, 247
gladiatorial equipment 127, 149, 238–9, 241, 260
gladii 6, 8, 12, 14, 24, 29, 30, 49, 80, 81, 82, 84, 85, 86, 87, 88, 90, 96, 107, 111, 127, 142, 153, 156, 171, 178, 180, 182, 183, 200, 213, 224, 225, 226, 227, 244, 269, 276
    hispaniensis 14, 30, 49, 84, 88, 153, 276
    pugnatorius 128
glandes 44, 276
Glanum monument 7, 8, 10–12, 24, 32, 36, 39, 49, 52
glue 25, 101
goatskin 45, 108, 150, 184, 191
gold 8, 24, 32, 41, 44–6, 48, 52, 54, 77, 81, 92, 98, 108, 162, 169, 175, 177, 185, 194, 198, 203, 205, 206, 214, 217, 222, 237, 246, 248, 258, 260, 270, 275–6
gorgons 30, 33, 43, 51, 107, 115, 122, 124, 135, 150, 205, 247
gorgoneiones 54, 107, 124, 135–6, 171, 198, 223
Gospel 267
governors 88, 260–1, 275
Granada Museum 42, 261, 279
gravestones 13, 24, 30, 67, 68, 82, 98, 100, 107, 112, 123, 127, 135–7, 140, 146, 151, 159, 160, 171, 172, 173, 177, 178, 180, 183–184, 197, 213, 214, 216, 219, 221, 245, 251, 253–4, 271; *see also* tombstones

Great Trajanic Frieze 66–7, 71, 81, 118, 200, 203, 204–6, 209–10, 212, 222, 258, 272
greaves 18, 30, 38, 43, 58, 84, 94, 112, 115, 125, 137, 140, 143, 150–1, 197, 241, 251, 276
Greco-Roman 11, 36, 115, 123, 136, 144, 198, 208, 223, 271
Greece 3–5, 87, 88, 90, 114, 139, 191, 219, 266, 269, 281
Greeks 6, 22, 38, 43, 45, 52, 54, 57, 138, 141, 143, 197, 219, 272
Gryneum 139
guardsmen 92, 229, 256
    imperial 63, 81, 94, 200, 203, 205, 208, 208, 209, 210, 212, 213, 217, 222, 245, 258–9
    city 193, *193*
Guisborough 185, 187, 256
Guttmann collection 8, 171, 249, 269

H

habitus 270
    gallici 54
Hadrian 64, 107, 111, 124, 164, 175, 198, 221–2, 243, 246, 251, 260, 267
Hadrian's Wall 64, 66, 140, 270, 272
hairstyle of soldiers *167*, 212, *226–7*, 258
Haltern 243, 245
haluq 213
Ham Hill 125
hammers 111, 173, 247
hand-thrown stones 143
Hannibal 66, 236
harnesses 30
    horse 49, 52–53, *122*, 136, 152, 167, 176, *180*, 193–4, *203*, 246, 250, 252, 256, 276
    ass 175
hastae 5, 6, 12, 48, 67, 73, 77, 143, 152, 167, 178–9, 180, 182, 197, 200, 204, 240, 247, 252, 522, 276
    amentata 74
    donatica 48
    longa 12
    prepilata 255
    pura 48, 178–9, 276
    navalis 58, *226*, *227*
    summa imperii 46, 179, 238, 268
hastati 5–6, 27, 46, 235
hastiliarii 128
Hauran 268
Hebron *118*, 120, 206
Hellenic 27, 37, 77, 112, *112*, 122, 129, 222, 241, 281
Hellenistic 5, 8, 10, 32, 33, 36, 36, 37, 38, 39, 44, 45, 49, 51, *51*, 52, 57, 58, 66–7, 89, *94*, 102, 123, 129, 140, 169, 187, 192, 194, 209, 217, 243, 259
helmets xiii, xiv, 8, 10, 15, 18, 23, 27, 29, 30, 32–8, 39, 41, 43–5, 49, *51*, 51, 53–4, 57–8, 68, 70, 77, 79, 80, 81, 87, 88–90, 94–5, *102*, *104*, 107, 108, 109–21, 127, 129, 137–8, 140, 152, *154*, 156, 158–60, *160*, 162, *162–5*, 164, 166–7, *168*, 169, 171, *172*, 175, 178–80, 184–95, 197–8, *201–3*, 205–10, 212, 217, 219, *223*, 224–5, 236–41, 244, 246–8, 250–4, 256–9, 271, 275–7, 281
    Agen-Port 8, *23*, 27, *30*, 35, *36*, 49, 114, 120, *180*, 253
    arming cap 219
    Attic 27, 36, 38, 44–5, 49, 58, *81*, 90, *104*, *111–12*, *114*, 120, *179*, 185, *186*, 188, 192, *203*, *205*, 206, 208, 208, 212, 239, 248, 250
    aventails 162
    Boeotian-Pseudocorinthian 36

Boeotian 49, 239
browband 35, 111, *111*, *115*, *118*, *180*, 185, *186*, 208, 254
Buggenum type 8, *15*, 34, 57, 58, *81*, 109, 111, *225*, 237, 247
carrying systems 118, 120–1, 159
cavalry 49, 51, *111*, 152, *154*, 158–9, 162, *168*, *180*, *183*, 184–91, 194–5, 197, *203*, 206, 208, *208*, 256
cheek guards 8, 34, 35, 36, *36*, 37, 57, 68, *81*, *89*, 90, 109, 111, *111*, 112, 114, *115*, *118*, 120, *160*, 162, *184*, 185, *203*, *219*, 244, 248; *see also bucculae*
chin straps 8, 35, 37, 44, 90, 109, 111, *111*, *115*, *118*, 162, 193, 257; *see also vinculum*
classification 32, *112*, 158, 237, 257
coifs 37
conical 33, 121, 160, 162, 164, *164*, *191*, 219
Coolus type 8, *15*, 35, 37, 44, 49, 51, 102, 109, 111, *112*, 121, *127*, 140, 158, *178*, *180*, 184, 234, 238, 244, 247–8, 256
covers 38, 68, *111*
crests 8, 10, 30, *33*, 37, 38, 45, 49, 52, 58, 68, 90, 107, *112*, *116*, 120, *120*, 121, *127*, 152, 159, *180*, 187, *188*, *192*, 194, *203*, 206, 208, 217, 224, 241, 246–7, 250, 258, 275
    cristae 275
    cristae transversae 30, 37, *93*, *116*, 121, 275
    diadema 111, 112, *179*, 184, 185, *190*, 206, 248, 254, 258
    eagle-headed 187, *188*, *191*, *192*
    hairy (embossed or applied) 88, *104*, 185, *188*, *190*, *195*, 197–8
    horned 8, 10, *154*, 275
    Imperial-Gallic *112*, 114, *115*, 121, 206, 224, 248
    Imperial-Italic 114, *118*, 206
    infantry 8, 10, *15*, 18, 27, 29, 30, 32–8, 39, 41, 43–5, 68, 70, 77, 79, 80, 8, *95*, *102*, 107, 108, 109–21, 158–9, 237–8, 248, 250–3
    lining 37, *111*, 121, 187, 219
    masks *15*, 29, 37, 171, *172*, 185, 187, *187*, 188–91, 194, *195*, 197–8
    Montefortino 27, 33–4, *34*, 35, 36, 37, 208, *225*, 238, 241, 247, 258, 271
    Phrygian 10, 187, 208, *208*
    plumes 37, 38, 45, 68, 90, *102*, 120–1, 156, *180*, 194, *203*, 206, 208, *208*, 241, 246, 248, 258, 275
    pseudo-Attic 184–5
    pseudo-Corinthian 32, 36, 58, 87, *94*, 114, *115*, 208–10, *223*, 241, 259
    reinforcing bars 120–1, 258
    Spangenhelm 70, *121*, 160, 162
    'sports' *195*
    Toledo *112*, *116*, 159, 248
    Weisenau *15*, 68, 90, 111, *112*, 114–21, *160*, *201*, *205*, 206, 253, 258
Heracles knot 58
Herculaneum *42*, 208, *208*, 239, 254
    soldier 224, 246
Hercules 123, 176
High Rochester 251
Hippika Gymnasia 159, 194–8, 276
Hippopotamus skin 167
Hispania 152, 271
    Citerior 3, 249
    Ulterior 3
Historia Augusta 63, 66, 175, 267
hoards 186
    Market Harborough 185
    Ulpia Trajana Sarmizegetusa 175, *193*, 243, 253, 256

hobnails 56, 224
Hochrhein 273
Hod Hill 67, 85, 125, 245, 257
Hofheim 72
horn 41, *88*, 141–2, 192, 212, 256
horses 3, 48, 52–3, *156*, *161*, 167, 175, 184, 193–4, 197–8, *203*, 256, 268
    archers 4, 164, 169, 221
    harnesses 39, 49, 52–3, 152, 167, 176, *180*, 187, *191*, *193*, 193–4, *203*, 240, 244, 246, 250, 252, 256, 268, 276
Housesteads 164, 165, 253, 270
Hungary 242, 255
hunting 7, 8, *13*, 54, 139, 144, 151–2, 183, 251, 268, 277
Hutcheson Hill 254
Hyginus or Pseudo-Hyginus 63, 242, 267
Hyperanor 253, 259

I

iacula 48, 152, 164, 255
Iberian 12, 24, 34, 37, 204, 271
Iberians 4, 6, *18*, 43–5, 53, 200, 217, 236, 247, 275, 277
Illyrians 6
imaginiferes 169, 171, 254, 276
imago 169
immunes 5, 65, *179*, 255, 276
impedimenta 45, 276
imperatores 5, 46, 52, 59, 63, 66
imperia 3, 5, 12, 32, 46, 276
India 64
Indo-European 11, 235
infantry 5, 12, *15*, 22, 29, 39, 41, 43–4, 49, 58, 65–7, 74, 80, 86, 88, 105, 125, 128, *128*, *138*, 142–4
infula 44
inlay 32, 97, 123, 156, 245–6
inscriptions 43, 65, 80, 104, 107, 109, 115, 121–2, 158, 178–9, 200, 271; *see also* epigraphy
insignia 8, 10, 20, 24, 29, 37, 46, 49, 77, 88, 107, 176, 179, *203*, 205, 237, 275–6
Insus 178, *180*, *192*
Inveresk 97
Inverness *180*
iron 6, 7, 8, 12, 20, 24–5, 29, 32, 35, 37–9, 41, 44, 49, 52, 67, 68, 72–3, 80, 86, 87, 92, 97–8, 101, 105, *114*, *118*, 120, 122, 124–5, 128–32, 135, 139–40, 142, *153*, 158, 160, *160*, 162, 171, 173, 175, 184–7, 191–4, 197, 198, 200, *203*, 204, 206, 208, 210–12, 236, 238, 244–5, 247, 250–4, 256–8, 268, 275–7
Iruna 249
Isidorus of Seville 3, 63, 100, 222, 265
Istanbul 72, *95*, 109, *111*, 112, *178*, *188*, *218*, 281
Italia 249, 270, 271
Italic 3, 6, 7, 8, 25, 27, 33–8, 42, 49, 58, *81*, 97, 109, 111–12, 114, *118*, 120, 122, 158, 194, 206, 208, 224, *225*, 236–7, 239, 245, 269
Italy 4, 49, 64–6, 81, 107, *144*, *167*, *205*, 214, 221, 225, 237, 242, 251, 258, 273, 279
Itanus 237
Iturean 6, 43, 160
Iulia Gens 36, 53
Iulius C. Caesar *see* Caesar
Iulius Magnus 247
Iulius Primus 194
ivory 11, 24, 49, 54, *86*, 92, 97, *110*, *141*, 153, 173, 176, 183, 191, 204, 210, 212, 246
Iža 249

J

jacula 164, 182
javelins 5, 7, 25, 43, 44, 48, 57, *73*, 74,
    143, 152, 158, 164, 167, 182, *192*,
    194, 236, 239, 252, 255
    Moorish 48
Jazyges 64, 66, *88*, 160, 162, 198
Jerusalem 64, *179*, *204*, 222, 273
Jewish *204*, 258–9, 265, 273
John the Evangelist 63, 197, 257, 259,
    267
Josephus 63, 73, 77, 80, 101, *110*, 122,
    149, 153, 182, 184, 187, *194*, 197,
    204, *222*, 242–4, 247–8, 251, 252,
    255–6, 261, 265, 270
Judaea 63–4, 206, 249
Jugurtha 3, 32, *33*, 267
Jupiter *15*, 32, 46, 107–8
Justinian 114, 265
Juvenal 3, 63, 177, 265

K

Kalkriese 20, 63, 67, 74, 92, 128,
    130–1, *131*, 171, 250
Karaagatsch 162, *164*
Karanis 261
karbatinai 222, 224
kardiophylaces 27
Kasir Ibrahim *see* Qasr Ibrim
kassida 198
Kastellvicus des Rainau-Buch 129
kastron 237
kataphraktos 275
Kladovo 92, *94*, 97, 98, *128*, 128, *179*,
    179, *186*
Kleinwinterheim *179*, *179*, 255
knives 156, 173
Koblenz-Weiler-Bubenheim 185
Kolstolna Pri Dunai 98
Koptos 254
Kostol *15*, *187*, 194, 198
Kowel *239*
kranê 182
kranes 110
Kranj 6, 271
kremasmata 136, 145, *226–7*
Krinolaos 254
Krokodilô 224, 254, 269
krossenos 54
Kunzing 151

L

La Almoina 7
La Caridad *see* Caminreal
La Tène 14, 15, 22, 35, 44, 49, 73, 97,
    112, 156, 182, 271
lamina 210
lamnae 12, 14, 210
    levisatares 210
lancea 45, 48, 73, 79, 152, 175, 179,
    182, 200
    pugnatoria 152
lancers 198
lances 73, 101, 166, 179, 270
lancets 173
Lanuvium 8, 51, 248
lapides missiles 44, *44–5*
lappets *33*, 39, 41, 51, 58, 123, 135–6,
    142, 173, *226*, 248, 254; *see also*
    pteryges, kremasmata
laticlavii 5, 214
Latin xi, xii, 46, *82*, 107, 151, 158, 178,
    212–13, 218–19, 229, 235, 243,
    249, 263–8
Latina (Via) 49
Latinised 158
laurel
    crowns 32, 48, 152, 169, *174*, 175,
        177, 185, *188*, 198, 208
    leaves 46, 175, 177, 246

law
    Latin 243
lead 37, 44, 45, 164, 204, 257, 276
leather 11, 13, 43, 68, 147, *148*, 224, 280
    production centres 108
legati 5, *23*, *37*, 38, 51, 63, 65–6, *124*,
    145, 240, 243, 276–7
leggings 151, 221, 277
legionarii (legionaries) 4, 12, *15*, 16, 20,
    38, 39, 41, 67, 68, 70, 73, 76, 78, ,
    79, *80*, 81, *81*, 85, 97, 99, 100–1,
    105, *106*, 107, *108*, 110, 114, 121,
    121, 123, 125, *126*, 134, 142,
    143, 145, 150, *150*, 151, 152, 153,
    156–9, 167, 171, 174, 204, 210,
    213, 214, *216*, *219*, 224, 229, 235,
    243, 247, 252, 269, 271, 275–7
legionary cavalry 256
legiones 5, 20, 22, 29, 32, 38, 43, 46, 54,
    64–5, 107, 108, *109*, 169, 173,
    179, 235, 242, 243, 249, 275–7
    Gemella 43
    I, IX, X, XI, XII, XIII, XIV, XV,
        XXI, XXVI, XXVII, XXX,
        XXXVI, XXXVIII 235–6
    I Adiutrix 174, 242, 243, 259
    I Italica 210, 242, 254, 269
    I Minervia 108, 242
    II Adiutrix 176, 247, 259
    II Augusta 15, 72, 242, 243, 247
    II Italica 104, 129, 261
    II Trajana 210
    III Cyrenaica 210
    III Martia *30*, 53
    III Scythica 86
    IIII 112
    IV Macedonica 105, *115*, 242
    V Alaudae 8, 58, *112*, 235, 242
    VI, VIII or IX *30*, 235
    VI Ferrata 175
    VI Victrix 242
    VII Claudia Regina 255
    VII Pia Fidelis 136
    VIII 46
    VIII Augusta 67, *67*, 68, 140, 247,
        255, 259, 260
    IX Hispana 122, 246
    X Legio 22, 32, *36*, 46, 53, 237
    XI 58
    XI Claudia Pia Fidelis 247–8, 254
    XII Fulminata 75, 107, 129
    XIII and XIV 43
    XIII Gemina Martia Victrix 85, 101,
        178, *192*, 242, 246
    XIIII Gemina 63, 171, 242, 245, 254
    XV Apollinaris 140, 176
    XV Primigenia 72, 245
    XVI Flavia Firma 209
    XVII, XVIII and XIX 63, 135
    XX Valeria Victrix 63, *82*, 136, 140,
        159
    XXII Primigenia 245
    XXX Ulpia Victrix 128, 242
Leiden 190, 258, 272, 280
Levantine archers 162, *163*
levis armatura 65, *86*, *110*, 138, 143, 242
lex 258
lexicons
    Sudae 14, 236
    Hesychios 261, 265, 267
Licaius 152, 153, 259
Licinius Murena 51
lictores 24, *30*, 46, *46*, 176, 237, 239, 276
lineae 214, 276
linen 11, 13, 25, 129, 139–42, *144*, 146,
    175, 192, 212–13, 214, 221–2
linothorax 39
lions
    motif 51–2, 122, 135, 175, 185, 197,
        254
    skins 77, *102*, 139, 171, 222, *223*, 240
literary sources 9, 13, *116*, 217, 220,
    229, 239

lituus 176
Livy 12, 25, 49, 54, 217, 236–7, 240–1,
    265
Lonchês 73
London *137*, *144*, *180*, 208, 249, 261,
    263, 264, 268–73, 281
Longinus Cassius 4
Lorarius, T.F. 24, *30*, 176
loricae xiv, *33*, 38, *38*, 39, *42*, 51, *81*, *82*,
    99, *115*, *122*, 123, 127–9, 135–6,
    139–41, 143–4, 148, *153*, 159,
    159, 203, 205, 224, 226–7, 238,
    248–51, 269, 273, 276
    hamis conserta 171, *203*, 210
    lintea 124, 139
    plumata 142, *142*, 162, 198
Lucanus 3, 38, 45, 48, 265
Luccius Faustus 171, 173, 254
Lucullus 4, 32, 41, 51, 54, 266
Lunca Mureşului 185
lunulae 46, *70*, 98, 100, *118*, 171, 194,
    203, *213*
Lyon 208, 267
Lydus 3, 8, 43, 239, 240, 265

M

Macedonia 3, 39, 104, 281
Macedonian *10*, *45*, 198, 217
Macedonians 6, 43, 86, 143
machairai 45, 143, 144, 182, 236, 276
Macrinus 212, 267
Madrid 250, 270, 271
Magdalensberg 20
Main 271
Mainz 14, *14*, *15*, 22, 34, 67, 68, 72, 81,
    82, *84*, 85, 86, 92, *127*, 173, 179,
    182, 200, 204, 206, 210, 244–5,
    248, 254, 257, 268, 270, 273
    pedestal relief *137*, 152, 157–8, 173,
        214, 224, 250
    Weisenau 120
malleoli 222
manduas 214
manicae 52, *70*, *76*, *79*, 149, 247, 251; *see*
    also armour, arm protections
manipuli 169
Mannheim 35, 44, 49, 224, 237–8
Mantua *176*, *226*, 214
manuscript 241
marble 123, 222
Marcellus Theatre 32
Marcomanni 64
Marcomannic Wars 66, 76, 87, *88*, *90*,
    104, 125, 129, 134, 142
Marcus Aurelius 63–4, 87, 89, 92, 128,
    140, 143, *144*, 158, 192, 194, 200,
    221, 250, 254, 265, 267
Marcus Aurelius Column 13, 74, *75*,
    76, 78, 80, *106*, 107–8, *114*,
    116, 120, 123, 128–9, 133–4,
    136–7, 152, 158–9, 200, *206*, 212,
    220, 250
marines *15*, 57–9, 65, 224–228, 275
Marius 3–6, 8, 15, 25, *29*, 29, 45–46,
    48, 53, 56, 266, 269
Mars 8, *27*, 38, 53, 121, 140, 150, 157,
    179, *180*, *188*, 191, *196*, *223*, 238,
    241, 255, 270
Marseille 129
Marsian War 8
Marsica 192
Martialis 3, 63
Masada 64, 107, *109*, 212, 213, 258
Maternus 200
Matrica 88
Mauretania 4, 32, *33*, 63
    Tingitana *194*, 249
mausoleums 13
    Julii *10–12*, 24, *102*
    Munatius Plancus 8, *23*, 24
Mautern 249
Mavilly 191

medallions 49, 197, 276
Medina, Duke of 250
Mediterraean 3, 11, 54, 57, 92, 212,
    229, 271
Mehrum 97
Meleagros *13*, *55*, 114
Mesopotamia 4, 64, 269
Metellus Quintus 240
metopae 8, *23*, 24, 32, 49, 51, 67, 70, *71*,
    76–7, 79–81, 81, 85, *85*, 87, *105*,
    121, 122, 125, *126*, *150*, *170*, *183*,
    191, 248, 249, 252–3
Mihovo 81
Milan 268–72
milites xii, 7, *8*, *10*, 12, 15, *18*, *29*, 32,
    36, 38, 39, 41, *43*, 53–4, 57, 68,
    70, 72, 74, 79, 80, *81*, 85, 86–7,
    90, 94, 98, 99, *106*, 111, 114, *115*,
    122, *124*, *126*, 128–9, 134–5,
    137–8, 142, *142*, 144, *148*, 151,
    164, *167*, 175, 177, *204*, 208, 210,
    214, 217, 218, 235, 240, 252, 255,
    260, 266, 272, 275–7
    gregarius 29, 38, 54, 77, 130, 249, 276
    legionis 5, 158, 160, *209*, 245, 247, 276
    ostensionalis 123, *177*
Minerva *90*, 108, *188*, *196*, 248, 251
missiles 25, 34, 44, 141, 164, *182*, 252
Mithra Tauroctonus 195
Mithraeum of Santa Maria Capuavetere
    194, *195*
Mithridates 3–4
Moesia 63, 142, 243
    Superior 280–1
    Inferior 249, 269, 281
Mogontiacum 200, 204; *see also* Mainz
Mokronog Group 81
Mondragon 43, 239
Monimus 217, 253
Mons Albanus 48
Mons Claudianus *191*, *192*, 212–14,
    218–19, *219–20*, 254, 271, 281
Montanus Capito *see* Capito, M.
Montefortino xiv 8, *27*, 33–7, 39, 41,
    44, 57, 58, *94*, *102*, 109, *111*, 208,
    225, 238, 241, 247, 258, 271
mosaics xi–xii, 13, 32, 52–3, *118*, 130,
    167, 200, 205, 217–18, 220, 222,
    225, 241, 250, 258–9, 268
moulds 137
Mouriés 8, 14
mouthpieces 257
Mules Mariani 45
mummy portraits 100, *101*, *148*, 149,
    212, 217, 220, 269
Musei Capitolini *33*, *145*, *223*, 269
Museo Archeologico Nazionale di
    Napoli *136*, 222, 251, 272, 279
Museo Nazionale Romano 28, 41, *89*,
    106, 143, *179*, *207*, 279
musical instruments 176
musicians 6, *46*, 48, 64, *124*, 176, 200
Musius, Cn. 171, 177
Musov 128
mussolina 214

N

Nahal Ever 213, 217
nails 25, 68, 101, 105, 140, 222, 224,
    228, 240, 253
Naples 92, *136*, 142, 214, 228, 268, 272
Napoleon III 44
Narbonensis 4, *8*, 24, 32, 39, 58, 249,
    280
nationes 66, 241, 276
nautae 57, 59, 224, 276
Nawa 112, *113*, 129, 268
Nero 63, 65, *94*, 167, *167*, 217, 224, 246,
    259, 267, 269
Nerva 64, 114, 222, *223*
Nervii 4, *8*, 240
Netherlands 80, 280

Neuss 109, 249, 272
Neviodunum 97
Newstead 72, 74, 85, 99, 129, 131, 133, 134, 140, 146, 147, 149–50, 182, 185, 190, 193–4, 204, 211, 247, 256–7, 269
niello 92, 97, 100, 123, 129, 245–6, 258
Niger 111, 192, 194
nimbus 164
Nitra 98
Njimegen 92, 109, 156–7, 184, 190, 247–8
nodulus 82
Nonnius Balbus 42
Noricum 63–64, 81, 249
Notitia Dignitatum 104, 108, 129
Novae 94, 210, 211, 214, 245, 248–9, 269–70, 273, 280
Novaesium 197, 249, 272; see also Neuss
Noviomagus 120, 122, 156, 157, 196, 208
Nubian 212–13
Numantia 22
numeri 66, 108, 152, 162–9, 198, 221, 243, 254, 275, 276
Numidians 6, 32, 43, 48, 53, 167, 242

O

Oberaden 7, 14, 24, 67, 68, 243
Oberammergau 245
Octavian 58, 239, 261; see also Augustus
Octavianus 3, 5, 32, 46, 58, 63, 66, 238
ocreae 43, 107, 150–1, 251, 276
Odes 265
Oescus 249
officers xiii, 4–7, 8, 22, 24, 32, 36, 38–9, 43, 45–6, 49, 52–4, 56, 58, 64–6, 80, 88, 92, 96–8, 102, 107, 112, 113, 121–2, 129, 135, 138, 139, 140, 145, 150–1, 168–9, 176, 179, 179, 194, 212–14, 217, 220, 224, 229, 239, 242, 258, 275–7
officia 276
  consularis 179
officina coactiliaria 140, 268
ollula 175
optiones 64, 65, 136–7, 225, 226, 228, 260, 276
oppida 38, 276
Opus Agriculturae 266
opus interrasile 68, 86, 92
order of battle against the Alans 263
ordo equestris 65, 276
ordo militaris 259
ordo senatorius 276
ordones 276
Ordovices 63
oriental armour 147, 272
Origo 250, 276
ostraka 169, 254, 261, 269
  B3 – US 61 K224 224, 261
Ostrov 187, 188, 191, 194, 272, 281
Osuna 7, 14–15, 18, 22, 25, 29, 37, 38, 43, 236
Otho 63
Ouroux sur la Saône 7
ovatio 48, 256
Ovidius 63

P

Padova 53, 212
paenulae 54, 57, 71
painting xii, 13, 8, 13, 24–5, 30, 32, 37, 39, 45, 51–4, 94, 107, 130, 135–6, 145, 145, 204, 208, 218–19, 238–9, 241, 253, 258, 259, 271
Palatine Hill xi, 235
Palestine 4, 137, 242
Palestrina 32, 118, 205, 217, 222, 225, 259

palintona toxa 160
Palladius 63, 266
pallia 214, 217, 276
Palmyra 66, 168
Palmyrene 160, 169, 218, 218
paludamenta 8, 54, 145, 214, 217–18, 259, 276
Pamukkale 144, 148
Pannonia 63–64, 88, 112, 142, 173, 218, 243–4, 249, 270
  Inferior 280
  Superior 280
papilla 175
papyrus 25, 218, 228
  BGU 1564 213, 217
  Michigan VIII 467 261
  Ryl. 189 (128p) 258
parapleuridia 256
Paris 136, 208, 224, 228, 249, 263, 266, 268–72, 281
Parma 212
parmae 48, 51, 51, 127, 252, 255, 256
  bruttiana 5, 29, 157, 275
  equestris 49, 51, 154, 167, 171, 184, 276
  velitaris 25
Parthia 64, 110, 112
Parthians 13, 63–4, 110, 112, 129–30, 160, 169, 193, 194, 198, 212, 219, 221, 235, 240, 269
paterae 175, 255, 272, 276
pattern-welding 14
Patrassos 281
Patrologia
  Greca 264
  Latina 266
Pausanias 63, 122, 139, 141, 266
Pécs 268, 270
pectorales 122
peltae 143, 276
pendants 68, 88, 100, 153, 194, 203, 250, 252
  heart shaped 100, 252
  ivy leaf 203
  pelta shaped 194
  straps 100, 180, 191, 194, 203, 252
Peregrini 66, 277
perimeridia 256
perizoma 221–2, 260, 276
perones 56, 122, 276
Persia 64
Persian 24, 52, 64, 219, 221, 266, 275
Pertinax 130, 146, 243, 267
Petilius Secundus 72, 245
Petronell-Carnuntum 197
Petronius Arbiter 63, 222, 266
Petronius Classicus 251
peytrals 197
phalerae 30, 46, 48–9, 52, 71, 123, 123, 127, 135, 139, 140, 149, 169, 171, 176, 177, 177, 178, 180, 191, 193–4, 198, 201, 205, 240, 248, 255, 276
phecasia 222
phecasiati milites 261
pickaxes see dolabrae
pila xiv, 5–7, 8, 10, 12, 24, 67, 68–70, 72–3, 127, 152, 182, 200, 203–4, 204, 205, 225, 244, 252, 269, 276–7
  binding 203–4
  butts 7, 204
  collets 7, 67
  handgrip 67, 204
  heads 67, 71, 72, 204
  heavy 6, 7, 67, 68, 204
  light 6, 7, 67, 72, 157
  muralia 7, 276
  origin 6, 236
  penetrative power 204
  shanks 6, 7, 67, 72, 73, 204
  socketed 7, 67
  spike-tanged 7

tanged 7, 67, 68
  use 6, 7, 24, 70, 72
  weighted spheroid 71, 204, 204, 218
  wooden rivets 6, 7
  wooden shafts 6, 7, 67, 68, 204
pileus pannonicus 218, 220
pilos 13, 218–19, 260, 276
pilus 276
pinecone 141
Pliny the Elder 8, 46, 100, 140, 167, 168, 177, 200, 206, 218, 220, 266
Pliny the Younger 255, 266
Plutarch 12, 32, 41, 266
Polybius 3, 6, 12, 25, 27, 29, 37, 51, 266
Pompeii 8, 24, 36, 37, 39, 44, 46, 48, 51, 92, 94, 98, 118, 145, 146, 151, 208, 218–219, 224, 238–9, 241, 254, 258, 261
  House of the Cryptoporticus 52
  House of Fabius Rufus 49, 208
  House of the Impluvium 32
  House of the Vetti 54, 94, 136
Pompeius the Great 3–4, 8, 12, 34, 38–39, 43, 51–2, 54, 56, 58, 235
Pompeius Sextus 59
Porolissum 74, 216, 281
Portonaccio Sarcophagus 89, 90, 106, 143–4, 144, 192, 261
posterior 5, 276–7
postsignani 65, 276
praefecti 63, 242, 277
  alae 243
  castrorum 65, 178, 179, 242, 277
  classis 58–9
  cohortis 95, 243
  equitum 6, 239
  evocatorum 6
  praetorii 65, 77, 212
  vigilum 65
praesidia 167, 168, 277
Praetorian Guard 30, 63, 65–7, 71–2, 81, 81, 93–4, 106, 107, 110, 118, 123, 171, 171, 172, 179, 179, 200–13, 217–18, 220–2, 245, 247, 248, 258–9, 260, 268, 272
praetoriani 65, 106, 124, 277
primi ordines 5, 277
primus pilus 5, 64–5, 236, 277
princeps 63, 65, 81, 277
principales 5, 6, 65, 277
principia 173, 277
profectio 179, 250
prometopidia 52, 256
propaganda monuments xiii, 10
pteryges 27, 30, 39, 41, 51, 54, 58, 68, 70, 77, 82, 84, 102, 122–5, 129, 135–6, 139–40, 142, 144–6, 159, 167, 169, 173, 210, 221, 223, 225, 226–7, 248, 250, 254, 256, 277
Ptolemaic 25, 26, 52, 205, 259, 272
Ptolemy xiv, 4
pugiones 24, 30, 44, 80, 84, 96, 97, 100, 153, 153, 159, 171, 173, 205, 224–5, 226–7, 228, 237, 245, 269, 277
Punic Wars 3, 6, 44, 57, 239, 268
purple
  colour used in dress and armour 8, 24, 39, 51, 90, 100, 108, 118, 193–4, 205, 217–18, 260
  feathers and plumes 37, 81, 203, symbol of luxury and command 33, 46, 54 193, 212, 214, 218, 237, 276
  Tyrian purple 218, 247, 268
purses 44, 100, 147, 224
puttees 276

Q

Qasr Ibrim 143, 144, 222
Quadi 64, 88, 142

quaestores 5, 277
Quintana Ridonda 34
Quintilianus 3, 8, 29, 30, 53, 267
quivers 44, 160, 163, 164, 182, 198, 246

R

Raeti Gesati 252
Raetia 63–4, 167, 242, 249
Rainach-Buch 129
Ramesses III 253
ram's head decoration 255
rank see insignia
Ravenna 224, 226, 272, 279
rawhide 90, 137–8, 169, 240
Rennes 152, 256
Reinheim 270
Reins 193, 240, 246
remiges 57
Renaissance 13
Res Gestae Divi Augusti 63, 255, 263
Res Publica 3, 229, 235
Rheingönheim 85, 98, 244, 246
Rhine 4, 34, 67, 68, 85, 86, 121, 123, 129, 146, 149, 203, 213, 242, 244, 248, 259
Rhineland 152, 159, 184
Rhodians 6, 44
Rhoxolani 161, 162, 162, 191, 198
Rhutenian 43
Ρωμαικα 263
Romania 66, 73, 74, 85, 269, 271–3, 281
Romanius Capito 256
Romanus 256
Rome 3–4, 6, 10, 28, 32, 33, 35, 37, 45, 48, 51, 57, 63–67, 70, 75–6, 78, 80, 89, 94, 95, 96, 99, 106, 122, 145, 154, 166, 169, 171, 177, 179, 187, 191, 194, 203, 206, 207, 209, 210, 216, 217, 222, 223, 228, 229, 241, 250, 257, 259, 260, 265, 268–73, 276, 279
Römisch-Germanisch Zentralmuseum Mainz (RGZM) 270
Romulus 235
Rottweil 183, 193
Rufinus S.225, 228, 261
rufuli 5
rufus 217
Rufus F. 49, 145, 208
rumices 252

S

Saalburg 224, 243
Saarland 270
Saar-Pfalz-Kreis 270
Sabeans 63
Sabine 32
Sabinus 66
sacella 173, 27
Sacrovir 15, 22, 63, 149, 247
saddles 193
  horns 52, 180, 193
  saddlecloth 52, 180, 193
saga 13, 30, 51, 54, 139, 166, 167, 176, 180, 191, 260, 277
sagacorticia 219
sagittari 44
sagittariorum 160, 164, 243, 253, 259
sagula 54, 164, 277
  gregalis 54
  virgatum et lucens 218
sagum see saga
sailors 57–9, 219, 224–6, 228, 242, 276
Saintes 152, 160, 250, 252, 255, 271
St Gregorio al Celio 8

St Peonios 220
St Remy 7, *10*, 22, 24, 32, 38; *see also* Glanum
Salassi 63
Saldum 245
Sallustius Crispus 3
Sallustius 25, 49
Salo 245
Salona *127*, 153, *153*
San Vittorino dell'Aquila 247
Saône 6, 7, 14, 24, *118*, 129, 179, 220, 269
Saltire 68
Samnite 25, 39, 42, 272, 237
sarabara 194, 277
sarcinae 45, 145, 175, 255
sarcophagi 159
Sarmatian type *79*, 88, 179, *191*, *216*
Sarmatians 63, 64, 66, 87, 88, 141, 142, *191*, 198, 200, 210, 251, 268, 269
Saturninus Aurelius 221
Satyricon 205, 222, 266
scabbards 20, 44, 85, 92, 96, 97, 156, 205, 246
Scaeva Caesius 39
Scafa 107, 111, 121, 149, 169
scarfs 54, *203*, 218, 220, 225, 260
Schaan 35
Scipio Caecilius 54
Scipio Cornelius Nasica 34
scorpions *203*, 205, 206, 259
Scotland 64, 72, 182
sculptors 66, 67, 160, 249
sculpture 11, 12, 13, 25, 29, *30*, 32, 34, 37, *37*, 43, 49, 52, 54, 58, 67, *70*, *72*, *90*, *93*, 100, 101, *102*, *106*, *111*, *116*, 122, 123, 130, 135, 136, 140, 146, 147, 151, 156, *156*, 177, *179*, *180*, 185, 205, 212, 213, 214, 220, 222, *223*, 224, *226*, 228, 241, 249, 250, 259, 269, 271, 272
scuta 5, 8, 25, 29, 32, 44, 49, 52, 72, 77, 79, 101, 107, 127, 175, 206, 240, 255, 277
scutarii 108
scutati 44, 277
Scythian *191*, 194, 198, 221
secures *38*, 46, 276, 205
Seleucid 52, 272
semaforos 64
semicinctium 221
semi-rigid scale 128
semispatha 224
senate 3, 5, 59, 237, 266
Seneca 3, 241, 261, 266, 267
Septimius, Caius 137
Septimius Severus 242, 267
sequanica 220
Serbia 85, *97*, *102*, 123, 243, 245, 246, 247, 254, 273, 280, 152, *187*
Serbian 271
Sermo 214, 259, 263
Sertorian Wars 237
Sertorius 4, 12, 14, 34, 39, 54, 266
Sertorius Festus, Q. 124, 125, 151, 173
Sertorius Firmus 173, 254
seviri equitum Romanorum 65
Sextus Pedius 242
shields 5, 6, 7, *8*, *13*, 24, 25, *26*, 29, 32, 37, 39, 44, 45, 48, 49, *51*, 54, 57, 58, *71*, 73, 75, 80, *81*, *90*, 101, *104*, 105, 107, *108*, 108, 109, *118*, *124*, *127*, 137, 138, 140, 143, 149, *156*, 157, 160, 164, 171, *174*, 175, 177, 182, 184, 197, *201*, 205, 206, 208, 209, 224, 237, 239, 240, 243, 244, 246, 247, 252, 255, 259, 275, 277
  binding 105, *109*
  blazons 209
  borders *104*
  bosses 32, 137, 247
  Celtic 25, 43, 44, 152
covering *147*
covers 107, 184
curved 25, 68, 101, 105, 157, 184, 277
flat 105, 157, 184, 206
handgrip 25, 32, 101, 105, 107, 157, 184, *203*, 252
hexagonal 49, *144*, *203*, 206, 224
oval 52, 58, 105, 129, 157, 158, 167, 171, 184, 194, 197, 205, 206, 210, 247, 249, 256
oxhide *109*
plank 25, 43, 101, 105, 157
rectangular 68, 105, 134, 145, 157, *168*, 205, 206, 224, 247, 259
rhomboid *15*, 32
round 5, 43, 77, *102*, *105*, 107, 139, 140, 158, 192, 228, 275, 276
silver 8, 49
trapezoidal 105
umbones 15, 25, 29, 44, 58, 68, *90*, *104*, 105, 107, *107*, *109*, *156*, 157, 158, 162, 184, *196*, 277
wicker 29
Sicily 3, 39
sidus Iulium 32, 36, 39, 49, 238
Siemiechów 114, 270
signa 5, 13, *30*, 46, 49, 59, 63, 70, 107, *127*, 169, *170*, 171, 173, *201*, 208, 239, 240, 246
signalling 24, 225, 275
signiferes 5, 46, 64, 70, 71, 102, 105, 168–9, 171, 172, 173, 180, 201, 208, 214, 254, 258, 276–7
Silei 152
Silius Attonis 159, 252, 256
silver 8, *30*, 32, 41, 44, 45, 46, 49, 54, 81, 85, 90, 92, 97, 98, 98, 100, *104*, 114, *116*, 116, 120, 135, 162, 169, 171, 177, 179, 185, *186*, *187*, *191*, 194, 198, *203*, 206, 217, 224, 245, 246, 248, 252, 275, 276
Silvius Italicus 3, 267
Silures 63
sinew 141, 160
siphonarii 64
Sirmium 74, 85, *111*, *125*, 128, 254
Sisak/Siscia 14, 34, *34*, 96, 97, *116*, 120, 131, 243, 244, 247, 248, 249, 271
slaves 39, 57, 66
slingers 6, 34, 43, 44, 58, 160, 164, *166*
slings 143
slingshots *166*
Slovakia 242
Slovenia 81, 97, 236
Smihel 14, 236
Smyrna 220
snakes 124, *188*
Social War 3, 6, *8*, 25
socii 6
socks 6, *90*, 166, 221, 222
soliferrea 252
Sora 8, 25, *29*, 37, 92, *112*, *127*, 140, 149, 169, *225*, 256, 272, 279
Sorano 272
Soranus 164
Soria 34
Scusse 167, 270
Spain 3, 4, 14, 15, 24, 34, *34*, 38, *45*, 212, 246, 250, 279
Spanish 3, 4, 32, 63, 97, 217, 245, 254, 272
Spartacus 4, 39, 46, 48
spathae 87, 153, 156, 183, 277
spears 5, 7, 8, 12, 37, 48, 49, 57, 58, 74, 77, 80, 143, 144, 152, *152*, 158, *164*, 177, 182, 224, 228, 240, 252, 255, 257, 276
speculatores 179, 255, 260, 277
sphendone 44
sphendonitai 58
spicula 74
spinning 109
spolia 160, 260
spurs 52, 275
squamae 70, 76, 106, 124, 126, 127, 128, 128, 130, 140, 149, 162, 169, 173, 198, 203, 212, 256
  piscis 124
  plumata 124, 212
Sremska Mitrovica 74; *see also* Sirmium
staffs 8, 24, *30*, 46, 48, 88, 157, 167, 176, 179, 205, 237, 275, 276, 277
standard-bearers 5, 6, *33*, 64, *70*, 71, 169, 171, 173, 176, 200
standards 5, 12, 22, 24, 45, 46, 48, 49, 68, 71, 96, 107, 128, 136, 169, 171, 173, 179, *191*, 197, 200, 217, 242, 268
stars 32, 167, 217, 242, 246
Statius 63, 98, 129, 246, *249*, 267
statuettes 45, 220
status 36, 131, 213, 220, 222, 225, 245
steel 14, 41, 73, 243, 247
stelae *30*, 151, 159, 192, 200, 228, 255, 256, 259
stele 49, 51, 52, *95*, 137, *176*, 192, *213*, 221, *226*, 240, 242, 260, 261, 277, 279
Steppe/Steppes *191*, 198
Stilicho diptych xi
Stillfried *80*, 133, 134, *134*
Strabo 3, 48, 240, 267
Strageath 176
Stratagemata 265
stratiothes 249
strator 222
Straubing 237
studs *70*, 100, *112*, 156, 159, 246
subarmales 41, 54, 146, *147*, 159
subligacula 54, 277
subligares 221
subligaria 221
subpaenulae 219
subuclae 219
Suda 14, 236, 267
sudarium 54
Suebi 242
Suetonius 3, 32, 46, 63, 139, 140, 141, 214, 267
Sulla 3, 4, *8*, *33*, 34, 35, 36, 39, 49, 51, 57, 236, 240, 264, 266
Sulpicius Celsus, Q. 95
superariae 219
Susa *41*, 130, 248, 250, 252, 270
Svilengrad 87, *90*, 142, 273
Svistov 249
Switzerland 14, 242, 273, 280
sword of Tiberius 204
swords 5, 6, 12, 14, 15, *18*, 20, 22, *23*, 24, *30*, 38, 39, 43, 45, 49, 54, 68, 80, *80*, *81*, 81, 84, 85
  battle 228
  blades 12, 14, *18*, 44, 45, 49, 81, 84, 85, *86*, 87, 88, 153, 182, 244, 245
  Boyer 14
  capuli 12, 15, 275
  Celtic 14, 44
  Delos 8
  eagle-headed pommels 92, *95*
  fittings 81
  frogs 98
  grips 24, 86, 87, 88, 92, 153, 183
  handguards 15, 156, 183
  handles 14, 85, 88, 92, 244
  Hispanic 15
inlaid decoration 92, 246
  lamnae 12, 14
  Mainz-type *22*, 81, 84
  morae 12, 15
  Mouries 8
  mucrones 12, 14, 153
  origins 24, 182
  Osuna 14, 15
  pommels *14*, 15, *23*, *30*, *44*, 49, 85, 86, 88, 88, 92
  Pompeii type *14*
  Republican
  ring-pommels 88, *88*, 92, 270, 275, *154*, 156, 183, 198, 204
  scabbards 12, 14, *14*, 15, 20, 24, *30*, 44, 45, 49, 54, 68, *71*, *80*, 81, 85, *86*, 87, 92, 96, 100, 125, 153, 156, 158, *180*, 183, 198, 204, 205, 224, 244, 246, 252, 257, 277
  short 43, 77
  suspension 20, 24, 81, 86, 92, 100, 204
  use 12, 14, 43, 87, 88, 92
  vaginae 12, 14, 15, 24, 49, *127*, 183, 205, 246, 277
symmachoi 45
Syria 4, 66, *116*, 139, 194
Syrian 6, 43, 112, 162, *163*, 164, 243, 253
Szokai 168

T

taberna 218, 277
tabulae 254, 277
  ansata 68, 108, 109, 179, 184, 277
  clesiana 242
  honestae missionis 252
  picta 13, 277
Tacfarinas 242
Tacitus 3, 43, 63, 107, 138, 141, 152, 153, 159, 166, 167, 208, 210, 217, 240, 260, 267
tapeta 193
taste 13, 54, 94, 136, 217, 249
Tekija 153, 156, 160, 246, 255
telae 25, 129
tents 175
  pegs 175
terminals 41, 100, 128, *180*, 204, 246
terracotta figure 44, 192
tesserae 6, 277
tesserarii 6, 64, 271, 277
testudo 105, 247, 252, 277
Teutoburgensis Saltus 249
Thames *180*, 245
Theilenhofen 120, 187
Thessalian/Thessalians 44, 193
thoraces 39, 51, 110, 122, 127, 129, 135, 248, 251
  folidotòs 124
  krikotòs 43
  laneus 140, 141, 214
  lineus 139
  linteus 8
  lepitodòs 41, 58, 124, 212
  stadios 42, 58, 122, 135, 226, 227, 277
thoracomachi 112, 139, 277
Thracians 43, 194, *213*
thunderbolts 32, 36, *71*, *203*
Tiberius 3, 63, 92, 97, *102*, 151, 159, 204, 205, 246, 258, 269
tibialia 141, 277
Tibiscum 87, 272
tinned *90*, 98, 100, 115, 125, 133, *196*
Titelberg 97
Titus 3, 64, *95*, 176, *179*, 187, 259, 264
tombstones 13, 24, 68, 85, 98, 107, 109, 130, 137, *146*, 149, 171, 175, *180*, 184, 185, 213, 217, 228, 241
tools 45, 121, 224, 270, 272
torques 48, 152, 167, 177, 178, 277

Tracht und Bewaffnung 271
Trajan 64, 66, 77, 81, *85*, 96, 108, *110*, *118*, 121, *124*, 133, 167, 171, 198, 200, 214, 222, 246, 268, 272
Trajan's Column 11, 13, 15, 66, 67, 70, *71*, *79*, *81*, 85, *99*, 100, *104*, 105, *105*, *108*, 108, 109, 112, *116*, *120*, 121, *121*, 122, 123, *124*, 129, 131, 134, *134*, 137, 138, *138*, *139*, 141, *141*, 142, 143, *143*, 145, *147*, 149, 152, 156, *156*, 157, *157*, *158*, 159, 160, *161*, *162*, 162, *163*, 164, *165*, 166, *166*, *167*, 167, 171, *172*, 173, *174*, 175, 176, *180*, *182*, 183, *183*, *184*, *185*, 192, 194, 198, 200, *201*, 206, 209, 210, 212, 213, 214, 221, 224, 225, 228, 244, 249, 250, 253, 254, 269
Trajan's Forum 66
trial pieces
triarii 5, 12, *27*, 235, 277
tribuni 8, 24, *27*, 30, 36, 39, 53, 54, 65–6, *94*, 98, 136, 145, *145*, 146, 246, 255, 277
  angusticlavius 277
  laticlavius 277
  militaris 53
Trier 176, 194
Trily 249
trophaea 228, 277
  Trajani 72, 93, 151, 205, 247, 269; see also Adamclisi
trousers 5, 6, 54, *68*, 140, 162, 166, *168*, *178*, *180*, 194, 198, 200, 221, *221*, 254, 275, 276, 277
tubae 46, 48, 176, 270, 277
tubicenes 6, *41*, 277
Tuchyna 97
tunicae 53, 140, 167, 176, 212–14, 218, 228, 260
  alba 217
  bracilis 228
  ferrea 238
  interior 214
  laticlavia 212
  militaris 13, *30*, 277
  nilotide 167
tunics 5, 6, 44, 53, 54, 57, 59, *90*, *102*, 140, *146*, 149, 164, 167, 173, 194, *203*, 212, 213, 214, 217, 218, 224, 240, 241, 253, 258, 259, 260
Turin 3, *65*, 81, *104*, 123, *124*, 151, *142*, 185, 208, 212, 268, 272, 279, 282
turmae 6, 65, 66, 178, 277
  ataluans 256
  patercliana 256

Tusculum 250
Tyne 107, 243, 247, 269, 270, 272

U

udones 222, 228
Ulpia Traiana Sarmizegetusa *73*, 74, *104*, 105, 171, 175, *192*, 193, 204, 243–4, 246, 248, 251, 253, 270
Ulpianus 221, 260
Ultra Limes 249
uniforms 8, *29*, 43, 46, 66, 67, *82*, 94, 107, 121, 152, 157, 160, 166, 200, *203*, 213, 217, 220, 221, 222, 225, 228, 276
urbana praefectura 65
urbaniciani 65, 200, 208
Urso 15, *18*, 25, 41, *43*
Usipetes 4
uteri 45

V

Vachéres warrior 44
Vaison la Romaine 248–9
Valencia 7
Valerius Albinus *213*
Valerius Crispus 67, *67*, 68, *112*, 137, 149, 173, 221, 259
Valerius Flaccus 46, 63, 108, 206, 252, 267
Valerius Genialis 197
Valerius, L. 244
Valerius Maximus 3, 8, 39, 54, 268
valetudinarium 173, *211*, 214, 254, 258, 269, 277
Valkenburg 157, 184, 270
Varro 3, 8, 32, 38, 48, 54, 63, 142, 213, 237, 238, 239, 240, 241, 245, 246, 248, 251, 259, 268
Varus 63, 66, 130, 135, 240, 242, 243, 250
Vatican 224
  Museum 52
Vechten *104*, 257
Vegetius 29, 30, 37, 63, 107, 108, 152, 171, 268, 275
velarium 261
velites 5, 25, 277
Velsen 245
venatores 167, 277
Venus Genetrix 39, 169, 194, 241
Vermand 254
Vernacula 235, 249
Verona 124, *127*, 173, 254
Verus 64, *104*, 129, 243, 254
verutum 252, 277

vestis militaris 107, 272, 277
Vesuvius 224, 270
veterani 64, 107, 272, 277
  veteranorum 65
vexilla 46, 48, 65, *154*, 170, 171, 178, 240, 261, 277
vexillarii 6, *170*, 277
vexillationes 66, 140, 160, *192*
vexilliferi 76, 171, 276
viatores 46
Victor 176, *176*, *178*, *188*, 247
victories 4, 5, 20, *30*, 32, *33*, 38, 45, 48, 59, 63, *110*, 122, 205, 208, 239, 242, 254, 261, 271
Victorinus Avrelius 208
vicus 129, 271, 277
Vienna 268, 269, 270
vincula 35, 90, 162, 220
Vindelici 63
vindicta 30, 46
Vindolanda *180*, 212, 218, 219, 220, 221, 222, 224
Vindonissa 68, *73*, 92, 98, 105, 108, *109*, *111*, 121, 125, *125*, *129*, 131, *131*, *132*, *133*, 135, *135*, 137, *137*, *138*, 138, *146*, 146, 147, *148*, 149, 151, *151*, 152, *152*, 156, *160*, *170*, 175, *175*, 176, 179, *182*, 183, *183*, *185*, *193*, 219, *219*, 221, *221*, 222, *222*, 243, 244, 245, 246, 247, 249, 270, 272, 273, 280
Vitellius 63, 166, *167*, 209, 260
Vites 30, *82*, 107, 121, 176, *213*, 277
Vize *188*, 192, 256
volsella 173
Volubilis 194, 249
Vozdizhenskaya Stanitsa 258
vulsella 173

W

Waal *190*, 256
War Museum in Belgrade 85, *86*, 280
warships 58
Warsaw 211, 254, 269–70, 280
Warta 270
watch 64, 277
watchmen 242
weapons 5, 6, 6, 7, 11, 12, 13, 14, *15*, 20, *20*, 22, 22, 24, 25, *29*, *30*, *33*, 37, 43, 48, 49, *51*, 54, 67, 70, *73*, 80, *81*, *104*, 104, 108, *112*, *118*, 123, *125*, *127*, 128, 129, 130, 139, 143, *149*, 150, 152, 153, *154*, 158, 160, 164, 166, 167, 175, 179, 182, *184*, 187, 198, 200, 212, 224, 229, 230, 236, 238,

244, 245, 246, 247, 252, 253, 260, 269, 270, 272, 276
Webster 130
Wehringen 88
Weiler *104*, 160, 185, 197, 256
Wicker 29, 34
Wiesbaden *68*, *112*, 137, 243, 257
Williams 264
Wilton crown 253
Windisch 249; *see also* Vindonissa
wings 8, 15, 29, 44, 46, 58, 107, 108, 169, 191, 258
wood 8, *14*, 15, 20, 43, *68*, 73, 74, *86*, 92, 97, 101, 105, 173, 183, 184, 193, 200, 204, 206, 236, 240, 245, 257
  alder 92
  ash 73, *182*, 200, 204, 243, 257
  birch 25, 46
  cornel *8*, 257
  haft 7, 67, 68
  hazel 73, *182*, 200
  oak 167
  pinecone 141
  plywood 25, 101, 105
  vine 277
wool 8, 25, 54, 59, *68*, *71*, 90, 129, 140, 146, 157, 158, 160, 166, 180, *203*, 212, 213, 214, 217, 218, 219, *219*, 220, 221, 222, 224
workshops 34, 67, *125*, 210, 245, 276
Worthing 268
wreaths 169, 171, 246, 254
  motif 92, 97
writing tablets 228

X

Xanten 185
  Wardt *104*, 152, 248
Xenophon 3, 63, 268

Y

Yugoslavia 97, 247

Z

Zagreb 14, *34*, 96, *116*, 121, 165, 204, 243, 253, 271, 273, 280
Zaragoza *34*, 44, *45*
zona 260
  militaris *33*, 51, 54, 77, 123, 225, 277
zonì 51, 94, 212
Zoomorphic style 198
Zugmantel 247